Julius Caesar

Commentaries on the Gallic War

Books 1-5 and 6.11-24

Julius Caesar
Commentaries on the Gallic War
Books 1–5 and 6.11–24

C. Iulii Caesaris
Commentarii Rerum Gestarum
De Bello Gallico

Text, Notes, Companion, and Vocabulary by

FRANCIS W. KELSEY

Revised and with a New Introduction by

REX STEM

Michigan Classical Press   ❧   Ann Arbor

Copyright © Rex Stem, 2017
All rights reserved.

ISBN 978-0-9799713-8-9

Published in the United States of America by
Michigan Classical Press
www.michiganclassicalpress.com

Manufactured in the United States of America

2019 2018 2017 4 3 2 1

A CIP catalogue record for this book is available from the Library of Congress.

Printed on acid-free paper ∞ by Thomson-Shore, Inc., Dexter, MI
www.thomsonshore.com

Image of F.W. Kelsey reproduced courtesy of the Kelsey Museum, University of Michigan.

Preface

This project was undertaken for the simple reason that I wanted to have undergraduate students of Latin read widely from Caesar's *Commentaries on the Gallic War* and no school commentary is in print from which I might do so. Commentaries on individual books of the Gallic War are available, and several new commentaries are appearing on the selections from the Gallic War that were chosen for the Advanced Placement Exam in Latin (introduced in spring 2013), but nothing that presents multiple books in their entirety for college level instruction.

Rather than reinvent the wheel, I am bringing back into print the best of the older school commentaries on the Gallic War, namely that published in 1918 by Francis W. Kelsey. The excellence of Kelsey's work is due to its rigor and completeness. Not only is the student presented with the complete text of over five (of the seven Caesarian) books of the Gallic War, but he or she also encounters a thorough grammatical (and sometimes historical) commentary, a complete Latin-English vocabulary for all the selections included, and an extensive Latin grammar keyed to the usage of Caesar (which also incorporates a description of the relevant geography and the military terms and practices of Caesar's time). The intermediate to advanced Latin student in a contemporary college classroom thus finds herein all he or she needs to make rapid progress in accurately comprehending Caesar's Latinity and narrative style. No other materials are needed.

The commentary is not interpretive, but focuses on improving the student's understanding of Latin grammar, syntax, and idiom. The notes are curt but rigorous, the vocabulary and grammar companion full and precise. The commentary regularly refers the student (by means of italicized numbers) to the grammar companion, and the companion itself is cross-referenced to the more advanced Latin grammars of Allen & Greenough and Bennett. Kelsey's work has remained the most complete student aid to reading Caesar since its publication in 1918, and it deserves to be revised and returned to the classroom.

My role in revising the manuscript involved several steps: proofreading the text files created by digitally scanning Kelsey's original text, limiting the even greater range of Kelsey's selections to Books 1-5 and 6.11-24 (and modifying the companion and vocabulary accordingly), and revising Kelsey's commentary and companion such that they are modernized and more accurately pitched to the needs of contemporary intermediate college Latin students (whom I teach every year). I then wrote an entirely new introduction within the context of current scholarship and with references to selected bibliography.

My revisions were student-tested by a group of undergraduates who volunteered to read and critique the complete text and commentary: Zac Bauman, Michael Boal, Keil Chase, Wesley Hanson, Aaron Heuckroth, and David Welch. Over a span of two academic years they made many suggestions to improve this book, and the collaboration was one of the most satisfying of my teaching career. Keil Chase also devoted many hours to standardizing and revising the text and notes; his speed and precision merit particular commendation. Other students and colleagues also helped with various aspects of the project: Carolyn Carey and Jennifer Devereaux in editing the commentary, Lester Stephens in clarifying the text, Alexandrea Sherman in revising the vocabulary, Barbara Craig in editing the Companion, Aislinn Melchior and Melissa Stem in improving the introduction, Christopher Craig in testing out a nearly finished version on his students in Tennessee. I owe the inspiration behind the whole project, as well as much of the original scanning and initial editing, to Giles Laurén. Ellen Bauerle and David Potter were instrumental in getting the book in its final form. I remain very grateful for all this help; whatever mistakes or obfuscations remain can only be attributed to my obtuseness in the face of so much good advice.

If you, as a reader or teacher of Caesar's Latin, discover errors in the text or commentary (whether simple typographical errors or mistakes of identification or description), I would appreciate learning of them (via email: srstem@ucdavis.edu) so that they could be corrected in a revised edition.

Table of Contents

Introductory Materials

Introduction to Caesar's *Commentaries on the Gallic War*

Reading from the Beginning

Julius Caesar is likely the most famous Roman of them all. His legacy transcends his life. Over the centuries he has become the archetype of the great man, especially the autocratic and imperialistic great man. He bestrode the narrow world like a colossus (Shakespeare, *Julius Caesar*, Act 1, Scene 2). His actions created metaphors we still use today: he crossed the Rubicon, but did not beware the Ides of March.

Caesar is most famous for his initiation of a civil war against the Senate of the Roman Republic, which he won, after which he became dictator for life, for which, in turn, he was assassinated as a tyrant by Brutus and Cassius. Was his assassination justified? Is murder the right response to a dictatorial threat to republican liberty? Are effective autocrats or unruly republics better for the common good? These questions have been debated, with Caesar as the test case, for the last two thousand years. Shakespeare's *Julius Caesar* captures the eye of the storm.

Hence what we know best about Caesar is that he was perceived to have become a tyrant and was killed for it. That is the end point of his story—a powerful and famous ending. And since we know how things end up, we have a tendency to read everything that happened before in light of that ending. This habit was already established when Caesar's ancient biographers summed up his life, and its appeal has never really waned.[1]

But there is an interpretive cost to reading back from the end, since the players within the historical drama at the time did not yet know the ending. During the nine years Caesar spent conquering Gaul, he could not have known that he would afterward prevail in a civil war but be killed for it. To read from the end is thus to skew the story as it unfolded, to obfuscate the contingencies of what happened, to add an inevitability that could only have emerged after the fact. A better way to understand Caesar's actions in the Gallic War is to read from the beginning and assess his understanding of events and his responses to them as they develop. This introduction, therefore, will not look forward to what happened after the Gallic War, and it will begin not from the end, but from the beginning, from Caesar's political position in Rome when his consulship ended and his command in Gaul began.[2]

Caesar in January 58 BC

The consulship was Rome's executive office, held jointly each year by two men. The attainment of the consulship was the peak of a successful political career. When Caesar was elected consul for the year 59 BC, the earliest year for which he was eligible, he added glory to his patrician lineage, especially since his father and grandfather had not reached the consulship. Moreover, during his year in office he oversaw significant legislative enactments, his closest two political associates—Pompey and Crassus—were among the most powerful men in Rome, and he had been granted the proconsulship

---

1   Suetonius, *Caesar* 30.5: "There are some who think that, seduced by the habit of command, he assessed his strength and that of his enemies and seized the opportunity to grasp the absolute power that he had wanted from an early age" (translation from Hurley 2011: 18). Plutarch, *Caesar* 69.1: "Caesar died after living fifty-six years in all. ... He had sought dominion and power all his days, and after facing so many dangers he had finally achieved them. And the only fruit it bore him was its name, and the perils of fame amid his envious fellow-citizens" (translation from Pelling 2011: 127).

2   Recommended starting points for engaging with Caesar's *Commentaries on the Gallic War*: Quinn 1982, Conte 1994: 225–33, Welch 1998, Kraus 2009. For gateways into *Gallic War* scholarship, see Welch and Powell 1998, Riggsby 2006, Grillo and Krebs 2017. Of older scholarship, Adcock 1956 remains an eloquent overview of Caesar as a man of letters, and the works of T. Rice Holmes (1907, 1914, 1931) are valuable on many points of detail. For Caesar's *Commentaries on the Civil War*, see Batstone and Damon 2006, Grillo 2012.

(governorship) of Cisalpine Gaul (what we regard today, roughly, as northern Italy), Transalpine Gaul (the Mediterranean coastal region of modern France, plus the Rhone River valley), and Illyricum (the coastal regions of the former Yugoslavia) for an unusually long period of five years. The responsibility for governing such a large area for so long was an enormous opportunity for further glory, especially in war, which the Romans particularly valued. From this perspective, to imagine Caesar in January of 58 is to picture him at the height of Rome's political class and preparing for a period abroad that would complement his domestic authority.

But the reality was different. Caesar's legislative enactments were tainted by his use of violence, intimidation, and disregard for protocol. Yet he was compelled to force the legislation through because he was beholden to Pompey and Crassus, with whose alliance he had secured election to the consulship. He was the junior member of the three, and they expected returns on their investment in him. All three became deeply resented among the Roman senatorial class, and Caesar, as their operational figurehead, most of all. Stalwarts in the Senate had vowed that he would be held accountable for the actions during his consulship that they regarded as unconstitutional. He was immune to formal accountability as long as he held his proconsulship, but he knew, even as he prepared to depart for Gaul, that he was facing a politically difficult return to Rome. The price of his success, in terms of public opinion, had been high, and the promise of his political future was clouded.

In early 58 it would have been hard to imagine that Caesar would end up richer than Crassus, a greater general than Pompey, and the most famous Roman of them all. But Caesar was resourceful, and he was willing to take risks with high stakes. During the civil war of Marius and Sulla, for example, Sulla ordered Caesar, then only 18 years old, to divorce his wife because of her close ties to the partisans of Marius. Caesar refused and went on the run to avoid Sulla's agents and the bounty on his head. Sulla eventually backed down. When Cicero had arrested five accomplices of Catiline in 63 BC, and the Senate was leaning toward sanctioning their execution, Caesar was the only one to speak against execution in favor of rigorous imprisonment and, at least temporarily, changed the majority opinion of the Senate. He was later confronted as a Catilinarian accomplice, but he stared down the opposition. He borrowed so much money in 63 BC for his campaign for the priestly office of *pontifex maximus* that he is reported to have told his mother on the morning of the election that he would return victorious or ruined. He returned victorious. After his praetorship in 61 BC, when he wished to set out to his governorship in Spain, his debts remained so high that his creditors refused to let him leave. Yet he secured sureties from Crassus, then conquered and plundered enough territory in Spain to pay all his debts. When it was time to set out for Gaul, therefore, Caesar had experienced potentially career-ending crises before, and he had found the means to overcome the challenges of each.[3]

Caesar's political challenges in early 58 BC were to restore his political reputation and to recapture the affection of the Roman people. He could not do so in person, for he would be absent from the city for five years (later extended to nine). Thus he needed a way to broadcast his voice from afar, to keep his achievements on behalf of the Roman people on their lips and in their imagination. His solution was to write his *Commentaries on the Gallic War*.

Caesar as Author: Writing the *Commentaries on the Gallic War*

Caesar was an able orator, reputed by some to be second only to Cicero in his generation. He also thought intensely about proper Latin usage and style of expression, as evidenced by the fact that in the midst of the Gallic War he wrote a treatise, dedicated to Cicero and yet challenging him, in defense of systematic precision in the use of language and vocabulary.[4] Thus it is not surprising that he

3   For Caesar's life up to the Gallic War, start with Suetonius, *Caesar* 1–23, and Plutarch, *Caesar* 1–15, after which the biographical chapters in Griffin 2009 provide good context while demonstrating how the ancient accounts can be challenged. Fuller accounts can be found at Goldsworthy 2006: 1–181 (more readable) and Gelzer 1968: 1–101 (more scholarly).

4   On Caesar as orator and writer, see Cicero, *Brutus* 251–62; Suetonius, *Caesar* 55–56; Quintilian 10.1.114. Regarding his treatise *On Analogy*, now lost, the best piece of evidence for its perspective (quoted at Aulus Gellius 1.10.4) is the advice: "just as you would avoid a rock in the sea, so you should avoid the unfamiliar and unusual word" (*ut tamquam scopulam, sic fugias inauditum atque insolens verbum*). See further Hall 1998, Fantham 2009,

would use his skills as a writer to support his achievements as a general and his needs as a politician. As a proconsul in the field, governing provinces and commanding armies, he would have sent official dispatches to the Senate reporting on his activities, and the tone of these dispatches, if the surviving examples (by Cicero: *Letters to Friends* 15.1, 15.2, and compare also 15.4) are representative, was declarative and not modest. It is a reasonable guess that Caesar's dispatches to the Senate were the initial drafts of what became his *Commentaries*, once he recognized the advantages of spreading a narrative of his achievements more widely.

If we assume that Caesar's *Commentaries*, although expressions of a literary style in their own right, were primarily intended as political documents, then this assumption affects when we imagine they were written and distributed. One school of thought, focused on Caesar at the Rubicon, suggests that he composed and distributed the whole narrative of his campaigns in Gaul (what we now call Books 1–7 of the *Commentaries*) at the end of the war, when he was seeking to return to Rome and was preparing for what would become his Civil War. The other school of thought, recognizing Caesar's immediate political needs during the war, is that he wrote an account of his deeds each year, in the autumn or winter after the campaigning season was over, and immediately sent copies to Rome. For this school, each book is the product of the year it describes, and was forged in the political circumstances of that year.[5]

Given my high estimation of Caesar's political shrewdness, I prefer annual and serial distribution to aggregate publication at the end. Corroborating evidence is circumstantial, yet collectively supports serial composition. There are claims made in the earlier books that later books contradict, and these claims could have been adjusted if the whole narrative were written together. The Nervii, for example, are said to be wiped out at 2.28, yet three years later they and their allies field an army of 60,000 (5.39, 5.49.1) and produce five thousand soldiers of their own two years after that (7.75.3). All Gaul is said to be pacified at 2.35.1 and 3.7.1, yet furious resistance breaks out in Book 5 while Book 7 describes the unified revolt of almost the whole of Gaul. Caesar's earlier claims appear overconfident, if not mistaken, and thus the sort of thing that he would have refrained from saying if he had had the chance (i.e., if the accounts of the earlier years were not already in circulation). In the year 56, Caesar's political opponents attempted to have his Gallic provinces stripped from him, and Cicero was eventually pressed to endorse Caesar's retention of his provinces before the Senate. Cicero's speech survives, with its fulsome depiction of Caesar's successes in Gaul (*On the Consular Provinces* 18–39, esp. 32–35) demonstrating the power of Caesar's political reach and the thoroughness of his engagement in his affairs back in Rome.[6] Such evidence makes it easier to believe that Caesar had already supplied his own account of his successes in Gaul to Roman audiences, and was not waiting until the end of the war to do so.[7]

After Caesar's death in 44 BC, one of his officers, Aulus Hirtius (one of the consuls of 43, who died in that year), wrote an account of Caesar's final two years in Gaul (51–50). In Hirtius' *Preface* to what we now call Book 8 of the *Commentaries on the Gallic War*, he explains that his book connects Caesar's account of the Gallic War to the beginning of Caesar's *Commentaries on the Civil War*. Hirtius' involvement suggests that he was then compiling a collected edition of Caesar's *Commentaries* on both the Gallic and Civil Wars, though his *Preface* reads as if Caesar's narratives are

and Garcea 2012.

5   The issue has been long debated: see Riggsby 2006: 9–11 for a summary, with further bibliography. Comparing Gelzer 1968: 171–72 (aggregate publication) to Goldsworthy 2006: 187–88 (serial publication) reveals how both sets of arguments can sound plausible. Even so, the scholarly trend since Wiseman 1998 favors serial publication.

6   For the context behind Cicero's *On the Consular Provinces*, see Grillo 2015. Osgood 2009 well demonstrates how intensely Caesar managed his correspondence to contribute to his public relations campaign during the Gallic War.

7   Note also Krebs 2013, who observes that several phrases and expressions in Lucretius' *On the Nature of Things* also appear in Caesar's *Commentaries on the Gallic War*, but only in Book 5 and after. Book 5 describes events of 54 BC, the year in which Lucretius' poem first became known to Caesar. The presence of Lucretian echoes in Caesar from that date, but not before, suggests that Book 5 was written after Caesar first read Lucretius, but that Books 1–4 were composed earlier, and most likely serially.

already well known on their own. He also records, in what is now one of our earliest and best pieces of evidence for the purpose and initial reception of Caesar's *Commentaries*, his assessment of Caesar's achievement as a writer (Book 8, *Preface* 4–7):

> *Constat enim inter omnes nihil tam operose ab aliis esse perfectum, quod non horum elegantia commentariorum superetur, qui sunt editi, ne scientia tantarum rerum scriptoribus deesset adeoque probantur omnium iudicio ut praerepta, non praebita, facultas scriptoribus videatur. Cuius tamen rei maior nostra quam reliquorum est admiratio, ceteri enim, quam bene atque emendate, nos etiam, quam facile atque celeriter eos perfecerit, scimus. Erat autem in Caesare cum facultas atque elegantia summa scribendi, tum verissima scientia suorum consiliorum explicandorum.*

> It is agreed among everyone that there has been nothing completed by anyone else so painstakingly that is not surpassed by the elegance of these commentaries, which were published so that knowledge of such great deeds would not be lacking to other writers, and they are esteemed in the judgment of everyone to such an extent that the means seems to have been forestalled rather than offered to those writers. Yet our admiration for this achievement is greater than that of others, for they know how well and correctly he completed them while we know how easily and quickly. Caesar possessed both the greatest means and elegance for writing and the truest knowledge for explicating his own thinking.

What Hirtius here makes explicit is the paradox at the heart of reading Caesar. He says that Caesar wrote these commentaries so that other writers would know what happened—we presume that those other writers are historians looking for first-hand accounts to be incorporated into formal histories—yet Caesar in fact foiled that purpose because his own account is so finished that any rewrite would fall short of the original. Caesar's text is thus more than it appears and not what it claims to be. Hirtius then offers two reasons why Caesar turned out to be the best narrator of his deeds: his skills as a writer and his perspective on events ("the truest knowledge for explicating his own thinking"). These reasons acknowledge Caesar's engagement in authorial persuasion and signal that Caesar is to be read more like a literary historian than a straightforward primary source.

This conclusion is strengthened by the other early testimonial we have for the reception of Caesar's commentaries among his contemporaries, this one from Cicero, in a dialogue written in 46 BC in which he and Brutus (Caesar's future assassin) are depicted as engaged in a discussion of Roman orators. Brutus transitions from Caesar's speeches to his commentaries, about which Cicero interjects (*Brutus* 262):

> *Tum Brutus: orationes quidem eius mihi vehementer probantur. compluris autem legi atque etiam commentarios, quos idem scripsit rerum suarum.*
>
> *Valde quidem, inquam, probandos; nudi enim sunt, recti et venusti, omni ornatu orationis tamquam veste detracta. Sed dum voluit alios habere parata, unde sumerent qui vellent scribere historiam, ineptis gratum fortasse fecit, qui illa volent calamistris inurere: sanos quidem homines a scribendo deterruit; nihil est enim in historia pura et inlustri brevitate dulcius.*

> Then Brutus said, "I highly esteem [Caesar's] orations. I have read several, and also his commentaries, which the same man wrote of his own deeds."
>
> "Very much indeed," I said, "ought they to be esteemed, for they are bare, natural, and graceful, with all the ornament of speech removed as if clothing. But while he wished that others, those who wished to write history, have the materials prepared from which they could draw, he perhaps did a favor for fools, those who would crimp them with curling-irons. Reasonable men, certainly, he deterred from writing, for there is nothing in history sweeter than clear and brilliant brevity."

Although Cicero is never unaware of Caesar's stature as his political and literary rival and thus there may be a double edge to this professed judgment, his point here is similar to that of Hirtius, namely that Caesar's apparent intention was to provide material for other historians, but that only a fool would seek to improve on Caesar's account. Employing a metaphor from the barber shop, Cicero claims that Caesar's style is so effective in its natural grace and brevity that any attempt to fluff it up with curling-irons would produce a less successful result. Another metaphor Cicero invokes is the heroic nudity common to ancient statuary, where the idealized body is more pleasing than a body fashionably dressed. By either metaphor, Cicero makes clear that he perceives Caesar's commentaries to be nothing less than finished history.

Both Cicero and Hirtius refer to Caesar's writing as "commentaries" (*commentarii*), which suggests that Caesar published them with that title.[8] Such a title aptly demonstrates the paradox Hirtius describes, for the title "Commentary," as best as we can reconstruct the genre without any other genuinely comparable examples surviving, seems to imply a loose collection of notes without claims to literary refinement.[9] To title a work a "Commentary" on events is thus to claim that the narrative is not yet proper history, lowering reader expectations for the level of sophistication to be found within. Such a title also allows an author to be selective about what is included, and Caesar limits his *Commentaries on the Gallic War* exclusively to events in Gaul (or Germany or Britain) relevant to that war. He does not discuss his personal life, for example, or politics in Rome. Moreover, he assumes a Roman audience who is already familiar with Roman institutions and the Roman army, and he makes no direct claims about the purpose or form of the work. He omits any introduction of himself as author: the opening paragraph of the text quickly describes the geography of Gaul and the following paragraph begins the narrative of events. The reader thus has to react to what the text says and does in order to interpret Caesar's authorial moves.

Form and Content, Style and Perspective

The judgments of Cicero and Hirtius stress that Caesar transcended what might have been expected of a first draft of the events of the Gallic War and presented what deserved to be regarded as the definitive account of these events. His success in doing so originates at the sentence level and percolates up through the themes of the whole work. Hence my analysis here will try to reflect that strategy and analyze in detail a few short passages near the beginning of the work in order to introduce its larger themes.

Consider, for example, the first time Caesar introduces himself. After an opening six chapters in which the geography of Gaul is surveyed and a plan is developed by the Helvetians (occupants of what is now Switzerland) to migrate across Gaul, the seventh chapter begins with Caesar entering the narrative and responding to these developments.

> *Caesari cum id nuntiatum esset, eos per provinciam nostram iter facere conari, maturat ab urbe proficisci et quam maximis potest itineribus in Galliam ulteriorem contendit et ad Genavam pervenit.* (1.7.1)

> When it had been announced to Caesar that they were attempting to make a march through our province, he hastens to depart from the city [Rome] and, with marches as great as is possible, pushes into Further Gaul and arrives at Geneva.

The sentence is declarative and straightforward. But it accomplishes more than it seems. First, the sentence depicts movement. The syntax flows smoothly from left to right (a circumstantial *cum*-clause introduces an indirect statement, then a present indicative main verb and two more main verbs in the present tense clearly linked by *et* and *et*), just as the action of the sentence involves Caesar leaving Rome in response to the news and hastening to Geneva. The speed is emphasized in the verbs

8   Kelsey 1905 demonstrates that Caesar's title was most likely *C. Iulii Caesaris Commentarii Rerum Gestarum* ("Commentaries on the Achievements of Gaius Julius Caesar"). The phrase *De Bello Gallico* ("on the Gallic War"), or some such similar phrase, was added by later copyists in order to distinguish these commentaries from those on the Civil War.

9   For a survey of the evidence for the genre and form of the *commentarius*, as well as how Caesar's *Commentarii* compare, see Riggsby 2006: 133–55. Kraus 2005 explores potential overlaps between the style of Caesar the man and the style of his *commentarius*.

(*maturat, contendit*; note also the choice to use the historic present) and we are also told that his marches were "as great as is possible" (*quam maximis potest*). Caesar does not characterize himself directly at all, yet he implicitly makes a positive impression on the reader as a quick and decisive leader: he makes it all the way from Rome to Geneva within one sentence of learning of the possible threat. Such speed and directness will be seen again and again; they are two vital reasons for Caesar's success.

The first word of the sentence is Caesar's name. First position provides emphasis, and Caesar is not modest about placing himself at the center of the action. He is undoubtedly the dominant figure of this sentence. Yet note that he does not make himself the subject of the sentence, even though his name is the first word. Rather, he stands in the dative case, for he presents himself as reacting to the news and then springing into action. From the start, then, Caesar is seen not to have provoked this conflict, nor even to have been aware of it until news of it was reported *to him*. But once he learned of the possible threat, he traveled as rigorously as possible to investigate it. He thus appears as a protector of Roman interests, nimble but not aggressive.

Most importantly, Caesar appears in the third person ("Caesar") not in the first person ("I"). It is crucial for reading this text to remember that the author of the narrative and the main actor of the narrative are the same person, yet Caesar clearly chose to blur that link. When Caesar refers to himself as author, in fact, he does so in the first person. At the beginning of the second book, for example, he refers back to something he mentioned at the end of the first book by saying "as we explained above" (*uti supra demonstravimus*; 2.1.1). The effect is that the author appears to be writing about the deeds of someone else, someone that the author has researched and is presenting for the reader's interest. This choice is one concrete example of how Caesar writes more like an actual historian than merely a commentator, and it clearly signals Caesar's literary awareness. Creating a distance between himself as actor and himself as author allows for variations in perspective, sometimes dramatic, in which the author can report something that the actor did not know at the moment, or in which the actor can be seen to be implementing plans that the author has not yet revealed. Far from being an indicator of any megalomaniacal schizophrenia, Caesar's split roles as actor and author provide him the tools to enhance his narrative by demonstrating that the performing of deeds and the recording of them are indeed different roles that require excellence in different skills.[10]

Also notable in this sentence is an indication that Caesar does not present himself as a neutral observer of events. He reveals his affiliation when he mentions that the Helvetians were attempting to make a march "through our province." Not "the Roman province," but "our province." "Our" is first person plural, thus Caesar the author presents himself as a Roman writing for his fellow Romans, as an author who expects his audience to share in Rome's possessions and Rome's interests. And if "our province" is at risk, then it is both natural and desirable to "us" that the magistrate in charge of governing it would respond immediately and capably to the threat. Caesar the author, in other words, assumes that his reading audience is on the side of Caesar the actor, who here represents Rome. This is a story about us and our province against them (*eos*) and their plans to interfere with our province. Hence this is a story with good guys and bad guys, a story for which the reader's patriotism is to be invoked in support of us, the good guys, the Romans.

In this one sentence, then, this first sentence in which we meet Caesar, we already have important clues that Caesar the actor is a leader of speed and purpose, that Caesar the author will depict the action in a seemingly detached style that embodies the businesslike actions to be narrated, and that Caesar in both roles presents himself as a Roman acting in support of Roman interests.

The first sentence of the chapter also frames the events that follow. An embassy of Helvetians approaches Caesar and asks his permission to cross the province. This is how Caesar responds:

> *Caesar, quod memoria tenebat, L. Cassium consulem occisum exercitumque eius ab Helvetiis pulsum et sub iugum missum, concedendum non putabat; neque homines inimico animo, data facultate per provinciam itineris faciundi, temperaturos ab iniuria et maleficio existimabat.* (1.7.4–5)

Caesar, because he remembered that the consul Lucius Cassius had been killed and his army

---

10   On the ramifications of Caesar's choice to refer to himself in the third person, see further Marincola 1997: 182–98, Batstone and Damon 2006: 143–46, Riggsby 2006: 150–55, Grillo 2011, Pelling 2013: 46–57.

routed by the Helvetians and sent under the yoke, was thinking that [the Helvetian request] ought not to be granted; he also judged that they, being men of hostile temper, if the opportunity for making a march through the province were granted, would not refrain from injury and wrongdoing.

The progression of the sentence reveals its design, which is to bring the reader through Caesar's train of thought and have the reader share in his conclusion. Caesar's name is again the first word but here the subject, for this is his thinking. Immediately after his name we find a causal clause, since his reasoning precedes his conclusion. The events of the causal clause (reported in indirect statement) are the killing of a Roman consul, the defeat of a Roman army, and the humiliation of that army. On the basis of this past history, which has not been mentioned in the text before, Caesar thinks that their request should not be granted. The Roman reader is likely to agree: why should Caesar trust men who have harmed Rome in the past?

The sentence then continues by expressing Caesar's judgment that the Helvetians, given that they are "men of hostile temper," would not refrain from further harming of Roman interests if (the ablative absolute functions as a conditional) Caesar grants their request. For the reader, the Helvetians' earlier actions seem to justify both their characterization as hostile and Caesar's mistrust of their intentions.

Moreover, once the reader conceives of events in an if-then pattern (i.e., if permission is granted, they will not refrain from wrongdoing), then the reader endorses Caesar's action in not granting permission and so preventing harm to the province. The way each half of the sentence is written greatly increases the likelihood that the reader endorses Caesar's conduct and accepts his understanding of these events. The Helvetians are untrustworthy because they are unlikely to be able to restrain themselves from riotous violence, thus Caesar is right to deny them their request and protect Roman property and territory. What reads as a description of Caesar's action at this particular moment is in fact the political and military foundation for the launching of his entire Gallic campaign.

The next chapter documents the responses of the two sides to Caesar's denial of the Helvetians' request to march through the province. Caesar engages the military machine that is the Roman army and puts them to work to thwart the Helvetian plan:

> *Interea ea legione, quam secum habebat, militibusque, qui ex provincia convenerant, a lacu Lemanno, qui in flumen Rhodanum influit, ad montem Iuram, qui fines Sequanorum ab Helvetiis dividit, milia passuum XVIIII murum in altitudinem pedum sedecim fossamque perducit. (1.8.1)*

Meanwhile, with that legion which he had with him, and with the soldiers who had assembled from the province, from Lake Leman, which flows into the Rhone River, to the Jura Mountains, which divide the territory of the Sequani from that of the Helvetii, an extent of nineteen miles, he constructs a rampart sixteen feet high and a trench.

Just as Caesar traveled from Rome to Geneva in one sentence, here his troops, in one sentence, build a rampart nineteen miles long and seal off the Roman province from the Helvetians. Moreover, the structure of the sentence again matches the event it depicts. The sentence opens with an ablative of means, followed by a relative clause, then another ablative of means, then another relative clause, then an ablative place from which, then a relative clause, then an accusative of place to which, then a relative clause. This repeated alternation between a piece of information and a relative clause that further contextualizes that information mimics the orderly repetition and accumulation of tasks that led to the construction of the rampart. The sentence, like the wall, is lengthy, but its development clear and effective.

Compare the Helvetian response:

> *Helvetii, ea spe deiecti, navibus iunctis ratibusque compluribus factis, alii vadis Rhodani, qua minima altitudo fluminis erat, non numquam interdiu, saepius noctu, si perrumpere possent, conati, operis munitione et militum concursu et telis repulsi, hoc conatu destiterunt. (1.8.4)*

> The Helvetians, cast down from that hope, having joined boats together and made several rafts, some at the fords of the Rhone, where the depth of the river was least, sometimes during the day, more often at night, having tested whether they were able to break through, repulsed by the line of defenses and by the rapid massing of soldiers and by missiles, desisted from this attempt.

The sentence depicts chaos and is itself chaotic. Some Helvetians fashion boats and attempt to cross the river on them. Others, it seems, try to cross on foot at fords. Their efforts come at all times of day and night and do not appear to be coordinated. A series of participial phrases (cast down, joined, made, tested, repulsed) represent the actions of the Helvetians, all of which lead to the final word of the sentence: they gave up. The first and last words of the sentence are its subject and verb (*Helvetii ... destiterunt*); all that comes between explains that final verb.

The contrast between Caesar's depiction of the actions of the Romans and the actions of the Helvetians goes far to demonstrate why the Romans successfully prevented the Helvetians from crossing the river. The Helvetians seem wild and unpredictable, unwilling to respect Roman attempts to restrain them unless compelled by force. The Romans appear capable and prepared to defend their territory, with a leader who directs them effectively. Thus does Caesar's sentence-level narrative capture his larger themes.[11]

Themes

The primary theme of the whole work, of course, is how the war was won. How leads to why, and Caesar has two sets of themes that suggest reasons for Rome's victory. The first set offers larger, more cultural reasons for Rome's superiority to Gaul, while the second set specifically depicts Caesar's army as a particularly effective agent of Roman power.

At various points, for example, Caesar characterizes Romans as superior to Gauls, both implicitly and explicitly.[12] Gauls are described as courageous in battle, and intent on defending their liberty, but they are also said to be rash and impulsive, quicker to start a fight than to stick with it, and not coordinated enough to implement a larger military strategy. The Romans, by contrast, are disciplined soldiers who know how to fight effectively because of their experience, their discipline, and their leadership. They are also more potent on the march (a river that the Gauls took twenty days to cross is crossed by the Romans in one; 1.13.2) and more advanced in their siege technology (one Gallic city laughs at the great size of the Roman siege engines until the engines begin moving toward them; 2.30–31). On these terms, any Roman army could have conquered Gaul.

Yet part of Caesar's purpose is to suggest that his leadership made that conquest more impressive and more thorough. Some elements of his narrative are directly concerned with displaying his own genius as a military leader. But he is not the only impressive figure. Individual centurions are noted for their extraordinary valor, as are officers under Caesar who enact effective strategies and display admirable fortitude.[13] Caesar's story, in other words, is about much more than him even though he plays the leading role. As he guides his reader to recognize over the course of the early books, the bond that formed between Caesar and his men eventually caused his army to be capable of offen-

11   For helpful demonstrations of how to read Caesar's style profitably, see Gotoff 1984, Williams 1985, James 2000, Kraus 2009: 165–71, Vasaly 2009: 245–51, Batstone and Damon 2006: 143–65. A trio of articles by Robert Brown (1999, 2004, 2013) is especially recommended.

12   For Caesar's presentation of the Gauls (and Germans and Britons) and their landscape, see Barlow 1998, Rawlings 1998, Erickson 2002, Krebs 2006, much of Riggsby 2006, Schadee 2008. For the historical integration of Gaul into the Roman Empire, see Woolf 1998; for the place of the Gauls in Roman imagination, see Williams 2001.

13   On Caesar's portrayal of himself, see Goldsworthy 1998, Riggsby 2006: 191–207, Kraus 2009: 168–71. For the role of Caesar's officers and centurions, see Marincola 1997: 212–13 and Welch 1998. For Caesar's depiction of battle scenes, see Lendon 1999 and 2015. For more about the Roman army and its practice of war in the time of Caesar, see Goldsworthy 2006: 190–96 and Gilliver 2002, followed by Goldsworthy 1996 and Potter 2010.

sive and defensive maneuvers that were as impressive as anything any Roman army had ever done. Caesar's planning, his quickness, his personal involvement, combined with the powers of endurance displayed by the soldiers, their tenacity under attack, and their willingness to sacrifice for the Roman cause—all of these qualities are manifestations of how Caesar depicts his model Roman army.

Caesar's goal as a commentator on his own deeds is to balance these levels of explanation, the general and the specific, and thereby put himself at the center of events yet have the events serve Rome. Roman readers would want Caesar to shine in every possible way, since that contributes to Roman glory, and the skills of the commander enhance the success of the army. Caesar can therefore describe his deeds in terms largely flattering to himself, yet depict himself as but an example of the successful traditions of Roman generalship that stretched back for centuries and led Rome to its dominance of the Mediterranean.[14] The way to measure Caesar's success as a writer, therefore, is not to interrogate how accurately he depicted events, but to ask how persuasively he explains to his Roman reader how and why the war was won.[15]

To come to the end. Caesar knew when he left for Gaul in 58 that his return to Rome would be politically difficult, and one of the reasons that he wrote his *Commentaries* was to ease that difficulty. Moreover, at the end of the war, when he sought to return to Rome with honor and to be assigned another military command, his *Commentaries* functioned as a justification for why he deserved one. Ultimately, he could not negotiate the return he sought and he forced the issue by crossing the Rubicon River, the southern boundary of Cisalpine Gaul that also marked the spatial boundary of his command, and marched into Italy with one of his legions. He thereby triggered civil war, and the struggle that followed has come to define Caesar more than the Gallic War has. Can we read the *Commentaries on the Gallic War* to understand Caesar's motivations and character in the civil war and after? Of course. But when we do, then we are reading from the end, after the context for Caesar's persuasion had changed, and not from the moment in which the persuasion was written. Thus we blur Caesar's literary strategies because of our skewed interest in his ultimate political goals.

But if we are right to believe that Caesar wrote what we now call Book 1 of the *Commentaries* in the winter of 58–57 BC, then we should read Book 1 in accordance with the challenges facing him at that moment. When his enemies were characterizing his consulship as a tyrannical trampling of the Senate and its traditions of governance,[16] the last thing Caesar would have wanted to do is to produce a narrative that was all about him, that displayed precisely the sense of superiority that his enemies were casting in his teeth. To study the *Commentaries on the Gallic War* for Caesar's innate self-centeredness is thus to regard him as a failed writer who could not suppress what his politics required him to suppress. Yet Caesar's undeniable political success argues against such failure, as does his manifest talent as a writer of narrative. To award Caesar the political acumen that he deserves requires instead that we read, warily, with the flow of his rhetoric. Let us explore how what we have fits with what Caesar needed, namely a narrative argument that emphasized his achievements in the service of Rome at the head of Roman army against a long-standing foe of the Roman people. Reading from the beginning allows one to appreciate how his literary form served his political cause.

---

14   Imagine, as a modern analogy, if America defeated France in the finals for the World Cup and then the coach of the American team wrote an account of the match with an openly patriotic tone. The cultural traditions of America and France would function as the backdrop to the particular reasons why the American team, as coached in this instance, was better than the French team. The coach's readership would be American fans of the team, and of the game, who wanted to better comprehend, and even to share in, their team's success. As fans, they would want to learn the inner workings of the team's victory and they would expect that interpretations of events would break in their favor. They would not want to be lied to, but they would give the coach the benefit of the doubt since, after all, he won. Such a scenario captures what I perceive Caesar to have been doing when he designed and wrote his *Commentaries on the Gallic War* for his Roman audience.

15   For considerations of Caesar's reliability in his *Commentaries on the Gallic War*, see Goldsworthy 2006: 185–90 and Damon 2007: 446–50. Note also the comment of Grillo 2011: 249: "[Caesar] 'solves' the problem of truth by not raising the question at all."

16   For Caesar's opposition, see Gelzer 1968: 79, 87–88 and Goldsworthy 2006: 168–81.

Debating Caesar's Achievement in the Gallic War

The Gallic War stretched over nine years, and it can be separated into three distinct phases: the initial conquest (58–56 BC), explorations from Gaul into Germany and Britain (55–54), and the eruption of a united Gallic resistance that necessitated a second Roman conquest (53–50). Caesar connects each year of the campaign through cause-and-effect relationships. His success against the Helvetians caused other Gallic tribes to seek his aid against the Germans who were occupying Gallic lands. His defeat of the Germans (at the end of Book 1) led him into central Gaul, where he met resistance from the Belgae and others in the northern region (Book 2). New resistance emerged in the third part of Gaul, Aquitania, in the following year (Book 3), and the next year saw a new German threat coming across the Rhine, which caused him to bridge the Rhine and explore Germany (the first half of Book 4). A similar sense of proactive exploration also led to two expeditions into Britain (Books 4 and 5). The winter after the return from Britain saw the origins of a widespread Gallic revolt, which at first caught Caesar by surprise (second half of Book 5), and which he was unable to root out (Book 6) until nearly the whole of Gaul unified against him and sparked a final, massive battle at Alesia (Book 7), followed by two years of mopping up (Hirtius' Book 8).

What the narrative of the war describes, in sum, is a vast amount of territory conquered by one army under one commander in one far-reaching war, achieved through a series of major victories, some under very difficult circumstances. After the second and fourth years of the war, the Roman Senate recognized Caesar with public celebrations of unprecedented length (2.35.4, 4.38.5), and the ancient historical tradition of the Gallic War after Caesar is strongly positive. Plutarch, for example, asserts that Caesar's generalship in Gaul demonstrated that he was the greatest of all Roman generals (*Caesar* 15). From the perspective of the ancient tradition, Caesar seems to have won the public relations battle that he designed his *Commentaries* to fight.[17]

Readers now, however, face two high hurdles to appreciating Caesar's achievement. One is a distaste for large-scale military violence. The massive numbers of Gallic casualties that Caesar reports are shocking and brutal to modern sensibilities, acts of genocide rather than justifiable conquest. The second is a distrust of political rhetoric. Caesar's attempt to lead his reader into adopting his perspective on events usually triggers an immediate sense of resistance in readers who have learned not to trust what politicians say about their own virtues.

These obstacles deserve to be faced directly. For the first, I would urge a sense of cultural relativism. The Romans embraced war as fundamental to their identity as Romans.[18] If we wish to understand Rome on its own terms, then the power of Caesar's warcraft deserves to be read and studied on its own terms. It is valuable to learn to embrace the perspective of a text without adopting it oneself. The same can be said of the second obstacle, since examining how Caesar seeks to persuade—particularly when one is wary of being persuaded—allows one to study persuasion itself, both what makes it effective and how it can be resisted. Because his persuasion is embodied within an unassuming style, he is easily read as a discerning reporter on events rather than as the agent of his own narrative. To resist his conclusions therefore requires that a reader remember the necessity to do so. Yet to appreciate him as a writer requires a reader who observes how he confounds that necessity.

17   For Caesar's success in influencing the later tradition of the Gallic War, see Welch 1998: 96–97, Osgood 2009: 349–53, and, in more detail, Pelling 1984 and 2011. Caesar's legacy overall was much more mixed (e.g., Pliny, *Natural History* 7.92): see further Pelling 2006, Wyke 2008, and the chapters (as well as the Introduction) on Caesar's reputation, ancient and modern, in Griffin 2009.

18   Collins 1972: 922–42, supported by Seager 2003, demonstrates that Caesar's aggressive imperialism was unlikely to have offended contemporary Roman attitudes (though Powell 1998 perceives defensiveness in Caesar's depiction of massacre).

Introduction to Kelsey's Commentary

The Purpose and Method of This Commentary

The purpose of this commentary, as revised, is to clarify the rules and patterns of Latin syntax for readers of Caesar's Latin at the intermediate or advanced college level. It does offer some historical details and background to the events described, but the focus is the explication of the grammar of the Latin. It does not offer literary or historiographical interpretation; it is not a commentary for scholars. It is for students and teachers of students, and it tries to anticipate and answer their questions through detailed explanation. It sometimes offers translations, literal and/or idiomatic, though it more often identifies the syntax of the word or phrase. The goal is that students can begin to read and understand Caesar's Latin with increasing proficiency and confidence. The notes are very heavy at the beginning, but gradually thin. Relative beginners should likely start reading from the beginning of Book 1, while relatively advanced students should still get a workout by reading Book 5. One can move at one's individual pace, or a class could read selections of different types from different books. The first five books of the *Commentaries* are included here in their entirety, plus chapters 11–24 of Book 6 (the discussion of Gallic and German customs). No other student commentary on Caesar's *Commentaries on the Gallic War* offers such breadth of text with such depth of grammatical coverage.

A major strength of this book is the inclusion, immediately after the text and commentary, of a full-scale Latin grammar keyed to Caesarian usage (called the "Companion to Caesar"). Notes in the commentary often include or consist of numbers in italics: these numbers are references to the section in the Companion that explains the grammatical or historical feature in question. The opening of Book 2, for example, begins *Cum esset Caesar*, and one finds in the commentary "**esset:** *185c.*" If one is not confident in explaining the form *esset* in this sentence, one can turn to the Companion, section 185, part c, and read a one-sentence summary, with two examples quoted from Caesar, of circumstantial *cum*-clauses (the note also includes reference to the explanations of this topic in Allen and Greenough's *New Latin Grammar* [AG] and Bennett's *New Latin Grammar* [B]). If one does not need the help, then one need not consult the Companion. In the commentary for 2.1.4, to take another example, one finds "**ad conducendos homines:** 'for hiring men,' i.e., mercenary soldiers; *230.3.*" The phrase is translated (primarily to explain the sense of *conducendos*), the sense of *homines* is then glossed, and the reference to the Companion (*230.3*) points you to an explanation, with two examples quoted from Caesar, of the use of gerundives in the accusative after *ad* to express purpose (also with further references to Allen and Greenough and to Bennett). Combined with the comprehensive vocabulary at the back of the book, the commentary and Companion are intended to provide the student, *within this book*, with everything needed to understand the grammar of Caesar's Latin text.

A particular strength of this book is the effort it applies to the understanding of passages in indirect discourse, especially extended indirect discourse, of which Caesar is rather fond in these *Commentaries*. Where there seemed to be pedagogical value in doing so, passages of indirect discourse are printed in italics as a visual cue to the reader to recognize the different syntax of these passages. Immediately below passages of extended indirect discourse (e.g., in chapter 13 of Book 1) is a rendering of those passages in direct form, with all words that would differ in indirect discourse printed in italics. A reader may thus start with the direct form, then study the differences from the indirect form, or translate the indirect discourse as Caesar wrote it with recourse to the direct form whenever clarification is needed.

Also included in the Companion, after the survey of grammar and syntax (chapters 1–249), are discussions of the geography of Gaul (chapters 250–66) and the Roman military (chapters 267–311). The presentation of military matters is intended to introduce students to the vocabulary and practices that were fundamental to the methods and organization of the Roman army in Caesar's time, with specific reference to Caesar's narrative. Caesar assumes such knowledge, thus his readers need to be aware of it. It is advisable that students read the geographical and military portions of the Companion early in their reading of Caesar.

This is an avowedly old-fashioned book. It originally appeared in 1918 and, though revised, its basic approach to reading Caesar's Latin is retained from a century ago. But as a student and then as a teacher, I have found it very useful for its ability to clarify Caesar's Latin, and thus to give confidence and speed to committed Latin students. There are certainly other methods, and other commentaries, by which to teach Caesar, and not all students will take to the method of this one. But as classicists well know, the new need not replace the old, especially when the old possesses the comprehensive thoroughness that this commentary does.

The Career of Francis W. Kelsey and the Development of This Commentary

Francis Willey Kelsey was a renowned figure in classical studies in the early twentieth century. He served as Professor of Latin at the University of Michigan from 1889 until his death in 1927, and served as president of the American Philological Association in 1906–7. He also served as president of the Archaeological Institute of America from 1907–12, and he was at least as prominent as an archaeologist as a literary scholar. He became one of the first American experts on the city of Pompeii due to his English edition (translated from German) of August Mau's *Pompeii: Its Life and Art* in 1899 (jointly revised with Mau for a second edition in 1902). Under his aegis Michigan undertook major excavations and acquired much of its artifact collection and its papyri. At his death a museum of antiquities at Michigan was created, later named the Kelsey Museum of Archaeology. He taught, traveled, fundraised, excavated, and promoted classical subjects and sites ceaselessly, and the story of his life reveals much about the modes and institutions by which the study of classical antiquity developed in America.

His origins were modest, but his impressive industry steadily led him to greater responsibilities. From a small farm in upstate New York, he graduated as a distinguished Classics major from the University of Rochester in 1880 and was immediately hired, at age 22, to teach at Lake Forest University, a small Presbyterian liberal arts college thirty miles north of Chicago in Lake Forest, Illinois.

In the decade from 1882–92, hence mostly during his years at Lake Forest before he moved to the University of Michigan in 1889, Kelsey produced a series of classroom commentaries: Cicero, *De Senectute* and *De Amicitia* (1882), three books of Lucretius (1884), Caesar's *Gallic War* (1886), the first four books of Xenophon's *Anabasis* (1889, with Andreas C. Zenos), *Selections from Ovid* (1891), *Select Orations and Letters of Cicero* (1892). All were designed with the immediate pedagogical needs of the day in mind but are still serviceable today. Kelsey revised these commentaries in updated editions for the rest of his career, above all the Caesar, which was the most successful and appeared in twenty-one editions up through 1927. In 1918, Kelsey produced a second school text of Caesar that abridged some sections of the *Gallic War* (the end of Book 5 and parts of Books 6 and 7) but added selections from the *Civil War* and a "Companion to Caesar." The Companion consists of four sections. The first, and by far the longest, is entitled "Essentials of Latin Grammar for the Study of Caesar," illustrated with examples from Caesar's text. The remaining three sections—"Gaius Julius Caesar," "The Geography of Caesar's Commentaries," and "The Roman Art of War in Caesar's Time"—are expanded from the introduction to his unabridged edition of the *Gallic War* (in its nineteenth edition in 1909).[19] Because of the pedagogical value of this Companion, it is Kelsey's 1918 edition (but here trimmed down to Books 1–5 and 6.11–24 of the *Gallic War*) that is the basis of this revised edition.[20]

Kelsey took the topic of pedagogy as seriously as other branches of his research, and he helped found the Michigan Classical Conference in 1895. The annual spring meetings of the group, attended by high school and college teachers from around the state, focused extensively on teaching. Some of the panels and essays written and delivered for these conferences were later edited and published by Kelsey in 1911 (revised edition, 1927) under the title *Latin and Greek in American Education*. The volume collects essays about the relevance of classical studies to medicine, engineer-

19   Pedley 2012 is the definitive biography of Kelsey. For the development of Kelsey's Caesar commentaries, see Pedley 2012: 28–31 and 236–37.
20   I have also trimmed out of this revised edition the section of the Companion devoted to the life of Caesar (chapters 244–280 in the 1918 edition).

ing, law, theology, and practical affairs, written both by academics and by successful members of each profession. Kelsey introduced the volume by advocating for a greater place for the study of Latin and Greek in American education, since he recognized even then the need for classical studies to assert its value. "In not a few institutions," he writes, "the idea of a 'liberal education' in the old sense is almost lost sight of; and as students elect their studies with a view to future utility, where Latin and Greek are not required they tend to be taken in college chiefly by those who purpose to become teachers." He then commences to assert the utility of Latin and Greek under several headings. Some of his arguments are too rooted in the culture of their time to be very compelling today, but others make a more timeless appeal to the higher value of learning Latin as a system of thought and expression. "As an instrument of training in the essentials of a working method," Kelsey declares, "no modern language and no science is the equal of Latin, either in the number and variety of mental processes which may be stimulated with a minimum of expenditure of effort, or in the ease and accuracy with which the results of those processes may be checked up, errors of observation or inference detected, and corrections made." Moreover, "whatever contributes to the student's grasp of the essential elements of vocabulary and structure adds to his power over language as an instrument of thought, and so to his effectiveness as a doer of the day's work." Such are the ideals that shaped the design of his school commentaries.[21]

In the opening pages of his 1918 Caesar commentary, however, Kelsey says little about his pedagogical principles.[22] What animates him far more, in both his Preface and his Introduction, is the context of World War I. The second paragraph of his Preface deserves to be quoted in full:

> America's entrance into the world conflict has aroused universal interest in warfare. Viewed in the light of the great struggle, Caesar's *Commentaries* take on a new interest. Modern armies have clashed on the battlefields of the Gallic War; modern camps are laid out in a way to suggest the manner of the Romans. The strategy of Joffre and of Hindenburg finds its prototype in that of Caesar, and modern armor, especially in types of helmet and breastplate, strikingly resembles that of ancient times. In countless ways—even to Caesar's statement, "Of all these the bravest are the Belgians"—the World War reproduces on a larger scale the campaigns of Caesar.

Kelsey then expands on these claims for the first two-thirds of his introduction. His first section compares "Warfare Ancient and Modern," and he provides specific discussions (with photographs and/or reconstructions) of "wolf-holes" at Alesia and Ypres, of trench digging tools, of the Roman pike and the contemporary hand grenade (which Americans were more accurate at throwing than Europeans "by reason of skill acquired in playing baseball"), plus several more. The second section, entitled "Caesar's Commentaries and the Great War," fills seven pages with specific points of contact between the two conflicts, ranging from geographical features to military actions. The most poignant comparison reveals the very similar shape and style of an excavated Gallic helmet and a contemporary French helmet, under which the caption reads: "This helmet was worn by Richard N. Hall, a graduate of the Ann Arbor high school and of Dartmouth College, who served in a volunteer ambulance corps

21   Kelsey 1927: 14, 19, 22–23. For the intellectual context behind Kelsey's perspective, see Winterer 2002: 110–57. Wyke 2012: 21–46 and 76–80 seeks to puncture the airy idealism behind the teaching of Caesar in Kelsey's era.

22   The first paragraph of the Preface reads: "This edition aims to interest the High School pupil in Caesar, to assist him by notes adapted to his stage of progress, and to facilitate his accomplishment of the second year of Latin work with appreciation of and respect for the subject, and with a firm foundation for further study." By comparison, in Kelsey's unabridged edition of the *Gallic War* he included two pages after the end of the notes (pages 435–36 in the nineteenth edition of 1909) where he offers his student-readers specific advice on how to read Caesar's Latin and sets a very high standard for what reading well requires (his standard would be just as admirable today). He begins: "The student of Caesar should give his attention to three things: the thought, translation, and explanation. A page of Caesar is not a mere exercise in parsing, contrived to discipline the mind and tax the patience of the student. It is a fragment of the world's literature."

in France and was killed by a shell on Christmas Eve, 1915."[23] To the high school student of 1918, Caesar's *Gallic War* had a new and terrible relevance.

The Latin Text

This edition is for students and is not a scholarly edition of Caesar's Latin text, but in the process of revising Kelsey's commentary I have also sought to update his text. I have compared Kelsey's text against the most recent scholarly edition, that by Wolfgang Hering (Teubner, 1987), and I have adopted the readings of Hering that I list below. Changes limited to punctuation are not noted. I adopted Hering's text when I felt that Latinity or sense were improved in ways that were relevant to the student reader for whom this edition is designed. Variants primarily involving word order or the choice between two close equivalents equally present in the tradition usually did not cause me to change Kelsey's text. Nor have I attempted to adjudicate about questions of orthography (e.g., *Garumna* vs. *Garunna* in I.1.2 or *eis* vs. *iis* in I.2.3 or *afficiebantur* vs. *adficiebantur* in I.2.4 or *Aeduo* vs. *Haeduo* in I.3.5 or *faciundi* vs. *faciendi* in I.7.5); in all such cases, I have simply retained Kelsey's text. For V.53–58, which was not included in Kelsey 1918, I have drawn text and notes from Kelsey 1909.

	Kelsey 1918	*Stem 2017 (with Hering 1987)*
I.11.4	quo Aedui, Ambarri	Ambarri
I.12.2	quartam fere	quartam vero
I.16.3	minus uti	uti minus
I.16.6	posset	possit
I.20.2	nec quemquam	neque quemquam
I.24.1	subducit	subduxit
I.25.5	passuum spatio, eo	passuum, eo
I.27.4	conferuntur, circiter	conferuntur nocte intermissa, circiter
I.31.1	fuerant	adfuerant
I.31.12	Admagetobrigae	ad Magetobrigam
I.35.2	dicendum	discendum
I.40.5	videbatur	videretur
I.40.6	inermos	inermes
I.40.7	superarint	superassent
I.41.1	innata est	inlata est
I.41.3	uti Caesari	uti per eos Caesari
I.41.4	ex Gallis	ex aliis
I.42.1	existimare	existimaret
I.43.1	a castris Ariovisti et Caesaris	a castris utriusque
I.43.4	pro magnis	a Romanis pro maximis
I.44.5	atque	idque
I.50.1	instruxit hostibus	instruxit hostibusque
I.51.3	in proelium	ad proelium
I.53.4	utraeque in ea fuga perierunt	utraque in ea fuga periit
II.2.1	inita	ineunte
II.2.6	comparata	provisa
II.4.5	sexaginta	milia sexaginta
II.5.6	munire	muniri
II.6.4	nuntium	nuntios

23   Kelsey 1918: xvii–xviii (Figures 10 and 11). See also Pedley 2012: 250–53 for the context of Hall's death and Kelsey's involvement in creating a Belgian relief fund during the war.

II.8.3	frontem	fronte
II.10.4	convenirent	convenire
II.11.3	his	eique
II.19.5	porrecta	prospectus ac
II.19.6	ut intra	ita ut intra
II.25.1	deserto loco	desertores
III.6.4	viderat	videbat
III.7.1	ita inita	inita
III.9.3	ad omnes	apud omnes
III.13.9	cum saevire ventus coepisset et se vento	cum se vento
III.15.1	circumsteterant	circumsisterent
III.15.4	opportuna	opportunitati
III.17.2	exercitum magnasque copias	exercitum
III.17.4	sevocabat	revocabat
III.20.1	quae, ut ante dictum est, tertia pars Galliae est	quae pars, ut ante dictum est, et regionum latitudine et multitudine hominum ex tertia parte Galliae est aestimanda
III.23.4	auctoritate	alacritate
III.26.1	velit	vellet
III.26.2	intritae	integrae
III.28.1	coeperunt	instituerunt
III.29.3	Lexoviisque, reliquis	Lexoviis reliquisque
IV.1.1	magna cum multitudine	magna multitudine
IV.1.4	ex finibus	suis ex finibus
IV.2.3	assuefecerunt	assuefaciunt
IV.3.1	posse	potuisse
IV.3.2	C	DC
IV.7.3	consuetudo	consuetudo haec
IV.7.5	possent	possint
IV.8.3	se Ubiis imperaturum	se ab Ubiis impetraturum
IV.9.3	arbitratur	arbitrabatur
IV.13.4	opportunissima	opportunissime
IV.14.2	perturbantur	perturbabantur
IV.16.6	ad auxilium	auxilium
IV.17.10	naves	trabes
IV.18.3	respondit	respondet
IV.22.3	quod	quicquid
IV.22.3	quaestori	id quaestori
IV.23.1	solvit	naves solvit
IV.23.3	montibus angustis	montium angustiis
IV.23.5	maxime ut	maximeque ut
IV.25.3	Atque	At
IV.25.6	proximis primi	proximis
IV.28.2	magno suo cum periculo	magno cum periculo
IV.30.1	ad Caesarem	ad ea, quae iusserat Caesar, facienda
IV.33.2	paulatim	paulum
IV.38.2	fuerant usi	erant usi
IV.38.2	pervenerunt	venerunt

V.3.5	familiaritate	auctoritate
V.7.1	tribuebat	tribuerat
V.8.1	rem frumentariam	rei frumentariae
V.8.2	reliquerat, ad solis occasum	relinquebat, solis occasu
V.11.4	posset	possit
V.13.2	Hibernia	Hibernia insula
V.13.3	subiectae	obiectae
V.13.3	sub bruma	sub brumam
V.14.3–5	[omitted]	atque omni parte … deducta est
V.16.3	[omitted]	equestris autem … periculum inferebat
V.19.2	effuderat, omnibus viis	effunderet, omnes viis notis
V.24.3	M. Crassum	M. Crassum quaestorem
V.25.4	cognoverat	cognoverit
V.25.5	quaestoreque	quaestoribusque
V.26.2	oppugnatum	oppugnanda
V.29.7	habere	haberet
V.34.2	[omitted]	erant et numero et virtute pugnandi pares
V.36.2	respondit	respondet
V.38.1	intermittit	iter intermittit
V.39.2	Huic	Hic
V.41.1	Tunc	Tum
V.42.3	esset	sunt
V.44.6	progrediendi	regrediendi
V.46.4	posset	possit
V.52.1	etiam	enim
V.53.1	oreretur [Kelsey 1909]	oriretur
V.54.4	voluntatum [Kelsey 1909]	voluntatis
V.56.2	consuerunt [Kelsey 1909]	coguntur
V.58.4	proterritis [Kelsey 1909]	perterritis
V.58.4	peterent [Kelsey 1909]	petant
VI.13.2	dicant nobilibus; quibus in hos	dicant; nobilibus in hos
VI.16.5	defecit	deficit
VI.21.4–5	[omitted]	Qui diutissime … corporis parte nuda
VI.23.9	sanctos	sanctosque
VI.24.4	qua ante, Germani	qua Germani

Outline of Books 1–5 and 6.11–24

Book I: 58 BC

1–29: Campaign against the Helvetii
    1–6: Events prior to Caesar's arrival; Helvetii decide to migrate
        1: The three parts of Gaul
        2–4: Rise and fall of Orgetorix, who proposes the migration
        5: Preparations for departure
        6: Determination of route; departure date of March 28
    7–12: Escalation into armed conflict
        7–8: Caesar hastens to Gaul, has one legion, denies the Helvetii passage
        9: Helvetii negotiate to travel through the territory of the Sequani
        10: Caesar recruits two legions, mobilizes three, sets out to stop the Helvetii
        11: Aedui and Allobroges ask for Roman aid against Helvetians
        12: Caesar destroys one quarter of the Helvetian force at the Arar River
    13–14: Helvetian embassy; speeches of Divico and Caesar
    15–22: Obstacles for Caesar as he pursues the Helvetians
        15: Small defeat for the Roman cavalry
        16: Caesar complains that the Aedui have not delivered promised grain
        17–18: Caesar learns of the duplicitous conduct of Dumnorix the Aeduan
        19–20: Caesar confronts Dumnorix but spares him for the sake of his loyal brother
        21–22: Miscommunication thwarts Caesar's attempt at a surprise attack
    23–29: Decisive defeat of the Helvetians
        23–24: Helvetians offer battle, Caesar forms his line
        25–26: Helvetians fight bravely but are completely defeated
        27–28: Caesar negotiates peace terms with the survivors; returns them home
        29: 368,000 Helvetians set out, 110,000 returned home
30–54: Campaign against Ariovistus and the Germans
    30–32: Caesar learns from the Aedui of the arrival and dominance of the Germans
    33–36: Initial negotiations with Ariovistus
        33–34: Caesar decides to intervene, asks Ariovistus to meet, is rebuffed
        35–36: Caesar makes demands by envoy, Ariovistus refuses to comply
    37–41: A near mutiny
        37–38: Caesar spurred to act, marches to Vesontio
        39: Panic and the threat of mutiny in the Roman camp
        40: Caesar defends his actions publicly, addresses fears
        41: Enthusiasm restored, the army sets out for Ariovistus
    42–47: Second round of negotiations with Ariovistus
        42: Conditions determined for a meeting
        43: Caesar relates his good faith, makes demands as before
        44: Ariovistus defends himself and his claim to his part of Gaul
        45: Caesar rebuts Ariovistus' claims to Gaul
        46–47: German misbehavior at the meeting, imprisoning of Roman envoys
    48–54: Decisive defeat of the Germans
        48–50: Placement of the opposing camps; Caesar offers battle
        51–52: Caesar provokes Germans to battle
        53: Germans defeated, Ariovistus escapes, envoys recovered
        54: Caesar ends the season with two notable victories

Book II: 57 BC

1–15: Campaign against the Belgae
    1–2: Caesar learns of preparations to fight the Romans, enlists two new legions
    3: His quick arrival causes the surrender of the Remi
    4: The Remi report on Belgic leaders and numbers

Book III: 57 and 56 BC

Book IV: 55 BC

32–35: Indecisive fighting
36: Caesar sails back to Gaul
37–38: The Morini attack some Romans after landing; a 20–day thanksgiving decreed

Book V: 54 BC

1–23: Second expedition into Britain
    1–7: Preliminaries
        1–2: Preparation of new fleet; Caesar's quieting of hostilities near Illyricum
        2–4: Caesar visits the Treveri, backs Cingetorix over Indutiomarus as their leader
        5: Fleet ready to depart to Britain
        6–7: Resistance of Dumnorix, who is pursued and killed
    8: Successful crossing
    9: First encounter with the British, capture of one of their strongholds
    10–11: Storm damages Roman fleet; Caesar beaches fleet and fortifies a new camp
    12–14: Ethnography and geography of Britain
    15–17: Skirmishes won by the Romans despite their shortage of cavalry
    18–21: Caesar advances, captures another stronghold
    22: Romans defend the fleet and camp from attack; Cassivellaunus seeks terms
    23: Caesar sails back to Gaul
24–58: Attacks of the Gauls upon Caesar's winter camps
    24–25: Distribution of legions into winter camps
    26–37: Attack of the Eburones on the camp of Sabinus and Cotta
        26–27: Initial attack; Ambiorix explains his actions and offers safe passage
        28–31: Dissension between Sabinus and Cotta; Sabinus prevails; legion sets out
        32–35: Romans ambushed and surrounded
        36–37: Deaths of Sabinus and Cotta; entire force destroyed
    38–45: Attack of the Nervii and Atuatuci on the camp of Quintus Cicero
        38: Ambiorix rouses the Nervii and Atuatuci with the story of his victory
        39–40: Initial attack; Romans fortify their camp
        41: Gauls explain themselves, offer Romans free passage; Cicero rejects offer
        42–43: Attack and siege intensifies; camp set afire
        44: Rivalry of Vorenus and Pullo
        45: News reaches Caesar of Cicero's situation
    46–52: Caesar relieves Cicero
        46–48: Caesar gathers two legions, marches to Cicero's aid
        49–51: Caesar draws the Gallic force onto himself, routs them
        52: Caesar arrives at Cicero's camp, dispenses praise and blame
    53–58: Attack of the Treveri on the camp of Labienus
        53–54: Caesar does his best to prevent further uprisings, partially successful
        55–56: Indutiomarus and the Treveri attack the camp of Labienus
        57–58: Indutiomarus defeated and killed; Gallic forces disperse

Book VI.11–24

11–20: Customs of the Gauls
    11: Gaul dominated by parties and factions
    12: Aedui and Sequani the leading peoples, but Remi rise in place of Sequani
    13–15: Druids and Knights, the two most important types of citizens
    16–17: Religious beliefs and customs
    18–19: Customs of time reckoning, family, marriage, burial
    20: Management of information
21–23: Customs of the Germans
    21–22: Private and domestic practices
    23: War and politics
24: Gauls and Germans compared

Bibliography

Adcock, F. E. 1956. *Caesar As Man of Letters*. Cambridge: Cambridge University Press.

Barlow, Jonathan. 1998. "Noble Gauls and Their Other in Caesar's Propaganda." In Welch and Powell 1998: 139–70.

Batstone, William W., and Cynthia Damon. 2006. *Caesar's Civil War*. Oxford: Oxford University Press.

Brown, Robert D. 1999. "Two Caesarian Battle-Descriptions: A Study in Contrast." *Classical Journal* 94: 329–57.

Brown, Robert D. 2004. "*Virtus Consili Expers*: An Interpretation of the Centurions' Contest in Caesar, *De Bello Gallico* 5.44." *Hermes* 132: 292–308.

Brown, Robert D. 2013. "Caesar's Description of Bridging the Rhine (*Bellum Gallicum* 4.16–19): A Literary Analysis." *Classical Philology* 108: 41–53.

Collins, John H. 1972. "Caesar as Political Propagandist." *Aufstieg und Niedergang der Römischen Welt* I.1: 922–66.

Conte, Gian Biagio. 1994. *Latin Literature: A History*. Baltimore: Johns Hopkins University Press.

Damon, Cynthia. 2007. "Rhetoric and Historiography." In W. Dominik and J. Hall, eds., *A Companion to Roman Rhetoric*. Oxford: Blackwell. 439–50.

Erickson, Brice. 2002. "Falling Masts, Rising Masters: The Ethnography of Virtue in Caesar's Account of the Veneti." *American Journal of Philology* 123: 601–22.

Fantham, Elaine. 2009. "Caesar as an Intellectual." In Griffin 2009: 141–56.

Garcea, Alessandro. 2012. *Caesar's De Analogia: Edition, Translation, and Commentary*. Oxford: Oxford University Press.

Gelzer, Matthias. 1968. *Caesar: Politician and Statesman*. Oxford: Blackwell.

Gilliver, Kate. 2002. *Caesar's Gallic Wars*. Oxford: Osprey Publishing.

Goldsworthy, Adrian. 1996. *The Roman Army at War: 100 BC – AD 200*. Oxford: Oxford University Press.

Goldsworthy, Adrian. 1998. "Instinctive Genius: The Depiction of Caesar the General." In Welch and Powell 1998: 193–219.

Goldsworthy, Adrian. 2006. *Caesar: Life of a Colossus*. New Haven: Yale University Press.

Gotoff, H. C. 1984. "Towards a Practical Criticism of Caesar's Prose Style." *Illinois Classical Studies* 9: 1–18.

Griffin, Miriam, ed. 2009. *A Companion to Julius Caesar*. Oxford: Wiley–Blackwell.

Grillo, Luca. 2011. "*Scribam ipse de me*: The Personality of the Narrator in Caesar's *Bellum Civile*." *American Journal of Philology* 132: 243–71.

Grillo, Luca. 2012. *The Art of Caesar's Bellum Civile: Literature, Ideology, and Community*. Cambridge: Cambridge University Press.

Grillo, Luca. 2015. *Cicero's De Provinciis Consularibus Oratio: Introduction and Commentary*. Oxford: Oxford University Press.

Grillo, Luca, and Christopher Krebs, eds. 2017. *The Cambridge Companion to the Writings of Julius Caesar*. Cambridge: Cambridge University Press.

Hall, Lindsay G. H. 1998. "*Ratio* and *Romanitas* in the *Bellum Gallicum*." In Welch and Powell 1998: 11–43.

Hering, Wolfgang, ed. 1987. *C. Iulii Caesaris Commentarii Rerum Gestarum, Vol. I: Bellum Gallicum*. Leipzig: B. G. Teubner.

Holmes, T. Rice. 1907. *Ancient Britain and the Invasions of Julius Caesar*. Oxford: Oxford University Press.

Holmes, T. Rice. 1914. *C. Iuli Caesaris Commentarii Rerum in Gallia Gestarum*. Oxford: Oxford University Press.

Holmes, T. Rice. 1931. *Caesar's Conquest of Gaul*. 2nd ed. (1st ed. 1911). Oxford: Oxford University Press.

Hurley, Donna W. 2011. *Suetonius: The Caesars, Translated with Introductions and Notes*. Indianapolis: Hackett.

James, Bryan. 2000. "Speech, Authority, and Experience in Caesar, *Bellum Gallicum* 1.39–41." *Hermes* 128: 54–64.

Kelsey, Francis W. 1905. "The Title of Caesar's Work on the Gallic and Civil Wars." *Transactions of the American Philological Association* 36: 211–38.

Kelsey, Francis W. 1909. *C. Iulii Caesaris Commentarii Rerum Gestarum; Caesar's Gallic War, with an Introduction, Notes, and Vocabulary.* 19th edition (1st ed. 1886). Boston: Allyn and Bacon.

Kelsey, Francis W. 1918. *C. Iulii Caesaris Commentarii Rerum Gestarum; Caesar's Commentaries: The Gallic War, Books I-IV, with selections from Books V-VII and from the Civil War; with an Introduction, Notes, a Companion to Caesar and a Vocabulary.* Boston: Allyn and Bacon.

Kelsey, Francis W. 1927. *Latin and Greek in American Education: With Symposia on the Value of Humanistic Studies.* Revised edition (1st ed. 1911). New York: Macmillan.

Kraus, Christina S. 2005. "Hair, Hegemony, and Historiography: Caesar's Style and Its Earliest Critics." In T. Reinhardt, M. Lapidge, and J. N. Adams, eds., *Aspects of the Language of Latin Prose.* Proceedings of the British Academy 129. Oxford: Oxford University Press. 97–115.

Kraus, Christina S. 2009. "*Bellum Gallicum.*" In Griffin 2009: 159–74.

Krebs, Christopher B. 2006. "Imaginary Geography in Caesar's *Bellum Gallicum.*" *American Journal of Philology* 127: 111–36.

Krebs, Christopher B. 2013. "Caesar, Lucretius, and the Dates of *De Rerum Natura* and the *Commentarii.*" CQ 63: 772–79.

Lendon, J. E. 1999. "The Rhetoric of Combat: Greek Military Theory and Roman Culture in Julius Caesar's Battle Descriptions." *Classical Antiquity* 18: 273–329.

Lendon, J. E. 2015. "Julius Caesar, Thinking About Battle and Foreign Relations." *Histos* 9: 1–28.

Marincola, John. 1997. *Authority and Tradition in Ancient Historiography.* Cambridge: Cambridge University Press.

Osgood, Josiah. 2009. "The Pen and the Sword: Writing and Conquest in Caesar's Gaul." *Classical Antiquity* 28: 328–58.

Pedley, John Griffiths. 2012. *The Life and Work of Francis Willey Kelsey: Archaeology, Antiquity, and the Arts.* Ann Arbor: University of Michigan Press.

Pelling, Christopher. 1984. "Plutarch on the Gallic Wars." *Classical Bulletin* 60: 88–103.

Pelling, Christopher. 2006. "Judging Julius Caesar." In Maria Wyke, ed., *Julius Caesar in Western Culture.* Oxford: Blackwell. 3–26.

Pelling, Christopher. 2011. *Plutarch: Caesar, Translated with an Introduction and Commentary.* Oxford: Oxford University Press.

Pelling, Christopher. 2013. "Xenophon's and Caesar's Third-Person Narratives – Or Are They?" In A. Marmodoro and J. Hill, eds., *The Author's Voice in Classical and Late Antiquity.* Oxford: Oxford University Press. 39–73.

Potter, David. 2010. "Caesar and the Helvetians." In G. G. Fagan and M. Trundle, eds., *New Perspectives on Ancient Warfare.* Leiden: Brill. 305–29.

Powell, Anton. 1998. "Julius Caesar and the Presentation of Massacre." In Welch and Powell 1998: 111–37.

Quinn, Betty Nye. 1982. "Caesar." In T. J. Luce, ed., *Ancient Writers: Greece and Rome, Volume I: Homer to Caesar.* New York: Scribners. 583–99.

Rawlings, Louis. 1998. "Caesar's Portrayal of Gauls as Warriors." In Welch and Powell 1998: 171–92.

Riggsby, Andrew M. 2006. *Caesar in Gaul and Rome: War in Words.* Austin: University of Texas Press.

Schadee, Hester. 2008. "Caesar's Construction of Northern Europe: Inquiry, Contact and Corruption in *De Bello Gallico.*" *Classical Quarterly* 58: 158–80.

Seager, Robin. 2003. "Caesar and Gaul: Some Perspectives on the *Bellum Gallicum.*" In F. Cairns and E. Fan-tham, eds., *Caesar Against Liberty? Perspectives on His Autocracy.* Cambridge: Francis Cairns. 19–34.

Vasaly, Ann. 2009. "Characterization and Complexity: Caesar, Sallust, and Livy." In A. Feldherr, ed., *The Cambridge Companion to the Roman Historians.* Cambridge: Cambridge University Press. 245–60.

Welch, Kathryn. 1998. "Caesar and His Officers in the Gallic War Commentaries." In Welch and Powell 1998: 85–110.

Welch, Kathryn, and Anton Powell, eds. 1998. *Julius Caesar as Artful Reporter: The War Commentaries as Political Instruments.* Swansea: Classical Press of Wales.

Williams, J. H. C. 2001. *Beyond the Rubicon: Romans and Gauls in Republican Italy.* Oxford: Oxford University Press.

Williams, Mark F. 1985. "Caesar's Bibracte Narrative and the Aims of Caesarian Style." *Illinois Classical Studies* 10: 215–26.

Winterer, Caroline. 2002. *The Culture of Classicism: Ancient Greece and Rome in American Intellectual Life, 1780–1910.* Baltimore: Johns Hopkins University Press.

Wiseman, T. P. 1998. "The Publication of *De Bello Gallico.*" In Welch and Powell 1998: 1–9.

Woolf, Greg. 1998. *Becoming Roman: The Origins of Provincial Civilization in Gaul.* Cambridge: Cambridge University Press.

Wyke, Maria. 2008. *Caesar: A Life in Western Culture.* Chicago: University of Chicago Press.

Wyke, Maria. 2012. *Caesar in the USA.* Berkeley and Los Angeles: University of California Press.

C. Iulii Caesaris
Commentarii Rerum Gestarum
De Bello Gallico

Julius Caesar
Commentaries on the Gallic War

Books I-V and VI.11-24

I.1: Geography of Gaul

1. 1 Gallia est omnis divisa in partes tres, quarum unam incolunt Belgae, aliam Aquitani, tertiam, qui ipsorum lingua Celtae, nostra Galli appellantur. 2 Hi omnes lingua, institutis, legibus inter se differunt. Gallos ab Aquitanis Garumna flumen, a Belgis Matrona et Sequana dividit. 3 Horum omnium fortissimi sunt Belgae, propterea quod a cultu atque humanitate provinciae longissime absunt, minimeque ad eos mercatores saepe commeant atque ea, quae ad effeminandos animos pertinent, important, proximique sunt Germanis, qui trans Rhenum incolunt, quibuscum continenter bellum gerunt. 4 Qua de causa Helvetii quoque reliquos Gallos virtute praecedunt, quod fere cotidianis proeliis cum Germanis contendunt, cum aut suis finibus eos prohibent aut ipsi in eorum finibus bellum gerunt.

[5 Eorum una pars, quam Gallos obtinere dictum est, initium capit a flumine Rhodano; continetur Garumna flumine, Oceano, finibus Belgarum; attingit etiam ab Sequanis et Helvetiis flumen Rhenum; vergit ad septentriones. 6 Belgae ab extremis Galliae finibus oriuntur; pertinent ad inferiorem partem fluminis Rheni; spectant in septentrionem et orientem solem. 7 Aquitania a Garumna flumine ad Pyrenaeos montes et eam partem Oceani, quae est ad Hispaniam, pertinet; spectat inter occasum solis et septentriones.]

1 **Gallia:** *2a; 255.* **Gallia omnis:** 'Gaul as a whole,' contrasted with Gaul in the narrower sense, i.e., Celtic Gaul; Celtic Gaul also is often called *Gallia; 256b.* **omnis:** *25a; 80b.* **divisa:** 'divided,' the perfect passive participle of *divido* used as a predicate adjective; *148c.* **in:** 'into'; *124a.* **partes:** *17b.* **tres:** *37b; 245c.* **quarum:** 'of which'; *47.* Why genitive? *97a.* **unam:** sc. *partem,* 'one (part)'; *23a.* Look up the three 'parts' of Gaul on Map Gallia. **incolunt:** 'inhabit'; *55.* **Belgae:** *19e; 256a.* **aliam** (partem): 'another (part),' less precise than *alteram* (*partem*), 'a second (part),' which might have been used; *23a.* **Aquitani:** sc. *incolunt; 89a.* **tertiam, qui:** = *tertiam partem ei incolunt, qui,* 'those inhabit a third part who'; *164a.* **ipsorum:** 'their own'; lit. 'of themselves'; *46.* **ipsorum lingua:** 'in their own language'; *131a.* **Celtae:** sc. *appellantur; 88; 256b.* **nostra:** *nostra lingua* = Latin; *157c.* **appellantur:** *53.*

2 **lingua, institutis, legibus:** 'in respect to language, institutions, and laws'; *142a; 234a.* **inter se:** 'from one another'; *159.* **differunt:** *69b.* **Garumna:** sc. *dividit,* 'separates.' **flumen:** *12e; 91a.* Derivation? *74d.* **Matrona:** *261.* **dividit:** singular number; why? *173a.*

3 **Horum:** *42b; 97a.* **fortissimi:** 'the bravest'; *27a.* **propterea:** adverb ('on this account') closely connected with *quod* ('namely that'), the two words together being translated 'because.' Three reasons are given for the bravery of the Belgians; the *–que* of *minimeque* attaches the second reason and the *–que* of *proximique* the third; *233b.* **cultu:** 'mode of life,' referring to the outward appearances of civilization; *20.* **atque:** *233a.* **humanitate:** 'refinement' in intellectual interests and in feeling; *10f.* **provinciae:** 'of the Province'; *94a; 259.* **longissime absunt:** 'are furthest removed'; *34a; 66a; 183a.* **minime . . . saepe:** 'very rarely'; lit. 'least often'; *35.* **eos:** *44; 160b.* **mercatores:** 'traders' from the Province, especially from Massilia, followed the course of the Rhone, the Saône, and the Loire, so that naturally they did not often go so far north as the Belgian country. **commeant:** 'make their way to', lit. 'go and come'; *53.* **ea:** 'those things,' object of *important; 160c.* Caesar seems to have had in mind particularly the importation of wine (II.15, IV.2). **ad effeminandos animos:** 'to weaken the courage', lit. 'to make minds effeminate'; *230.3.* **animos:** *6a; 92a.* **pertinent:** 'tend'; *54.* **important:** *53; 175a.* **proximique sunt:** 'and they are nearest'; *33; 233b.* **Germanis:** why dat.? *108a.* **trans:** here 'on the other side of'; *122a.* **quibuscum:** *125c.* **continenter:** 'continually'. **bellum gerunt:** 'they wage war'; *6a; 55.*

4 **Qua de causa:** 'For this reason'; *167.* **quoque:** 'also.' **reliquos:** 'the rest of the'; *171a.* **Gallos:** only the inhabitants of Celtic Gaul are meant; no comparison with the Belgians and the Aquitanians is implied; *113a.* **virtute:** 'in valor'; *142a.* **praecedunt:** 'excel'; *113b.* **fere cotidianis proeliis:** 'in (lit. 'by means of') almost daily battles'; *131a.* **cum:** the preposition *cum* is distinguished from the conjunction *cum* by the sense and the connection. **contendunt:** 'contend'; *55.* **cum:** *185a.* **aut . . . aut:** 'either . . . or'; *235b.* **suis:** 'their own,' referring to the Helvetians; *158a.* **finibus:** 'country'; lit. 'boundaries'; *14b; 127a.* **eos:** translate as if *Germanos,* 'the Germans', in order to avoid using 'them' and 'they' with reference to two different peoples in the same sentence. **prohibent:** 'are keeping (the Germans) out.' **ipsi:** 'themselves'; *162a.* There is no detailed record of these border raids. **eorum:** translate as if *Germanorum.* **finibus:** *124a.*

5 **Eorum . . . septentriones:** there is reason for believing that this passage (I.1.5-7) was not written by Caesar but was added after his time by someone who thought it worthwhile to give with greater detail the boundaries

of the three divisions of Gaul mentioned by Caesar at the beginning of the chapter. When it is omitted, the transition from the statement about the Helvetians in I.1.4 to the activities of the Helvetian leader Orgetorix at I.2.1 becomes easy and natural. Translation: 5 'One part of Gaul taken as a whole (lit. 'of them'), which it has been said the Celts occupy, takes its beginning at the river Rhone; it is bounded by the Garumna (*Garonne*) river, the Ocean, and the territory of the Belgians; it also reaches from the Sequanians and Helvetians to the river Rhine; it lies to the north. 6 (The country of) the Belgians commences at the most distant borders of (Celtic) Gaul and extends to the lower part of the river Rhine; it faces north and east. 7 Aquitania extends from the Garumna (*Garonne*) river to the Pyrenees mountains and that part of the Ocean which is near to Spain; it faces northwest.'

I.2-29: Campaign against the Helvetii

Orgetorix persuades his countrymen to migrate.

2. 1 Apud Helvetios longe nobilissimus fuit et ditissimus Orgetorix. Is, M. Messala, M. Pisone consulibus, regni cupiditate inductus coniurationem nobilitatis fecit et civitati persuasit ut de finibus suis cum omnibus copiis exirent; 2 *perfacile esse, cum virtute omnibus praestarent, totius Galliae imperio potiri.* 3 Id hoc facilius eis persuasit, quod undique loci natura Helvetii continentur: una ex parte flumine Rheno, latissimo atque altissimo, qui agrum Helvetium a Germanis dividit; altera ex parte monte Iura altissimo, qui est inter Sequanos et Helvetios; tertia, lacu Lemanno et flumine Rhodano, qui provinciam nostram ab Helvetiis dividit. 4 His rebus fiebat ut et minus late vagarentur et minus facile finitimis bellum inferre possent; qua ex parte homines bellandi cupidi, magno dolore afficiebantur. 5 Pro multitudine autem hominum et pro gloria belli atque fortitudinis angustos se fines habere arbitrabantur, qui in longitudinem milia passuum CCXL, in latitudinem CLXXX patebant.

1 **Apud:** *122a.* **longe:** *153b.* **nobilissimus:** 'highest in rank'; *27a.* **ditissimus:** *31.* **Orgetorix:** *10c; 245a.* **M. Messala, M. Pisone consulibus:** 'in the year that Marcus Messala and Marcus Piso were consuls,' lit. 'with M. Messala and M. Piso (being) consuls,' i.e., what we would call 61 BC. This consular naming formula is the regular means for distinguishing the year in the Roman Republican calendar; *240a.* The phrase is an ablative absolute, which usually includes a noun and a participle in the ablative, but which can include two nouns (as here) or a noun and an adjective in the ablative, especially when the connection between the two ablatives is one of 'being'. In fact, classical Latin lacks a participle for the verb 'to be' (*esse*), thus an expression of 'being' has to be added when translating phrases like this ablative absolute; *144b1.* **M.:** = *Marco; 19a.* **regni:** 'for kingly power,' objective genitive; *6a; 102.* **cupiditate:** 'by a desire'; *10f; 135a.* **inductus:** '(having been) led on'; *148b; 226b.* **coniurationem:** 'conspiracy'; *12c.* **nobilitatis:** lit. 'of the nobility,' here regarded as a collective noun; in sense = 'among the nobles'; *10f; 92b; 98a.* **fecit:** *57b.* **civitati:** *10f; 105.* **ut . . . exirent:** 'to go out,' 'to migrate.' What kind of clause? *199a5.* **cum omnibus copiis:** 'with all (their) belongings'; *137a.* **exirent:** plural because *civitati,* '(his) state,' to which the unexpressed subject refers, is thought of as if it were *civibus,* 'the people of (his) state'; *68b; 173b; 238h.*

2 **perfacile . . . potiri:** indirect quotation (thus marked by italic type), dependent on the idea of saying in *persuasit; 212a; 212c5; 213b.* **perfacile esse:** '(saying) that it was exceedingly easy.' The subject of *esse* is *potiri,* 'to obtain possession of'; *222b.* Why is *perfacile* neuter? *148d.* **virtute:** *142a.* **omnibus:** *107a.* **praestarent:** *53; 184a.* **totius Galliae:** 'of the whole (of) Gaul'; *23; 102.* **imperio:** 'sovereignty.' Why ablative? *131c.* **potiri:** *60; 61a4.*

3 **Id:** acc.; 'that (course)'; *117a; 160c.* **hoc:** neuter ablative singular, 'because of this,' referring to what follows, as explained by *quod,* '(namely) because'; *135a; 161a.* **facilius:** 'the more easily'; *34a.* **eis:** *44; 105.* **undique:** 'on all sides.' **loci natura:** 'by natural features,' lit. 'by the nature of the place'; *131a.* **continentur:** 'are hemmed in'; why indicative? *183a.* **una ex parte:** 'on one side,' the north side; *126c.* **flumine:** *131a.* **latissimo:** 'very wide'; *153a.* **altissimo:** here 'very deep,' but in the next line 'very high.' **qui:** the antecedent is *Rheno; 163a.* **agrum:** here 'territory.' **a Germanis:** 'from (the territory of) the Germans'; *127c; 251.* **altera:** for *secunda,* 'second,' as often. **monte Iura:** 'by the Jura range'; *mons* refers sometimes to a single mountain, sometimes to a group or chain of mountains, or to a moderate elevation. **tertia:** sc. *ex parte.* **lacu:** *20b.* **Rhodano:** the part of the Rhone just below Geneva; see Map 1. **provinciam:** *259.* **nostram:** i.e., *Romanam; 157c.* **Helvetiis:** *251.* Caesar does not deem it necessary to give the boundary on the fourth or east side, in the Alps.

4 **His rebus:** 'Because of these conditions,' lit. 'these things'; *135a.* **fiebat:** 'it came about'; *70a.* **ut . . . possent:** subject of *fiebat; 203.1.* **et . . . et:** *233a.* **minus late vagarentur:** 'they were more restricted in their movements,' lit. 'wandered less broadly,' than they wished; *177a.* **minus:** *35.* **finitimis:** '(their) neighbors'; *107b; 154a.* **inferre:** *69b.* **possent:** *66b.* **qua ex parte:** 'and on that account,' *ex parte* is here used idiomatically and not in the same sense as just above in I.2.3; *167.* **homines:** in apposition to the subject of *afficiebantur,* '(being) men'; *12b;*

91b. bellandi: 'of waging war'; 53; 230.1. **cupidi:** 'fond (of)'; 22b. **afficiebantur:** 57b. **dolore:** 11d; 136b. 5**Pro:** 'In proportion to'; 125a. **multitudine hominum:** '(their) population'; how lit.? The number was 263,000 (I.29). **autem:** 236b. **gloria belli atque fortitudinis:** '(their) reputation for war (lit. 'of war') and for bravery'; 102. **angustos fines:** 'small (lit. 'narrow') territories'; 113a. **se habere:** 'that they had'; 178; 213a. **arbitrabantur:** 'they thought,' lit. 'were thinking'; 175a. **qui:** i.e., *fines*. **in longitudinem:** 'in length'; 76. **milia passuum:** 'miles.' Lengths of the Roman 'pace' and Roman 'mile'? 243. **milia:** 38a; 118a. **passuum:** 20b; 97a. **CCXL:** 36; 38b. **latitudinem:** 'breadth'; 81. **CLXXX:** *centum octoginta*, sc. *milia passuum*; 38b. As the actual distance across the Helvetian territory was about 80 Roman miles, it has been suggested that Caesar wrote LXXX, *octoginta*, which was changed to CLXXX by an error in copying. **patebant:** 'extended'; 54. The territory occupied by the Helvetians comprised close to the whole of the modern Swiss cantons of Vaud, Neuchâtel, Basel, Freiburg, Bern, Solothurn, and Aargau. At an earlier period the Helvetians had lived north of the Rhine, but they had been forced to the south side by the Germans.

They make preparations; Orgetorix forms a conspiracy.

3. 1 His rebus adducti et auctoritate Orgetorigis permoti constituerunt ea, quae ad proficiscendum pertinerent, comparare, iumentorum et carrorum quam maximum numerum coemere, sementes quam maximas facere, ut in itinere copia frumenti suppeteret, cum proximis civitatibus pacem et amicitiam confirmare. 2 Ad eas res conficiendas biennium sibi satis esse duxerunt; in tertium annum profectionem lege confirmant. 3 Ad eas res conficiendas Orgetorix deligitur. Is sibi legationem ad civitates suscepit. 4 In eo itinere persuadet Castico, Catamantaloedis filio, Sequano, cuius pater regnum in Sequanis multos annos obtinuerat et a senatu populi Romani amicus appellatus erat, ut regnum in civitate sua occuparet, quod pater ante habuerat; 5 itemque Dumnorigi Aeduo, fratri Diviciaci, qui eo tempore principatum in civitate obtinebat ac maxime plebi acceptus erat, ut idem conaretur, persuadet, eique filiam suam in matrimonium dat. 6 Perfacile factu esse illis probat conata perficere, propterea quod ipse suae civitatis imperium obtenturus esset; non esse dubium, quin totius Galliae plurimum Helvetii possent; se suis copiis suoque exercitu illis regna conciliaturum confirmat. 7 Hac oratione adducti inter se fidem et ius iurandum dant; et, regno occupato per tres potentissimos ac firmissimos populos, totius Galliae sese potiri posse sperant.

1**adducti, permoti:** agree with the unexpressed subject of *constituerunt*. **auctoritate:** 'by the influence'; 135a. **permoti:** 'stirred to action.' **constituerunt:** 'they (i.e., *Helvetii*) determined,' followed by **comparare** 'to make ready'; 221a. **ea:** 'those things'; after *comparare*; 113a; 160c. **ad proficiscendum:** 'for departing'; 230.3. **pertinerent:** subjunctive in a relative clause of characteristic; 194a. **iumentorum:** 'draft-animals'; horses, mules, and oxen; 98a. **carrorum:** two-wheeled 'carts,' drawn largely by oxen. **quam maximum:** 'the largest possible'; 153c. **coemere:** 'to buy up.' **coemere, facere, confirmare:** after *constituerunt*; 221a. **sementes quam maximas:** 'as large sowings as possible'; 14b; 153c. **in itinere:** 'on the way'; 18c. **copia frumenti suppeteret:** 'there might be an adequate supply of grain,' lit. 'a supply of grain might be at hand.' **suppeteret:** 196a. **proximis:** 'neighboring,' lit. 'nearest'; 33. **pacem et amicitiam:** '(relations of) peace and friendship.' **confirmare:** '(and) to strengthen'; 234a.

2**Ad ... conficiendas:** gerundive construction, 'to complete these preparations,' lit. 'for those things to be completed'; 230.3. **biennium satis esse:** 'that two years was sufficient'; 212d; 214a. **biennium:** 79b. **sibi:** 'for them'; 40b; 158a. **duxerunt:** here a verb of thought; 'they reckoned'; 213a. **in:** 'for.' **profectionem:** '(their) departure'; 157a. **confirmant:** historical present in place of which should logically be a past tense, 'they fixed'; 175b. Other historical presents in this chapter are *deligitur, persuadet, dat, probat, confirmat, dant, sperant.*

3**Ad ... conficiendas:** just as above in I.3.2. **deligitur:** 'is (was) chosen'; 175b. **sibi ... suscepit:** 'took upon himself'; 107a. **legationem ad civitates:** 'the office of envoy to the states'; 150d.

4**Castico:** 105. **Catamantaloedis:** 99. **filio, Sequano:** 91a. **pater:** 11b. **regnum:** 'the chief authority'; at this time there was no hereditary or absolute monarchy among the Gauls; 1; 258a. **annos:** 118a. **populi Romani amicus:** 'friend of the Roman people'; 88. Such titles were conferred as a recognition of services rendered, or as a means of gaining favor. **sua:** 157b. **ut ... occuparet:** 'to seize'; 199a5; 177b. **quod:** here a relative pronoun (i.e., not 'because'); 47; 163a.

5**item:** 'also.' **Dumnorigi:** 10c; 105. **fratri:** 11e. **Diviciaci:** 19d. **eo tempore:** 'at that time'; 147a. **principatum:** 'the foremost place'; it is not indicated whether the dominant position of Dumnorix among the Aeduans was due wholly to his influence or whether he was at that time also holding some office. **civitate:** '(his) state,' i.e., the Aeduan state. **obtinebat:** force of the imperfect? 175a. **maxime acceptus:** 'very acceptable'; 30. **plebi:** 108a. **ut idem conaretur:** 'to attempt the same thing'; the construction is similar to that of **ut ... occuparet** above; 61a1; 199a5. **idem:** 45; 117a. **ei:** 104a. **dat:** 67a; 175b.

6 **Perfacile ... possent:** indirect quotation (thus marked in italic type) depending on *probat*; 213a. **Perfacile:** in predicate after *esse* (as in I.2.2); 212c5. **factu:** 'to do,' lit. 'in respect to the doing,' the ablative form of the supine; 232. **esse:** 214a. **illis probat:** 'he (Orgetorix) showed them'; 104a. **conata:** '(their) undertakings'; 157a. **perficere:** 'to carry through'; subject of *esse*; 57b; 79b; 222b. **suae:** 'his own,' emphatic; 157b. **imperium:** 'the sovereign power'; 74b. **obtenturus esset:** 'he was going to seize'; 63. Why subjunctive? 214a. **non esse dubium:** 'that there was no doubt.' **dubium:** in predicate; neuter because the subject of *esse* is a clause. **quin .. . possent:** 'that the Helvetians were the most powerful (people) in all Gaul,' lit. 'were able the most (i.e., to the greatest extent) of the whole (of) Gaul'; 201b. **Galliae:** 97b. **plurimum:** neuter accusative used substantively; 32; 118b. **se suis copiis:** 'that he with his own means'; 131a; 157b. **exercitu:** here not exactly 'army' but 'armed retinue,' like that with which Orgetorix afterwards overawed the judges, as related in I.4.2. **illis:** 104a. **illis regna conciliaturum:** sc. *esse*, 'that he would get kingships for them'; 89c. **confirmat:** 'he (Orgetorix) assured (them).'

7 **inter se:** 159. **fidem et ius iurandum:** 'an oath-bound pledge of good faith,' lit. 'good faith and oath'; hendiadys; 13h; 238d. **regno occupato:** ablative absolute, lit. 'with the supreme power having been seized'; 144a, b3. **potentissimos ac firmissimos:** 'very powerful and very firmly established'; 153a. **populos:** the Helvetians, the Sequanians, and the Aeduans. **Galliae:** after *potiri*; 131d. **sese posse sperant:** 'they hoped that they would be able'; 213a. **potiri:** after *posse*; 221a.

The conspiracy is revealed; Orgetorix dies.

4. 1 Ea res est Helvetiis per indicium enuntiata. Moribus suis Orgetorigem ex vinculis causam dicere coegerunt; damnatum poenam sequi oportebat, ut igni cremaretur. 2 Die constituta causae dictionis Orgetorix ad iudicium omnem suam familiam, ad hominum milia decem, undique coegit, et omnes clientes obaeratosque suos, quorum magnum numerum habebat, eodem conduxit; per eos, ne causam diceret, se eripuit. 3 Cum civitas, ob eam rem incitata, armis ius suum exsequi conaretur, multitudinemque hominum ex agris magistratus cogerent, Orgetorix mortuus est; 4 neque abest suspicio, ut Helvetii arbitrantur, quin ipse sibi mortem consciverit.

1 **Ea res:** 'The matter,' i.e., Orgetorix's scheme; lit. 'that thing'; 160d. **Helvetiis:** why dat.? 104a. **per indicium:** 'through (the agency of) informers,' lit. 'through information'; 92b; 123a. **est enuntiata:** 'was reported'; 172a. **Moribus suis:** 'In accordance with their customs,' as distinguished from Roman procedure; 136c. **ex vinculis:** 'in chains'; 126c. **causam dicere:** 'to plead his case'; 221a. **damnatum:** agrees with *eum* understood as object of *sequi*, '(him having been) condemned'; implicitly, the participle is also conditional, '(him) if condemned'; 209. **poenam:** subject of *sequi*, 'the penalty,' defined by the following *ut*-clause. **oportebat:** 73a, b. **damnatum poenam sequi oportebat:** 'if condemned, the penalty would inevitably follow,' lit. 'it was necessary that the penalty follow him, having been condemned.' **igni:** 14b; 131a. **ut igni cremaretur:** 'of being burned by fire,' lit. 'that he be burned by fire'; 203.4. The Gauls punished some offenses by burning alive, and sometimes offered human sacrifices (VI.16, 19).

2 **Die constituta:** 'On the day appointed'; 21a; 147a. **dictionis:** dependent on *Die*, 'for the pleading'; 102. **iudicium:** 'the (place of) judgment,' 'the trial.' **familiam:** here = 'slaves,' lit. 'body of slaves,' taken collectively (one's 'family' included all members of the household, not just immediate relations, and the numbers described here indicate that the larger sense of *familia* is being referred to). **ad:** 'about,' with adverbial force when modifying words of number such as *decem*; Caesar often gives a round number where it is impossible to be exact. **hominum:** 12b; 97a. **milia:** appositive of *familiam*; 38a; 91a. **clientes:** 'retainers'; 17c. **obaeratos:** 'debtors.' In Gaul debtors who were unable to pay might be forced into bondage (VI.13). **eodem:** 'to the same place,' the place of judgment. **conduxit:** 'brought,' lit. 'led together.' **per eos:** 'with their help,' lit. 'by means of them'; 123a. **diceret:** 196a. **ne ... eripuit:** 'he rescued himself in order that he might not plead his case'; i.e., Orgetorix overawed the judges so that they did not dare proceed with the trial.

3 **incitata:** 'aroused'; 148b. **ius suum:** 'its right' to call traitors to account. **exsequi:** 'enforce'; 200b. **conaretur, cogerent:** note the force of the imperfect tense and the subjunctive mood; 185c. **hominum:** 98a. **agris:** 'the country'; 7a; 130a. **magistratus:** 'the public officials'; here evidently the local officers are meant; 82b. **mortuus est:** 'died'; 57c; 176a.

4 **neque abest suspicio:** 'and the suspicion is not lacking'; 12c; 233a. **ut:** followed by the indicative, 'as'; see Vocab. **quin ... consciverit:** 'that he committed suicide,' lit. 'that he himself inflicted death upon himself'; 201b. **mortem:** 17c.

The Helvetians complete their preparations to migrate.

5. 1 Post eius mortem nihilo minus Helvetii id, quod constituerant, facere conantur, ut e finibus suis exeant. 2 Ubi iam se ad eam rem paratos esse arbitrati sunt, oppida sua omnia, numero ad duodecim, vicos ad quadringentos, reliqua privata aedificia incendunt; 3 frumentum omne, praeter quod secum portaturi erant, comburunt, ut, domum reditionis spe sublata, paratiores ad omnia pericula subeunda essent; trium mensium molita cibaria sibi quemque domo efferre iubent. 4 Persuadent Rauracis et Tulingis et Latobrigis, finitimis, uti, eodem usi consilio, oppidis suis vicisque exustis, una cum eis proficiscantur; Boiosque, qui trans Rhenum incoluerant et in agrum Noricum transierant Noreiamque oppugnarant, receptos ad se socios sibi asciscunt.

1 **Post:** *122a.* **eius:** i.e., *Orgetorigis.* **nihilo minus:** 'nonetheless,' lit. 'by nothing less'; *140.* **id quod:** *160c.* **conantur:** *175b.* **ut . . . exeant:** explains *id*; *203.4.* From the fact that, notwithstanding the treason and death of Orgetorix, the Helvetians carried out the plan of migrating, it is evident that behind the movement there was a general cause stronger than the influence of any individual. It seems probable that this cause was the pressure of the Germans, with whom, as stated in I.1.4, the Helvetians were constantly at war.
2 **Ubi iam:** 'As soon as,' lit. 'When now.' **paratos:** 'ready,' a predicate adjective (i.e., not the verbal form *paratos esse*); *148c.* **oppida:** 'fortified towns'; *6a.* **numero:** *142a; 85.* **ad:** adverb, as in I.4.2. **vicos:** 'villages,' unfortified. **quadringentos:** 'four hundred'; *36.* **reliqua:** *171a.* **privata aedificia:** 'buildings belonging to individuals,' not in the walled towns or villages. **incendunt:** 'they set fire to.'
3 **praeter quod:** i.e., *praeter id* (*frumentum*) *quod.* **secum:** 'with them'; *125c.* **portaturi erant:** 'they were going to carry'; *63.* **comburunt:** 'they burned'; *175b.* **domum:** 'home'; *119b.* **reditionis:** 'of a return'; *12c; 102.* **spe:** *21.* **spe sublata:** 'the hope having been taken away'; *144b3.* **subeunda:** 'undergo,' lit. 'to be undergone,' a gerundive in agreement with *pericula* (i.e., not the passive periphrastic *subeunda essent*); *68b; 230.3.* **essent:** *196a.* **trium:** *37b.* **mensium:** *14b.* **trium mensium:** 'for (lit. 'of') three months'; *100a.* **molita cibaria:** 'ground rations.' The grain was to be ground to coarse flour before starting, in contrast with the Roman custom of carrying unground grain on campaigns (277). **quemque:** *49a; 170b.* **domo:** *20c; 130b.* **efferre:** *69b.* **sibi quemque efferre iubent:** '(and) they ordered each one for himself to carry away'; *200b; 234a.* On an allowance of three quarters of a pound of coarse flour per day for each person, more than 12,000 tons would be needed to feed 368,000 people (I.29) for 90 days. If each cart carried a ton, more than 12,000 carts would have been required to transport the supplies, and perhaps half as many more for other purposes. If we reckon 20 feet to a cart, 18,000 carts in single file would form a line 68 miles long.
4 **Rauracis:** why dat.? *105.* The Rauraci, Tulingi, and Latobrigi were apparently north of the Helvetians (Map 1), and particularly exposed to the attacks of the Germans; hence their readiness to join the Helvetians in migrating. **et . . . et:** *234a.* **finitimis:** '(their) neighbors'; *91a; 157a.* **uti . . . proficiscantur:** translate by an infinitive, as *ut . . . exirent* in I.2.1; *61a3; 199a5.* **usi:** 'adopting'; lit. 'having used'; *61a3; 228a.* **consilio:** 'plan'; *131c.* **oppidis suis vicisque exustis:** 'having burned their towns and villages,' lit. 'their towns and villages having been burned'; *144b2.* **una:** adverb. **eis:** *Helvetiis*; *137a; 160b.* **agrum Noricum:** 'the territory of the Norici,' corresponding, in general, with the western part of Austria south of the Danube, between Bavaria and Hungary. **transierant:** 'had passed over'; *68b.* **oppugnarant:** 'had taken by storming'; *300.* Full form? *64a1.* **Boiosque . . . receptos ad se socios sibi asciscunt:** lit. '(the Helvetians) associate to themselves the Boii, having been (previously) received to themselves as allies,' i.e., the Helvetians convince their established allies, the Boii, to migrate with them; *228a.* Note how the main verb is present in tense, the participle perfect, and the relative clauses pluperfect, which allows the actions involving the Boians to be put in a clear chronological order. **socios:** *115a.*

Of two possible routes they choose to go through the Province.

6. 1 Erant omnino itinera duo, quibus itineribus domo exire possent: unum per Sequanos, angustum et difficile, inter montem Iuram et flumen Rhodanum, vix qua singuli carri ducerentur, mons autem altissimus impendebat, ut facile perpauci prohibere possent; 2 alterum per provinciam nostram, multo facilius atque expeditius, propterea quod inter fines Helvetiorum et Allobrogum, qui nuper pacati erant, Rhodanus fluit, isque non nullis locis vado transitur. 3 Extremum oppidum Allobrogum est, proximumque Helvetiorum finibus, Genava. Ex eo oppido pons ad Helvetios pertinet. Allobrogibus sese vel persuasuros, quod nondum bono animo in populum Romanum viderentur, existimabant, vel vi coacturos, ut per suos fines eos ire paterentur. 4 Omnibus rebus ad profectionem comparatis, diem dicunt, qua die ad ripam Rhodani omnes conveniant. Is dies erat a. d. v. Kal. Apr., L. Pisone, A. Gabinio consulibus.

1 **Erant:** 'There were'; *90a.* **duo:** *37b.* **itineribus:** redundant; *165a; 134a.* **domo:** as in I.5.3. **possent:** the subjunctive mood indicates a relative clause of characteristic; *194a.* **unum . . . alterum:** sc. *iter* (*erat*); *91c.* **per Sequanos:** *251.* **difficile:** *29.* **inter . . . Rhodanum:** on the right bank of the Rhone. There was no route across the Jura range practicable for so large a force, while the passage down the left bank of the Rhine, and westward between the Jura and the Vosges Mountains (Map 1), was left out of consideration, not only (we may assume) because it was less direct, but also because it was exposed to the attacks of Ariovistus (whose influence is revealed in I.31). **vix:** 'hardly.' **qua:** 'where'; translate as if the order were *qua vix.* **singuli:** 'one at a time,' see Vocab. **ducerentur:** 'could (lit. 'would') be drawn along'; subjunctive in another clause of characteristic, the relative adverb *qua* having the force of a relative pronoun. The narrowest point of the route is at the "Mill-Race Gorge" (Pas de l'Écluse), 19 Roman miles (about 17.5 English miles; *243b*) below Geneva (see Map 2). **mons altissimus:** Mt. Crédo, now pierced by a tunnel, 2.5 miles long, through which passes the railroad from Geneva to Lyons. **autem:** 'moreover'; *236a, b.* **impendebat:** 'was looming over'; *54.* The indicative mood reveals that this clause, which is the second geographical consideration introduced by *qua* ('where'), is a statement of fact rather than of characteristic. **perpauci:** 'very few' men, posted on the heights above the road. Force of *per*? *79b* and Vocab. **prohibere:** sc. *eos.* **possent:** *197a.*

2 **alterum:** sc. *iter* (*erat*), as above with *unum.* **provinciam nostram:** *157c; 259.* **multo:** 'much,' lit. 'by much'; *140.* **facilius:** *29.* **expeditius:** 'more convenient.' **Allobrogum:** *19e.* **nuper:** 'recently,' in 61 BC, after a revolt; the Allobroges were first conquered by Q. Fabius Maximus, in 121 BC (I.45). **pacati erant:** 'had been subdued'; *53; 192.* **isque:** 'and it (the Rhone)'; *160b.* **non nullis:** 'some,' lit. 'not none'; *23a.* **locis:** *6c; 145c.* **vado transitur:** 'is fordable,' lit. 'is crossed by a ford'; *68c; 134a.*

3 **Extremum:** 'The most remote,' lit. 'utmost,' from the point of view of Rome; *33.* **finibus:** *108a.* **pons:** *17c.* **Helvetios:** *251.* **pertinet:** 'reaches across.' **Allobrogibus:** *105.* **vel . . . vel:** 'either . . . or'; *235b.* **sese . . . persuasuros:** sc. *esse,* indirect statement after *existimabant; 89c; 213a; 214a.* **quod:** 'because.' **nondum . . . viderentur:** 'did not yet seem,' i.e., to the Helvetians, and this attributed reasoning renders *viderentur* in the subjunctive mood; *183a. Videor* is commonly to be understood as 'seem' rather than the literal passive 'be seen'; see Vocab. **bono animo:** 'kindly disposed,' lit. 'with a good disposition'; in predicate after *viderentur; 143b.* **in:** here 'toward.' **vi:** 'by force'; *18a.* **coacturos:** i.e., *sese* (the Helvetians) *eos* (the Allobroges) *coacturos esse,* also in indirect statement after *existimabant.* **ut . . . paterentur:** 'to permit' (from *patior*), substantive clause after *persuasuros* (*esse*), *coacturos* (*esse*); *199a.* **eos:** translate as if *Helvetios;* see I.1.4. **ire:** *68a.*

4 **Omnibus . . . comparatis:** 'when all preparations had been completed'; *144b2.* How lit.? **dicunt:** 'they appointed.' **qua die:** 'on which'; *147a; 165a.* **ad ripam:** 'on the bank' across from the Province; the north bank of the Rhone. **conveniant:** 'they should assemble'; subjunctive of purpose, as if *qua* were *ut ea,* 'that on that day'; *193.* **dies:** gender? *21a.* **a. d. v. Kal. Apr.:** *ante diem quintum Kalendas Apriles,* 'the fifth day before the Calends of April,' March 28 by our calendar; *241a, b.* **L. Pisone, A. Gabinio consulibus:** 58 BC (cf. I.2.1); *144b1; 240a.*

Caesar hastens to Geneva and parleys with the Helvetians.

7. 1 Caesari cum id nuntiatum esset, eos per provinciam nostram iter facere conari, maturat ab urbe proficisci et quam maximis potest itineribus in Galliam ulteriorem contendit et ad Genavam pervenit. 2 Provinciae toti quam maximum potest militum numerum imperat (erat omnino in Gallia ulteriore legio una); pontem, qui erat ad Genavam, iubet rescindi. 3 Ubi de eius adventu Helvetii certiores facti sunt, legatos ad eum mittunt nobilissimos civitatis, cuius legationis Nammeius et Verucloetius principem locum obtinebant, qui dicerent *sibi esse in animo sine ullo maleficio iter per provinciam facere, propterea quod aliud iter haberent nullum; rogare ut eius voluntate id sibi facere liceat.* 4 Caesar, quod memoria tenebat, L. Cassium consulem occisum exercitumque eius ab Helvetiis pulsum et sub iugum missum, concedendum non putabat; 5 neque *homines inimico animo, data facultate per provinciam itineris faciundi, temperaturos ab iniuria et maleficio* existimabat. 6 Tamen, ut spatium intercedere posset, dum milites, quos imperaverat, convenirent, legatis respondit *diem se ad deliberandum sumpturum; si quid vellent, ad Id. April. reverterentur.*

1 **Caesari:** *19c; 245e.* **nuntiatum esset:** *185c.* **eos . . . conari:** infinitive clause of indirect discourse in apposition with *id;* the gist of the report, in the direct form, was *Helvetii per provinciam nostram iter facere conantur; 214a.* **maturat:** 'he hastened.' **urbe:** Rome, which by way of distinction was *the* city; *17b.* **quam maximis potest itineribus:** 'with the utmost possible speed', lit. 'with marches as great as is possible'; *153c.* **Galliam ulteriorem:** here including the Province, Caesar's immediate destination; *255; 259.* **ad:** 'to the vicinity of'; *120a.* **pervenit:** 'came,' lit. 'comes through.' If, as Plutarch says, Caesar arrived at the Rhone on the eighth day after leaving Rome, he must have traveled at the rate of about 100 Roman miles (about 92 English miles; *243b*) per day.

2 **Provinciae . . . imperat:** 'he levied upon the Province,' i.e., he drafted men to serve in his army; *105; 106a.* **militum:** *10b;* legionary soldiers are meant. **legio:** this 'legion' was the Tenth, afterwards famous; *267e.* **pontem . . . rescindi:** 'that the bridge be broken down'; *200b.*

3 **adventu:** *20b.* **certiores facti sunt:** 'were informed,' lit. 'were made more certain'; *115c.* **legatos:** 'as envoys'; predicate accusative; *6a; 115a.* **mittunt:** 'sent'; *175b.* **nobilissimos:** 'the most distinguished men'; *154a.* **cuius legationis:** 'and in this delegation,' lit. 'of which delegation'; *167.* **principem:** 'foremost'; *26b; 10b.* **qui dicerent:** 'who were to say', 'in order to say'; *193a.* **sibi . . . liceat:** *212a-c.* **sibi esse in animo:** 'that it was their intention'; lit., 'that it was in the mind to them'; *sibi* is a dative of possession; *111; 178; 214a.* **sine ullo maleficio:** 'without any wrongdoing,' i.e., without doing any harm; *125a; 23a.* **facere:** subject of *esse; 222b.* **haberent:** *214a.* **nullum:** emphatic position; *245d.* **rogare:** sc. *se,* '(and) that they requested'; *215; 234a.* **eius voluntate:** 'with his consent'; *138.* **ut . . . liceat:** 'that permission might be granted,' lit. 'that it be permitted'; subjunctive already in the direct form; *73b; 199a4.* **facere:** *222a.*

4 **memoria tenebat:** 'he remembered,' lit. 'he was holding by means of memory'; *131a; 183a.* **L.:** = *Lucium; 19a.* **occisum:** sc. *esse,* 'had been killed'; *89c; 213a.* **exercitum:** 'army'; *20; 74b.* **pulsum:** sc. *esse,* 'had been routed'; *178.* **sub iugum:** 'under the yoke,' made by setting two spears upright and placing a third on them horizontally, as a cross-piece; under this captured soldiers were made to pass, bending forward, as a token of complete submission and humiliation. The defeat of Cassius by the Helvetians took place in 107 BC; *124a.* **concedendum** (esse) **non putabat:** 'was not thinking that the request ought to be granted,' lit. 'that it ought to be conceded'; *63; 73e.*

5 **neque:** translate as if *et non.* **homines:** subject of *temperaturos* (*esse*), after *existimabat.* **inimico animo:** 'of hostile temper'; *143a.* **data facultate:** lit. 'with the opportunity having been given,' an ablative absolute equivalent to *si facultas data esset,* 'if opportunity should have been granted'; *144b4.* **itineris faciundi:** 'of marching,' lit. 'of making a march'; *64b; 230.1; 102.* **temperaturos:** sc. *esse,* 'would refrain.'

6 **Tamen:** 'nevertheless'; *236a.* **spatium:** nominative, 'a space,' here an interval of time. **intercedere:** 'intervene'; *221a.* **posset:** *196a.* **dum:** 'until.' **convenirent:** 'should assemble'; *190b.* **diem:** 'some time,' lit. 'a day.' **se:** *158a.* **ad deliberandum:** 'for consideration'; *230.3.* **sumpturum:** sc. *esse,* 'would take'; *214a.* **quid:** 'anything'; *168.* **vellent, reverterentur:** 'they wanted', 'they should return'; in the direct form *si vultis, revertimini; 206.2; 218.1a; 216.* **Id. April.:** *Idus Apriles,* April 13; *241.*

Caesar prevents the Helvetians from entering the Province.

8. 1 Interea ea legione, quam secum habebat, militibusque, qui ex provincia convenerant, a lacu Lemanno, qui in flumen Rhodanum influit, ad montem Iuram, qui fines Sequanorum ab Helvetiis dividit, milia passuum XVIIII murum in altitudinem pedum sedecim fossamque perducit. 2 Eo opere perfecto, praesidia disponit, castella communit, quo facilius, si, se invito, transire conarentur, prohibere possit. 3 Ubi ea dies, quam constituerat cum legatis, venit, et legati ad eum reverterunt, negat se *more et exemplo* populi Romani posse iter ulli per provinciam dare; et, si vim facere conentur, prohibiturum ostendit. 4 Helvetii, ea spe deiecti, navibus iunctis ratibusque compluribus factis, alii vadis Rhodani, qua minima altitudo fluminis erat, non numquam interdiu, saepius noctu, si perrumpere possent, conati, operis munitione et militum concursu et telis repulsi, hoc conatu destiterunt.

1 **Interea:** 'meanwhile,' i.e., while the more distant troops levied on the Province were gathering at the Rhone and the Helvetians were waiting for Caesar's answer. **legione, militibus:** looked upon as instruments rather than as agents; *131b; 126a.* **secum:** *125c.* **qui . . . influit:** while Caesar's statement is not incorrect, modern geographers consider Lake Geneva as an enlargement of the Rhone, applying the name 'Rhone' also to the principal feeder entering the lake at the upper end. **Helvetiis:** *251.* **milia:** *118a; 243b; 38a.* **XVIIII:** *undeviginti; 36; 38b.* **murum:** 'a rampart'; *1.* **in altitudinem pedum sedecim:** 'sixteen feet high,' lit. 'to a height of sixteen feet.' **pedum:** *10b; 100a.* **fossam:** 'trench.' **perducit:** 'he constructed'; *175b.* For much of the distance between Lake Geneva and Mill-Race Gorge (17.5 English miles, see note on I.6.1), the left bank of the Rhone is steep enough to make extensive fortifying unnecessary. What Caesar did was, apparently, to make the slopes hard to surmount by cutting the face down from the top for sixteen feet and throwing the dirt out toward the river in such a way as to produce the effect of a rampart and trench; palisades were probably driven in along the edge of the bluff. See Map 2.

2 **Eo opere perfecto:** 'When this work had been finished'; *13e; 144b2.* **praesidia:** 'detachments' of troops. **disponit:** 'he stationed at intervals'; *79d.* **castella:** 'redoubts'; their probable location is shown on Map 2. **communit:** 'he strongly fortified.' **quo:** why used in place of *ut? 193b.* **se invito:** 'without his permission,' lit. 'with him (being) unwilling'; *144a.* Note how this clause is nested within the others: an ablative absolute within a

conditional clause within a purpose clause. **conarentur:** *177b; 220.* **prohibere:** sc. *eos.*

3 **ea dies:** April 13; see I.7.5. **reverterunt:** 'returned'; *79d.* **negat:** = 'deny', i.e., 'say that it is not so.' Hence, as often, it is best translated by transferring the negation to the following indirect statement and treating it as *dicit . . . non.* **more et exemplo:** 'custom and precedent'; *136c.* **iter:** i.e., permission to make a march. **ulli:** *23a;* here used as a noun, 'to anyone.' **vim facere:** 'use force'; *18a.* **conentur,** (se eos) **prohibiturum** (esse): in the direct form, *si conabimini, prohibebo; 215; 218.1a.*

4 **ea spe deiecti:** 'cast down from that hope'; *57b.* **spe:** *127a.* **navibus iunctis ratibusque compluribus factis:** 'joined boats together,' attempting to make a floating bridge, 'and made a number of rafts' for poling across. How lit.? *144b2.* **alii:** 'others,' i.e., separate from those who were trying to cross with boats and rafts. **vadis:** *134a.* **minima:** *32.* **non numquam:** 'sometimes.' **interdiu:** 'by day.' **saepius:** *35.* **noctu:** 'at night.' **si perrumpere possent:** indirect question after *conati,* '(to see) whether they could break through'; *204.4.* **conati:** 'having tried', deponent participle, in agreement with *Helvetii,* both those in boats and rafts and the others (*alii*) on foot; *61a1.* **operis munitione:** lit. 'by the fortification of their (line of) work,' i.e., the line of defenses (*murus, fossa, castella*) produced by their work; *opus* in such a context indicates works of military engineering. **concursu:** 'by the running together' of Roman defenders at the locations of the Helvetians' attempted crossings; *20b.* **telis:** i.e., thrown by the Romans. **repulsi:** 'having been forced back,' another participle in agreement with *Helvetii* and *alii.* **hoc conatu destiterunt:** 'they gave up (lit. 'desisted from') this attempt'; *127a.*

The Helvetians obtain an agreement to go through the territory of the Sequani.

9. 1 Relinquebatur una per Sequanos via, qua, Sequanis invitis, propter angustias ire non poterant. 2 His cum sua sponte persuadere non possent, legatos ad Dumnorigem Aeduum mittunt, ut, eo deprecatore, a Sequanis impetrarent. 3 Dumnorix gratia et largitione apud Sequanos plurimum poterat, et Helvetiis erat amicus, quod ex ea civitate Orgetorigis filiam in matrimonium duxerat, et cupiditate regni adductus novis rebus studebat et quam plurimas civitates suo beneficio habere obstrictas volebat. 4 Itaque rem suscipit et a Sequanis impetrat, ut per fines suos Helvetios ire patiantur, obsidesque uti inter sese dent, perficit: Sequani, ne itinere Helvetios prohibeant; Helvetii, ut sine maleficio et iniuria transeant.

1 **Relinquebatur:** 'There was left'; *90a.* **una via:** nominative, 'only the way,' described in I.6.1. **qua:** *134a.* **Sequanos:** *251.* **Sequanis invitis:** *144b3.* **angustias:** 'the narrowness' (lit. 'the narrows') of the road through Mill-Race Gorge.

2 **His:** the Sequani; *105.* **sua sponte:** 'of their own accord', 'by their own influence'; *17d; 157b.* **possent:** *66b; 184a.* **eo deprecatore:** 'through his mediation,' lit. 'with him being the mediator'; *144b6.* **impetrarent:** 'they might gain their request'; *177b; 196a.*

3 **gratia et largitione:** 'on account of his popularity and lavish giving'; *135a.* **plurimum poterat:** 'had very great influence,' lit. 'was able to a very great degree'; *118b.* A fuller account of Dumnorix is given in I.18, where we learn that he had practical control of the revenues of the Aeduans and was bitterly opposed to Caesar. **Helvetiis:** *108a.* **Orgetorigis . . . duxerat:** see I.3.5. **novis rebus studebat:** 'was eager for a revolution,' lit. 'new things'; *105.* **quam plurimas:** 'as many . . . as possible'; *153c.* **suo beneficio obstrictas:** 'placed under obligation to himself,' lit. 'bound by his own service (to them).' **volebat:** *71.*

4 **ut . . . patiantur:** substantive clause containing the object of his request; *199a8.* **obsidesque uti inter sese dent, perficit:** 'and brought about that they give hostages between them.' Hostages were exchanged as a pledge of good faith; if that faith was later violated, the hostages were liable to be abused or killed. **uti . . . dent:** substantive clause of result after *perficit; 203.3.* **Sequani** (obsides dant), **Helvetii** (obsides dant): these clauses are in apposition with the subject of *dent* and explain the exchange of hostages from the perspective of each side; *91c.* **itinere:** *127a.* **ne . . . prohibeant, ut . . . transeant:** clauses of purpose, expressing the terms of the agreement for the ratification of which the exchange of hostages was arranged.

Caesar, learning of their plan, brings five legions from Italy.

10. 1 Caesari renuntiatur, Helvetiis esse in animo per agrum Sequanorum et Aeduorum iter in Santonum fines facere, qui non longe a Tolosatium finibus absunt, quae civitas est in provincia. 2 *Id si fieret, intellegebat magno cum periculo provinciae futurum, ut homines bellicosos, populi Romani inimicos, locis patentibus maximeque frumentariis finitimos haberet.* 3 Ob eas causas ei munitioni, quam fecerat, T. Labienum legatum praefecit; ipse in Italiam magnis itineribus contendit, duasque ibi legiones conscribit, et tres, quae circum Aquileiam hiemabant, ex hibernis educit; et, qua proximum iter in ulteriorem

Galliam per Alpes erat, cum his quinque legionibus ire contendit. 4 Ibi Ceutrones et Graioceli et Caturiges, locis superioribus occupatis, itinere exercitum prohibere conantur. 5 Compluribus his proeliis pulsis, ab Ocelo, quod est oppidum citerioris provinciae extremum, in fines Vocontiorum ulterioris provinciae die septimo pervenit; inde in Allobrogum fines, ab Allobrogibus in Segusiavos exercitum ducit. Hi sunt extra provinciam trans Rhodanum primi.

1 **renuntiatur:** impersonal, 'it was reported (back) to Caesar'; the prefix *re-* implies that men had been sent out by him and now returned with the information; *79d.* **Helvetiis esse in animo:** also impersonal (and the subject of *renuntiatur*): 'it was the Helvetians' intention,' lit. '(that) it was in the mind to the Helvetians'; cf. I.7.3. **non longe ... absunt:** the territories of the Santones were on the west coast, more than 100 miles from the nearest point of the Province; see Map Gallia. If the Helvetians should reach their destination, they would be further from the Province than when they started, yet even at that distance, claims Caesar, they might become dangerous neighbors. **quae civitas:** 'a state which,' the state of the Tolosates; *165c.*
2 **Id:** the migration to the territory of the Santones, referring back to *iter ... facere.* **fieret ... futurum** (esse): a condition in indirect discourse after *intellegebat*; in the direct form, *fiet ... erit; 70a; 218.1a.* **cum:** *136a.* **provinciae:** 'for the Province'; *102.* **ut ... haberet:** 'to have,' lit. 'that it (the Province) have'; substantive clause of result; *203.1.* **bellicosos:** 'warlike'; *75f.* **inimicos:** here a noun in apposition to *homines; 91a.* **locis ... finitimos:** *108a; 115.* **patentibus:** 'open' to attack, not being protected by natural barriers. **frumentariis:** 'productive' of grain; *30.*
3 **munitioni:** *107b; 74b.* **T.:** = *Titum; 19a.* **legatum:** 'lieutenant-general'; *273a.* **praefecit:** 'placed in command (of)'; *57b.* **Italiam:** Cisalpine Gaul is here meant; *252b.* **duas legiones:** the 11th and 12th; *267e.* **conscribit:** 'enlisted' by conscription. **tres:** sc. *legiones,* the 7th, 8th, and 9th. **circum:** 'in the neighborhood of,' lit. 'around'; the winter-quarters were not in the town; *122a.* **Aquileiam:** a Roman colony near the head of the Adriatic Sea. **ex hibernis:** *127c; 295.* **qua:** 'where.' **ulteriorem Galliam:** *255.* **Alpes:** *260.* **cum:** *137b.*
4 **Ibi:** i.e., in the Alps; Caesar's route lay over the pass of Mt. Genèvre (see Map 1). **locis superioribus occupatis:** *144b2.* **itinere:** *127a.*
5 **Compluribus proeliis:** 'by means of several battles'; *131a.* **his pulsis:** 'driving them off'; how lit.? *144b2; 160b.* **ab:** here 'from.' **citerioris provinciae:** 'nearer' from the viewpoint of Rome; *253.* **extremum:** i.e., most westerly. **ulterioris provinciae:** *259.* **pervenit:** 'passed through'; *175b.* **inde:** trace Caesar's route from Ocelum on Map 1. **exercitum:** three trained legions from near Aquileia, and two legions of recruits just levied in Cisalpine Gaul (the 11th and 12th), with which was joined the tenth legion, released from guarding the fortification below Geneva; for the campaign against the Helvetians Caesar had thus 6 legions, collectively about 22,000 men, besides cavalry. Light-armed troops, used in later years, are not mentioned in Book I; *267e.* **Hi:** Segusiavi. **trans Rhodanum:** Caesar probably crossed the Rhone by a pontoon bridge, a short distance above the junction with the Arar. The Segusiavi were clients of the Aeduans, hence on good terms with the Romans. Most of their territory was on the west side of the Rhone, but they seem to have occupied also the narrow corner between the Rhone and the Arar.

The Aeduans, Ambarri, and Allobroges seek Caesar's aid against the Helvetians.
11. 1 Helvetii iam per angustias et fines Sequanorum suas copias traduxerant, et in Aeduorum fines pervenerant eorumque agros populabantur. 2 Aedui, cum se suaque ab eis defendere non possent, legatos ad Caesarem mittunt rogatum auxilium: 3 *ita se omni tempore de populo Romano meritos esse, ut, paene in conspectu exercitus nostri, agri vastari, liberi eorum in servitutem abduci, oppida expugnari non debuerint.* 4 Eodem tempore Ambarri, necessarii et consanguinei Aeduorum, Caesarem certiorem faciunt *sese, depopulatis agris, non facile ab oppidis vim hostium prohibere.* 5 Item Allobroges, qui trans Rhodanum vicos possessionesque habebant, fuga se ad Caesarem recipiunt, et demonstrant *sibi praeter agri solum nihil esse reliqui.* 6 Quibus rebus adductus Caesar non exspectandum sibi statuit, dum, omnibus fortunis sociorum consumptis, in Santonos Helvetii pervenirent.

1 **angustias:** see I.9.1 and I.6.1-2. It must have taken Caesar 7 or 8 weeks to go to Cisalpine Gaul, gather his forces there, and bring them across the Province to the north side of the Rhone. Meanwhile the Helvetians, with their throng of women and children and their loaded carts, had slowly threaded the narrow Mill-Race Gorge and had advanced, in all, only about 100 miles. **suas copias traduxerant:** 'had led their forces across (the mountains).' **Aeduorum fines:** on the west side of the Arar, which the front end of the Helvetian host already had crossed. See Map 1. **populabantur:** 'were laying waste'; *61a1; 175a.*

2 **sua:** 'their possessions'; *154a.* **possent:** *184a.* **rogatum:** 'to ask for', the supine of purpose after a verb of motion; *231a.* **auxilium:** 'help'; *231b.*

3 **ita,** etc: indirect quotation (thus marked in italic type). **Direct form:** ita (*nos*) omni tempore de populo Romano *meriti sumus,* ut, paene in conspectu exercitus *tui,* agri vastati, liberi *nostri* in servitutem abduci, oppida expugnari non *debuerint.* **ita . . . ut:** 'in such a way . . . that'; *197.* **se omni tempore de populo Romano meritos esse:** '(saying) that they had at all times merited (fair treatment) from the Roman people'; *213b.* More than 60 years before, in 121 BC, the Aeduans had been recognized by treaty as *socii populi Romani,* 'allies of the Roman people'. **nostri:** *157c.* **agri, liberi, oppida:** subjects of *non debuerint.* **vastari, abduci, expugnari:** *221a.* **liberi eorum:** 'their children'. **servitutem:** 'slavery', the penalty of capture; *10f.* **non debuerint:** 'ought not'; perfect subjunctive after (i.e., chronologically prior to) the historical present *mittunt;* *177; 197b.* The perfect tense of *debuerint,* followed by present infinitives, thus sets the action of the infinitives in the past. In English, however, since the verb 'ought' is defective and has no perfect tense, the perfect tense of *debuerint* has to be transferred to the infinitives: 'ought not to have been laid waste . . . ought not to have been led away . . . ought not to have been taken by assault'; *249b.*

4 **necessarii:** 'relatives', including connections by marriage; *91a; 154a.* **consanguinei:** 'kinsmen', comprising only blood relations. **depopulatis agris:** *144b2;* here the deponent participle is felt as passive; *59b.* **ab oppidis:** *127b.* **prohibere:** *213a.*

5 **trans Rhodanum:** i.e., on the north side of the Rhone, probably west of the Mill-Race Gorge. **fuga:** *136b.* **se recipiunt:** lit. 'withdraw themselves'. **demonstrant:** 'stated'; *175b.* **sibi . . . nihil esse reliqui:** 'that they had nothing left'; *213a.* **sibi:** *111.* **agri solum:** 'the bare ground', lit. 'the soil of the field'. **reliqui:** used as a noun, a partitive genitive dependent on *nihil* ('nothing of a remainder'; 'nothing (of) left'); *97a.*

6 **Quibus:** *167.* **non exspectandum sibi:** sc. *esse,* '(that) he ought not to wait', lit. '(that) it should not be waited for by him'; *73e; 89c; 213a.* **sibi:** *110.* **dum . . . pervenirent:** *190b.* **fortunis:** here 'possessions', 'property'. **omnibus fortunis sociorum consumptis:** *144b2.* **Santonos:** 'the (country of) the Santoni', who were previously (I.10.1) referred to as the 'Santones'; *19e; 282.*

Caesar cuts to pieces one division of the Helvetians at the Arar.

12. 1 Flumen est Arar, quod per fines Aeduorum et Sequanorum in Rhodanum influit incredibili lenitate ita ut oculis, in utram partem fluat, iudicari non possit. Id Helvetii ratibus ac lintribus iunctis transibant. 2 Ubi per exploratores Caesar certior factus est tres iam partes copiarum Helvetios id flumen traduxisse, quartam vero partem citra flumen Ararim reliquam esse, de tertia vigilia cum legionibus tribus e castris profectus ad eam partem pervenit, quae nondum flumen transierat. 3 Eos impeditos et inopinantes aggressus, magnam partem eorum concidit; reliqui sese fugae mandarunt atque in proximas silvas abdiderunt. 4 Is pagus appellabatur Tigurinus; nam omnis civitas Helvetia in quattuor pagos divisa est. 5 Hic pagus unus, cum domo exisset, patrum nostrorum memoria L. Cassium consulem interfecerat et eius exercitum sub iugum miserat. 6 Ita sive casu sive consilio deorum immortalium, quae pars civitatis Helvetiae insignem calamitatem populo Romano intulerat, ea princeps poenas persolvit. 7 Qua in re Caesar non solum publicas, sed etiam privatas iniurias ultus est, quod eius soceri L. Pisonis avum, L. Pisonem legatum, Tigurini eodem proelio, quo Cassium, interfecerant.

1 **Flumen est Arar:** 'There is a river, the Arar'; *90a.* **Arar:** now Saône (pronounced sōn); *18e.* **per fines:** for a part of its course the Arar formed the boundary between the Aeduans and the Sequanians. **incredibili lenitate:** 'of incredible sluggishness'; *143a.* **incredibili:** *74f.* **oculis:** 'with the eye'; *92a; 131a.* **in utram partem:** 'in (lit. 'into') which direction'; *23a.* **fluat:** *204.3.* **iudicari:** 'to be determined'; *221a.* **possit:** the subject is the indirect question *in . . . fluat,* but it is easiest to translate as impersonal: 'it is not able to be determined'; *197b.* **lintribus iunctis:** 'by (means of) small boats fastened together'; the floats thus constructed, as well as the rafts, could be easily poled across in the still water; *15a; 131a.* It is also plausible to conceive of the phrase as an ablative absolute; *144b6.*

2 **exploratores:** 'scouting parties'; *287.* **tres . . . traduxisse:** translate as if *Helvetios iam* ('already') *duxisse tres partes* ('three quarters') *copiarum trans id flumen;* *114a.* **citra:** 'on this side of', i.e., the east side; *122a.* **Ararim:** *18e.* **de tertia vigilia:** *242d.* **legionibus tribus:** around ten to twelve thousand men; *137b.* **castris:** probably not far from Sathonay, east of the Saône, above its junction with the Rhone; see Map 1. **profectus:** *61a3.*

3 **Eos:** *160b.* **impeditos et inopinantes:** The Helvetians were completely surprised and had no chance to form a line of battle; the Roman soldiers plied their short swords rapidly and effectively; *282e.* **aggressus:** 'attacking'; *57c; 226c.* **reliqui:** *154a; 171a.* **mandarunt:** = *mandaverunt;* lit. 'committed themselves (*sese*) to flight', i.e.,

'took to flight'; *64a1.* **in:** translate as 'in' (lit. 'into') on account of the idea of motion in *abdiderunt,* as if, i.e., they (went) 'into the nearest woods' (and) 'concealed themselves.'

4 **pagus:** 'canton,' properly a territorial division, but here referring to its inhabitants. **Tigurinus:** *148a.* **civitas:** *257a.* **divisa:** *148c.*

5 **domo:** *130b.* **exisset:** *68b; 185c.* **memoria:** 'within the memory'; *147b.* **L. Cassium . . . miserat:** see I.7.4.

6 **sive . . . sive:** *235b.* **casu:** 'by chance'; *20; 135a.* **deorum:** *8d.* **quae pars civitatis Helvetiae . . . ea:** translate as if *ea pars civitatis Helvetiae quae; 165c.* **populo:** *107.* **princeps persolvit:** 'was the first to pay,' lit. 'first paid'; *152b.* **poenas:** *92a.*

7 **Qua:** *167.* **non solum . . . sed etiam:** *236d.* **ultus est:** *61a3.* **quod:** causal, i.e., 'because.' **quod . . . interfecerant:** i.e., *quod Tigurini, eodem proelio quo Cassium (interfecerant), interfecerant Lucium Pisonem legatum, avum Lucii Pisonis, eius* (Caesar's) *soceri.* Lucius Calpurnius Piso, consul in 58 BC, was the father of Caesar's fourth wife, Calpurnia. **soceri:** *7b.* **proelio:** *147b.*

Caesar bridges the Arar and crosses; the Helvetians send envoys.

13. 1 Hoc proelio facto, reliquas copias Helvetiorum ut consequi posset, pontem in Arari faciendum curat atque ita exercitum traducit. 2 Helvetii, repentino eius adventu commoti, cum id, quod ipsi diebus XX aegerrime confecerant, ut flumen transirent, illum uno die fecisse intellegerent, legatos ad eum mittunt; cuius legationis Divico princeps fuit, qui bello Cassiano dux Helvetiorum fuerat. 3 Is ita cum Caesare egit: *si pacem populus Romanus cum Helvetiis faceret, in eam partem ituros atque ibi futuros Helvetios, ubi eos Caesar constituisset atque esse voluisset; 4 sin bello persequi perseveraret, reminisceretur et veteris incommodi populi Romani et pristinae virtutis Helvetiorum. 5 Quod improviso unum pagum adortus esset, cum ei, qui flumen transissent, suis auxilium ferre non possent, ne ob eam rem aut suae magnopere virtuti tribueret aut ipsos despiceret; 6 se ita a patribus maioribusque suis didicisse ut magis virtute contenderent quam dolo aut insidiis niterentur. 7 Quare ne committeret, ut is locus, ubi constitissent, ex calamitate populi Romani et internecione exercitus nomen caperet aut memoriam proderet.*

Direct form (I.13.3-7): 3 Si pacem populus Romanus cum Helvetiis *faciet,* in eam partem *ibunt* atque ibi *erunt* Helvetii, ubi eos (*tu*) *constitueris* atque esse *volueris;* 4 sin bello persequi *perseverabis, reminiscere* et veteris incommodi populi Romani et pristinae virtutis Helvetiorum. 5 Quod improviso unum pagum adortus *es,* cum ei, qui flumen *transierant,* suis auxilium ferre non possent, *noli* ob eam rem aut *tuae* magnopere virtuti *tribuere* aut *nos despicere;* 6 (*nos*) ita a patribus maioribusque *nostris didicimus,* ut magis virtute *contendamus* quam dolo aut insidiis *nitamur.* 7 Quare *noli committere* ut is locus, ubi *constiterimus* [future perfect], ex calamitate populi Romani et internecione exercitus nomen *capiat* aut memoriam *prodat.*

1 **Hoc proelio facto:** *144b2.* **consequi:** 'to pursue'; *61a3.* **posset:** *196a.* **pontem faciendum curat:** 'he (Caesar) had a bridge built,' lit. 'provided for a bridge to be made'; *229b.* It was doubtless a pontoon bridge, designed and built by the engineers, *fabri,* enrolled in the legions; *270b.* **in:** 'over,' lit. 'on.'

2 **cum . . . intellegerent:** translate as if *cum intellegerent illum* (Caesar) *uno die fecisse* ('had accomplished') *id quod,* etc.; *178; 185c.* **XX:** viginti; *38b.* **ut flumen transirent:** a substantive clause explaining *id;* translate as if a noun: '(namely) the crossing of the river,' lit. 'that they cross the river'; *203.4.* **cuius legationis:** 'and of this delegation'; *167.* **princeps:** *10b.* **bello Cassiano:** 'in the war with Cassius,' lit. 'in the Cassian war'; *147b.* Since the defeat of Cassius took place in 107 BC, Divico must have been at least 70 or 80 years old at the time of which Caesar was writing, 58 BC.

3 **cum Caesare egit:** 'conferred with Caesar'; *137c.* **faceret, ituros** (esse), **futuros** (esse): *89c; 218.1a.* **ubi:** = 'where' (refers back to *ibi*). **constituisset, voluisset:** future perfect indicative in the direct form, since the action is prior to that of the future tense of the apodosis. In indirect discourse, indicative verbs in subordinate clauses shift in mood to subjunctive, and the tense of the subjunctive demonstrates relative time to that of the main verb. Since the main verb of speaking here is the perfect *egit,* the pluperfect subjunctive is necessary to maintain priority to the action of the main verb; *177a; 214a; 246.*

4 **Sin:** 'But if,' suggesting a second condition in contrast to the first. **bello:** *131a.* **persequi:** sc. *eos,* 'to assail (them)'; *61a3; 221a.* **perseveraret:** '(Caesar) should continue.' **reminisceretur:** indirect command (i.e., an imperative in the direct form), 'he should remember'; *216* (or, like a jussive subjunctive, 'let him remember'; *180b*). **veteris:** *26a.* **incommodi:** the defeat of Cassius. Why genitive? *103a.*

5 **Quod:** 'The fact that'; *198b.* **pagum:** see I.12.4. **adortus esset, transissent:** *214a.* **suis:** 'to their own (countrymen)'; *154a.* **possent:** subjunctive also in the direct form; *185c.* **ne ob eam rem aut suae magnopere**

virtuti tribueret aut ipsos despiceret: 'he should neither attribute very much to his own virtue on account of the fact (that he had attacked one canton unexpectedly, when . . .), nor should he look down upon them.' **ne . . . tribueret, despiceret:** negated indirect commands (i.e., the negative form of the imperative in the direct form), which can also be translated 'let him neither attribute . . . nor look down'); *216.* **rem:** the 'fact' expressed by the clause *Quod . . . adortus esset.* **aut . . . aut:** 'either . . . or' (*235*), but here negated by *ne* and so best translated as 'neither . . . nor.' **magnopere:** adverb, here taking the place of a direct object. **virtuti:** *104b.* **ipsos:** 'them,' i.e., *Helvetios; 162b.*

6 **ita . . . ut:** *197b.* **maioribus:** 'forefathers'; *154a.* **didicisse:** 'had learned'; *178.* **ut . . . contenderent:** 'to fight,' lit. '(such) that they fight'; *197a.* **magis:** 'rather'; *35.* **quam** (ut) **niterentur:** 'than to rely upon.' **dolo aut insidiis:** 'deceit or ambushes'; *131c.*

7 **Quare:** *237a.* **ne committeret, ut is locus . . . nomen caperet:** 'he should not cause that place to take its name,' lit. 'he should not bring it about (or 'let him not bring it about') that that place take its name.' **committeret:** cf. *tribueret, I.13.5.* **ut . . . caperet:** substantive clause of result; *203.3.* **ubi constitissent:** 'where they had taken their stand' (from *consisto*) in order to fight the Romans. **populi Romani:** 'for the Roman people'; *102.* **internecione:** 'annihilation.' **exercitus:** 'of an army,' i.e., Caesar's army. **aut:** negated by the *ne* preceding *committeret.* **memoriam proderet:** i.e., *memoriam calamitatis posteris proderet;* 'should he hand down the memory (of the disaster to posterity).' Divico thus concludes, as Caesar reports his embassy, with a taunting threat.

Caesar lays down conditions; the Helvetians reject them.

14. 1 His Caesar ita respondit: *eo sibi minus dubitationis dari, quod eas res, quas legati Helvetii commemorassent, memoria teneret, atque eo gravius ferre, quo minus merito populi Romani accidissent;* 2 *qui si alicuius iniuriae sibi conscius fuisset, non fuisse difficile cavere; sed eo deceptum, quod neque commissum a se intellegeret, quare timeret, neque sine causa timendum putaret.* 3 *Quod si veteris contumeliae oblivisci vellet, num etiam recentium iniuriarum, quod, eo invito, iter per provinciam per vim temptassent, quod Aeduos, quod Ambarros, quod Allobrogas vexassent, memoriam deponere posse?* 4 *Quod sua victoria tam insolenter gloriarentur, quodque tam diu se impune iniurias tulisse admirarentur, eodem pertinere.* 5 *Consuesse enim deos immortales, quo gravius homines ex commutatione rerum doleant, quos pro scelere eorum ulcisci velint, his secundiores interdum res et diuturniorem impunitatem concedere.* 6 *Cum ea ita sint, tamen, si obsides ab eis sibi dentur, uti ea, quae polliceantur, facturos intellegat, et si Aeduis de iniuriis, quas ipsis sociisque eorum intulerint, item si Allobrogibus satisfaciant, sese cum eis pacem esse facturum.* 7 Divico respondit: *Ita Helvetios a maioribus suis institutos esse, uti obsides accipere, non dare, consuerint; eius rei populum Romanum esse testem.* Hoc responso dato, discessit.

Direct form (I.14.1-6): 1 *Eo mihi minus dubitationis datur, quod eas res, quas commemoravistis, memoria teneo, atque eo gravius fero, quo minus merito populi Romani acciderunt;* 2 *qui si alicuius iniuriae sibi conscius fuisset, non fuit difficile cavere; sed eo deceptus est, quod neque commissum (esse) a se intellegebat, quare timeret, neque sine causa timendum (esse) putabat.* 3 *Quod si veteris contumeliae oblivisci volo, num etiam recentium iniuriarum, quod, me invito, iter per provinciam per vim temptavistis, quod Aeduos, quod Ambarros, quod Allobrogas vexavistis, memoriam deponere possum?* 4 *Quod vestra victoria tam insolenter gloriamini, quodque tam diu vos impune iniurias tulisse admiramini, eodem pertinet.* 5 *Consuerunt enim di immortales, quo gravius homines ex commutatione rerum doleant, quos pro scelere eorum ulcisci volunt, his secundiores interdum res et diuturniorem impunitatem concedere.* 6 *Cum haec ita sint, tamen, si obsides a vobis mihi dabuntur, uti ea, quae pollicemini, vos facturos (esse) intellegam, et si Aeduis de iniuriis, quas ipsis sociisque eorum intulistis, item si Allobrogibus satisfacietis, vobiscum pacem faciam.*

1 **His:** *104b.* **eo:** from *is,* ablative of cause, 'because of this,' i.e., 'for this reason,' explained by the following *quod*-clause ('namely because . . .'); *135a; 160c.* **sibi . . . dari:** '(that) he had less hesitation' (i.e., about his present course of action), lit. 'less of hesitation is given to him'; *97b.* **sibi:** *158a; 104a.* **commemorassent:** *64a1.* **memoria teneret:** cf. *I.7.4; 131a.* **eo gravius** (se eas res) **ferre, quo minus merito populi Romani accidissent:** correlative expression of degree of difference, lit. 'that (he) bore (these things) more heavily by that degree (*eo*) by which (*quo*) they had happened less deservedly to the Roman people,' i.e., he was upset about them to the same degree that they were undeserved, hence highly upset; *140.* **minus merito populi Romani:** lit. 'less in accordance with (that which was) deserved of the Roman people,' *136c.* **accidissent:** *214a.*

2 **qui:** = *populus Romanus,* 'it' or 'they'; *167.* **si:** past contrary to fact condition; *208.* **alicuius iniuriae sibi conscius fuisset:** 'had been conscious of any injustice on its part,' i.e., of committing any wrongdoing. **alicuius:** from *aliqui; 49a.* **iniuriae:** *102.* **sibi:** lit. 'to itself,' in the sense of 'on its part'; *109a.* **fuisse:** why *fuit* in the

direct form? *208b.* **cavere:** 'to take precautions' (lit. 'to be on guard') against reprisals, which the Roman people would have expected if they had in any way wronged the Helvetians. **eo . . . quod:** as in I.14.1. **deceptum:** *eum* (i.e., *populum Romanum*) *deceptum esse,* '(that) they had been deceived.' **quod neque . . . putaret:** 'because they understood that nothing had been done by them for which they should fear and they thought that they ought not to be afraid without cause.' **commissum:** sc. *esse,* impersonal, but most easily translated with *neque* as if *et nihil commissum esse.* **quare timeret:** regard *quare* as if *propter quod,* referring back to *neque commissum,* thus introducing a relative clause of characteristic, '(of the sort that) on account of which they (the Roman people) should fear,' subjunctive also in the direct form; *194a* (or one can regard *quare* as introducing an indirect question; *204.3*). **neque timendum:** sc. *esse,* impersonal, lit. 'it ought not to be feared'; *73e.*

3 **Quod:** translate 'Even' or 'But'; lit. 'as to which,' referring to the thought of the preceding sentence; *118d.* **veteris contumeliae:** 'the old insult,' i.e., the destruction of Cassius's army in 107 BC; *103a.* **vellet:** *218.1a.* **num . . . posse:** *179b1.* **num etiam . . . posse:** 'was he also able'; *num* introduces a question to which the expected answer is "no." **recentium iniuriarum:** dependent on *memoriam* near the end of the sentence; 'of fresh outrages,' specified in the following appositional clauses introduced by *quod,* '(namely) the fact that'; *198b.* **eo invito:** *eo = Caesare,* 'against his will,' lit. 'with him (being) unwilling'; *144b5.* **per provinciam per vim:** note the two different senses of *per:* 'though the province' (spatial) vs. 'through force' (i.e., by means of force). **temptassent:** *64a1; 214a.* **quod, quod, quod:** emphatic repetition, sc. *vexassent* with all three; *89a; 239a.* **Allobrogas:** *19f.* **deponere:** 'put aside'; *221a.*

4 **Quod . . . quodque:** 'The fact that . . . and the fact that'; the two clauses introduced by *quod* (and linked by *–que*) stand as subject of *pertinere; 198b; 214a.* **sua victoria:** 'because of their victory' over the Romans under Cassius in 107 BC; *135a.* **insolenter:** 'arrogantly'; *34a.* **gloriarentur:** 'they were boasting'; *214a.* **tam diu se impune iniurias tulisse:** 'that they for so long had perpetrated wrongs without punishment'; indirect discourse within the *quodque . . . admirarentur* clause. **admirarentur:** 'they marveled'; *61a1.* **eodem pertinere:** 'pointed to the same conclusion (lit. 'to the same place'),' i.e., were further indications of impending retribution for the wrongs they had committed.

5 **Consuesse enim deos immortales, quo gravius homines ex commutatione rerum doleant, quos pro scelere eorum ulcisci velint, his secundiores interdum res et diuturniorem impunitatem concedere:** reorganized into English word order, this sentence would read: *enim deos immortales, quo homines doleant gravius ex commutatione rerum, consuesse interdum concedere secundiores res et diuturniorem impunitatem his quos velint ulcisci pro eorum scelere.* **Consuesse:** 'are accustomed'; *64a2; 176b; 214a.* **deos:** *8d.* **quo . . . doleant:** purpose clause; *193b.* **gravius:** *34a.* **ex commutatione rerum:** 'from their reversal of fortune,' lit. 'from the changing of things.' **scelere:** *13e.* **ulcisci:** *223b.* **his:** 'to those,' antecedent of *quos* six words prior. **diuturniorem impunitatem:** 'a more prolonged escape from punishment'; *76b; 106a.* **concedere:** 'to grant,' after *Consuesse,* the first word in the sentence; *221a; 113b.*

6 **Cum:** 'although'; *187.* **ea:** *haec* in the direct form; *160a.* **tamen:** *236a.* **uti . . . intellegat:** purpose clause that incorporates an indirect statement that incorporates a relative clause. **ea:** object of *facturos (esse),* with which supply *eos* as subject. **polliceantur:** *61a2.* **Aeduis, Allobrogibus:** dat. after *satisfaciant; 105.* **de:** 'for.' **ipsis:** the Aeduans. **sociis:** the Ambarri. **satisfaciant:** 'they should make restitution'; *79b.*

7 **Direct form:** Ita *Helvetii* a maioribus suis *instituti sunt,* uti obsides accipere, non dare, consuerint; *huius rei populus Romanus est testis.* **institutos esse:** 'were formed.' **uti . . . consuerint:** 'that they were accustomed'; *64a2; 197b.* **esse testem:** 'was a witness.' **Hoc responso dato:** 'after making this reply,' lit. 'with this reply having been given'; *144b2.* **discessit:** 'he (Divico) departed.'

The Helvetians resume their march and defeat Caesar's cavalry; Caesar follows.

15. 1 Postero die castra ex eo loco movent. Idem facit Caesar equitatumque omnem, ad numerum quattuor milium, quem ex omni provincia et Aeduis atque eorum sociis coactum habebat, praemittit, qui videant, quas in partes hostes iter faciant. 2 Qui, cupidius novissimum agmen insecuti, alieno loco cum equitatu Helvetiorum proelium committunt et pauci de nostris cadunt. 3 Quo proelio sublati Helvetii, quod quingentis equitibus tantam multitudinem equitum propulerant, audacius subsistere non numquam et novissimo agmine proelio nostros lacessere coeperunt. 4 Caesar suos a proelio continebat, ac satis habebat in praesentia hostem rapinis, pabulationibus populationibusque prohibere. 5 Ita dies circiter quindecim iter fecerunt, uti inter novissimum hostium agmen et nostrum primum non amplius quinis aut senis milibus passuum interesset.

1 **Postero:** 'the following'; *33.* **movent:** sc. *Helvetii; 175b.* **Idem:** neuter accusative; *45.* **equitatum:** 'his cav-

alry'; *157a; 269b.* **coactum habebat:** 'had collected'; *229a.* **qui videant:** 'to see'; relative clause of purpose; *193a.* **videant:** plural because the subject *qui* is plural, on account of the idea of *equites* in the antecedent *equitatum; 164d; 238h.* **quas … faciant:** indirect question; *204.2.* **quas in partes:** 'in what direction'; how lit.? *48b.*

2 **Qui:** '(and) those men'; *167.* **cupidius:** 'too eagerly'; *153a.* **novissimum agmen:** 'the last (part of the) column' of the Helvetians, i.e., the rearguard; *27b; 12e; 152a.* **insecuti:** *61a3.* **alieno loco:** 'on unfavorable ground,' lit. 'in an unsuitable place,' probably a place too hilly for easy mobility; *145c.* **pauci:** presumably the rest safely retreated. **de nostris:** translate as if *nostrorum; 97d.*

3 **sublati:** 'elated'; see *tollo* in the Vocab. **quod:** causal. **quingentis:** *36.* **equitibus:** *131b.* **audacius:** *34a.* **subsistere:** 'to halt and make a stand'; i.e., attack the Romans following them. **non numquam:** 'sometimes,' perhaps even 'often' (litotes; *239g*), lit. 'not never.' **novissimo agmine:** 'with their rearguard'; *131b.* **proelio:** *131a.* **nostros:** 'our men'; *154a.* **lacessere:** 'to harass.' **coeperunt:** *72b.*

4 **suos:** 'his soldiers'; *154a.* **a proelio:** *127b.* **satis habebat:** 'considered (it) sufficient'; the object of *habebat* is *prohibere,* and *satis* is used as a predicate accusative; *115a.* **in praesentia:** 'for the present.' **rapinis, pabulationibus populationibusque:** 'from pillaging, foraging, and laying waste' the country; *92a; 127a.*

5 **Ita:** *197b.* **dies:** *118a.* **nostrum primum** (agmen): 'the first (part of) our column,' i.e., the vanguard; *288.* **amplius:** 'more,' here the neuter nominative form of the comparative adjective functioning as a substantive, i.e., the subject of *interesset; 154a.* **quinis, senis:** distributive, 'five or six miles' each day; *36.* **milibus:** *38a; 129a; 243b.* **interesset:** 'intervened'; *66a.*

The Aeduans do not bring the grain they promised.

16. 1 Interim cotidie Caesar Aeduos frumentum, quod essent publice polliciti, flagitare. 2 Nam propter frigora, non modo frumenta in agris matura non erant, sed ne pabuli quidem satis magna copia suppetebat, 3 eo autem frumento, quod flumine Arari navibus subvexerat, propterea uti minus poterat, quod iter ab Arari Helvetii averterant, a quibus discedere nolebat. 4 Diem ex die ducere Aedui; conferri, comportari, adesse dicere. 5 Ubi se diutius duci intellexit et diem instare, quo die frumentum militibus metiri oporteret, convocatis eorum principibus, quorum magnam copiam in castris habebat, in his Diviciaco et Lisco, qui summo magistratui praeerat, quem 'vergobretum' appellant Aedui, qui creatur annuus et vitae necisque in suos habet potestatem, graviter eos accusat, 6 quod, cum neque emi neque ex agris sumi possit, tam necessario tempore, tam propinquis hostibus, ab eis non sublevetur, praesertim cum, magna ex parte eorum precibus adductus, bellum susceperit; multo etiam gravius, quod sit destitutus, queritur.

1 **Aeduos, frumentum:** *116a.* **quod essent polliciti:** 'which (he said) they had promised'; Caesar the writer presents the statement of Caesar the commander as if it were quoted from someone else; *183a; 214b.* **flagitare:** historical infinitive, 'kept demanding'; *182.*

2 **frigora:** 'the (times of) cold,' the spring being later than in Italy; *92c.* **frumenta:** the plural is used by Caesar of standing grain; 'crops of grain.' **matura:** 'ripe.' **ne pabuli quidem satis magna copia suppetebat:** lit. 'not even of fodder was a sufficiently great supply available'; fodder was required for the baggage animals as well as the horses of the cavalry. **ne … quidem:** 'not even'; *237c.*

3 **autem:** *236a.* **frumento:** after *uti; 131c.* **flumine:** 'by (way of) the river'; *134a.* **navibus:** *131a.* **Arari:** *18e.* **subvexerat:** 'he had brought up.' **propterea … quod:** cf. I.1.3; do not translate *propterea* until you get to *quod.* **averterant:** the Helvetians had at first followed the valley of the Arar (*Saône*) northward, but now 'had turned away from the Arar' and passed westward into the valley of the Liger (*Loire*), avoiding the mountainous country opposite the place where they had crossed the Arar; see Map 1. **a quibus:** translate closely after the antecedent *Helvetii.*

4 **Diem ex die ducere:** sc. *eum,* 'were putting him off from day to day.' **Diem:** *118a.* **ducere, dicere:** historical infinitives; *182.* **conferri, comportari, adesse:** sc. *frumentum,* in indirect discourse after *dicere;* 'that (the grain) was being collected, that it was being brought, that it was at hand'; climax, with asyndeton; *238a; 239d.*

5 **diutius:** 'too long'; *153a.* **instare:** 'was near'; *178; 213a.* **die:** *165a.* **frumentum:** object of *metiri.* **metiri:** 'to measure out'; *61a4; 222a.* How often did the soldiers receive grain? *277.* **oporteret:** *73a, b; 214a.* **convocatis eorum principibus:** 'having called together their leading men'; how lit.? *144b2.* **in his Diviciaco et Lisco:** sc. *convocatis;* Caesar could have written *in quibus (principibus) Diviciacus et Liscus erant,* but he chose this variation within this series of relative clauses. **summo:** *33.* **magistratui:** *107a; 82b.* **praeerat:** 'held'; *66a.* **vergobretum:** 'vergobret'; *115a; 258a.* Meaning? See Vocab. **qui:** 'who'; the antecedent is *vergobretum.* **annuus:** 'annually'; *151.* **vitae necisque:** 'of life and death'; *102.* **in suos:** 'over his countrymen'; *154a.* **graviter eos accusat:** the brief main clause of this long sentence; *175b.*

6 **emi:** 'be purchased'; *55.* **neque ... neque:** *233a.* **possit:** sc. *frumentum; 220.* **tam necessario tempore:** 'at so necessary a time'; *147a.* **tam propinquis hostibus:** *144b2.* **non sublevetur:** with *quod,* 'because (as he said) he received no help from them,' lit. 'was not helped by them'; *214b.* See I.16.1, *quod essent polliciti.* **praesertim cum:** 'especially since'; *184b.* **magna ex parte:** 'in great measure.' **eorum precibus:** 'by their entreaties'; *135a.* **adductus:** the participle carries forward the causal force of the clause: 'especially since he had undertaken the campaign because he had been prevailed upon by their entreaties'; *227a1.* **bellum:** 'the campaign' against the Helvetians. **multo:** *140.* **quod:** causal. **sit destitutus:** translate as if pluperfect, 'he had been abandoned,' since the time is past relative to that of **queritur,** which is a historical present, 'he complained'; *177b; 214b.*

Liscus discloses treachery.

17. 1 Tum demum Liscus, oratione Caesaris adductus, quod antea tacuerat, proponit: *esse non nullos, quorum auctoritas apud plebem plurimum valeat, qui privatim plus possint quam ipsi magistratus.* 2 *Hos seditiosa atque improba oratione multitudinem deterrere, ne frumentum conferant, quod debeant:* 3 *praestare, si iam principatum Galliae obtinere non possint, Gallorum quam Romanorum imperia perferre;* 4 *neque dubitare debere, quin, si Helvetios superaverint Romani, una cum reliqua Gallia Aeduis libertatem sint erepturi.* 5 *Ab eisdem nostra consilia, quaeque in castris gerantur, hostibus enuntiari; hos a se coerceri non posse.* 6 *Quin etiam, quod necessariam rem coactus Caesari enuntiarit, intellegere sese, quanto id cum periculo fecerit, et ob eam causam, quam diu potuerit, tacuisse.*

> *Direct form* (I.17.1-2, 5-6): 1 *Non nulli sunt,* quorum auctoritas apud plebem plurimum *valet,* qui privatim plus *possunt* quam ipsi magistratus. 2 *Hi* seditiosa atque improba oratione multitudinem *deterrent,* ne frumentum conferant, quod *(conferre) debent;* [3 *(dicunt)* praestare ... ; 4 neque dubitare debere, quin ... sint erepturi]. 5 Ab eisdem *tua* consilia, quaeque in castris *geruntur,* hostibus *enuntiantur; hi a me* coerceri non *possunt.* 6 Quin etiam, quod necessariam rem coactus *tibi enuntiavi, intellego,* quanto id cum periculo *fecerim,* et ob eam causam, quam diu *potui, tacui.*

1 **quod:** as antecedent supply *id* with *proponit; 160c.* **tacuerat:** 'had kept to himself'; how lit.? **proponit:** 'brought forward, (saying) that,' i.e., 'declared'; *213a.* **esse non nullos:** 'that there were some men,' lit. 'not none'; *90a; 212.* **plurimum valeat:** 'carried very great weight'; *32; 118b.* **privatim:** 'as private individuals'; *77.* **plus possint:** 'had more power.' Gallic leaders could control multitudes of personal adherents (cf., e.g., I.4.2); *257; 258.*

2 **deterrere:** 'were holding back' by inspiring fear. **oratione:** 'talk.' **ne ... conferant:** 'from furnishing,' a clause of hindering or preventing; *201a.* **conferant:** plural because of the idea of plurality in *multitudinem; 173b.* **debeant:** 'they ought' (to furnish), lit. 'they owed,' i.e., they were under obligation to furnish.

3 **praestare ... erepturi:** parenthetical indirect quotation within the indirect quotation attributed to Liscus, summarizing the line of argument (*oratione,* I.17.2) by which the anti-Roman leaders influenced the Aeduan populace; '(saying) that it was better,' etc. Hence I.17.3-4 represent a double layer of indirect discourse: within the claims Caesar attributes to Liscus are the claims Liscus attributes to these powerful private individuals. The indirect speech attributed to Liscus resumes at I.17.5. **praestare:** impersonal. **si iam ... non possint:** 'if they (the Aeduans) could no longer'; *218.1a.* Formerly, and for a considerable period, the Aeduans had been the leading people in Gaul (VI.13). **Gallorum:** 'of Gauls,' i.e., over the Helvetians. **imperia:** 'the commands'; plural as referring to the acts of a sovereign power. **perferre:** 'to endure,' subject of *praestare.*

4 **neque dubitare debere:** sc. *se,* 'and they (the Aeduan populace) ought not to doubt.' **quin ... sint erepturi:** 'that they (the Romans) were going to take away'; a clause of doubting that would be subjunctive also in direct discourse; *201c; 63.* **superaverint:** 'should have overpowered'; *218.1b; 219.* **una:** adverb, 'together.' **Aeduis:** dative after *erepturi sint; 109b.*

5 **nostra:** from the Roman point of view. **quaeque:** the *–que* is the connective, while *quae* introduces an indirect question; *204.2.* **quaeque ... gerantur:** 'and whatever is done,' lit. 'and what things are done.' **enuntiari:** both *consilia* and *quae in castris gerantur* are the subjects of this infinitive. **se:** Liscus. **coerceri:** 'be restrained'; Liscus' authority as vergobret, including 'power of life and death' (I.16.5), was here of no avail.

6 **Quin etiam:** 'moreover.' **quod ... enuntiarit:** 'as to the fact that he had reported'; a substantive clause introduced by *quod; 198c.* **necessariam rem:** 'pressing matter.' **coactus:** 'under compulsion,' lit. 'having been compelled,' by reason of the vehemence of Caesar's complaints (I.16.5-6) and his position as the highest Aeduan official. **enuntiarit:** *64a1.* **quanto cum periculo:** 'with how much danger,' introduces an indirect question; *204.3.* **id:** refers back to the clause *quod ... enuntiarit; 160c.* **periculo:** *137c.* **fecerit:** translate as if pluperfect, since *intellegere* is historical present (compare *tacuisse,* even though *potuerit,* like *fecerit,* is perfect subjunctive).

41

ob eam causam: 'on account of this reason,' i.e., the danger. **quam diu:** 'as long as.' **tacuisse:** intransitive, sc. *se* as subject; 'he had kept silent.'

Caesar learns that Dumnorix is the traitor.

18. 1 Caesar hac oratione Lisci Dumnorigem, Diviciaci fratrem, designari sentiebat; sed, quod pluribus praesentibus eas res iactari nolebat, celeriter concilium dimittit, Liscum retinet. 2 Quaerit ex solo ea, quae in conventu dixerat; dicit liberius atque audacius. Eadem secreto ab aliis quaerit, reperit esse vera: 3 *ipsum esse Dumnorigem, summa audacia, magna apud plebem propter liberalitatem gratia, cupidum rerum novarum. Complures annos portoria reliquaque omnia Aeduorum vectigalia parvo pretio redempta habere, propterea quod, illo licente, contra liceri audeat nemo.* 4 *His rebus et suam rem familiarem auxisse et facultates ad largiendum magnas comparasse;* 5 *magnum numerum equitatus suo sumptu semper alere et circum se habere,* 6 *neque solum domi, sed etiam apud finitimas civitates largiter posse, atque huius potentiae causa matrem in Biturigibus homini illic nobilissimo ac potentissimo collocasse;* 7 *ipsum ex Helvetiis uxorem habere, sororem ex matre et propinquas suas nuptum in alias civitates collocasse.* 8 *Favere et cupere Helvetiis propter eam affinitatem, odisse etiam suo nomine Caesarem et Romanos, quod eorum adventu potentia eius deminuta et Diviciacus frater in antiquum locum gratiae atque honoris sit restitutus.* 9 *Si quid accidat Romanis, summam in spem per Helvetios regni obtinendi venire; imperio populi Romani non modo de regno, sed etiam de ea, quam habeat, gratia desperare.* 10 Reperiebat etiam in quaerendo Caesar, quod proelium equestre adversum paucis ante diebus esset factum, initium eius fugae factum a Dumnorige atque eius equitibus (nam equitatui, quem auxilio Caesari Aedui miserant, Dumnorix praeerat), eorum fuga reliquum esse equitatum perterritum.

Direct form (I.18.3-9): 3 *Ipse est Dumnorix,* summa audacia, magna apud plebem propter liberalitatem gratia, *cupidus* rerum novarum. Complures annos portoria reliquaque omnia Aeduorum vectigalia parvo pretio redempta *habet,* propterea quod, illo licente, contra liceri *audet* nemo. 4 His rebus et suam rem familiarem *auxit* et facultates ad largiendum magnas *comparavit.* 5 Magnum numerum equitatus suo sumptu semper *alit* et circum se *habet;* 6 neque solum domi, sed etiam apud finitimas civitates largiter *potest,* atque huius potentiae causa matrem in Biturigibus homini illic nobilissimo ac potentissimo *collocavit;* 7 *ipse* ex Helvetiis uxorem *habet,* sororem ex matre et propinquas suas nuptum in alias civitates *collocavit.* 8 *Favet* et *cupit* Helvetiis propter eam affinitatem, *odit* etiam suo nomine Caesarem et Romanos, quod adventu potentia eius *deminuta* (*est*) et Diviciacus frater in antiquum locum gratiae atque honoris *est* restitutus. 9 Si quid accidat Romanis, summam in spem per Helvetios regni obtinendi *veniat;* imperio populi Romani non modo de regno, sed etiam de ea, quam *habet,* gratia *desperat.*

1 **oratione:** *131a.* **Dumnorigem:** *10c.* **Diviciaci:** *19d; 258c.* **designari:** *213a.* **quod:** causal. **pluribus praesentibus:** 'with many persons present'; *144b2.* **res:** 'matters,' i.e., the real reasons why the state of the Aeduans had not made good its promises. **iactari:** *223a.* **celeriter:** 'quickly,' so as to shut off discussion; *34a.* **concilium:** 'the assembly' of leading Aeduans (*principibus,* I.16.5). **retinet:** '(but) detained'; *238a.*

2 **Quaerit ex** (eo) **solo ea, quae:** '(Caesar) asked him alone about what,' lit. 'he inquired from him alone about those things which'; *116c.* **dicit:** sc. *Liscus.* **liberius:** 'more freely'; *34a.* **secreto:** 'privately'; *34b.* **esse vera:** sc. *ea,* 'that they (Liscus's statements) were true'; *148c.*

3 For the indirect quotation, see *212.* **ipsum:** in predicate, 'that Dumnorix was the very man,' as Caesar had surmised (I.18.1); *162a.* **summa audacia:** '(a man) of (lit. 'with') the utmost audacity'; *143a.* **annos:** *118a.* **portoria:** 'tolls,' levied chiefly, we may assume, upon goods passing through the country along the roads and rivers. **reliqua:** *171a.* **vectigalia:** 'revenues' in general; *vectigal* (derived from *vectus,* participle of *veho*) means that which is 'brought in' to the public treasury; *16d.* **pretio:** 'price'; *141.* **redempta habere:** translate as if *habere* were an auxiliary verb: '(he) had bought up'; *229a.* The Aeduan revenues, apparently, were 'bought up' as among the Romans; that is, the task of collecting taxes was sold at auction to the highest bidder, who guaranteed to the state a certain sum, did the collecting through his agents, and kept for himself all that he could make above the amount paid into the public treasury and the costs of collection. **illo licente:** 'when he made a bid'; *144a.* **contra:** here an adverb. **liceri:** 'to bid,' deponent; *61a2.* Since no one dared to bid against Dumnorix, he could obtain the right to collect the taxes on terms very favorable to himself.

4 **rebus:** *131a.* **et ... et:** *233a.* **rem familiarem:** 'private fortune.' **auxisse:** '(he) had increased.' **ad largiendum:** 'for bribery'; *61a4; 230.3.* **comparasse:** *64a1.*

5 **suo sumptu:** 'at his own expense.' **alere:** 'maintained.'

6 **neque:** translate as if *et non*; *233a.* **solum:** 'only'; *236d.* **domi:** *20c; 146.* **largiter posse:** 'had great influence';

lit. 'was able to a large extent'; *118b*. **huius potentiae causa:** *135b*. **Biturigibus:** *10c*. **homini:** *107b*. **illic nobil-issimo ac potentissimo:** 'the most noble and powerful man in that place,' in apposition to *in Biturigibus homini*. **collocasse:** sc. *nuptum*, as also just below in I.18.7: '(he) had placed his mother with a man (in order to marry),' i.e., he arranged for her marriage; *64a*; *231a*.

7 **ipsum:** '(he) himself,' Dumnorix. **uxorem:** a daughter of Orgetorix (I.3.5); *13d*. **sororem ex matre:** 'half-sister, on his mother's side.' **suas propinquas:** 'his female relatives.' **nuptum:** 'in order to marry (them)'; supine of purpose after *collocasse*; *231a*. **in:** 'among,' lit. 'into,' from the sense of motion in *collocasse*.

8 **Favere et cupere:** '(he) was favorable and wished well to.' **Helvetiis:** *105*. **odisse etiam:** '(and he) also hated'; *72*. **suo nomine:** 'on his own account,' lit. 'in his own name,' i.e., 'for his own (personal) reasons.' **quod:** causal. **deminuta** (sit): 'had been lessened.' **in antiquum locum:** 'to his former position,' which the rise of Dumnorix had obscured.

9 **Si quid accidat, . . .** (se) **venire:** a condition of possible realization in indirect speech; *218.2*. **quid:** *49a*; *168*. **accidat:** here used of something unfavorable; the expression 'if anything should happen to him' has a similar underlying suggestion. **per:** 'with the help of'; *123a*. **regni obtinendi:** *102*; *230.1*. **imperio populi Romani:** 'under the rule of the Roman people'; *138*. **non modo . . . sed etiam:** *236d*. **de regno:** 'of the kingship.'

10 **quaerendo:** gerund; *230.4*. **quod proelium equestre adversum . . . esset factum:** 'as to the fact that the cavalry battle had turned out adversely'; a substantive clause introduced by *quod*, cf. *quod . . . enuntiarit* in I.17.6; *198c*. **adversum:** in agreement with *proelium*, but predicative and adverbial; *151*. **paucis ante diebus:** *140*. **initium:** 'the beginning.' **fugae:** i.e., the flight that caused the battle to turn out adversely. **factum:** sc. *esse*; infinitive in indirect discourse after *reperiebat*. The implication is that Dumnorix treacherously started to flee with the Aeduan contingent, which then precipitated a general rout. **equitatui:** dative after *praeerat*; *107a*. **auxilio Caesari:** double dative, 'as an aid to Caesar'; *112b*. **fuga:** *135a*. **esse perterritum:** 'had been thrown into a panic'; another infinitive (the subject of which is *reliquum equitatum*) after *reperiebat*.

Convinced of the treachery of Dumnorix, Caesar consults his brother Diviciacus.

19. 1 Quibus rebus cognitis, cum ad has suspiciones certissimae res accederent, quod per fines Sequanorum Helvetios traduxisset, quod obsides inter eos dandos curasset, quod ea omnia, non modo iniussu suo et civitatis, sed etiam inscientibus ipsis, fecisset, quod a magistratu Aeduorum accusaretur, satis esse causae arbitrabatur, quare in eum aut ipse animadverteret, aut civitatem animadvertere iuberet. 2 His omnibus rebus unum repugnabat, quod Diviciaci fratris summum in populum Romanum studium, summam in se voluntatem, egregiam fidem, iustitiam, temperantiam cognoverat; nam, ne eius supplicio Diviciaci animum offenderet, verebatur. 3 Itaque prius quam quicquam conaretur, Diviciacum ad se vocari iubet et, cotidianis interpretibus remotis, per C. Valerium Troucillum, principem Galliae provinciae, familiarem suum, cui summam omnium rerum fidem habebat, cum eo colloquitur; 4 simul commonefacit quae, ipso praesente, in concilio Gallorum de Dumnorige sint dicta, et ostendit quae separatim quisque de eo apud se dixerit. 5 Petit atque hortatur, ut sine eius offensione animi vel ipse de eo, causa cognita, statuat, vel civitatem statuere iubeat.

1 **Quibus rebus cognitis:** 'having found out these things'; how lit.? **accederent:** here, as often, to be translated as passive, 'were added.' **quod . . . traduxisset:** the first of four substantive clauses that define *certissimae res* and are introduced by *quod*, which is best translated 'the fact that'; substantive clauses introduced by *quod* usually take the indicative, but here the verbs are attracted into the subjunctive because they are subordinated to a circumstantial *cum*-clause; *198b*; *220*. **obsides dandos curasset:** 'had arranged that hostages be given'; *229b*. **inter eos:** between the two peoples, the Sequanians and the Helvetians. **iniussu suo et civitatis:** 'without his own (Caesar's) authorization and that of the state' of the Aeduans; *135b*; *157d*. **inscientibus ipsis:** 'without their knowledge,' lit. 'with themselves not knowing'; *ipsis = Caesare et Aeduis*; *144b2*. **magistratu Aeduorum:** Liscus, the vergobret (I.16.5). **satis . . . causae:** *97b*. **esse:** 'that there was'; *90a*. **arbitrabatur:** the main verb of this sentence. **quare in eum ipse animadverteret:** 'on account of which he himself should punish him,' lit. 'should give attention to him'; *quare = propter quam*, introducing the equivalent of a relative clause of characteristic; *194a*. **aut . . . aut:** *235*.

2 **rebus:** *105*. **unum:** 'one consideration'; *154a*. **repugnabat:** 'was resisting,' lit. 'was fighting back against.' **quod:** introduces a substantive clause that explains *unum*: 'one thing . . . namely that'; *198b*. **Diviciaci fratris:** this possessive genitive should be understood with all the accusative nouns that follow: *studium, voluntatem, fidem, iustitiam, temperantiam*. **temperantiam:** *238a*. **cognoverat:** 'was familiar with'; *176b*. **eius:** translate as if *Dumnorigis*. **offenderet:** with *ne*, 'that he might offend'; *202*. **verebatur:** 'he was afraid'; *61a2*.

3 **quicquam:** *49a.* **conaretur:** *189b.* **Diviciacum vocari:** 'that Diviciacus be summoned'; *223a.* **cotidianis interpretibus:** 'the ordinary (lit. 'daily') interpreters.' Diviciacus evidently did not speak Latin nor Caesar Celtic; *10e.* **per:** *123a.* **Galliae provinciae:** *259.* **cui summam omnium rerum fidem habebat:** 'in (lit. 'to') whom he had the utmost confidence in (lit. 'of') all matters.' **eo:** Diviciacus.

4 **quae:** *48a; 204.2.* **ipso:** Diviciacus. **separatim:** *77.* **quisque:** *49a.* **apud se:** 'in his (Caesar's) presence'; *158a.*

5 **Petit atque hortatur:** sc. *Diviciacum; 60.* **ut . . . statuat, iubeat:** substantive clauses representing indirect commands; *199a.* **eius:** dependent on *animi;* translate with *sine offensione:* 'without offense to (lit. 'of') his (Diviciacus') spirit.' **vel . . . vel:** *235a, b.* **ipse . . . statuat:** lit., 'that he (Caesar) himself pass judgment'; the connection with the preceding *hortatur* shows that the underlying thought is: 'to permit him (Caesar), having heard the case, to pronounce judgment on Dumnorix (*de eo*), or direct the state (of the Aeduans) to pronounce judgment.' **causa cognita:** *144b2.*

Moved by Diviciacus' plea, Caesar pardons Dumnorix, but warns him.

20. 1 Diviciacus, multis cum lacrimis Caesarem complexus, obsecrare coepit, ne quid gravius in fratrem statueret: 2 *scire se, illa esse vera, neque quemquam ex eo plus quam se doloris capere, propterea quod, cum ipse gratia plurimum domi atque in reliqua Gallia, ille minimum propter adulescentiam posset, per se crevisset;* 3 *quibus opibus ac nervis non solum ad minuendam gratiam, sed paene ad perniciem suam uteretur. Sese tamen et amore fraterno et existimatione vulgi commoveri.* 4 *Quod si quid ei a Caesare gravius accidisset, cum ipse eum locum amicitiae apud eum teneret, neminem existimaturum, non sua voluntate factum; qua ex re futurum, uti totius Galliae animi a se averterentur.* 5 Haec cum pluribus verbis flens a Caesare peteret, Caesar eius dextram prendit; consolatus rogat, finem orandi faciat; tanti eius apud se gratiam esse ostendit, uti et rei publicae iniuriam et suum dolorem eius voluntati ac precibus condonet. 6 Dumnorigem ad se vocat, fratrem adhibet; quae in eo reprehendat, ostendit; quae ipse intellegat, quae civitas queratur, proponit; monet, ut in reliquum tempus omnes suspiciones vitet; praeterita se Diviciaco fratri condonare dicit. Dumnorigi custodes ponit, ut, quae agat, quibuscum loquatur, scire possit.

1 **multis cum lacrimis:** *136a.* **complexus:** 'embracing'; *61a3; 226c.* **quid:** substantive form (= *aliquid*); *49a; 117a; 168.* **gravius:** *153a.* **statueret:** *199a4.*

2 **scire se:** '(saying) that he knew'; *213b; 178.* **neque quemquam:** 'and that not anyone'; *49a; 168.* **ex eo:** 'on account of that fact'; *160c.* **plus doloris:** *25b; 97b.* **ipse:** Diviciacus. **gratia:** *135a.* **plurimum:** sc. *posset,* in parallel to *minimum posset* in the subsequent phrase; *118b.* **domi:** i.e., *in Aeduis; 20c; 146.* **ille:** Dumnorix. **minimum:** *32; 118b.* **adulescentiam:** Dumnorix apparently was considerably younger than Diviciacus. **per se crevisset:** '(Dumnorix) had increased (in resources and strength) through his help'; *123a.*

3 **quibus:** 'and these'; *167.* **opibus:** 'resources'; after *uteretur; 131c.* **nervis:** lit. 'sinews' or 'tendons,' here used metaphorically as tools for exerting strength. **ad minuendam gratiam:** 'to lessen his (Diviciacus's) popularity'; *230.3.* **fraterno:** i.e., *fratris;* 'by affection for his brother.' **existimatione vulgi:** 'by public opinion'; how lit.? *6b.*

4 **Quod:** *118d.* **quid:** nominative (= *aliquid*); *168.* **ei:** = *Dumnorigi.* **a Caesare:** 'at the hands of Caesar.' **accidisset, existimaturum** (esse): condition of fact in indirect discourse; *218.1b.* **cum:** 'while'; *185c.* **eum locum amicitiae apud eum:** 'such a relation of friendship with Caesar'; how lit.? **non factum:** sc. *esse,* 'that it was not done,' after *existimaturum* (*esse*); *213a.* **sua:** referring to Diviciacus. **sua voluntate:** *136c.* **futurum:** sc. *esse,* 'it would come about'; the subject is *uti . . . averterentur; 203.1.*

5 **cum . . . peteret:** *185c.* **pluribus verbis:** 'with very many words'; i.e., 'at great length'; *138.* **flens:** *226a; 227b.* **dextram:** sc. *manum.* **consolatus rogat:** 'reassuring (Diviciacus) he asked (him)'; *61a1; 226c.* **finem orandi faciat:** 'to make an end of his pleading,' sc. *ut* before *finem; 199a4; 200a.* **orandi:** gerund; *230.1.* **tanti eius apud se gratiam esse:** 'that his (*eius* refers to Diviciacus) influence with himself (*se* refers to Caesar) was so great,' lit. 'of so great account'; *101.* **uti . . . condonet:** *197b.* **et . . . et:** *233a.* **rei publicae:** *102.* **eius voluntati:** 'in response to his wishes'; dative of indirect object on account of the meaning 'give' or 'present' in *condonet; 104a.* **condonet:** this verb has the sense of giving something (in the accusative) over to someone or something (in the dative) in the sense of overlooking or forgiving it for the sake of that person.

6 **fratrem adhibet:** 'he called in his brother (Diviciacus).' **quae . . . reprehendat:** *48a; 204.2.* **in eo:** 'in regard to him.' **intellegat:** = *sciat.* **civitas:** i.e., of the Aeduans, whose agreement to furnish grain had been sabotaged. **monet:** 'he warned (Dumnorix).' **in reliquum tempus:** 'for the future.' **vitet:** 'he should avoid'; *199a3.* **praeterita:** neuter plural, lit. 'things having been passed over,' i.e., 'the past'; *154a.* **Diviciaco fratri:** dative indirect object of *condonare,* as just above, with the sense 'for the sake of Diviciacus, his brother'; *104a.* **custodes:** 'watchers,' corresponding with the detectives of our day, for Dumnorix was not imprisoned. **agat:** *204.2.* **quibuscum:** *125c.*

Caesar plans to crush the Helvetians by a double surprise.

21. 1 Eodem die ab exploratoribus certior factus, hostes sub monte consedisse milia passuum ab ipsius castris octo, qualis esset natura montis et qualis in circuitu ascensus, qui cognoscerent, misit. 2 Renuntiatum est facilem esse. De tertia vigilia Titum Labienum, legatum pro praetore, cum duabus legionibus et eis ducibus, qui iter cognoverant, summum iugum montis ascendere iubet; quid sui consilii sit, ostendit. 3 Ipse de quarta vigilia eodem itinere, quo hostes ierant, ad eos contendit equitatumque omnem ante se mittit. 4 P. Considius, qui rei militaris peritissimus habebatur et in exercitu L. Sullae et postea in M. Crassi fuerat, cum exploratoribus praemittitur.

1 **Eodem die:** 'on the same day' that he had summoned the council of Gallic leaders in camp (I.16.5), and had had the interviews with Diviciacus and Dumnorix. **exploratoribus:** 287. **hostes ... octo:** 213a. The Helvetians were now in the valley of the Liger (*Loire*), southeast of Bibracte; see Map 1. **sub monte:** 'at the foot of a height'; 124a. **consedisse:** 'had encamped.' **milia passuum:** 118a; 243. **qualis ... misit:** translate as if (in English word order), *misit (exploratores) qui cognoscerent qualis esset natura montis et qualis (esset) in circuitu ascensus.* **qualis esset natura montis:** indirect question, 'of what sort the nature of the mountain was'; 204.3. **in circuitu ascensus:** 'the ascent from the opposite side,' lit. 'the ascent in the going around.' Caesar planned a flank movement, with a surprise attack upon the Helvetians from two sides at once; a Roman force, following a circuitous route, would from the rear secretly ascend the height at the foot of which the Helvetians were encamped, and charge down upon them from above, while Caesar with the rest of the army attacked them in front. **qui cognoscerent:** 193a.

2 **esse:** sc. *ascensum.* **de tertia vigilia:** 242c, d. **legatum pro praetore:** when a lieutenant-general was given a special responsibility to act outside the presence of the commander, he was designated 'lieutenant-general in place of the commander'; 273. **eis ducibus:** 'with those as guides,' referring to the patrols previously sent out. **summum iugum montis:** 'the highest ridge of the height,' which was apparently long and uneven. **ascendere:** 200b. **quid sui consilii sit:** 'what his plan was,' lit. 'what is of his plan,' indirect question; 97b; 204.2.

3 **itinere, quo:** 134a. **eos:** = *hostes.* **equitatum:** the cavalry were to put initial pressure on the enemy; 288.

4 **rei militaris:** 'in (lit. 'of') the art of war'; 21b; 102. **peritissimus:** 148c; 153a. This favorable characterization of Considius preemptively justifies why Caesar chose him for so important a reconnoiter. **L. Sullae, M. Crassi:** both of high repute as generals, Sulla for his services first in the war with Jugurtha in Africa, then in the Social War, and in the East; Crassus, for his decisive defeat of Spartacus; 19a. **M. Crassi:** sc. *exercitu.*

The plan miscarries because of false information.

22. 1 Prima luce, cum summus mons a Labieno teneretur, ipse ab hostium castris non longius mille et quingentis passibus abesset, neque, ut postea ex captivis comperit, aut ipsius adventus aut Labieni cognitus esset, 2 Considius equo admisso ad eum accurrit, dicit *montem, quem a Labieno occupari voluerit, ab hostibus teneri; id se a Gallicis armis atque insignibus cognovisse.* 3 Caesar suas copias in proximum collem subducit, aciem instruit. Labienus (ut erat ei praeceptum a Caesare, ne proelium committeret, nisi ipsius copiae prope hostium castra visae essent, ut undique uno tempore in hostes impetus fieret), monte occupato, nostros exspectabat proelioque abstinebat. 4 Multo denique die per exploratores Caesar cognovit et montem a suis teneri et Helvetios castra movisse et Considium, timore perterritum, quod non vidisset, pro viso sibi renuntiavisse. 5 Eo die, quo consuerat intervallo, hostes sequitur, et milia passuum tria ab eorum castris castra ponit.

1 **summus:** 152a. **passibus:** 129a. **abesset, cognitus esset:** 185c. **neque ... aut ... aut:** these conjunctions effectively combine into 'and neither ... nor'; 233a; 235. **ut ... comperit:** 'as he ascertained'; the indicative verb underscores the validity of the claim, for Caesar wants it to be recognized that his plan could have succeeded. **captivis:** 'prisoners.' **Labieni:** sc. *adventus.*

2 **equo admisso:** 'with his horse at top speed'; how lit.? 144b7. **accurrit:** 'hastened'; how lit.? **occupari:** *occupo,* meaning 'seize' or 'take possession of' is generally much stronger than its English derivative 'occupy'; 81. **voluerit:** 214a. **Gallicis armis:** 309. **insignibus:** 'insignia,' from the neuter noun *insigne.*

3 **in:** 'onto.' **subducit:** 'led up.' **aciem instruit:** 'drew up a line of battle'; 297a. **ut erat ... impetus fieret:** an explanatory parenthesis, with its components tightly conjoined: 'as it had been ordered ... not to ... unless ... so that ...'. **erat ei praeceptum:** 'he had been ordered,' lit. 'it had been ordered to him'; the subject is **ne proelium committeret,** 'not to commit to battle'; 73d; 199b. **nisi ... visae essent:** 218.1b. **prope:** 122a. **ut ... fieret:** purpose clause; 196a. **impetus:** nominative. **nostros:** the troops with Caesar; 154a. **proelio:** 127a.

4 **Multo die:** 'late in the day,' ablative of time when. **timore:** 'fear,' used especially of a cowardly fear. **perterri-**

tum: 'thoroughly frightened'; *79b.* **quod:** as antecedent supply an *id* as the object of *renuntiavisse; 160c.* **pro viso:** 'as seen'; *154a.*

5 **quo consuerat intervallo:** = *eo intervallo, quo sequi consuerat* (= *consueverat*), but more succinctly = 'at the customary interval'; this was five or six miles (I.15.5); *138; 165c.*

Caesar turns to go to Bibracte for supplies; the Helvetians pursue and attack.

23. 1 Postridie eius diei, quod omnino biduum supererat, cum exercitui frumentum metiri oporteret, et quod a Bibracte, oppido Aeduorum longe maximo et copiosissimo, non amplius milibus passuum XVIII aberat, rei frumentariae prospiciendum existimavit; iter ab Helvetiis avertit ac Bibracte ire contendit. 2 Ea res per fugitivos L. Aemilii, decurionis equitum Gallorum, hostibus nuntiatur. 3 Helvetii, seu quod timore perterritos Romanos discedere a se existimarent, eo magis quod pridie, superioribus locis occupatis, proelium non commisissent, sive eo, quod re frumentaria intercludi posse confiderent, commutato consilio atque itinere converso, nostros a novissimo agmine insequi ac lacessere coeperunt.

1 **Postridie eius diei:** 'the next day,' lit. 'on the after-day of this day'; *94c.* **quod ... et quod:** 'because ... and because.' **biduum supererat:** 'two days remained.' **cum:** lit. 'when,' but more freely 'before'; *185c.* **metiri:** *61a4; 277.* **oporteret:** *73a.* **Bibracte:** *16c.* **oppido:** *91a; 262b.* **longe:** *153b.* **milibus:** *129a.* **rei frumentariae:** 'the supply of grain,' or, more generally, 'supplies'; *105.* **prospiciendum** (sibi esse): 'that he ought to provide for,' lit. 'that it ought to be provided for'; *73e.* **Bibracte:** here accusative; *119a.*

2 **fugitivos:** 'runaway slaves'; deserters from an army were called *perfugae* (I.28.2); *74g.* **L.:** *19a.* Lucius Aemilius was a Roman officer in charge of a squad of Gallic horsemen. **decurionis:** 'decurion'; *269c.*

3 **seu quod ... sive eo, quod:** 'whether because ... or because of this, (namely) because'; *eo* being explained by the following *quod*-clause; *135a; 235.* **Romanos discedere:** indirect statement after *existimarent.* **existimarent:** a subjunctive verb in a causal clause indicates that the author attributes the explanation to another party; *183a.* **eo magis quod:** 'all the more (because of this, namely) because'; another causal *eo* explained through a subsequent *quod*; this causal clause supplements the reason given above (starting in *seu quod*). **pridie:** 'on the day before.' **superioribus locis occupatis:** referring to the maneuver of Labienus (I.21.2-3); *144b5.* **re frumentaria:** *127a.* **intercludi posse:** sc. *Romanos.* **confiderent:** 'were confident'; *183a; 213a.* **commutato, converso:** *144a; 239c.* **a:** *126c; 288.*

Romans and Helvetians prepare for battle; the Helvetians advance.

24. 1 Postquam id animum advertit, copias suas Caesar in proximum collem subduxit equitatumque, qui sustineret hostium impetum, misit. 2 Ipse interim in colle medio triplicem aciem instruxit legionum quattuor veteranarum; 3 atque supra se in summo iugo duas legiones, quas in Gallia citeriore proxime conscripserat, et omnia auxilia collocari ac totum montem hominibus compleri, et interea sarcinas in unum locum conferri et eum ab eis, qui in superiore acie constiterant, muniri iussit. 4 Helvetii, cum omnibus suis carris secuti, impedimenta in unum locum contulerunt; ipsi, confertissima acie reiecto nostro equitatu, phalange facta sub primam nostram aciem successerunt.

1 **Postquam:** 'after'; *188.* **id:** *113c.* **collem:** the hill of Armecy, about 16 miles southeast of Mt. Beuvray (the site of ancient Bibracte), and not far from the village of Montmort. See Map 3, A. **qui sustineret:** *193a.*

2 **interim:** 'meanwhile,' while the cavalry were holding back the enemy; it must have taken Caesar at least two hours to change over his marching column, which was five or six miles long, into battle lines. **in colle medio:** *152a.* **triplicem aciem:** the four legions stood side by side, with the cohorts of each legion arranged in three lines (297). The triple line was not straight, but followed the contour of the hillside, and was about an English mile in length; see Map 3, B-B. **legionum:** *98a.* **veteranarum:** 'veteran'; *267d, e.*

3 **supra se:** Caesar was near the front. **summo:** *152a.* **legiones ... collocari:** the object of *iussit* at the end of the sentence. **legiones, quas ... conscripserat:** the 11th and 12th legions; see I.10.3; *253.* **auxilia:** *268.* **ac:** 'and (thus).' **hominibus:** *131b.* By occupying the gently rounding crest of the hill, Caesar strengthened his position in case his battle lines, posted halfway up the slope, should be forced back. **interea:** 'in the meantime,' while the troops were taking their positions. **sarcinas:** 'packs'; *290.* **eum:** sc. *locum.* **eis:** i.e., the two legions most recently conscripted. **muniri:** 'be fortified,' by a trench and a rampart formed from the earth thrown out of the trench. The trench, which for a part of the distance was double, has been traced by excavations; the earthen rampart has disappeared. The line of defense thus hastily made on the highest part of the hill was semicircular in shape (Map 3, A).

4 **secuti:** *226c.* **impedimenta:** 'baggage'; *74d.* After the Helvetian fighting men turned back in order to attack

Caesar, the long line of carts turned and came back also and formed a great corral, probably at the spot marked "Helvetian Corral" on Map 3. **ipsi:** the fighting men, as distinguished from the old men, women, and children with the baggage. **confertissima acie:** *131a.* **reiecto nostro equitatu:** *144b2.* **phalange facta:** the Gauls, forming in 'a compact mass' (*phalanx* is not a technical term here), probably fifteen to twenty men deep, moved forward slowly but with almost irresistible momentum; those in the front rank held their large shields so that these would overlap, presenting a firm barrier to the enemy; *18f.* **sub:** the Helvetians advanced uphill and so 'up against' the first line, see Map 3, E-E.; *124a.*

The Romans charge, forcing the Helvetians back.

25. 1 Caesar, primum suo, deinde omnium ex conspectu remotis equis, ut, aequato omnium periculo, spem fugae tolleret, cohortatus suos proelium commisit. 2 Milites, e loco superiore pilis missis, facile hostium phalangem perfregerunt. Ea disiecta, gladiis destrictis in eos impetum fecerunt. 3 Gallis magno ad pugnam erat impedimento, quod, pluribus eorum scutis uno ictu pilorum transfixis et colligatis, cum ferrum se inflexisset, neque evellere neque, sinistra impedita, satis commode pugnare poterant, 4 multi ut, diu iactato bracchio, praeoptarent scutum manu emittere et nudo corpore pugnare. 5 Tandem vulneribus defessi, et pedem referre et, quod mons suberat circiter mille passuum, eo se recipere coeperunt. 6 Capto monte et succedentibus nostris, Boii et Tulingi, qui hominum milibus circiter XV agmen hostium claudebant et novissimis praesidio erant, ex itinere nostros ab latere aperto aggressi, circumvenire, et, id conspicati, Helvetii, qui in montem sese receperant, rursus instare et proelium redintegrare coeperunt. 7 Romani conversa signa bipertito intulerunt; prima et secunda acies, ut victis ac summotis resisteret, tertia, ut venientes sustineret.

1 **suo:** sc. *equo remoto*; *144b2.* **deinde:** *237b.* **omnium equis:** 'the horses of all' the mounted officers and Caesar's staff, not of the cavalry. **suo, omnium:** *157d.* **aequato omnium periculo:** *144b6.* **tolleret:** *196a.* **cohortatus suos:** it was customary for Roman commanders to address their soldiers just before committing them to battle; *228a.*

2 **e loco superiore pilis missis:** 'hurling their pikes,' with precision and terrible effect, 'from their higher position' on the slope; *282d; 144b6.* **perfregerunt:** 'broke up.' **Ea** (phalange) **disiecta, gladiis destrictis:** two more ablative absolutes; *282e.* **impetum fecerunt:** the first-line soldiers probably allowed the Helvetians to approach within 60 feet before hurling their pikes and charging.

3 **Gallis magno . . . impedimento:** double dative, 'a great hindrance (lit. 'for a great hindrance') to the Gauls'; *112.* **erat:** the subject is the following *quod*-clause; *198b.* **quod . . . neque evellere neque . . . pugnare poterant:** this clause describes two things the Helvetians were unable to do, while the reasons why they were unable to do them are explained in additional subordinate clauses (an ablative absolute and a *cum*-clause in the first case, another ablative absolute in the second). **scutis:** *309.* **uno ictu pilorum:** 'by the one strike of the pikes,' i.e., in the initial volley of pikes right before the Romans' charge. **transfixis et colligatis:** 'pierced and pinned together'; *144b2.* **ferrum:** the 'iron' of the pike (*282d*) was long enough to pierce two or more overlapping shields and was of soft metal, so that it would bend easily; its hard barbed point also hindered withdrawal. **se inflexisset:** 'had become bent,' lit. 'had bent itself'; *185c.* **evellere:** 'to pull (the pike) out.' **sinistra impedita:** 'since the left hand,' which carried the shield, 'was hampered'; *144b3.*

4 **multi:** emphatic position, subject of *praeoptarent*; *245d.* **ut:** 'so that,' introducing a clause of result; *197a.* **iactato bracchio:** 'having jerked their arm back and forth' in the effort to pull the bent pike iron out of their shields; how lit.? *144b2.* **praeoptarent:** 'preferred.' **manu:** *127a.* **emittere:** 'to drop.' **nudo:** 'unprotected' by a shield.

5 **vulneribus:** *13e; 135a.* **defessi:** 'exhausted.' **pedem referre:** 'to fall back,' lit. 'to bear back the foot'; *79d.* **quod mons suberat:** 'because there was a height nearby,' southwest of the hill of Armecy; see Map 3; *66a.* **mille:** *38a.* **eo:** adverb, 'to that place.' **se recipere:** 'to retreat,' lit. 'to take themselves back.'

6 **Capto monte et succedentibus nostris:** note the temporal distinction in the participles: after the Helvetians had seized the top of the height, the Romans were advancing up the slope; see Map 3, F-F; *144b2.* **Boii et Tulingi:** see I.5.4. **hominum:** *97a.* **milibus:** *131a.* **agmen hostium claudebant:** 'were at the end of (lit. 'were enclosing') the enemy's marching column.' **novissimis** (= *novissimo agmini*) **praesidio:** *112b.* **ex itinere:** 'from the march,' i.e., changing from marching order to fighting order as they came up. As the long column of emigrants had started out that morning, the 15,000 Boians and Tulingians formed the vanguard. When the order passed along the column to halt and turn back (I.23.3), they became the rearguard and thus were several miles away when the battle commenced. As the non-combatants were forming a corral with the carts, they marched by it and reached the field of battle just as the Romans were following the retreating Helvetians. **ab**

latere aperto: 'on the exposed flank'; *126c*. Since the shield was carried on the left arm, 'the exposed side' of the soldier was the right side, whence the expression was carried over to a body of soldiers in action. In the present instance, the three Roman lines, still retaining, in the confusion of battle, their distinct formation, were following the stubbornly resisting Helvetians toward the southwest from their original position, when the Boians and Tulingians came against them from the west, thus 'attacking' the Romans on the right flank. See Map 3, H. **circumvenire**: 'to move around them,' so as to fall upon the Romans in the rear; sc. *coeperunt*, which can be drawn forward and repeated from the last word in the sentence. **conspicati**: *226c*. **redintegrare**: 'to renew,' i.e., again assuming the offensive; see Map 3, G-G.

7 **conversa signa bipertito intulerunt**: 'turned and advanced the standards (lit. 'advanced the standards having been turned'; *228a; 285*) in two divisions'; one division facing straight ahead (**prima et secunda acies**), the other (**tertia acies**) facing the Boians and Tulingians. Strictly speaking, only the third line changed front (Map 3, D); the first and second lines were already in position to meet the new attack of the Helvetians (Map 3, C-C). **resisteret**: *196a*.

victis ac summotis: 'those who had been beaten and driven back'; *105; 154a; 227a4*. **tertia**: sc. *acies; 91c*.

The Helvetians are totally defeated; Caesar pursues the fleeing.

26. 1 Ita ancipiti proelio diu atque acriter pugnatum est. Diutius cum sustinere nostrorum impetus non possent, alteri se, ut coeperant, in montem receperunt, alteri ad impedimenta et carros suos se contulerunt. 2 Nam hoc toto proelio, cum ab hora septima ad vesperum pugnatum sit, aversum hostem videre nemo potuit. 3 Ad multam noctem etiam ad impedimenta pugnatum est, propterea quod pro vallo carros obiecerant et e loco superiore in nostros venientes tela coniciebant, et non nulli inter carros rotasque mataras ac tragulas subiciebant nostrosque vulnerabant. 4 Diu cum esset pugnatum, impedimentis castrisque nostri potiti sunt. Ibi Orgetorigis filia atque unus e filiis captus est. 5 Ex eo proelio circiter hominum milia CXXX superfuerunt eaque tota nocte continenter ierunt, nullam partem noctis itinere intermisso; in fines Lingonum die quarto pervenerunt, cum et propter vulnera militum et propter sepulturam occisorum nostri, triduum morati, eos sequi non potuissent. 6 Caesar ad Lingonas litteras nuntiosque misit, *ne eos frumento neve alia re iuvarent; qui si iuvissent, se eodem loco, quo Helvetios, habiturum.* Ipse, triduo intermisso, cum omnibus copiis eos sequi coepit.

1 **ancipiti proelio**: 'in two battles,' lit. 'by means of a two-headed battle'; *131a*. **ancipiti**: *26b*. **acriter**: *34a*. **pugnatum est**: impersonal passive; *73d*. **diutius**: *35*. **impetus**: accusative. **possent**: sc. *hostes; 185c*. **alteri, alteri**: 'those on one side' (i.e., *Helvetii*), 'those on the other' (*Boii et Tulingi*); *91c; 154a; 171b*. **carros**: arranged for defense around the corral (Map 3). **se contulerunt**: 'retreated,' still fighting; there was no disorderly rout.

2 **Nam**: *237a*. **proelio**: *147b*. **cum**: 'although'; *187*. **hora**: *242a*. **vesperum**: 'evening'; *7b*. **aversum**: 'turned' in flight. Caesar speaks with evident admiration of the bravery of the enemy.

3 **Ad multam noctem**: 'until late at night'; *17b; 152a*. **ad**: here 'at' or 'by.' **pro vallo carros obiecerant**: 'had arranged their carts in front as a rampart.' **loco superiore**: the top of the carts. **coniciebant**: 'kept hurling', the imperfect tense here emphasizes the repeated nature of the action. **rotas**: 'wheels.' These in many cases were doubtless solid disks of wood, which Roman weapons would not pierce. **mataras ac tragulas**: 'spears and darts'; *309*. **subiciebant**: notice the force of *sub-*, 'kept throwing from below' as the Roman soldiers attacked the rampart of carts. **vulnerabant**: 'were wounding'; there must have been moonlight, or at least clear starlight, else the Gauls could not have aimed their weapons so well.

4 **castris**: 'encampment,' i.e., the corral of wagons; *131c*. **e filiis**: translate as if *filiorum; 97d*. **captus est**: *172b*.

5 **CXXX**: *centum triginta; 36; 38b*. **nocte**: *147c*. **ierunt**: 'they went,' i.e., they set out from the site from the battle, seeking refuge; *68a*. **partem**: *118a*. **intermisso**: *144b2*. As the survivors seemingly traveled at night only during the first night, the thought in *nullam ... intermisso* is substantially the same as that in *ea ... ierunt*. **fines Lingonum**: more than fifty miles north of the battlefield. **cum**: *184a*. **sepulturam**: 'burial.' **occisorum**: 'the slain,' both Roman and Gaul; *154a*. **triduum**: 'for (a period of) three days'; *118a*.

6 **Lingonas**: *19f*. **litteras**: 'letters.' **nuntios**: 'messages,' to be delivered orally. **ne**: '(saying) that they should not'; *213b; 212a*. **eos**: translate as if *Helvetios*. **iuvarent**: 'supply,' lit. 'aid'; *216*. **qui si**: = *et illi si*, 'and if they'; *167*. **iuvissent**: sc. *eos = Helvetios; 218.1b*. **se ... habiturum**: in full, *se eos (= Lingonas) eodem loco, quo Helvetios haberet, habiturum esse*. **eodem loco**: metaphorical, 'in the same position.'

The Helvetians beg for terms; one division tries to escape.

27. 1 Helvetii, omnium rerum inopia adducti, legatos de deditione ad eum miserunt. 2 Qui cum eum in itinere convenissent seque ad pedes proiecissent suppliciterque locuti flentes pacem petissent, atque eos in eo loco, quo tum essent, suum adventum exspectare iussisset, paruerunt. 3 Eo postquam

Caesar pervenit, obsides, arma, servos, qui ad eos perfugissent, poposcit. 4 Dum ea conquiruntur et conferuntur nocte intermissa, circiter hominum milia VI eius pagi, qui Verbigenus appellatur, sive timore perterriti, ne, armis traditis, supplicio afficerentur, sive spe salutis inducti, quod in tanta multitudine dediticiorum suam fugam aut occultari aut omnino ignorari posse existimarent, prima nocte e castris Helvetiorum egressi ad Rhenum finesque Germanorum contenderunt.

1 **inopia:** 'lack'; *131a.* **legatos:** 'envoys.' **deditione:** '(unconditional) surrender.'
2 **Qui:** *167.* **convenissent:** *113b.* **flentes:** *227b.* **eos:** = *Helvetios*, not *legatos.* **essent:** attracted into the subjunctive; cf. *vellent* in I.28.1; *220.* **iussisset:** *185c; 200b.*
3 **Eo:** adv., 'to that place.' **postquam:** *188a.* **qui perfugissent:** *194a.*
4 **ea:** comprising *obsides, arma, (fugitivos) servos;* neuter plural under the same rule of agreement as predicate adjectives; *150b.* **conquiruntur:** historical present after *dum; 190a.* **conferuntur:** *69b.* **nocte intermissa:** 'with night having intervened,' lit. 'with night having been let in between'; *144b2.* **VI:** = *sex; 36.* **sive . . . sive:** *235b.* **perterriti:** describes the *milia VI; 150c; 238h.* **ne:** 'that'; *202.* **armis traditis:** 'after giving up their arms'; *144b2.* **quod . . . existimarent:** *183b.* **in tanta multitudine:** i.e., *cum* ('since') *tanta multitudo dediticiorum esset.* **dediticiorum:** 'of those who had surrendered.' **prima:** *152a.*

Caesar captures the fugitives, and sends the rest (except for the Boians) back to their homeland.
28. 1 Quod ubi Caesar resciit, quorum per fines ierant, his uti conquirerent et reducerent, si sibi purgati esse vellent, imperavit; reductos in hostium numero habuit; 2 reliquos omnes, obsidibus, armis, perfugis traditis, in deditionem accepit. 3 Helvetios, Tulingos, Latobrigos in fines suos, unde erant profecti, reverti iussit; et, quod, omnibus frugibus amissis, domi nihil erat, quo famem tolerarent, Allobrogibus imperavit ut eis frumenti copiam facerent; ipsos oppida vicosque, quos incenderant, restituere iussit. 4 Id ea maxime ratione fecit, quod noluit eum locum, unde Helvetii discesserant, vacare, ne propter bonitatem agrorum Germani, qui trans Rhenum incolunt, e suis finibus in Helvetiorum fines transirent et finitimi Galliae provinciae Allobrogibusque essent. 5 Boios, petentibus Aeduis, quod egregia virtute erant cogniti, ut in finibus suis collocarent, concessit; quibus illi agros dederunt, quosque postea in parem iuris libertatisque condicionem atque ipsi erant, receperunt.

1 **Quod:** accusative; *167.* **Quod ubi Caesar resciit:** 'When Caesar found this out,' referring to the flight of the Verbigens; *188a.* **quorum:** precedes its antecedent *his*, which is in the dative after *imperavit; 105.* **quorum per fines ierant, his:** 'those through whose territory they (the Verbigens) had gone.' **reducerent:** *199a1.* **sibi:** 'in his sight'; *109a.* **purgati:** 'free from guilt'; *221b.* **vellent:** in indirect discourse as a part of the command; in the direct form, *si vultis; 71.* **reductos:** sc. *eos*, 'after they had been brought back'; how lit.? *227a4.* **in hostium numero:** 'as enemies'; how lit.? The 6000 Verbigens were probably massacred, as a terrible warning, but they may have been sold into slavery.
2 **reliquos:** *171a.* **accepit:** *57a.*
3 **suos:** *157b.* **unde:** = *e quibus.* **erant profecti:** *61a3.* **frugibus amissis:** 'since all the produce of the fields was gone'; no crops had been planted this season. How lit.? *144b3.* **domi:** locative, 'at home,' i.e., in their own country; *146.* **erat:** sc. *eis.* **quo famem tolerarent:** 'by which they could endure their hunger'; *194a.* **facerent:** 'furnish'; why subjunctive? *199a1.* **oppida, vicos:** see I.5.2. **quos:** *163c.*
4 **ea maxime ratione . . . quod:** 'especially for this reason, (namely) because'; *161a.* **noluit:** *71; 223a.* **unde:** = *e quo.* **bonitatem:** 'good quality'; *76a.* **transirent:** *196a.* As the Helvetians were now reduced to about one third of their former number, much of their land must have been left unoccupied, and was probably soon seized upon by German immigrants. **Galliae provinciae:** *108a; 259.* The northernmost part of the Province was held by the Allobroges; see Map 1.
5 **Boios:** emphatic position (*245d*); for sense, order thus: *Aeduis* (dative after *concessit*), *petentibus ut Boios in finibus suis collocarent, quod (Boii) egregia virtute (esse) cogniti erant, (Caesar) concessit.* The Aeduans, hard pressed in their strife with the Sequanians, desired an accession of strength. **virtute:** *143b.* **collocarent:** *199a6.* **concessit:** 'he granted' the request. **quibus:** the Boians; translate as if *et eis; 167.* **quosque:** = *et eos.* **parem . . . atque:** 'the same as'; *233c.* **receperunt:** 'they admitted.'

The number of the Helvetians and their allies.
29. 1 In castris Helvetiorum tabulae repertae sunt, litteris Graecis confectae, et ad Caesarem relatae, quibus in tabulis nominatim ratio confecta erat, qui numerus domo exisset eorum, qui arma ferre possent, et item separatim pueri, senes mulieresque. 2 Quarum omnium rerum summa erat capitum

Helvetiorum milia CCLXIII, Tulingorum milia XXXVI, Latobrigorum XIIII, Rauracorum XXIII, Boiorum XXXII; ex his, qui arma ferre possent, ad milia XCII. Summa omnium fuerunt ad milia CCCLXVIII. 3 Eorum, qui domum redierunt, censu habito, ut Caesar imperaverat, repertus est numerus milium C et X.

1 **castris:** the corral of wagons. **tabulae:** 'tablets,' such as those generally used for business documents. These were of light-colored wood, and made with a rim like that of a slate. The surface inside the rim was coated with a thin layer of wax, on which writing was done with a pointed stilus. The writing appeared on the wood, which showed through wherever the stilus had scraped away the wax. **litteris Graecis confectae:** 'written in Greek characters,' which were used also by the Druids (VI.14.3). On account of the antiquity of Massilia (262a), the Greek alphabet must have become familiar to the inhabitants of southern Gaul at an early date. **relatae:** sc. *sunt*; 69b. **tabulis:** *165a.* **nominatim:** 'by name'; 77. **qui:** interrogative adjective; 48b. **domo:** 130b. **exisset:** 68b; 204.2. **qui ... possent:** 194a. **pueri:** 'children'; 7a. **senes:** 18b. **mulieres:** 11c.

2 **Quarum:** 167. **rerum:** 'items,' here used of persons; Caesar was thinking of the numbers rather than the personality. **summa:** 'the sum,' i.e., the aggregate number. **capitum Helvetiorum:** translate as if *Helvetiorum*; we say "so many head" of livestock, not of human beings. **CCLXIII:** *ducenta sexaginta tria;* 37b, d; 38b. **XXXVI,** etc.: 36; 37b. **qui arma ferre possent:** i.e., *ei, qui arma ferre possent* (194a), *erant.* **ad:** adverb, 'approximately.' **fuerunt:** plural on account of the influence of the predicate noun *milia;* 173b.

3 **Eorum ... numerus milium C et X:** emphatic word order due to the desire to withhold the number until the very end of the sentence; read for sense as: *numerus eorum qui domum redierunt ... repertus est (esse) milium C et X.* **domum:** 119b. **redierunt:** 'returned'; 68b. **censu:** 'a census'; 80b. **ut:** 'as,' as often when *ut* is followed by an indicative verb. **C et X:** Caesar thus leaves it to the reader to comprehend that over 250,000 people did not return from the Helvetians' attempted emigration. His inclusion of his discovery of the precise numbers on these tablets demonstrates not only the staggering human cost of Caesar's intervention, but also his willingness to take unflinching responsibility for it.

I.30-54: Campaign against Ariovistus and the Germans

The Gallic leaders congratulate Caesar, request a conference.

30. 1 Bello Helvetiorum confecto, totius fere Galliae legati, principes civitatum, ad Caesarem gratulatum convenerunt: 2 *intellegere sese, tametsi pro veteribus Helvetiorum iniuriis populi Romani ab his poenas bello repetisset, tamen eam rem non minus ex usu terrae Galliae quam populi Romani accidisse,* 3 *propterea quod eo consilio, florentissimis rebus, domos suas Helvetii reliquissent, uti toti Galliae bellum inferrent imperioque potirentur, locumque domicilio ex magna copia deligerent, quem ex omni Gallia opportunissimum ac fructuosissimum iudicassent, reliquasque civitates stipendiarias haberent.* 4 Petierunt, uti sibi concilium totius Galliae in diem certam indicere idque Caesaris voluntate facere liceret; *sese habere quasdam res, quas ex communi consensu ab eo petere vellent.* 5 Ea re permissa, diem concilio constituerunt et iure iurando, ne quis enuntiaret, nisi quibus communi consilio mandatum esset, inter se sanxerunt.

1 **Galliae:** Celtic Gaul; 256b. **principes:** 10b. **civitatum:** 10f; 257. **gratulatum:** supine; 231a.

2 **Intellegere sese, tametsi:** '(saying) that they understood that, although'; 212c1; 213b. **iniuriis:** with two genitives, *Helvetiorum* (subjective; 95) and *populi* (objective; 102); translate 'wrongs done to the Roman people by the Helvetians.' **poenas:** 'punishment'; 92a. **bello:** 131a. **repetisset:** = *repetivisset,* 'had exacted,' lit. 'had sought in return'; 64a3; 214a. **rem:** 'achievement.' **ex usu terrae Galliae:** 'to the advantage of the territory of Gaul'; *ex usu* should also be understood with *populi Romani.*

3 **eo consilio:** 'with this design,' explained by the following *uti*-clauses, '(namely) in order to ...'; 138. **florentissimis rebus:** 'though their circumstances were exceedingly prosperous'; 144b5; 153a. **domos:** 20c. **uti .. . haberent:** a series of substantive clauses that explain *eo consilio;* 203.4 (which could also be understood as purpose clauses; 196a). **imperio:** 74b; 131c. **domicilio:** 'for habitation'; 112a. **copia:** sc. *locorum.* **quem:** *locum* is the antecedent; '(that) place which.' **opportunissimum ac fructuosissimum:** 'the most suitable and the most productive'; 75f. **iudicassent:** 64a1. **stipendiarias:** predicative, 'tributary (to them)'; 115b.

4 **Petierunt, uti sibi ... liceret:** 'they asked permission'; how lit.? **sibi:** plural; after *liceret;* 105. **in:** 'for.' **indicere:** 'to appoint'; 222a. **id:** 160c. **voluntate:** 138. **liceret:** 73b. **sese habere:** 213b. **ab eo:** 116b.

5 **concilio:** 112b. **iure iurando:** 13h; 131a. **ne quis:** 'that no one,' lit. 'that not anyone'; 49a; 168. **enuntiaret:** 'should make known (its proceedings).' **nisi quibus:** i.e., *nisi ut illi enuntiarent, quibus ... mandatum esset* (imper-

sonal), 'except those to whom the task should have been assigned'; *73d.* **inter se sanxerunt:** *159.*

Direct form (I.30.2-3): *Intellegimus,* tametsi pro veteribus Helvetiorum iniuriis populi Romani ab his poenas bello *repetieris,* tamen eam rem non minus ex usu terrae Galliae quam populi Romani accidisse, propterea quod eo consilio, florentissimis rebus, domos suas Helvetii *reliquerunt,* uti toti Galliae bellum inferrent, etc.

Caesar is urged by Diviciacus to defend Gaul against Ariovistus.

31. 1 Eo concilio dimisso, idem principes civitatum, qui ante adfuerant, ad Caesarem reverterunt petieruntque, ut sibi secreto, in occulto, de sua omniumque salute cum eo agere liceret. 2 Ea re impetrata, sese omnes flentes Caesari ad pedes proiecerunt: *non minus se id contendere et laborare, ne ea, quae dixissent, enuntiarentur, quam uti ea, quae vellent, impetrarent, propterea quod, si enuntiatum esset, summum in cruciatum se venturos viderent.* 3 Locutus est pro his Diviciacus Aeduus: *Galliae totius factiones esse duas; harum alterius principatum tenere Aeduos, alterius Arvernos.* 4 *Hi cum tantopere de potentatu inter se multos annos contenderent, factum esse, uti ab Arvernis Sequanisque Germani mercede arcesserentur.* 5 *Horum primo circiter milia XV Rhenum transisse; postea quam agros et cultum et copias Gallorum homines feri ac barbari adamassent, traductos plures; nunc esse in Gallia ad centum et XX milium numerum.* 6 *Cum his Aeduos eorumque clientes semel atque iterum armis contendisse; magnam calamitatem pulsos accepisse; omnem nobilitatem, omnem senatum, omnem equitatum amisisse.* 7 *Quibus proeliis calamitatibusque fractos, qui et sua virtute et populi Romani hospitio atque amicitia plurimum ante in Gallia potuissent, coactos esse Sequanis obsides dare nobilissimos civitatis et iure iurando civitatem obstringere, sese neque obsides repetituros, neque auxilium a populo Romano imploraturos, neque recusaturos, quo minus perpetuo sub illorum dicione atque imperio essent.* 8 *Unum se esse ex omni civitate Aeduorum, qui adduci non potuerit, ut iuraret aut liberos suos obsides daret.* 9 *Ob eam rem se ex civitate profugisse et Romam ad senatum venisse auxilium postulatum, quod solus neque iure iurando neque obsidibus teneretur.* 10 *Sed peius victoribus Sequanis quam Aeduis victis accidisse, propterea quod Ariovistus, rex Germanorum, in eorum finibus consedisset tertiamque partem agri Sequani, qui esset optimus totius Galliae, occupavisset, et nunc de altera parte tertia Sequanos decedere iuberet, propterea quod paucis mensibus ante Harudum milia hominum XXIIII ad eum venissent, quibus locus ac sedes pararentur.* 11 *Futurum esse paucis annis, uti omnes ex Galliae finibus pellerentur atque omnes Germani Rhenum transirent; neque enim conferendum esse Gallicum cum Germanorum agro, neque hanc consuetudinem victus cum illa comparandam.* 12 *Ariovistum autem, ut semel Gallorum copias proelio vicerit, quod proelium factum sit ad Magetobrigam, superbe et crudeliter imperare, obsides nobilissimi cuiusque liberos poscere, et in eos omnia exempla cruciatusque edere, si qua res non ad nutum aut ad voluntatem eius facta sit.* 13 *Hominem esse barbarum, iracundum, temerarium; non posse eius imperia diutius sustineri.* 14 *Nisi quid in Caesare populoque Romano sit auxilii, omnibus Gallis idem esse faciendum, quod Helvetii fecerint, ut domo emigrent, aliud domicilium, alias sedes, remotas a Germanis, petant, fortunamque, quaecumque accidat, experiantur.* 15 *Haec si enuntiata Ariovisto sint, non dubitare, quin de omnibus obsidibus, qui apud eum sint, gravissimum supplicium sumat.* 16 *Caesarem, vel auctoritate sua atque exercitus, vel recenti victoria, vel nomine populi Romani, deterrere posse, ne maior multitudo Germanorum Rhenum traducatur, Galliamque omnem ab Ariovisti iniuria posse defendere.*

Direct form (I.31.3-16): 3 Galliae totius factiones *sunt duae;* harum alterius principatum *tenent Aedui,* alterius, *Arverni.* 4 Hi cum tantopere de potentatu inter se multos annos contenderent, *factum est,* uti ab Arvernis Sequanisque Germani mercede arcesserentur. 5 Horum primo circiter milia XV Rhenum *transierunt;* postea quam agros et cultum et copias Gallorum homines feri ac barbari *adamarunt* (= *adamaverunt*), *traducti sunt* plures; nunc *est* in Gallia ad centum et XX milium *numerus.* 6 Cum his *Aedui* eorumque clientes semel atque iterum armis *contenderunt;* magnam calamitatem *pulsi acceperunt;* omnem nobilitatem, omnem senatum, omnem equitatum *amiserunt.* 7 Quibus proeliis calamitatibusque *fracti,* qui et sua virtute et populi Romani hospitio atque amicitia plurimum ante in Gallia *potuerant, coacti sunt* Sequanis obsides dare nobilissimos civitatis et iure iurando civitatem obstringere, sese neque obsides repetituros, neque auxilium a populo Romano imploraturos, neque recusaturos, quo minus perpetuo sub illorum dicione atque imperio essent. 8 *Unus ego sum,* ex omni civitate Aeduorum, qui adduci non *potuerim,* ut *iurarem* aut liberos *meos* obsides *darem.* 9 Ob eam rem ex civitate *profugi,* et Romam ad senatum *veni* auxilium postulatum, quod solus neque iure iurando neque obsidibus *tenebar.* 10 Sed peius victoribus Sequanis quam Aeduis victis *accidit,* propterea quod Ariovistus, rex Germanorum, in eorum finibus *consedit* (*183a*), tertiamque partem agri Sequani, qui *est* optimus totius Galliae, *occupavit*; et nunc de altera parte tertia Sequanos decedere *iubet*, propterea quod paucis mensibus ante Harudum milia hominum XXIIII ad eum *venerunt*, quibus locus ac sedes *parentur*. 11 Paucis annis omnes ex Galliae finibus *pellentur*, atque omnes Germani Rhenum *transibunt*; neque enim *conferendus est Gallicus* (*ager*) cum Germanorum agro, neque *haec consuetudo* victus cum illa *comparanda* (*est*). 12 *Ariovistus* autem, ut semel Gallorum copias proelio *vicit*, quod proelium factum *est* ad Magetobrigam, superbe et crudeliter *imperat*, obsides nobilissimi cuiusque liberos *poscit*, et in eos omnia exempla cruciatusque *edit*, si qua res non ad nutum aut ad voluntatem eius facta *est*. 13 *Homo est barbarus, iracundus, temerarius*; non *possunt* eius imperia diutius sustineri. 14 Nisi quid in *te* populoque Romano *erit* auxilii, omnibus Gallis idem *est* faciendum, quod Helvetii *fecerunt*, ut domo emigrent, aliud domicilium, alias sedes, remotas a Germanis, petant, fortunamque, quaecumque accidat, experiantur. 15 Haec si enuntiata Ariovisto *erunt*, non *dubito*, quin de omnibus obsidibus, qui apud eum *sint*, gravissimum supplicium sumat. 16 *Tu*, vel auctoritate *tua* atque exercitus, vel recenti victoria, vel nomine populi Romani, deterrere *potes*, ne maior multitudo Germanorum Rhenum traducatur, Galliamque omnem ab Ariovisti iniuria *potes* defendere.

1 **concilio:** where this council was held we are not informed; perhaps at Bibracte. **idem:** nominative plural; *45*. **petierunt . . . liceret:** as in I.30.4. **secreto:** 'privately,' as a protection against betrayal. **in occulto:** 'in a secret place,' as a precaution against spies. **cum eo:** *137c*. **agere:** 'to confer.'

2 **flentes:** *227b*. **Caesari:** translate as if *Caesaris*; *109a*. **non . . . viderent:** *213b*. **Direct form:** non minus id *contendimus* et *laboramus*, ne ea, quae *dixerimus*, enuntientur, quam uti ea, quae *velimus* (*220*), impetremus, propterea quod, si enuntiatum *erit*, summum in cruciatum *nos venturos* (*esse*) videmus. **non minus se id contendere et laborare, ne ea . . . enuntiarentur, quam uti . . . impetrarent:** 'that they strove and toiled no less (for) this,' explained by the following *ne*-clause (*117a*): '(namely) that those things should not be disclosed, than (for this, namely) that they should obtain . . . .' **dixissent:** future perfect in the direct form. **enuntiatum esset:** impersonal: 'if disclosure should have been made.' **venturos:** *89c*.

3 **Galliae:** Celtic Gaul; *256b*. **factiones:** here 'leagues' rather than 'parties,' because made up of states. **alterius . . . alterius:** *23b*; *171b*. **Arvernos:** a powerful state, southwest of the country of the Aeduans. See Map Gallia.

4 **de potentatu:** 'for supremacy.' **annos:** *118a*. **contenderent:** *185c*. **factum esse:** the subject is *uti . . . arcesserentur*; translate 'it had come about'; *203.1*. **Sequanis:** these entered into alliance with the Arvernians because of their hatred of the Aeduans. The strife between the Sequanians and the Aeduans arose from the fact that the Arar for a part of its course formed the boundary between the two states, and each claimed the exclusive right to levy tolls on passing vessels. **mercede:** 'for pay'; *141*. **arcesserentur:** in order to contend more effectively against the Aeduans, the Sequanians hired Germans to fight for them.

5 **Horum:** *Germanorum*. **transisse:** *113b*. **postea quam:** *188a*; *214a*. **copias:** here 'resources' or 'wealth.' **homines:** 'these men,' i.e., the 15,000 Germans just mentioned. **adamassent:** 'had formed an eager desire for,' lit. 'had come to love' (*ad + amo*); *64a1*. **traductos:** *89c*. **plures:** sc. *Germanos*. **numerum:** sc. *Germanorum*.

6 **clientes:** 'dependents,' here referring to dependent states. **semel atque iterum:** in English idiom, 'time and again,' lit. 'once and again.' **pulsos:** in agreement with the understood *Aeduos* that is the subject of *accepisse*. **omnem nobilitatem,** etc.: the activity of Aeduan men of rank recorded in Book VII shows that this statement, if accurately reported, was greatly exaggerated. **senatum:** *258b*. **equitatum:** collective, 'knights,' mentioned last as the broadest term in the enumeration; apparently the 'nobles' were a subdivision of the 'knights,' preeminent on account of aristocratic birth as well as the possession of large resources; *257b*.

7 **fractos:** in agreement with *eos* (*Aeduos*) understood as subject of *coactos esse* and antecedent of *qui*. **hospitio:** 'relation of hospitality,' less close than the relation implied in *amicitia*. Both relations were established by treaties between states; when *hospitium* was established between two states, each was bound to entertain the other's representatives at public expense. **atque:** force? *233a*. **plurimum ante potuissent:** 'had previously possessed the greatest power'; *118b*. **obsides:** accusative, 'as hostages'; *115a*. **nobilissimos:** as in I.7.3. **iure iurando:** *13h*. **sese neque obsides repetituros:** sc. *esse*, 'that they would neither try to get the hostages back'; the content of the oath (*sese . . . essent*) would be in indirect discourse even if the context were in the direct form; *213b*. **imploraturos:** sc. *esse*, 'solicit'; *89c*. **recusaturos:** sc. *esse*, 'refuse.' **quo minus . . . essent:** 'to be'; a clause of refusing; *201a*. **perpetuo:** 'forever'; *34b*. **illorum:** translate as if *Sequanorum*. **dicione:** 'sway.'

8 **Unum se esse:** 'that he (Diviciacus) was the only one.' **potuerit:** perfect subjunctive already in the direct form; *194a*. **ut iuraret:** 'to take the oath'; *199a5*. **liberos suos obsides:** *115a*.

9 **profugisse:** 'had fled.' **Romam:** *119a*. **postulatum:** 'to demand'; a strong word, justified by the urgency of the cause and the friendly relations between the Aeduan state and Rome; *231a, b*.

10 **peius:** 'a worse fate,' lit. 'worse thing'; neuter accusative subject of *accidisse*; *32*; *154a*. **victoribus:** here an adjective, 'victorious.' **victoribus . . . victis:** *239c*. **rex:** *91a*. **Germanorum:** apparently Swabians (I.37.3). **oc-**

cupavisset: 'had seized,' in the rich level country west of the Rhine, in modern Alsace. **de altera parte tertia:** 'from a second third-part.' **decedere:** 'to withdraw'; *200b*. **mensibus:** *140*. **Harudum:** *19e*. **locus ac sedes:** 'places of habitation'; how lit.? *15b*. **pararentur:** 'were to be provided'; *193a*.

11 **Futurum esse:** 'it would come about'; the subject is the following *uti*-clause; *203.1*. **annis:** *147a*. **omnes:** sc. *Galli*. **conferendum esse:** 'is to be compared'; *229c*. **Gallicum:** sc. *agrum*. Caesar means that the land in Gaul is incomparably better than that in Germany; we usually state such comparisons in the opposite way. **consuetudi-nem victus:** 'standard of living.' **hanc:** *Gallicam*. **illa:** 'that (of the Germans).' **comparandam:** *89c*.

12 **Gallorum:** the Aeduans and their allies. **copias:** here 'forces.' **ut semel:** 'as soon as,' lit. 'when once.' **vicerit, imperare, poscere, edere:** representing perfects and presents in the direct form, used for vividness; the pluper-fect and perfect or imperfect in the direct form might have been expected, and in translation past tenses should be used; *188a*. **quod proelium:** 'a battle which'; *165a*. **ad Magetobrigam:** 'near to Magetobriga'; where the place was we do not know. **nobilissimi cuiusque:** 'of every man of high rank'; *170a*. **imperare:** here intransi-tive. **in eos omnia exempla cruciatusque edere:** 'inflicted all kinds of exemplary punishments and tortures upon them'; i.e., these punishments were intended as warning examples to deter others from opposition or resistance. **qua:** *49a; 168*. **ad nutum:** 'at his nod,' i.e., at the slightest intimation of his desires.

13 **iracundum:** 'quick-tempered.' **temerarium:** 'reckless.'

14 **quid . . . auxilii:** 'some help'; *97b; 168*. **omnibus Gallis idem esse faciendum:** 'all the Gauls would have to do the same thing,' lit. 'the same thing would have to be done by all the Gauls'; *110; 229c*. **idem:** subject of *faci-endum esse*, explained both by the relative clause *quod Helvetii fecerint* and by the appositive clause *ut . . . emigrent (et) . . . petant . . . –que . . . experiantur; 203.4*. **ut . . . emigrent:** '(namely) to emigrate,' lit. 'that they emigrate.' **domo:** *130b*. **fortunamque, quaecumque accidat, experiantur:** 'and to put their fortune to the test, whatever (fortune) might occur'; i.e., to try their luck, come what may. **quaecumque:** indefinite relative; *50a*.

15 **Haec:** the things currently being reported to Caesar, as well as the appeal to him. **non dubitare:** sc. *se*, 'he (Diviciacus) had no doubt.' **quin . . . sumat:** 'that he (Ariovistus) would inflict'; *201c*. **de:** 'upon.'

16 **auctoritate:** *131a*. **exercitus:** '(that) of his army'; *157d*. **deterrere ne maior multitudo Germanorum Rhe-num traducatur:** 'to prevent a larger host of Germans from being brought across the Rhine'; *201a*. **Rhenum:** why accusative? *114b*. **Ariovisti:** *95*.

The lot of the Sequani, showing what might happen to all.

32. 1 Hac oratione ab Diviciaco habita, omnes, qui aderant, magno fletu auxilium a Caesare petere coeperunt. 2 Animadvertit Caesar unos ex omnibus Sequanos nihil earum rerum facere, quas ceteri facerent, sed tristes, capite demisso, terram intueri. Eius rei quae causa esset, miratus, ex ipsis quaesiit. 3 Nihil Sequani respondere, sed in eadem tristitia taciti permanere. Cum ab his saepius quaereret, neque ullam omnino vocem exprimere posset, idem Diviciacus Aeduus respondit: 4 *hoc esse miseri-orem et graviorem fortunam Sequanorum quam reliquorum, quod soli ne in occulto quidem queri neque auxilium implorare auderent, absentisque Ariovisti crudelitatem, velut si coram adesset, horrerent,* 5 *prop-terea quod reliquis tamen fugae facultas daretur, Sequanis vero, qui intra fines suos Ariovistum recepissent, quorum oppida omnia in potestate eius essent, omnes cruciatus essent perferendi.*

Direct form (I.32.4-5): 4 Hoc *est* miserior et gravior fortuna Sequanorum quam reliquorum, quod soli ne in oc-culto quidem queri neque auxilium implorare *audent*, absentisque Ariovisti crudelitatem, velut si coram *adsit,* horrent, 5 propterea quod reliquis tamen fugae facultas *datur,* Sequanis vero, qui intra fines suos Ariovistum *receperunt,* quorum oppida omnia in potestate eius *sunt,* omnes cruciatus *sunt* perferendi.

1 **fletu:** 'weeping'; shedding of tears by men was much more common among the Gauls and Romans than among us.

2 **unos:** 'alone'; *23a*. **nihil:** 'none'; how lit.? **ceteri:** *171a*. **facerent:** *214a; 213a*. **tristes:** *151*. **capite demisso:** 'with bowed heads'; how lit.? *144b7*. **quae:** *48b*. **esset:** *204.2*. **miratus:** *226c*. **quaesiit:** *116c*.

3 **respondere, permanere:** *182*. **taciti:** *148c*. **saepius:** 'again and again'; how lit.? *153a*. **quaereret, posset:** Cae-sar is the subject; *185c*. **neque:** = *et non; 233a*. **vocem:** 'utterance'; *10c*.

4 **hoc:** 'On this account,' explained by the following *quod*-clause (cf. I.2.3); *135a*. **miseriorem:** 'more wretched'; *22d*. **ne . . . quidem:** *237c*. **auderent:** with *ne . . . quidem* and *neque:* 'not even in secret did they dare to complain nor to solicit aid'; *62*. **absentis:** 'in his absence'; how lit.? **velut si:** 'just as if.' **adesset:** subjunctive also in the direct form; *210*.

5 **reliquis:** 'to the rest' of the Celtic Gauls; *171a*. **tamen:** 'at any rate,' as a last resource. **fugae facultas:** 'the opportunity for flight'; *102*. **Sequanis . . . essent perferendi:** 'the Sequanians . . . had to endure'; how lit.? *229c; 110*. **oppida omnia:** exaggeration, for the Sequanians still held Vesontio (*Besançon*), which was their strongest fortified place (I.38). **omnes:** 'all possible.'

Caesar, claiming reasons of state, promises his help against Ariovistus.

33. 1 His rebus cognitis, Caesar Gallorum animos verbis confirmavit pollicitusque est sibi eam rem curae futuram; *magnam se habere spem, et beneficio suo et auctoritate adductum Ariovistum finem iniuriis facturum.* 2 Hac oratione habita, concilium dimisit. Et secundum ea multae res eum hortabantur, quare sibi eam rem cogitandam et suscipiendam putaret; in primis, quod Aeduos, fratres consanguineosque saepe numero a senatu appellatos, in servitute atque dicione videbat Germanorum teneri, eorumque obsides esse apud Ariovistum ac Sequanos intellegebat; quod in tanto imperio populi Romani turpissimum sibi et rei publicae esse arbitrabatur. 3 Paulatim autem Germanos consuescere Rhenum transire, et in Galliam magnam eorum multitudinem venire, populo Romano periculosum videbat; 4 neque sibi homines feros ac barbaros temperaturos existimabat, quin, cum omnem Galliam occupavissent, ut ante Cimbri Teutonique fecissent, in provinciam exirent atque inde in Italiam contenderent, praesertim cum Sequanos a provincia nostra Rhodanus divideret; quibus rebus quam maturrime occurrendum putabat. 5 Ipse autem Ariovistus tantos sibi spiritus, tantam arrogantiam sumpserat, ut ferendus non videretur.

1 **sibi . . . futuram:** sc. *esse*, 'that this matter should have his attention'; how lit.? *112b.* **magnam se habere spem:** *213b.* **beneficio suo:** Caesar's kindness, when he was consul (59 BC), in helping secure recognition of Ariovistus by the Roman Senate; Caesar reminds Ariovistus of this later (I.35.2, 43.4-5). **Ariovistum:** the subject of *facturum* (*esse*); modified by the participial phrase *et beneficio suo et auctoritate adductum.* **iniuriis:** *104a.* **facturum:** sc. *esse*, after *habere spem*, which is used in place of *sperare*; *89c; 213a.*

2 **secundum ea:** prepositional phrase; 'besides those considerations'; *122a; 160c.* **quare:** translate as if *propter quas* (cf. *quare* in I.14.2, 19.1). **sibi:** *110.* **cogitandam:** sc. *esse*, 'ought to be taken into consideration.' **putaret:** *194a.* **in primis:** 'first of all'; how lit.? **quod . . . videbat:** *198b.* **fratres:** predicate accusative after *appellatos*; *88b.* **consanguineos:** 'kin,' implying blood-relationship, while *fratres*, like our term 'brethren,' might be used as a title implying close relations without kinship. The use of the title here may imply that the Aeduans claimed descent from the Trojans, as did the Romans. **numero:** with *saepe* (*saepenumero* is in fact often printed together as one word), 'repeatedly'; *142a; 85.* **quod . . . esse arbitrabatur:** '(a state of affairs) which he judged to be'; the antecedent of *quod* is the thought expressed by the infinitive clauses depending on *videbat* and *intellegebat.* **in . . . Romani:** 'in view of the greatness of the power (lit. 'the so great power') of the Roman people.' **turpissimum:** 'exceedingly disgraceful'; *148c; 153a.* **sibi:** *108a.*

3 **autem:** 'moreover' introduces the second reason (*in primis* above introduced the first); *236a.* **Paulatim . . . videbat:** for sense, order thus: *videbat autem (esse) periculosum populo Romano Germanos paulatim consuescere Rhenum transire et in Galliam magnam eorum multitudinem venire:* 'he saw that it was full of danger . . . for the Germans gradually to become accustomed . . . and for their great host to come . . .'; *Germanos consuescere* and *multitudinem venire* are the subject of an *esse* to be understood after *videbat; 213a.* **periculosum:** 'full of danger'; *148d; 75f.*

4 **feros ac barbaros:** adjectives modifying *homines*, the accusative subject of *temperaturos*, that strongly characterize the Germans. **sibi . . . temperaturos:** sc. *esse*, 'would hold back,' lit. 'restrain themselves'; *105.* **quin . . . in provinciam exirent:** 'from going out (of Gaul and) into the Province'; *201a.* **ut:** 'as'; *188b; 214a.* **ut . . . fecissent:** related in thought with *exirent* and *contenderent.* **Cimbri Teutonique:** in the closing years of the second century BC, the Cimbrians and Teutons swept over Celtic Gaul and passed into the Province, from which the Cimbrians made their way into Cisalpine Gaul. The Teutons were annihilated in a fierce battle at Aquae Sextiae (now *Aix*), about 20 miles north of Massilia, by Gaius Marius in 102 BC, and a year later the Cimbrians met a similar fate at Vercellae, in Cisalpine Gaul, northeast of Turin. See Map Gallia. **Italiam:** here including Cisalpine Gaul; *252b.* **praesertim cum:** *184b.* **Sequanos:** *251.* **Rhodanus:** '(only) the Rhone,' i.e., the Rhone is to be understood as a slight protection against an invading host. **quibus rebus:** dative after *occurrendum; 107a; 167.* **quam maturrime:** *34a; 153c.* **occurrendum:** sc. *sibi esse:* 'that he ought to meet,' lit. 'that it ought to be met by him'; *110; 229c.*

5 **tantos spiritus:** 'such insolent airs'; *20b.* **ferendus non:** 'unbearable'; how lit.?

Caesar invites Ariovistus to a conference; he is rebuffed.

34. 1 Quam ob rem placuit ei, ut ad Ariovistum legatos mitteret, qui ab eo postularent, uti aliquem locum, medium utriusque, colloquio deligeret: *velle sese de re publica et summis utriusque rebus cum eo agere.* 2 Ei legationi Ariovistus respondit: *si quid ipsi a Caesare opus esset, sese ad eum venturum fuisse; si quid ille se velit, illum ad se venire oportere.* 3 Praeterea, *se neque sine exercitu in eas partes Galliae venire* *audere, quas Caesar possideret, neque exercitum sine magno commeatu atque molimento in unum locum contrahere posse. 4 Sibi autem mirum videri, quid in sua Gallia, quam bello vicisset, aut Caesari aut omnino populo Romano negotii esset.*

Direct form (I.34.2-4): 2 Si quid *mihi* a Caesare opus esset, ad eum *venissem*; si quid ille *me vult*, illum ad *me* venire *oportet*. 3 Praeterea, neque sine exercitu in eas partes Galliae, quas Caesar *possidet*, venire *audeo*, neque exercitum sine magno commeatu atque molimento in unum locum contrahere *possum*. 4 *Mihi* autem mirum *videtur*, quid in *mea* Gallia, quam bello *vici*, aut Caesari aut omnino populo Romano negotii *sit*.

1 **placuit ei:** 'he (Caesar) resolved,' lit. 'it was pleasing to him.' **ut . . . mitteret:** with *placuit*; 'to send'; *199a7*. **postularent:** *193a.* **aliquem:** *49a.* **medium utriusque:** 'midway between them'; lit. 'the middle place of each'; *51; 102; 152.* **colloquio:** 'for a conference'; *112a.* **deligeret:** *199a4.* **velle sese:** '(stating) that he wished'; *213b.* **summis utriusque rebus:** 'affairs of the utmost importance to both,' lit. 'the greatest things of each.'
2 **si . . . fuisse:** *208c.* **si quid ipsi a Caesare opus esset:** 'if he himself had wanted anything of Caesar,' lit. 'if anything were necessary to himself from Caesar'; *132b.* **quid se:** 'anything of himself (Ariovistus)'; *116d.*
3 **Praeterea:** 'furthermore.' Ariovistus was seemingly over near the Rhine, a long distance from Caesar, who was probably in the vicinity of Bibracte. **commeatu:** 'store of supplies.' **atque:** *233a.* **molimento:** 'great effort' in accumulating supplies as well as in mobilizing his forces; for the army of Ariovistus, so long as it was scattered in small detachments, could live off the country.
4 **mirum:** 'a cause for wonder'; *148d.* **bello:** *131a.* **quid . . . Caesari . . . negotii esset:** subject of *videri*; 'what business Caesar had,' lit. 'what of business there was to Caesar'; *204.2.* **aut . . . aut:** *235a.* **Caesari, populo:** *111.* **negotii:** *97b.*

Caesar through envoys makes demands of Ariovistus.

35. 1 His responsis ad Caesarem relatis, iterum ad eum Caesar legatos cum his mandatis mittit: 2 quoniam, tanto suo populique Romani beneficio affectus, cum in consulatu suo rex atque amicus a senatu appellatus esset, hanc sibi populoque Romano gratiam referret, ut, in colloquium venire invitatus, gravaretur, neque de communi re discendum sibi et cognoscendum putaret, haec esse, quae ab eo postularet: 3 primum, ne quam multitudinem hominum amplius trans Rhenum in Galliam traduceret; deinde, obsides, quos haberet ab Aeduis, redderet, Sequanisque permitteret, ut, quos illi haberent, voluntate eius reddere illis liceret; neve Aeduos iniuria lacesseret, neve his sociisque eorum bellum inferret. 4 Si id ita fecisset, sibi populoque Romano perpetuam gratiam atque amicitiam cum eo futuram; si non impetraret, sese, quoniam, M. Messala, M. Pisone consulibus, senatus censuisset, uti, quicumque Galliam provinciam obtineret, quod commodo rei publicae facere posset, Aeduos ceterosque amicos populi Romani defenderet, se Aeduorum iniurias non neglecturum.

Direct form (I.35.2-4): 2 Quoniam, tanto *meo* populique Romani beneficio affectus, cum in consulatu *meo* rex atque amicus a senatu appellatus *est*, (Ariovistus) hanc *mihi* populoque Romano gratiam *refert*, ut, in colloquium venire invitatus, *gravetur*, neque de communi re discendum sibi et cognoscendum *putet*, haec *sunt*, quae ab eo *postulo*. 3 Primum, (*postulo*) ne (*Ariovistus*) quam multitudinem hominum amplius trans Rhenum in Galliam *traducat*; deinde, obsides, quos *habet* ab Aeduis, *reddat*, Sequanisque *permittat*, ut (*obsides*), quos hi habent, voluntate eius reddere illis *liceat*; neve Aeduos iniuria *lacessat*, neve his sociisque eorum bellum *inferat*. 4 Si id ita *fecerit*, *mihi* populoque Romano perpetua gratia atque amicitia cum eo *erit*; si non *impetrabo*, quoniam, M. Messala, M. Pisone consulibus, senatus *censuit*, uti, quicumque Galliam provinciam obtineret, quod commodo rei publicae facere posset, Aeduos ceterosque amicos populi Romani defenderet, Aeduorum iniurias non *neglegam*.

1 **his mandatis:** 'this message,' lit. 'these instructions' to the envoys, which were to be presented orally, and are here summarized; *212c4.*
2 **quoniam:** 'since.' **tanto suo populique Romani beneficio affectus:** 'although treated with so great kindness by himself and the Roman people'; how lit.? *157d; 227a3.* **cum . . . esset:** explains what the *beneficium* was. **consulatu suo:** in the previous year; see I.33.1. **rex . . . a senatu:** cf. I.3.4. The truth seems to be that in the strife between the Aeduans and Ariovistus the Roman Senate thought it the best policy to be allies with both sides. The Senate therefore continued to profess friendship for the Aeduans, but after they sustained a crushing defeat at Magetobriga (I.31.6-8, 12) it courted Ariovistus. To what extent Caesar was responsible for the conferring of the titles on Ariovistus in 59 BC we do not know. **hanc . . . gratiam referret:** 'he renders such gratitude'; *183a;*

214a. **ut ... gravaretur:** '(such) that he ... felt burdened'; a substantive clause of result explaining *gratiam*; *203.4.* **in:** 'to.' **invitatus:** 'when he had been invited'; *227a3.* **neque ... discendum sibi et cognoscendum putaret:** continues the result clause after *gratiam referret*: 'and he did not think that he ought to learn about and come to understand.' **de communi re:** 'about a matter of mutual interest.' **discendum sibi:** sc. *esse*; *73e*; *110.* **haec esse:** 'these were the things'; *161a*; *160c.* These two words are the main clause of the sentence; everything prior to them is part of the causal clause (*quoniam*) that leads to this statement of Caesar's consequent demands.

₃ **primum, ne ... traduceret; deinde ... redderet:** 'first, not to lead across ... ; second, to return ...'; *199a4*; *237b.* **quam:** *49a*; *168.* **hominum:** *98a.* **redderet, permitteret:** sc. *ut*; *200a.* **Sequanis permitteret ut ... reddere illis liceret:** 'to grant to the Sequanians that it be permitted to them to return'; *permitteret* and *liceret* approach redundancy. **quos:** supply *obsides* as the object of *reddere* and the antecedent of *quos*. **voluntate:** *138.* **reddere:** *222a.* **neve ... lacesseret:** 'nor to harass'; Caesar continues his list of demands; *199a4.*

₄ **fecisset, futuram** (esse): *fecerit* (future perfect) and *erit* in the direct form; *218.1b.* **sibi:** *111.* **perpetuam:** 'lasting.' **M. Messala, M. Pisone consulibus:** 61 BC; *240a*; *238a.* **censuisset:** 'decreed'; *183a*; *214a.* **uti ... defenderet:** *199a7*; *177b.* **quicumque:** *50a.* **provinciam:** 'as a province'; *115a.* **obtineret:** 'was holding,' in the sense of governing. **quod:** 'so far as,' lit. 'with respect to that which'; *194f.* **commodo rei publicae:** *138*; *102.* **se:** repeated from *sese* above. **neglecturum:** sc. *esse*, 'he would not leave unnoticed,' a threat sufficiently forceful, although veiled.

Ariovistus replies, claiming prior rights in Gaul and defying Caesar.

36. ₁ Ad haec Ariovistus respondit: *ius esse belli, ut, qui vicissent, eis, quos vicissent, quem ad modum vellent, imperarent; item populum Romanum victis non ad alterius praescriptum, sed ad suum arbitrium, imperare consuesse.* ₂ *Si ipse populo Romano non praescriberet, quem ad modum suo iure uteretur, non oportere se a populo Romano in suo iure impediri.* ₃ *Aeduos sibi, quoniam belli fortunam temptassent et armis congressi ac superati essent, stipendiarios esse factos.* ₄ *Magnam Caesarem iniuriam facere, qui suo adventu vectigalia sibi deteriora faceret.* ₅ *Aeduis se obsides redditurum non esse; neque his neque eorum sociis iniuria bellum illaturum, si in eo manerent, quod convenisset, stipendiumque quotannis penderent; si id non fecissent, longe eis fraternum nomen populi Romani afuturum.* ₆ *Quod sibi Caesar denuntiaret, se Aeduorum iniurias non neglecturum, neminem secum sine sua pernicie contendisse.* ₇ *Cum vellet, congrederetur; intellecturum, quid invicti Germani, exercitatissimi in armis, qui inter annos XIIII tectum non subissent, virtute possent.*

Direct form (I.36.1-7): ₁ Ius *est* belli, ut, qui *vicerint*, eis, quos *vicerint*, quem ad modum *velint, imperent*; item *populus Romanus* victis non ad alterius praescriptum, sed ad suum arbitrium, imperare *consuevit.* ₂ Si *ego* populo Romano non *praescribo*, quem ad modum suo iure *utatur*, non *oportet me* a populo Romano in *meo* iure impediri. ₃ *Aedui mihi*, quoniam belli fortunam *temptaverunt* et armis congressi ac superati *sunt, stipendiarii facti sunt.* ₄ Magnam *Caesar* iniuriam *facit*, qui suo adventu vectigalia *mihi* deteriora *faciat.* ₅ Aeduis obsides non *reddam*; neque his neque eorum sociis iniuria bellum *inferam*, si in eo *manebunt*, quod *convenit*, stipendiumque quotannis *pendent*; si id non *fecerint* (future perfect), longe eis fraternum nomen populi Romani aberit. ₆ Quod *mihi* Caesar *denuntiat*, se Aeduorum iniurias non neglecturum, *nemo mecum* sine sua pernicie *contendit.* ₇ Cum *volet*, *congrediatur*! *Intelleget*, quid invicti Germani, exercitatissimi in armis, qui inter annos XIIII tectum non *subierunt*, virtute *possint.*

₁ **ius esse belli:** 'that it was a law of war'; the law is then stated as a substantive clause; *203.4.* **ut, qui vicissent, ... imperarent:** the relative clause functions as the subject of *imperarent*; 'that those who had conquered should rule over.' **eis:** after *imperarent*; *105.* **qui vicerit, quos vicerint, quem ad modum vellent:** relative clauses of characteristic; *194a.* **quem ad modum:** 'in whatever way,' lit. 'according to which manner': in full, *ad (eum) modum ad quem.* **victis:** *227a4.* **alterius:** *23b.*

₂ **populo Romano:** *107.* **quem ad modum:** 'in what way'; *quem* is here interrogative, introducing an indirect question; *48b*; *204.3.* **suo:** 'its own.' **oportet:** *73a.* **suo:** 'his own,' the reflexive reflects its subject.

₃ **congressi** (essent): 'had contended'; *57c.* **stipendiarios:** 'subject to the payment of tribute'; *148c.*

₄ **Magnam:** emphatic position; *245d.* **qui:** 'since he'; *194c.* **suo:** refers to Caesar. **vectigalia:** see I.18.3. **sibi:** refers to Ariovistus. **deteriora:** Caesar's arrival had given the Aeduans the courage to refuse to pay tribute to Ariovistus.

₅ **iniuria:** 'wrongfully'; *136b.* **in eo manerent, quod convenisset:** 'they should abide by (lit. 'in') that which had been agreed upon.' **stipendium:** 'tribute.' **quotannis:** *79b.* **penderent:** 'should pay'; originally 'weigh out,' a meaning appropriate to an earlier time when payments were made in uncoined metal. There is a similar development of meaning in the English "pound sterling." **longe eis . . . afuturum:** sc. *esse*, 'would be far from (benefiting) them.' **eis:** dative; *109b.* **fraternum nomen populi Romani:** 'the title (lit. 'name') Brethren of the Roman People.'

6 **Quod . . . denuntiaret:** 'As for Caesar's warning to him,' i.e., to Ariovistus; how lit.? *198c.* **se . . . neglecturum:** explains the warning introduced by *quod . . . denuntiaret* by repeating the language of the end of I.35.4. **se:** Caesar. **secum:** with Ariovistus. **sua:** 'his own,' referring to *neminem.*

7 **congrederetur:** 'let him come on'; *216.* **intellecturum:** *eum* (= *Caesarem*) *intellecturum esse*; *215.* **quid Germani . . . virtute possent:** 'what valor the Germans had'; how lit.? *118b.* **invicti:** 'unconquered.' **exercitatissimi:** 'most thoroughly trained.' **inter:** 'during'; with *annos*, stronger than the simple accusative of time. **XIIII:** *36; 38b.* **tectum:** 'roof.' **subissent:** *113b.* **virtute:** *142a.*

Caesar hears further complaints, marches toward Ariovistus.

37. 1 Haec eodem tempore Caesari mandata referebantur, et legati ab Aeduis et a Treveris veniebant: 2 Aedui questum, quod Harudes, qui nuper in Galliam transportati essent, fines eorum popularentur, *sese, ne obsidibus quidem datis, pacem Ariovisti redimere potuisse;* 3 Treveri autem, *pagos centum Sueborum ad ripas Rheni consedisse, qui Rhenum transire conarentur; his praeesse Nasuam et Cimberium fratres.* 4 Quibus rebus Caesar vehementer commotus maturandum sibi existimavit, ne, si nova manus Sueborum cum veteribus copiis Ariovisti sese coniunxisset, minus facile resisti posset. 5 Itaque re frumentaria, quam celerrime potuit, comparata, magnis itineribus ad Ariovistum contendit.

1 **eodem tempore . . . et:** 'at the same time as,' lit. 'at the same time . . . also'; the phrase correlates the events.
2 **Aedui:** sc. *veniebant.* **questum:** *231a; 61a3.* **Harudes:** see I.31.10. **transportati essent:** 'had been brought over' by Ariovistus. **popularentur:** 'were (as they said) laying waste'; *214b.* **sese:** '(reporting) that they'; *213b.* **ne obsidibus quidem datis:** 'not even by the giving of hostages'; *144b6.* **redimere:** 'to purchase' or acquire through exchange.
3 **Treveri:** i.e., *Treveri dicebant.* **Sueborum:** an account of the ancient Swabians is given in IV.1. **conarentur:** *193a.* **his:** *107a.* **praeesse:** *66a.* **Nasuam:** *19d.*
4 **vehementer commotus:** 'greatly disturbed,' a strong expression. Caesar does not often give us an insight into his feelings, which adds weight to those occasions on which he does. **maturandum sibi:** sc. *esse*, 'that he ought to make haste,' how lit.? *73e.* **ne . . . minus facile resisti posset:** lit. 'lest it be less easily able to be withstood,' but the double negative (*ne . . . minus*) combines to mean 'so that it would be easier to withstand'; *73c; 196b.* **sese coniunxisset:** 'should have united,' lit. 'conjoined themselves'; *218.1b.*
5 **quam celerrime potuit:** 'as quickly as possible'; *153c.* **comparata:** *144b2.* **magnis itineribus:** 'by forced marches'; *289; 18c.* Where Caesar was when the negotiations with Ariovistus were begun, and from where he went to meet Ariovistus, cannot be determined. It seems probable that he overtook the survivors of the Helvetians near the site of Dijon (see Map 1), that from there he came back to Bibracte for the Gallic Council, and that from some point near Bibracte 'the forced marches' eastward began, as indicated on Map 1.

Hearing that Ariovistus has designs on Vesontio, Caesar hastens there.

38. 1 Cum tridui viam processisset, nuntiatum est ei, Ariovistum cum suis omnibus copiis ad occupandum Vesontionem, quod est oppidum maximum Sequanorum, contendere, triduique viam a suis finibus processisse. 2 Id ne accideret, magnopere sibi praecavendum Caesar existimabat. 3 Namque omnium rerum, quae ad bellum usui erant, summa erat in eo oppido facultas, 4 idque natura loci sic muniebatur, ut magnam ad ducendum bellum daret facultatem, propterea quod flumen Dubis, ut circino circumductum, paene totum oppidum cingit; 5 reliquum spatium, quod est non amplius pedum sescentorum, qua flumen intermittit, mons continet magna altitudine, ita, ut radices montis ex utraque parte ripae fluminis contingant. 6 Hunc murus circumdatus arcem efficit et cum oppido coniungit. 7 Huc Caesar magnis nocturnis diurnisque itineribus contendit, occupatoque oppido ibi praesidium collocat.

1 **tridui:** translate as if *trium dierum*; *100a.* **viam:** 'march'; *118a.* **occupandum:** gerundive; the gerund in the accusative would not have a direct object; *230.3.* **quod:** why not *qui*, to agree in gender with *Vesontionem*? *164c.* **suis finibus:** in the country taken from the Sequanians, in Upper Alsace. But the report was unfounded, for if

Ariovistus had marched as the report indicated he would have reached Vesontio before Caesar.

2 **Id:** the seizure of Vesontio by Ariovistus. **accideret:** *196b.* **sibi praecavendum:** sc. *esse*, 'that he ought to take precautions'; *110; 73e.*

3 **ad bellum:** 'for war.' **usui:** 'useful'; how lit.? *112a.* **facultas:** 'abundance.'

4 **id:** *oppidum.* **natura loci:** cf. I.2.3. **ad ducendum bellum:** 'for prolonging the war,' at any rate until Ariovistus could bring the new Swabian hordes (I.37.3) to his assistance; *230.3.* **facultatem:** 'capability.' **ut circino circumductum:** 'as though drawn around by a pair of compasses.' **paene cingit:** 'almost encircles.' The Dubis (modern *Doubs*, 'Black River') here bends into the form of a loop, leaving only one side of the town (*reliquum spatium*) not surrounded by it; and this space is taken up by a high hill, the top of which forms an irregular plateau.

5 **spatium:** object of *continet.* **pedum sescentorum:** 'than six hundred feet' in breadth; a genitive of measure is here used instead of a comparative ablative, *quam* being omitted after *amplius*; *100a; 129b.* **sescentorum:** the distance across the neck of the loop from the river to the river again is about 1600 Roman feet; but the distance which needed to be fortified, measured across the top of the plateau, was only 600 feet. **qua flumen intermittit:** 'where the river leaves a space between' its loop, thus forming a neck of land. **mons:** see I.2.3. **continet:** 'holds together,' i.e., 'fills.' **altitudine:** about 400 feet above the river; *143a.* **ita, ut:** *197b.* **radices montis:** object of *contingant*; 'the roots of the mountain,' i.e., 'the base.' **ripae:** nominative. **contingant:** 'touch.'

6 **Hunc murus circumdatus arcem efficit et cum oppido coniungit:** 'a wall, extended around this (mountain), renders (the mountain) a citadel and joins (it) with the town.' **arcem:** *115a.*

7 **nocturnis diurnisque:** 'by night and by day'; *76b.* Caesar probably arrived at Vesontio soon after the middle of August.

Panic seizes Caesar's army on account of fear of the Germans.

39. 1 Dum paucos dies ad Vesontionem rei frumentariae commeatusque causa moratur, ex percontatione nostrorum vocibusque Gallorum ac mercatorum, qui ingenti magnitudine corporum Germanos, incredibili virtute atque exercitatione in armis esse praedicabant (saepe numero sese cum his congressos ne vultum quidem atque aciem oculorum dicebant ferre potuisse), tantus subito timor omnem exercitum occupavit, ut non mediocriter omnium mentes animosque perturbaret. 2 Hic primum ortus est a tribunis militum, praefectis, reliquisque, qui, ex urbe amicitiae causa Caesarem secuti, non magnum in re militari usum habebant; 3 quorum alius alia causa illata, quam sibi ad proficiscendum necessariam esse diceret, petebat, ut eius voluntate discedere liceret; non nulli pudore adducti, ut timoris suspicionem vitarent, remanebant. 4 Hi neque vultum fingere neque interdum lacrimas tenere poterant; abditi in tabernaculis, aut suum fatum querebantur aut cum familiaribus suis commune periculum miserabantur. 5 Vulgo totis castris testamenta obsignabantur. Horum vocibus ac timore paulatim etiam ei, qui magnum in castris usum habebant, milites centurionesque, quique equitatui praeerant, perturbabantur. 6 Qui se ex his minus timidos existimari volebant, non se hostem vereri, sed angustias itineris et magnitudinem silvarum, quae intercederent inter ipsos atque Ariovistum, aut rem frumentariam, ut satis commode supportari posset, timere dicebant. 7 Non nulli etiam Caesari nuntiabant, cum castra moveri ac signa ferri iussisset, non fore dicto audientes milites neque propter timorem signa laturos.

1 **ad:** *120a.* Only a 'garrison' (*praesidium*) was stationed in the citadel; the rest of the army was encamped 'near' the town. **rei . . . causa:** 'for the sake of the grain supply and (other) provisions'; *135b.* **moratur:** '(Caesar) was delaying'; *190a.* **ex percontatione:** 'in consequence of (lit. 'out of') the questioning.' **vocibus:** here 'stories'; *10c.* **mercatorum:** many traders accompanied the army, to trade with friendly natives as well as to purchase loot from the soldiers and supply them with extras not provided in the army rations. **magnitudine, virtute, exercitatione:** *143b.* **corporum:** *92a; 13f.* Caesar elsewhere (IV.1) speaks of the 'huge size' of the Germans, who, by contrast in stature, seemed larger to the Romans than they would have seemed to us. **exercitatione:** 'practiced skill.' **praedicabant:** 'were declaring.' **saepe numero:** see I.33.2. **cum his congressos:** 'having engaged with them (the Germans)'; *congressos* modifies *sese*, the accusative subject of *potuisse* in indirect discourse after *dicebant.* **vultum . . . ferre:** 'to endure their countenance,' i.e., the sight of their faces. **aciem oculorum:** 'the fierce look of their eyes,' lit. 'the keenness of their eyes.' The idea is that the speakers claimed to be unable to look the Germans in the eye when faced with the intensity of their gaze. **tantus . . . ut:** *197b.* **timor:** 'panic'; used of a groundless, cowardly fear. **non mediocriter:** 'in no slight degree'; litotes; *239g.* **mentes animosque:** 'hearts and minds.'

2 **Hic:** sc. *timor.* **ortus est a:** 'started with,' lit. 'arose from.' **tribunis militum:** 'military tribunes'; *274.* **praefectis:** not the 'cavalry prefects' (*269c*), but 'subsidiary officials' in various positions of slight responsibility, chiefly, we may assume, in connection with the light-armed troops. Caesar's financial and political relations made it expedient for him to furnish military appointments for a number of aristocratic young men who had had no military experience, but wanted a taste of it because that was considered the proper thing. These were in a different class from Publius Crassus, for example, and other young Romans of high social position with Caesar, who took their work very seriously and became excellent officers. **urbe:** Rome. **amicitiae causa:** *135b.* Caesar is politic as well as polite in ascribing to personal friendship the presence of these men in his army. **non magnum:** *239g.* **re militari:** 'warfare.'

3 **quorum:** i.e., those described in the first part of this sentence, those with whom the panic first started; *167.* **alius, alia causa:** repetition of *alius* in different cases results in a distributive sense: 'one man with one reason, another man with another reason,' i.e., each man in the group had his own reason; *171c.* **alia causa illata:** *144b2.* **quam:** *causa* is the antecedent; accusative as the subject of an indirect statement (*quam esse necessariam*) after *diceret.* **ad proficiscendum:** *230.3.* **diceret:** *214b.* **quorum alius . . . petebat:** 'each man of this group, having offered his own reason, which he said was for him a necessary reason to depart, was seeking.' **ut . . . liceret:** 'that it be permitted (to him)'; *199a4.* **eius voluntate:** 'with his (Caesar's) approval'; *138.* **non nulli:** 'some' or 'several,' lit. 'not none.' **pudore:** 'by a sense of shame.' **vitarent:** *196a.* **remanebant:** 'remained' in camp, after the exodus of the others.

4 **abditi:** 'shutting themselves up'; *174.* **aut suum fatum querebantur:** 'they were either bewailing their fate.'

5 **Vulgo:** adverb, 'generally.' **totis castris:** 'throughout the camp'; *145c.* **obsignabantur:** 'were being sealed,' referring to the process by which wax tablets, on which wills were ordinarily written, were sealed up. **in castris:** 'in the army' is the corresponding phrase in English. **milites, centuriones, qui equitatui praeerant:** these groups are in apposition to *ei, qui magnum in castris usum habebant.* **centuriones:** 'the centurions'; *275a.* **quique:** *et (ei) qui;* cavalry prefects and decurions are meant; *269c.*

6 **Qui ex his:** (*ei*) *ex his, qui;* 97d. **se . . . existimari:** *223a.* **volebant:** *71.* **non se vereri:** 'that they were not afraid of,' indirect statement after *dicebant,* the last word of the sentence, and matched with the subsequent statement *sed . . . timere.* **angustias:** the gorges in the valley of the Dubis (*Doubs*), through which the most direct route led northeast to the region where Ariovistus was. **rem:** object of *timere,* where a nominative, subject of *posset,* might have been expected; prolepsis; *238g.* **ut:** 'that not'; *202.*

7 **signa ferri:** 'the standards to be carried,' i.e., that the army should advance; *284; 285.* **iussisset:** subjunctive in a subordinate clause in indirect discourse after *nuntiabant,* the pluperfect tense here standing for a future perfect indicative in the direct form; *214a.* **non fore dicto audientes milites:** 'that the soldiers would not obey the command'; lit. 'would not be listeners to the thing said.' **fore:** here = *futuros esse; 52.* **dicto:** *105.* **neque . . . signa laturos:** sc. *esse,* 'nor would they advance'; the same idiom as *signa ferri* above.

Caesar addresses the centurions.

40. 1 Haec cum animadvertisset, convocato consilio, omniumque ordinum ad id consilium adhibitis centurionibus, vehementer eos incusavit; primum, quod, aut quam in partem, aut quo consilio ducerentur, sibi quaerendum aut cogitandum putarent: 2 *Ariovistum, se consule, cupidissime populi Romani amicitiam appetisse; cur hunc tam temere quisquam ab officio discessurum iudicaret? 3 Sibi quidem persuaderi, cognitis suis postulatis atque aequitate condicionum perspecta, eum neque suam neque populi Romani gratiam repudiaturum. 4 Quod si, furore atque amentia impulsus, bellum intulisset, quid tandem vererentur? aut cur de sua virtute aut de ipsius diligentia desperarent? 5 Factum eius hostis periculum patrum nostrorum memoria, cum, Cimbris et Teutonis a Gaio Mario pulsis, non minorem laudem exercitus, quam ipse imperator, meritus videretur; factum etiam nuper in Italia, servili tumultu, quos tamen aliquid usus ac disciplina, quae a nobis accepissent, sublevarent. 6 Ex quo iudicari posse, quantum haberet in se boni constantia, propterea quod, quos aliquamdiu inermes sine causa timuissent, hos postea armatos ac victores superassent. 7 Denique hos esse eosdem Germanos, quibuscum saepe numero Helvetii congressi, non solum in suis, sed etiam in illorum finibus, plerumque superassent; qui tamen pares esse nostro exercitui non potuerint. 8 Si quos adversum proelium et fuga Gallorum commoveret, hos, si quaererent, reperire posse, diuturnitate belli defatigatis Gallis, Ariovistum, cum multos menses castris se ac paludibus tenuisset neque sui potestatem fecisset, desperantes iam de pugna et dispersos subito adortum, magis ratione et consilio quam virtute vicisse. 9 Cui rationi contra homines barbaros atque imperitos locus fuisset, hac ne ipsum quidem sperare nostros exercitus capi posse. 10 Qui suum timorem in rei frumentariae simulationem angustiasque itineris conferrent, facere arroganter, cum aut de officio imperatoris desperare aut praescribere viderentur. 11 Haec sibi esse* *curae; frumentum Sequanos, Leucos, Lingones sumministrare, iamque esse in agris frumenta matura; de iti-nere ipsos brevi tempore iudicaturos.* 12 *Quod non fore dicto audientes neque signa laturi dicantur, nihil se ea re commoveri; scire enim, quibuscumque exercitus dicto audiens non fuerit, aut, male re gesta, fortunam de-fuisse, aut, aliquo facinore comperto, avaritiam esse convictam; suam innocentiam perpetua vita, felicitatem Helvetiorum bello esse perspectam.* 13 *Itaque se, quod in longiorem diem collaturus fuisset, repraesentaturum et proxima nocte de quarta vigilia castra moturum, ut quam primum intellegere posset, utrum apud eos pudor atque officium, an timor, plus valeret.* 14 *Quod si praeterea nemo sequatur, tamen se cum sola decima legione iturum, de qua non dubitaret, sibique eam praetoriam cohortem futuram.* 15 Huic legioni Caesar et indulserat praecipue et propter virtutem confidebat maxime.

Direct form (I.40.2-14): 2 *Ariovistus, me* consule, cupidissime populi Romani amicitiam *appetiit*; cur hunc tam temere quisquam ab officio discessurum (esse) *iudicet*? 3 *Mihi* quidem *persuadetur*, cognitis *meis* postu-latis atque aequitate condicionum perspecta, eum neque *meam* neque populi Romani gratiam repudiaturum (esse). 4 *Quod si* (*Ariovistus*), furore atque amentia impulsus, bellum *intulerit*, quid tandem *vereamini*? aut cur de *vestra* virtute aut de *mea* diligentia *desperetis*? 5 *Factum* (*est*) eius hostis periculum patrum nostrorum memoria, cum, Cimbris et Teutonis a Gaio Mario pulsis, non minorem laudem exercitus, quam ipse imper-ator, meritus *videbatur*; factum (*est periculum*) etiam nuper in Italia, servili tumultu, quos tamen aliquid usus ac disciplina, quae a nobis *acceperant, sublevabant.* 6 *Ex* quo iudicari *potest*, quantum *habeat* in se boni constan-tia, propterea quod, quos aliquamdiu inermes sine causa *timuistis*, hos postea armatos ac victores *superavistis.* 7 *Denique hi sunt idem* Germani, quibuscum saepe numero Helvetii congressi, non solum in suis, sed etiam in illorum finibus, plerumque *superaverunt*; qui tamen pares esse nostro exercitui non *potuerunt.* 8 *Si* quos adversum proelium et fuga Gallorum *commovet*, hi, *si* *quaerent*, reperire *poterunt*, diuturnitate belli defatigatis Gallis, Ariovistum, cum multos menses castris se ac paludibus tenuisset neque sui potestatem fecisset, (*eos = Gallos*) desperantes iam de pugna et dispersos subito adortum, magis ratione et consilio quam virtute vicisse. 9 *Cui* rationi contra homines barbaros atque imperitos locus *fuit*, hac ne *ipse* quidem *sperat* nostros exercitus capi posse. 10 *Qui* suum timorem in rei frumentariae simulationem angustiasque itineris *conferunt, faciunt* arroganter, cum aut de officio imperatoris desperare aut praescribere *videantur.* 11 *Haec mihi* sunt curae: fru-mentum *Sequani, Leuci,* Lingones *sumministrant*, iamque *sunt* in agris frumenta matura; de itinere *ipsi* brevi tempore *iudicabitis.* 12 *Quod* (*milites*) non fore dicto audientes neque signa laturi dicuntur, nihil ea re *commo-veor; scio* enim, quibuscumque exercitus dicto audiens non fuerit, aut, male re gesta, fortunam defuisse, aut, aliquo facinore comperto, avaritiam esse convictam: *mea innocentia* perpetua vita, *felicitas* Helvetiorum bello *est perspecta.* 13 *Itaque*, quod in longiorem diem collaturus *fui, repraesentabo*; et *hac* nocte de quarta vigilia castra *movebo*, ut quam primum intellegere *possim*, utrum apud *milites* pudor atque officium, an timor, plus *valeat.* 14 *Quod si* praeterea nemo *sequetur*, tamen *ego* cum sola decima legione *ibo*, de qua non *dubito, mihique ea praetoria cohors erit.*

---

1 **ordinum:** 'companies'; *12d.* A Roman legion was divided into ten cohorts, with each cohort containing three maniples, and each maniple divided into two companies. Hence there were 60 companies in a legion, over each of which was a centurion; *267c.* **centurionibus:** ordinarily only the centurions of first rank, the six centurions of the first cohort of each legion, were invited to a war-council. But on this occasion all the centurions of the six legions (360 in number) were brought together, doubtless with the lieutenants and other higher officers, not for deliberation, but for an address by the commander in chief. **quod . . . putarent:** 'because (as he told them) they thought'; *214b.* **quam, quo:** *48b; 204.2.* **consilio:** 'plan.' **sibi quaerendum** (esse) **aut cogitandum** (esse): the subject is the preceding pair of indirect questions; 'that they should be the ones to inquire or consider'; how lit.? *73e.*

2 **Ariovistum,** etc.: Caesar shifts from reporting his reason for his rebuke of the soldiers to reporting the oral arguments he delivered. **se consule:** 'during his consulship'; *144b1.* Caesar had been consul in 59 BC and undertook the Gallic War in the following year. Caesar has already stressed Ariovistus' relationship to Rome at I.33.1 and I.35.2. **hunc . . . discessurum:** sc. *esse*, indirect discourse after *iudicaret.* **quisquam:** subject of *iudicaret; 49a; 168.* **ab officio:** 'from the obligation' of his friendship. **iudicaret:** deliberative subjunctive in a rhetorical question; *179b2.*

3 **Sibi quidem persuaderi:** 'he at least was persuaded'; how lit.? *106b.* **cognitis suis postulatis:** 'once his demands became known'; *postulatis* is a noun not a participle; *144b2.* **aequitate:** 'fairness.' **eum:** = *Ariovistum.* **suam:** *157d.* **repudiaturum:** sc. *esse*, 'would reject'; infinitive in indirect discourse after *persuaderi.*

4 **Quod si:** 'but if'; *118d.* **impulsus:** 'carried away.' **quid tandem vererentur:** 'what, after all, were they to fear?'; another deliberative subjunctive (so also *desperarent*); *179b2; 61a2.*

5 **Factum** (esse) **eius hostis periculum:** 'A trial had been made of that enemy,' i.e., of the Germans. **memoria:** *147b.* **Cimbris, Teutonis:** see the note on I.33.4. **meritus:** for *meritus esse*; with *videretur*, 'was seen to have earned'; *148e.* **factum etiam:** sc. *esse eius hostis periculum*; the *etiam* ('also') further indicates that Caesar is introducing a second example. **nuper:** 'recently.' Among the centurions present there were probably a number who had served as soldiers in the war with Spartacus, the term of military service being twenty years; *267a.* **servili tumultu:** = *tumultu servorum*, 'at the time of the uprising of the slaves', 73-71 BC; referring to the insurrection led by Spartacus, the gladiator, who had a succession of victories for two years but was ultimately crushed. Caesar implies that among the gladiators and other slaves serving under Spartacus there were many of Germanic origin. **tumultu:** why ablative? *147b.* **quos:** the antecedent is the implied *servorum*; *164b.* **quos tamen aliquid usus ac disciplina, quae a nobis accepissent, sublevarent:** 'whom nevertheless the practice and training which they had gained from us aided to some extent.' Caesar argues that the reasons for the initial success of Spartacus' forces (and in particular, it seems, of the Germans among those forces) were the practice (*usus*) and training (*disciplina*) that they had learned from Romans. Yet even with that training, they were nevertheless (*tamen*) defeated once a genuine trial was made of them by Roman forces. **aliquid:** *118b.* **quae:** neuter pl.; *163c.*

6 **Ex quo iudicari posse:** 'from which it can be judged.' **quantum haberet in se boni constantia:** 'how great an advantage there is in steadfastness,' lit. 'how much of good steadfastness has in itself'; this indirect question is the subject of *posse*; *204.3.* **boni:** *97b.* **quos:** the antecedent is the *hos* (*servos Germanos*) six words later. **inermes:** '(while) unarmed,' referring to the slaves in the earlier stages of the insurrection, before they were able to supply themselves with weapons. **timuissent, superassent:** the subject, specifically, are those in Caesar's audience who had fought in the slave revolt, but Caesar speaks as if his entire audience had done so. **armatos:** 'equipped with arms.' **victores:** referring to the slaves' initial success in the revolt, which would have increased their confidence.

7 **Denique:** 'Finally,' closing the argument about the Germans. **quibuscum:** 'with whom'; cf. I.1.4; *125c.* **congressi:** 'had engaged (in battle) and,' lit. 'having engaged'; *228a.* **illorum:** = *Germanorum*. **plerumque superassent:** 'generally defeated.' **qui tamen:** *Helvetii* is the antecedent; 'yet who'; *236a.*

8 **Si quos adversum proelium et fuga Gallorum commoveret:** 'if the Gauls' adverse battle and flight were alarming any (of them).' Caesar turns the argument from the Germans in general to Ariovistus in particular, seeking to diminish his notable victory against the Gauls. **quos:** i.e., anyone in Caesar's audience; *168; 49a.* **adversum proelium:** referring to their defeat by Ariovistus at Magetobriga; see I.31.12. **commoveret:** singular despite the two subjects; *172b.* **hos:** refers back those identified in *quos*, and makes them the subject of the main clause. **si quaererent:** 'if they would inquire,' the imperfect subjunctive stands for a future indicative, in the direct form, in the protasis of a condition of fact; *206; 218.1a.* **diuturnitate belli defatigatis Gallis:** 'when the Gauls had become exhausted by the length of the war'; *144b2.* **menses:** *118a.* **castris se ac paludibus tenuisset:** 'had remained in camp and in the marshes,' lit. 'held himself back by means of'; placing his camp in the marshes made it more difficult for him to be approached or attacked; *131a.* **neque sui potestatem fecisset:** 'and had given (them) no opportunity for himself,' i.e., no opportunity to attack or capture him. **sui:** *102.* **desperantes iam de pugna et dispersos subito adortum, magis ratione et consilio quam virtute vicisse:** i.e., *Ariovistum . . . subito adortum* (*eos = Gallos*) *desperantes iam de* ('of') *pugna et dispersos, vicisse* (*eos*) *ratione et consilio* ('by cunning and strategy') *magis quam virtute*. **adortum:** *226c.*

9 **Cui rationi contra homines barbaros atque imperitos locus fuisset, hac ne ipsum quidem sperare nostros excercitus capi posse:** 'not even (Ariovistus) himself could hope that our armies (would) be caught (i.e., deceived) by the (cunning) which had a place (lit. 'to which a place had been') against barbarous and unskilled men.' **Cui rationi . . . hac:** i.e., *hac ratione, cui*, 'by the (lit. 'this') cunning . . . (to) which'; *165c.* **Cui:** dative of possession; *111.* **contra:** here a preposition. **ipsum . . . sperare . . . posse:** the main clause. **nostros exercitus capi:** indirect discourse after *sperare*.

10 **Qui . . . conferrent:** this clause describes the group who are the subject of the main verb *facere*, i.e., *eos, qui . . . conferrent, facere*. For Caesar's characterization of their motivation, see I.39.6. **suum timorem in rei frumentariae simulationem . . . conferrent:** 'ascribed their fear to a pretended anxiety about supplies.' **cum . . . viderentur:** *184a.* **praescribere:** sc. *officium imperatoris*.

11 **sibi curae:** *112b.* **frumenta:** how different from *frumentum*? Cf. I.16.2. **ipsos . . . iudicaturos:** sc. *esse*, 'they themselves (the members of Caesar's audience) will decide;' *ipsos* contrasts with *sibi*.

12 **Quod . . . dicantur:** sc. *milites* as subject; cf. I.39.7. **Quod:** 'As to the fact that'; *198c.* **neque signa laturi** (esse) **dicantur:** lit. '(soldiers) are said not to be going to advance the standards'; *148e; 172d; 224a; 285.* **nihil:** 'not at all'; *118c.* **scire:** sc. *se*; *215.* **quibuscumque . . . esse perspectam:** this sentence explains two things that Caesar claims to know about commanders whose armies mutiny: either their poor conduct led to bad luck, or their greed was seen to have tempted them to criminal action. The structure of the sentence first defines its

subject as pertaining to commanders whose troops do not obey them, then provides the alternate reasons (*aut ... aut*) for mutiny, each conveyed by a causal ablative absolute followed by the resulting action expressed as an indirect statement after *scire*. **quibuscumque exercitus dicto audiens non fuerit, aut, male re gesta, fortunam defuisse, aut:** 'whichever (commanders) an army did not obey, either their luck failed (them) because of a thing done poorly, or.' **dicto audiens:** an idiom that expresses a single concept, 'obedient' (lit. 'listening to the thing said'), which is followed by the dative (*quibuscumque*); *50a; 108a.* **male re gesta:** *144b3.* **fortunam:** the Romans were superstitious in avoiding anything that seemed unlucky. **defuisse:** sc. *eis* as the antecedent of *quibuscumque; 109b; 66a.* **aliquo:** from *aliqui; 49a.* **facinore:** 'crime'; *13f; 144b3.* **avaritiam:** 'greed,' the underlying cause of the crimes committed by generals, according to Caesar. **esse convictam:** 'had been clearly proved' against them. **suam ... esse perspectam:** the concluding claim that disproves the possibility of the two circumstances just described. **suam:** emphatic position; *157b.* **innocentiam:** 'integrity,' freedom from the corruption implied in *avaritiam.* **perpetua vita:** 'during his entire life'; *147c.* **felicitatem:** 'good fortune'; both this word and *innocentiam* are subjects of *esse perspectam.* **Helvetiorum bello:** 'in the war with (lit. 'of') the Helvetians.'
13 **longiorem:** 'more distant.' **collaturus fuisset:** 'he had been going to put off'; *63; 69b.* **repraesentaturum (esse):** sc. *id,* antecedent of *quod;* 'he would do at once (that) which.' **de quarta vigilia:** *242d.* **quam primum:** *153c.* **posset:** *196a.* **utrum ... an:** *204.1.* **plus valeret:** 'should have more influence' with them; *118b.*
14 **Quod si:** 'even if'; *118d.* **sequatur:** *218.1a.* **non dubitaret:** 'he entertained no doubts.' **eam praetoriam cohortem futurum:** 'it would be the general's bodyguard,' to which a general (originally called *praetor*) was entitled.
15 **legioni:** *105; 267e.* **indulserat:** 'had favored.' **praecipue:** 'especially'; emphatic position; *244a.* **confidebat maxime:** 'had the fullest confidence.'

Fear and mutiny change to enthusiasm; Caesar advances.

41. 1 Hac oratione habita, mirum in modum conversae sunt omnium mentes, summaque alacritas et cupiditas belli gerendi inlata est; 2 princepsque decima legio per tribunos militum ei gratias egit, quod de se optimum iudicium fecisset, seque esse ad bellum gerendum paratissimam confirmavit. 3 Deinde reliquae legiones cum tribunis militum et primorum ordinum centurionibus egerunt, uti per eos Caesari satisfacerent; *se neque umquam dubitasse neque timuisse, neque de summa belli suum iudicium, sed imperatoris esse existimavisse.* 4 Eorum satisfactione accepta, et itinere exquisito per Diviciacum, quod ex aliis ei maximam fidem habebat, ut milium amplius quinquaginta circuitu locis apertis exercitum duceret, de quarta vigilia, ut dixerat, profectus est. 5 Septimo die, cum iter non intermitteret, ab exploratoribus certior factus est, Ariovisti copias a nostris milibus passuum quattuor et XX abesse.

1 **Hac oratione habita:** *144b2.* **mirum in modum:** 'in a remarkable way.' **omnium:** including not only the officers but also the soldiers, to whom the speech was promptly reported by the centurions. **summa alacritas:** 'the utmost enthusiasm.' **gerendi:** *102; 230.1.*
2 **princeps:** adjective; *152b.* **per:** *123a.* **tribunos militum:** *274.* **ei gratias egit:** 'conveyed thanks to him.' **fecisset:** why subjunctive? *183a.* **gerendum:** *230.3.*
3 **reliquae:** *171a.* **primorum ordinum centurionibus:** 'the centurions of first rank,' apparently the six centurions of the first cohort in each legion. **egerunt:** 'arranged.' **uti ... satisfacerent:** 'to apologize'; *199a8.* **per:** 'with the help of.' **se:** '(declaring) that they'; *213b.* **dubitasse:** *64a1.* **neque:** translate as if *et non.* **de summa belli iudicium:** 'the judgment concerning the supreme (plan) for the war.' **suum, imperatoris:** in predicate after *esse;* 'was not their (business), but (the business) of the commander'; *94d; 157d.*
4 **quod ... habebat:** 'because he (Caesar) had.' **ei:** 'in him'; *109a.* **ut ... duceret:** 'such that he could lead'; explains *itinere; 203.4.* **milium amplius quinquaginta circuitu:** '(although) with a detour (lit. 'a going around') of more than fifty miles,' in order to avoid the dangerous defiles of the Doubs valley; see I.39.6. **milium quinquaginta:** sc. *passuum.* Why genitive? *100a; 129b.* **locis apertis:** 'through open country,' lit. 'in open places,' marching first north, and then northeast, between the Jura and the Vosegus mountains; see Map 1; *145c.*
5 **Septimo die:** Caesar had probably covered about 120 miles since leaving Vesontio. He was now in the valley of the Rhine, never previously entered by a Roman general with an army. **iter:** accusative, 'the march.' **exploratoribus:** *287.* **nostris:** sc. *copiis.* **milibus:** *147c.* **XX:** viginti; *36; 38b.*

Ariovistus suggests a conference, which is arranged.

42. 1 Cognito Caesaris adventu, Ariovistus legatos ad eum mittit: *quod antea de colloquio postulasset, id* *per se fieri licere, quoniam propius accessisset seque id sine periculo facere posse existimaret.* 2 Non respuit condicionem Caesar, iamque eum ad sanitatem reverti arbitrabatur, cum id, quod antea petenti denegasset, ultro polliceretur; 3 magnamque in spem veniebat, pro suis tantis populique Romani in eum beneficiis, cognitis suis postulatis, fore, uti pertinacia desisteret. Dies colloquio dictus est ex eo die quintus. 4 Interim saepe cum legati ultro citroque inter eos mitterentur, Ariovistus postulavit, ne quem peditem ad colloquium Caesar adduceret: *vereri se, ne per insidias ab eo circumveniretur; uterque cum equitatu veniret; alia ratione sese non esse venturum.* 5 Caesar, quod neque colloquium interposita causa tolli volebat, neque salutem suam Gallorum equitatui committere audebat, commodissimum esse statuit, omnibus equis Gallis equitibus detractis, eo legionarios milites legionis decimae, cui quam maxime confidebat, imponere, ut praesidium quam amicissimum, si quid opus facto esset, haberet. 6 Quod cum fieret, non irridicule quidam ex militibus decimae legionis dixit: *plus, quam pollicitus esset, Caesarem facere; pollicitum, se in cohortis praetoriae loco decimam legionem habiturum, ad equum rescribere.*

1 **quod . . . , id . . . fieri licere:** '(that) he was permitting that thing to happen which . . . '; i.e., *id* is the antecedent of *quod*. **postulasset, accessisset:** supply 'Caesar' as subject in order to avoid using 'he' with reference to two persons. **postulasset:** *64a1.* **per se:** with *licet* = 'so far as he was concerned.' **facere posse:** 'could do.'
2 **non respuit:** 'did not reject.' **ad sanitatem:** 'to his senses'; *157a.* **petenti:** sc. *sibi.* **denegasset:** 'he (Ariovistus) had refused.' **ultro:** 'of his own accord.'
3 **magnamque in spem veniebat:** 'and he was coming to have great hopes,' lit. 'into a great hope.' **pro:** 'in return for.' **suis populique:** *157d.* See I.35.2 and I.43.4. **cognitis suis postulatis:** cf. I.40.3. **fore:** infinitive (= *futurum esse*) in indirect discourse after *spem*, as if Caesar had written *sperabat*; the subject is *uti . . . desisteret*; *225; 203.1.* **pertinacia:** *127a.* **colloquio:** *112a.* **ex eo die quintus:** emphatic position; 'the fifth day from that day.'
4 **ultro citroque:** 'back and forth' between the headquarters of the two commanders. **mitterentur:** *185c.* **quem peditem:** 'any foot soldier'; *49a; 10d.* **vereri se:** '(saying) that he was afraid'; *213b.* **ne:** 'that'; *202.* **veniret:** 'should come'; jussive subjunctive, *veniat* in the direct form; *216.* **alia ratione:** 'on any other condition'; *136c.*
5 **colloquium . . . tolli:** *223a.* **tolli:** 'be done away with.' **interposita causa:** *144b6.* **Gallorum equitatui:** see I.15.1. **esse:** infinitive in indirect discourse after *statuit*, the subject is *imponere*, with *commodissimum*, 'the most expedient (thing),' in predicate; *222b; 148d.* **Gallis equitibus:** 'from the Gallic horsemen'; *109b.* **equis detractis:** *144b2.* **eo:** adv., 'to that place,' = *in eos (equos)*, 'onto them.' **cui:** 'in which'; *105.* **quam:** *153c.* **imponere:** 'to mount.' **si quid opus facto esset:** 'if there should be any need of action.' **quid:** *118b.* **facto:** *132a.* **haberet:** *196a.*
6 **Quod cum fieret:** 'While this was being done'; *185c.* **non irridicule:** 'not without wit'; *239g.* **quidam:** *168.* **plus:** object of *facere*; 'was doing more' for the legion. **pollicitum:** 'having promised'; sc. *eum*, referring to Caesar, subject of *rescribere.* **se . . . habiturum:** 'that he would consider;' this indirect statement restates what Caesar had promised; see I.40.14. **ad equum rescribere:** lit. 'is transferring (them) to a horse'; the phrase has a double meaning: 'is transferring (them) to the cavalry,' which would be a demotion for a legionary soldier, or 'is transferring (them) to the equestrian order,' which would elevate them to a much more significant social status; in the contrast (yet in the presumption of the latter sense) lies the point of the joke.

Caesar and Ariovistus meet; Caesar justifies his demands.

43. 1 Planities erat magna et in ea tumulus terrenus satis grandis. Hic locus aequo fere spatio a castris utriusque aberat. 2 Eo, ut erat dictum, ad colloquium venerunt. Legionem Caesar, quam equis devexerat, passibus ducentis ab eo tumulo constituit. Item equites Ariovisti pari intervallo constiterunt. 3 Ariovistus, ex equis ut colloquerentur et praeter se denos ut ad colloquium adducerent, postulavit. 4 Ubi eo ventum est, Caesar initio orationis sua senatusque in eum beneficia commemoravit, quod rex appellatus esset a senatu, quod amicus, quod munera amplissime missa; quam rem et paucis contigisse et a Romanis pro maximis hominum officiis consuesse tribui docebat: 5 *illum, cum neque aditum neque causam postulandi iustam haberet, beneficio ac liberalitate sua ac senatus ea praemia consecutum.* 6 Docebat etiam, quam veteres quamque iustae causae necessitudinis ipsis cum Aeduis intercederent, 7 quae senatus consulta, quotiens quamque honorifica, in eos facta essent, ut omni tempore totius Galliae principatum Aedui tenuissent, prius etiam quam nostram amicitiam appetissent: 8 *populi Romani hanc esse consuetudinem, ut socios atque amicos non modo sui nihil deperdere, sed gratia, dignitate, honore auctiores velit esse; quod vero ad amicitiam populi Romani attulissent, id eis eripi quis pati posset?* 9

Postulavit deinde eadem, quae legatis in mandatis dederat: *ne aut Aeduis aut eorum sociis bellum infer-ret; obsides redderet; si nullam partem Germanorum domum remittere posset, at ne quos amplius Rhenum transire pateretur.*

1 **Planities:** 'plain' of Alsace, between the Vosges (*Vosegus*) mountains and the Rhine; *21a.* **erat:** *90a.* **tumulus terrenus:** 'an earthy mound,' whose sides, free from rocks and ledges, furnished an easy ascent for horsemen. This has been identified as the hill of Plettig, an elevation of oval shape about 24 miles southwest of Strasbourg, between the villages of Epfig and Dambach; it rises in isolation more than 160 feet above the surrounding plain. **aequo fere spatio aberat:** 'was about equally distant,' lit. 'distant by a generally equal interval'; *147c.*
2 **ut erat dictum:** 'as had been agreed.' **equis devexerat:** 'had conveyed on horseback,' lit. 'by means of horses'; *131a.* **passibus:** *147c.* **ducentis:** *36; 37d.* How many feet in 200 paces? *243b.* **intervallo:** *138.*
3 **ex equis:** 'on horseback,' lit. 'from their horses'; *126c.* **denos:** 'ten men each'; *36; 85.* **adducerent:** *199a4.*
4 **Ubi eo ventum est:** 'when they had come to that place,' lit. 'when it was come,' impersonal passive; *73d.* **initio:** *147b.* **sua senatusque:** *157d.* **beneficia:** explained by the appositional *quod*-clauses following; see I.35.2, I.42.3. **quod rex appellatus esset:** '(namely the fact) that he had been called king'; not a causal clause but a statement of fact, yet subjunctive because it is being reported; *198b; 214b.* **rex:** *88a.* **amicus:** sc. *appellatus esset;* *89a.* **munera:** what these 'presents' were, we do not know. **amplissime:** 'in richest measure'; *34a.* **missa:** sc. *essent.* **quam rem:** 'and that this recognition,' lit. 'thing'; *167.* **et . . . et:** *233a.* **paucis:** *105; 154a.* **pro maximis hominum officiis:** 'in return for men's greatest services.' **docebat:** 'he stated.'
5 **illum . . . consecutum:** sc. *esse; 213b.* **cum neque aditum neque causam postulandi iustam haberet:** 'although he had neither (a means of) approach (to the Senate) nor a just reason for asking.' These circumstances suggest the significance of Caesar's own actions on Ariovistus' behalf, but why Caesar asserts that Ariovistus' claim was not just is unknown. **beneficio:** *135a.* **sua:** *157b.* **praemia:** 'distinctions.'
6 **etiam:** 'also,' marking the transition to a new argument. **quam veteres quamque iustae causae necessitudinis ipsis cum Aeduis intercederent:** 'how old and how just (were the) reasons for a close relationship (that) existed between themselves and (lit. 'with') the Aeduans'; an indirect question; *204.3.* **veteres:** *26a.* **necessitudinis:** *12d.* **ipsis:** i.e., *Romanis;* why dat.? *107a.*
7 **quae senatus consulta quotiens quamque honorifica in eos facta essent:** 'what (were the) decrees of the Senate – how often and how complimentary – (that) had been passed in their behalf'; *204.2.* **quae:** *48b.* **quamque:** = *et quam.* **honorifica:** *31.* **ut:** 'how'; *204.3.* **omni tempore:** see I.11.3. **prius etiam quam:** 'even before'; *189a; 220.* **nostram:** *157c.*
8 **hanc:** for *hoc; 164c.* **ut . . . velit:** 'to desire'; explaining *hanc; 203.4; 71.* **socios atque amicos . . . deperdere, sed . . . auctiores esse:** accusatives and infinitives after *velit; 223a1.* **non modo . . . sed:** *236d.* **sui nihil deperdere:** 'should lose nothing of what they had,' lit. 'of their own'; *97a; 154a.* **gratia:** *142a.* **quod . . . attulissent, id eis eripi quis pati posset:** i.e., *quis posset pati id, quod . . . attulissent, eis eripi?* The reference is to the power and independence of the Aeduans in former times. **attulissent:** 'had brought'; *69b.* **eis:** dative, 'from them'; *109b.* **posset:** a rhetorical question posed with a deliberative subjunctive (*possit* in the direct form); *179b2.*
9 **Postulavit eadem:** 'he made the same demands'; *117a.* **dederat:** 'he had entrusted'; see I.35; *67a.* **ne . . . inferret, redderet, ne . . . pateretur:** indirect commands that explain *eadem; 216.* **domum:** *119b.* **remittere:** 'send back.' **posset:** *218.1a.* **at:** 'at any rate'; *236a.* **quos:** *168.*

Ariovistus uncompromisingly justifies his demands.

44. 1 Ariovistus ad postulata Caesaris pauca respondit, de suis virtutibus multa praedicavit: 2 *transisse Rhenum sese non sua sponte, sed rogatum et arcessitum a Gallis; non sine magna spe magnisque praemiis domum propinquosque reliquisse; sedes habere in Gallia ab ipsis concessas, obsides ipsorum voluntate datos; stipendium capere iure belli, quod victores victis imponere consuerint.* 3 *Non sese Gallis, sed Gallos sibi bellum intulisse; omnes Galliae civitates ad se oppugnandum venisse ac contra se castra habuisse; eas omnes copias a se uno proelio pulsas ac superatas esse.* 4 *Si iterum experiri velint, se iterum paratum esse decertare; si pace uti velint, iniquum esse de stipendio recusare, quod sua voluntate ad id tempus pependerint.* 5 *Amicitiam populi Romani sibi ornamento et praesidio, non detrimento, esse oportere, idque se hac spe petisse. Si per populum Romanum stipendium remittatur et dediticii subtrahantur, non minus libenter sese recusaturum populi Romani amicitiam, quam appetierit.* 6 *Quod multitudinem Germanorum in Galliam traducat, id se sui muniendi, non Galliae impugnandae causa, facere; eius rei testimonium esse, quod nisi rogatus non venerit, et quod bellum non intulerit, sed defenderit.* 7 *Se prius in Galliam venisse quam populum Romanum. Numquam ante hoc tempus exercitum populi Romani Galliae provinciae finibus egressum.* 8 *Quid sibi* *vellet? Cur in suas possessiones veniret? Provinciam suam hanc esse Galliam, sicut illam nostram. Ut ipsi concedi non oporteret, si in nostros fines impetum faceret, sic item nos esse iniquos, quod in suo iure se interpellaremus. 9 Quod fratres a senatu Aeduos appellatos diceret, non se tam barbarum neque tam imperitum esse rerum, ut non sciret, neque bello Allobrogum proximo Aeduos Romanis auxilium tulisse, neque ipsos in his contentionibus, quas Aedui secum et cum Sequanis habuissent, auxilio populi Romani usos esse. 10 Debere se suspicari, simulata Caesarem amicitia, quod exercitum in Gallia habeat, sui opprimendi causa habere. 11 Qui nisi decedat, atque exercitum deducat ex his regionibus, sese illum non pro amico, sed pro hoste, habiturum. 12 Quod si eum interfecerit, multis sese nobilibus principibusque populi Romani gratum esse facturum (id se ab ipsis, per eorum nuntios, compertum habere), quorum omnium gratiam atque amicitiam eius morte redimere posset. 13 Quod si decessisset et liberam possessionem Galliae sibi tradidisset, magno se illum praemio remuneraturum et, quaecumque bella geri vellet, sine ullo eius labore et periculo confecturum.*

Direct form (I.44.2-13): 2 Transii Rhenum non mea sponte, sed rogatus et arcessitus a Gallis; non sine magna spe magnisque praemiis domum propinquosque reliqui; sedes habeo in Gallia ab ipsis concessas, obsides ipsorum voluntate datos; stipendium capio iure belli, quod victores victis imponere consuerunt. 3 Non ego Gallis, sed Galli mihi bellum intulerunt; omnes Galliae civitates ad me oppugnandum venerunt ac contra me castra habuerunt; eae omnes copiae a me uno proelio pulsae ac superatae sunt. 4 Si (Galli) iterum experiri volunt, iterum paratus sum decertare; si pace uti volunt, iniquum est de stipendio recusare, quod sua voluntate adhuc pependerunt. 5 Amicitiam populi Romani mihi ornamento et praesidio, non detrimento, esse oportet, idque (eam) hac spe petii. Si per populum Romanum stipendium remittetur et dediticii subtrahentur, non minus libenter recusabo (206) populi Romani amicitiam, quam appetii. 6 Quod multitudinem Germanorum in Galliam traduco, id mei (39) muniendi (causa), non Galliae impugnandae causa, facio; eius rei testimonium est, quod nisi rogatus non veni, et quod bellum non intuli, sed defendi. 7 Ego prius in Galliam veni quam populus Romanus. Numquam ante hoc tempus exercitus populi Romani Galliae provinciae finibus egressus est. 8 Quid mihi vis? Cur in meas possessiones venis? Provincia mea est haec Gallia, sicut illa (Gallia) vestra (provincia est). Ut mihi concedi non oporteat, si in vestros fines impetum faciam, sic item vos estis iniqui, quod me in meo iure interpellatis. 9 Quod fratres a senatu Aeduos appellatos (esse) dicis, non tam barbarus neque tam imperitus rerum sum, ut non sciam, neque bello Allobrogum proximo Aeduos Romanis auxilium tulisse, neque ipsos in his contentionibus, quas Aedui mecum et cum Sequanis habuerunt, auxilio populi Romani usos esse. 10 Debeo suspicari, simulata te amicitia, quod exercitum in Gallia habes, mei opprimendi causa habere. 11 Nisi decedes, atque exercitum deduces ex his regionibus, te non pro amico, sed pro hoste, habebo. 12 Quod si te interfecero, multis nobilibus principibusque populi Romani gratum faciam (id ab ipsis, per eorum nuntios, compertum habeo), quorum omnium gratiam atque amicitiam tua morte redimere possum. 13 Quod si decesseris et liberam possessionem Galliae mihi tradideris, magno te praemio remunerabor et, quaecumque bella geri voles, sine ullo tuo labore et periculo conficiam.

1 **postulata:** 'demands.' **pauca:** sc. *verba*, object of *respondit*; 154a. **suis:** emphatic; 157b. **virtutibus:** 'merits.' **multa praedicavit:** 'had much to say'; how lit.?

2 **rogatum:** 'because he had been asked'; 227a1. **non sine:** 239g. **reliquisse, habere, capere:** sc. *se* (Ariovistus) as subject. **ipsis:** the Gauls. **concessas:** 'which had been ceded'; 227a4. **obsides:** i.e., *se habere sedes et obsides*; 238a. **voluntate:** 138. **iure:** 'in accordance with the rights (lit. 'right') of war'; 13g; 136c. **quod:** the antecedent is *stipendium*. **victis:** 'the vanquished'; 227a4. **consuerint:** 64a2; 194a.

3 **sese Gallis . . . Gallos sibi:** 239b. **castra habuisse:** 'had fought'; how lit.? **uno proelio:** see I.31.12.

4 **paratum decertare:** 'ready to fight it out'; 148c; 221c. **uti:** present infinitive of *utor*, 'to enjoy'; followed by what case? 131c. **iniquum:** 'unfair.' Why neuter? 148d. **de stipendio recusare:** 'to refuse to pay the tribute,' lit. 'to refuse regarding the tribute.' **sua:** i.e., of the Gauls; they, however, told a different story, as we learn from I.31.10.

5 **sibi ornamento:** 112b. **ornamento et praesidio, non detrimento:** 'a source of prestige and a protection, not a loss.' **oportere esse:** 'ought to be,' lit. 'it was proper that it be,' the subject of *oportere* is *amicitiam . . . esse*. **petisse:** sc. *eam*, 'had sought it,' i.e., Roman friendship. **per:** 123a. **subtrahantur:** 'should be snatched from under' his control. The *dediticii* were 'prisoners of war,' held as hostages to force the payment of tribute.

6 **Quod . . . traducat:** 'As to the fact that he brought over'; 198c. **multitudinem:** 120,000, according to I.31.5. **id:** the object of *facere*, referring back to the *quod*-clause. **sui muniendi, non Galliae impugnandae causa:** take the *causa* with both gerundives; *causa* literally means 'for the sake of' but can effectively be understood as 'in order to'; 230.1. **testimonium:** 'proof'; in predicate with *esse*, to which the *quod*-clauses stand as subject. **quod:** 'the fact that'; 198b. **nisi rogatus:** 'without being asked.'

7 **Galliam:** Celtic Gaul (*256b*), as in I.44.8; the Province had been under Roman control since 121 BC; *259*. **finibus:** *127a*.

8 **Quid sibi vellet:** 'what did he (Caesar) want with regard to him (Ariovistus)?'; *109a*; *217a*. **hanc Galliam:** 'this (part of) Gaul,' toward the Rhine. **illam nostram:** *illam Galliam esse nostram provinciam*. **Ut . . . sic item:** 'Just as . . . so likewise.' **ipsi concedi non oporteret:** 'no concession ought to be made to him (Ariovistus),' lit. 'it ought not be conceded.' **non oporteret, si . . . faceret:** *non oporteat, si . . . faciam* in the direct form, a condition of possible realization; *207.1*. **quod:** causal. **se interpellaremus:** 'we were obstructing him.'

9 **Quod . . . diceret:** 'As to the fact that he (Caesar) said.' **fratres:** *88a*. Cf. I.33.2. **appellatos:** sc. *esse*. **imperitum rerum:** 'unversed in affairs'; *102*. **tam . . . ut:** *197b*. **bello:** only three years before, in 61 BC; *147b*. **ipsos . . . Aedui:** since the Aedui are being referred to in both instances, translate as if *Aeduos . . . ei* ('they'). **contentionibus:** 'struggles.' **secum:** *cum Ariovisto*.

10 **Debere se suspicari:** 'that he had good reason to suspect'; how lit.? **simulata amicitia:** 'under the guise of friendship'; how lit.? *144b5*. **quod:** 'because.' **sui opprimendi causa:** *230.1*. **habere:** sc. *eum* (i.e., *exercitum*) 'was keeping (it there).'

11 **Qui:** Caesar; *167*. **deducat:** 'withdraw.' **habiturum:** sc. *esse*.

12 **Quod:** 'moreover'; *118d*. **gratum esse facturum:** 'would perform a favor,' lit. 'would become pleasing.' **id:** 'that fact'; *160c*. **compertum habere:** translate as if *comperisse*; *229a*. **quorum omnium gratiam atque amicitiam:** 'the gratitude and friendship of all of whom'; *97c*. **eius:** Caesar's. **morte:** *131a*. It is not impossible that Ariovistus had been in communication with Caesar's enemies; but whether he spoke the truth or not, he was evidently familiar with the party strifes and jealousies at this time in Roman politics.

13 **Quod:** 'On the other hand'; *118d*. **liberam:** i.e., without interference. **Galliae:** Celtic Gaul, as above. **illum:** translate as if *Caesarem*. **remuneraturum:** sc. *esse*, 'he would compensate'; *61a1*. **quaecumque bella geri vellet:** this phrase forms the object of *confecturum* (*esse*). **quaecumque:** *50a*. **eius:** 'on the part of Caesar.' If Caesar will withdraw, Ariovistus will fight his battles for him. The offer causes Ariovistus to seem somewhat less defiant than in I.36.

Caesar continues to defend his position.

45. 1 Multa a Caesare in eam sententiam dicta sunt, quare negotio desistere non posset: *neque suam neque populi Romani consuetudinem pati, uti optime meritos socios desereret, neque se iudicare, Galliam potius esse Ariovisti quam populi Romani.* 2 *Bello superatos esse Arvernos et Rutenos a Quinto Fabio Maximo, quibus populus Romanus ignovisset neque in provinciam redegisset neque stipendium imposuisset.* 3 *Quod si antiquissimum quodque tempus spectari oporteret, populi Romani iustissimum esse in Gallia imperium; si iudicium senatus observari oporteret, liberam debere esse Galliam, quam, bello victam, suis legibus uti voluisset.*

> *Direct form (I.45.1-3):* 1 Neque *mea* neque populi Romani *consuetudo patitur*, uti optime meritos socios *deseram*, neque *iudico*, Galliam potius esse *tuam* quam populi Romani. 2 Bello *superati sunt* Arverni et Ruteni a Quinto Fabio Maximo, quibus populus Romanus *ignovit*, neque (*eos*) in provinciam *redegit*, neque (*eis*) stipendium *imposuit*. 3 Quod si antiquissimum quodque tempus spectari *oportet*, populi Romani iustissimum *est* in Gallia imperium; si iudicium senatus observari *oportet*, *libera debet* esse *Gallia*, quam, bello victam, suis legibus uti *voluit*.

1 **in eam sententiam, quare . . . non posset:** 'to this purpose, (namely) why he could not.' **negotio:** *127a*. **posset:** *204.3*. **neque**, etc.: *213b*. **suam, populi:** *157d*. **uti . . . desereret:** after *pati*; *199a6*. **optime meritos socios:** 'allies who deserved the best treatment.' **neque:** 'and not.' **esse Ariovisti:** 'belonged to Ariovistus'; *94d*.

2 **Bello:** *131a*. **Arvernos, Rutenos:** conquered in 121 BC, but not included in the Province excepting a small division of the Ruteni, called *Ruteni provinciales*; see Map Gallia. **quibus:** *105*; *167*. **ignovisset:** the Romans with good reason had 'pardoned' them: their country, lying beyond the Cévennes mountains, could have been held only with the greatest difficulty. **in provinciam redegisset:** 'had not reduced (them) into a province,' i.e., forced them, formally, into the Roman administrative structure.

3 **Quod si:** 'And if'; *118d*. **antiquissimum quodque tempus:** 'each oldest time,' i.e., the oldest precedent on each side for involvement in Gaul; *170a*; *49a*. **populi Romani iustissimam esse in Gallia imperium:** i.e., *imperium populi Romani in Gallia esse iustissimam*. **iustissimum:** 'entirely justified.' **observari:** 'to be regarded'; *249b*. **quam . . . voluisset:** the subject of *voluisset* is an understood *senatus*; the antecedent of *quam* is *Galliam*. **victam:** 'although it had been conquered'; *227a3*. **suis:** 'its own,' referring to *Galliam*, the subject of *uti*, the present infinitive of *utor*.

The conference is abruptly ended by hostile actions of the German cavalry.

46. 1 Dum haec in colloquio geruntur, Caesari nuntiatum est, equites Ariovisti propius tumulum accedere et ad nostros adequitare, lapides telaque in nostros conicere. 2 Caesar loquendi finem facit seque ad suos recepit suisque imperavit, ne quod omnino telum in hostes reicerent. 3 Nam etsi sine ullo periculo legionis delectae cum equitatu proelium fore videbat, tamen committendum non putabat, ut, pulsis hostibus, dici posset, eos ab se per fidem in colloquio circumventos. 4 Postea quam in vulgus militum elatum est, qua arrogantia in colloquio Ariovistus usus omni Gallia Romanis interdixisset, impetumque ut in nostros eius equites fecissent, eaque res colloquium ut diremisset, multo maior alacritas studiumque pugnandi maius exercitui iniectum est.

1 **geruntur:** translate by a past tense; *190a.* **tumulum:** referred to in I.43.1; *123b.* The German cavalry were about a thousand Roman feet from the hill (I.43.2), the tenth legion at an equal distance. **adequitare:** 'were riding up (to).'

2 **ne quod omnino telum ... reicerent:** 'not to hurl back any missile at all'; *168.*

3 **legionis:** 'to the legion,' lit. 'for'; *102.* **delectae:** 'chosen' in the sense that he had selected them to be mounted on horseback (I.42.5). **cum equitatu proelium fore videbat:** 'he saw that a battle with the (enemy) cavalry would be.' **committendum** (esse) **non putabat:** 'he was thinking that (battle) ought not to be joined.' **ut ... dici posset:** 'so (i.e., 'such') that it could be said,' a clause of result; *197a.* **pulsis hostibus:** *144b4.* **eos ... circumventos:** sc. *esse*, indirect speech after *dici*; *eos = hostes.* **per fidem:** 'through a pledge of good faith,' used to entrap them.

4 **Postea quam:** *188a.* **vulgus:** 'rank and file'; *6b.* **elatum est:** 'it had been made known,' lit. 'carried out'; the subject is the series of indirect questions that follow; *69b.* **qua arrogantia ... Ariovistus usus:** 'with what arrogance Ariovistus,' lit. 'Ariovistus, having employed what arrogance'; *131c; 204.2.* **omni Gallia Romanis interdixisset:** 'had prohibited (to) the Romans from all Gaul.' **Gallia:** *127a.* **Romanis:** a dative of reference idiomatic after *interdico*; *109c.* **impetumque ut in nostros eius equites fecissent:** i.e., *et ut eius equites fecissent impetum in nostros.* **ut:** 'how.' **fecissent, diremisset:** *204.3.* **pugnandi:** 'for fighting'; *102; 230.1.* **exercitui:** *107a.* **iniectum est:** were (lit. 'was') infused'; *172b.*

Ariovistus seeks to reopen negotiations, but throws Caesar's envoys into chains.

47. 1 Biduo post Ariovistus ad Caesarem legatos mittit: *velle se de his rebus, quae inter eos agi coeptae neque perfectae essent, agere cum eo; uti aut iterum colloquio diem constitueret aut, si id minus vellet, e suis legatis aliquem ad se mitteret.* 2 Colloquendi Caesari causa visa non est, et eo magis, quod pridie eius diei Germani retineri non potuerant, quin in nostros tela conicerent. 3 Legatum e suis sese magno cum periculo ad eum missurum et hominibus feris obiecturum existimabat. 4 Commodissimum visum est Gaium Valerium Procillum, C. Valerii Caburi filium, summa virtute et humanitate adulescentem, cuius pater a C. Valerio Flacco civitate donatus erat, et propter fidem et propter linguae Gallicae scientiam, qua multa iam Ariovistus longinqua consuetudine utebatur, et quod in eo peccandi Germanis causa non esset, ad eum mittere, et una M. Metium, qui hospitio Ariovisti utebatur. 5 His mandavit, ut, quae diceret Ariovistus, cognoscerent et ad se referrent. 6 Quos cum apud se in castris Ariovistus conspexisset, exercitu suo praesente conclamavit: *quid ad se venirent? an speculandi causa?* Conantes dicere prohibuit et in catenas coniecit.

1 **Biduo post:** 'two days later,' lit. 'later by two days'; *140.* **velle,** etc.: *212c4; 213b.* **Direct form:** *Volo de his rebus, quae inter nos agi coeptae neque perfectae sunt, tecum agere;* (*rogo*) *uti aut iterum colloquio diem constituas, aut, si id minus velis, e tuis legatis aliquem ad me mittas.* **coeptae** (essent): *72c.* **uti ... constitueret:** i.e., (*se rogare*), *uti* (*Caesar*) *... constitueret*; the idea of asking is implied in *velle se ... agere cum eo*; *199a4.* **minus:** translate as if *non.* **e legatis:** *97d.* **suis:** *Caesaris.* **aliquem:** *49a.* Ariovistus wanted Caesar to send not a messenger but one of his highest officers (*legati*).

2 **causa visa non est:** 'there did not seem (to be any) reason'; *90b.* **et eo magis, quod:** 'especially because,' lit. 'and the more on this account, because'; *eo* being an ablative of cause that is then explained by the following *quod*-clause; *135a.* **diei:** *94c.* **quin ... conicerent:** 'from hurling'; *201a.*

3 **Legatum e suis sese magno cum periculo ad eum missurum ... existimabat:** i.e., (*Caesar*) *existimabat ... sese missurum* (*esse*) *legatum e suis ad eum* (= *Ariovistum*) *magno cum periculo.* **Legatum e suis:** 'an envoy from his staff,' i.e., one of his officers. **magno cum periculo:** *136a.* **hominibus:** *107a.*

4 **Commodissimum visum est Gaium Valerium Procillum ... ad eum mittere:** i.e., *visum est commodissi-*

mum mittere Gaium Valerium Procillum ad eum (Ariovistum); 222a. **C.:** = *Gai; 19a.* **Valerii:** *8a.* **virtute:** *143a.*
adulescentem: 'a young man.' **C. Valerio Flacco:** governor of the Province of Gaul in 83 BC. **civitate donatus erat:** 'had been presented with citizenship'; Roman citizenship was often conferred upon foreigners who had rendered some service. In this case the Gaul *Caburus* took the First Name and Clan Name of *C. Valerius Flaccus*, to whom he was indebted for the distinction, and was known as *C. Valerius Caburus; 19a, b.* **qua multa Ariovistus utebatur:** 'which Ariovistus spoke fluently,' lit. 'which (language) Ariovistus used much'; *multa* is an adjective modifying *qua (lingua)*, but is best understood adverbially. **consuetudine:** 'practice'; *135a.* **et quod:** 'and because,' continuing the list of causes above in *et propter . . . et propter.* **quod . . . non esset:** 'because (as he thought) there was not'; *183a.* **in eo:** 'in his case.' **peccandi causa:** '(any) reason for doing wrong,' i.e., for harming him, since Procillus was a Gaul. **una:** adv., 'together,' i.e., with Procillus. **utebatur:** 'enjoyed.' Metius may have been received and entertained by Ariovistus in the course of the negotiations which in 59 BC culminated in the recognition of the German ruler by the Roman Senate (I.35.2).

5 **His mandavit, ut . . . cognoscerent:** 'he commissioned them to learn,' lit. 'He entrusted to them that they learn'; *105; 199a1.* **quae diceret Ariovistus:** object of *cognoscerent* and *referrent.*

6 **exercitu suo praesente:** *144b2.* **conclamavit:** 'he called out loudly.' **quid:** 'why'; *118e.* **venirent:** *217a.* **an speculandi causa:** '(was it) in order to act as spies?'; *179a2; 230.1.* **Conantes** (eos) **dicere prohibuit:** 'when they tried to speak he stopped them,' lit. 'he checked them trying to speak,' because he wished his army to believe that they were spies; *227a5.*

Ariovistus moves camp so as to cut off Caesar's supplies.

48. 1 Eodem die castra promovit et milibus passuum sex a Caesaris castris sub monte consedit. 2 Postridie eius diei praeter castra Caesaris suas copias traduxit et milibus passuum duobus ultra eum castra fecit eo consilio, uti frumento commeatuque, qui ex Sequanis et Aeduis supportaretur, Caesarem intercluderet. 3 Ex eo die dies continuos quinque Caesar pro castris suas copias produxit et aciem instructam habuit, ut, si vellet Ariovistus proelio contendere, ei potestas non deesset. 4 Ariovistus his omnibus diebus exercitum castris continuit, equestri proelio cotidie contendit. 5 Genus hoc erat pugnae, quo se Germani exercuerant. Equitum milia erant sex, totidem numero pedites velocissimi ac fortissimi, quos ex omni copia singuli singulos suae salutis causa delegerant; cum his in proeliis versabantur. 6 Ad eos se equites recipiebant; hi, si quid erat durius, concurrebant, si qui, graviore vulnere accepto, equo deciderat, circumsistebant; 7 si quo erat longius prodeundum aut celerius recipiendum, tanta erat horum exercitatione celeritas, ut iubis equorum sublevati cursum adaequarent.

1 **promovit:** '(Ariovistus) moved forward.' **milibus passuum sex:** 'at six miles'; *147c.* How far by our measurement? *243a, b.* **Caesaris castris:** Caesar's camp has been identified between Gemar and Ostheim, about 35 miles southwest of Strasbourg. See Map 4, LARGE CAMP.

2 **diei:** *94c.* **praeter:** 'beyond.' **praeter . . . traduxit:** Ariovistus's line of march, as suggested on Map 4, probably skirted or traversed the foothills of the Vosges in such a way that Caesar could not attack him while executing this movement. **castra fecit:** the camp of Ariovistus, probably at the place so marked on Map 4, was favorably located for defense. **uti . . . intercluderet:** explains *consilio; 196a.* **frumento:** *127a.* Ariovistus thought that by cutting off Caesar's supplies he could force Caesar to withdraw, or else to fight on ground of his own choosing. **qui:** *163c.* **supportaretur:** subjunctive by attraction; *220.*

3 **dies continuos quinque:** *118a.* **aciem instructam:** 'his army drawn up' in triple line, as indicated on Map 4, Caesar's First Position; *297a.* **ut:** 'so that'; *196a.* **vellet:** *220.* **ei . . . deesset:** 'he did not lack opportunity'; how lit.? *239g.*

4 **diebus:** *147c.* **exercitum:** the German infantry, as we see from the next line. **castris:** 'within the camp'; *131a.* **equestri proelio:** 'with cavalry skirmishing.' **contendit:** *238a.*

5 **Genus pugnae:** 'The kind of fighting,' i.e., the method. **hoc:** *161a.* **quo se Germani exercuerant:** 'in which the Germans had trained themselves.' **erant:** *90a.* **numero:** *142a; 85.* **pedites:** sc. *erant; 10d.* **velocissimi:** 'the fastest.' **quos ex omni copia singuli singulos suae salutis causa delegerant:** 'each one of whom (i.e., the foot-soldiers), out of the whole force, each one (of the horsemen) had chosen for the sake of his own safety,' i.e., for his protection. **singuli singulos:** distributive adjectives are often reciprocal and they are regarded as plural collectives even when, as here, they refer to groups of one: 'each single horseman had chosen a single infantryman.' **singulos:** agrees with *quos; 36.* **versabantur:** here deponent, '(the horsemen) were moving about' with their paired foot-soldiers such that the pair moved together.

6 **eos, hi:** the foot-soldiers. **se recipiebant:** i.e., after the cavalry charged forward, they would then draw back

and regroup with their infantry partners. **si quid erat durius, concurrebant:** general condition of fact, i.e., the condition describes a customary or repeated sequence of actions and *si* effectively means 'whenever'; *205.2.* **quid durius:** 'anything rather hard'; *153a.* **concurrebant:** 'they rushed together' to the point of difficulty. **si qui ... deciderat, circumsistebant:** another general condition, 'whenever anyone had fallen, they would gather round him'; *205.4.* **qui:** 'anyone'; *49a, b.* **graviore vulnere accepto:** *144a3.* **equo:** *127a.*

7 **si quo erat longius prodeundum aut celerius recipiendum:** 'if it was necessary to advance in any direction unusually far, or to retreat with special swiftness.' **quo:** adv., indefinite after *si* (cf. *aliquo*), 'to any place.' **erat prodeundum:** lit. 'it had to be gone forth'; *73e.* **longius, celerius:** *153a.* **erat:** *90a.* **exercitatione:** *135a.* **ut . . . adaequarent:** *197b.* **iubis equorum:** 'by the manes of the horses.' **sublevati:** 'supporting themselves'; *174.* **cursum adaequarent:** 'they kept up with the running' of the horses. Caesar afterwards employed German horsemen as mercenaries and they rendered him very effective service, such as at the siege of Alesia in 52 BC.

Caesar fortifies a camp beyond Ariovistus, reopening the road.

49. 1 Ubi eum castris se tenere Caesar intellexit, ne diutius commeatu prohiberetur, ultra eum locum, quo in loco Germani consederant, circiter passus sescentos ab his, castris idoneum locum delegit acieque triplici instructa ad eum locum venit. 2 Primam et secundam aciem in armis esse, tertiam castra munire iussit. 3 Hic locus ab hoste circiter passus sescentos, uti dictum est, aberat. Eo circiter hominum numero sedecim milia expedita cum omni equitatu Ariovistus misit, quae copiae nostros terrerent et munitione prohiberent. 4 Nihilo setius Caesar, ut ante constituerat, duas acies hostem propulsare, tertiam opus perficere iussit. 5 Munitis castris, duas ibi legiones reliquit et partem auxiliorum; quattuor reliquas in castra maiora reduxit.

1 **eum:** Ariovistus. **se:** object of *tenere*. **ne ... prohiberetur:** see I.48.2; *196a.* **eum locum:** Map 4, CAMP OF ARIOVISTUS. **loco:** *165a.* **his:** *Germanis.* **castris:** *108a; 291.* **idoneum:** 'suitable.' **acie triplici:** *297a.*

2 **castra:** this camp on Map 4 is called the 'Small Camp,' *castra minora*, in order to distinguish it from the 'Large Camp,' *castra maiora*. The two camps were around two miles apart; both were on somewhat higher ground. Caesar's object in establishing the smaller camp, only a little more than half a mile from the Germans, was to keep open the road to Vesontio, and so maintain communication with his base of supplies. **munire:** 'fortify'; *200b; 293.*

3 **Eo:** adv., 'to that place.' **hominum ... expedita:** translate as if *sedecim milia hominum expeditorum*. **expedita:** 'light-armed.' **quae copiae:** 'in order that these forces'; *193a.*

4 **Nihilo setius:** 'nevertheless,' lit. 'by nothing the less'; *140.* **duas:** i.e., *primam et secundam.*

5 **auxiliorum:** *268.* **reliquas:** sc. *legiones*. How many men, probably, in the six legions? *267b, e.*

The Germans, Caesar learns, dare not fight before the new moon.

50. 1 Proximo die, instituto suo, Caesar e castris utrisque copias suas eduxit paulumque a maioribus castris progressus aciem instruxit hostibusque pugnandi potestatem fecit. 2 Ubi ne tum quidem eos prodire intellexit, circiter meridiem exercitum in castra reduxit. Tum demum Ariovistus partem suarum copiarum, quae castra minora oppugnaret, misit. 3 Acriter utrimque usque ad vesperum pugnatum est. Solis occasu suas copias Ariovistus, multis et illatis et acceptis vulneribus, in castra reduxit. 4 Cum ex captivis quaereret Caesar, quam ob rem Ariovistus proelio non decertaret, hanc reperiebat causam, quod apud Germanos ea consuetudo esset, ut matres familiae eorum sortibus et vaticinationibus declararent, utrum proelium committi ex usu esset necne; *eas ita dicere:* 5 *non esse fas Germanos superare, si ante novam lunam proelio contendissent.*

1 **instituto suo:** 'in accordance with his usual practice' (I.48.3); *136c.* **utrisque:** *51.* **aciem:** Map 4, Caesar's Second Position. **potestatem fecit:** 'gave an opportunity.'

2 **ne ... quidem:** *237c.* **prodire:** *68b.* **meridiem:** 'midday.' **quae:** translate as if *ut ea*; *193a.*

3 **Acriter ... pugnatum est:** 'Fiercely the battle was fought'; *73d.* **usque ad:** '(all the way) up to.' **Solis occasu:** 'At sunset'; *147a.* **multis et illatis et acceptis vulneribus:** Caesar emphasizes the equal intensity of the fight on both sides.

4 **ex:** *116c.* **quam ob rem:** 'for what reason'; *204.2.* How lit.? **proelio non decertaret:** 'would not fight a decisive battle,' lit. 'fight to the finish by means of battle'; *131a.* Ariovistus had used only a part of his forces. **hanc causam:** explained by the following appositional *quod*-clause; *161a; 198b.* **ea consuetudo esset:** 'it was the

custom'; *214b.* **matres familiae eorum:** 'their matrons,' lit. 'their mothers of the family,' married women who were believed to have prophetic powers. **sortibus:** 'by means of the casting of lots'; *17c.* **vaticinationibus:** 'prophetic utterances.' **declararent:** *203.2.* **utrum proelium committi ex usu esset necne:** 'whether it was expedient that battle be joined, or not.' **utrum . . . necne:** 'whether . . . or not'; *204.1.* **ex usu:** 'expedient,' lit. 'of advantage.' **eas ita dicere:** indirect quotation of what the captives said the matrons declared; *213b.*

5 **non . . . contendissent:** indirect quotation, depending on *dicere.* **non esse fas:** '(that) it was not allowed' by divine right, i.e., it was not the gods' will. **Germanos superare:** '(that) the Germans prevail,' i.e., be victorious; accusative and infinitive after *non esse fas.* **novam lunam:** 'the new moon' of September 18, 58 BC, according to modern computations.

Taking advantage of the Germans' reluctance, Caesar forces an engagement.

51. 1 Postridie eius diei Caesar praesidio utrisque castris, quod satis esse visum est, reliquit; omnes alarios in conspectu hostium pro castris minoribus constituit, quod minus multitudine militum legionariorum pro hostium numero valebat, ut ad speciem alariis uteretur; ipse, triplici instructa acie, usque ad castra hostium accessit. 2 Tum demum necessario Germani suas copias castris eduxerunt generatimque constituerunt, paribus intervallis, Harudes, Marcomanos, Tribocos, Vangiones, Nemetes, Sedusios, Suebos, omnemque aciem suam raedis et carris circumdederunt, ne qua spes in fuga relinqueretur. 3 Eo mulieres imposuerunt, quae ad proelium proficiscentes passis manibus flentes implorabant, ne se in servitutem Romanis traderent.

1 **diei:** *94c.* The date was about September 14. **praesidio utrisque castris:** a dative of purpose and a dative of indirect object, 'as a garrison for each camp'; *112a; 104a.* **quod:** as antecedent sc. *id*, object of *reliquit.* **alarios:** 'auxiliaries'; the light-armed troops, called *alarii* ('wing-men') because usually stationed on the wings (*alae*) of an army; *268.* **quod:** causal. **minus multitudine valebat:** 'was weaker in respect to his force'; how lit.? *118b.* **pro:** 'in comparison with.' **ad speciem:** 'for show' in order to hide from the enemy his weakness in heavy infantry; Ariovistus would take the *alarios* for *legionarios.* **uteretur:** *196a.* **triplici acie:** the front formed by the legions must have been at least a mile long. The probable arrangement of the legions in order of battle is indicated in Map 4; in the rear line only two cohorts to each legion are shown, for the reason that one cohort was probably drawn off for the guard duty indicated at the beginning of this chapter (*praesidio*); *297.*
2 **necessario:** adverb, 'of necessity.' **castris:** *127a.* **generatim:** 'by tribes,' the soldiers of each tribe being formed into a body by themselves. **intervallis:** *138.* **Harudes . . . Suebos:** objects of *constituerunt.* **aedis et carris:** 'with wagons,' probably covered, 'and carts.' **circumdederunt:** 'encircled,' on the rear and wings, as indicated in Map 4. **ne qua spes in fuga relinqueretur:** 'so that not any hope for (lit. 'in') flight would be left'; *196a.* **qua:** *168.*
3 **Eo:** 'thereon,' upon the wagons and carts. **mulieres:** acc., *11c.* **proficiscentes:** sc. *eos; 227a4.* **passis manibus:** 'with outstretched hands'; *144b2.* **flentes:** nom., *227b.* **ne . . . traderent:** *199a4.* **Romanis:** *104a.*

Desperate fighting, hand-to-hand; the Roman left, wavering, is reinforced.

52. 1 Caesar singulis legionibus singulos legatos et quaestorem praefecit, uti eos testes suae quisque virtutis haberet; 2 ipse a dextro cornu, quod eam partem minime firmam hostium esse animadverterat, proelium commisit. 3 Ita nostri acriter in hostes, signo dato, impetum fecerunt, itaque hostes repente celeriterque procurrerunt, ut spatium pila in hostes coniciendi non daretur. 4 Reiectis pilis, comminus gladiis pugnatum est. At Germani, celeriter ex consuetudine sua phalange facta, impetus gladiorum exceperunt. 5 Reperti sunt complures nostri, qui in phalanga insilirent et scuta manibus revellerent et desuper vulnerarent. 6 Cum hostium acies a sinistro cornu pulsa atque in fugam conversa esset, a dextro cornu vehementer multitudine suorum nostram aciem premebant. 7 Id cum animadvertisset P. Crassus adulescens, qui equitatui praeerat, quod expeditior erat quam ei, qui inter aciem versabantur, tertiam aciem laborantibus nostris subsidio misit.

1 **singulis legionibus singulos legatos . . . praefecit:** 'he placed . . . one *legatus* in command of each legion'; for the paired *singulis singulos*, see I.48.5. Caesar had six legions (*267e*); hence over each of five legions he put a lieutenant (*legatus*), and over the sixth he placed the quaestor (*273b*). **testes:** 'as witnesses'; *115a.* **quisque:** 'each' legionary soldier; *170b.*
2 **a dextro cornu:** 'on the right wing'; *126c.* **eam partem hostium:** the German left wing, opposite the Roman right. **minime firmam:** sc. *partem*, 'the weakest part.'

3 **Ita:** modifies *acriter*, 'so fiercely'; *34a*. **signo:** given on the trumpet; *286a1*. **itaque:** = *et ita*; the *ita* modifies *repente celeriterque*. **spatium:** a 'space,' either of time or distance. **pila:** object of *coniciendi* (i.e., the gerund takes a direct object and does not undergo gerundival attraction); *230.1*; *282d*.

4 **Reiectis pilis ... pugnatum est:** 'they threw aside their pikes and fought'; how lit.? *144b2*; *73d*. **gladiis:** *282e*. **ex:** 'in accordance with.' **phalange:** 'a compact mass,' like the formation adopted by the Helvetians; see I.24.4. **exceperunt:** 'received,' in the sense of 'withstood.' The Germans apparently did not hurl their spears but relied upon their shields and swords; the German sword was longer than the Roman, and single-edged.

5 **complures nostri:** 'many men on our side'; how lit.? *97c*. **phalanga:** *18f*. **insilirent:** 'leaped (upon)'; *194a*. **desuper:** 'from above.' In hand-to-hand fighting the Roman soldier, parrying blows with his own shield, generally tried to strike with his sword under or around the shield of the enemy. In this case the shields of the Germans were interlocked in a close formation, and Caesar's men in their eagerness, as they rushed on the foe, sprang up, pulled back the enemy's shields from the top, and stabbed with their short swords from above.

6 **a sinistro cornu:** 'on their left wing,' facing the Roman right, where Caesar was; *126c*. **pulsa** (esset), **conversa esset:** why subjunctive? *187*. **a dextro cornu:** opposite the Roman left. **multitudine:** *131b*.

7 **P. Crassus:** See Vocab. under *Crassus* (2). **adulescens:** 'young,' so called to distinguish him from his father and from his older brother, who was afterwards with Caesar in Gaul; see Vocab. under *Crassus* (3). **equitatui:** *107*. **quod expeditior erat quam ei, qui:** 'because he was more unencumbered than those who.' Since the cavalry was not fighting, Crassus was freer to look about and see where help was most needed. **ei, qui inter aciem versabatur:** i.e., the officers of the legions. **inter aciem:** 'amidst the line of battle.' **tertiam aciem:** the 'third line' was usually kept as a reserve force until needed; *297b*. **laborantibus:** 'who were hard pressed'; *227a4*. **nostris, subsidio:** *112b*.

Caesar is victorious; the captive envoys are rescued.

53. 1 Ita proelium restitutum est, atque omnes hostes terga verterunt neque prius fugere destiterunt, quam ad flumen Rhenum, milia passuum ex eo loco circiter quinquaginta, pervenerunt. 2 Ibi perpauci aut, viribus confisi, tranare contenderunt aut, lintribus inventis, sibi salutem reppererunt. 3 In his fuit Ariovistus, qui, naviculam deligatam ad ripam nactus, ea profugit; reliquos omnes consecuti equites nostri interfecerunt. 4 Duae fuerunt Ariovisti uxores, una Sueba natione, quam domo secum eduxerat, altera Norica, regis Voccionis soror, quam in Gallia duxerat, a fratre missam; utraque in ea fuga periit. Duae filiae; harum altera occisa, altera capta est. 5 C. Valerius Procillus, cum a custodibus in fuga, trinis catenis vinctus, traheretur, in ipsum Caesarem hostes equitatu insequentem incidit. 6 Quae quidem res Caesari non minorem quam ipsa victoria voluptatem attulit, quod hominem honestissimum provinciae Galliae, suum familiarem et hospitem, ereptum e manibus hostium, sibi restitutum videbat, neque eius calamitate de tanta voluptate et gratulatione quicquam fortuna deminuerat. 7 Is, se praesente, de se ter sortibus consultum dicebat, utrum igni statim necaretur an in aliud tempus reservaretur; sortium beneficio se esse incolumem. 8 Item M. Metius repertus et ad eum reductus est.

---

1 **restitutum est:** 'was restored'; the language implies that the Roman left wing was ceasing to fight when the reserves were sent to its aid. **neque prius fugere destiterunt, quam:** 'and they did not cease to flee until'; *189a*.

2 **viribus:** *135a*. **confisi:** *62*; *226c*. **tranare:** 'to swim across'; *221a*. **lintribus:** *15a*.

3 **In his:** 'among these.' **naviculam:** diminutive; 'a small boat.' **deligatam:** 'tied.' **nactus:** 'coming upon'; *61a3*; *226c*. **ea:** 'in it'; *131a*. Ariovistus seems to have died not long afterwards (V.29). **omnes:** accusative, modifies *reliquos*. **equites:** *299*. **interfecerunt:** the slain numbered 80,000, according to Plutarch (*Life of Caesar*, 19.12).

4 **Duae uxores:** the Germans ordinarily had but one wife. **una** (uxor), **altera:** *91c*. **natione:** 'by birth'; how lit.? *142a*. **duxerat:** i.e., *in matrimonium duxerat*, 'had married.' **a fratre:** 'by her brother,' i.e., Voccio. **utraque:** *51*. **filiae:** sc. *fuerunt*; *89a*. **altera, altera:** *171b*. **occisa:** sc. *est*; *89b*.

5 **Procillus:** see I.47.4. **trinis catenis:** 'with three chains'; *37e*. **vinctus:** 'bound.' Principal parts of *vincio* and *vinco*? **traheretur:** 'was being dragged along.' **hostes:** object of *insequentem*.

6 **Quae res:** 'and this circumstance'; *167*. **Caesari:** *104a*. **attulit:** *69b*. **quod ... videbat:** explains *quae res*, '(namely) that he saw (that).' **honestissimum:** 'very honorable'; *honestus*, from *honor*, is never 'honest.' **hospitem:** 'guest-friend'; *10d*. **restitutum:** sc. *esse*; *213a*. **neque:** = *et non*. **eius calamitate:** 'by his (Procillus') destruction'; *131a*. **de tanta:** 'from his (so) great.' **gratulatione:** '(reason for) thankfulness.' **quicquam fortuna deminuerat:** with the negative in *neque*, 'fortune had not detracted,' lit. 'had not lessened anything at all'; *168*; *117a*.

7 **Is ... dicebat:** the remainder of this sentence consists of Procillus' report. **se praesente:** 'in his presence,' lit.

'with him (being) present.' **sortibus consultum:** sc. *esse*, 'the lots were consulted'; see I.50.4. How lit.? *73d;* *131a.* **utrum . . . an:** *204.1.* **igni:** *14b.* **statim:** *77.* **necaretur:** 'should be killed.' 8 **M. Metius:** I.47.4. **eum:** *Caesarem.*

His army in winter quarters, Caesar sets out for North Italy.

54. 1 Hoc proelio trans Rhenum nuntiato, Suebi, qui ad ripas Rheni venerant, domum reverti coeperunt; quos ubi, qui proximi Rhenum incolunt, perterritos senserunt, insecuti magnum ex his numerum occiderunt. 2 Caesar, una aestate duobus maximis bellis confectis, maturius paulo quam tempus anni postulabat, in hiberna in Sequanos exercitum deduxit; 3 hibernis Labienum praeposuit; ipse in citeriorem Galliam ad conventus agendos profectus est.

1 **Suebi . . . venerant:** see I.37.3. **quos ubi, qui proximi Rhenum incolunt, perterritos senserunt:** translate as if *et ubi ei, qui proximi Rhenum incolunt, eos* (i.e., *Suebos*) *perterritos* (*esse*) *senserunt.* **Rhenum:** *123b.* **insecuti:** *226c.* **ex his:** *97d.*
2 **aestate:** 'summer'; *147a.* The defeat of the Helvetians took place near the end of June, that of Ariovistus the second week in September. With not more than 35,000 soldiers, including cavalry and light-armed troops, Caesar had overcome two forces several times as large as his own. **maturius:** *34a.* **hiberna:** 'winter quarters'; *293-5.* **Sequanos:** *251.* The region in which the battle was fought had probably formed a part of the Sequanian territory but had been ceded to Ariovistus.
3 **hibernis:** probably at Vesontio, which possessed great advantages as a military base, as explained in I.38. **praeposuit:** 'put in charge of'; *107b.* **citeriorem Galliam:** *253.* **ad conventus agendos:** 'to conduct assizes', i.e., courts and other legal proceedings. The governor of a province from time to time visited its principal cities in order to preside over provincial courts for the administration of justice. In Cisalpine Gaul, moreover, Caesar would be nearer Rome and so enabled to keep in touch with political conditions there.

BOOK II

II.1-15: Campaign against the Belgians

The Belgians form a league against Caesar.

1. 1 Cum esset Caesar in citeriore Gallia, ita uti supra demonstravimus, crebri ad eum rumores afferebantur, litterisque item Labieni certior fiebat, omnes Belgas, quam tertiam esse Galliae partem dixeramus, contra populum Romanum coniurare obsidesque inter se dare: 2 *coniurandi has esse causas: primum, quod vererentur, ne, omni pacata Gallia, ad eos exercitus noster adduceretur;* 3 *deinde, quod ab non nullis Gallis sollicitarentur,* partim qui, ut Germanos diutius in Gallia versari noluerant, ita populi Romani exercitum hiemare atque inveterascere in Gallia moleste ferebant, partim qui mobilitate et levitate animi novis imperiis studebant; 4 ab non nullis etiam, quod in Gallia a potentioribus atque eis, qui ad conducendos homines facultates habebant, vulgo regna occupabantur, qui minus facile eam rem imperio nostro consequi poterant.

1 **esset:** *185c.* **citeriore Gallia:** *124a; 253.* **ita uti:** 'just as.' **supra:** 'above,' i.e., referring to a preceding part of the work, in this case the last chapter of Book I. **demonstravimus:** *156.* Caesar the *writer* sometimes speaks in the first person, but always presents Caesar the *general* in the third. **crebri:** 'frequent,' an adjective agreeing with *rumores*, but with the force of an adverb; *151.* **afferebantur:** force of the imperfect? *175a.* **litteris:** *131a.* **certior fiebat:** 'he was informed'; how lit.? **dare:** *213a; 214a.* **Belgas:** *19e; 256a.* **quam:** subject accusative with *esse*, = *quos*, 'who,' attracted to the feminine singular to agree with *partem* in the predicate; *164c; 251.* **Galliae:** here Transalpine Gaul, as in I.1.1, which is the passage referred to in *dixeramus*. **dixeramus:** *214c.* **coniurare:** 'were conspiring,' according to the Roman point of view. **inter se dare:** *159.*

2 **coniurandi . . . sollicitarentur:** summary of the statement made in the dispatch from Labienus; *212c3.* **Direct form:** Coniurandi *hae* sunt causae: primum, quod *verentur*, ne, omni pacata Gallia, ad eos exercitus noster *adducatur*; deinde, quod ab non nullis Gallis *sollicitantur*. **has:** 'as follows,' lit. 'these'; *161a.* **coniurandi causas:** explained by the appositional *quod*-clauses following; *230.1; 198b; 214a.* **primum, deinde:** *237b.* **ne:** 'that'; *202.* **omni pacata Gallia:** = *si Gallia omnis pacata esset*; *144b4.* **Gallia:** Celtic Gaul, bordering the Belgian country on the south; the Romans remained in possession of a considerable portion of Celtic Gaul after the defeat of the Helvetians and Ariovistus (the actions described in Book I); *256b.* **ad eos:** the fear of a Roman invasion was justified, as subsequent events prove; the "conspiracy" of the Belgians was the natural effort of a spirited people to defend their liberties against anticipated encroachment. **noster:** *157c.*

3 **sollicitarentur:** 'were being stirred up.' **partim qui:** 'partly (by those) who.' Caesar here shifts to direct statements, presenting as facts, on his own authority, details reported by Labienus. **ut . . . ita:** 'as . . . so'; *188b.* **diutius:** *153a.* **Germanos versari:** *223a1.* **inveterascere:** 'should become established,' lit. 'grow old.' **novis imperiis:** 'a change of rulers'; *105.* How lit.? **non nullis:** i.e., powerful nobles; sc. *sollicitabantur*.

4 **a potentioribus:** 'by the more powerful'; *154a.* **ad conducendos homines:** 'for hiring men,' i.e., mercenary soldiers; *230.3.* **facultates:** 'the means.' **vulgo:** adv., 'commonly.' **regna occupabantur:** 'kingships were seized,' though *regnum* here is not necessarily a formal kingship, but more generally the condition of supreme power; *258c.* **qui:** 'and these men.' **minus facile:** 'less easily.' **eam rem:** 'that object,' the obtaining of supreme power. **imperio nostro:** 'under our sovereignty'; *138.*

Caesar raises two new legions, marches to Belgian territory.

2. 1 His nuntiis litterisque commotus, Caesar duas legiones in citeriore Gallia novas conscripsit et, ineunte aestate, in ulteriorem Galliam qui deduceret, Q. Pedium legatum misit. 2 Ipse, cum primum pabuli copia esse inciperet, ad exercitum venit. 3 Dat negotium Senonibus reliquisque Gallis, qui finitimi Belgis erant, uti ea, quae apud eos gerantur, cognoscant seque de his rebus certiorem faciant. 4 Hi constanter omnes nuntiaverunt, manus cogi, exercitum in unum locum conduci. 5 Tum vero dubitandum non existimavit, quin ad eos proficisceretur. 6 Re frumentaria provisa, castra movet diebusque circiter quindecim ad fines Belgarum pervenit.

1 **nuntiis litterisque:** cf. I.26.6. **duas legiones:** the thirteenth and fourteenth. Caesar now had eight legions, numbered VII to XIV; *267a, e, f.* **ineunte aestate:** 'at the beginning of the warm season,' probably the latter part of May; how lit.? *68b; 144b1.* **ulteriorem Galliam:** *255.* **qui** (eas) **deduceret:** 'to lead them,' probably over the Great Saint Bernard pass; *193a.* **legatum:** *273a.* Pedius was a son of Caesar's sister Julia.

2 **pabuli copia:** 'the supply of forage,' which was needed for the numerous draft animals used for the transportation of military stores, as well as for the horses of the cavalry and the officers. **cum primum:** *185c.* **inciperet esse:** 'began to be,' i.e., was available. **exercitum:** probably stationed at or near Vesontio; see Map 1. Caesar could move much faster on his own than if he had led the two newly drafted legions himself.
3 **Dat negotium Senonibus:** 'he directed the Senones,' lit. 'he gave the task to'; *104a; 175b.* **reliquis:** *171a.* **Belgis:** *108a.* **uti ... cognoscant ... faciant:** *199a1.* **apud eos:** i.e., *apud Belgas.* **gerantur:** *220.* **se:** *158a.*
4 **constanter:** 'uniformly,' i.e., with agreement between the reports. **manus cogi:** 'bodies of troops' among the Belgians 'were being gathered'; accusative and infinitive after *nuntiaverunt.* **locum:** why not ablative? *124a.*
5 **dubitandum non:** sc. *esse sibi,* 'that he ought not to hesitate'; *73e.* **quin ... proficisceretur:** *201c.* **ad:** 'against.' **eos:** *Belgas.*
6 **Re frumentaria provisa:** 'having provided for a supply of grain'; *144b2.* How lit.? **castra movet:** 'he broke camp'; *175b.* **diebus:** *147a.* **circiter:** adverb with *quindecim.* **ad fines pervenit:** 'he reached the territories,' lit. 'he came through to.' The probable route is indicated on Map 1.

The Remi submit, and give information about the other Belgians.

3. 1 Eo cum de improviso celeriusque omni opinione venisset, Remi, qui proximi Galliae ex Belgis sunt, ad eum legatos Iccium et Andecumborium, primos civitatis, miserunt, 2 qui dicerent: *se suaque omnia in fidem atque potestatem populi Romani permittere, neque se cum reliquis Belgis consensisse, neque contra populum Romanum coniurasse,* 3 *paratosque esse et obsides dare et imperata facere et oppidis recipere et frumento ceterisque rebus iuvare.* 4 *Reliquos omnes Belgas in armis esse, Germanosque, qui cis Rhenum incolant, sese cum his coniunxisse,* 5 *tantumque esse eorum omnium furorem, ut ne Suessiones quidem, fratres consanguineosque suos, qui eodem iure et isdem legibus utantur, unum imperium unumque magistratum cum ipsis habeant, deterrere potuerint, quin cum his consentirent.*

Direct form (II.3.2-5): 2 *Nos nostraque omnia in fidem atque potestatem populi Romani permittimus;* neque cum reliquis Belgis *consensimus,* neque contra populum Romanum *coniuravimus,* 3 *paratique sumus* et obsides dare et imperata facere et (*te*) oppidis recipere et (*te*) frumento ceterisque rebus iuvare. 4 *Reliqui* omnes *Belgae* in armis *sunt, Germanique,* qui cis Rhenum *incolunt,* sese cum his *coniunxerunt;* 5 *tantusque est* eorum omnium *furor,* ut ne Suessiones quidem, fratres consanguineosque *nostros,* qui eodem iure et isdem legibus *utuntur,* unum imperium unumque magistratum *nobiscum habent,* deterrere *potuerimus,* quin cum his consentirent.

1 **Eo:** = *ad fines Belgarum.* **de improviso:** 'unexpectedly'; ablative singular neuter of the adjective used as a noun, forming with *de* an adverbial phrase like the English 'all of a sudden.' **celerius omni opinione:** 'more quickly than any one had expected,' lit., 'than every expectation'; *129a.* **venisset:** *185c.* **Remi:** the name survives in Reims, the modern name of the city occupying the site of the ancient capital of the Remi, Durocortorum. **Galliae:** Celtic Gaul; *256b.* Why dative? *108a.* **ex Belgis:** translate as if *inter Belgas.* **legatos:** 'as envoys'; *115a.* **primos:** 'the leading men'; *154a.* **civitatis:** of the Remi.
2 **qui dicerent:** 'to say'; *193a.* **se,** etc.: *212c3.* **se suaque omnia:** lit. 'themselves and all their own things.' **permittere:** sc. *se* as subject; *214a.* **coniurasse:** = *coniuravisse; 64a1.*
3 **paratos:** adjective, in predicate. **et, et:** *234a.* **dare, facere,** (eum) **recipere,** (eum) **iuvare:** after *paratos; 221c.* **imperata facere:** 'to obey (his) orders,' lit. 'to do the things having been commanded'; *157a.* **oppidis:** 'in (their) towns'; how lit.? *131a.* **frumento:** *131a.*
4 **cis Rhenum:** 'on this side of the Rhine,' i.e., the west side; Caesar writes from the point of view of the Province.
5 **tantum:** adjective, in predicate. **eorum omnium:** *Belgarum et Germanorum.* **ne ... quidem:** *237c.* **Suessiones:** object of *deterrere.* The name survives in Soissons. **suos:** 'their own,' referring to the Remi. **qui:** the subject of both *utantur* and *habeant.* **iure:** '(body of) rights'; *13g; 131c.* **isdem:** *45.* **potuerint:** *197a, b.* **quin consentirent:** 'from uniting'; *201a.*

Report of the Remi on the history and forces of the Belgians.

4. 1 Cum ab eis quaereret, quae civitates quantaeque in armis essent et quid in bello possent, sic reperiebat: *plerosque Belgas esse ortos a Germanis, Rhenumque antiquitus traductos, propter loci fertilitatem ibi consedisse,* 2 *Gallosque, qui ea loca incolerent, expulisse, solosque esse, qui patrum nostrorum memoria, omni Gallia vexata, Teutonos Cimbrosque intra suos fines ingredi prohibuerint;* 3 *qua ex re fieri, uti* *earum rerum memoria magnam sibi auctoritatem magnosque spiritus in re militari sumerent.* 4 De numero eorum omnia se habere explorata Remi dicebant, propterea quod, propinquitatibus affinitatibusque coniuncti, quantam quisque multitudinem in communi Belgarum concilio ad id bellum pollicitus sit, cognoverint: 5 *plurimum inter eos Bellovacos et virtute et auctoritate et hominum numero valere; hos posse conficere armata milia centum, pollicitos ex eo numero electa milia sexaginta, totiusque belli imperium sibi postulare.* 6 *Suessiones suos esse finitimos; fines latissimos feracissimosque agros possidere.* 7 *Apud eos fuisse regem nostra etiam memoria Diviciacum, totius Galliae potentissimum, qui cum magnae partis harum regionum, tum etiam Britanniae, imperium obtinuerit; nunc esse regem Galbam; ad hunc propter iustitiam prudentiamque summam totius belli omnium voluntate deferri;* 8 *oppida habere numero XII, polliceri milia armata L; totidem Nervios, qui maxime feri inter ipsos habeantur longissimeque absint;* 9 *XV milia Atrebates, Ambianos X milia, Morinos XXV milia, Menapios VII milia, Caletos X milia, Veliocasses et Viromanduos totidem, Atuatucos XVIIII milia;* 10 *Condrusos, Eburones, Caerosos, Paemanos,* qui uno nomine Germani appellantur, *arbitrari se posse armare ad XL milia.*

Direct form (II.4.1-3): 1 *Plerique Belgae sunt orti* a Germanis, Rhenumque antiquitus *traducti,* propter loci fertilitatem *hic consederunt,* 2 Gallosque, qui *haec* loca *incolebant, expulerunt; solique sunt,* qui patrum nostrorum memoria, omni Gallia vexata, Teutonos Cimbrosque intra suos fines ingredi prohibuerint; 3 qua ex re *fit,* uti earum rerum memoria magnam sibi auctoritatem magnosque spiritus in re militari *sumant.*

Direct form (II.4.5-10): 5 Plurimum inter eos *Bellovaci* et virtute et auctoritate et hominum numero *valent; hi possunt* conficere armata milia centum; *polliciti* (*sunt*) ex eo numero electa milia sexaginta, totiusque belli imperium sibi *postulant.* 6 Suessiones *nostri sunt finitimi;* fines latissimos feracissimosque agros *possident.* 7 Apud eos *fuit rex* nostra etiam memoria *Diviciacus,* totius Galliae *potentissimus,* qui cum magnae partis harum regionum, tum etiam Britanniae, imperium *obtinuit;* nunc est *rex Galba;* ad hunc propter iustitiam prudentiamque *summa* totius belli omnium voluntate defertur; 8 oppida *habent* numero XII, *pollicentur* milia armata L; totidem *Nervii,* qui maxime feri inter ipsos *habentur* longissimeque *absunt;* 9 XV milia Atrebates, *Ambiani* X milia, *Morini* XXV milia, *Menapii* VII milia, *Caleti* X milia, Veliocasses et *Viromandui* totidem, *Atuatuci* XVIIII milia; 10 Condrusos, Eburones, Caerosos, Paemanos, qui uno nomine Germani appellantur, *arbitramur* posse armare ad XL milia.

1 **ab eis:** *116c.* **quaereret:** why subjunctive? **quae civitates quantaeque in armis essent:** 'which states were in arms and how large they were'; the –*que* of *quantaeque* joins *quae* and *quantae* as two indirect questions, both of which have *essent* as their verb; *48b; 204.2.* **quid . . . possent:** 'what strength they had,' lit. 'to what degree they were able'; *118b.* **sic:** 'as follows.' **plerosque Belgas:** '(that) most of the Belgians'; *97c.* **a Germanis:** *128b.* The Belgians were of Celtic stock, but had formerly lived on the east side of the Rhine, hence the belief that they were of Germanic origin. **Rhenum:** accusative after *tra*(*ns*) in *traductos; 114a.* **antiquitus:** adv., 'in ancient times.' **ibi:** in Gaul.

2 **expulisse, esse:** *Belgas* is still the subject. **solosque esse, qui:** 'and were the only (people of Gaul) who'; *solos* is in predicate. **memoria:** *147b.* **omni Gallia vexata:** 'when Gaul as a whole was ravaged' by the Cimbrians and Teutons: see I.33.4; *144b2; 255.* **ingredi:** 'from entering'; Caesar uses the infinitive with subject-accusative after *prohibeo; 223a3.* **prohibuerint:** the perfect subjunctive in a relative clause of characteristic (*194a*) is retained from the direct form.

3 **qua ex re:** 'and in consequence of this achievement'; *167.* **fieri, uti . . . sumerent:** *203.1.* **memoria:** *135a.* **in re militari:** 'in respect to the art of war.' **sumerent:** why imperfect? *177a.*

4 **eorum:** *Belgarum.* **omnia se habere explorata:** '(that) they possessed complete information,' lit. 'they held all things investigated'; *229a.* **propterea quod:** see I.1.3. **propinquitatibus affinitatibusque:** 'by blood relationships and intermarriages'; *76a.* **coniuncti:** *227a1.* **quantam quisque multitudinem . . . pollicitus sit:** 'how great a host each one (i.e., each representative from each state or tribe) . . . had promised'; *204.3.* **cognoverint:** the subjunctive mood marks this clause as subordinate to the indirect statement *omnia se habere explorata; 214a.*

5 **plurimum, etc.:** *212c3.* **plurimum Bellovacos valere:** '(that) the Bellovaci were the most powerful'; *118b.* **virtute:** *135a.* **conficere:** 'muster'; *57b.* **armata milia:** translate as if *milia hominum armatorum.* **pollicitos:** *89b.* **electa milia sexaginta:** 'sixty thousand picked men.' **totius:** *23a.*

6 **suos finitimos:** 'their neighbors,' neighbors of the Remi. **feracissimos:** 'very productive'; *27a; 153a.* **possidere:** as subject-accusative supply *eos,* i.e., *Suessiones.*

7 **fuisse:** 'that there had been'; *90a.* **Diviciacum:** this king of the Suessiones is not to be confused with Divici-

acus the Aeduan, who is mentioned in the next chapter. **cum . . . tum:** 'not only . . . but also'; *186b.* **regionum:** dependent on *partis*, which limits *imperium*. **Britanniae:** not the whole of Britain, probably only a portion of the island along the southeast coast; *263.* **esse regem Galbam:** translate as if *Galbam esse regem*; *19d.* **ad hunc . . . deferri:** '(that) upon him . . . was conferred'; *69b.* **summam:** 'the supreme command', accusative subject of *deferri* (i.e., *not* an adjective in agreement with *prudentiam*). **voluntate:** *138.*

8 **habere, polliceri:** sc. *eos* (*Suessiones*). **numero:** *142a; 85.* **XII, L, etc.:** *38b, 36.* **milia armata:** see II.4.5. **totidem:** sc. *milia armata polliceri.* **Nervios:** the Nervians, and the other peoples named, can be located on Map 1. **maxime feri:** in predicate; *30.* **ipsos:** the Belgians in general, not the Nervians. **habeantur, absint:** vivid use of the present tense where the imperfect (since *cognoverint* above introduces the indirect discourse) might have been expected. **absint:** from the country of the Remi.

9 **Atrebates:** sc. *polliceri.* **Ambianos:** in the region of modern Amiens. **XVIIII:** *undeviginti; 36.*

10 **qui . . . appellantur:** *214c.* **Germani:** perhaps so called because, although of Celtic stock, they had been the last of the Belgians to move from the east side of the Rhine to the Belgian country. **uno:** 'a common.' **se:** the Remi; *158a.* **ad:** adverb, often found with numerals: 'about.'

Caesar, taking hostages from the Remi, crosses the Axona and encamps.

5. 1 Caesar, Remos cohortatus liberaliterque oratione prosecutus, omnem senatum ad se convenire principumque liberos obsides ad se adduci iussit. Quae omnia ab his diligenter ad diem facta sunt. 2 Ipse, Diviciacum Aeduum magnopere cohortatus, docet, quanto opere rei publicae communisque salutis intersit, manus hostium distineri, ne cum tanta multitudine uno tempore confligendum sit: 3 *id fieri posse, si suas copias Aedui in fines Bellovacorum introduxerint et eorum agros populari coeperint.* His mandatis eum ab se dimittit. 4 Postquam omnes Belgarum copias in unum locum coactas ad se venire vidit, neque iam longe abesse, ab eis, quos miserat, exploratoribus et ab Remis cognovit, flumen Axonam, quod est in extremis Remorum finibus, exercitum traducere maturavit atque ibi castra posuit. 5 Quae res et latus unum castrorum ripis fluminis muniebat et, post eum quae erant, tuta ab hostibus reddebat et, commeatus ab Remis reliquisque civitatibus ut sine periculo ad eum portari possent, efficiebat. 6 In eo flumine pons erat. Ibi praesidium ponit et in altera parte fluminis Q. Titurium Sabinum legatum cum sex cohortibus relinquit; castra in altitudinem pedum duodecim vallo fossaque duodeviginti pedum muniri iubet.

1 **Remos . . . prosecutus:** 'encouraging the Remi and attending (to them) in gracious words'; how lit.? *226c.* **senatum:** *258b; 75b.* **principum:** *10b.* **obsides:** 'as hostages'; *88a.* **Quae omnia:** 'And all of these things'; *167.* **diligenter:** *34a.* **ad diem:** 'promptly,' lit. 'to the day.'

2 **Diviciacum:** see II.4.7 and I.18, 20, 31, etc. **quanto opere:** 'how greatly,' lit. 'with what great trouble,' an ablative of manner that is effectively an interrogative adverb (sometimes written as *quantopere*; compare *magnopere* three words earlier). **rei publicae:** *Romanorum.* **communis:** of Romans and Aeduans. **intersit:** this impersonal verb means 'it is a concern' or 'it is important' and takes a genitive of the thing concerned (here *rei publicae:* 'for the State'); *103e.* **intersit:** why subjunctive? *204.3.* **manus distineri:** subject of *intersit;* 'that the enemy's forces be kept apart'; *222c; 79d.* **ne . . . confligendum sit:** 'that it might not be necessary to fight'; *73e; 196a.*

3 **id:** refers to *manus distineri*, 'that (object)'; *213b; 160c.* **in . . . introduxerint:** 'should have led into'; the perfect subjunctive here reflects the future perfect indicative in the direct form; *218.1b.* **His mandatis:** *144b2.*

4 **coactas . . . venire:** 'had been brought together and were coming'; *228a.* **vidit:** more vivid than *intellexit;* thus do we use the word 'see' of things understood but not perceived with the eyes; *188a.* **neque:** translate as if *et non*, and put the *non* with *abesse.* **abesse:** sc. *eas* (= *copias*); dependent on *cognovit.* **ab eis, quos miserat, exploratoribus:** read as if *ab eis exploratoribus quos miserat.* **exploratoribus:** *287.* **flumen, exercitum:** *114a.* **Axonam:** now the *Aisne;* see Map 1. **quod:** the antecedent is *flumen.* **extremis finibus:** 'the most remote part of the country'; *152a.* **ibi castra posuit:** Caesar 'encamped' on the north side of the Axona, about a mile and a half northeast of the present village of Berry-au-Bac; see Map 5.

5 **Quae res:** 'and this thing,' i.e., the placement of his camp; *167.* **et . . . et:** *233d.* **ripis:** *131a; 291b.* **et, post eum quae erant, tuta . . . reddebat:** 'and was rendering safe (those places) which were behind him'; sc. *ea loca* as the antecedent of *quae.* **tuta:** *115b.* **commeatus . . . ut . . . portari possent, efficiebat:** 'brought it about that supplies could be brought'; *203.3.*

6 **In:** 'across.' **erat:** *90a.* **praesidium:** at D on Map 5. **in altera parte:** on the south side of the Axona; see Map 5, C. Caesar now had both ends of the bridge well guarded. In consequence, he was able to get provisions from his allies across the river, to set a watch on the Remi (the sincerity of whose professions of loyalty was not beyond

question), and, finally, to keep open an avenue of retreat in case of disaster. **sex cohortibus:** about how many men? *267c.* **pedum:** *100a.* The measurement of twelve feet included both the height of the bank formed by the earth thrown out of the trench and that of the row of palisades along the outer edge; *293.* **vallo:** ablative of means after *muniri*; *131a.* **duodeviginti pedum:** eighteen Roman feet broad, measured across the top; the trench, with sloping sides, was probably about ten feet deep. Excavations have discovered traces of this rampart and trench.

The Belgians attack Bibrax, a town of the Remi.

6. 1 Ab his castris oppidum Remorum, nomine Bibrax, aberat milia passuum VIII. Id ex itinere magno impetu Belgae oppugnare coeperunt. Aegre eo die sustentatum est. 2 Gallorum eadem atque Belgarum oppugnatio est haec. Ubi, circumiecta multitudine hominum totis moenibus, undique in murum lapides iaci coepti sunt, murusque defensoribus nudatus est, testudine facta portas succendunt murumque subruunt. 3 Quod tum facile fiebat. Nam cum tanta multitudo lapides ac tela conicerent, in muro consistendi potestas erat nulli. 4 Cum finem oppugnandi nox fecisset, Iccius Remus, summa nobilitate et gratia inter suos, qui tum oppido praefuerat, unus ex eis, qui legati de pace ad Caesarem venerant, nuntios ad eum mittit, *nisi subsidium sibi summittatur, sese diutius sustinere non posse.*

1 **nomine:** 'by name'; *142a.* **milia passuum VIII:** *118a; 243b.* **ex itinere:** 'from the line of march,' attacking the town as soon as they reached it; see Vocab. under *iter.* **sustentatum est:** *73d.*
2 **Gallorum eadem atque Belgarum oppugnatio:** 'the Gauls' (method of) storming (fortified places), (which is) the same as (that) of the Belgians'; *233c.* **est haec:** 'is as follows,' lit. 'is this'; *161a.* **circumiecta multitudine:** *144b2.* **moenibus:** the indirect object of the action described in *circumiecta*; *104a.* **iaci:** *57b.* **coepti sunt:** *72c.* **defensoribus:** 'of its defenders'; *127a.* **testudine facta:** 'having made a tortoise roof,' in the Roman fashion; *144b2; 305.* **succendunt:** 'they,' the attacking host, 'set on fire'; *175c.*
3 **Quod tum:** 'And this (outcome), on that occasion,' referring to the burning of the gates, and undermining of the walls, of Bibrax. **conicerent:** *173b; 184a.* **consistendi potestas:** 'the ability to remain standing,' lit. 'for standing'; *230.1.* **erat nulli:** translate as if *nemini*, 'no one had,' lit. 'there was to none,' dative of possession; *12d; 111.*
4 **fecisset:** *185c.* **Iccius:** see II.3.1; the next few clauses (up to *nuntium ad se mittit*) are all in apposition and convey information about Iccius. **summa nobilitate:** 'a man of'; *143a.* **inter suos:** 'among his countrymen'; *154a.* **oppido:** *107a.* **tum praefuerat:** i.e., *praepositus erat et tum praeerat.* **ex eis:** *97d.* **legati:** in predicate after *venerant*; 'as envoys.' **nisi:** '(saying) that unless'; *213b.* **sibi:** 'to them,' the beleaguered inhabitants of Bibrax. **summittatur:** 'should be sent to their relief'; *218.1a.* **sustinere:** intransitive, 'hold out.'

Caesar relieves Bibrax; the Belgians march toward his camp.

7. 1 Eo de media nocte Caesar, isdem ducibus usus, qui nuntii ab Iccio venerant, Numidas et Cretas sagittarios et funditores Baleares subsidio oppidanis mittit; 2 quorum adventu et Remis cum spe defensionis studium propugnandi accessit, et hostibus, eadem de causa, spes potiundi oppidi discessit. 3 Itaque paulisper apud oppidum morati agrosque Remorum depopulati, omnibus vicis aedificiisque, quo adire potuerant, incensis, ad castra Caesaris omnibus copiis contenderunt et a milibus passuum minus duobus castra posuerunt; quae castra, ut fumo atque ignibus significabatur, amplius milibus passuum VIII in latitudinem patebant.

1 **Eo:** toward Bibrax. **de:** *242d.* **isdem:** 'the same men'; *45; 131c.* **ducibus:** 'as guides,' predicative; *131f.* **usus:** *226c.* **nuntii:** construed as *legati* at the end of the previous chapter. **Numidas et Cretas sagittarios et funditores Baleares:** bowmen and slingers; *268.* **Cretas:** *19f.* **subsidio, oppidanis:** *112b.* **oppidanis:** 'the inhabitants of the town.' **mittit:** *175b.*
2 **quorum adventu:** 'at the arrival of whom'; *147b.* **et Remis . . . et hostibus:** 'for the Remi, on the one hand . . . for the enemy, on the other hand'; *109a, b; 233a.* **cum spe defensionis studium propugnandi accessit:** '(along) with the hope of defense there came an eagerness to come out fighting.' **spe:** *137c.* **accessit:** *accedo* is often, as here, used as the passive of *addo.* **eadem de causa:** 'for the same reason.' **potiundi oppidi:** *64b; 102; 230.1.* **discessit:** Caesar's choice of verbs highlights the contrast: *cum spe accessit* set against *spes discessit.*
3 **paulisper:** 'for a short time.' **morati, depopulati:** sc. *hostes* as subject of *contenderunt; 61a1.* **vicis, aedificiis:** in agreement with *incensis* (cf. I.5.2); *144b2.* **quo:** adverb; translate as if *ad quae*, 'to which they could go,' i.e., within a reasonable range. **omnibus copiis:** *137b.* **a milibus passuum minus duobus:** 'less than two miles away,' i.e., 'at (lit. 'from') a distance of thousands of paces less than two (thousands).' The Roman point of view

differs from ours in such phrases. **quae castra:** 'and this camp,' marked CAMP OF THE BELGIANS on Map 5, while Caesar's camp is at A; *167*. **fumo:** 'by the smoke.' **significabatur:** 'was indicated'; *73d*. **milibus:** why ablative? *129a*. **VIII:** *38b; 36*. **patebant:** 'extended.'

Caesar adds to the fortifications of his camp, awaits attack.

8. 1 Caesar primo et propter multitudinem hostium et propter eximiam opinionem virtutis proelio supersedere statuit; 2 cotidie tamen equestribus proeliis, quid hostis virtute posset et quid nostri auderent, periclitabatur. 3 Ubi nostros non esse inferiores intellexit, loco pro castris ad aciem instruendam natura opportuno atque idoneo, quod is collis, ubi castra posita erant, paululum ex planitie editus, tantum adversus in latitudinem patebat, quantum loci acies instructa occupare poterat, atque ex utraque parte lateris deiectus habebat, et in fronte leniter fastigatus paulatim ad planitiem redibat, 4 ab utroque latere eius collis transversam fossam obduxit circiter passuum quadringentorum et ad extremas fossas castella constituit ibique tormenta collocavit, ne, cum aciem instruxisset, hostes, quod tantum multitudine poterant, ab lateribus pugnantes, suos circumvenire possent. 5 Hoc facto, duabus legionibus, quas proxime conscripserat, in castris relictis, ut, si quo opus esset, subsidio duci possent, reliquas VI legiones pro castris in acie constituit. Hostes item suas copias ex castris eductas instruxerant.

1 **eximiam opinionem virtutis:** 'their extraordinary reputation for bravery'; *102*. **proelio supersedere:** 'to refrain from battle'; *127a*.

2 **equestribus proeliis:** 'cavalry skirmishes,' as distinguished from a regular engagement, with infantry. **quid hostis virtute posset et quid nostri auderent:** *118b*. **virtute:** *142a*. **periclitabatur:** 'kept trying (to find out)'; *175d*.

3 **loco . . . idoneo:** ablative absolute, translate as if *cum locus* ('since the space') . . . *opportunus atque idoneus esset*; *144b3*. **pro:** 'in front of.' **ad aciem instruendam:** *230.3*. **natura:** 'naturally,' lit. 'by nature.' **atque:** *233a*. **quod . . . redibat:** explains why the ground in front of the camp was well adapted for forming a line of battle. **castra:** Map 5, A. **paululum ex planitie editus:** 'a little elevated from the plain.' **is collis . . . tantum adversus in latitudinem patebat, quantum loci acies instructa occupare poterat:** 'that hill, (on the side) facing (the enemy), extended in width to just the extent of space as a line of battle, drawn up, could occupy.' **adversus:** adjective, 'facing,' agreeing with *collis*. **tantum:** *118a*. **quantum:** correlative with *tantum*, and object of *occupare*, having *loci* dependent on it. **loci:** translate as if dependent on *tantum*; *97a*. The long, gently sloping hillside, broad enough to afford room for a Roman triple line, is shown on Map 5, between the Miette brook and the narrowing crest of the hill southwest of Caesar's camp; six legions are there shown in order of battle. **ex utraque parte:** = 'on either side,' the side of the camp toward the river, and the opposite side. **lateris deiectus:** 'steep slopes,' lit. 'slopes for a flank'; *13e*. **habebat:** *collis* is still the subject. **in fronte:** 'in front' of the camp, on the southwest side. **leniter fastigatus:** 'sloping gently.' **planitiem:** the level ground between the hill and the river above and below Berry-au-Bac. **redibat:** here 'descended,' lit. 'was coming back to.'

4 **transversam fossam obduxit:** 'he extended a trench crosswise,' that is, at right angles with the length of the hill. Starting from opposite corners of the camp, Caesar prolonged two lines of entrenchments at right angles to the sides, each about a third of a mile in length. One ran down the south slope of the hill, toward the Aisne, the bed of which in Caesar's time is indicated on the plan by the broken line. The other ran down the north slope, toward the Miette brook; both are indicated on Map 5 by red lines (a, b). At the ends of these entrenchments he constructed forts (*castella*) (B B), where he stationed troops with artillery engines (*tormenta*). His purpose was to guard against a flank movement on the part of the enemy, by which they might reach the rear of the camp and attack from behind while his forces were engaged in front. **passuum quadringentorum:** 'four hundred paces' in length; how lit.? *100a*. How far by our measurement? *243b*. **ad extremas fossas:** 'at the ends of the trenches'; *152a*. **castella:** Map 5, B B. **tormenta:** 'artillery,' such as were used in siege operations; *303*. **instruxisset:** *220*. **quod tantum multitudine poterant:** 'because they were so strong in numbers'; why indicative? *183a*. **tantum:** *118b*. **multitudine:** *142a*. **ab lateribus:** 'on the flanks'; *126c*. **pugnantes:** with *hostes*. **suos:** 'his men'; *154a*. A glance at Map 5 shows how well designed the trenches were to protect against an attack upon the right end of the battle line, and block access to the rear, which was otherwise protected by the river. **possent:** *196a*.

5 **duabus legionibus:** the thirteenth and fourteenth, enrolled a few months before; see II.2.1. Generally, as in this instance, Caesar exposed his veterans to the brunt of the battle, leaving recruits, whose powers had not been fully tested, as a reserve force; *267d, f*. **relictis:** *144b2*. **quo:** after *si* = 'at any point.' **esset:** *220*. **subsidio:** 'as a reserve force'; *112a*. **acie:** undoubtedly a triple line; *297*. **eductas instruxerant:** 'had led forth and drawn up'; *228a*. For the relative position of the two armies, see Map 5.

The Belgians attempt to cross the Axona and attack Titurius.

9. 1 Palus erat non magna inter nostrum atque hostium exercitum. Hanc si nostri transirent, hostes exspectabant; nostri autem, si ab illis initium transeundi fieret, ut impeditos aggrederentur, parati in armis erant. 2 Interim proelio equestri inter duas acies contendebatur. Ubi neutri transeundi initium faciunt, secundiore equitum proelio nostris, Caesar suos in castra reduxit. 3 Hostes protinus ex eo loco ad flumen Axonam contenderunt, quod esse post nostra castra demonstratum est. 4 Ibi, vadis repertis, partem suarum copiarum traducere conati sunt, eo consilio, ut, si possent, castellum, cui praeerat Q. Titurius legatus, expugnarent pontemque interscinderent; 5 si minus potuissent, agros Remorum popularentur, qui magno nobis usui ad bellum gerendum erant, commeatuque nostros prohiberent.

1 **Palus:** the marshy ground along the Miette brook, indicated on Map 5. **erat:** *90a.* **nostrum atque hostium exercitum:** 'our army and that of the enemy'; *157d.* **Hanc:** *paludem.* **si:** after *exspectabant:* 'were waiting (to see) whether'; *204.4.* **nostri autem, si ab illis initium transeundi fieret, ut impeditos aggrederentur, parati in armis erant:** *nostri autem parati in armis erant, ut, si ab illis (hostibus) initium transeundi (paludem) fieret, (eos,* the enemy engaged in crossing over, hence at a disadvantage) *impeditos aggrederentur.* **fieret:** *220.* **aggrederentur:** *57c.* Why subjunctive? *196a.*
2 **proelio:** *131a.* **contendebatur:** *73d.* **neutri:** nom. pl., 'neither side'; each side was waiting for the other to assume the offensive; *23a.* **secundiore equitum proelio nostris:** lit. 'with the battle of the cavalries being more favorable to us'; *144b5.* **nostris:** *108a.*
3 **protinus:** 'at once.' **eo loco:** on the opposite side of the marsh from the Romans. **quod:** *flumen.* **demonstratum est:** 'it has been shown'; see II.5.4-5. **post nostra castra:** 'behind our camp.'
4 **vadis:** shallow places, suitable for fording, are still found in the Aisne, between the mouth of the Miette brook and the village of Pontavert; for the route of the attacking forces see Map 5, H H. **eo consilio:** 'with this design,' explained by the appositive *ut*-clauses following; *135a; 203.4.* **possent:** *220.* **castellum:** on the south bank of the river; see II.5.6 and Map 5, C. The Belgians planned to storm the fort from the rear. The attempt was justified, from the military point of view; for the destruction of the bridge would have made Caesar's position extremely difficult.
5 **minus:** translate as if *non.* **potuissent:** change of tense from *possent,* 'if they could,' to *potuissent* 'if (having made the attempt) they should have been unsuccessful.' **popularentur, prohiberent:** sc. *ut,* the clauses also being in apposition with *consilio.* **nobis, usui:** *112b.* **commeatu:** *127a.*

Caesar prevents their crossing; they decide to disperse.

10. 1 Caesar, certior factus ab Titurio, omnem equitatum et levis armaturae Numidas, funditores sagittariosque pontem traducit atque ad eos contendit. 2 Acriter in eo loco pugnatum est. Hostes impeditos nostri in flumine aggressi magnum eorum numerum occiderunt; 3 per eorum corpora reliquos audacissime transire conantes multitudine telorum reppulerunt; primos, qui transierant, equitatu circumventos interfecerunt. 4 Hostes, ubi et de expugnando oppido et de flumine transeundo spem se fefellisse intellexerunt, neque nostros in locum iniquiorem progredi pugnandi causa viderunt, atque ipsos res frumentaria deficere coepit, consilio convocato, constituerunt, optimum esse, domum suam quemque reverti, et, quorum in fines primum Romani exercitum introduxissent, ad eos defendendos undique convenire, ut potius in suis quam in alienis finibus decertarent et domesticis copiis rei frumentariae uterentur. 5 Ad eam sententiam cum reliquis causis haec quoque ratio eos deduxit, quod Diviciacum atque Aeduos finibus Bellovacorum appropinquare cognoverant. His persuaderi, ut diutius morarentur neque suis auxilium ferrent, non poterat.

1 **certior factus:** 'having been informed' of the enemy's attempted movement. **equitatum, pontem:** *114a.* As Caesar's camp was south of the Miette and east of the bridge over the Axona, he could send his cavalry across the bridge without danger of interference, and from the south side of the river could attack the enemy in the act of crossing. **levis armaturae Numidas, funditores sagittariosque:** 'the Numidians of light equipment'; translate 'the light-armed Numidians,' namely 'slingers and bowmen'; *268; 100a.* **funditores:** probably provided with leaden bullets, though such are not mentioned by Caesar. **eos:** *hostes.*
2 **in eo loco:** where the enemy started to cross the river; marked on Map 5 by crossed swords. **pugnatum est:** *73d.* **aggressi:** *226c.*
3 **per eorum corpora reliquos audacissime transire conantes:** 'the rest, (while) trying most bravely to cross (the river) through the bodies of those (already slain).' The bravery of these Belgians, recorded by Caesar with

evident admiration, justifies his characterization at the beginning of Book I (I.1.3). **reppulerunt:** from *repello*; the subject remains *nostri*. **equitatu:** *131b*. **circumventos interfecerunt:** 'surrounded and killed'; *228a*.
4 **Hostes:** the main body of the enemy, which remained inactive while a detachment (*partem suarum copiarum*, II.9.4) tried to cross the river. **et de . . . et de:** 'both regarding . . . and regarding'. **oppido:** Bibrax; see II.6-7; *230.4*. **spem se fefellisse:** 'that their hope had deceived them'. **neque:** translate as if *et . . . non*. **nostros:** the six legions that had been formed in order of battle and then led back to camp (II.8.5, 9.2). **locum iniquiorem:** the swampy territory between the two camps. **pugnandi causa:** *230.1*; *94b*. **ipsos:** *hostes*; the object of *deficere*. **deficere:** 'to fail'; *57b*. As the Gauls for the most part engaged only in short campaigns, their arrangements for supplies were often sketchy. **consilio:** 'a conference' of the leaders. **optimum esse:** 'that it was best'. The subject of *esse* is the infinitive clause *quemque reverti*, and *optimum* is in predicate; *148d*. **domum suam:** 'to his own home'; *119b*. **et . . . convenire:** sc. *quemque*, a continuation of the thought initiated by *optimum esse*. **quorum in fines . . . ad eos defendendos:** *eos* is the antecedent of *quorum*, 'to defend those . . . into whose territory'; *230.3*. **introduxissent:** *220*. **potius quam:** 'rather than'. **alienis:** = *aliorum*, 'of others', as opposed to **domesticis**, 'their own', i.e., what they have at home. **decertarent:** *196a*. **copiis:** 'supplies'; *131c*.
5 **cum reliquis causis:** 'together with the rest of these reasons'; *137a*; *171a*. **ratio:** 'consideration', explained by the appositive clause *quod* ('that') . . . *cognoverant*; *198b*. **Diviciacum:** see II.5.2-3. **finibus:** *105*. **cognoverant:** 'they knew'; *176b*. **His:** the Bellovaci; *105*. **His persuaderi . . . non poterat:** 'These could not be persuaded', lit. 'it could not be persuasive to them'; *106b*. **ut morarentur:** 'to stay' with the united Belgian force; *199a5*. Caesar's plan of dividing the forces of the Belgians, suggested in II.5, was thus successful. **neque:** 'and not'.

The Belgians retreat in disorder; Caesar pursues them with great slaughter.

11. 1 Ea re constituta, secunda vigilia magno cum strepitu ac tumultu castris egressi, nullo certo ordine neque imperio, cum sibi quisque primum itineris locum peteret et domum pervenire properaret, fecerunt, ut consimilis fugae profectio videretur. 2 Hac re statim Caesar per speculatores cognita, insidias veritus, quod, qua de causa discederent, nondum perspexerat, exercitum equitatumque castris continuit. 3 Prima luce, confirmata re ab exploratoribus, omnem equitatum, qui novissimum agmen moraretur, praemisit eique Q. Pedium et L. Aurunculeium Cottam legatos praefecit; T. Labienum legatum cum legionibus tribus subsequi iussit. 4 Hi, novissimos adorti et multa milia passuum prosecuti, magnam multitudinem eorum fugientium conciderunt, cum ab extremo agmine, ad quos ventum erat, consisterent fortiterque impetum nostrorum militum sustinerent, 5 priores, quod abesse a periculo viderentur, neque ulla necessitate neque imperio continerentur, exaudito clamore perturbatis ordinibus omnes in fuga sibi praesidium ponerent. 6 Ita sine ullo periculo tantam eorum multitudinem nostri interfecerunt, quantum fuit diei spatium; sub occasum solis destiterunt seque in castra, ut erat imperatum, receperunt.

1 **re:** 'conclusion', i.e., to disperse. **secunda vigilia:** *242c*; *147a*. **strepitu:** 'uproar'; *136a*. **castris:** shown on Map 5; *127a*. **nullo certo ordine neque imperio:** ablative of attendant circumstance, explaining *magno . . . tumultu*, and in turn explained by the causal clause *cum . . . properaret*; 'with no fixed order nor chain of command'; *138*. **sibi quisque:** *170b*. **primum:** 'the foremost'. **peteret:** *184a*. **fecerunt, ut . . . profectio videretur:** substantive clause of result, 'they acted such that their departure seemed'; *203.3*. **fugae:** *108a*.
2 **per:** *123a*. **speculatores:** 'spies'; *287*. **veritus:** *226c*. **quod:** 'since'. **qua de causa:** 'for which reason', i.e., 'why'. **discederent:** *204.2*. **castris:** translate 'in camp'; *131a*.
3 **Prima luce:** 'at day break'; *152a*. **re:** 'the fact' that the Belgian host had actually dispersed. **exploratoribus:** *287*. **qui novissimum agmen moraretur:** 'to delay the rear guard' of the retreating Belgians; *193a*. **eique:** = *equitatuique*; *107b*. **Pedium:** see II.2.1. **legatum:** *273a*.
4 **Hi:** 'these men', the legionaries under Labienus; the cavalry had gone ahead to retard the Belgian rear till the Roman infantry could catch up with it. **milia:** *118a*. **eorum fugientium:** 'of them as they fled'. **cum:** introduces a series of clauses that explain why the Roman legionaries were able to kill so many of the retreating Belgians; *184a*. **ab extremo agmine:** sc. *ei Belgae*, '(those Belgians) at the end of the column'; *126c*; *152a*. **agmine:** here used not of an orderly marching column but of a mass of soldiers in flight. **ad quos ventum erat:** 'to whom it had been come', i.e., 'the Roman soldiers had come'; *73d*. **consisterent:** 'were making a stand'.
5 **priores:** '(while) those nearer the front' of the Belgian column; *154a*; *33*. **viderentur:** the verb of a causal clause subordinate to the extended causal *cum*-clause; *220*. **exaudito clamore:** 'when they had heard the shouting' behind them; *144b2*. **ordinibus:** 'ranks'. **sibi:** *109a*. **praesidium ponerent:** 'sought safety', lit. 'were placing protection'. **ponerent:** with *cum*, as *consisterent*, *sustinerent*.

6 **quantum fuit diei spatium:** 'as great as the space of the day was,' i.e., as long as daylight permitted; *quantum* is correlative with *tantam*. **ut erat imperatum:** *73d*.

Noviodunum, besieged by Caesar, surrenders.

12. 1 Postridie eius diei Caesar, prius quam se hostes ex terrore ac fuga reciperent, in fines Suessionum, qui proximi Remis erant, exercitum duxit et magno itinere ad oppidum Noviodunum contendit. 2 Id ex itinere oppugnare conatus, quod vacuum ab defensoribus esse audiebat, propter latitudinem fossae murique altitudinem, paucis defendentibus, expugnare non potuit. 3 Castris munitis, vineas agere, quaeque ad oppugnandum usui erant, comparare coepit. 4 Interim omnis ex fuga Suessionum multitudo in oppidum proxima nocte convenit. 5 Celeriter vineis ad oppidum actis, aggere iacto turribusque constitutis, magnitudine operum, quae neque viderant ante Galli neque audierant, et celeritate Romanorum permoti, legatos ad Caesarem de deditione mittunt et, petentibus Remis, ut conservarentur, impetrant.

1 **diei:** *94c.* **se reciperent:** 'could rally,' lit. 'recover themselves'; why subjunctive? *189b.* **in fines Suessionum:** see Map 1. Having scattered the great host of united Belgians, Caesar proceeds to the reduction of the different states one by one. **Remis:** *108a.* **magno itinere:** 'by a forced march'; *289.* **Noviodunum:** = "Newtown"; thought to have been on the hill of Pommiers, near the modern city of Soissons.
2 **ex itinere:** see Vocab. under *iter.* **oppugnare:** *300.* **vacuum ab:** 'destitute of.' **esse:** i.e., *id* (*oppidum*) *esse vacuum.* **latitudinem fossae:** the wider the 'moat,' the more difficult the filling of it so as to gain access to the wall. **latitudinem fossae murique altitudinem:** *239c.* **paucis defendentibus:** 'though there were but few defending it'; *144b5.*
3 **Castris:** probably on high ground east of Pommiers, where traces of a Roman camp, thought to date from Caesar's time, have been discovered. **vineas agere:** sc. *coepit*, as at the end of the sentence: 'he began to move forward the arbor sheds'; *302a.* **quaeque:** = *et* (*ea*) *quae*, with *ea* being the antecedent of *quae* as well as the object of *comparare.* **usui:** 'of use.' Why dative? *112a.*
4 **omnis . . . Suessionum multitudo:** 'the whole multitude of the Suessiones,' i.e., all the Suessiones who had originally fled. **proxima nocte:** the night following the day on which Caesar reached Noviodunum, encamped, and commenced preparations for besieging the town.
5 **vineis:** 'arbor sheds,' open at the ends, were rapidly constructed, and placed in parallel rows which began outside the range of the enemy's weapons and were extended to the edge of the moat; *144b2.* **aggere iacto:** lit. 'with the filling having been cast'; this dirt 'filling' was carried under the lines of the arbor sheds and 'cast' into the moat so as to level it up and make it possible to roll the towers close to the city wall. **turribus:** 'towers'; *302b.* **magnitudine, celeritate:** *135a.* **operum:** 'siege-works.' **petentibus Remis:** 'at the request of the Remi'; how lit.? **ut conservarentur:** after *petentibus*, 'that they should be spared'; *199a4.*

The Suessiones submit; Caesar marches against the Bellovaci.

13. 1 Caesar, obsidibus acceptis primis civitatis atque ipsius Galbae regis duobus filiis, armisque omnibus ex oppido traditis, in deditionem Suessiones accipit exercitumque in Bellovacos ducit. 2 Qui cum se suaque omnia in oppidum Bratuspantium contulissent, atque ab eo oppido Caesar cum exercitu circiter milia passuum V abesset, omnes maiores natu, ex oppido egressi, manus ad Caesarem tendere et voce significare coeperunt, *sese in eius fidem ac potestatem venire neque contra populum Romanum armis contendere.* 3 Item, cum ad oppidum accessisset castraque ibi poneret, pueri mulieresque ex muro passis manibus suo more pacem ab Romanis petierunt.

1 **obsidibus:** 'as hostages'; predicative, after *acceptis*; *88b.* **primis:** 'the foremost men'; *154a*; *144b2.* **Galbae:** see II.4.7. **Bellovacos:** translate as if *in fines Bellovacorum*; *251.*
2 **Qui cum:** 'when they,' i.e., the Bellovaci; *167.* **oppidum:** 'stronghold'; not a city but a fortified place of refuge, occupied only in time of danger. **maiores natu:** 'the old men'; how lit.? *142a.* **egressi:** 'came out and'; *228a.* **tendere:** 'to stretch out.' **in eius fidem:** 'under his protection'; *124a.* **venire:** *213b.* **neque:** translate as if *et . . . non.* **contendere:** 'struggle' any longer.
3 **accessisset:** *185c.* **pueri:** 'children,' not 'boys' merely. **passis manibus:** 'with hands outstretched'; *144b2.* Principal parts of *pando* and *patior?* **more:** with *passis*; *136c.*

Diviciacus presents the case of the Bellovaci.

14. 1 Pro his Diviciacus (nam post discessum Belgarum, dimissis Aeduorum copiis, ad eum reverterat) facit verba: 2 *Bellovacos omni tempore in fide atque amicitia civitatis Aeduae fuisse; impulsos ab suis principibus, qui dicerent, Aeduos, a Caesare in servitutem redactos, omnes indignitates contumeliasque perferre, et ab Aeduis defecisse et populo Romano bellum intulisse.* 3 *Qui eius consilii principes fuissent, quod intellegerent, quantam calamitatem civitati intulissent, in Britanniam profugisse.* 4 *Petere non solum Bellovacos, sed etiam pro his Aeduos, ut sua clementia ac mansuetudine in eos utatur.* 5 *Quod si fecerit, Aeduorum auctoritatem apud omnes Belgas amplificaturum, quorum auxiliis atque opibus, si qua bella inciderint, sustentare consuerint.*

> *Direct form* (II.14.2-5): 2 *Bellovaci omni tempore in fide atque amicitia civitatis Aeduae* fuerunt; *impulsi ab suis principibus, qui* dicebant, *Aeduos, a* te *in servitutem redactos, omnes indignitates contumeliasque perferre, et ab Aeduis* defecerunt *et populo Romano bellum* intulerunt. 3 *Qui eius consilii principes* fuerant, *quod* intellegebant, *quantam calamitatem civitati intulissent, in Britanniam* profugerunt. 4 Petunt *non solum* Bellovaci, *sed etiam pro his* Aedui, *ut* tua *clementia ac mansuetudine in eos* utaris. 5 *Quod si* feceris, *Aeduorum auctoritatem apud omnes Belgas* amplificabis; *quorum auxiliis atque opibus, si qua bella* inciderunt, *sustentare* consuerunt.

1 **Pro:** 'on behalf of.' **his:** *Bellovacis.* **discessum:** see II.11.1. **Aeduorum copiis:** see II.5.2-3 and II.10.5. **eum:** Caesar. **facit verba:** 'made a plea'; how lit.?

2 **Bellovacos,** etc.: *213b; 212c1.* **omni tempore:** 'at all times'; cf. I.11.3. **dicerent:** 'kept saying'; *175a.* **omnes indignitates contumeliasque:** 'every kind of ill-treatment and insult'; *92c.* **et . . . et:** *233a.* **defecisse:** 'had revolted'; *57b.*

3 **Qui:** as antecedent supply *eos* with *profugisse.* **principes:** here = *auctores,* 'advisers.' **quantam calamitatem civitati intulissent:** indirect question after *intellegerent; 204.3.*

4 **petere, utatur:** vivid use of present tenses where past tenses might have been expected. **clementia:** 'mercifulness,' the quality which leads a man to treat with kindness those against whom he has grounds of offense. **mansuetudine:** 'compassion,' the quality that makes one able to realize the sufferings of others. **in:** 'toward.'

5 **si fecerit, . . . (se) amplificaturum** (esse): Caesar is the subject; the perfect subjunctive *fecerit* represents the future perfect indicative *feceris* in the direct form; *218.1b.* **quorum auxiliis atque opibus:** 'with whose aid and resources'; *quorum* refers to the Belgians. **si qua bella inciderint, sustentare:** 'to sustain whatever wars occurred,' lit. 'if any wars occurred.' **qua:** after *si,* 'any'; *168; 49a.* **consuerint:** the Aedui are the subject; *176b.*

Caesar makes terms with the Bellovaci and Ambiani, learns about the Nervians.

15. 1 Caesar, honoris Diviciaci atque Aeduorum causa, sese eos in fidem recepturum et conservaturum dixit; et quod erat civitas magna inter Belgas auctoritate atque hominum multitudine praestabat, DC obsides poposcit. 2 His traditis omnibusque armis ex oppido collatis, ab eo loco in fines Ambianorum pervenit; qui se suaque omnia sine mora dediderunt. 3 Eorum fines Nervii attingebant; quorum de natura moribusque Caesar cum quaereret, sic reperiebat: 4 *nullum aditum esse ad eos mercatoribus; nihil pati vini reliquarumque rerum ad luxuriam pertinentium inferri, quod his rebus relanguescere animos eorum et remitti virtutem existimarent;* 5 *esse homines feros magnaeque virtutis; increpitare atque incusare reliquos Belgas, qui se populo Romano dedidissent patriamque virtutem proiecissent;* 6 *confirmare, sese neque legatos missuros neque ullam condicionem pacis accepturos.*

> *Direct form* (II.15.4-6): 4 *Nullus aditus est ad eos mercatoribus; nihil* patiuntur *vini reliquarumque rerum ad luxuriam pertinentium inferri, quod his rebus relanguescere animos eorum et remitti virtutem* existimant. 5 Sunt *homines* feri *magnaeque virtutis;* increpitant *atque* incusant *reliquos Belgas, qui se populo Romano* dediderint *patriamque virtutem* proiecerint; 6 confirmant, *sese neque legatos missuros* (esse) *neque ullam condicionem pacis accepturos* (esse).

1 **honoris:** dependent on *causa;* 'out of regard for Diviciacus'; *94b.* **Diviciaci:** dependent on *honoris; 102.* **in fidem:** as in II.13.2. **quod erat civitas magna inter Belgas auctoritate:** 'because the state (of the Bellovaci) was with great prestige among the Belgians.' **magna auctoritate:** *143b.* **hominum multitudine praestabat:** 'had the greatest population,' lit. 'was surpassing in (respect to) their multitude of men'; *142a.* **DC:** *sescentos; 36.* The fact that for the sake of his Aeduan supporters Caesar had spared the Bellovaci did not prevent him from exacting a large number of hostages to bind them in their pledge of submission.

2 **collatis:** *69b.* **eo loco:** Bratuspantium. For Caesar's route, see Map 1.

3 **Eorum:** the Ambiani. **Nervii attingebant:** 'the (country of the) Nervians bordered,' lit. 'touched upon'; *251.* **de natura:** *116c.*

4 **nullum,** etc.: *212c3.* **aditum:** 'access.' **esse:** *175c.* **mercatoribus:** *111.* **pati:** sc. *eos* (*Nervios*) as subject; *60.* **nihil vini:** 'no wine,' lit. 'nothing of wine'; the partitive genitive continues in *reliquarumque rerum . . . pertinentium; 97a.* **ad luxuriam pertinentium:** 'which contribute to luxurious living'; how lit.? **rebus:** *135a.* **relanguescere:** 'become weak.' **virtutem:** 'valor,' the manifestation of courage in brave deeds. **existimarent:** *183a.*

5 **magnae virtutis:** genitive of quality taking the place of an adjective, hence connected by *-que* with *feros; 100a.* **increpitare atque incusare:** sc. *eos,* 'that they upbraided and condemned.' **reliquos:** *171a.* **qui:** 'because they'; *194c.*

6 **sese:** refers to *eos* understood as subject of *confirmare,* 'they (the Nervii) asserted that they.' **missuros:** sc. *esse;* indirect discourse after *confirmare.*

II.16-28: Battle against the Nervii at the Sabis

The Nervians, Atrebatians, and Viromanduans await Caesar at the Sabis.

16. 1 Cum per eorum fines triduum iter fecisset, inveniebat ex captivis: *Sabim flumen a castris suis non amplius milia passuum X abesse;* 2 *trans id flumen omnes Nervios consedisse adventumque ibi Romanorum exspectare una cum Atrebatibus et Viromanduis, finitimis suis* (nam his utrisque persuaserant, uti eandem belli fortunam experirentur); 3 *exspectari etiam ab his Atuatucorum copias, atque esse in itinere;* 4 *mulieres, quique per aetatem ad pugnam inutiles viderentur, in eum locum coniecisse, quo propter paludes exercitui aditus non esset.*

1 **eorum:** *Nerviorum.* **triduum:** = *tres dies; 118a.* **iter fecisset:** 'had advanced'; for the route, see Map 1. **inveniebat:** = *quaerendo cognoscebat.* **Sabim,** etc.: *212c3.* **Sabim:** accusative like *turrim; 14c.* **milia:** why not ablative? *129b; 118a.*

2 **trans id flumen:** they crossed over to the south side of the Sabis (now often referred to by its modern name, Sambre), which flows in an easterly direction into the Meuse; *261.* **his utrisque:** 'both these peoples'; *51; 23a.* The combined forces of the Nervians, Atrebatians, and Viromanduans were estimated at 75,000 (II.4.7-9). **nam . . . experirentur:** *214c.*

3 **copias:** 'forces,' the subject of *exspectari.* **in itinere:** 'on the way.'

4 **mulieres, quique:** = *mulieres et eos, qui,* with *mulieres* and *eos* being objects of *coniecisse.* **per aetatem:** 'by reason of age.' **inutiles:** predicative, 'useless.' **eum locum:** perhaps in the vicinity of the modern city of Mons. **coniecisse:** the Nervii and their allies are the understood subject. **quo:** adverb, = *ad quem.* **exercitui:** *111.* **esset:** relative clause of characteristic; *194a; eum locum . . . quo . . . exercitui aditus non esset* = 'the (sort of) place to which an army has no access.'

They plan to surprise the Romans on the march.

17. 1 His rebus cognitis, exploratores centurionesque praemittit, qui locum idoneum castris deligant. 2 Cum ex dediticiis Belgis reliquisque Gallis complures, Caesarem secuti, una iter facerent, quidam ex his, ut postea ex captivis cognitum est, eorum dierum consuetudine itineris nostri exercitus perspecta, nocte ad Nervios pervenerunt atque his demonstrarunt: *inter singulas legiones impedimentorum magnum numerum intercedere, neque esse quicquam negotii, cum prima legio in castra venisset reliquaeque legiones magnum spatium abessent, hanc sub sarcinis adoriri;* 3 *qua pulsa impedimentisque direptis, futurum, ut reliquae contra consistere non auderent.* 4 Adiuvabat etiam eorum consilium, qui rem deferebant, quod Nervii antiquitus, cum equitatu nihil possent (neque enim ad hoc tempus ei rei student, sed, quicquid possunt, pedestribus valent copiis), quo facilius finitimorum equitatum, si praedandi causa ad eos venissent, impedirent, teneris arboribus incisis atque inflexis, crebrisque in latitudinem ramis enatis, et rubis sentibusque interiectis, effecerant, ut instar muri hae saepes munimentum praeberent, quo non modo non intrari, sed ne perspici quidem posset. 5 His rebus cum iter agminis nostri impediretur, non omittendum sibi consilium Nervii existimaverunt.

1 **qui . . . deligant:** 'in order to choose'; *193a; 291a, b.* **castris:** *108a.*

2 **ex . . . Gallis:** after *complures; 97d.* **dediticiis:** the Suessiones (II.13.1), the Bellovaci (II.15.1), and the Ambiani (II.15.2). **secuti:** *226c.* **facerent:** *185c.* **quidam:** *168.* **ut:** 'as.' **consuetudine . . . perspecta:** *144b2.* **eorum dierum consuetudine itineris nostri exercitus:** 'the custom of the march of our army of those days,' i.e., the three days when Caesar was advancing into the country of the Nervians (II.16.1). **demonstrarunt:** *64a1.* **im-**

pedimentorum: *271; 74d.* **numerum:** 'quantity.' **neque esse quicquam negotii:** 'and that it was no trouble,' lit. 'and it was not anything of trouble'; *97b; 168; 49a.* **esse:** the subject is *adoriri;* 'it was no trouble to attack'; *222b.* **castra:** the place selected for a camp; the camp would not be fortified until the legions arrived; *292; 293.* **spatium:** *118a.* **hanc:** *legionem,* i.e., the first legion. **sarcinis:** 'packs.' The plan was to attack the first legion to come up, just as it reached the place chosen for encampment, before the soldiers could deposit their packs and get themselves ready for fighting; *290.*

3 **qua pulsa:** 'when this (legion) had been routed'; *144b2.* **futurum:** sc. *esse,* the subject is *ut ... auderent;* 'it would be that'; *203.1.* **reliquae:** sc. *legiones.* **contra:** adverb.

4 **Adiuvabat etiam eorum consilium, qui rem deferebant:** 'was also aiding the plan of those who were report-ing this information (*rem*).' But what is the subject of *adiuvabat?* The whole clause **quod Nervii ... effecer-ant:** 'the fact that the Nervii had brought it about'; *198b.* **antiquitus:** adv., 'long ago.' **cum ... possent:** *184a.* **equitatu:** *142a.* **nihil:** *118c.* **neque enim:** 'and in fact ... not.' **ei rei student:** 'they give attention to that thing (the cavalry)'; *105.* **quicquid possunt, pedestribus valent copiis:** 'to whatever degree they are able, they are strong in infantry forces.' **quicquid:** *118b.* **copiis:** *142a.* **quo ... impedirent:** *193b.* **praedandi causa:** 'in order to plunder'; *230.1.* **venissent:** *220.* **teneris ... inflexis:** 'cutting into young trees and bending them over'; how lit.? *144b2.* **in latitudinem:** 'at the sides,' lit. 'in(to) width.' **ramis enatis:** with *crebris,* 'letting the branches grow thickly,' lit. 'with thick branches having been grown out'; *151; 61a3.* **rubis sentibusque interiectis:** 'planting briars and thorn-bushes in the intervening spaces'; how lit.? **effecerant, ut ... praeberent:** *203.3.* **instar muri:** 'like a wall,' lit. 'the likeness of a wall'; *instar,* indeclinable, is in apposition to *munimentum; 94b.* **hae saepes:** 'these hedges,' nominative; *15b.* **munimentum:** 'line of defense'; *74d.* **praeberent:** 'provided.' **quo non modo non intrari, sed ne perspici quidem posset:** 'into which one could not only not enter, but through which one could not even see,' lit. 'to where it could not only not be entered, but not even seen through'; *73d; 237c.* **quo:** adverb = *in quod* (*munimentum*). By cutting into young trees near the root they were able to bend these down to a horizontal position without killing them. The stem of the tree would then increase in size very slowly, but along the trunk branches would grow out, above and on the sides (*in latitudinem*). In the spaces along the line of defense not filled by trees thus trained, briars and thorn-bushes were planted. The whole formed a living and impenetrable hedge. Similar hedges are still found in this region.

5 **Nervii existimaverunt:** the main clause of the sentence, which introduces an indirect statement that incor-porates a *cum*-clause. **impediretur:** *184a.* **non omittendum sibi consilium:** 'they ought not to disregard this plan.' How lit.? **omittendum:** *89c; 73e.* **sibi:** *110.* **consilium:** the plan of attack proposed above in II.17.2-3.

The Romans make camp on a height sloping to the river.

18. 1 Loci natura erat haec, quem locum nostri castris delegerant. Collis ab summo aequaliter declivis ad flumen Sabim, quod supra nominavimus, vergebat. 2 Ab eo flumine pari acclivitate collis nasce-batur adversus huic et contrarius, passus circiter CC infimus apertus, ab superiore parte silvestris, ut non facile introrsus perspici posset. 3 Intra eas silvas hostes in occulto sese continebant; in aperto loco secundum flumen paucae stationes equitum videbantur. Fluminis erat altitudo pedum circiter trium.

1 **Loci natura erat haec, quem locum nostri castris delegerat:** translate as if *natura loci, quem nostri castris delegerant, erat haec.* **haec:** 'as follows'; *161a.* **locum:** *165a.* **castris:** *112a.* The site has been identified, on the left or north bank of the Sabis (*Sambre*), in France, near the Belgian frontier, opposite the city of Hautmont; Map 6, A. **Collis:** on which the camp was laid out. **ab summo aequaliter declivis:** 'sloping evenly from the top.' **supra:** II.16.1. **nominavimus:** 'we have mentioned by name'; *156.* **vergebat:** 'was inclining.'

2 **Ab eo:** 'from the'; *160d.* **pari acclivitate:** 'with similar upward slope'; *143a.* **nascebatur:** 'arose.' **adversus huic et contrarius:** 'facing this (hill) and opposite (to it),' on the south side of the Sabis; the highest part of the second hill is at B on Map 6. **huic:** *108a.* **passus:** *118a.* **CC:** *ducentos; 36.* How far? *243b.* **infimus:** 'at the lower edge' of the hill, along the river. **apertus:** free from woods. **ab superiore parte silvestris:** 'wooded on the up-per portion'; *126c.* **ut:** 'so that'; *197a.* **introrsus:** 'within.'

3 **aperto loco:** indicated on Map 6, between the river and the broken line marking the northern limit of the woods. **secundum:** preposition, 'along.' **stationes:** 'pickets,' i.e., small units of men with defensive responsibili-ties. **videbantur:** translate as passive. **pedum:** *100b.* **trium:** *37b.*

A furious attack is made on the Romans while they are fortifying the camp.

19. 1 Caesar, equitatu praemisso, subsequebatur omnibus copiis; sed ratio ordoque agminis aliter se habebat ac Belgae ad Nervios detulerant. 2 Nam quod hostibus appropinquabat, consuetudine sua

Caesar VI legiones expeditas ducebat; post eas totius exercitus impedimenta collocarat; 3 inde duae legiones, quae proxime conscriptae erant, totum agmen claudebant praesidioque impedimentis erant. 4 Equites nostri, cum funditoribus sagittariisque flumen transgressi, cum hostium equitatu proelium commiserunt. 5 Cum se illi identidem in silvas ad suos reciperent ac rursus ex silva in nostros impetum facerent neque nostri longius, quam quem ad finem prospectus ac loca aperta pertinebant, cedentes insequi auderent, interim legiones VI, quae primae venerant, opere dimenso castra munire coeperunt. 6 Ubi prima impedimenta nostri exercitus ab eis, qui in silvis abditi latebant, visa sunt, quod tempus inter eos committendi proelii convenerat, ita ut intra silvas aciem ordinesque constituerant atque ipsi sese confirmaverant, subito omnibus copiis provolaverunt impetumque in nostros equites fecerunt. 7 His facile pulsis ac proturbatis, incredibili celeritate ad flumen decucurrerunt, ut paene uno tempore et ad silvas et in flumine et iam in manibus nostris hostes viderentur. 8 Eadem autem celeritate adverso colle ad nostra castra atque eos, qui in opere occupati erant, contenderunt.

1 **equitatu praemisso:** 288. **omnibus copiis:** 137b. **ratio ordoque:** 'principle of arrangement,' lit. 'principle and arrangement,' hendiadys; 238d. **aliter se habebat ac Belgae:** 'were different from what the Belgians,' lit. 'was holding itself otherwise than the Belgians.' **habebat:** 173a. **ac:** 233c.

2 **quod:** causal. **hostibus:** 105. **consuetudine sua:** 'in accordance with his usual practice,' when in the enemy's country; 136c. **VI:** 38b. The legions were those numbered 7-12. **expeditas:** predicative, 'in light order'; without the packs (*sarcinae*), which in such cases were doubtless carried with the heavy baggage; 115b. **impedimenta:** 271. **collocarat:** full form? 64a1.

3 **duae legiones:** numbered 13 and 14 (see II.2.1). **proxime:** 35. **praesidio, impedimentis:** 112b; 288.

4 **transgressi:** to the south side of the Sabis. **cum:** 137c. **equitatu:** the cavalry (II.18.3) must have been furnished by the Atrebatians and Viromanduans, not by the Nervians (II.17.4).

5 **identidem:** 'repeatedly.' **suos:** the enemy's infantry, concealed in the woods (II.18.3). **reciperent:** 175d. **neque:** translate as if *et . . . non*. **longius:** 'further.' **quem ad finem:** = *ad eum finem ad quem*, 'to the limit to which.' **prospectus:** 'line of sight.' **loca aperta pertinebant:** 'the open ground was extending.' **cedentes:** sc. *eos* (*hostes*), object of *insequi*; 'as they retreated.' **primae venerant:** 'had been the first to come up'; 152b. **opere dimenso:** 'having measured off the work'; 144b2; 59b; 293.

6 **prima impedimenta:** 'the first part of the baggage train'; Map 6; 152a. **nostri exercitus:** genitive. **abditi latebant:** '(having been) concealed, were hidden.' **visa sunt:** passive in meaning. **quod tempus:** i.e., *tempus* (in thought an appositive of the clause *Ubi . . . visa sunt*, but attracted into the relative clause) . . . *quod convenerat*, 'the time which had been agreed on,' lit. 'which time'; 165b. **committendi proelii:** dependent on *tempus*, 230.1. **ita ut:** 'just as.' **ipsi sese confirmaverant:** 'had encouraged one another.' **copiis:** 137b. **nostros equites:** who had crossed the river (above: II.19.4).

7 **incredibili:** 74f. **decucurrerunt:** 'they ran down' the sloping ground between the edge of the forest and the river. **ut:** 'so that'; 197a. **tempore:** 'instant.' **ad silvas:** 'near the woods,' whence they had just emerged. **in manibus nostris:** in English idiom, 'upon us'; how lit.? **viderentur:** 'they were seen.'

8 **adverso colle:** '(although) the hill (was) facing (them)'; 144b5. **occupati:** 'engaged'; 148c. **contenderunt:** the Belgians may have covered the distance between the woods on the south side of the Sabis and the site of the Roman camp in ten minutes; the distance is about two-thirds of an English mile.

Discipline and training enable the soldiers to meet the emergency.

20. 1 Caesari omnia uno tempore erant agenda: vexillum proponendum, quod erat insigne, cum ad arma concurri oporteret; signum tuba dandum; ab opere revocandi milites; qui paulo longius aggeris petendi causa processerant, arcessendi; acies instruenda, milites cohortandi, signum dandum. 2 Quarum rerum magnam partem temporis brevitas et incursus hostium impediebat. 3 His difficultatibus duae res erant subsidio, scientia atque usus militum, quod superioribus proeliis exercitati, quid fieri oporteret, non minus commode ipsi sibi praescribere, quam ab aliis doceri poterant, et quod ab opere singulisque legionibus singulos legatos Caesar discedere, nisi munitis castris, vetuerat. 4 Hi propter propinquitatem et celeritatem hostium nihil iam Caesaris imperium exspectabant, sed per se, quae videbantur, administrabant.

1 **Caesari:** emphatic, hence placed at the beginning; 110; 229c. **vexillum:** 'the flag'; 284b3. **proponendum, dandum, revocandi,** etc.: sc. *erat, erant*; 229c. **quod erat insigne, cum ad arma concurri oporteret:** 'which was the sign that the soldiers should arm,' lit. 'which was the signal when there ought to be a running together to arms.' **insigne:** here the noun, not the adjective. **ad arma concurri:** 73d. **oporteret:** 73c. **tuba:** 'with the

trumpet'; the signal was to 'fall in'; *286a1*. **opere:** the 'work' of constructing the camp. **revocandi** (erant): 'had to be recalled.' **qui:** as antecedent sc. *ei* (*milites*), subject of *arcessendi* (*erant*). **paulo longius:** 'a little further' than usual; *140*. **aggeris:** 'material' for the rampart, in this case probably wood; *230.1*; *293*. **arcessendi** (erant): 'had to be sent for.' **cohortandi** (erant): see I.25.1. **signum dandum** (erat): 'the signal' for battle 'had to be given'; *286c*.

2 **Quarum:** *167*. **temporis brevitas et incursus hostium:** *239c*. **brevitas:** 'the shortness.' **incursus:** 'the on-rush.' **impediebat:** *173a*.

3 **His ... subsidio:** 'Two things served to offset these disadvantages,' explained by *scientia ... poterant* and *quod ab opere ... vetuerat*; how lit.? *112b*. **quod:** 'the fact that'; *198b*. **superioribus proeliis exercitati, quid fieri oporteret, non minus commode ipsi sibi praescribere, quam ab aliis doceri poterant:** translate as if *ipsi, superioribus proeliis exercitati, poterant praescribere sibi quid fieri oporteret non minus commode quam poterant doceri ab aliis*. **oporteret:** *204.2*. **et quod:** 'and the fact that'; this clause explains the second circumstance that offset the Romans' difficulties; *198b*. **singulis legionibus singulos legatos discedere:** 'the several lieutenants to depart from their respective legions,' i.e., 'each lieutenant to depart from his individual legion'; see I.48.5. **discedere:** *200b*. **nisi munitis castris:** 'unless with the camp fortified,' i.e., until the work was done; *144b2*.

4 **Hi:** the *legatus* in charge of each legion. **nihil:** adverbial accusative; *118c*. **per se:** 'on their own responsibility.' **quae videbantur:** '(those things) which seemed good,' which is often the sense when *videor* is used absolutely. These veterans knew what to do when they saw the enemy coming, and did not lose their heads.

They form hurriedly; under Caesar's encouragement they fight desperately.

21. 1 Caesar, necessariis rebus imperatis, ad cohortandos milites, quam in partem fors obtulit, decucurrit et ad legionem decimam devenit. 2 Milites non longiore oratione cohortatus, quam uti suae pristinae virtutis memoriam retinerent neu perturbarentur animo hostiumque impetum fortiter sustinerent, 3 quod non longius hostes aberant, quam quo telum adigi posset, proelii committendi signum dedit. 4 Atque in alteram partem item cohortandi causa profectus pugnantibus occurrit. 5 Temporis tanta fuit exiguitas hostiumque tam paratus ad dimicandum animus, ut non modo ad insignia accommodanda, sed etiam ad galeas induendas scutisque tegimenta detrahenda tempus defuerit. 6 Quam quisque ab opere in partem casu devenit quaeque prima signa conspexit, ad haec constitit, ne in quaerendis suis pugnandi tempus dimitteret.

1 **necessariis rebus imperatis:** 'having given (only) the indispensable orders.' **quam in partem:** = *in eam partem, in quam,* 'into that part (of the army) into which chance offered,' i.e., he simply ran to those nearest him, a statement introduced to explain why Caesar came first to the tenth legion, which, as the most experienced, had least need of the general's presence; *69b*. **decucurrit:** Caesar was perhaps near the northeast corner of the camp (Map 6, A) when he started to rush down the slope to where the troops were forming.

2 **non longiore oratione ... quam uti:** 'with a speech not longer than (what it took to say) that.' **uti ... sustinerent:** substantive clauses giving the gist of the words of exhortation; *199a2*. **neu perturbarentur animo:** we might say 'and keep cool'; how lit.? *142a*; *199d*.

3 **quod ... aberant:** gives the reason for *signum dedit*. **quam quo:** 'than (the distance) to which'; *194b*. **adigi:** present passive infinitve of *adigo*. **signum:** see II.20.1.

4 **alteram partem:** 'another part' of the hastily formed line; apparently Caesar went across to the right wing, where the seventh and twelfth legions were. See Map 6. **pugnantibus occurrit:** 'he met up with men (already) fighting'; *107a*; *175b*.

5 **Temporis ... exiguitas:** 'so short was the time.' How lit.? **hostium:** dependent on *animus*; *233b*; *245d*. **ad insignia accommodanda:** 'for fitting on their decorations,' particularly the crests, which were taken off from the helmets on the march. In battle it was important that the crests be in place, for by differences of these in form and color the different legions and cohorts could be distinguished. **ad galeas induendas:** 'for putting on their helmets'; *282a*. **scutisque tegimenta detrahenda:** 'for drawing the coverings off the shields,' which were protected by coverings against moisture; *127a*; *282c*.

6 **Quam quisque ab opere in partem casu devenit quaeque prima signa conspexit, ad haec constitit:** translate as if: *Quam in partem quisque devenit casu ab opere et ad haec signa quae prima conspexit, constitit*. **Quam ... in partem:** 'Into which part (of the battle-line).' **opere:** the work of building the camp. **ad:** 'near to.' **constitit:** 'he took his stand.' Under ordinary circumstances it was a serious offense for a soldier to be found in a maniple in which he did not belong. **in quaerendis suis:** sc. *signis*; *284b2*. **dimitteret:** 'lose'; *196a*.

22. 1 Instructo exercitu, magis ut loci natura deiectusque collis et necessitas temporis, quam ut rei militaris ratio atque ordo postulabat, cum diversae legiones aliae alia in parte hostibus resisterent, saepibusque densissimis, ut ante demonstravimus, interiectis prospectus impediretur, neque certa subsidia collocari, neque quid in quaque parte opus esset provideri, neque ab uno omnia imperia administrari poterant. 2 Itaque in tanta rerum iniquitate fortunae quoque eventus varii sequebantur.

1 **magis ut . . . quam ut:** 'more as . . . than as'; take *postulabat* with both phrases. **loci:** 'of the ground.' **diversae:** 'separated.' **aliae alia in parte:** fuller expression of the thought in *diversae*; 'one at one point, another at another'; *171c.* **resisterent, impediretur:** *184a.* **densissimis:** 'very thick'; *153a.* **ante:** see II.17.4. **prospectus:** 'the view' over the field of battle. **certa subsidia collocari** (poterant): 'could reserves be posted at fixed points,' lit. 'could fixed reserves be posted,' i.e., the movements of the enemy were so obscured by the thickets that Caesar could not tell where reserve forces could be posted to advantage. **certa:** *151.* **quid . . . opus esset:** *132b; 204.2.* **quaque:** from *quisque.* **provideri:** sc. *poterat,* 'could be foreseen,' the subject is provided by the whole clause *quid in quaque parte opus esset.* **uno:** 'one person.'

2 **in tanta rerum iniquitate:** 'under so disadvantageous conditions,' lit. 'in so great an unevenness of things.' **fortunae:** dependent on *eventus.* **quoque:** just as the conditions were uneven, so 'also' were the outcomes. **eventus varii:** 'various outcomes.'

Two legions drive the Atrebatians across the river, two force back the Viromanduans, but two are outflanked by the Nervians.

23. 1 Legionis VIIII et X milites, ut in sinistra parte aciei constiterant, pilis emissis cursu ac lassitudine exanimatos vulneribusque confectos Atrebates (nam his ea pars obvenerat) celeriter ex loco superiore in flumen compulerunt et, transire conantes insecuti, gladiis magnam partem eorum impeditam interfecerunt. 2 Ipsi transire flumen non dubitaverunt et, in locum iniquum progressi, rursus resistentes hostes, redintegrato proelio, in fugam coniecerunt. 3 Item alia in parte diversae duae legiones, XI et VIII, profligatis Viromanduis, quibuscum erant congressae, ex loco superiore, in ipsis fluminis ripis proeliabantur. 4 At totis fere castris a fronte et a sinistra parte nudatis, cum in dextro cornu legio XII et, non magno ab ea intervallo, VII constitisset, omnes Nervii confertissimo agmine duce Boduognato, qui summam imperii tenebat, ad eum locum contenderunt; 5 quorum pars ab aperto latere legiones circumvenire, pars summum castrorum locum petere coepit.

1 **VIIII, X:** *nonae, decimae; 38b.* **milites:** nominative. **ut . . . constiterant:** 'as they had taken their stand,' i.e., 'given that they had ended up.' **aciei:** *21b.* For the position of the legions see Map 6. **pilis emissis:** 'having hurled their pikes'; *282d.* **lassitudine:** 'fatigue,' resulting from the three-quarter mile dash first downhill to the river, then across the river, and uphill again to the Roman line. **exanimatos:** 'who were out of breath'; *227a1.* **vulneribus confectos:** 'worn out by wounds,' referring to those struck by the pikes. **Atrebates:** accusative. **his:** *107a.* **ea pars:** i.e., the Roman left wing, of which Labienus was in command. **loco superiore:** the Romans, being nearer the top of the hill, were on higher ground. **conantes:** sc. *eos* (*Atrebates*), object of *insecuti.* **impeditam:** by the crossing of the river.

2 **Ipsi:** the soldiers of the ninth and tenth legions. **transire:** *201b.* **locum iniquum:** the 'ground' south of the Sabis, sloping back from the river and in part covered with woods; Map 7. **hostes:** object of *coniecerunt.* **redintegrato proelio:** 'they (the Romans) renewed the battle and'; *144b2.*

3 **alia in parte:** the Roman center, in front of the camp. See Map 7. **diversae:** 'separated,' i.e., 'in different places,' not, as ordinarily, forming a continuous line. **quibuscum:** *125c.* **proeliabantur:** 'were continuing the battle'; *175a.*

4 **a:** *126c.* **nudatis:** not only the 8th and 11th legions in front, but the 9th and 10th legions on the left of the camp, had abandoned their positions to pursue the enemy, leaving the camp 'unprotected' except on the right, where the 12th and 7th legions stood. **cum:** 'since'; *184a.* **XII:** *duodecima.* **non:** with *magno; 239g.* **intervallo:** *138.* **VII:** (*legio*) *septima.* **constitisset:** why singular? *173a.* **omnes Nervii:** their fighting force was estimated by the Remi at 50,000 (II.4.8), but is later reported as 60,000 (II.28.2). **confertissimo agmine:** a mass formation, like that of the Helvetians (I.24.4); called a 'column' (*agmen*), rather than a 'battle-line' (*acies*) because it was still advancing, not yet having divided in order to deliver the attack at two points. **duce Boduognato:** 'led by Boduognatus'; how lit.? *144b2.* **summam imperii:** 'the supreme command.'

5 **quorum pars . . . pars:** 'and a part of these (Nervians) . . . , (while) a part'; *167.* **ab aperto latere:** 'on the exposed flank,' i.e., the right flank. **legiones:** the 7th and 12th. **summum castrorum locum:** 'the height on which the camp was'; how lit.?

The Roman camp is taken; seemingly all is lost.

24. 1 Eodem tempore equites nostri levisque armaturae pedites, qui cum eis una fuerant, quos primo hostium impetu pulsos dixeram, cum se in castra reciperent, adversis hostibus occurrebant ac rursus aliam in partem fugam petebant; 2 et calones, qui ab decumana porta ac summo iugo collis nostros victores flumen transisse conspexerant, praedandi causa egressi, cum respexissent et hostes in nostris castris versari vidissent, praecipites fugae sese mandabant. 3 Simul eorum, qui cum impedimentis veniebant, clamor fremitusque oriebatur, aliique aliam in partem perterriti ferebantur. 4 Quibus omnibus rebus permoti, equites Treveri, quorum inter Gallos virtutis opinio est singularis, qui auxilii causa a civitate ad Caesarem missi venerant, cum multitudine hostium castra nostra compleri, legiones premi et paene circumventas teneri, calones, equites, funditores, Numidas diversos dissipatosque in omnes partes fugere vidissent, desperatis nostris rebus, domum contenderunt; 5 Romanos pulsos superatosque, castris impedimentisque eorum hostes potitos, civitati renuntiaverunt.

1 **levis armaturae pedites:** 'footsoldiers of light armor,' by which Caesar means slingers and bowmen: see II.19.4. **cum eis una:** 'together with them,' the cavalry. **quos . . . pulsos dixeram:** sc. *pulsos esse*, indirect statement after *dixeram*, lit. 'whom I had said to have been routed,' but more smoothly 'whom, as I said, had been routed.' **dixeram:** see II.19.6-7. **recipierent:** force of *re-*? *79d.* **adversis hostibus:** 'the enemy facing (them),' i.e., they were meeting the enemy face-to-face; *107a.* The Nervians came up so rapidly that they were already entering the Roman camp at the time when Caesar's cavalry and light-armed troops, which had been routed on the other side of the Sabis, were just coming back to it again. The descriptive force of the imperfects in this chapter adds to the vividness of the picture.
2 **calones:** 'camp-servants,' chiefly, we may assume, servants of officers. **ab decumana porta:** 'at the rear gate' of the camp, which, since the hill sloped toward the river, was on the highest part of the hill. Map 7, C C; *294a.* **nostros:** the 9th and 10th legions. **praedandi causa egressi:** i.e., they were leaving the camp by the rear gate to hunt for plunder. **hostes . . . versari:** 'that the enemy were moving about.' **praecipites:** 'headlong'; *151.*
3 **eorum, qui:** the drivers of the baggage-train, just coming up; behind it were the 13th and 14th legions bringing up the rear. See Map 7. **oriebatur:** *61b; 173a.* **alii aliam in partem:** 'some in one direction, others in another'; *171c.* **ferebantur:** 'were rushing,' lit. 'were being carried'; *174.*
4 **virtutis opinio:** 'reputation for courage,' meant of the Treveri as a whole, not merely of the cavalry. **singularis:** 'extraordinary'; the implication is that the Treveran horsemen went away not by reason of cowardice but because they thought the day hopelessly lost. **auxilii causa:** Caesar must have made an agreement with the Treveri before starting on this campaign. **civitate:** personified, hence with *a*; *126a.* **cum . . . vidissent:** *185c.* **castra compleri:** the first in a series of indirect statements dependent upon *vidissent*. **legiones:** the 7th and 12th; see Map 7. **diversos dissipatosque:** 'separated,' one body of troops from another, 'and scattered.' **desperatis nostris rebus:** 'despairing of our victory'; *144b3.*
5 **pulsos, superatos:** sc. *esse.* **castris, impedimentis:** after *potitos (esse)*; *131c.*

Caesar rushes into the fight, calls centurions by name, and renews the battle.

25. 1 Caesar ab X legionis cohortatione ad dextrum cornu profectus, ubi suos urgeri signisque in unum locum collatis XII legionis confertos milites sibi ipsos ad pugnam esse impedimento vidit, quartae cohortis omnibus centurionibus occisis signiferoque interfecto, signo amisso, reliquarum cohortium omnibus fere centurionibus aut vulneratis aut occisis, in his primipilo P. Sextio Baculo, fortissimo viro, multis gravibusque vulneribus confecto, ut iam se sustinere non posset, reliquos esse tardiores et non nullos ab novissimis desertores proelio excedere ac tela vitare, hostes neque a fronte ex inferiore loco subeuntes intermittere et ab utroque latere instare et rem esse in angusto vidit, neque ullum esse subsidium, quod summitti posset; 2 scuto ab novissimis uni militi detracto, quod ipse eo sine scuto venerat, in primam aciem processit centurionibusque nominatim appellatis, reliquos cohortatus, milites signa inferre et manipulos laxare iussit, quo facilius gladiis uti possent. 3 Cuius adventu spe illata militibus ac redintegrato animo, cum pro se quisque in conspectu imperatoris etiam in extremis suis rebus operam navare cuperet, paulum hostium impetus tardatus est.

1 **Caesar:** the beginning of a complex sentence which extends to *possent* at the end of II.25.2. The principal clause has for its subject *Caesar*, with which the participles *profectus* and *cohortatus* agree; for its predicate it has the verbs *processit* and *iussit*. The leading subordinate clause is *ubi . . . vidit*, which is so expanded by the intro-

duction of details that *vidit* is repeated for the sake of clarity. These details are expressed in part by infinitives with subject-accusatives dependent on *vidit,* in part by ablatives absolute, and in part by the minor clauses *ut . . . posset* and *quod . . . posset.* **ab X legionis cohortatione:** = *ab decima legione, quam cohortatus erat.* Caesar's account of his personal part in this battle, which was interrupted by his description of the progress of the fighting (II.22-24) is here resumed from II.21.1-4. **X:** *38b; 36.* **suos urgeri:** 'that his men were hard pressed.' **signisque:** the *-que* connects *urgeri* and *esse; signis* refers to 'the standards' of the maniples; *284b2.* **signis in unum locum collatis:** *144b3.* **XII:** *duodecimae.* **XII legionis confertos milites:** 'the soldiers of the twelfth legion, crowded together'; *milites* is the subject of *esse;* the reason for their crowding is explained in the immediately preceding ablative absolute. The crowding, which exposed them all the more to the missiles of the enemy, and their consequent losses, were no doubt in part due to their lack of experience in fighting; this legion, raised in 58 BC (I.10.3), had been in service only a year. During the battle with the Helvetians it guarded the baggage and had no part in the fray. **sibi ipsos ad pugnam esse impedimento:** 'were themselves a hindrance to themselves for fighting'; *112b; 178.* **quartae cohortis:** at the front, perhaps at the end of the first line; *297a.* **centurionibus occisis:** the first of several consecutive ablatives absolute. **signifero:** 'the standard-bearer.' Each cohort had three standards, of which there were thirty in the legion. Here the reference probably is to the standard-bearer who carried the standard of the first maniple of the cohort, which was looked upon as the standard of the cohort; *284b2.* **in his:** 'among them.' **primipilo:** 'the first centurion' of the first cohort, hence regarded as the first centurion of the legion; *275b.* **multis gravibusque:** 'many severe wounds'; *152c.* **confecto:** 'exhausted'; with *primipilo.* Baculus did not die, but lived to establish the reputation of being one of the bravest, if not the most brave, among Caesar's men. **ut:** 'so that'; *197a.* **reliquos:** sc. *centuriones;* Caesar here switches back to accusative and infinitive constructions preceding the second occurrence of *vidit.* **tardiores:** 'less active,' having lost their initiative. **ab novissimis:** 'in the rear ranks'; *126c.* **proelio:** *127a.* **tela vitare:** i.e., were falling back out of the range of missiles. **hostes neque a fronte ex inferiore loco subeuntes intermittere et ab utroque latere instare:** 'that both in front the enemy did not cease coming up from the lower ground (i.e., along the river) and on both flanks were pressing'; see Map 7. The Nervians outnumbered the men of the 12th and 7th legions five or six to one. **neque . . . et:** *233d.* **rem esse in angusto:** 'that matters had reached a crisis,' lit. 'that the situation was in a narrow spot.' **subsidium:** 'reserve force'; the 13th and 14th legions were not yet available, because too far off. **posset:** *194a.*

2 **scuto ab novissimis uni militi detracto:** 'snatching a shield from a soldier in the rear ranks'; how lit.? *144b2.* **uni:** here 'a,' weaker than 'one'; *23a.* **militi:** *109b.* **quod:** causal. **eo:** adverb, '(to) there.' **sine scuto:** in battle even commanders may have carried shields, for protection in an emergency. **nominatim:** Caesar's personal knowledge of his men was always an important factor in his success. **signa inferre:** 'to advance'; *285.* **manipulos laxare:** 'to open up the ranks,' lit. 'to spread out the companies.' **quo:** *193b.*

3 **Cuius:** *167.* **illata:** *69b.* **militibus:** why dative? *107b.* **pro se quisque:** 'each one according to his ability'; *170b.* **etiam in extremis suis rebus:** 'even under conditions of the utmost peril to himself'; how lit.? **operam navare:** 'to do his best,' lit. 'to engage his task energetically.' **cuperet:** *184a.*

Caesar directs the formation of a double front; Labienus sends reinforcements.

26. 1 Caesar, cum VII legionem, quae iuxta constiterat, item urgeri ab hoste vidisset, tribunos militum monuit, ut paulatim sese legiones coniungerent et conversa signa in hostes inferrent. 2 Quo facto, cum alii aliis subsidium ferrent, neque timerent, ne aversi ab hoste circumvenirentur, audacius resistere ac fortius pugnare coeperunt. 3 Interim milites legionum duarum, quae in novissimo agmine praesidio impedimentis fuerant, proelio nuntiato, cursu incitato in summo colle ab hostibus conspiciebantur, 4 et T. Labienus castris hostium potitus et ex loco superiore, quae res in nostris castris gererentur, conspicatus, X legionem subsidio nostris misit. 5 Qui cum ex equitum et calonum fuga, quo in loco res esset, quantoque in periculo et castra et legiones et imperator versaretur, cognovissent, nihil ad celeritatem sibi reliqui fecerunt.

1 **iuxta constiterat:** the 7th legion 'had made their stand nearby' the 12th, on the right wing; see Map 6. **vidisset:** *185c.* **ut . . . inferrent:** 'that the (two) legions gradually draw together, face about, and advance against the enemy,' lit. 'join themselves and advance the turned standards against the enemy'; *199a.* Probably one legion simply took up a position behind the other, facing in the opposite direction, so that the rear of both was secure. **conversa signa:** *285; 228a.*

2 **ferrent:** *184a.* **neque:** translate as if *et . . . non.* **ne:** *202.* **aversi:** 'those in the rear,' lit. 'those turned away'; the new formation is shown on Map 7.

3 **legionum duarum:** the 13th and 14th; see Map 7. **in novissimo agmine:** i.e., in the original marching column, as undertaken that morning before the battle began. **praesidio impedimentis:** *112b.* **cursu incitato:**

'having quickened their pace,' lit. 'with a run having been incited,' i.e., once they were aware of the battle, they hastened to join it. **summo colle:** 'the top of the hill' back of the Roman camp; *152a.*

4 **castris:** *131c.* **loco superiore:** the height on which the Belgian camp was located; Map 7, B. To this height Labienus with the 9th and 10th legions had pursued the Atrebates (II.23.1-2). The probable lines of flight and pursuit are indicated on Map 7. **quae:** *48b.* **gererentur:** *204.2.* **conspicatus:** as binoculars had not yet been invented, Labienus saw with the unaided eye; the distance from camp to camp across the valley was over a mile. **X:** *decimam.* **subsidio nostris:** *112b.*

5 **Qui cum . . . cognovissent:** 'and when they (the soldiers of the Tenth) realized'; *167; 185c.* **Qui:** plural from the idea of *milites* in *legionem.* **quo in loco res esset:** 'how matters stood'; how lit.? *204.2.* **versaretur:** *172b; 204.3.* **nihil ad celeritatem sibi reliqui fecerunt:** 'they spared no effort in regard to speed,' lit. 'they made nothing of a remainder for themselves with regard to speed.' **sibi:** *109a.* **reliqui:** partitive genitive; *97a.*

The Romans gain a complete victory, though the enemy fight with courage.

27. 1 Horum adventu tanta rerum commutatio est facta, ut nostri, etiam qui vulneribus confecti procubuissent, scutis innixi proelium redintegrarent, calones, perterritos hostes conspicati, etiam inermes armatis occurrerent, 2 equites vero, ut turpitudinem fugae virtute delerent, omnibus in locis pugnando se legionariis militibus praeferrent. 3 At hostes etiam in extrema spe salutis tantam virtutem praestiterunt, ut, cum primi eorum cecidissent, proximi iacentibus insisterent atque ex eorum corporibus pugnarent; 4 his deiectis et coacervatis cadaveribus, qui superessent, ut ex tumulo, tela in nostros conicerent et pila intercepta remitterent; 5 ut non nequiquam tantae virtutis homines iudicari deberet ausos esse transire latissimum flumen, ascendere altissimas ripas, subire iniquissimum locum, quae facilia ex difficillimis animi magnitudo redegerat.

1 **etiam qui:** *etiam (ei) qui,* 'even those who.' **procubuissent:** 'had sunk down'; *220.* **scutis:** *131c.* **ut . . . redintegrarent, occurrerent, praeferrent:** three result clauses, the first two in asyndeton; *197b; 238a.* **perterritos hostes:** sc. *esse,* 'that the enemy had become panic-stricken.' **inermes:** with *calones;* placed, for the sake of contrast, next to *armatis;* 'unarmed, rushed against armed (men).'

2 **vero:** *236a.* **delerent:** *196a.* **virtute:** *131a.* **pugnando:** *230.4.* **militibus:** *107b.* **se praeferrent:** 'show themselves superior to,' i.e., 'surpass.' In regular circumstances, the cavalry was rated by the Romans of secondary importance; *269.*

3 **etiam in extrema spe salutis:** 'even in their last hope of safety.' **primi eorum:** 'their foremost ranks'; how lit.? *154a.* **iacentibus insisterent:** 'were standing upon the fallen'; *227a4.* **ex:** *126c.*

4 **coacervatis cadaveribus:** 'when their bodies had been heaped' on those of the Nervians that had first fallen. **qui:** as antecedent supply *ei,* subject of *conicerent.* **superessent:** *220.* **ut ex tumulo:** 'as from a mound.' **conicerent:** 'continued to hurl'; *175.* **pila intercepta remitterent:** 'were throwing back the pikes they had caught,' lit. 'the pikes having been intercepted.' **conicerent, remitterent:** in the same construction as *insisterent, pugnarent;* *197b.*

5 **ut non nequiquam tantae virtutis homines iudicari deberet ausos esse:** a result clause, presenting Caesar's conclusion; 'so that it ought not to be judged that men of so great valor dared in vain'; i.e., they fought in a manner worthy of their heroic advance. **tantae virtutis:** *100a.* **homines . . . ausos esse:** accusative and infinitive after *iudicari;* *62.* **latissimum:** *153a.* **altissimas:** the banks are steep where the Nervians crossed. **quae:** 'things (referring to the actions expressed in the preceding infinitives) which, from things most difficult, their greatness of mind had rendered easy.' **facilia:** *115b.*

Caesar spares the remnant of the Nervians.

28. 1 Hoc proelio facto, et prope ad internecionem gente ac nomine Nerviorum redacto, maiores natu, quos una cum pueris mulieribusque in aestuaria ac paludes coniectos dixeramus, hac pugna nuntiata, cum victoribus nihil impeditum, victis nihil tutum arbitrarentur, 2 omnium, qui supererant, consensu legatos ad Caesarem miserunt seque ei dediderunt; et in commemoranda civitatis calamitate, ex DC ad tres senatores, ex hominum milibus LX vix ad D, qui arma ferre possent, sese redactos esse dixerunt. 3 Quos Caesar, ut in miseros ac supplices usus misericordia videretur, diligentissime conservavit suisque finibus atque oppidis uti iussit et finitimis imperavit, ut ab iniuria et maleficio se suosque prohiberent.

1 **Hoc proelio facto:** 'now that this battle was over'; how lit.? **prope ad internecionem:** 'nearly to utter destruc-

tion.' Six years later, however, the Nervians were expected to send a force of 6000 warriors to Alesia (VII.75.3). **redacto:** 'reduced.' **maiores natu:** 'the elders,' lit. 'those greater in birth'; *142a.* **aestuaria:** here 'tidal marshes,' surrounded by salt water at high tide. **coniectos:** cf. *quos . . . pulsos dixeram* in II.24.1; *89c.* **dixeramus:** see II.16.4. **cum . . . arbitrarentur:** *184a.* **nihil impeditum:** 'that there was nothing to oppose,' lit. 'nothing obstructed.' **victis:** *227a4.* **nihil tutum:** 'no safety,' lit. 'nothing safe.'

2 **omnium:** dependent on *consensu.* **et . . . dixerunt:** translate as if: *dixerunt, in commemoranda civitatis calamitate, sese redactos esse ex DC (senatoribus) ad tres senatores, ex hominum milibus LX vix ad D, qui arma ferre possent.* **in commemoranda:** 'in enumerating'; *230.4.* **DC:** *sescentis (senatoribus).* Reckoning the Nervian army at 60,000 (10,000 more than the Remi reported; II.4.8), 600 *senatores* would average one to every 100 men. **D:** *quingentos,* modified by *vix ad,* 'to barely.' Exaggeration on the part of the suppliants was to be expected. **qui . . . possent:** relative clause of characteristic; *194a.*

3 **Quos:** direct object of *conservavit*; *167.* **ut . . . videretur:** *196a.* **in:** 'toward.' **usus:** sc. *esse,* after *videretur,* in agreement with the subject (Caesar): 'so that he might seem to have employed'; *221b.* **misericordia:** 'compassion'; cf. II.14.4; *131c.* **suisque finibus atque oppidis uti iussit:** 'and he ordered (them) to enjoy their territories and towns'; *200b.* **finitimis:** *105.* **ut . . . prohiberent:** *199a1.* **iniuria et maleficio:** 'wrongdoing and ill treatment' of the weak remnant of the Nervians.

II.29-33: Capture of the Stronghold of the Atuatuci

The Atuatuci gather in one stronghold.

29. 1 Atuatuci, de quibus supra scripsimus, cum omnibus copiis auxilio Nerviis venirent, hac pugna nuntiata, ex itinere domum reverterunt; 2 cunctis oppidis castellisque desertis, sua omnia in unum oppidum, egregie natura munitum, contulerunt. 3 Quod cum ex omnibus in circuitu partibus altissimas rupes deiectusque haberet, una ex parte leniter acclivis aditus in latitudinem non amplius ducentorum pedum relinquebatur; quem locum duplici altissimo muro munierant; tum magni ponderis saxa et praeacutas trabes in muro collocabant. 4 Ipsi erant ex Cimbris Teutonisque prognati, qui, cum iter in provinciam nostram atque Italiam facerent, eis impedimentis, quae secum agere ac portare non poterant, citra flumen Rhenum depositis, custodiam ex suis ac praesidium VI milia hominum una reliquerunt. 5 Hi post eorum obitum multos annos a finitimis exagitati, cum alias bellum inferrent, alias illatum defenderent, consensu eorum omnium pace facta, hunc sibi domicilio locum delegerunt.

1 **supra:** see II.16.3. **cum:** *185c.* **omnibus copiis:** 19,000 men, if they reached the estimate of the Remi (II.4.9); *136b.* **auxilio Nerviis:** *112b.* **ex itinere:** see Vocab., under *iter.*

2 **castellis:** 'fortresses'; small fortified places, perhaps occupied only in time of danger. **oppidum:** 'stronghold,' like that of the Bellovaci in II.13.2. Some locate this stronghold on the hill where now the citadel of Namur is, at the junction of the Meuse and the Sambre and across the Sambre from the city of Namur; see Map 8. Others, considering the hill at Namur too small, prefer, as the site of the stronghold, the hill of Falhize, which lies on the north bank of the Meuse, opposite the town of Huy, 19 miles below Namur. **egregie:** 'outstandingly.'

3 **Quod cum:** 'and although this (stronghold)'; *187*; *167.* **ex omnibus in circuitu partibus:** 'on all sides going round in a circle.' **rupes deiectusque:** 'cliffs and slopes.' **leniter acclivis aditus:** 'a gently rising approach.' If the stronghold was on the hill across from Namur, this narrow 'approach' was on the southwest side. **pedum:** the case is not influenced by *amplius*; *100a*; *129b.* **duplici:** 'double'; *26a.* **ponderis:** *100a.* **praeacutas trabes:** 'beams sharpened at the ends'; *17c.* **in:** 'on.' **collocabant:** 'they were placing,' at the time (*tum*) when Caesar came up; the change of tense from the pluperfect (*munierant*) is to be noted.

4 **Cimbris Teutonisque:** see I.33.4. **prognati:** 'descended'; *128b.* **provinciam:** *259.* **eis impedimentis . . . depositis:** *144b2.* **impedimentis:** 'animals and goods'; the use of *agere,* 'drive,' with *portare,* suggests that cattle or horses as well as portable possessions are here included. **citra flumen Rhenum:** 'on this side of the Rhine river,' i.e., on the west side, from the Roman perspective. **custodiam . . . ac praesidium:** 'as a guard and garrison' of the *impedimenta* and the place, respectively; *115a.* **ex suis:** i.e., *sex milia hominum ex suis*; *97d.* **una:** adv., 'together,' i.e., 'in the same place.'

5 **Hi:** the 6000 Atuatuci, subject of *delegerunt,* the last word of the sentence. **eorum:** the great host of the Cimbrians and Teutons. **obitum:** 'destruction,' at Aquae Sextiae in 102 BC and at Vercellae in 101 BC. **alias . . . alias:** 'sometimes . . . sometimes.' **illatum defenderent:** sc. *bellum,* the opposite perspective on the exact phrase just used (*bellum inferrent*), lit. 'they were defending (against) a war having been brought against (them).' **consensu:** *138.* **eorum omnium:** 'of them all,' including the Atuatuci and their neighbors. **sibi domicilio:** *112b.* **locum:** 'district.'

Caesar besieges the stronghold; the Atuatuci ridicule the siege-works.

30. 1 Ac primo adventu exercitus nostri crebras ex oppido excursiones faciebant parvulisque proeliis cum nostris contendebant; 2 postea vallo pedum XII, in circuitu XV milium crebrisque castellis circummuniti oppido sese continebant. 3 Ubi, vineis actis, aggere exstructo, turrim procul constitui viderunt, primum irridere ex muro atque increpitare vocibus, quod tanta machinatio a tanto spatio institueretur: 4 *quibusnam manibus aut quibus viribus, praesertim homines tantulae staturae* (nam plerumque omnibus Gallis prae magnitudine corporum suorum brevitas nostra contemptui est), *tanti oneris turrim in muro sese collocare posse confiderent?*

1 **primo adventu:** 'at the first arrival', i.e., *primo post adventum tempore*, 'in the initial period after the arrival'; *147b.* **exercitus nostri:** genitive. **crebras excursiones:** 'frequent sallies', a sally being a sudden rush out of a fixed position. **parvulis:** note the diminutive; *76c.*
2 **vallo, castellis:** these (linked by the *-que* of *crebrisque*) formed the line of contravallation; see Map 8. **pedum XII:** in height; *38b; 100a.* **XV milium:** sc. *pedum*, though Caesar in such cases elsewhere has *passuum*. A circuit of three Roman miles seems to satisfy the conditions; *243b.* **circummuniti:** 'hemmed in,' lit. 'fortified all around,' by the wall and forts constructed by the Romans. **oppido:** *131a.*
3 **vineis actis:** *302a.* **aggere exstructo:** '(and) after an embankment had been built up'; *301.* **turrim:** *14b; 302b.* **irridere atque increpitare:** 'they (the Atuatuci) were jeering and taunting,' the historical infinitives add vividness; *182.* **vocibus:** *131a.* **quod tanta machinatio . . . institueretur:** 'because (as they said) so big a siege-machine was being constructed'; *214b.* **a tanto spatio:** 'so far off,' lit. 'at so great an interval'; *126c.*
4 **quibusnam . . . confiderent:** *213b; 212c6.* **Quibusnam manibus:** 'by what hands, indeed'; *48c.* **viribus:** *18a.* **homines tantulae staturae:** the diminutive *tantulae* is scornful, '(being) men of so small a stature,' or 'such little chaps'; *91b; 100a.* **nam . . . est:** *214c.* **plerumque:** adv., 'generally'. **Gallis, contemptui:** both datives, 'is a source of contempt for all the Gauls'; *112b.* **oneris:** 'weight'; *13e.* **confiderent:** 'did they believe'; *217a.*

Frightened by the approach of the tower, they seek peace.

31. 1 Ubi vero moveri et appropinquare moenibus viderunt, nova atque inusitata specie commoti, legatos ad Caesarem de pace miserunt, qui, ad hunc modum locuti, 2 *non se existimare, Romanos sine ope deorum bellum gerere, qui tantae altitudinis machinationes tanta celeritate promovere possent, se suaque omnia eorum potestati permittere* dixerunt; 3 *Unum petere ac deprecari: si forte pro sua clementia ac mansuetudine, quam ipsi ab aliis audirent, statuisset, Atuatucos esse conservandos, ne se armis despoliaret.* 4 *Sibi omnes fere finitimos esse inimicos ac suae uirtuti invidere; a quibus se defendere, traditis armis, non possent.* 5 *Sibi praestare, si in eum casum deducerentur, quamvis fortunam a populo Romano pati, quam ab his per cruciatum interfici, inter quos dominari consuessent.*

1 **moveri:** sc. *turrim.* **moenibus:** *105.* **viderunt:** Atuatuci. **specie:** 'sight'; *21b.* **qui:** subject of *dixerunt*, the last word of II.31.2. **ad hunc modum:** 'in the following way'; *161a.* **locuti:** introduces the indirect speech *non . . . possent*, while the subsequent indirect statement *se . . . permittere* is governed by *dixerunt* at the end of II.32.2.
2 **non:** understand with *sine ope*. **ope:** 'help.' **deorum:** *8d.* **qui:** 'since they (the Romans)'; *194c.* **se suaque omnia:** the object of *permittere*, but assume *se* also as the subject of *permittere*. **eorum:** of the Romans.
3 **Unum:** 'one thing (only),' explained by *ne . . . despoliaret*. **deprecari:** 'begged (for mercy).' **pro:** 'in accordance with.' **clementia ac mansuetudine:** cf. II.14.4. **audirent:** 'they kept hearing about'; *audivissent*, implying a single instance, would have been less complimentary. **conservandos:** sc. *esse*, accusative and infinitive after *statuisset*. **si statuisset . . . , ne despoliaret:** 'if he should have resolved . . . , (then) let him not strip them of their arms'; in the direct form, *si statueris* (future perfect) . . . *noli nos armis despoliare*; *218.1b; 216.* **armis:** *127a.*
4 **Sibi:** after *inimicos*. **virtuti:** *105.* **a:** 'from,' here in the sense of 'against.' **traditis armis:** i.e., *si arma tradita essent; 144b4.*
5 **praestare:** here impersonal, 'it was better.' **eum casum:** 'such an unfortunate circumstance,' involving a choice between the mercy of the Romans and the treatment of their neighbors. **quamvis fortunam:** 'any fortune whatever'; *49a.* **a:** 'at the hands of.' **pati:** subject of *praestare; 222b.* **dominari:** 'to exercise dominion'; *61a1.* **consuessent:** *64a2.*

Caesar sets the conditions for surrender, but the Atuatuci secretly keep back arms.

32. 1 Ad haec Caesar respondit: *se magis consuetudine sua quam merito eorum civitatem conservaturum,*

*si, prius quam murum aries attigisset, se dedidissent; sed deditionis nullam esse condicionem nisi armis tra-
ditis. 2 Se id, quod in Nerviis fecisset, facturum finitimisque imperaturum, ne quam dediticiis populi Romani
iniuriam inferrent. 3 Re nuntiata ad suos, illi se, quae imperarentur, facere dixerunt.* 4 Armorum magna
multitudine de muro in fossam, quae erat ante oppidum, iacta, sic ut prope summam muri aggerisque
altitudinem acervi armorum adaequarent, et tamen circiter parte tertia, ut postea perspectum est,
celata atque in oppido retenta, portis patefactis, eo die pace sunt usi.

1 **consuetudine sua:** 'in accordance with his practice' of mercifully treating a prostrate foe; *136c.* **merito eorum:** 'because of their merit,' i.e., what they deserved; *135a.* **civitatem conservaturum, si, prius quam . . .
attigisset, se dedidissent:** in the direct form, *civitatem conservabo, si, prius quam . . . attigerit* (future perfect), *vos
dedideritis* (future perfect). **aries:** 'battering-ram'; it was a rule of war that besieged cities which did not capitu-
late before the battering-ram touched the walls should, when captured, be given over to destruction; *10e; 302c.*
armis traditis: *144b2.*

2 **id, quod:** *160c.* **in:** 'in the case of.' **facturum:** *89c.* **ne . . . inferrent:** *199a1.* **quam:** *168; 49a.* **dediticiis populi
Romani:** 'those who have surrendered to the Roman people,' lit. 'the (surrendered) subjects of'; *107b.*

3 **quae:** sc. *ea,* the object of *facere,* as antecedent. **imperarentur:** *214a.* **se . . . facere dixerunt:** 'they said that
they were carrying out'; vivid use of the present tense where the future might have been expected.

4 **multitudine:** 'quantity'; with *iacta; 144b2.* **fossam:** Map 8, C. **sic ut . . . adaequarent:** *197b.* **summam muri
aggerisque altitudinem:** 'the full height of the wall and the embankment'; *152a.* The 'embankment' had been
prolonged to the edge of the moat; the deep space between the end of the 'embankment' and the 'wall,' from the
bottom of the moat up, was nearly filled with weapons. **acervi:** nominative plural, 'heaps.' **et tamen:** 'and yet',
i.e., even though they dropped heaps of weapons over the walls. **parte tertia:** sc. *armorum.* **ut postea perspectum est:** 'as was ascertained later.' Caesar can thus explain now what was hidden from him at the time. **celata,
retenta:** with *parte tertia; 144b2.* **patefactis:** 'thrown open.' **pace sunt usi:** 'they enjoyed peace.'

They attack, are defeated, and sold into slavery.

33. 1 Sub vesperum Caesar portas claudi militesque ex oppido exire iussit, ne quam noctu oppidani
a militibus iniuriam acciperent. 2 Illi, ante inito, ut intellectum est, consilio, quod, deditione facta,
nostros praesidia deducturos aut denique indiligentius servaturos crediderant, partim cum eis, quae
retinuerant et celaverant, armis, partim scutis ex cortice factis aut viminibus intextis, quae subito, ut
temporis exiguitas postulabat, pellibus induxerant, tertia vigilia, qua minime arduus ad nostras munitiones ascensus videbatur, omnibus copiis repente ex oppido eruptionem fecerunt. 3 Celeriter, ut ante
Caesar imperaverat, ignibus significatione facta, ex proximis castellis eo concursum est, 4 pugnatum-
que ab hostibus ita acriter est, ut a viris fortibus in extrema spe salutis iniquo loco contra eos, qui ex
vallo turribusque tela iacerent, pugnari debuit, cum in una virtute omnis spes salutis consisteret. 5
Occisis ad hominum milibus IIII, reliqui in oppidum reiecti sunt. 6 Postridie eius diei refractis portis,
cum iam defenderet nemo, atque intromissis militibus nostris, sectionem eius oppidi universam Caesar vendidit. 7 Ab eis, qui emerant, capitum numerus ad eum relatus est milium LIII.

1 **Sub:** 'towards.' **vesperum:** *7b.* **ne . . . acciperent:** *196a.* **quam:** *168; 49a* (as in II.32.2). **a:** as in II.31.4.

2 **ante inito, ut intellectum est, consilio:** 'having formed a plan (lit. 'with a plan having been entered into') beforehand, as was understood (afterward).' **quod . . . crediderant:** causal, explaining what led to the plan being
formed. **praesidia deducturos:** sc. *esse,* 'would withdraw the garrisons' from the forts and the line of circumval-
lation, where the Roman sentries kept watch. **denique:** 'at any rate.' **indiligentius:** 'less carefully'; *153a.* **servaturos:** sc. *esse,* 'would maintain' the garrisons. **partim . . . partim:** 'partly . . . partly,' i.e., some were outfitted in
one way, and some were outfitted in a different way. **cum:** with *armis,* and understood with *scutis.* **ex cortice:** 'of
bark'; *98b.* **aut viminibus intextis:** 'or (of) wicker-work,' lit. 'withes interwoven.' **quae . . . induxerant:** 'which
they had covered'; the antecedent of *quae* is *scutis.* **tertia vigilia:** *242c.* **qua:** adv., 'where.' **minime arduus:** 'least
steep'; *30.* **ascensus:** implies that the Roman line of contravallation, at the point it was attacked, was on ground
somewhat above the level of the plain, so that the enemy, after rushing down from the town, had to advance up
a height in order to storm the Roman fortifications. **copiis:** *137b.* **eruptionem:** 'sortie,' i.e., a sudden and collective attack from a fixed position.

3 **ignibus:** 'by fire-signals'; *131a.* **significatione:** 'warning.' **eo:** to the point attacked. **concursum est:** 'the soldiers rushed,' lit. 'it was rushed together'; *73d.*

4 **ita:** here does not introduce a result clause. **ut . . . pugnari debuit:** a generalizing description in the indicative:

'as it ought to have been fought'; *249b.* **in extrema spe salutis:** cf. II.27.3. **iniquo loco:** *145c.* **vallo:** the Roman line of contravallation. **turribus:** stationed at intervals along the line of contravallation, as on the rampart around a camp. **iacerent:** *194a.* **in una virtute:** 'in valor alone.'

5 **ad:** adverb, 'about,' modifying *quattuor* (IIII).

6 **diei:** *94c.* **refractis:** 'had been burst in'; how lit.? **cum:** *184a.* **iam:** 'any longer.' **sectionem universam:** '(their) confiscated goods all together,' i.e., at auction in one lot. In such cases the buyers who joined in the bid afterwards divided up the purchase among themselves for resale in smaller lots. Such wholesale buyers accompanied Roman armies. In this instance the booty included not only everything that the captured Atuatuci had, but the people themselves, who were sold into slavery. Caesar does not fail to acknowledge that he can be thoroughly ruthless.

7 **qui emerant:** 'who had purchased' the enormous lot. **capitum:** 'of persons,' lit. 'of heads.' **milium:** agrees with *capitum,* after *numerus.* **LIII:** *quinquaginta trium; 38b; 36.* Some of the Atuatuci, however, were still left in the country; cf. V.38.1, V.39.3.

II.34-35: Successful Closing of the Year

Maritime states in northwestern Gaul submit to Publius Crassus.

34. 1 Eodem tempore a P. Crasso, quem cum legione una miserat ad Venetos, Venellos, Osismos, Coriosolitas, Esuvios, Aulercos, Redones, quae sunt maritimae civitates Oceanumque attingunt, certior factus est, omnes eas civitates in dicionem potestatemque populi Romani esse redactas.

1 **P.:** *19a.* **Crasso:** see Vocab. under *Crassus,* (2). **legione una:** the 7th, which must have started for western Gaul soon after the battle of the Sabis. **miserat:** Caesar is the subject, as also of *factus est* below. **Venetos:** see III.8. **Venellos:** for the location of the Venelli and other peoples mentioned, see Map Gallia. **Coriosolitas:** *19f.* **quae:** *164c.* **Oceanum:** the Atlantic; see Vocab.

German tribes offer submission; the army goes into winter quarters; a thanksgiving is decreed at Rome.

35. 1 His rebus gestis, omni Gallia pacata, tanta huius belli ad barbaros opinio perlata est, uti ab eis nationibus, quae trans Rhenum incolerent, legati ad Caesarem mitterentur, qui se obsides daturas, imperata facturas pollicerentur. 2 Quas legationes Caesar, quod in Italiam Illyricumque properabat, inita proxima aestate ad se reverti iussit. 3 Ipse, in Carnutes, Andes, Turonos, quaeque civitates propinquae his locis erant, ubi bellum gesserat, legionibus in hiberna deductis, in Italiam profectus est. 4 Ob easque res ex litteris Caesaris dierum XV supplicatio decreta est, quod ante id tempus accidit nulli.

1 **tanta huius belli ... opinio perlata est:** 'the reputation of this campaign that reached ... was so great,' lit. 'so great a reputation of this war was carried through.' **incolerent:** *220.* **se:** feminine, taking the gender of *nationibus;* hence *daturas* and *facturas* (sc. *esse*) are feminine. **pollicerentur:** *193a.*

2 **Quas:** *167.* **quod:** causal. **Italiam:** here including Cisalpine Gaul; *252b.* **inita proxima aestate:** 'at the beginning of the following summer,' lit. 'with the next summer having been entered into'; *144b1.*

3 **in Carnutes, Andes, Toronos:** take with *legionibus in hiberna deductis; 251.* See Map Gallia. **quaeque civitates:** *et in eas civitates quae; 165c.* **hiberna:** *293.*

4 **easque:** *233b.* **ex:** 'after receipt of.' **litteris:** 'dispatches' to the Roman Senate, reporting his victories. **supplicatio:** 'a solemn thanksgiving,' services of prayer to avert misfortune as well as giving of thanks to the gods for victory. Usually such services lasted only three or four days; the longest previous 'thanksgiving' was of twelve days, decreed after Pompey had ended the war with Mithridates. **quod:** sc. *id,* '(a thing) which,' referring to the fact stated in the preceding clause. If, by comparison, Caesar had written *quae,* then *supplicatio* would be its specific antecedent, whereas the choice of *quod* emphasizes that the idea of the whole preceding clause is the antecedent. **nulli:** emphatic final position; = *nemini; 12d.*

BOOK III

III.1-6: Operations in the Alps

Caesar stations Galba with a small force in the Alps; Galba locates his winter quarters in Octodurus.
1. 1 Cum in Italiam proficisceretur Caesar, Ser. Galbam, cum legione XII et parte equitatus, in Nantuates, Veragros, Sedunosque misit, qui a finibus Allobrogum et lacu Lemanno et flumine Rhodano ad summas Alpes pertinent. 2 Causa mittendi fuit, quod iter per Alpes, quo magno cum periculo magnisque cum portoriis mercatores ire consuerant, patefieri volebat. 3 Huic permisit, si opus esse arbitraretur, uti in his locis legionem hiemandi causa collocaret. 4 Galba, secundis aliquot proeliis factis castellisque compluribus eorum expugnatis, missis ad eum undique legatis obsidibusque datis et pace facta, constituit cohortes duas in Nantuatibus collocare et ipse cum reliquis eius legionis cohortibus in vico Veragrorum, qui appellatur Octodurus, hiemare; 5 qui vicus, positus in valle, non magna adiecta planitie, altissimis montibus undique continetur. 6 Cum hic in duas partes flumine divideretur, alteram partem eius vici Gallis concessit, alteram, vacuam ab his relictam, cohortibus ad hiemandum attribuit. Eum locum vallo fossaque munivit.

1 **proficisceretur:** Caesar 'was departing' on the trip referred to in II.35.3; *185c*. The events of Book III, as a whole, belong to the year 56 BC, but the uprising of the Alpine tribes narrated in chapters 1-6 took place in the latter part of the autumn and early winter of 57 BC. **Italiam:** Cisalpine Gaul; *252b*. **Ser.:** = *Servium*; *19a*. **Galbam:** see Vocab. under *Galba*, (1). **XII:** *duodecima*; *38b*. Caesar had eight legions, numbered VII to XIV inclusive; *267e, f*. **Nantuates:** *251*. The states mentioned can be found on Map 1. **summas Alpes:** 'the highest part of the Alps'; *152a*.
2 **mittendi:** *230.1*. **iter:** 'the route' to Italy, over the pass now known as the Great St. Bernard. **quo:** 'on which (route).' **periculo:** the danger arose not so much from the precipitous way over the mountains as from the hostility of the natives. These lived in part by plundering and by levying tolls (*portoria*; cf. I.18.3) on the goods of traders going over the pass. **patefieri:** 'be made open,' i.e., open without interference; the subject is *iter*; *70b*; *223a*.
3 **Huic:** Galba. **opus esse:** 'that it was necessary.' **arbitraretur:** *220*. **legionem:** the 12th legion had suffered so severely in the battle of the Sabis (II.25) that Caesar would hardly have stationed it at so difficult a post if he had anticipated serious opposition. **collocaret:** *199a6*.
4 **proeliis factis . . . pace facta:** the ablative absolutes indicate successive events. First come the engagements, then the taking of strongholds; later, the sending of envoys, then the giving of hostages; finally, the ratification of peace. **eorum:** the Alpine peoples'. **cohortes duas:** how many men? *267c*. **in Nantuatibus:** perhaps where St. Maurice now is, on the upper Rhone; *251*. **cum:** *137a*. **reliquis cohortibus:** doubtless the two strongest cohorts were detailed for the separate post; how many men the remaining eight contained is difficult to estimate. **vico:** how different from *oppidum*? **Octodurus:** near Martigny, see Map 1. **hiemare:** sc. *constituit*.
5 **qui:** *167*. **valle:** 'valley.' **non magna:** *239g*. **adiecta:** 'adjoining,' lit. 'having been joined to.'
6 **Cum:** *184a*. **hic:** sc. *vicus*. **flumine:** the Dranse, which flows into the Rhone, from the south, at the point where the Rhone turns northwest toward Lake Geneva. **alteram . . . alteram:** *171b*. **Gallis:** *107b*. **vacuam:** predicative, after *relictam*; Galba expelled the inhabitants from the part of Octodurus which was on the west bank of the Dranse, and turned the dwellings into winter quarters; *88b*.

There is a sudden uprising of the inhabitants.
2. 1 Cum dies hibernorum complures transissent, frumentumque eo comportari iussisset, subito per exploratores certior factus est, ex ea parte vici, quam Gallis concesserat, omnes noctu discessisse, montesque, qui impenderent, a maxima multitudine Sedunorum et Veragrorum teneri. 2 Id aliquot de causis acciderat, ut subito Galli belli renovandi legionisque opprimendae consilium caperent: 3 primum, quod legionem, neque eam plenissimam, detractis cohortibus duabus et compluribus singillatim, qui commeatus petendi causa missi erant, absentibus, propter paucitatem despiciebant; 4 tum etiam, quod propter iniquitatem loci, cum ipsi ex montibus in vallem decurrerent et tela conicerent, ne primum quidem impetum suum posse sustineri existimabant. 5 Accedebat quod suos ab se liberos abstractos obsidum nomine dolebant, et Romanos non solum itinerum causa, sed etiam perpetuae possessionis culmina Alpium occupare conari et ea loca finitimae provinciae adiungere sibi persuasum habebant.

1 **hibernorum:** 'of (life in) winter quarters.' **transissent:** *68b; 185c.* **eo:** to the part of the town used for winter quarters. **iussisset:** sc. *Galba.* **exploratores:** *287.* **concesserat:** *214c.* The Gauls occupied the part of the town on the east bank. **impenderent:** *214a.* **a:** with the ablative of agent because of the idea of *homines* in *multitudo; 126b.*

2 **Id:** explained by the clause *ut . . . caperent; 203.4.* **aliquot de causis:** 'for several reasons'; Caesar then goes on to list them: *primum, quod* ('first because') *. . . tum etiam, quod* ('then also because'), etc. **renovandi:** 'for renewing.' *102; 230.1.*

3 **neque eam plenissimam:** 'and that not at its most full,' i.e., 'not even at full strength'; *161c.* The reasons for its depletion are explained by the following ablative absolutes. **compluribus:** sc. *militibus.* **singillatim:** 'as individuals,' not sent out as cohorts or maniples. **commeatus petendi causa:** *230.1.*

4 **tum etiam:** *deinde* is more common as correlative with *primum; 237b.* **cum:** *184a.* **ipsi:** *Galli.* **ne primum quidem impetum suum:** the subject of *posse sustineri,* 'not even their first assault'; *237c.*

5 **Accedebat quod:** 'there was the additional fact that'; *accedit,* as if *additur,* can have an impersonal passive sense of 'there is added'; this sentence thus continues Caesar's listing of the reasons for the Alpine uprising. **quod . . . dolebant:** *198b.* **abstractos:** 'had been taken away'; *89c; 223a2.* **nomine:** 'under the name'; *136b.* **Romanos . . . conari:** accusative and infinitive after *sibi persuasum habebant.* **itinerum causa:** cf. III.1.2. **possessionis:** also after *causa.* **culmina:** 'summits,' commanding the passes; *12e.* **finitimae provinciae:** *107b; 259.* **adiungere:** 'to annex,' complementary infinitive with *conari; 221a.* **sibi persuasum habebant:** 'were convinced (that),' lit. 'had (it) persuaded (to) themselves (that)'; *229a.* **persuasum:** predicative, in agreement with the infinitive clause *Romanos . . . conari,* object of *habebant; 148d.*

Galba, calling a council, decides not to retreat.

3. 1 His nuntiis acceptis, Galba, cum neque opus hibernorum munitionesque plene essent perfectae, neque de frumento reliquoque commeatu satis esset provisum, quod, deditione facta obsidibusque acceptis, nihil de bello timendum existimaverat, consilio celeriter convocato, sententias exquirere coepit. 2 Quo in consilio, cum tantum repentini periculi praeter opinionem accidisset ac iam omnia fere superiora loca multitudine armatorum completa conspicerentur, neque subsidio veniri neque commeatus supportari, interclusis itineribus, possent, prope iam desperata salute, non nullae eius modi sententiae dicebantur, ut, impedimentis relictis eruptione facta, isdem itineribus, quibus eo pervenissent, ad salutem contenderent. 3 Maiori tamen parti placuit, hoc reservato ad extremum consilio, interim rei eventum experiri et castra defendere.

1 **His nuntiis:** see II.2.1. **neque . . . neque:** 'not . . . and not.' **opus hibernorum munitionesque:** 'the work on the winter quarters,' in general, 'and the fortifications' (see III.1.6). **plene essent confectae:** 'had been fully finished.' **perfectae:** agreement? *172b.* **de:** 'for.' **satis esset provisum:** 'sufficient provision had been made,' lit. 'it had been sufficiently provided for'; *73d.* **quod:** causal, explaining why the previous two circumstances were so. **nihil . . . timendum:** sc. *esse,* '(that) nothing was to be feared'; *73e.* **consilio:** doubtless of the centurions; cf. I.40.1. **sententias exquirere:** 'to ask for opinions' regarding the best course to pursue.

2 **Quo:** *167.* **cum . . . possent:** *184a.* **tantum repentini periculi:** 'so great danger suddenly,' lit. 'so much of sudden danger'; *97b.* **praeter opinionem:** 'contrary to expectation.' **completa:** sc. *esse,* participle here used as a predicate adjective, '(to be) filled up'; *221b.* **subsidio:** *112a.* **veniri:** impersonal passive infinitive after an implied *posset; 73d.* **neque subsidio veniri:** sc. *posset,* 'and help could not come,' lit. 'and there was not able to be a coming as a source of aid.' **interclusis itineribus:** *144b3.* **prope:** adv., 'nearly.' **prope iam desperata salute:** *144b2.* **eius modi:** 'of the following sort'; *100a.* **ut . . . contenderent:** explains *eius modi; 203.4.* **isdem:** *45.* **itineribus:** *134a.* **pervenissent:** *220.* **ad salutem:** 'to (a place of) safety.'

3 **Maiori parti placuit:** 'the majority decided,' lit. 'it was pleasing to the greater part'; *73c.* **hoc . . . consilio:** i.e., the proposal to expedite their escape; *144b2.* **ad extremum:** 'to the last'; *154a.* **rei eventum experiri:** 'to await (lit. 'put to the test') the outcome of the situation.'

The inhabitants, superior in numbers, make a furious attack.

4. 1 Brevi spatio interiecto, vix ut eis rebus, quas constituissent, collocandis atque administrandis tempus daretur, hostes ex omnibus partibus, signo dato, decurrere, lapides gaesaque in vallum conicere. 2 Nostri primo integris viribus fortiter repugnare neque ullum frustra telum ex loco superiore mittere, et quaecumque pars castrorum nudata defensoribus premi videbatur, eo occurrere et auxilium ferre; 3 sed hoc superari, quod diuturnitate pugnae hostes defessi proelio excedebant, alii integris viribus succedebant. 4 Quarum rerum a nostris propter paucitatem fieri nihil poterat, ac non modo defesso ex pugna excedendi, sed ne saucio quidem eius loci, ubi constiterat, relinquendi ac sui recipiendi facultas dabatur.

1 **Brevi spatio interiecto:** 'after a brief interval,' lit. 'with a brief space (of time) having been put in between.' **vix ut:** 'scarely (enough of an interval) so that'; *197a.* **eis rebus . . . collocandis atque administrandis:** *230.2.* **constituissent:** *220.* **decurrere, conicere:** historical infinitives; *182.* **gaesa:** Gallic 'javelins'; *309.*

2 **integris:** 'unimpaired'; *22f; 135a.* **repugnare, mittere, occurrere, ferre:** also historical infinitives. **neque ullum frustra telum . . . mittere:** 'and they were not sending any missile in vain,' i.e., they achieved some damaging effect from every throw. **ex loco superiore:** i.e., the rampart of the camp. **quaecumque pars:** 'whatever part'; *50a; 192.* **nudata defensoribus:** 'having been stripped of its defenders'; *127a.* **eo:** = *in eam partem;* 'to that part they rushed.'

3 **hoc superari, quod:** 'they were overcome because of this, namely that'; *135a; 182.* **defessi:** '(when) exhausted.' **proelio:** *127a.* **alii:** '(and) others'; *238a.* **viribus:** *143a.* **succedebant:** 'were taking their places.'

4 **rerum:** dependent on *nihil; 97a.* **non modo defesso:** translate as if *non modo non defesso;* 'not only not to one (who was) exhausted,' i.e., one on the Roman side; *236d; 154a.* **ex pugna excedendi:** dependent on *facultas dabatur,* 'was the opportunity given for withdrawing from the battle.' **sed ne saucio quidem:** 'but not even to one (who was) wounded'; *154a; 237c.* **eius loci . . . relinquendi ac sui recipiendi:** likewise dependent on *facultas dabatur:* 'for abandoning that place . . . and retreating'; *230.1.*

The Romans, in dire straits, resolve upon a sally.

5. 1 Cum iam amplius horis sex continenter pugnaretur ac non solum vires, sed etiam tela nostros deficerent, atque hostes acrius instarent languidioribusque nostris vallum scindere et fossas complere coepissent, resque esset iam ad extremum perducta casum, 2 P. Sextius Baculus, primi pili centurio, quem Nervico proelio compluribus confectum vulneribus diximus, et item C. Volusenus, tribunus militum, vir et consilii magni et virtutis, ad Galbam accurrunt atque unam esse spem salutis docent, si, eruptione facta, extremum auxilium experirentur. 3 Itaque, convocatis centurionibus, celeriter milites certiores facit, paulisper intermitterent proelium ac tantum modo tela missa exciperent seque ex labore reficerent; post, dato signo, ex castris erumperent atque omnem spem salutis in virtute ponerent.

1 **Cum iam . . . pugnaretur:** 'when fighting had now been going on'; *175f; 73d.* **horis:** *129a.* **deficerent:** 'were failing,' in the sense of 'were lacking to.' **acrius:** *34a.* **languidioribus nostris:** 'as our men became weaker'; how lit.? *144b3.* **vallum scindere:** 'to tear down the rampart' by pulling up the palisades along the outer edge. **fossas:** plural because the parts of the moat on the four sides are thought of as separate trenches. **iam ad extremum casum:** i.e., the moment deferred at III.3.3 (*ad extremum*) had arrived. **perducta:** with *esset; 185c.*

2 **P. Sextius Baculus, primi pili centurio:** 'the chief centurion,' i.e., the first centurion of the first cohort, hence regarded as the first centurion of the legion; *275b.* **quem . . . confectum** (esse) **diximus:** 'whom, (as) we said, had been exhausted'; see II.25.1. **Nervico proelio:** 'in the battle with the Nervians,' lit. 'in the Nervian battle'; *147b.* The battle had taken place not long before (see II.19-28). **Volusenus:** the suggestion was evidently made first by Baculus to his ranking officer, Volusenus, who hurried with him to Galba. **tribunus:** *274.* **consilii magni:** 'of excellent judgment'; *100a.* **unam esse spem salutis . . . si:** '(that) the only hope of safety was if they, by making a sally, put their ultimate reserve to the test'; the *si*-clause explains what their only hope is. **facta eruptione:** *144b6.* **extremum auxilium:** i.e., their only hope for safety is to challenge their ultimate reserve, namely their own courage.

3 **centurionibus:** how many ordinarily in 8 cohorts? *275b.* **milites certiores facit:** 'he (Galba) informed the soldiers,' through the centurions. **intermitterent proelium:** 'to stop fighting,' lit. 'let them discontinue the battle,' an indirect command reporting what would have been issued as a direct command (in the imperative) to the soldiers; *216.* **tantum modo tela missa exciperent:** 'only to parry,' with their shields, 'the missiles hurled' by the enemy, in order to save their strength for the sortie. **post:** adv., 'afterward.' **erumperent:** 'to burst forth,' suddenly assuming the offensive; *216.*

The Romans prevail; but Galba withdraws to the Province.

6. 1 Quod iussi sunt, faciunt, ac subito, omnibus portis eruptione facta, neque cognoscendi, quid fieret, neque sui colligendi hostibus facultatem relinquunt. 2 Ita, commutata fortuna, eos, qui in spem potiundorum castrorum venerant, undique circumventos intercipiunt; et ex hominum milibus amplius XXX, quem numerum barbarorum ad castra venisse constabat, plus tertia parte interfecta, reliquos perterritos in fugam coniciunt ac ne in locis quidem superioribus consistere patiuntur. 3 Sic, omnibus hostium copiis fusis armisque exutis, se in castra munitionesque suas recipiunt. 4 Quo proelio facto, quod saepius fortunam temptare Galba nolebat, atque alio se in hiberna consilio venisse meminerat, aliis occurrisse rebus videbat, maxime frumenti commeatusque inopia permotus, postero die, omnibus eius vici aedificiis incensis, in provinciam reverti contendit, 5 ac, nullo hoste prohibente aut iter demorante, incolumem legionem in Nantuates, inde in Allobroges, perduxit, ibique hiemavit.

1 **Quod iussi sunt, faciunt:** *id, quod facere iussi sunt, faciunt; 160c.* **portis:** *134a; 294a.* **cognoscendi:** after *facultatem; 102; 230.1.* **quid fieret:** after *cognoscendi; 204.2.* **sui colligendi:** 'of collecting their forces (lit. 'themselves'),' scattered on all sides of the camp, in order to resist the four mass attacks launched from the four gates; *154b.*

2 **eos . . . circumventos intercipiunt:** 'they surrounded and cut off those'; *intercipio* here means 'cut short the life of'; *228a.* **potiundorum:** *64b.* **ex . . . interfecta:** translate as if: *plus tertia parte interfecta, ex amplius triginta hominum milibus, quem numerum barbarorum ad castra venisse constabat.* **ex:** *97d.* **amplius, plus:** *129b.* **quem numerum barbarorum . . . venisse constabat:** 'which number of natives was agreed (i.e., well known) to have come'; *constat* is often impersonal, followed by accusative and infinitive (lit. 'and it is agreed that this number had come'). **quem numerum:** *165b.* **plus tertia parte interfecta:** on this reckoning the Roman soldiers on average killed three to five Gauls apiece. It seems hardly credible that a force of more than 30,000 men, attacking under conditions very favorable to themselves, could have been beaten off even by a Roman force less than one tenth as large; perhaps the estimate of the number of the enemy was exaggerated. **ne in locis quidem superioribus:** 'not even on the heights' surrounding the valley; see III.1.5.

3 **fusis:** 'routed.' **armisque exutis:** 'and deprived of their weapons,' which they must have left behind in their hasty flight; *exutis* agrees with *copiis*, while *armis* is ablative of separation after *exutis; 127a.*

4 **Quo proelio facto:** 'after this battle'; how lit.? **quod:** causal. **saepius:** 'too often'; *153a.* **se . . . venisse:** accusative and infinitive after *meminerat*, 'he was mindful (that).' **alio . . . consilio:** 'with one design,' stated in III.1.2; *138.* **aliis occurrisse rebus videbat:** '(but) he perceived that (he) had run into different conditions,' the *alio consilio* draws a contrast with *aliis rebus* ('one' . . . 'another'; *171c*), implying the impossibility of carrying out the original design with the force at his disposal. **permotus:** with *maxime*; causal in force, capping the ideas in the preceding *quod*-clause; *227a1.* **eius vici:** Octodurus, of which the part assigned to the natives, as well as that occupied by the Romans (III.1.6), was now burned.

5 **iter demorante:** 'delaying his march'; *61a1.* **incolumem:** predicative, 'in safety.'

III.7-16: Campaign against the Veneti

Crassus, wintering near the Ocean, sends to the nearest states for grain.

7. 1 His rebus gestis, cum omnibus de causis Caesar pacatam Galliam existimaret, superatis Belgis, expulsis Germanis, victis in Alpibus Sedunis, atque inita hieme in Illyricum profectus esset, quod eas quoque nationes adire et regiones cognoscere volebat, subitum bellum in Gallia coortum est. 2 Eius belli haec fuit causa. P. Crassus adulescens cum legione VII proximus mare Oceanum in Andibus hiemabat. 3 Is, quod in his locis inopia frumenti erat, praefectos tribunosque militum complures in finitimas civitates frumenti commeatusque petendi causa dimisit; 4 quo in numero est T. Terrasidius missus in Esuvios, M. Trebius Gallus in Coriosolitas, Q. Velanius cum T. Silio in Venetos.

1 **omnibus de causis:** with *existimaret*, 'had every reason to think,' lit. 'in regard to all reasons.' **pacatam:** sc. *esse.* **Galliam:** *256b.* **superatis Belgis:** see II.1-33. **expulsis Germanis:** see I.30-54. **Sedunis:** of the Alpine tribes the Seduni, as the most important, are alone mentioned. **inita hieme:** 'at the beginning of winter'; how lit.? *68b; 144b1.* **profectus esset:** still after *cum.* **subitum:** *151.* **coortum est:** 'broke out,' lit. 'arose'; *61b.*

2 **haec:** 'as follows'; *161a.* **adulescens:** cf. I.52.7 and Vocab. under *Crassus,* (2). **proximus mare Oceanum:** 'very near to the (Atlantic) Ocean,' *proximus* here acts as a preposition.

3 **praefectos:** 'subsidiary officers'; cf. I.39.2. **tribunos militum:** *274.*

4 **Coriosolitas:** *19f; 251.* The peoples mentioned can be found on Map 9.

The Veneti detain his representatives and lead a revolt.

8. 1 Huius est civitatis longe amplissima auctoritas omnis orae maritimae regionum earum, quod et naves habent Veneti plurimas, quibus in Britanniam navigare consuerunt, et scientia atque usu rerum nauticarum reliquos antecedunt, et in magno impetu maris atque aperto paucis portibus interiectis, quos tenent ipsi, omnes fere, qui eo mari uti consuerunt, habent vectigales. 2 Ab his fit initium retinendi Silii atque Velanii, quod per eos suos se obsides, quos Crasso dedissent, recuperaturos existimabant. 3 Horum auctoritate finitimi adducti — ut sunt Gallorum subita et repentina consilia — eadem de causa Trebium Terrasidiumque retinent; et celeriter, missis legatis, per suos principes inter se coniurant, *nihil, nisi communi consilio, acturos eundemque omnes fortunae exitum esse laturos:* 4 reliquasque civitates sollicitant, ut in ea libertate, quam a maioribus acceperint, permanere, quam Romanorum servitutem perferre malint. 5 Omni ora maritima celeriter ad suam sententiam perducta, communem legationem ad P. Crassum mittunt: *si velit suos recuperare, obsides sibi remittat.*

1 **Huius est civitatis longe amplissima auctoritas:** translate as if *auctoritas huius civitatis est longe amplissima.* **Huius civitatis:** of the Venetans, the last state mentioned in III.7. **omnis orae maritimae regionum earum:** 'of the entire sea-coast in (lit. 'of') these regions,' *omnis orae maritimae* is a contracted expression for *omnium civitatum orae maritimae,* 'of all the states of the sea-coast.' **et . . . et . . . et:** after the causal *quod,* listing the reasons that explain their *auctoritas; 233d.* **in . . . navigare:** 'to make the voyage to.' The Venetans had developed an extensive carrying business between Gaul and Britain. **Britanniam:** *263.* **consuerunt:** *64a2; 176b.* **scientia:** *142a.* **rerum nauticarum:** 'nautical matters.' **reliquos:** *171a.* **antecedunt:** 'excel.' **in magno impetu maris atque aperto paucis portibus interiectis:** 'with (only) a few ports placed amidst the force of a great and open sea,' lit. 'in the great and open force of the sea'; *144b3.* **quos:** *portibus* is the antecedent. **omnes:** object of *habent,* antecedent of *qui.* **eo mari:** the modern Bay of Biscay; *16b; 131c.* **vectigales:** 'subject to tribute'; predicative; *115a, b.* On account of the violence of the sea, and the fewness of the harbors, navigators were obliged to take refuge in the harbors of the Venetans, who charged them tolls.

2 **Ab his fit initium retinendi Silii atque Velanii:** 'These (Venetans) took the first step by detaining Silius and Velanius,' lit. 'a beginning was made by these (Venetans) of detaining'; see III.7.4 for Silius and Velanius. **per eos:** i.e., in exchange for Silius and Velanius; *123a.* **suos se obsides . . . recuperaturos:** i.e., *se recuperaturos (esse) suos obsides.* **dedissent:** *214a.*

3 **finitimi:** nominative. **ut:** 'since,' an explanatory parenthesis outlining what Caesar sees as a general truth. The fickleness of the Gauls is again asserted by Caesar at III.19.6. **inter se:** *159.* **nihil . . . acturos eundemque omnes fortunae exitum esse laturos:** translate as if *se acturos (esse) nihil . . . et (se) omnes laturos esse eundem exitum fortunae; 213b.* **eundemque omnes fortunae exitum esse laturos:** 'and they all would bear the same outcome of fortune,' i.e., they would endure whatever happened together equally.

4 **reliquas:** *171a.* **ut . . . malint:** *199a2; 71.* **acceperint:** *220.* **quam:** '(rather) than.'

5 **si . . . remittat:** in the direct form: *si vis tuos recuperare, obsides nobis remitte; 218.1a; 216.*

Caesar orders ships built; the coastal states prepare for war.

9. 1 Quibus de rebus Caesar a Crasso certior factus, quod ipse aberat longius, naves interim longas aedificari in flumine Ligeri, quod influit in Oceanum, remiges ex provincia institui, nautas gubernatoresque comparari iubet. 2 His rebus celeriter administratis, ipse, cum primum per anni tempus potuit, ad exercitum contendit. 3 Veneti reliquaeque item civitates, cognito Caesaris adventu, simul quod, quantum in se facinus admisissent, intellegebant, legatos — quod nomen apud omnes nationes sanctum inviolatumque semper fuisset — retentos ab se et in vincula coniectos, pro magnitudine periculi bellum parare et maxime ea, quae ad usum navium pertinent, providere instituunt, hoc maiore spe, quod multum natura loci confidebant. 4 Pedestria esse itinera concisa aestuariis, navigationem impeditam propter inscientiam locorum paucitatemque portuum sciebant, 5 neque nostros exercitus propter inopiam frumenti diutius apud se morari posse confidebant; 6 *ac iam ut omnia contra opinionem acciderent, tamen se plurimum navibus posse, Romanos neque ullam facultatem habere navium, neque eorum locorum, ubi bellum gesturi essent, vada, portus, insulas novisse;* 7 ac longe aliam esse navigationem in concluso mari atque in vastissimo atque apertissimo Oceano perspiciebant. 8 His initis consiliis, oppida muniunt, frumenta ex agris in oppida comportant, naves in Venetiam, ubi Caesarem primum esse bellum gesturum constabat, quam plurimas possunt, cogunt. 9 Socios sibi ad id bellum Osismos, Lexovios, Namnetes, Ambiliatos, Morinos, Diablintes, Menapios asciscunt; auxilia ex Britannia, quae contra eas regiones posita est, arcessunt.

1 **certior factus:** here participial, 'having been informed,' lit. 'having been made more certain.' **longius:** 'too far

away'; *153a*. Caesar was probably in Cisalpine Gaul; for the revolt of the Venetans came to a head in the early spring, and in April of 56 BC Caesar met Pompey and Crassus at Luca. **naves longas:** 'galleys'; *306a*. **interim:** 'meanwhile,' pending his return to the army. **aedificari:** 'be built.' **Ligeri:** the Loire; *18e*. See Maps 9 and 10. **quod influit in Oceanum:** explains why, although the Venetans were strong on the ocean, the ships were ordered to be built on the Loire. **remiges:** 'rowers.' **nautas:** 'sailors.' **gubernatores:** 'steersmen,' who managed the rudders; *306b*; *84*. The fighting on these ships was to be done by legionaries (III.14.3).

2 **cum primum per anni tempus potuit:** 'as soon as he was able during the time of the year'; *185b*. Caesar probably rejoined the army in May.

3 **simul quod:** '(and) at the same time because,' i.e., this is the second reason given, the first having been explained in the causal ablative absolute *cognito Caesaris adventu*; *144b3*. **quantum in se facinus admisissent:** 'how great a crime they had committed,' lit. 'into how great a crime they had admitted themselves'; *se* refers to the subject of *admisissent*; *204.3*. **legatos . . . retentos ab se et in vincula coniectos:** sc. *esse* with *retentos* and *coniectos*; this accusative and infinitive clause stands in apposition as an explanation of their *facinus*, '(namely that) envoys had been detained,' etc. **legatos . . . quod nomen:** 'envoys, a title (lit. 'name') which'; *165b*. **instituunt:** takes the complementary infinitives *parare* and *providere*; *Veneti reliquaeque item civitates* is the subject; *175b*. **hoc maiore spe, quod:** 'with their hope greater on this account, (namely) because.' **hoc:** *135a*. **spe:** *138*. **multum confidebant:** 'had much confidence'; *118b*. **natura:** *135a*.

4 **Pedestria esse itinera concisa aestuariis . . . sciebant:** 'they knew that the land routes were cut by inlets of the sea,' (lit. 'by estuaries,' areas of land flooded at high tide), making progress of an army difficult; see Map 10. **navigationem:** 'navigation,' by the Romans; sc. *esse*; *81*. **inscientiam locorum:** 'lack of knowledge of the country.'

5 **neque:** translate as if *et . . . non*. **diutius:** 'for too long.'

6 **ac . . . novisse:** a brief summary in indirect discourse; 'and (they believed) that,' etc.; *212c6*. **ut omnia . . . acciderent:** with *iam*, 'even granting that everything turned out'; *acciderent* would also be subjunctive in direct discourse; *191b*. **plurimum posse:** cf. I.3.6. **navibus:** *142a*. **facultatem navium:** 'supply of ships,' lit. 'capability of ships.' **eorum locorum:** 'of those areas.' **ubi:** = *in quibus*. **gesturi essent:** *63*.

7 **longe aliam esse navigationem in . . . atque in:** '(that) navigation was far different on . . . than on'; *233c*. **in concluso mari:** 'on a confined sea,' referring to the Mediterranean, which has only slight tides. **mari:** *16b*.

8 **frumenta:** unthreshed 'grain,' just ripening in the fields, hurriedly cut and transported into the towns; see I.16.2. The time was near the beginning of July. **constabat:** see III.6.2. **quam plurimas possunt:** with *naves*; *153c*.

9 **Socios:** 'as allies'; *115a*. **Osismos,** etc.: these states can be found on Map Gallia. **auxilia ex Britannia:** aid furnished by the Britons gave Caesar a pretext later for invading the island (IV.20). **contra eas regiones:** 'opposite these regions,' i.e., facing Gaul across what we would call the English Channel.

Caesar considers it equally important to check this uprising and to distribute his forces so as to prevent revolts elsewhere.

10. 1 Erant hae difficultates belli gerendi, quas supra ostendimus, sed multa tamen Caesarem ad id bellum incitabant: 2 iniuria retentorum equitum Romanorum, rebellio facta post deditionem, defectio datis obsidibus, tot civitatum coniuratio, in primis ne, hac parte neglecta, reliquae nationes sibi idem licere arbitrarentur. 3 Itaque cum intellegeret omnes fere Gallos novis rebus studere et ad bellum mobiliter celeriterque excitari, omnes autem homines natura libertati studere et condicionem servitutis odisse, prius quam plures civitates conspirarent, partiendum sibi ac latius distribuendum exercitum putavit.

1 **Erant:** *90a*. **supra:** III.9, the previous chapter. **multa:** 'many things,' nominative, after which follows a series of nominatives in apposition: *iniuria, rebellio, defectio, coniuratio*.

2 **iniuria retentorum equitum Romanorum:** 'the injury done by the detention of Roman equestrians,' lit. 'the injury of the Roman equestrians having been detained,' referring to the detained envoys (III.8.2-3), who, as the other tribunes in Caesar's army, had the rank of *equites*. The participle *retentorum* is here best translated as a noun; *96*; *228b*. **defectio:** 'a revolt.' **datis obsidibus:** *144b5*. **in primis:** idiomatic: 'especially,' lit. 'among the first things.' **ne . . . arbitrarentur:** the clause is also in apposition with *multa*; '(the fear) that,' etc.; *202*. **hac parte neglecta:** 'if this part (of Gaul) were overlooked,' i.e., allowed to revolt without punishment; *144b4*. **idem licere:** accusative and infinitive after *arbitrarentur*; 'that the same thing was permitted.' **licere:** *73b*.

3 **cum:** *184a*. **novis rebus studere:** 'were eager for a change of rule,' lit. 'new things'; *105*. **mobiliter:** 'easily.' **excitari:** 'were stirred.' **natura libertati studere:** 'have a natural desire for liberty'; how lit.? **odisse:** *72b*; *176b*.

prius quam: with the subjunctive also in direct discourse; *189b.* **plures civitates conspirarent:** 'more states should league together.' **partiendum** (esse) **sibi ac latius distribuendum** (esse) **exercitum:** 'that he ought to divide up his army (lit. 'that his army ought to be divided up by him') and distribute (it) more widely,' in order to hold all parts of the country in check; *73e; 110.*

11. 1 Itaque T. Labienum legatum in Treveros, qui proximi flumini Rheno sunt, cum equitatu mittit. 2 Huic mandat, Remos reliquosque Belgas adeat atque in officio contineat, Germanosque, qui auxilio a Belgis arcessiti dicebantur, si per vim navibus flumen transire conentur, prohibeat. 3 P. Crassum, cum cohortibus legionariis XII et magno numero equitatus, in Aquitaniam proficisci iubet, ne ex his nationibus auxilia in Galliam mittantur ac tantae nationes coniungantur. 4 Q. Titurium Sabinum legatum cum legionibus tribus in Venellos, Coriosolitas Lexoviosque mittit, qui eam manum distinendam curet. 5 D. Brutum adulescentem classi Gallicisque navibus, quas ex Pictonibus et Santonis reliquisque pacatis regionibus convenire iusserat, praeficit et, cum primum possit, in Venetos proficisci iubet. Ipse eo pedestribus copiis contendit.

1 **Treveros:** see Map Gallia; *251.* **proximi:** here followed by the dative; *108a.*
2 **adeat:** *sc. ut; 200a; 199a1.* **in officio:** 'in allegiance,' i.e., their duty to acknowledge their submission. **auxilio:** *112a.* **arcessiti** (esse) **dicebantur:** 'were said to have been summoned'; *148e; 214c.* **conentur:** *220.*
3 **XII:** *duodecim;* Crassus had a legion and two cohorts of infantry. **Aquitaniam:** *256c.* **Galliam:** Celtic Gaul; *256b.* As the Aquitanians were of different stock, their relations with their Celtic neighbors seem ordinarily not to have been very close. **ne . . . mittantur:** *196a.*
4 **qui eam manum distinendam curet:** 'in order to keep their forces at a distance,' lit. 'to provide for their band to be kept apart'; *193a.* **distinendam:** *79d; 229b.*
5 **D.:** *19a.* **classi:** 'fleet,' built on the Loire (III.9.1-2). **Gallicis navibus:** used as supply ships. **possit:** indicative in the direct form. **eo:** *in Venetos.* **copiis:** *137b.*

The capture of the strongholds of the Veneti proves fruitless.

12. 1 Erant eius modi fere situs oppidorum, ut, posita in extremis lingulis promunturiisque, neque pedibus aditum haberent, cum ex alto se aestus incitavisset (quod bis accidit semper horarum XII spatio), neque navibus, quod, rursus minuente aestu, naves in vadis afflictarentur. 2 Ita utraque re oppidorum oppugnatio impediebatur; 3 ac si quando, magnitudine operis forte superati, extruso mari aggere ac molibus atque his oppidi moenibus adaequatis, suis fortunis desperare coeperant, magno numero navium appulso, cuius rei summam facultatem habebant, omnia sua deportabant seque in proxima oppida recipiebant; 4 ibi se rursus isdem opportunitatibus loci defendebant. 5 Haec eo facilius magnam partem aestatis faciebant, quod nostrae naves tempestatibus detinebantur, summaque erat vasto atque aperto mari, magnis aestibus, raris ac prope nullis portibus, difficultas navigandi.

1 **eius modi . . . ut:** ' of such a character that'; *100b; 197b.* **situs:** nominative plural. **posita:** participle, agreeing with *oppida* to be understood as the subject of *haberent.* **in extremis lingulis promunturiisque:** 'at the ends of tongues of land,' relatively low, 'and promontories,' high points of land, projecting into the sea; *152a.* **neque pedibus . . . neque navibus:** both with *aditum haberent.* **pedibus:** 'by land'; how lit.? *131a.* **aditum:** i.e., for an attacking army. **cum ex alto se aestus incitavisset:** 'when the tide had rushed in (lit. 'spurred itself on') from the deep.' **quod:** '(a thing) which,' referring to the preceding clause; hence neuter. **bis . . . spatio:** At the height of summer, the day is longer than the cycle of the tides, thus there can be two tides within one day. **horarum:** the long 'hours' of the summer days; *242.* **spatio:** 'within the period'; *147c.* **rursus minuente aestu:** 'at ebb tide'; how lit.? *144b2.* **afflictarentur:** 'would be damaged,' in case they should be over the shallow places when the tide went out.
2 **utraque re:** 'by both conditions,' both the rising and the ebbing of the tide.
3 **quando:** after *si,* 'at any time.' **operis:** = *munitionum,* explained by what follows. **superati:** agrees with *oppidani,* understood as subject of *coeperant.* **extruso mari aggere ac molibus atque his oppidi moenibus adaequatis:** 'when the sea had been shut out by massive dikes and when these (dikes) had been built up to a level with the walls of the town.' Starting from the nearest point of land that at high tide remained above water, the Romans extended toward the town two massive parallel embankments, or dikes, working whenever the tide would allow, since at high tide the enclosed space would be under water. Having prolonged their dikes almost to the city, they filled in the last stretch when the tide was low, and shut out the water from both sides, thus giving

a dry avenue of approach between the dikes from the adjacent country to the town. But by the time they were ready to attack, using each embankment as an *agger* (301), the townspeople had already departed by ship; see Map 10, A. **extruso mari:** *144b2.* **aggere ac molibus:** 'by massive dikes'; hendiadys; lit. 'by an embankment and masses (used as dams)'; *238d.* **moenibus:** *107a.* **fortunis:** dative; *109a.* **appulso:** 'having been brought up' to the threatened town. **cuius rei summam facultatem habebant:** *cuius rei* instead of *quarum* (*navium*), 'of which (thing) they had the greatest abundance.' **deportabant:** repeated action, 'they would carry off'; *175d.* 4 **isdem:** *45.* **opportunitatibus:** 'advantages.' **defendebant:** *175d.*

5 **eo facilius ... quod:** '(the) more easily because of this, namely that.' **magnam partem aestatis:** *118a.* **detinebantur:** in the Loire (III.9.1). **summa ... difficultas:** *245d.* **vasto atque aperto mari:** the first of three causal ablative absolutes, explaining why the difficulty was so great; *144b3.* There is an implied contrast with the more sheltered and almost tideless waters of the Mediterranean. **raris ac prope nullis:** 'infrequent, in fact, almost entirely lacking'; how lit.?

Advantages of the sea-going Venetan ships over Roman galleys.

13. 1 Namque ipsorum naves ad hunc modum factae armataeque erant: carinae aliquanto planiores quam nostrarum navium, quo facilius vada ac decessum aestus excipere possent; 2 prorae admodum erectae, atque item puppes, ad magnitudinem fluctuum tempestatumque accommodatae; 3 naves totae factae ex robore ad quamvis vim et contumeliam perferendam; 4 transtra, ex pedalibus in altitudinem trabibus, confixa clavis ferreis digiti pollicis crassitudine; 5 ancorae pro funibus ferreis catenis revinctae; 6 pelles pro velis alutaeque tenuiter confectae, sive propter lini inopiam atque eius usus inscientiam, sive eo – quod est magis veri simile – quod tantas tempestates Oceani tantosque impetus ventorum sustineri ac tanta onera navium regi velis non satis commode posse arbitrabantur. 7 Cum his navibus nostrae classi eius modi congressus erat, ut una celeritate et pulsu remorum praestaret; reliqua pro loci natura, pro vi tempestatum illis essent aptiora et accommodatiora. 8 Neque enim his nostrae rostro nocere poterant (tanta in eis erat firmitudo), neque propter altitudinem facile telum adigebatur, et eadem de causa, minus commode copulis continebantur. 9 Accedebat, ut, cum se vento dedissent, et tempestatem ferrent facilius et in vadis consisterent tutius et, ab aestu relictae, nihil saxa et cautes timerent; quarum rerum omnium nostris navibus casus erat extimescendus.

1 **Namque ipsorum naves:** closely connected with the end of III.12, explaining the navigational challenges facing the Romans; 'And (the Venetans do not have the same difficulty in navigating these waters) since their ships.' **ad hunc modum:** 'in the following way.' **armatae:** 'equipped.' **carinae:** 'keels'; sc. *erant*. **aliquanto planiores:** 'somewhat flatter,' so that the ships were more flat-bottomed than the Roman galleys; *140.* **quam:** 'than (the keels).' **quo:** *193b.* **decessum aestus:** 'the ebbing of the tide.'

2 **prorae admodum erectae:** 'the prows were very high'; sc. *erant* in this and the following clauses. **puppes:** 'sterns.' **fluctuum:** 'of sea-waves.' **accommodatae:** '(having been) adapted.'

3 **totae:** 'wholly'; *151.* **robore:** 'oak'; *13f.* **quamvis:** 'no matter how great,' lit. 'any you please'; *49a.* **vim et contumeliam:** 'violence and buffeting'; *230.3.*

4 **transtra, ex pedalibus in altitudinem trabibus, confixa clavis ferreis digiti pollicis crassitudine:** 'the cross-timbers, (made) out of beams a foot thick (lit. 'in height'), (were) fastened (to the sides) with iron bolts with the thickness of a thumb (lit. 'of the digit of the thumb').' **trabibus:** *17c.* **crassitudine:** *143a.*

5 **ancorae:** 'anchors,' like those in use today. **pro funibus:** 'instead of ropes.' As the Romans used only cables of rope, the chain cables of the Venetans seemed noteworthy. **revinctae:** '(were) fastened.'

6 **pelles:** 'hides.' **velis:** 'sails' of canvas. **alutae tenuiter confectae:** 'leather worked thin.' **sive propter ... sive eo, quod:** *235a, b.* **lini:** 'flax.' **eius:** *lini.* **eo:** 'on this account,' explained by *quod ... arbitrabantur*; *135a.* **quod est magis veri simile:** 'which is more probable,' this *quod* is relative and refers to the thought of the following *quod*-clause, which is causal after *eo*. **veri simile:** *108b.* **impetus:** 'gusts.' **sustineri, regi:** both infinitives are to be taken with *velis non satis commode posse.* **tanta onera navium:** 'such heavy vessels,' lit. 'the so great loads of the ships.' **onera:** *13e.* **regi:** 'be managed,' lit. 'be ruled.' **velis:** 'with (canvas) sails.'

7 **Cum:** here 'with.' **nostrae classi congressus erat:** 'the encounter of our fleet,' lit. 'the encounter to our fleet was', *classi* being dative of possession; *111.* **eius modi ... ut:** 'such ... that,' lit. 'of this sort, namely that'; *100b*; *197b.* **una:** 'only.' **una celeritate et pulsu remorum:** 'in respect to speed alone and the stroke of its oars'; *142a.* Propulsion by oars gave to the galley a rapidity and freedom of movement. **praestaret:** understand *nostra classis* as subject. **reliqua:** '(while) the rest,' lit. 'the remaining things,' i.e., everything else regarding the fleet's design; *171a.* **pro:** 'in regard to.' **illis essent aptiora:** 'was more suitable for them (the Venetan ships),' still part of the result clause introduced by *ut.* **illis:** *108a.*

8 **his:** the Venetan ships; *105.* **nostrae:** sc. *naves.* **rostro:** 'by ramming,' lit. 'with the beak'; *306c; 307.* **nocere:** 'do injury.' **telum adigebatur:** 'could a missile be thrust (up) toward then,' lit. 'was a missile being thrust.' The galleys were built relatively low, and light. **copulis continebantur:** 'could they be held with grappling hooks,' thrown out from a galley to catch and hold a hostile ship so that the Romans could board it; *307.*

9 **Accedebat, ut:** 'there was the additional fact that'; *203.1.* **se vento dedissent:** 'they (the Venetan ships) ran before the wind,' lit. 'they had given themselves over to the wind.' **ferrent:** 'they would weather.' **consisterent:** 'would remain,' lit. 'come to a halt.' **tutius:** *34b.* **aestu:** personified, hence with *ab*; *126b.* **relictae:** the Venetan ships, being flat-bottomed, when left by the tide settled easily and safely on the ground. **nihil:** = emphatic *non*; *118c.* **navibus:** *110.* **casus erat extimescendus:** 'the occurrence was greatly to be feared'; *229c.*

Caesar's fleet, commanded by Brutus, arrives; a sea battle ensues.

14. 1 Compluribus expugnatis oppidis, Caesar, ubi intellexit frustra tantum laborem sumi neque hostium fugam, captis oppidis, reprimi neque eis noceri posse, statuit exspectandam classem. 2 Quae ubi convenit ac primum ab hostibus visa est, circiter CCXX naves eorum, paratissimae atque omni genere armorum ornatissimae, profectae ex portu nostris adversae constiterunt; 3 neque satis Bruto, qui classi praeerat, vel tribunis militum centurionibusque, quibus singulae naves erant attributae, constabat, quid agerent aut quam rationem pugnae insisterent. 4 Rostro enim noceri non posse cognoverant; turribus autem excitatis, tamen has altitudo puppium ex barbaris navibus superabat, ut neque ex inferiore loco satis commode tela adigi possent et missa a Gallis gravius acciderent. 5 Una erat magno usui res praeparata a nostris, falces praeacutae insertae affixaeque longuriis, non absimili forma muralium falcium. 6 His cum funes, qui antemnas ad malos destinabant, comprehensi adductique erant, navigio remis incitato, praerumpebantur. 7 Quibus abscisis, antemnae necessario concidebant, ut, cum omnis Gallicis navibus spes in velis armamentisque consisteret, his ereptis, omnis usus navium uno tempore eriperetur. 8 Reliquum erat certamen positum in virtute, qua nostri milites facile superabant, atque eo magis, quod in conspectu Caesaris atque omnis exercitus res gerebatur, ut nullum paulo fortius factum latere posset; 9 omnes enim colles ac loca superiora, unde erat propinquus despectus in mare, ab exercitu tenebantur.

1 **frustra:** see III.12.2. **captis oppidis, reprimi:** sc. *posse,* 'could be checked by taking the towns'; *144b6.* **neque eis noceri posse:** 'nor could harm be done to them'; *106b; 105.* **exspectandam:** in full, *sibi exspectandam esse.*

2 **Quae:** *167.* **convenit:** 'arrived,' lit. 'came as a body.' **CCXX:** *ducentae et viginti; 38b; 36.* **paratissimae:** 'fully ready'; *153a.* **omni genere armorum:** 'with every kind of equipment,' i.e., everything needed to make a ship ready for action; *133.* **ornatissimae:** 'completely fitted out.' **nostris adversae constiterunt:** 'they took up a position facing (lit. 'opposite to') our (ships).' The sea battle probably took place in the bay of Quiberon, Caesar's army being drawn up in sight on the heights of St. Gildas. The courses of the fleets may be traced on Map 10.

3 **neque satis Bruto . . . constabat:** 'and it was not sufficiently clear to Brutus'; *73c.* **tribunis militum centurionibusque:** the legionaries on the Roman galleys were under their regular officers. How many galleys participated in the battle we do not know. **quibus singulae naves erant attributae:** 'to whom the ships had been individually assigned,' i.e., distributively, one by one. **quid agerent:** 'what they were to do'; *217b.*

4 **Rostro:** as in III.13.8. **noceri:** sc. *eis,* the enemy's ships, cf. just above in III.14.1. **turribus excitatis:** 'even though the towers had been erected' on the Roman ships; *144b5; 306d.* **ex:** 'on'; *126c.* **neque . . . et:** 'both . . . not . . . and'; *233a.* **inferiore loco:** the decks and towers of the Roman vessels. **adigi:** cf. III.13.8. **possent:** *197a.* **missa:** sc. *tela.* **gravius:** 'with greater force,' because thrown from a considerable height down upon the decks of the galleys.

5 **magno usui:** 'very useful'; how lit.? *112a.* **praeparata:** participle, '(having been) made ready beforehand.' **falces:** in apposition to *una res; 17c; 91a.* **falces praeacutae insertae affixaeque longuriis:** 'hooks sharpened at the ends, inserted into (the ends of) long poles and fastened to (them).' **non absimili forma muralium falcium:** = *forma non absimili formae* (*108b*) *muralium falcium,* 'with a shape not unlike that of wall hooks'; *143a; 238b.* **muralium falcium:** used on long poles to pull stones out of walls; *302c.*

6 **His:** sc. *falcibus; 131a.* **cum:** 'whenever'; *186a.* **funes:** 'the cables,' of rope. **qui antemnas ad malos destinabant:** 'which fastened the sail-yards to the masts.' **adducti erant:** 'had been pulled taut.' **navigio remis incitato:** 'when the ship' that had caught its hook in the enemy's rigging 'was driven forward with its oars'; *144b2.* **praerumpebantur:** '(the cables of the enemy ship) were severed,' lit. 'broken off in front.'

7 **abscisis:** 'cut off.' **concidebant:** 'fell down.' **cum:** *184a.* **Gallicis navibus:** 'for the Gallic ships,' dative; *109a.* **armamentis:** 'rigging'; they had no oars. **his ereptis:** *144b4.* **usus:** 'control.' **uno:** translate as if *eodem.* **eriperetur:** *197a.*

8 **Reliquum:** emphatic position; *245d.* **certamen:** 'contest.' **erat positum in:** 'depended on'; how lit.? **qua:** *142a.* **eo:** 'on this account'; *135a.* **res:** 'the struggle.' **paulo fortius:** 'unusually brave,' lit. 'a little braver (than usual).' **factum:** 'deed.' **posset:** *197a.* Once an enemy ship had been immobilized, then the Roman legionaries would storm it, fighting what was effectively an infantry battle on the deck of the ship. Not only was this the type of fighting in which they held the advantage (cf. the Venetan advantages described in III.13), but it also formed a spectacle for those watching from shore.

9 **omnes colles et loca superiora:** the heights of St. Gildas; see Map 10. **unde erat propinquus despectus in mare:** 'from which there was a nearby view over the sea'; the *de-* of *despectus* implying a view from an elevation.

Roman courage, ingenuity, and good luck win the day.

15. 1 Deiectis, ut diximus, antemnis, cum singulas binae ac ternae naves circumsisterent, milites summa vi transcendere in hostium naves contendebant. 2 Quod postquam barbari fieri animadverterunt, expugnatis compluribus navibus, cum ei rei nullum reperiretur auxilium, fuga salutem petere contenderunt. 3 Ac iam conversis in eam partem navibus, quo ventus ferebat, tanta subito malacia ac tranquillitas exstitit, ut se ex loco movere non possent. 4 Quae quidem res ad negotium conficiendum maxime fuit opportunitati; 5 nam singulas nostri consectati expugnaverunt, ut perpaucae ex omni numero noctis interventu ad terram pervenerint, cum ab hora fere IIII usque ad solis occasum pugnaretur.

1 **cum:** *186a.* **singulas binae ac ternae naves circumsisterent:** 'two or (lit. 'and') three galleys were surrounding a single ship' of the enemy. We are not to suppose that Caesar's fleet outnumbered that of the Venetans; the Romans simply concentrated their forces on one vessel at a time, instead of engaging the whole line of the enemy at once. **singulas:** sc. *naves.* **binae:** *36.* **transcendere in:** 'to board,' in the nautical sense. **contendebant:** *175d.*

2 **Quod:** translate as if *et hoc*; *quod* and *fieri* are accusative and infinitive after *animadverterunt.* **ei rei nullum reperiretur auxilium:** 'no remedy,' i.e., counter-tactic, 'was discovered against this action,' i.e., the boarding of their vessels by the legionaries.

3 **quo:** translate as if *in quam* after *in eam partem.* **ventus ferebat:** 'the wind was blowing,' lit. 'was bearing (them).' **malacia ac tranquillitas:** 'calm and stillness.' **exstitit:** 'ensued'; in the latter part of summer a morning wind in these regions is often followed by a calm in the afternoon; *176a; 173a.* **non possent:** relying entirely on sails, the Venetans were helpless when the wind failed them.

4 **res:** 'circumstance.' **opportunitati:** *112a.*

5 **singulas:** sc. *naves,* '(their ships) one by one.' **consectati:** 'pursuing'; *226c.* **numero:** *97d.* **interventu:** 'because of the coming'; *135a.* **cum:** 'although'; *187.* **hora IIII:** i.e., *hora quarta,* a little before ten o'clock by our reckoning; the battle took place toward the end of summer, before the autumnal equinox; *242a, b.*

The captive Veneti are sold into slavery as a warning.

16. 1 Quo proelio bellum Venetorum totiusque orae maritimae confectum est. 2 Nam cum omnis iuventus, omnes etiam gravioris aetatis, in quibus aliquid consilii aut dignitatis fuit, eo convenerant, tum, navium quod ubique fuerat, in unum locum coegerant; 3 quibus amissis, reliqui neque quo se reciperent, neque quem ad modum oppida defenderent, habebant. Itaque se suaque omnia Caesari dediderunt. 4 In quos eo gravius Caesar vindicandum statuit, quo diligentius in reliquum tempus a barbaris ius legatorum conservaretur. Itaque, omni senatu necato, reliquos sub corona vendidit.

1 **Quo proelio:** *131a; 167.* **bellum Venetorum:** 'war with (lit. 'of') the Venetans.' **totius orae maritimae:** see III.8.1

2 **cum . . . tum:** *186b.* **gravioris aetatis:** 'more advanced age'; *143a.* **aliquid consilii aut dignitatis:** 'any judgment or influence,' lit. 'anything of'; *97b.* **fuit:** *90a.* **eo:** to the country of the Venetans. **navium quod ubique fuerat:** i.e., *id navium, quod eis ubique fuerat,* 'all the ships that they had had anywhere,' lit. 'that (much) of ships which had been (to them) everywhere'; *97b.*

3 **quibus amissis:** i.e., in the battle against the Romans; both the men and the ships. **reliqui:** 'those who survived'; how lit.? **neque quo . . . neque quem ad modum:** 'neither a place to which . . . nor a means by which (lit. 'neither where . . . nor how').' **quo se reciperent:** indirect deliberative question; it would have the subjunctive also as a direct question; *217b.* **suaque omnia:** 'and all they had'; how lit.?

4 **eo . . . quo:** 'on this account . . . in order that,' an ablative of cause leading to a comparative purpose clause introduced by *quo*; *193b.* **eo gravius . . . quo diligentius:** to be understood correlatively, 'the more severely by

that degree by which the more diligently.' **gravius vindicandum:** sc. *esse*, 'that a severer punishment ought to be inflicted,' lit. 'that it ought be punished more severely.' **in reliquum tempus:** 'for the future.' **ius legatorum:** 'the right(s) of ambassadors,' whose bodies were to be considered inviolable. **omni senatu necato:** 'killed all the senate and'; how lit.? *144b2; 258b.* **sub corona:** 'into slavery,' lit. 'under the wreath,' referring to the wreath placed on the heads of captives sold at auction. These maritime states were thereby so reduced in strength that they afterwards gave Caesar no trouble.

III.17-19: Expedition of Sabinus against the Venelli

Sabinus encamps in the country of the Venelli and feigns fear.

17. 1 Dum haec in Venetis geruntur, Q. Titurius Sabinus cum eis copiis, quas a Caesare acceperat, in fines Venellorum pervenit. 2 His praeerat Viridovix ac summam imperii tenebat earum omnium civitatum, quae defecerant, ex quibus exercitum coegerat; 3 atque his paucis diebus Aulerci Eburovices Lexoviique, senatu suo interfecto, quod auctores belli esse nolebant, portas clauserunt seque cum Viridovice coniunxerunt; 4 magnaque praeterea multitudo undique ex Gallia perditorum hominum latronumque convenerat, quos spes praedandi studiumque bellandi ab agri cultura et cotidiano labore revocabat. 5 Sabinus idoneo omnibus rebus loco castris sese tenebat, cum Viridovix contra eum duorum milium spatio consedisset cotidieque, productis copiis, pugnandi potestatem faceret, ut iam non solum hostibus in contemptionem Sabinus veniret, sed etiam nostrorum militum vocibus non nihil carperetur; 6 tantamque opinionem timoris praebuit, ut iam ad vallum castrorum hostes accedere auderent. 7 Id ea de causa faciebat, quod cum tanta multitudine hostium, praesertim eo absente, qui summam imperii teneret, nisi aequo loco aut opportunitate aliqua data, legato dimicandum non existimabat.

1 **Venetis:** *251.* **geruntur:** translate by a past tense; *190a.* **eis copiis:** three legions, as related in III.11.4. **in fines Venellorum:** the probable route of Sabinus is shown on Map 9.

2 **Viridovix:** *19d.* **summam imperii:** 'the chief command,' lit. 'the height of power.' Viridovix not only commanded the forces of the Venellans, but was commander in chief of all the forces raised by the revolting states.

3 **his paucis diebus:** 'within the few days' after the arrival of Sabinus; *147a; 160d.* **Aulerci Eburovices:** one name; see Map 9. **auctores belli:** 'supporters of the war'; why nominative? *221b.* **nolebant:** plural because *senatu* is thought of as *senatoribus; 173b.* **portas clauserunt:** the shutting of city gates on the approach of an army was a virtual declaration of war.

4 **perditorum:** 'desperate,' lit. 'ruined.' **latronum:** 'bandits.' **spes praedandi:** 'the hope of plundering'; *230.1.*

5 **idoneo omnibus rebus loco:** 'in a location suitable in all respects'; *145c; 142a.* **castris:** *131a.* The camp of Sabinus was probably near the small river Sée, in the southern part of the Venellan territory; see Map 9. **cum:** *187.* **duorum milium spatio:** 'at an interval of (only) two miles'; *147c.* **ut:** 'so that'; *197a.* **non solum ... sed etiam:** *236d.* **hostibus:** 'in the eyes of the enemy'; *109a.* **vocibus:** *131a.* **non nihil:** 'rather sharply,' lit. 'not to no extent'; *118c; 239g.*

6 **opinionem:** 'impression'; *81.* **praebuit:** 'exhibited.'

7 **Id:** the holding of the Roman soldiers in camp. **faciebat:** sc. *Sabinus.* **quod ... non existimabat:** causal, explanatory of *ea de causa.* **cum:** here 'with.' **eo absente, qui:** 'in the absence of him (Caesar) who'; *144b3.* **teneret:** *214a.* **nisi:** i.e., *nisi dimicaret.* **aequo loco:** 'advantageous position'; sc. *dato.* **144b2. legato dimicandum:** sc. *esse,* 'a lieutenant ought to contend,' lit. 'it ought to be contended by a lieutenant'; *73e; 110.*

By a ruse he leads the enemy to attack him.

18. 1 Hac confirmata opinione timoris, idoneum quendam hominem et callidum delegit, Gallum, ex eis, quos auxilii causa secum habebat. 2 Huic magnis praemiis pollicitationibusque persuadet, uti ad hostes transeat, et, quid fieri velit, edocet. 3 Qui ubi pro perfuga ad eos venit, timorem Romanorum proponit; quibus angustiis ipse Caesar a Venetis prematur, docet, 4 neque longius abesse, quin proxima nocte Sabinus clam ex castris exercitum educat et ad Caesarem auxilii ferendi causa proficiscatur. 5 Quod ubi auditum est, conclamant omnes occasionem negotii bene gerendi amittendam non esse, ad castra iri oportere. 6 Multae res ad hoc consilium Gallos hortabantur: superiorum dierum Sabini cunctatio, perfugae confirmatio, inopia cibariorum, cui rei parum diligenter ab eis erat provisum, spes Venetici belli, et quod fere libenter homines id, quod volunt, credunt. 7 His rebus adducti, non prius

Viridovicem reliquosque duces ex concilio dimittunt, quam ab his sit concessum, arma uti capiant et ad castra contendant. 8 Qua re concessa, laeti, ut explorata victoria, sarmentis virgultisque collectis, quibus fossas Romanorum compleant, ad castra pergunt.

1 **callidum:** 'crafty.' **Gallum:** in apposition to *hominem*, 'a Gaul.' **ex eis:** *97d.* **auxilii causa:** i.e., among his auxiliary forces.
2 **persuadet:** *175b.* **edocet:** parallel to *persuadet*, which is followed by an indirect command (*199a5*), while *edocet* is followed by an indirect question (*204.2*).
3 **Qui:** *167.* **pro perfuga:** 'as (if) a deserter.' **venit:** *188a.* **quibus angustiis:** 'in what difficulties,' lit. 'straits'; *204.2*
4 **neque longius abesse, quin proxima nocte Sabinus ... educat:** translate as if: *neque longius abesse proxima nocte, quin Sabinus ... educat*, 'and that no later than on the following night Sabinus would lead,' lit. 'and that it was not more distant than that on the following night Sabinus would lead'; clauses that involve doubt, hindrance, or (as here) delay, especially when negated, introduce *quin*-clauses; *201b.*
5 **Quod ubi auditum est:** 'when this was heard,' *quod* refers to Gallus' 'report' to the enemy. **ad castra iri oportere:** 'that they ought to go to the camp,' lit. 'that it was right that there be a going to the camp,' *iri* is the present passive infinitive of *eo*, here used impersonally; *68d; 73d.*
6 **superiorum:** 'preceding.' **cunctatio:** the first in a series of nominatives that explain *multae res.* **confirmatio:** 'the assurance.' **cui rei ... erat provisum:** 'for which thing provision had been made,' lit. 'it had been provided.' **quod fere ... credunt:** a statement of a general truth rounds out Caesar's listing of the *multae res* that urged the Gauls to attack: 'the fact that men generally believe'; *198b; 175c.* **volunt:** sc. *credere.*
7 **dimittunt:** the subject are all those who had gathered in assembly in order to hear the report of the 'deserter.' **prius ... quam ab his sit concessum:** 'until it had been granted by these men'; *189b.* **capiant:** *199a6.*
8 **laeti:** 'joyfully'; *151.* **ut explorata victoria:** 'as if victory were (already) confirmed,' lit. 'just as with victory having been confirmed'; *144b2.* **sarmentis virgultisque collectis:** 'they gathered branches and brushwood and'; how lit.? I.e., bundles of shoots and bushes were tied together for convenience in handling. **quibus ... compleant:** translate as if *ut eis ... compleant*; *193a; 131a.*

Sabinus achieves surprise and wins a decisive victory.

19. 1 Locus erat castrorum editus et paulatim ab imo acclivis circiter passus mille. Huc magno cursu contenderunt, ut quam minimum spatii ad se colligendos armandosque Romanis daretur, exanimatique pervenerunt. Sabinus, suos hortatus, cupientibus signum dat. 2 Impeditis hostibus propter ea, quae ferebant, onera, subito duabus portis eruptionem fieri iubet. 3 Factum est opportunitate loci, hostium inscientia ac defatigatione, virtute militum et superiorum pugnarum exercitatione, ut ne unum quidem nostrorum impetum ferrent ac statim terga verterent. 4 Quos impeditos integris viribus milites nostri consecuti, magnum numerum eorum occiderunt; reliquos equites consectati, paucos, qui ex fuga evaserant, reliquerunt. 5 Sic, uno tempore, et de navali pugna Sabinus et de Sabini victoria Caesar certior factus est, civitatesque omnes se statim Titurio dediderunt. 6 Nam ut ad bella suscipienda Gallorum alacer ac promptus est animus, sic mollis ac minime resistens ad calamitates perferendas mens eorum est.

1 **Locus:** 'site.' **editus et paulatim ab imo acclivis circiter passus mille:** 'elevated and gradually sloping from the bottom for about one mile,' i.e., the camp sat atop a hill and the ascent to it was about one mile in length on a gradual slope. **passus:** *118a.* **Huc:** up the slope to the camp. **magno cursu:** i.e., at full speed. **quam minimum spatii:** 'as little time as possible'; *97b; 153c.* **exanimati:** 'breathless,' i.e., out of breath from their running. **hortatus:** see *I.25.1; 226c.* **cupientibus:** sc. *eis*, i.e., those desiring the signal to begin the fight.
2 **onera:** see *III.18.8.* **duabus portis:** sc. *castrorum*; probably the gates on the right and left sides of the camp; *294a; 134a.*
3 **Factum est ... ut:** 'the result was ... that,' lit. 'it happened ... that'; *203.1.* **opportunitate:** the first of several ablatives of cause that explain why things happened the way they did; *135a.* **ne unum quidem nostrorum impetum:** 'not even one charge of our men,' i.e., they did not withstand the initial assault; *237c.* **ferrent:** sc. *hostes* as subject. **ac:** 'but'; *234b.*
4 **consecuti:** *226c.* **reliquos:** 'the rest' of the Gauls not slain by the legionaries. **equites:** sc. *nostri.* **paucos:** '(only) a few'; *154a.*
5 **Sabinus:** sc. *certior factus est.* **Titurio:** i.e., Q. Titurius Sabinus, for the full name see *III.11.4; 19b.* The sub-

jugation of these states was now complete; the submission reported the previous year (II.34) had been only nominal.

6 **ut . . . sic:** 'just as . . . so.' **alacer:** *24.* **mollis:** 'yielding.' **resistens:** participle, with *minime*, 'not at all resisting,' lit. 'capable of resistance.' Caesar again comments on the fickleness of the Gauls (cf. III.8.3, 10.3; IV.5.2-3).

III.20-27: Campaign of Crassus against the Aquitani

Crassus, entering Aquitania, meets a force of the Sotiates.

20. 1 Eodem fere tempore P. Crassus, cum in Aquitaniam pervenisset, quae pars, ut ante dictum est, et regionum latitudine et multitudine hominum ex tertia parte Galliae est aestimanda, cum intellegeret in eis locis sibi bellum gerendum, ubi paucis ante annis L. Valerius Praeconinus legatus, exercitu pulso, interfectus esset, atque unde L. Manlius proconsul, impedimentis amissis, profugisset, non mediocrem sibi diligentiam adhibendam intellegebat. 2 Itaque re frumentaria provisa, auxiliis equitatuque comparato, multis praeterea viris fortibus Tolosa et Carcasone et Narbone, quae sunt civitates Galliae provinciae finitimae his regionibus, nominatim evocatis, in Sotiatium fines exercitum introduxit. 3 Cuius adventu cognito Sotiates, magnis copiis coactis, equitatuque, quo plurimum valebant, in itinere agmen nostrum adorti, primum equestre proelium commiserunt; 4 deinde, equitatu suo pulso atque insequentibus nostris, subito pedestres copias, quas in convalle in insidiis collocaverant, ostenderunt. Hi, nostros disiectos adorti, proelium renovarunt.

1 **P. Crassus:** with twelve cohorts and a large body of cavalry (III.11.3). The cavalry would have been of no use to Caesar in the campaign against the Venetans, but could be employed by Crassus to advantage in the mountainous regions of Aquitania. **quae pars . . . ex tertia parte Galliae est aestimanda:** 'which (i.e., Aquitania) is to be regarded as one of the three parts of Gaul,' lit. 'which part is to be regarded as of the third part of Gaul,' i.e., as one third of the whole. **ut ante dictum est:** see I.1.1. **latitudine:** *142a.* Aquitania, in fact, is geographically the smallest of the three parts of Gaul that Caesar identifies. **cum:** *184a.* **sibi bellum gerendum:** sc. *esse*, lit. 'that war was to be waged by him.' **ubi:** = *in quibus*, refers back to *in eis locis*. **paucis ante annis:** twenty-two years before (*140*), in 78 BC. In that year Praeconinus, mentioned only here, and Lucius Manlius, proconsul of the Province, were routed by Hirtuleius, the quaestor of Sertorius (about whom, cf. III.23.5). **unde:** = *e quibus*. **L.:** *19a.* **non mediocrem:** 'no ordinary'; *239g.* **sibi:** *110.*

2 **comparato:** *144b2; 172b.* **viris fortibus . . . evocatis:** veteran soldiers who, having served their time (20 years), were living in the Province; *267a.* **Tolosa:** *127a; 262a.* **Galliae provinciae finitimae:** *finitimae* agrees with *civitates, Galliae provinciae* genitive after *civitates.* **nominatim:** requests to reenter the service were sent to the veterans individually. **evocatis:** lit. 'called out,' but in sense more like 'invited back.' **Sotiatium:** see Map 9; *19e.*

3 **Cuius:** Sabinus; *167.* **equitatuque:** to be understood, given how it is explained by *quo plurimum valebant*, with *adorti; 131a.* The *–que* thus links the two participial actions in the sentence so far: the ablative *coactis* (part of the ablative absolute *magnis copiis coactis*) and the nominative *adorti.* **quo:** *142a.* **plurimum:** *118b.*

4 **subito:** apparently the flight of the cavalry was a ruse, to draw the pursuing Romans into the enclosed valley (*convalle*) where the infantry of the Sotiates was in ambush. **Hi:** referring to *pedestres copias*.

In a fierce fight he defeats them and captures their city.

21. 1 Pugnatum est diu atque acriter, cum Sotiates, superioribus victoriis freti, in sua virtute totius Aquitaniae salutem positam putarent, nostri autem, quid sine imperatore et sine reliquis legionibus, adulescentulo duce, efficere possent, perspici cuperent; tandem confecti vulneribus hostes terga verterunt. 2 Quorum magno numero interfecto, Crassus ex itinere oppidum Sotiatium oppugnare coepit. Quibus fortiter resistentibus, vineas turresque egit. 3 Illi, alias eruptione temptata, alias cuniculis ad aggerem vineasque actis (cuius rei sunt longe peritissimi Aquitani, propterea quod multis locis apud eos aerariae securaeque sunt), ubi diligentia nostrorum nihil his rebus profici posse intellexerunt, legatos ad Crassum mittunt, seque in deditionem ut recipiat, petunt. Qua re impetrata, arma tradere iussi faciunt.

1 **victoriis:** *131e.* **cum Sotiates . . . putarent, nostri autem . . . cuperent:** the paired causal clauses explain why

the battle was fought so fiercely; *184a.* **quid ... possent, perspici cuperent:** 'were desiring that it be observed what they were able'; the indirect question is the the subject of *perspici*; *204.2.* **sine imperatore:** i.e., *sine Caesare.* **adulescentulo duce:** 'with a youth as leader,' referring to Crassus; *144b2.*

2 **ex itinere:** see Vocab. under *iter.* **oppidum:** identified with Sôs, the name of which is derived from *Sotiates.* **oppugnare:** Crassus tried to take the town by sudden storming; *300.* **vineas, turres:** the arbor-sheds and towers used for besieging; *302.*

3 **Illi:** the Sotiates. **alias ... alias:** 'at one time ... at another.' **cuniculis:** 'tunnels,' underground passageways from which the Roman works could be undermined, so that they would fall in, or could be set on fire. **cuius rei sunt longe peritissimi Aquitani:** 'at (lit. 'of') which thing (i.e., the driving of tunnels) the Aquitani are by far the most skilled'; *102.* **locis:** *145c.* **aerariae:** 'copper mines.' **secturae:** 'excavations,' probably open cuts from which iron ore was taken, as distinguished from the more elaborate tunnels of the copper mines. Remains of ancient copper and iron mines have been found in the region of the Sotiates. **sunt:** *90a.* **diligentia:** *135a.* **his rebus:** 'by these devices'; *131a.* **seque in deditionem ut recipiat, petunt:** translate as if *et petunt ut recipiat se in deditionem.* **iussi faciunt:** 'they, having been ordered, do (what they were ordered).'

Adiatunnus with a devoted band makes a sortie, is captured.

22. 1 Atque in ea re omnium nostrorum intentis animis, alia ex parte oppidi Adiatunnus, qui summam imperii tenebat, cum DC devotis, quos illi 'soldurios' appellant — 2 quorum haec est condicio, uti omnibus in vita commodis una cum eis fruantur, quorum se amicitiae dediderint; si quid his per vim accidat, aut eundem casum una ferant aut sibi mortem consciscant 3 (neque adhuc hominum memoria repertus est quisquam, qui, eo interfecto, cuius se amicitiae devovisset, mortem recusaret) — 4 cum his Adiatunnus eruptionem facere conatus, clamore ab ea parte munitionis sublato, cum ad arma milites concurrissent vehementerque ibi pugnatum esset, repulsus in oppidum tamen, uti eadem deditionis condicione uteretur, a Crasso impetravit.

1 **in:** 'upon.' **intentis animis:** *144b2.* **summam imperii:** see III.17.2. **DC:** *sescentis*; *38b.* **devotis:** 'faithful followers.' **soldurios:** 'the vow-beholden.'

2 **quorum haec est condicio:** 'whose agreement (i.e., in order to be included in the *soldurii*) is this.' **uti ... fruantur:** *203.4.* **omnibus in vita commodis:** 'all their advantages in life'; *131c.* **una:** adv., 'together.' **quorum se amicitiae dederint:** 'to whose friendship they have given themselves'; the antecedent of *quorum* is *eis.* **dediderint:** *220.* **si quid his ... accidat:** cf. I.18.9. **vim:** 'violence.' **ferant:** sc. *ut*, in parallel with *uti ... fruantur* above. **sibi mortem consciscant:** cf. I.4.4.

3 **adhuc:** 'up to this time.' **memoria:** *147b.* **recusaret:** *194a.*

4 **his:** = *devotis* in III.22.1, resuming the narrative interrupted by the long explanation. **sublato:** 'raised,' from *tollo.* **repulsus:** *227a3.* **uti ... uteretur:** after *impetravit*; *199a8.* **eadem:** 'the same' as the rest. **impetravit:** 'obtained (by request),' i.e., 'accomplished.'

Proceeding further, Crassus finds a formidable army.

23. 1 Armis obsidibusque acceptis, Crassus in fines Vocatium et Tarusatium profectus est. 2 Tum vero barbari, commoti, quod oppidum et natura loci et manu munitum paucis diebus, quibus eo ventum erat, expugnatum cognoverant, legatos quoque versus dimittere, coniurare, obsides inter se dare, copias parare coeperunt. 3 Mittuntur etiam ad eas civitates legati, quae sunt citerioris Hispaniae finitimae Aquitaniae; inde auxilia ducesque arcessuntur. 4 Quorum adventu magna cum alacritate et magna hominum multitudine bellum gerere conantur. 5 Duces vero ei deliguntur, qui una cum Q. Sertorio omnes annos fuerant summamque scientiam rei militaris habere existimabantur. 6 Hi consuetudine populi Romani loca capere, castra munire, commeatibus nostros intercludere instituunt. 7 Quod ubi Crassus animadvertit, suas copias propter exiguitatem non facile diduci, hostem et vagari et vias obsidere et castris satis praesidii relinquere, ob eam causam minus commode frumentum commeatumque sibi supportari, in dies hostium numerum augeri, non cunctandum existimavit, quin pugna decertaret. 8 Hac re ad consilium delata, ubi omnes idem sentire intellexit, posterum diem pugnae constituit.

1 **in fines Vocatium et Tarusatium:** i.e., further south and west, closer to the Pyrenees and Spain.

2 **quod ... cognoverant:** causal, explaining the reason why the enemy were *commoti.* **oppidum:** *oppidum*

Sotiatium, III.21.2. **et natura loci et manu:** the two ways by which the *oppidum* was *munitum*, i.e., the natural defenses of the town had been strengthened by fortifications built by hand. **munitum:** *227a3.* **paucis diebus, quibus:** 'within a few days after (lit. within which)'; *147a.* **eo:** adverb. **ventum erat:** *73d.* **expugnatum:** sc. *esse*; its subject is *oppidum*. **cognoverant:** *176b.* **quoque versus:** 'in all directions.' **coniurare:** 'to take oaths together,' as a means of forming bonds of loyalty.

3 **citerioris Hispaniae:** *94d; 265.* **finitimae:** agrees with *quae.*

4 **adventu:** *147b.* **hominum:** *98a.* **gerere conantur:** 'they tried to wage,' i.e., 'they undertook to start.'

5 **Duces:** in predicate, *ei* is the subject; *88a.* **vero:** 'but.' **una cum:** 'together with.' **Q. Sertorio:** a military leader of the popular party in the civil war between Marius and Sulla. After Sulla's victorious return to Rome, Sertorius organized an army in Spain, and held his own against the Sullan government for ten years before he was killed in 72 BC. **omnes annos:** 'during all (those) years,' 82-72 BC, when Sertorius had an army in the field.

6 **consuetudine populi Romani:** *136c.* **loca capere:** 'to choose locations' for encampment. **commeatibus:** *127a.*

7 **Quod:** 'this (circumstance),' namely the actions described in the following accusative and infinitive clauses. **diduci:** 'separated,' or 'spread out,' so as to cope at all points with the numerically superior enemy. **hostem et vagari et:** '(but) that the enemy both roamed' at will 'and.' **castris:** the enemy camp; *104a.* **satis praesidii:** *97b.* **in dies:** 'day by day.' **non cunctandum:** sc. *esse sibi*, 'that he ought not to delay,' how lit.? **quin pugna decertaret:** 'to fight it out by means of a battle,' i.e., 'to fight a decisive battle'; clauses that involve doubt, hindrance, or (as here) delay, especially when negated, introduce *quin*-clauses (so also III.18.4); *201b.*

8 **omnes idem sentire:** 'that all held the same opinion'; *117a.*

Forming battle order, he waits, then attacks the enemy's camp.

24. 1 Prima luce productis omnibus copiis, duplici acie instituta, auxiliis in mediam aciem coniectis, quid hostes consilii caperent, exspectabat. 2 Illi, etsi propter multitudinem et veterem belli gloriam paucitatemque nostrorum se tuto dimicaturos existimabant, tamen tutius esse arbitrabantur, obsessis viis, commeatu intercluso, sine ullo vulnere victoria potiri, 3 et, si propter inopiam rei frumentariae Romani sese recipere coepissent, impeditos in agmine et sub sarcinis infirmiores animo adoriri cogitabant. 4 Hoc consilio probato ab ducibus, productis Romanorum copiis, sese castris tenebant. 5 Hac re perspecta Crassus, cum sua cunctatione atque opinione timoris hostes nostros milites alacriores ad pugnandum effecissent, atque omnium voces audirentur, *exspectari diutius non oportere, quin ad castra iretur,* cohortatus suos, omnibus cupientibus, ad hostium castra contendit.

1 **duplici acie:** not so strong as the customary triple line, but necessary here because the Roman force was so greatly outnumbered by the enemy; *297.* **duplici:** *26a.* **auxiliis:** the auxiliary troops were usually stationed upon the wings; in this instance they were placed at the middle of the line because Crassus did not have confidence in them (III.25.1). **quid consilii:** 'what (of a) plan'; *97b.* **caperent:** 'would adopt'; *204.2.* **exspectabat:** 'was waiting (to see).'

2 **multitudinem:** estimated at 50,000 (III.26.6). **paucitatem:** the whole force under the command of Crassus (see III.11.3, 20.2) can hardly have amounted to 10,000 men. **tuto:** *34b.* **tutius esse ... potiri:** *tutius* is predicative with *esse*, of which the subject is *potiri*, 'that it was safer to obtain'; *222b; 148d.* **obsessis viis:** 'having blocked the roads (and)'; how lit.? *238a.* **potiri:** *131c.*

3 **sese recipere:** 'to retreat.' **impeditos:** sc. *eos (Romanos).* **sarcinis:** *290.* **infirmiores animo:** paired with *impeditos*, 'less courageous'; how lit.? *142a.* **adoriri cogitabant:** 'they were intending to attack.'

4 **productis Romanorum copiis:** *144b5.* **castris:** *131a.*

5 **cum ... effecissent, ... audirentur:** *184a.* **opinione:** 'impression.' **hostes:** nominative. **alacriores:** *115b.* **omnium:** i.e., *omnium militum.* **audirentur, exspectari diutius non oportere:** 'were heard (saying) that they ought not to wait any longer'; *213b.* **quin:** see III.23.7. **ad castra iretur:** see III.18.5; *68d; 73d; 201b.* **omnibus cupientibus:** *144b3.* **ad hostium castra:** this is the only attack of the Romans on a fortified camp recorded in the Gallic War.

He learns that the enemy's rear gate is not well guarded.

25. 1 Ibi cum alii fossas complerent, alii multis telis coniectis defensores vallo munitionibusque depellerent, auxiliaresque, quibus ad pugnam non multum Crassus confidebat, lapidibus telisque subministrandis et ad aggerem caespitibus comportandis speciem atque opinionem pugnantium praeberent; cum item ab hostibus constanter ac non timide pugnaretur telaque ex loco superiore missa non frustra acciderent, 2 equites, circumitis hostium castris, Crasso renuntiaverunt, non eadem esse diligentia ab decumana porta castra munita facilemque aditum habere.

1 **alii ... alii:** *milites Romani; 171b.* **fossas:** see III.5.1. **vallo:** constructed in the Roman fashion (III.23.6); *127a; 293.* **quibus:** dative; *105.* **non multum:** *118b.* **lapidibus ... sumministrandis:** 'by supplying stones,' etc., ablatives of means; *230.4.* **ad aggerem:** *sc. faciendum.* The rampart of the enemy's camp was so high that the Romans began to make a sloping mound up to it, like the *agger* used in besieging a town. **caespitibus:** 'chunks of sod'; *10d.* **speciem ... pugnantium:** 'the appearance and impression of fighting men.' **ex loco superiore missa:** 'because thrown from higher ground,' i.e., the top of the rampart of their camp; *227a1.*

2 **circumitis hostium castris:** 'having ridden around the enemy's camp,' how lit.? **esse ... castra munita:** indirect statement after *renuntiaverunt.* **eadem diligentia:** *136b.* **ab decumana porta:** 'on the side of the rear gate'; *126c; 294a.* Note that this entire chapter is one sentence.

Surprising the enemy by a rear attack, he routs them.

26. 1 Crassus, equitum praefectos cohortatus, ut magnis praemiis pollicitationibusque suos excitarent, quid fieri vellet, ostendit. 2 Illi, ut erat imperatum, eductis eis cohortibus, quae, praesidio castris relictae, integrae ab labore erant, et longiore itinere circumductis, ne ex hostium castris conspici possent, omnium oculis mentibusque ad pugnam intentis, celeriter ad eas, quas diximus, munitiones pervenerunt, 3 atque, his prorutis, prius in hostium castris constiterunt, quam plane ab his videri aut, quid rei gereretur, cognosci posset. 4 Tum vero, clamore ab ea parte audito, nostri, redintegratis viribus, quod plerumque in spe victoriae accidere consuevit, acrius impugnare coeperunt. 5 Hostes undique circumventi, desperatis omnibus rebus, se per munitiones deicere et fuga salutem petere contenderunt. 6 Quos equitatus apertissimis campis consectatus, ex milium L numero, quae ex Aquitania Cantabrisque convenisse constabat, vix quarta parte relicta, multa nocte se in castra recepit.

1 **equitum praefectos:** *269c.* **ut ... excitarentur:** *199a2.* **suos:** the cavalrymen, on whom the success of the surprise depended. **quid fieri vellet:** *204.2.*

2 **Illi:** the cavalry prefects, who guided cohorts of infantry to the rear of the enemy's camp. It is possible that the cavalrymen took the legionaries with them on their horses in order to transport them quickly by a roundabout way. **ut erat imperatum:** 'as they were ordered,' lit. 'as it had been ordered (to them).' **praesidio castris:** *112b.* **relictae:** *227a1.* **et:** connects *eductis* and *circumductis.* **longiore:** *153a.* **possent:** *196a.* **omnium:** *hostium.* **oculis ... intentis:** *144b2.* **eas, quas diximus, munitiones:** i.e., those on the rear side of the enemy's camp (III.25.2).

3 **prorutis:** 'thrown down.' **constiterunt:** 'stood.' **prius ... quam:** *189b.* **plane:** 'clearly.' **videri:** sc. *possent,* 'they could be seen.' **quid rei gereretur, cognosci posset:** 'they could comprehend what was going on,' lit. 'it was able to be comprehended (by them) what of a thing was being conducted.' **quid rei:** *97b; 204.2.*

4 **clamore ... audito:** from the shouting at the rear of the camp the Romans fighting in front knew that the attack there was in progress, and were inspired to greater efforts. **quod plerumque in spe victoriae accidere consuevit:** relative clause referring to the thought in *redintegratis viribus,* 'which (thing) is accustomed to happen in the hope of victory'; *176b.*

5 **desperatis omnibus rebus:** 'in utter despair'; how lit.? *144b2.* **se per munitiones deicere:** 'to throw themselves down (to the ground) all along the fortifications.' **contenderunt:** 'struggled.'

6 **apertissimis:** 'wide and open.' Cf. *153a.* **campis:** *145c.* **consectatus:** *226c.* **ex milium L numero, quae ex Aquitania Cantabrisque convenisse constabat, vix quarta parte relicta:** translate the latter part first: 'with scarcely a fourth part left out of the 50,000 (in number) which are agreed to have gathered out of Aquitania and the Cantabrians.' **numero:** *142a.* **quae:** subject accusative of *convenisse;* the antecedent is *milium.* **multa nocte:** 'late at night'; *152a.* Compare *multo die* in I.22.4.

Crassus receives the submission of other Aquitanian states.

27. 1 Hac audita pugna, maxima pars Aquitaniae sese Crasso dedidit obsidesque ultro misit; quo in numero fuerunt Tarbelli, Bigerriones, Ptianii, Vocates, Tarusates, Elusates, Gates, Ausci, Garumni, Sibusates, Cocosates; 2 paucae ultimae nationes, anni tempore confisae, quod hiems suberat, hoc facere neglexerunt.

1 **ultro:** 'voluntarily,' the adverb implies doing something unexpected or additional of one's own volition. **quo in numero:** lit. 'in which number,' but more naturally 'in the number of whom,' or 'among whom.' **Tarbelli,** etc.: see Map 9. The Tarbelli have left a trace of their name in modern Tarbes; the Bigerriones, in Bagnères de

Bigorre, a source for fresh water in the Pyrenees; the Elusates, in Eauze; the Ausci, in Auch; the Sibusates, in Saubusse.

2 **paucae ultimae nationes:** i.e., *paucae nationes, quae ultimae erant;* 'a few very remote peoples.' **tempore:** *135a.* **quod:** causal.

III.28-29: Campaign against the Morini and the Menapii

Caesar proceeds against the Morini and the Menapii.

28. 1 Eodem fere tempore Caesar, etsi prope exacta iam aestas erat, tamen, quod, omni Gallia pacata, Morini Menapiique supererant, qui in armis essent neque ad eum umquam legatos de pace misissent, arbitratus id bellum celeriter confici posse, eo exercitum duxit; qui longe alia ratione ac reliqui Galli bellum gerere instituerunt. 2 Nam quod intellegebant, maximas nationes, quae proelio contendissent, pulsas superatasque esse, continentesque silvas ac paludes habebant, eo se suaque omnia contulerunt. 3 Ad quarum initium silvarum cum Caesar pervenisset castraque munire instituisset, neque hostis interim visus esset, dispersis in opere nostris, subito ex omnibus partibus silvae evolaverunt et in nostros impetum fecerunt. 4 Nostri celeriter arma ceperunt eosque in silvas reppulerunt et, compluribus interfectis, longius impeditioribus locis secuti, paucos ex suis deperdiderunt.

1 **Eodem fere tempore:** 'about the same time' that Crassus completed the reduction of Aquitania, perhaps in the latter part of August. The narrative of Caesar's own military operations, interrupted at III.16, is here resumed. **prope exacta:** 'almost completed.' **omni Gallia:** 'Gaul as a whole.' **supererant, qui:** 'were the (only) remaining (peoples) who.' **essent:** *194a.* **neque:** translate as if *et non.* **arbitratus:** *226c.* **eo:** adverb. **exercitum duxit:** the distance traversed in the march from the sea-coast of the country of the Venetans to the northern coasts of Gaul could hardly have been less than 400 English miles. **qui:** '(but) they'; *167.* **longe alia ratione ac reliqui Galli:** 'in a way far different from (that of) the rest of the Gauls'; *233c.*
2 **continentes:** 'continuous,' i.e., unbroken expanses of land. **habebant:** coordinate with *intellegebant;* sc. *quod.* **eo:** *in eas* (*silvas ac paludes*).
3 **initium:** 'the edge,' lit. 'the beginning.' **neque hostis:** still after *cum,* 'and (when) the enemy had not.' **in opere:** of fortifying the camp. **evolaverunt:** 'flew forth.'
4 **longius:** 'too far'; *153a.* **impeditioribus locis:** 'in places (that were) much obstructed' by trees and marshes.

Hiding in forests, favored by rains, they elude him.

29. 1 Reliquis deinceps diebus Caesar silvas caedere instituit et, ne quis inermibus imprudentibusque militibus ab latere impetus fieri posset, omnem eam materiam, quae erat caesa, conversam ad hostem collocabat et pro vallo ad utrumque latus exstruebat. 2 Incredibili celeritate magno spatio paucis diebus confecto, cum iam pecus atque extrema impedimenta a nostris tenerentur, ipsi densiores silvas peterent, eius modi sunt tempestates consecutae, uti opus necessario intermitteretur et continuatione imbrium diutius sub pellibus milites contineri non possent. 3 Itaque vastatis omnibus eorum agris, vicis aedificiisque incensis, Caesar exercitum reduxit et in Aulercis Lexoviis reliquisque item civitatibus, quae proxime bellum fecerant, in hibernis collocavit.

1 **Reliquis diebus:** of the summer. **deinceps:** 'in succession.' **caedere:** 'to cut down.' **ne quis . . . impetus:** 'so that no attack'; *49a; 196a.* **imprudentibus:** 'off their guard.' *144b2.* **materiam:** 'material,' here 'timber.' **conversam ad hostem:** 'turned toward the enemy.' **pro vallo:** 'as a rampart.' **extruebat:** 'built (it) up.' As the Romans advanced they felled trees, and placed them, with the tops outwards, at either side of the space which they cleared, thus forming an effective defense against the lurking foe.
2 **confecto:** 'cleared,' lit. 'accomplished.' **iam . . . tenerentur:** 'were already in our hands.' **pecus:** 'cattle'; *13f.* **extrema impedimenta:** 'the rear of their baggage-train'; *152a.* **ipsi:** the people themselves, as distinguished from their possessions; as Caesar cut his way through the woods, they retreated further and further into the forest; *238a.* **eius modi . . . uti:** *197b.* **eius modi sunt tempestates consecutae:** 'there followed storms of such a sort.' **continuatione:** *135a.* **imbrium:** 'rainstorms'; *15c.* **sub pellibus:** 'in tents'; how lit.? *295a.*
3 **Aulercis,** etc.: see Map 9. **Lexoviis:** see III.11.4. **reliquisque civitatibus:** Venetans (chapters 12-16), Venellans (17-19), and Sotiates (20-27). **proxime:** 'most recently.'

BOOK IV

IV.1-15: Campaign against the Usipetes and Tencteri

Pressed by the Suebi, the Usipetes and Tencteri enter Gaul; customs and prowess of the Suebi.

1. 1 Ea, quae secuta est, hieme, qui fuit annus Cn. Pompeio, M. Crasso consulibus, Usipetes Germani et item Tencteri magna multitudine hominum flumen Rhenum transierunt, non longe a mari, quo Rhenus influit. 2 Causa transeundi fuit, quod, ab Suebis complures annos exagitati, bello premebantur et agri cultura prohibebantur. 3 Sueborum gens est longe maxima et bellicosissima Germanorum omnium. 4 Hi centum pagos habere dicuntur, ex quibus quotannis singula milia armatorum bellandi causa suis ex finibus educunt. Reliqui, qui domi manserunt, se atque illos alunt; 5 hi rursus in vicem anno post in armis sunt, illi domi remanent. 6 Sic neque agri cultura nec ratio atque usus belli intermittitur. 7 Sed privati ac separati agri apud eos nihil est, neque longius anno remanere uno in loco colendi causa licet. 8 Neque multum frumento, sed maximam partem lacte atque pecore vivunt, multumque sunt in venationibus; 9 quae res, et cibi genere et cotidiana exercitatione et libertate vitae (quod, a pueris nullo officio aut disciplina assuefacti, nihil omnino contra voluntatem faciunt) et vires alit et immani corporum magnitudine homines efficit. 10 Atque in eam se consuetudinem adduxerunt, ut locis frigidissimis neque vestitus praeter pelles habeant quicquam, quarum propter exiguitatem magna est corporis pars aperta, et laventur in fluminibus.

1 **hieme:** *12a; 147a.* **qui:** in agreement not with the antecedent *hieme*, but with the predicate noun *annus; 164c.* **annus:** 55 BC; Pompey and Crassus entered upon their consulship January 1 of that year. The winter of 56-55 BC, according to the calendar in use, fell wholly in 55 BC; for the Roman calendar in use had fallen so far behind that January 1 of the official year came on November 30 of the solar year. The calendar was corrected in 46 BC by Julius Caesar. **consulibus:** *240a.* **Germani:** appositive of both *Usipetes* and *Tencteri.* **quo:** = *in quod.* The horde of Usipetes and Tencteri is thought to have crossed the Rhine near Xanten or Emmerich, below Cologne, in the region where the Rhine receives the Lippe as tributary (see Map 11).

2 **transeundi:** *68b.* **quod:** *198b.* **annos:** *118a.* **cultura:** *127a.*

3 **Sueborum gens:** the Suebi are the ancestors of the modern Swabians; see Map Gallia.

4 **pagos:** 'districts' or 'villages' within a region or adminstrative area. **singula milia:** 'a thousand each'; if each district furnished a thousand warriors, the armed force of the Swabians would have reached 100,000 men. **bellandi:** *230.1.* **suis ex finibus educunt:** invasion of neighboring territory is implied. **qui domi manserunt:** 'who (each year) have remained at home.' **illos:** 'the others'; those in the field.

5 **hi, illi:** 'the latter' (i.e., the second group described in IV.1.4, namely those who stayed at home), 'the former' (namely those who went out to fight); *161b.* **in vicem:** 'in turn.' **anno:** *140.*

6 **cultura:** *131a.* **nec:** = *et* (with *sic*) *non* (with *intermittitur*). **ratio ... belli:** 'the pursuit of war in theory and practice'; how lit.? **intermittitur:** *173a.*

7 **privati ac separati:** 'assigned to an individual and marked off' by boundaries; the land was held in common. **agri nihil:** 'no land'; *97a.* **anno:** *129a.* **remanere:** *222a.* **colendi causa:** 'in order to till the soil'; how lit.? *230.1.* Changes of location were doubtless made each year in order to obtain the best results from the farming.

8 **frumento:** ablative of means; translate with *vivunt,* 'they live on grain'; how lit.? **partem:** *118c.* **lacte:** 'milk'; *10g.* **pecore:** *13f.* **multum sunt in venationibus:** 'devote much time to hunting'; how lit.? **multum:** 'to a great extent'; *118b.* **venationibus:** *92a.*

9 **quae res:** 'this circumstance,' their devotion to hunting; *167.* **et cibi genere:** 'both by reason of the kind of food' obtained by hunting; *135a.* **quod:** causal, introducing a parenthesis that explains their *libertas.* **a pueris:** 'from childhood,' lit. 'from (the time they were) boys.' **nullo officio aut disciplina:** ablative with *assuefacti,* 'habituated to no obligation or training'; how lit.? *139.* **et ... et:** *233a.* **vires:** *18a.* **alit, efficit:** *quae res* is the subject. **immani:** with *magnitudine;* 'huge.' **homines:** predicate accusative, with *eos* understood as object of *efficit.* Cf. I.39.1.

10 **in eam se consuetudinem adduxerunt:** 'they have trained themselves to this custom'; how lit.? **locis frigidissimis:** '(even) in the coldest places'; *145c.* **ut ... habeant:** substantive clause that explains *eam consuetudinem; 203.4.* **neque vestitus ... quicquam:** 'no clothing,' lit. 'not anything of clothing.' **vestitus:** *97b.* **quicquam:** *49a.* **quarum:** *pelles* is the antecedent, to be taken with *propter exiguitatem.* **laventur:** 'bathe,' a passive used reflexively; *174.*

2. 1 Mercatoribus est aditus magis eo, ut, quae bello ceperint, quibus vendant, habeant, quam quo ullam rem ad se importari desiderent. 2 Quin etiam iumentis, quibus maxime Galli delectantur quaeque
impenso parant pretio, Germani importatis non utuntur, sed quae sunt apud eos nata, parva atque
deformia, haec cotidiana exercitatione, summi ut sint laboris, efficiunt. 3 Equestribus proeliis saepe
ex equis desiliunt ac pedibus proeliantur, equosque eodem remanere vestigio assuefaciunt, ad quos
se celeriter, cum usus est, recipiunt; 4 neque eorum moribus turpius quicquam aut inertius habetur
quam ephippiis uti. 5 Itaque ad quemvis numerum ephippiatorum equitum quamvis pauci adire audent. 6 Vinum omnino ad se importari non patiuntur, quod ea re ad laborem ferendum remollescere
homines atque effeminari arbitrantur.

1 **Mercatoribus . . . desiderent:** translate as if: *Mercatoribus est aditus (ad Suebos) magis eo, ut habeant (eos)*
quibus vendant (ea) quae bello ceperint, quam quo desiderent ullam rem importari ad se. **Mercatoribus est aditus:**
'Traders have access,' lit. 'There is access to traders'; *111.* **magis eo, ut:** 'more on this account, namely so that.'
ceperint: *220.* (eos) **quibus vendant:** '(those) to whom they may sell'; *194a.* **habeant:** *196a.* **quam quo:** =
quam eo quod, 'than for the reason that'; *183c.* **desiderent:** 'desire.'
2 **Quin etiam:** 'moreover.' **iumentis:** with *utuntur,* emphatic by position; *131c; 245d.* The word can describe
any 'beasts of burden,' but here horses alone are meant. **quibus maxime Galli delectantur:** 'in which the Gauls
especially take delight.' **quaeque impenso parant pretio:** 'and which they obtain at a high price'; *141.* So great
was the interest of the Gauls in horses that they developed choice breeds, and Gallic horses were in demand
in Rome. The horse figures prominently on Gallic coins. **quibus . . . efficiunt:** translate as if: *efficiunt cotidiana*
exercitatione ut haec (iumenta), quae nata sunt apud eos parva atque deformia, sint summi laboris. **deformia:** 'un-
sightly.' **summi laboris:** '(capable) of the greatest endurance'; *100b.* **sint:** *203.3.*
3 **pedibus:** 'on foot.' **eodem vestigio:** 'on the same spot' where they have been left; *145c.* **assuefaciunt:** takes
accusative (*equos*) and infinitive (*remanere*): 'habituate their horses to remain.' **cum usus est:** 'when it is necessary'; *186a.*
4 **neque . . . quicquam:** *168.* **eorum moribus:** 'according to their view'; how lit.? *136c.* **inertius:** 'more indolent.' **habetur:** 'is regarded.' **ephippiis:** 'saddle-cloths,' padding spread over the horse's back; *131c.*
5 **ad quemvis numerum:** 'to whatever number'; *49a.* **ephippiatorum:** 'riding with saddle-cloths.' **quamvis**
pauci: 'however few' in number; *quamvis* is an adverb. Caesar claims that a band of German cavalry, no matter
how small, would always dare to attack an enemy riding with saddle-cloths, no matter how numerous, because
the mere presence of saddle-cloths among the enemy was such an indication of softness that the Germans could
be confident of success.
6 **Vinum . . . ad se importari:** cf. II.15.4. **re:** *135a.* **remollescere:** 'lose their vigor,' lit. 'become soft again.'

3. 1 Publice maximam putant esse laudem, quam latissime a suis finibus vacare agros; hac re significari, magnum numerum civitatum suam vim sustinere non potuisse. 2 Itaque una ex parte a Suebis
circiter milia passuum DC agri vacare dicuntur. 3 Ad alteram partem succedunt Ubii, quorum fuit
civitas ampla atque florens, ut est captus Germanorum; ei paulo sunt eiusdem generis ceteris humaniores, propterea quod Rhenum attingunt, multumque ad eos mercatores ventitant, et ipsi propter
propinquitatem Gallicis sunt moribus assuefacti. 4 Hos cum Suebi, multis saepe bellis experti, propter
amplitudinem gravitatemque civitatis finibus expellere non potuissent, tamen vectigales sibi fecerunt
ac multo humiliores infirmioresque redegerunt.

1 **Publice:** 'for a people,' lit. 'publicly.' **laudem:** *88a.* **quam:** *153c.* **vacare agros:** 'that the lands be unoccupied,'
this accusative and infinitive clause is the subject of *esse.* **hac re significari, magnum numerum civitatum:** still
after *putant,* '(they think that) by this circumstance (i.e., *quam latissime a suis finibus vacare agros*) it is indicated
that a great number of states'; the subject of *significari* is the accusative and infinitive clause following.
2 **una ex parte:** 'on one side.' The east side is meant, and the country left vacant was probably Bohemia, from
which the Boii had withdrawn; cf. I.5.4. The name *Boii* survives in 'Bohemia.' **Suebis:** *251.* **milia:** *118a.* **DC:**
38b; 36. **agri:** nominative plural; *172d.*
3 **Ad alteram partem:** 'to the opposite (lit. 'other') side,' toward the Rhine. **succedunt:** 'come next,' i.e., are
the closest people. **fuit:** the perfect tense implies that the condition described no longer exists. **ut est captus**
Germanorum: 'according to the German standard,' lit. 'considering how the notion of the Germans is'; *ut* here
introduces a qualification of the claim that the Ubian state was *ampla* and *florens,* since the German notion of
prosperity was lower than the Roman one. **captus:** here the 4th declension noun. **eiusdem generis ceteris:**

'than the rest of this same people (i.e., the Germans)'; *129a.* **humaniores:** 'more civilized.' **multum ventitant:** 'freely come and go'; *78a.* **sunt assuefacti:** 'have become familiar with'; *139.* Caesar further compares Gallic and German customs at VI.11-24.

4 **Hos:** *Ubios,* object of *expellere.* **cum:** *187.* **multis saepe bellis experti:** 'having tested (them) often by means of many wars.' **gravitatem:** 'importance.' **civitatis:** of the Ubii. **finibus:** *127a.* **vectigales:** predicate accusative, 'made (them) tributary'; *115b.* **multo:** *140.* **redegerunt:** from *redigo,* 'rendered (them).'

By strategy the Usipetes and Tencteri overcome the Menapii.

4. 1 In eadem causa fuerunt Usipetes et Tencteri, quos supra diximus, qui complures annos Sueborum vim sustinuerunt; ad extremum tamen, agris expulsi et multis locis Germaniae triennium vagati, ad Rhenum pervenerunt, 2 quas regiones Menapii incolebant. Hi ad utramque ripam fluminis agros, aedificia vicosque habebant; 3 sed, tantae multitudinis aditu perterriti, ex eis aedificiis, quae trans flumen habuerant, demigraverunt et cis Rhenum, dispositis praesidiis, Germanos transire prohibebant. 4 Illi, omnia experti, cum neque vi contendere propter inopiam navium neque clam transire propter custodias Menapiorum possent, reverti se in suas sedes regionesque simulaverunt 5 et, tridui viam progressi, rursus reverterunt atque, omni hoc itinere una nocte equitatu confecto, inscios inopinantesque Menapios oppresserunt, 6 qui, de Germanorum discessu per exploratores certiores facti, sine metu trans Rhenum in suos vicos remigraverant. 7 His interfectis navibusque eorum occupatis, prius quam ea pars Menapiorum, quae citra Rhenum erat, certior fieret, flumen transierunt atque, omnibus eorum aedificiis occupatis, reliquam partem hiemis se eorum copiis aluerunt.

1 **In eadem causa:** 'in the same condition' of subjection to the Swabians. **quos supra diximus:** 'whom we spoke of above'; see IV.1.1-2. **annos:** *118a.* **ad extremum tamen:** 'in the end, however.' **multis locis Germaniae:** 'over many parts of Germany,' lit. 'in many places'; *145c.* **triennium:** used instead of *tres annos.*
2 **quas regiones:** '(to) the districts which'; in full, *ad eas regiones quas*; *165c.* **ad utramque ripam:** '(adjacent) to both banks.' **aedificia, vicos:** cf. I.5.2.
3 **tantae multitudinis:** their number, as reported at IV.15.3, was 430,000. **trans flumen:** on the east side of the Rhine; Caesar writes from the point of view of one in Gaul. **Germanos transire:** 'the Germans from crossing'; *223a3.*
4 **Illi:** *Germani.* **reverti se:** 'that they were returning,' accusative and infinitive after *simulaverunt.*
5 **tridui:** translate as if *trium dierum; 100a.* **viam:** *118a.* **nocte:** *147a.* **equitatu:** *131b.* **oppresserunt:** 'surprised.'
6 **trans:** to the east side. **remigraverant:** 'had moved back.'
7 **occupatis:** 'seized.' **fieret:** *189b.* **partem:** *118a.* **eorum:** the Menapii on the west side of the Rhine. **eorum copiis:** 'with their supplies.'

Caesar fears the effect of this victory upon the fickle Gauls.

5. 1 His de rebus Caesar certior factus et infirmitatem Gallorum veritus, quod sunt in consiliis capiendis mobiles et novis plerumque rebus student, nihil his committendum existimavit. 2 Est enim hoc Gallicae consuetudinis, uti et viatores, etiam invitos, consistere cogant et, quid quisque eorum de quaque re audierit aut cognoverit, quaerant, et mercatores in oppidis vulgus circumsistat, quibusque ex regionibus veniant quasque ibi res cognoverint, pronuntiare cogat. 3 His rebus atque auditionibus permoti, de summis saepe rebus consilia ineunt, quorum eos in vestigio paenitere necesse est, cum incertis rumoribus serviant et plerique ad voluntatem eorum ficta respondeant.

1 **infirmitatem:** 'fickleness.' Cf. III.19.6. **veritus:** *226c.* **rebus:** *105.* **nihil his committendum:** sc. *esse,* 'that no trust at all should be placed in them'; *73e.* **nihil:** = emphatic *non; 118c.*
2 **Est enim hoc Gallicae consuetudinis, uti . . . cogant:** 'for it is a custom of the Gauls to compel,' lit. 'this is (characteristic) of Gallic custom, namely that they compel.' **consuetudinis:** *100b.* **uti cogant, quaerant, circumsistat, cogat:** explain *hoc; 203.4.* **viatores:** 'travelers,' on country roads. **invitos:** *151.* **cogant:** the subject is supplied in thought from *Gallicae,* as if it were *Gallorum.* **quid:** *204.2.* **eorum:** *97a.* **quaque:** *49a.* **audierit:** *64a3.* **vulgus:** *6b.* **quibusque:** = *quibus* (48b) + *-que.* **quasque:** = *quas* + *-que; 204.2.* **pronuntiare:** '(them) to declare.'
3 **rebus atque auditionibus:** 'reports and hearsay.' **summis:** 'of the utmost importance.' **quorum eos paenitere necesse est:** 'of which they must repent'; how lit.? *103c.* **in vestigio:** 'in an instant.' **paenitere:** subject of *est;*

73a. **serviant:** 'they (the Gauls) subject themselves'; *184a.* **plerique:** 'most,' i.e., most of those traders whom they question, thus the subject of *respondeant* is different than the subject of *serviant.* **ad eorum voluntatem:** 'according to the inclination of those (asking the questions).' **ficta respondeant:** 'give as answers things having been invented.'

He resolves to fight the Usipetes and Tencteri.
6. 1 Qua consuetudine cognita, Caesar, ne graviori bello occurreret, maturius, quam consuerat, ad exercitum proficiscitur. 2 Eo cum venisset, ea, quae fore suspicatus erat, facta cognovit; 3 *missas lega-tiones ab non nullis civitatibus ad Germanos invitatosque eos, uti ab Rheno discederent; omniaque, quae postulassent, ab se fore parata.* 4 Qua spe adducti, Germani latius iam vagabantur et in fines Eburonum et Condrusorum, qui sunt Treverorum clientes, pervenerant. 5 Principibus Galliae evocatis, Caesar ea, quae cognoverat, dissimulanda sibi existimavit eorumque animis permulsis et confirmatis, equi-tatuque imperato, bellum cum Germanis gerere constituit.

1 **graviori:** 'more serious,' in case the fickle Gauls and the Germans should unite against him; *153a.* **bello:** *107a.* **occurreret:** *196a.* **maturius:** 'earlier' in the spring, perhaps in the first part of April; *34a.* **exercitum:** divided up for winter quarters among the Lexovii and other states in the autumn of 56 BC (III.29.3); now probably brought together again near the lower Seine, in advance of Caesar's arrival.
2 **Eo:** = *ad exercitum.* **ea, quae fore suspicatus erat, facta:** sc. *esse,* '(that) those things had been done which he had suspected would be done.' **fore:** = *futura esse,* lit. 'would be,' but here with the sense of 'would be done.'
3 **missas, invitatos:** sc. *esse.* **eos:** *Germanos.* **uti ab Rheno discederent:** 'to depart from the Rhine,' i.e., to pro-ceed toward the interior of Gaul in order to help drive the Romans out; *199a.* **omniaque:** 'and (with the prom-ise) that everything'; *213b.* This sentence is thus a deeper level of indirect speech: 'Caesar learned that (level 1) embassies had been sent (who promised) that (level 2) everything would be.' **postulassent:** future perfect in-dicative in the direct form; *64a1.* **fore parata:** 'would be prepared,' a substitute for the future infinitive passive.
4 **Qua spe:** 'by this prospect'; *167.* **Eburonum, Condrusorum,** etc.: see Map Gallia.
5 **dissimulanda:** sc. *esse,* 'ought to be kept secret.' **sibi:** *110.* **permulsis:** 'having soothed'; how lit.? *144b2.* **im-perato:** here 'levied.' **constituit:** here not 'determined,' but 'announced his intention'; he had previously made up his mind.

He marches near to the Germans, who parley, assert their rights in Gaul, and request lands.
7. 1 Re frumentaria comparata equitibusque delectis, iter in ea loca facere coepit, quibus in locis esse Germanos audiebat. 2 A quibus cum paucorum dierum iter abesset, legati ab his venerunt, quorum haec fuit oratio: 3 *Germanos neque priores populo Romano bellum inferre, neque tamen recusare, si lacessantur, quin armis contendant, quod Germanorum consuetudo haec sit a maioribus tradita, quicum-que bellum inferant, resistere neque deprecari. Haec tamen dicere, venisse invitos, eiectos domo;* 4 *si suam gratiam Romani velint, posse eis utiles esse amicos; vel sibi agros attribuant vel patiantur eos tenere, quos armis possederint:* 5 *sese unis Suebis concedere, quibus ne di quidem immortales pares esse possint; reliquum quidem in terris esse neminem, quem non superare possint.*

Direct Form: 3 *Germani* neque priores populo Romano bellum *inferunt,* neque tamen *recusant,* si *lacessentur,* quin armis contendant, quod Germanorum consuetudo haec *est* a maioribus tradita, quicumque bellum *inferunt,* resistere neque deprecari. Haec tamen *dicimus,* (*nos*) venisse invitos, eiectos domo. 4 si (*vos Ro-mani*) *nostram* gratiam *vultis, possumus vobis* utiles esse amicos; vel *nobis* agros *attribuite* vel *patimini* (*nos*) eos (*agros*) tenere, quos armis *possedimus.* 5 unis Suebis *concedimus,* quibus ne di quidem immortales pares esse *possint; reliquus* quidem in terris *est nemo,* quem non superare *possimus.*

1 **delectis:** 'selected.' **iter facere:** 'to march.' **locis:** *165a.*
2 **quibus:** 'these (places)'; *167.* **paucorum dierum iter abesset:** 'he was a journey of a few days distant'; *118a; 243c.* **dierum:** *100a.* **quorum haec fuit oratio:** 'whose plea was as follows'; *161a.*
3 **Germanos neque ... neque tamen:** '(that) the Germans were not ... but nor were they.' **priores:** *152b.* **lacessantur:** present, used for greater vividness, where a past tense might have been expected; *218.1a.* **quin armis contendant:** 'to contend with arms,' after *recusare; 201a.* **quod:** causal. **quicumque:** *50a.* **resistere:** sc. *eis* (*105*), as antecedent of *quicumque;* the infinitive explains *consuetudo haec,* 'this custom was handed down,

namely to resist whoever.' **neque deprecari:** 'and not to beg for mercy.' **haec:** 'this,' lit. 'these things'; explained by what follows: '(namely) that they had come.' **dicere, venisse:** sc. *se*; *215.* **eiectos:** 'because they had been driven forth'; *227a1.* **domo:** *127a.*

4 **posse, tenere:** sc. *se*; *215.* **attribuant, patiantur:** *216.* **possederint:** from *possido.*

5 **unis:** 'alone'; *23a.* **quibus . . . possent:** *194a.* **di:** *8d; 237c.* **reliquum in terris neminem:** 'no one else on earth,' lit. 'no one remaining (out of those) in the lands'; *12d.* **esse neminem, quem:** 'there was no one whom'; *194a.*

Caesar insists that they go back to Germany; the parley continues.

8. 1 Ad haec Caesar, quae visum est, respondit; sed exitus fuit orationis: *sibi nullam cum his amicitiam esse posse, si in Gallia remanerent; 2 neque verum esse, qui suos fines tueri non potuerint, alienos occupare; neque ullos in Gallia vacare agros, qui dari, tantae praesertim multitudini, sine iniuria possint; 3 sed licere, si velint, in Ubiorum finibus considere, quorum sint legati apud se et de Sueborum iniuriis querantur et a se auxilium petant; hoc se ab Ubiis impetraturum.*

1 **quae visum est:** sc. *ea quae visum est respondere,* '(those things) which it seemed proper (to respond);' *quae* is the direct object of the implied *respondere,* while *visum est* is impersonal (and thus has the sense of 'it seemed good/proper'). Caesar does not give the whole of his answer, which perhaps followed the same line of argument as his statement to Ariovistus (I.45). **sibi nullam cum his amicitiam esse posse:** in the direct form, *mihi nulla cum vobis amicitia esse potest,* 'I can have no friendly relations with you'; *111; 212c1.*

2 **verum:** consistent with what is true, 'a fair thing.' **qui:** for antecedent supply *eos* as subject-accusative with *occupare.* **alienos:** sc. *fines;* 'of others.' **possint:** the present tense is used for the sake of vividness.

3 **licere:** sc. *eis,* followed by an infinitive, 'it was permitted (to them) to'; *73b.* **apud se:** 'with him.' **Sueborum iniuriis:** see IV.3.3-4. **hoc se ab Ubiis impetraturum:** sc. *esse,* 'that he would obtain this from the Ubii.'

9. 1 Legati haec se ad suos relaturos dixerunt et, re deliberata, post diem tertium ad Caesarem reversuros; interea ne propius se castra moveret, petierunt. 2 Ne id quidem Caesar ab se impetrari posse dixit. 3 Cognoverat enim magnam partem equitatus ab eis, aliquot diebus ante, praedandi frumentandique causa ad Ambivaritos trans Mosam missam; hos exspectari equites atque eius rei causa moram interponi arbitrabatur.

1 **haec se ad suos relaturos dixerunt:** translate as if: *dixerunt se relaturos (esse) haec ad suos.* **post diem tertium:** 'in three days,' but in reality 'in two days,' for in such expressions the Romans inclusively counted the days with which a period began and ended, hence 'today, tomorrow, and the next day' equal three days. **propius se:** *123b.* **moveret:** *199a4.*

2 **id:** the accusative subject of *posse impetrari.* **ab:** 'from.' **impetrari:** 'granted,' lit. 'obtained by (their) request.'

3 **diebus:** *140.* **frumentandi causa:** 'to forage'; how lit.? **trans:** 'across' to the west side of the Mosa (*Meuse*); the main body of their force, and Caesar, were on the east side, between the Meuse and the Rhine. **hos exspectari equites:** in order that, upon their return, an attack with all their forces might be made upon the Romans. **rei:** the return of the cavalry. **interponi:** 'introduced.'

Description of the Rhine region.

[**10.** 1 Mosa profluit ex monte Vosego, qui est in finibus Lingonum, et parte quadam ex Rheno recepta, quae appellatur Vacalus, insulam efficit Batavorum, 2 neque longius ab eo milibus passuum LXXX in Oceanum influit. 3 Rhenus autem oritur ex Lepontiis, qui Alpes incolunt, et longo spatio per fines Nantuatium, Helvetiorum, Sequanorum, Mediomatricorum, Tribocorum, Treverorum citatus fertur 4 et, ubi Oceano appropinquavit, in plures diffluit partes, multis ingentibusque insulis effectis (quarum pars magna a feris barbarisque nationibus incolitur, 5 ex quibus sunt, qui piscibus atque ovis avium vivere existimantur), multisque capitibus in Oceanum influit.]

1 On account of certain difficulties and inconsistencies in this chapter many think that it was not written by Caesar, but added later by someone who wished to supply a geographical background for this part of the narrative; the Meuse, for example, does not rise in the Vosges mountains, and the Rhine could hardly have flowed through the country of the Nantuates. If the chapter is omitted, there is an easy transition from IV.9 to IV.11. Transla-

tion: 1 'The Meuse flows forth out of the Vosges mountains, which are in the country of the Lingones; receiving from the Rhine an affluent, which is called the Waal, it forms (with this) the island of the Batavians, 2 and not further from this than eighty miles it flows into the Ocean. 3 The Rhine, moreover, rises in the country of the Lepontii, who dwell in the Alps, and in a long course flows rapidly through the territories of the Nantuates, the Helvetii, the Sequani, the Mediomatrici, the Triboci, and the Treverans; 4 and, where it approaches the Ocean, it divides up into several branches, forming many large islands. Of these (islands) a considerable portion are inhabited by wild and savage tribes, 5 some of whom are believed to live on fish and birds' eggs. (The Rhine) flows into the Ocean through many mouths.'

The parley, Caesar concludes, is being continued merely to gain time.

11. 1 Caesar cum ab hoste non amplius passuum XII milibus abesset, ut erat constitutum, ad eum legati revertuntur; qui in itinere congressi magnopere, ne longius progrederetur, orabant. 2 Cum id non impetrassent, petebant, uti ad eos equites, qui agmen antecessissent, praemitteret eosque pugna prohiberet, sibique ut potestatem faceret in Ubios legatos mittendi; 3 *quorum si principes ac senatus sibi iure iurando fidem fecisset, ea condicione, quae a Caesare ferretur, se usuros* ostendebant; *ad has res conficiendas sibi tridui spatium daret.* 4 Haec omnia Caesar eodem illo pertinere arbitrabatur, ut, tridui mora interposita, equites eorum, qui abessent, reverterentur; tamen *sese non longius milibus passuum IIII, aquationis causa, processurum eo die dixit;* 5 *huc postero die quam frequentissimi convenirent, ut de eorum postulatis cognosceret.* 6 Interim ad praefectos, qui cum omni equitatu antecesserant, mittit, qui nuntiarent, ne hostes proelio lacesserent et, si ipsi lacesserentur, sustinerent, quoad ipse cum exercitu propius accessisset.

1 **Caesar:** after denying the request of the Germans to delay (IV.9.1-2), Caesar evidently had marched toward them. **XII:** *38b; 36.* **milibus:** *129a.* **ut erat constitutum:** the agreement was that the envoys should return in three days (IV.9.1); *73d.* **qui:** 'and they'; *167.* **congressi:** sc. *cum eo,* 'meeting him'; *57c; 226c.* **progrederetur:** *199a4.*

2 **antecessissent:** *220; 288.* **praemitteret:** here without a direct object, 'that he send (word) forward to those cavalry.' **pugna:** *127a.* **sibique ut potestatem faceret:** 'and that he would give to them the opportunity.' **mittendi:** gerund; genitive after *potestatem; 230.1.*

3 **quorum:** *Ubiorum.* **iure iurando fidem fecisset:** 'should have made a pledge by means of an oath'; *13h.* **fecisset:** agrees with *senatus,* the nearer subject; *172b.* **ea condicione, quae a Caesare ferretur, se usuros:** 'that they would accept that condition which was proposed by Caesar,' namely that they be settled in Ubian territory (see IV.8.3). **condicione:** *131c.* **daret:** indirect command in place of the imperative *da* in the direct form; *216.*

4 **eodem illo:** 'to the (lit. 'that') same end.' **ut . . . reverterentur:** 'namely that,' explaining *eodem illo; 203.4.* **abessent:** see IV.9.3; *220.* **aquationis causa:** 'in order to get water'; *94b.*

5 **huc:** i.e., to the place where he would stop for water. **quam frequentissimi:** 'in the greatest possible numbers,' lit. 'in as great numbers as possible'; *153c.* **convenirent:** *convenite* in the direct form; *216.* **cognosceret:** *196a.*

6 **praefectos:** *269c.* **equitatu:** *137a.* **qui nuntiarent:** '(men) to convey the order'; *193a.* **sustinerent:** sc. *ut; 200a.* The Roman cavalry were ordered to act on the defensive. **accessisset:** subjunctive also in the direct form; *190c.*

The German cavalry surprises and routs the cavalry of Caesar; the bravery of Piso the Aquitanian.

12. 1 At hostes, ubi primum nostros equites conspexerunt, quorum erat V milium numerus, cum ipsi non amplius DCCC equites haberent, quod ei, qui frumentandi causa erant trans Mosam profecti, nondum redierant, nihil timentibus nostris, quod legati eorum paulo ante a Caesare discesserant atque is dies indutiis erat ab his petitus, impetu facto celeriter nostros perturbaverunt; 2 rursus his resistentibus, consuetudine sua ad pedes desiluerunt, subfossisque equis compluribusque nostris deiectis, reliquos in fugam coniecerunt atque ita perterritos egerunt, ut non prius fuga desisterent, quam in conspectum agminis nostri venissent. 3 In eo proelio ex equitibus nostris interficiuntur IIII et LXX, 4 in his vir fortissimus, Piso Aquitanus, amplissimo genere natus, cuius avus in civitate sua regnum obtinuerat, amicus a senatu nostro appellatus. 5 Hic cum fratri, intercluso ab hostibus, auxilium ferret, illum ex periculo eripuit, ipse, equo vulnerato, deiectus, quoad potuit, fortissime restitit; 6 cum circumventus, multis vulneribus acceptis, cecidisset, atque id frater, qui iam proelio excesserat, procul animadvertisset, incitato equo se hostibus obtulit atque interfectus est.

1 **ubi primum:** *188c.* **nostros equites:** the Roman cavalry had apparently advanced in the direction of the German camp. **V milium:** *269b; 100a.* **cum:** *187.* **DCCC:** *octingentos; 38b; 36.* **equites:** *129b.* **quod . . . redierant:** causal, explaining why their cavalry were so few. **ei . . . profecti:** see IV.9.3. **timentibus nostris:** *144b2.* **quod . . . petitus:** causal, explaining why the Romans were caught off guard. **indutiis:** 'for a truce'; *112a.* **impetu facto:** 'charged and'; how lit.? *144b2.*

2 **rursus:** 'again,' i.e., after they were initially thrown on the defensive. **his:** the Roman cavalry. **consuetudine:** *136c.* **sua:** *157b.* **ad pedes desiluerunt:** 'they jumped down to the ground' from their horses. **subfossis . . . deiectis:** 'and they stabbed the horses (of our cavalry) from underneath and dismounted quite a number of our men and'; how lit.? **reliquos:** sc. *nostros.* **fuga:** *127a.* **agminis:** the main force. **venissent:** subjunctive by attraction; *189a; 220.*

3 **ex equitibus:** *97d.* **IIII et LXX:** *quattuor et septuaginta; 38b.* The result of the skirmish showed the superiority of the German over the Gallic cavalry. Later in the war Caesar would hire German horsemen and make effective use of them against the Gauls (VII.80).

4 **Piso:** a Roman name, probably conferred on some Aquitanian with Roman citizenship; cf. I.47. **genere:** *128a.* **amicus:** cf. I.3; *88a.*

5 **deiectus:** 'although thrown' from his horse, he continued to fight on foot; *227a3.* **potuit:** *190c.*

6 **id:** 'that (event),' i.e., the death of his brother. **proelio:** *127a.* **incitato equo:** *144b2.* **se hostibus obtulit:** 'he hurled himself upon the enemy.' Many instances of individual bravery and devotion are recorded by Caesar.

The German leaders come to offer apology; Caesar detains them.

13. 1 Hoc facto proelio Caesar neque iam sibi legatos audiendos neque condiciones accipiendas arbitrabatur ab eis, qui per dolum atque insidias, petita pace, ultro bellum intulissent; 2 exspectare vero, dum hostium copiae augerentur equitatusque reverteretur, summae dementiae esse iudicabat; 3 et, cognita Gallorum infirmitate, quantum iam apud eos hostes uno proelio auctoritatis essent consecuti, sentiebat; quibus ad consilia capienda nihil spatii dandum existimabat. 4 His constitutis rebus et consilio cum legatis et quaestore communicato, ne quem diem pugnae praetermitteret, opportunissime res accidit, quod postridie eius diei mane, eadem et simulatione et perfidia usi, Germani frequentes, omnibus principibus maioribusque natu adhibitis, ad eum in castra venerunt, 5 simul, ut dicebatur, sui purgandi causa, quod contra atque esset dictum et ipsi petissent, proelium pridie commisissent, simul ut, si quid possent, de indutiis fallendo impetrarent. 6 Quos sibi Caesar oblatos gavisus, illos retineri iussit; ipse omnes copias castris eduxit equitatumque, quod recenti proelio perterritum esse existimabat, agmen subsequi iussit.

1 **Hoc facto proelio:** 'after this battle'; how lit.? **audiendos:** *89c.* **ab:** 'from'; Caesar had arranged to take up their proposals on the following day (see IV.11.5). **per dolum atque insidias:** to be taken closely with *petita pace;* i.e., what made their attack treacherous was the fact that they had sought peace immediately before. **ultro:** i.e., without provocation. **bellum intulissent:** 'had made an attack.'

2 **exspectare:** subject of *esse; 222b.* **dum:** 'until', with the subjunctive also in the direct form; *190b.* **summae dementiae esse:** 'that it was the height of folly,' lit. 'was of the greatest madness'; *100b.*

3 **infirmitate:** see IV.5.1. **quantum . . . auctoritatis:** 'how much (of) prestige'; *97b; 204.3.* **hostes . . . essent consecuti:** 'the (German) enemy had gained.' **quibus:** translate as if *et eis.* **ad consilia capienda:** *230.3.* **nihil spatii:** 'no time'; *97a.*

4 **consilio:** 'decision,' explained by the appositive clause *ne . . . praetermittet,* 'not to let any chance to fight pass'; lit. 'that he would not let pass any day of battle.' **cum legatis:** *137c.* **quaestore:** *273b.* **quod:** explains *res,* 'namely that'; *198b.* **diei:** *94c.* **mane:** 'early in the morning.' **eadem:** 'the same' as before. **perfidia:** 'treachery.' To justify his own course Caesar accuses the Germans of bad faith. But if they did not mean what they said, why did so many of them trust themselves to Caesar's power? The collision on the previous day could well have been precipitated without the approval of the leaders of the German host. **Germani frequentes:** 'a large number of Germans,' lit. 'Germans in large numbers.'

5 **simul . . . simul:** 'both . . . and'; each of which is followed by an expression of purpose, but note that the first takes the form of *causa* plus the gerundive while the second is an *ut* clause with the subjunctive. **ut dicebatur:** 'as was alleged.' **sui purgandi causa:** 'in order to clear themselves'; *154b; 230.1.* **quod contra atque esset dictum:** 'because, contrary to what had been said.' **contra atque:** 'otherwise than' or 'contrary to what'; *233c.* **proelium commisissent:** '(as they admitted) they had started the battle'; *183a.* **si quid possent:** 'if to any

extent they could'; *118b.* **de indutiis fallendo:** the gerund *fallendo* is explained by the prepositional phrase *de indutiis,* 'by playing false in the matter of the truce,' i.e., by falsely claiming that they did not intentionally violate the truce. **impetrarent:** 'they might obtain their request,' i.e., a truce during which they could solicit pledges of good faith from the Ubians.

6 **Quos:** *167.* **oblatos:** sc. *esse; 69b.* **gavisus:** 'rejoicing'; *62; 226c.* **agmen subsequi:** 'to follow the main force,' i.e., to bring up the rear, instead of leading the van, as the cavalry usually did; *288.*

Surprising the leaderless German host, he utterly destroys it.

14. 1 Acie triplici instituta et celeriter VIII milium itinere confecto, prius ad hostium castra pervenit, quam, quid ageretur, Germani sentire possent. 2 Qui omnibus rebus subito perterriti, et celeritate adventus nostri et discessu suorum neque consilii habendi neque arma capiendi spatio dato, perturbabantur, copiasne adversus hostem ducere, an castra defendere, an fuga salutem petere praestaret. 3 Quorum timor cum fremitu et concursu significaretur, milites nostri, pristini diei perfidia incitati, in castra irruperunt. 4 Quo loco, qui celeriter arma capere potuerunt, paulisper nostris restiterunt atque inter carros impedimentaque proelium commiserunt; 5 at reliqua multitudo puerorum mulierumque (nam cum omnibus suis domo excesserant Rhenumque transierant) passim fugere coepit; ad quos consectandos Caesar equitatum misit.

1 **Acie triplici:** *297a.* **VIII:** *38b.* **itinere:** the army probably marched in three parallel columns, which deployed as they neared the camp of the enemy. The country must have been open and fairly level for such a deployment to have been feasible. **prius . . . quam . . . possent:** the subjunctive *possent* reveals both that Caesar arrived before the Germans were aware, and that he acted with the intention of doing so; *189b.* **quid ageretur:** *204.2.*
2 **et . . . et:** 'both . . . and'; *233a.* **celeritate, discessu:** ablatives of cause to be understood with the ablative absolute *spatio dato* at the end of the clause. **suorum:** the German leaders who had gone to Caesar and were held by him under guard. **consilii . . . capiendi:** gerundive and gerund in coordinate construction after *spatio,* 'a space (of time) for'; *230.1.* **perturbabantur:** 'were (too) confused (to decide).' **ne . . . an . . . an:** 'whether . . . or . . . or'; *204.1.* **ducere:** *222a.* **praestaret:** here used impersonally, 'it was better.'
3 **Quorum:** the German host; *167.* **cum:** *185c.* **pristini diei:** 'of the previous day.' **irruperunt:** 'burst into.'
4 **Quo loco:** *castris Germanorum.* **restiterunt:** the subject is an implied *ei,* antecedent of *qui.* **inter carros:** the German camp, like that of the Helvetians (see I.26), was a corral protected by carts.
5 **at:** *236a.* **reliqua multitudo puerorum mulierumque:** 'the rest of the host (consisting) of women and children'; *98a.* **cum:** here the preposition, not the conjunction, in accordance with the sense and the connection. **excesserant:** i.e., *Usipetes et Tencteri.* **quos:** the antecedent is *multitudo; 164d.* Caesar's conduct in detaining the German leaders, who had come to him under a flag of truce, and then attacking and pursuing the leaderless host without mercy, seems treacherous and unlike his ordinary procedure. It is perhaps to be explained by the fact that he was fighting Germans not Gauls, for he presents the Germans as outside of civilization and thus perhaps less deserving of the protections of conventional warfare.

15. 1 Germani, post tergum clamore audito, cum suos interfici viderent, armis abiectis signisque militaribus relictis, se ex castris eiecerunt, 2 et cum ad confluentem Mosae et Rheni pervenissent, reliqua fuga desperata, magno numero interfecto, reliqui se in flumen praecipitaverunt atque ibi timore, lassitudine, vi fluminis oppressi perierunt. 3 Nostri ad unum omnes incolumes, perpaucis vulneratis, ex tanti belli timore, cum hostium numerus capitum CCCCXXX milium fuisset, se in castra receperunt. 4 Caesar eis, quos in castris retinuerat, discedendi potestatem fecit. 5 Illi, supplicia cruciatusque Gallorum veriti, quorum agros vexaverant, remanere se apud eum velle dixerunt. His Caesar libertatem concessit.

1 **Germani:** the warriors who armed for defense when the camp was attacked (IV.14.4). **clamore:** 'the shrieking' of the women and children, part of whom were cut down by the legionaries entering the camp, part by the cavalry after they had fled from the camp.
2 **Mosae:** the Meuse, but possibly *Mosellae* (the Moselle) was written but corrupted to *Mosae* in the manuscript tradition. If so, it seems probable that the German camp was south of the Moselle and that the fleeing warriors came to the region of Coblenz, which lies in the angle formed by the Moselle as it enters the Rhine. **reliqua fuga desperata:** 'abandoning hope of further flight'; how lit.? *144b2.* **flumen:** the Rhine, at Coblenz. **lassitudine:** in consequence of the fighting and running.

3 **ad unum:** 'to a man,' emphasizing *omnes*. **incolumes:** predicative, 'unharmed.' **ex tanti belli timore:** '(freed) from the fear aroused by (lit. 'fear of') so great a war'; the reason for their fear is explained by the following *cum*-clause; the phrase seems to apply generally to the whole sentence: 'they returned to camp safe from the fear' generated because of the enemy's large numbers. **cum:** 'since'; *184a*. **capitum . . . fuisset:** 'had amounted to 430,000'; cf. I.29.2; *100b*. **CCCCXXX:** = *quadringentorum triginta*; *38b*; *36*. If, as among the Helvetians, one fourth were fighting-men, the Usipetes and Tencteri mustered an army of more than 130,000. The number seems greatly exaggerated.

4 **quos in castris retinuerat:** i.e., the crowd of German leaders whom he had detained in the Roman camp (see IV.13.6). **discedendi potestatem fecit:** 'allowed (them) to depart,' lit. 'made an opportunity for departing.'

5 **Gallorum:** 'at the hands of the Gauls'; *95*. **veriti:** *61a2*; *226c*. **libertatem:** 'leave' to stay. They probably entered his service as mercenaries.

IV.16-19: First Expedition into Germany

Caesar resolves to cross the Rhine and enter Germany.

16. 1 Germanico bello confecto, multis de causis Caesar statuit sibi Rhenum esse transeundum; quarum illa fuit iustissima, quod, cum videret Germanos tam facile impelli, ut in Galliam venirent, suis quoque rebus eos timere voluit, cum intellegerent et posse et audere populi Romani exercitum Rhenum transire. 2 Accessit etiam quod illa pars equitatus Usipetum et Tencterorum, quam supra commemoravi praedandi frumentandique causa Mosam transisse neque proelio interfuisse, post fugam suorum se trans Rhenum in fines Sugambrorum receperat seque cum eis coniunxerat. 3 Ad quos cum Caesar nuntios misisset, qui postularent, eos, qui sibi Galliaeque bellum intulissent, sibi dederent, responderunt: 4 *Populi Romani imperium Rhenum finire; si, se invito, Germanos in Galliam transire non aequum existimaret, cur sui quicquam esse imperii aut potestatis trans Rhenum postularet?* 5 Ubii autem, qui uni ex Transrhenanis ad Caesarem legatos miserant, amicitiam fecerant, obsides dederant, magnopere orabant, ut sibi auxilium ferret, quod graviter ab Suebis premerentur: 6 *Vel, si id facere occupationibus rei publicae prohiberetur, exercitum modo Rhenum transportaret; id sibi auxilium spemque reliqui temporis satis futurum.* 7 *Tantum esse nomen atque opinionem eius exercitus, Ariovisto pulso et hoc novissimo proelio facto, etiam ad ultimas Germanorum nationes, uti opinione et amicitia populi Romani tuti esse possint.* 8 Navium magnam copiam ad transportandum exercitum pollicebantur.

1 **quarum:** *97a*. **illa:** *161a*. **quod . . . voluit:** explains *illa* (*causa*); *198b*. **ut . . . venirent:** 'to come'; *199a5*. **suis quoque rebus:** 'for their own interests also'; *rebus* is dative after *timere*. **eos timere:** accusative and infinitive after (*Caesar*) *voluit*, the main verb of the *quod* clause. **exercitum:** subject of *posse* and *audere*.

2 **Accessit etiam quod:** 'There was also the reason that'; *198b*. **supra:** see IV.9.3. **quam . . . transisse:** accusative and infinitive after *commemoravi*, 'which I related to have crossed' or 'which, as I related, had crossed.' **commemoravi:** for the first person, cf. *demonstravimus*, II.1.

3 **quos:** *Sugambros*. **postularent:** *193a*. **eos:** direct object of *dederent*. **dederent:** *200a*.

4 **imperium Rhenum finire:** *Rhenum* is the subject, *imperium* the object, of *finire*. **se invito:** cf. I.8.2. **aequum:** 'right'; in predicate, neuter, accusative, in agreement with the infinitive clause *Germanos transire*, which stands as object of *existimaret*, 'if (Caesar) judged (it) not right that the Germans cross.' **sui quicquam esse imperii aut potestatis trans Rhenum:** *quicquam* and *esse* are accusative and infinitive, *trans Rhenum* goes closely with *quicquam*, the genitives are predicative: 'that anything beyond the Rhine was under his authority or power'; *94d*. **postularet:** with *cur*, 'why should he claim'; *217a*.

5 **uni:** 'alone.' **ex Transrhenanis:** 'of the peoples across the Rhine'; *97d*. **miserant, fecerant, dederant:** *234a*; *238a*. **quod . . . premerentur:** *183a*.

6 **Vel:** *213b*; *235a*. **id facere:** 'from doing that'; *223a3*. **occupationibus rei publicae:** 'by the requirements of public business.' **exercitum, Rhenum:** *114a*. **modo:** 'only,' i.e., without Caesar himself. **transportaret:** *216*. **id:** 'that (movement).' **auxilium spemque reliqui temporis:** 'an aid (in the present) and a hope for the future,' lit. 'hope for the remaining time,' i.e., Caesar's deployment of the army across the river would bolster their reputation for the moment and for the longer term.

7 **opinionem:** 'reputation.' **eius:** 'his,' i.e., *Caesaris*. **Ariovisto pulso:** 'in consequence of the defeat of Ariovistus' (related in I.30-54); how lit.? *144b3*.

8 **ad transportandum exercitum:** *230.3*.

He builds a bridge across the Rhine.

17. 1 Caesar his de causis, quas commemoravi, Rhenum transire decreverat; sed navibus transire neque satis tutum esse arbitrabatur, neque suae neque populi Romani dignitatis esse statuebat. 2 Itaque, etsi summa difficultas faciendi pontis proponebatur propter latitudinem, rapiditatem altitudinemque fluminis, tamen id sibi contendendum, aut aliter non traducendum exercitum, existimabat. 3 Rationem pontis hanc instituit: tigna bina sesquipedalia, paulum ab imo praeacuta, dimensa ad altitudinem fluminis, intervallo pedum duorum inter se iungebat. 4 Haec cum, machinationibus immissa in flumen, defixerat fistucisque adegerat, non sublicae modo derecte ad perpendiculum, sed prone ac fastigate, ut secundum naturam fluminis procumberent, 5 his item contraria duo ad eundem modum iuncta, intervallo pedum quadragenum ab inferiore parte, contra vim atque impetum fluminis conversa, statuebat. 6 Haec utraque, insuper bipedalibus trabibus immissis, quantum eorum tignorum iunctura distabat, binis utrimque fibulis ab extrema parte distinebantur; 7 quibus disclusis atque in contrariam partem revinctis, tanta erat operis firmitudo atque ea rerum natura, ut, quo maior vis aquae se incitavisset, hoc artius illigata tenerentur. 8 Haec derecta materia iniecta contexebantur ac longuriis cratibusque consternebantur; 9 ac nihilo setius sublicae et ad inferiorem partem fluminis oblique agebantur, quae, pro ariete subiectae et cum omni opere coniunctae, vim fluminis exciperent; 10 et aliae item supra pontem mediocri spatio, ut, si arborum trunci sive trabes deiciendi operis causa essent a barbaris missae, his defensoribus earum rerum vis minueretur, neu ponti nocerent.

---

1 **commemoravi:** note how, in this sentence, Caesar appears in both the first and the third person at the same time. **navibus transire . . . esse arbitrabatur:** 'he thought that to cross in boats was'; *222b.* **tutum:** predicative; *148d.* Caesar was always careful to have the country in the rear of his army well secured, not only for the transportation of supplies but also to make a retreat if necessary. **suae, populi:** *157d.* **dignitatis esse:** 'would be consistent with (lit. 'characteristic of') the prestige'; *94d.*

2 **etsi:** *191a.* **proponebatur:** 'was put before (him).' **latitudinem:** between 1300 and 1600 feet in the region where Caesar built the bridge, that is, near Neuwied, between Coblenz and Andernach (see Map 11). **rapiditatem:** 'swiftness'; *76a.* **id sibi contendendum:** sc. *esse*, 'that he had to make the effort'; *110.* **aut:** *235a.*

3 **Rationem pontis hanc instituit:** 'he devised a plan for the bridge as follows'; *161a.* **tigna bina:** 'a pair of logs,' to be driven into the riverbed and used as posts to support the bridge; see Plates I and II, a a; *36.* **sesquipedalia:** 'a foot and a half thick.' **ab imo:** 'at the lower end'; *154a; 126c.* **dimensa ad altitudinem fluminis:** passive; 'measured off to (correspond with) the depth of the river,' the longer posts for use near the middle, the shorter for driving nearer the banks; *59b.* **intervallo pedum duorum:** 'at an interval of two feet,' i.e., two feet apart; *138.* **inter se:** 'together'; *159.* **iungebat:** sc. *Caesar*; the object is *tigna*. The two posts of each pair were apparently fastened together on the bank before they were driven into the riverbed.

4 **machinationibus immissa:** 'having been let down by mechanical devices,' presumably rafts equipped with cranes and adjustable ropes and pulleys; *228a.* **defixerat fistucisque adegerat:** 'had planted these firmly and driven (them) home with pile-drivers'; the pluperfect with *cum* implies repeated action; *186a.* **non sublicae modo:** 'not in the manner of an (ordinary) pile,' because ordinarily piles are driven in perpendicularly, while these pairs were driven with a slant. **derecte:** 'straight up and down.' **ad perpendiculum:** 'according to the plumb-line,' or, we might say, 'to the perpendicular,' i.e., in a straight line forming a 90 degree angle with the riverbed. **prone ac fastigate:** 'leaning forward and slanting.' **ut secundum naturam fluminis procumberent:** 'so that they leaned obliquely in conformity with (lit. 'according to') the direction of the current'; *122a.*

5 **his contraria:** 'opposite these'; *108a.* Plates I, II, a' a'. **duo:** sc. *tigna; bina* might have been used. **ad eundem modum:** 'in the same manner'; *45.* **quadragenum:** 'forty' Roman feet; *22c.* The distance must have been measured on the surface of the water; Plate I, A. **ab inferiore parte:** 'on the lower side,' i.e., downstream from the first pair. **contra vim atque impetum fluminis conversa:** 'turned against the force and rushing of the river.' As the first pair of posts slanted downstream, so the second pair slanted upstream; Plate I A, a a'. **statuebat:** '(Caesar) set.'

6 **Haec utraque . . . distinebantur:** 'the two pairs' of posts 'were held apart'; *51.* **insuper bipedalibus trabibus immissis, quantum eorum tignorum iunctura distabat:** 'with beams having the thickness of two feet, corresponding with the space between the posts' (of each pair) 'having been let in above.' The heavy crossbeam, or sill, is marked b b on Plates I, II. **quantum:** accusative of extent representing the idea of measure in *bipedalibus*; *118a.* **quantum eorum tignorum iunctura distabat:** lit. 'as much as the joining of those posts was distant;' the pairs of posts were driven in two feet apart, and this two foot beam corresponded to, and was inserted such that it would entirely fill, the two foot gap between the pairs. **binis utrimque fibulis ab extrema parte:** 'by a pair

of braces on each side' (i.e., on each pair of posts) 'at the very end,' i.e., attached at the end of the two-foot beam and forming a brace by also being attached to the piles. If these 'pairs of braces' were made of wood, they may have been like those represented in the Plates I and II, c c.

7 **quibus disclusis atque in contrariam partem revinctis:** 'with these (the two pairs of posts [*tigna*], one pair above and one below) kept (at the proper distance) apart, and braced (lit. 'bound back') in opposite directions,' the lower posts slanting upstream, the upper posts slanting downstream; *144b3*. **tanta erat operis firmitudo atque ea rerum natura, ut:** 'so great was the firmness of the structure, and such (was) the nature of things, that.' By 'the nature of things,' Caesar presumably refers to the physics of the water moving downstream. **quo maior vis aquae se incitavisset:** 'by which (degree) the force of the water had urged itself on greater'; *220*. **hoc artius illigata tenerentur:** 'by this (degree) they (the opposite pairs of posts, *tigna*) were bound and held together more closely.' **illigata:** lit. 'having been bound'; *228a*. **quo ... hoc:** correlative expression of degree of difference; *140*. The greater the force of the water upon the posts, the more that force compressed the two pairs of posts together.

8 **Haec ... contexebantur:** 'these (piers),' each one formed by fastening the crossbeam, two feet thick, securely to the pair of posts at either end, 'were joined.' As the bridge was designed to carry a moving load of cavalry and draft animals as well as infantry, and was obviously built hastily of rough timbers, with a wide margin of safety, we may suppose that the length of the crossbeams was not more than 25 feet, possibly not more than 20 feet; the number of piers was probably between sixty and seventy. **derecta materia iniecta:** 'with material' (presumably girders made of wood) 'having been laid on perpendicular,' i.e., at right angles to the piers and the direction of the current, laid in the direction that one would follow across the bridge; *92b; 144b6*. These girders are labeled d on Plates I and II. **longuriis:** 'with long poles,' laid on the girders, in the direction of the current; marked h on the Plates. **cratibus:** 'wickerwork,' woven of supple branches, laid over the long poles and taking the place of the planks on a modern bridge; marked i on the Plates. **consternebantur:** 'were covered.'

9 **nihilo setius:** 'nevertheless,' i.e., in order to assure the safety of the bridge still further; *140*. **sublicae et ad inferiorem partem fluminis oblique agebatur:** 'piles were also driven obliquely to the lower part (i.e., on the downstream side) of the river'; these piles, slanting upstream, braced the piers against the force of the current; marked e on the Plates. **et:** for *etiam*, 'also.' **quae ... exciperent:** 'in order that they receive,' i.e., help to withstand; *193a*. **pro ariete subiectae et cum omni opere coniunctae:** 'having been set underneath as a buttress and joined with the whole structure.'

10 **aliae:** i.e., *aliae sublicae agebantur*, marked f f on the Plates. These piles functioned as screens to protect the bridge against floating logs or other objects in the current liable to damage it. **mediocri spatio:** 'by a short distance,' with the *supra* of *supra pontem*; *140*. **trunci:** 'tree-trunks'; *81*. **trabes:** 'logs' or 'beams,' i.e., large pieces of wood. **deiciendi operis causa:** *230.1*. **essent missae:** *220*. **his defensoribus:** *his* refers to the *sublicae* personified as defenders, translate 'by these defenses.' **earum rerum:** the *trunci* and *trabes*. **neu:** 'and not'; lit. 'or not'; *196b*.

Entering Germany, Caesar finds some tribes submissive, but the Sugambrians flee.

18. 1 Diebus X, quibus materia coepta erat comportari, omni opere effecto, exercitus traducitur. 2 Caesar, ad utramque partem pontis firmo praesidio relicto, in fines Sugambrorum contendit. 3 Interim a compluribus civitatibus ad eum legati veniunt; quibus, pacem atque amicitiam petentibus, liberaliter respondet obsidesque ad se adduci iubet. 4 At Sugambri ex eo tempore, quo pons institui coeptus est, fuga comparata, hortantibus eis, quos ex Tencteris atque Usipetibus apud se habebant, finibus suis excesserant suaque omnia exportaverant seque in solitudinem ac silvas abdiderant.

1 **Diebus X, quibus:** 'within ten days from which (day)'; *quibus* should be understood as *ex quo die*. The plural form is strictly illogical, in that it should refer only to the first day on which material began to be collected, but *quibus* is, in effect, attracted into the plural by the *diebus*; *147a*. **comportari:** *72c*. The rapidity and skill with which the bridge was built bear witness to Caesar's genius in practical affairs as well as to the efficiency of his engineers and mechanics; *270b*.

2 **partem:** here = 'end.' **praesidio relicto:** 'having left a garrison'; *144b2*. See Plate II, g for a conception of how the camp protected the end of the bridge. **Sugambrorum:** the German end of the bridge led into the country of the Ubians; north of the Ubians were the Sugambrians (see Map Gallia).

3 **quibus:** indirect object after *respondit*. **quibus ... petentibus:** 'to whom ... (when they were) seeking.'

4 **At:** *236a*. **ex eo tempore, quo:** 'from that time at which.' **institui:** *72c*. **eo:** 'the'; *160d*. **fuga comparata:** 'taking to flight'; how lit.? **hortantibus eis, quos ... habebant:** 'at the instigation of those, whom (the Sugambri) had,' how lit.? In IV.15.2, it seemed that few of the Tencteri and the Usipetes had escaped (with the exception of

the cavalry who had not yet returned; IV.16.2), but Caesar here seems to suggest that some made it across the Rhine. **exportaverant:** 'had carried away.' **in solitudinem ac silvas:** cf. I.12.3; 'into the recesses of the forests'; *238d.*

He ravages the country of the Sugambrians, encourages the Ubians, returns to Gaul.

19. 1 Caesar, paucos dies in eorum finibus moratus, omnibus vicis aedificiisque incensis frumentisque succisis, se in fines Ubiorum recepit; atque his auxilium suum pollicitus, si ab Suebis premerentur, haec ab eis cognovit: 2 *Suebos, postea quam per exploratores pontem fieri comperissent, more suo concilio habito, nuntios in omnes partes dimisisse, uti de oppidis demigrarent, liberos, uxores suaque omnia in silvis deponerent, atque omnes, qui arma ferre possent, unum in locum convenirent;* 3 *hunc esse delectum medium fere regionum earum, quas Suebi obtinerent; hic Romanorum adventum exspectare atque ibi decertare constituisse.* 4 Quod ubi Caesar comperit, omnibus eis rebus confectis, quarum rerum causa traducere exercitum constituerat, ut Germanis metum iniceret, ut Sugambros ulcisceretur, ut Ubios obsidione liberaret, diebus omnino XVIII trans Rhenum consumptis, satis et ad laudem et ad utilitatem profectum arbitratus, se in Galliam recepit pontemque rescidit.

1 **eorum:** *Sugambrorum.* **moratus:** *226c.* **vicis aedificiisque:** for the distinction between them, see I.5.2. **frumentis succisis:** 'cut down the standing grain and'; how lit.? *144b2.* **si . . . premerentur:** indirect speech, from the idea of 'saying' in *pollicitus*; future indicative in the direct form; *213b.* **haec:** 'the following,' which Caesar summarizes indirectly.

2 **postea quam:** with the indicative in the direct form; *188a.* **more:** *136c.* **nuntios:** 'messengers.' **uti de oppidis demigrarent:** '(instructing people) to move away from the strongholds'; the substantive clause (and those that follow) is an indirect command that conveys the instructions of the messengers; *199a.* **qui . . . possent:** *194a.*

3 **hunc esse delectum medium fere:** '(that) this (place) had been chosen (being) nearly (at) the center'; *medium* agrees with *hunc*, which picks up from *unum in locum.* **hic:** adverb. **regionum:** *102.* **exspectare:** sc. *eos* (*Suebos*) as subject. **ibi:** 'at that point.'

4 **Quod:** 'this (information)'; *167.* **eis rebus confectis:** 'having accomplished those objects'; *144b3.* **rerum:** *165a.* **ut Germanis metum iniceret:** '(namely) to strike fear in the Germans'; an *ut*-clause in apposition to *rebus* after a verb of deciding, i.e., this clause (and those that follow) explain the objects (*res*) for the sake of which Caesar had decided to cross the Rhine; *203.4.* In reality Caesar accomplished very little by the march into Germany and he is here straining to justify an expedition barren of tangible results. **ut Sugambros ulcisceretur:** 'to take vengeance on the Sugambri,' apparently because they received the survivors of the Usipetes and Tencteri (IV.18.4). **obsidione:** 'from oppression,' lit. 'from siege'; the Ubii had been forced to pay tribute to the Swabians (IV.3.4); *127a.* **XVIII:** *38b; 36.* **profectum:** sc. *esse*, from *proficio*; the subject is *satis*; accusative and infinitive after *arbitratus.*

IV.20-38: First Expedition into Britain

Caesar resolves to invade Britain; he lacks information.

20. 1 Exigua parte aestatis reliqua, Caesar, etsi in his locis, quod omnis Gallia ad septentriones vergit, maturae sunt hiemes, tamen in Britanniam proficisci contendit, quod, omnibus fere Gallicis bellis, hostibus nostris inde sumministrata auxilia intellegebat 2 et, si tempus anni ad bellum gerendum deficeret, tamen magno sibi usui fore arbitrabatur, si modo insulam adisset, genus hominum perspexisset, loca, portus, aditus cognovisset; quae omnia fere Gallis erant incognita. 3 Neque enim temere praeter mercatores illo adit quisquam, neque eis ipsis quicquam praeter oram maritimam atque eas regiones, quae sunt contra Gallias, notum est. 4 Itaque vocatis ad se undique mercatoribus, neque quanta esset insulae magnitudo, neque quae aut quantae nationes incolerent, neque quem usum belli haberent aut quibus institutis uterentur, neque qui essent ad maiorem navium multitudinem idonei portus, reperire poterat.

1 **Exigua parte . . . reliqua:** ablative absolute. **aestatis:** it was now near the end of July. **hiemes:** in the plural, 'winter storms.' **omnis Gallia:** 'Gaul as a whole'; cf. I.1.1. **ad septentriones vergit:** 'lies toward the north,' in relation to the latitude of Italy; see Map 12. **Britanniam:** *263.* **quod . . . intellegebat:** the aid given by the

Britains to the Venetans (III.9) or to the other Gauls, e.g., to refugees from the Bellovaci (II.14), seems to have been slight, but it nevertheless furnished a plausible pretext for the invasion of Britain. **bellis:** *147b.* **inde:** *e Britannia.* **sumministrata:** *sc. esse.*

2 **si:** '(even) if.' **tempus anni:** i.e., the time remaining in the portion of the year suitable for campaigning. **deficeret:** 'was insufficient,' subjunctive because subordinate to *fore* (= *futurum esse*) in indirect statement. **sibi usui fore:** *112b.* **arbitrabatur:** *183a.* **adisset:** representing a future perfect indicative in a direct form (*si adiero, mihi usui erit*), here subordinated to *fore* in an indirect statement in secondary sequence, hence 'it would be advantageous if he had gone'; *218.1b.* **aditus:** 'approaches'; points, outside the regular harbors, where a landing could be made. **quae omnia fere:** 'nearly all of these things'; *167; 97c.* **incognita:** the Venetans at least must have been informed about Britain (III.8), but Caesar had destroyed them, and it was not to be expected that Gauls having the knowledge desired by Caesar would be free in imparting it to him.

3 **Neque enim ... quisquam:** 'for no one'; *168.* **temere:** 'rashly,' i.e., 'without good reason.' **illo:** adverb. **neque ... quicquam:** 'and nothing.' **eis ipsis:** the *mercatores*; *108a.* **Gallias:** plural because referring to the different regions: 'the various parts of Gaul.'

4 **quanta esset insulae magnitudo:** 'how great the magnitude of the island was'; indirect question after *reperire poterat* at the end of the sentence; *204.3.* **quae aut quantae nationes incolerent:** sc. *quae nationes eam incolerent aut quantae essent*; *204.2, 3.* **quem:** *48b.* **qui essent ... idonei portus:** understand *qui* with *portus; idonei* is predicative. **ad maiorem navium multitudinem:** i.e., for a fleet, whose requirements were very different from those of trading vessels coming to port singly or in small numbers; *153a.*

He sends Volusenus to Britain and makes preparations; he receives British envoys, sends Commius to Britain.

21. 1 Ad haec cognoscenda, prius quam periculum faceret, idoneum esse arbitratus C. Volusenum cum navi longa praemittit. 2 Huic mandat, ut, exploratis omnibus rebus, ad se quam primum revertatur. 3 Ipse cum omnibus copiis in Morinos proficiscitur, quod inde erat brevissimus in Britanniam traiectus. 4 Huc naves undique ex finitimis regionibus et, quam superiore aestate ad Veneticum bellum effecerat classem, iubet convenire. 5 Interim, consilio eius cognito et per mercatores perlato ad Britannos, a compluribus insulae civitatibus ad eum legati veniunt, qui polliceantur obsides dare atque imperio populi Romani obtemperare. 6 Quibus auditis, liberaliter pollicitus hortatusque ut in ea sententia permanerent, eos domum remittit; 7 et cum eis una Commium, quem ipse, Atrebatibus superatis, regem ibi constituerat, cuius et virtutem et consilium probabat et quem sibi fidelem esse arbitrabatur, cuiusque auctoritas in his regionibus magni habebatur, mittit. 8 Huic imperat, quas possit, adeat civitates horteturque ut populi Romani fidem sequantur, seque celeriter eo venturum nuntiet. 9 Volusenus, perspectis regionibus omnibus, quantum ei facultatis dari potuit, qui navi egredi ac se barbaris committere non auderet, quinto die ad Caesarem revertitur, quaeque ibi perspexisset, renuntiat.

1 **prius ... faceret:** 'before making the attempt'; *189b.* **idoneum:** substantive adjective in predicate, 'a suitable person.' **navi longa:** *306a.* **praemittit:** sc. *eum.*

2 **ut revertatur:** *199a1.* **quam primum:** *153c.*

3 **in Britanniam:** after *traiectus; 150d.* **traiectus:** 'passage'; see Map 11.

4 **Huc:** to the vicinity of modern Boulogne. **naves, classem:** direct objects of *iubet*, but note how *classem* has been absorbed into the end of the relative clause to which it is logically the antecedent; hence **quam ... classem** = *eam classem, quam; 165c.* **ad Veneticum bellum:** see III.11-15.

5 **polliceantur:** *193a.* **dare:** i.e., *se daturos esse; 178.* **imperio obtemperare:** 'submit to the authority'; *105.*

6 **liberaliter pollicitus:** 'having made generous promises,' presumably about the degree and duration of the protection he could offer them. **ut ... permanerent:** an indirect comment after *hortatus; 199a2.* **domum:** *119b.*

7 **una:** adverb, 'together with them.' **Commium:** object of *mittit*, the last word in the sentence; the relative clauses that follow describe Commius. **ipse:** Caesar. **Atrebatibus:** conquered in the battle at the Sabis, two years previously (II.23). **regem:** *115a.* **ibi:** among the Atrebatians. **magni habebatur:** 'was considered great,' lit. 'of great (value)'; *101.*

8 **possit:** sc. *adire.* Why subjunctive? *220.* **adeat, hortetur, nuntiet:** *200a.* **sequantur:** *199a2.* **se:** Caesar.

9 **quantum ei facultatis dari potuit:** 'to the degree that he had the opportunity,' lit. '(to the extent of) how great (of) an opportunity was able to be given to him'; *97b.* **qui ... non auderet:** 'since he ... did not dare'; *194c.* **navi:** *14b; 127a.*

He receives the submission of the Morini, assembles a fleet.

22. 1 Dum in his locis Caesar navium parandarum causa moratur, ex magna parte Morinorum ad eum legati venerunt, qui se de superioris temporis consilio excusarent, quod, homines barbari et nostrae consuetudinis imperiti, bellum populo Romano fecissent, seque ea, quae imperasset, facturos pollicerentur. 2 Hoc sibi Caesar satis opportune accidisse arbitratus, quod neque post tergum hostem relinquere volebat neque belli gerendi propter anni tempus facultatem habebat neque has tantularum rerum occupationes Britanniae anteponendas iudicabat, magnum eis numerum obsidum imperat. Quibus adductis, eos in fidem recepit. 3 Navibus circiter LXXX onerariis coactis contractisque, quot satis esse ad duas transportandas legiones existimabat, quicquid praeterea navium longarum habebat, id quaestori, legatis praefectisque distribuit. 4 Huc accedebant XVIII onerariae naves, quae ex eo loco a milibus passuum VIII vento tenebantur, quo minus in eundem portum venire possent; has equitibus distribuit. 5 Reliquum exercitum Q. Titurio Sabino et L. Aurunculeio Cottae legatis in Menapios atque in eos pagos Morinorum, a quibus ad eum legati non venerant, ducendum dedit; 6 P. Sulpicium Rufum legatum cum eo praesidio, quod satis esse arbitrabatur, portum tenere iussit.

1 **his locis:** in the country of the Morini, probably in the vicinity of modern Boulogne. **moratur:** *190a.* **qui se . . . excusarent:** 'to excuse themselves'; *193a.* **de superioris temporis consilio:** 'for their decision of the previous season,' 56 BC (III.28-29). **quod . . . fecissent:** 'because (as they said) they had made'; *183a.* **homines barbari:** '(being) uncivilized people'; *91b.* **consuetudinis:** Caesar presumably refers to the Roman 'custom' of treating with consideration peoples that submitted to Roman rule; *102.* **se . . . facturos:** sc. *esse,* accusative and infinitive after *pollicerentur,* which is another relative clause of purpose (the –*que* of *seque* links *pollicerentur* with *excusarent*). **imperasset:** *64a1; 214a.*

2 **belli gerendi:** after *facultatem.* **propter anni tempus:** it was already August, too late in the season to enter upon an extended campaign. **neque has tantularum rerum occupationes Britanniae anteponendas iudicabat:** 'and he judged that the engagements of such little affairs ought not to be given precedence over (the invasion of) Britain.' **has:** *160d.* **tantularum:** *76c.* **Britanniae:** *107a.* **eis . . . imperat:** 'he demands from them,' lit. 'commands to them'; *105.* **Quibus:** sc. *obsidibus.*

3 **Navibus onerariis:** 'transports'; these were sailing vessels, while the galleys were propelled by oars; *306a.* **LXXX:** *octoginta; 38b.* **coactis contractisque:** 'pressed into service and brought together' in a single harbor. **quot:** 'as many as.' **duas legiones:** the 7th and the 10th. The smallness of the force is consistent with Caesar's statement that the purpose of the expedition was not conquest but the obtaining of information. If the two legions, after three years of hard fighting, contained each about 3600 men (*267b*) fit for service, the total of 7200 men divided up among the 80 transports would have averaged 90 men to a ship. The vessels were not large; and the supplies, not merely provisions but tents and other equipment, must have taken up considerable space. **quicquid navium longarum:** 'whatever (of) long ships'; *97b.* **id:** = *quicquid . . . habebant.* **quaestori:** *273b.* **praefectis:** 'subsidiary officers.' The galleys seem also to have carried slingers, bowmen, and artillery (see IV.25).

4 **Huc accedebant:** 'in addition to this number there were'; how lit.? *90b.* **eo loco:** *portus Itius,* now Boulogne; see Map 11. **a:** 'at a distance of.' The small harbor eight Roman miles up the coast, where the 18 transports were detained, is now called Ambleteuse; Map 11 A. **quo minus:** 'so that . . . not'; *201a.* **eundem portum:** *portus Itius.* **equitibus:** the cavalry contingents of the two legions, 500 or 600 horsemen in all; *269a.* **equitibus distribuit:** the horsemen could more easily go across the country to the smaller harbor (IV.23.1).

5 **Reliquum exercitum:** five legions, if we assume that one legion was assigned to duty at the harbor; for Caesar had eight legions in all, and only two were required for the expedition. **in Menapios . . . ducendum:** 'to be led into (the territory of) the Menapii'; *229b.*

6 **eo praesidio, quod:** = *tanto praesidio, quantum.*

Caesar sails to Britain and makes preparation to land.

23. 1 His constitutis rebus, nactus idoneam ad navigandum tempestatem, tertia fere vigilia naves solvit equitesque in ulteriorem portum progredi et naves conscendere et se sequi iussit. 2 A quibus cum paulo tardius esset administratum, ipse hora diei circiter quarta cum primis navibus Britanniam attigit, atque ibi in omnibus collibus expositas hostium copias armatas conspexit. 3 Cuius loci haec erat natura, atque ita montium angustiis mare continebatur, uti ex locis superioribus in litus telum adigi posset. 4 Hunc ad egrediendum nequaquam idoneum locum arbitratus, dum reliquae naves eo convenirent, ad horam nonam in ancoris exspectavit. 5 Interim legatis tribunisque militum convocatis, et quae ex Voluseno cognovisset et quae fieri vellet ostendit, monuitque (ut rei militaris ratio maximeque ut maritimae res postularent) ut, cum celerem atque instabilem motum haberent, ad nutum et ad tempus omnes res ab eis administrarentur. 6 His dimissis, et ventum et aestum uno tempore nactus secundum, dato signo et sublatis ancoris, circiter milia passuum VII ab eo loco progressus, aperto ac plano litore naves constituit.

1 **nactus:** *61a3; 226c.* **tempestatem:** 'weather'; *tempestas* may imply good or bad weather according to the connection. **tertia fere vigilia:** 'about the third watch'; indefinite because the embarkation must have taken two or three hours; *242c.* **naves solvit:** 'got under way,' lit. 'released (the ships),' from Boulogne. The date was probably August 26. **ulteriorem portum:** Ambleteuse, northeast of Boulogne (see IV.22.4). **progredi:** i.e., by land. **naves conscendere:** 'to embark.'

2 **quibus:** 'them,' the cavalry; *167.* **paulo tardius:** 'a little too slowly,' probably due to the difficulty of getting the horses aboard; *153a.* **esset administratum:** '(this order) had been carried out'; *73d.* **hora quarta:** the beginning of 'the fourth hour' on August 26 in the latitude of Dover by Roman reckoning was about 8:30 a.m. by our time; *242b.* **Britanniam attigit:** 'reached (lit. 'touched upon') Britain,' near Dover; see Map 11. **expositas:** 'arrayed.'

3 **haec:** 'such.' **ita montium angustiis mare continebatur:** 'the sea was so bordered by the narrow spaces of the cliffs,' i.e., the cliffs were so close to the water that they left only narrow strips of land beween them and the water. The chalk cliffs near Dover run almost straight up from the water's edge. **locis superioribus:** i.e., the top of the cliffs. **litus:** 'shore'; *13f.*

4 **convenirent:** *190b.* **horam nonam:** the beginning of the ninth hour was about 2:20 p.m. by our time; *242b.* **in ancoris:** 'at anchor.'

5 **tribunis militum:** *274.* **et . . . et:** *233a.* **quae:** *204.2.* The information derived from Volusenus was probably to the effect that there was a good landing place further up the coast. **ut rei militaris ratio maximeque ut maritimae res postularent:** 'as military practice and especially as naval operations required'; *ut* here is 'as,' normally followed by the indicative, but here, even though parenthetical, felt to be subordinate to the indirect command following *monuit; 220.* **ut . . . omnes res ab eis administrarentur:** after *monuit,* 'that all orders be executed by them'; *199a.* **cum celerem atque instabilem motum haberent:** 'since (these conditions) involved quick and unsteady movement'; *184a.* **ad nutum:** 'at (his) nod,' i.e., at his command. **ad tempus:** 'at the (right) time.'

6 **secundum:** 'favorable,' both wind and tide bearing toward the northeast. **eo loco:** Dover. **progressus:** *226c.* **aperto ac plano litore:** between Walmer and Deal, about seven miles northeast of Dover; *145c.* **naves constituit:** 'he ran the ships aground,' lit. 'brought the ships to a halt.'

The legionaries attempt to land, the Britons resist fiercely.

24. 1 At barbari, consilio Romanorum cognito, praemisso equitatu et essedariis, quo plerumque genere in proeliis uti consuerunt, reliquis copiis subsecuti, nostros navibus egredi prohibebant. 2 Erat ob has causas summa difficultas, quod naves propter magnitudinem, nisi in alto, constitui non poterant; militibus autem, ignotis locis, impeditis manibus, magno et gravi onere armorum oppressis, simul et de navibus desiliendum et in fluctibus consistendum et cum hostibus erat pugnandum, 3 cum illi, aut ex arido aut paulum in aquam progressi, omnibus membris expeditis, notissimis locis, audacter tela conicerent et equos insuefactos incitarent. 4 Quibus rebus nostri perterriti, atque huius omnino generis pugnae imperiti, non eadem alacritate ac studio, quo in pedestribus uti proeliis consuerant, utebantur.

1 **essedariis:** 'chariot-fighters,' described more fully below in IV.33. **quo genere:** 'a type (of warrior) which'; *165b; 131c.* **reliquis copiis subsecuti:** 'having followed after with the rest of their forces'; the Britons followed by land, as near the shore as possible; *137b.* **navibus egredi:** 'from disembarking'; *223a3; 127a.*

2 **Erat:** *90a.* **has:** refers to what follows; *161a.* **in alto:** 'in deep (water)'; *154a.* **constitui:** 'be grounded,' so as to remain firm. **militibus . . . desiliendum (erat):** 'the soldiers . . . had to jump down'; how lit.? *73e; 110.* **ignotis locis:** '(being) on unfamiliar ground,' lit. 'in unknown places'; *145c.* **oppressis:** agrees with *militibus;* 'weighed down.' **et . . . et . . . et:** *238f.*

3 **cum:** 'while'; *187.* **illi:** *Britanni.* **ex arido:** 'from dry land,' compare *in alto* above. **membris:** 'limbs,' i.e., both their hands (free from having to carry any extra armament) and their legs (free from the waves). **notissimis locis:** 'thoroughly acquainted with the ground'; how lit.? *153a; 144b2.* **insuefactos:** 'trained' to fight in such conditions along the beach and even into the water.

4 **generis:** with *imperiti; 102.* **eadem:** *150a.* **quo:** *163c; 131c.* **pedestribus:** lit. 'on foot,' i.e., on land, where they would have their footing. **utebantur:** 'were displaying.'

The standard-bearer of the Tenth leaps overboard, bidding the others follow.

25. 1 Quod ubi Caesar animadvertit, naves longas, quarum et species erat barbaris inusitatior et motus ad usum expeditior, paulum removeri ab onerariis navibus et remis incitari et ad latus apertum hostium constitui, atque inde fundis, sagittis, tormentis hostes propelli ac summoveri iussit; quae res magno usui nostris fuit. 2 Nam, et navium figura et remorum motu et inusitato genere tormentorum permoti, barbari constiterunt ac paulum modo pedem rettulerunt. 3 At nostris militibus cunctantibus, maxime propter altitudinem maris, qui decimae legionis aquilam ferebat, obtestatus deos, ut ea res legioni feliciter eveniret, 'Desilite,' inquit, 'commilitones, nisi vultis aquilam hostibus prodere; ego certe meum rei publicae atque imperatori officium praestitero.' 4 Hoc cum voce magna dixisset, se ex navi proiecit atque in hostes aquilam ferre coepit. 5 Tum nostri, cohortati inter se, ne tantum dedecus admitteretur, universi ex navi desiluerunt. 6 Hos item ex proximis navibus cum conspexissent, subsecuti hostibus appropinquarunt.

1 **Quod:** 'this,' i.e., the situation described in the previous sentence; *167.* **naves longas:** 'galleys,' the subject of *removeri, incitari,* and *constitui,* all to be understood after *iussit.* **animadvertit:** *188a.* **species:** 'appearance.' **inusitatior:** 'less familiar.' Oar-driven galleys were not so well adapted to withstand the bufferings of northern waters as solidly built sailing vessels, such as those of the Venetans (see III.13-14); *306.* **motus ad usum expeditior:** 'the movement was easier for use,' i.e., for navigating, since the galleys could be driven faster, and in any direction. **ad latus apertum:** 'onto the exposed flank,' (i.e., the right flank of the enemy, because the shield was carried on the left arm and thus came to be thought of generally as the protected flank). The galleys were to be placed parallel with the shore. **inde:** = *e navibus longis.* **fundis:** 'with slings,' which hurled slingshots of lead (or something similar) as bullets. **sagittis:** 'arrows'; *268.* **tormentis:** 'artillery'; the word 'artillery' used to be applied to engines of war whose propulsion was derived from tension before it came to be restricted to cannon, which derive their propulsion from explosives. The 'torsioners' used on the galleys were probably small catapults, which Caesar elsewhere calls 'scorpions' (*303a*). **quae res:** 'and this maneuver.' **usui:** *112b.*
2 **figura:** the galleys were relatively long, narrow, and low. **paulum modo:** 'just a little,' from the water's edge.
3 **altitudinem:** the sailing vessels which had been run aground on the sandy bottom formed a line, irregular because of the variation in depth, at least two thirds of a mile long; the water where the bows were driven into the sand was probably up to the soldiers' necks. **qui:** as antecedent sc. *is,* subject of *inquit.* **aquilam:** 'eagle'; *284b1.* **obtestatus per deos ut:** *199a4.* **commilitones:** 'fellow-soldiers'; *93.* **vultis:** *71.* **ego:** *87b.* **certe:** 'at any rate.' **praestitero:** *176c.*
4 **cum:** *185c.* **voce:** *136b.* **magna:** 'loud.'
5 **cohortati inter se:** *159; 226c.* **dedecus:** 'disgrace,' the loss of the eagle of the legion; *13f.* **admitteretur:** 'be incurred'; *199a2.* **universi:** 'all together.'
6 **ex proximis navibus:** functions as the subject of *conspexissent:* 'those from the nearest ships.' **subsecuti:** 'they followed close after and'; how lit.? *228a.* **appropinquarunt:** *64a1.*

Finally the Romans force the enemy back and land.

26. 1 Pugnatum est ab utrisque acriter. Nostri tamen, quod neque ordines servare neque firmiter insistere neque signa subsequi poterant, atque alius alia ex navi, quibuscumque signis occurrerat, se aggregabat, magnopere perturbabantur; 2 hostes vero, notis omnibus vadis, ubi ex litore aliquos singulares ex navi egredientes conspexerant, incitatis equis impeditos adoriebantur, 3 plures paucos circumsistebant, alii ab latere aperto in universos tela coniciebant. 4 Quod cum animadvertisset Caesar, scaphas longarum navium, item speculatoria navigia, militibus compleri iussit et, quos laborantes conspexerat, his subsidia summittebat. 5 Nostri, simul in arido constiterunt, suis omnibus consecutis, in hostes impetum fecerunt atque eos in fugam dederunt; neque longius prosequi potuerunt, quod equites cursum tenere atque insulam capere non potuerant. Hoc unum ad pristinam fortunam Caesari defuit.

1 **Pugnatum est:** *73d.* **utrisque:** *51.* **ordines servare:** 'to keep the ranks.' **firmiter insistere:** 'to get a firm footing.' **signa:** *284b2.* **alius alia ex navi:** 'one from this ship, another from that'; *171c.* **quibuscumque signis oc-**

currerat, se aggregabat: 'was joining himself to whichever standards he had happened to meet,' the indefinite relative clause functions as the object of *aggregabat*, while *quibuscumque* is dative as the the object of *occurrerat*; *50a; 107a.*

2 **notis omnibus vadis:** *144b3.* **singulares:** 'one by one.' **conspexerant:** *188d.* **incitatis equis:** 'urging their horses forward'; *144b2.* **adoriebantur:** 'they would attack'; *175d.*

3 **plures paucos:** *plures hostes paucos Romanos.* **ab latere aperto:** 'on the exposed flank,' the right side, unprotected by a shield. **universos:** 'groups of soldiers,' contrasted with the individuals referred to in III.26.2.

4 **scaphas:** 'small boats,' carried on the galleys. **speculatoria navigia:** 'scouting vessels,' smaller and lighter than the galleys, without a beak, and designed for rapid movement. **his:** the antecedent of the preceding *quos.* **subsidia summittebat:** *subsidia* describes *scaphas* and *speculatoria navigia*, 'he was sending (the small boats and scouting vessels) as support.'

5 **in arido:** 'on dry ground'; *154a.* **constiterunt:** *188a.* **suis omnibus consecutis:** 'with all of their own comrades following after.' **neque:** 'but . . . not.' **longius:** 'very far.' **equites:** who set out from Ambleteuse (IV.23.1). **insulam capere:** 'to reach the island.' **Hoc unum ad pristinam fortunam Caesari defuit:** 'in this respect only was Caesar's usual good fortune incomplete,' lit. 'this one thing to his former good fortune was lacking to Caesar.' Thus does Caesar seek to cast a successful glow over a difficult undertaking.

The Britons offer to submit, and return Commius to Caesar.

27. 1 Hostes proelio superati, simul atque se ex fuga receperunt, statim ad Caesarem legatos de pace miserunt; obsides sese daturos, quaeque imperasset, facturos polliciti sunt. 2 Una cum his legatis Commius Atrebas venit, quem supra demonstraveram a Caesare in Britanniam praemissum. 3 Hunc illi e navi egressum, cum ad eos oratoris modo Caesaris mandata deferret, comprehenderant atque in vincula coniecerant; 4 tum, proelio facto, remiserunt. In petenda pace eius rei culpam in multitudinem contulerunt et, propter imprudentiam ut ignosceretur, petiverunt. 5 Caesar questus, quod, cum ultro, in continentem legatis missis, pacem ab se petissent, bellum sine causa intulissent, ignoscere se imprudentiae dixit obsidesque imperavit; 6 quorum illi partem statim dederunt, partem, ex longinquioribus locis arcessitam, paucis diebus sese daturos dixerunt. 7 Interea suos remigrare in agros iusserunt, principesque undique convenire et se civitatesque suas Caesari commendare coeperunt.

1 **simul atque se ex fuga receperunt:** 'as soon as they recovered (themselves) from their flight'; *188a.* **daturos:** *89c.* **quaeque,** etc.: i.e., *et ea, quae imperavisset, facturos esse; 214a.*

2 **Una:** adverb. **supra:** see IV.21.7. **quem supra demonstraveram . . . praemissum:** sc. *esse*, lit. 'whom I had explained above to have been sent in advance,' but it is smoother to render the main verb as a subordinate one, 'whom, as I explained above, had been sent in advance.' **demonstraveram:** for the first person, see II.1.1, and for Caesar as first and third person in the same sentence, see also IV.17.1.

3 **illi:** *hostes.* **oratoris modo:** 'in the manner of an envoy,' lit. 'of an orator.'

4 **proelio facto:** i.e., *post hoc proelium; 144b2.* **remiserunt:** sc. *eum.* **In petenda pace:** *230.4.* **eius rei culpam:** 'the blame for this thing,' namely, *quod Commius, orator Caesaris, comprehensus atque in vincula coniectus erat; 102.* **in multitudinem:** i.e., *in populum*, on their citizenry at large, as if the leaders had little choice but to follow the inclinations of popular will. **ignosceretur:** sc. *sibi*, 'that pardon be granted them'; *199a4; 106b.*

5 **questus:** *226c.* **quod . . . intulissent:** 'because (as he said) they had,' etc.; *183a.* **cum . . . petissent:** see IV.21.5; *187.* **continentem:** 'the continent,' i.e., Gaul. **sine causa:** from the Roman point of view; but the Romans would have considered the defense of the shores of Italy against an armed force a most noble action. Thus do conditions alter opinions. **ignoscere se:** 'that he was pardoning,' after *dixit.* **imprudentiae:** *105.*

6 **arcessitam:** i.e., *cum ea (pars) arcessita esset; 227a1.*

7 **suos:** 'their people'; the demobilization of the British host was ordered. **iusserunt:** the British envoys are the subject. **convenire:** *ad Caesarem.* **Caesari commendare:** 'to put under Caesar's protection.'

The ships with the cavalry are prevented from landing by a storm.

28. 1 His rebus pace confirmata, post diem quartum, quam est in Britanniam ventum, naves XVIII, de quibus supra demonstratum est, quae equites sustulerant, ex superiore portu leni vento solverunt. 2 Quae cum appropinquarent Britanniae et ex castris viderentur, tanta tempestas subito coorta est, ut nulla earum cursum tenere posset, sed aliae eodem, unde erant profectae, referrentur, aliae ad inferiorem partem insulae, quae est propius solis occasum, magno cum periculo deicerentur; 3 quae, tamen ancoris iactis, cum fluctibus complerentur, necessario adversa nocte in altum provectae continentem petierunt.

1 **His rebus:** the giving of hostages, the demobilization of the British host, and the presence of British leaders in Caesar's camp. **post diem quartum, quam est in Britanniam ventum:** = *quarto die postquam in Britanniam venit;* 'three days after' by our reckoning; cf. IV.9.1. **est ventum:** *73d.* **supra:** see IV.22.4. **demonstratum est:** 'mention has been made.' **sustulerant:** 'had taken on board.' **superiore portu:** Ambleteuse. **leni vento:** 'with a light breeze,' blowing north or northeast; *138.* **solverunt:** 'set sail.'

2 **Quae cum:** 'and when these (ships).' **ex castris:** Caesar's camp was on rising ground, not far from the shore, so that it commanded a wide view of the sea. **viderentur:** translate as passive. **tempestas:** 'storm,' a northeaster; cf. IV.23.1. **posset:** *197b.* **aliae ... aliae:** *171b.* **eodem, unde:** 'to the same place from which'; Ambleteuse. **referrentur:** sc. *ut.* **ad inferiorem partem insulae, quae est propius solis occasum:** i.e., to the south and the west from Caesar's landing place. See Map 11, A. **propius:** *123b.* **deicerentur:** 'were driven'; *57b.*

3 **quae, tamen ancoris iactis, cum:** 'nevertheless they anchored and when they'; how lit.? *167; 144b2.* **necessario:** adv., 'of necessity.' **adversa nocte:** 'in the face of the night,' a metaphorical form of expression transferred from physical space (as *adverso colle; 134a*) to time. **in altum provectae:** 'they put out to sea and'; how lit.? *226c; 228a.*

The fleet on the British shore is wrecked by a high tide.

29. 1 Eadem nocte accidit, ut esset luna plena, qui dies maritimos aestus maximos in Oceano efficere consuevit, nostrisque id erat incognitum. 2 Ita uno tempore et longas naves, quibus Caesar exercitum transportandum curaverat, quasque in aridum subduxerat, aestus complebat, et onerarias, quae ad ancoras erant deligatae, tempestas afflictabat, neque ulla nostris facultas aut administrandi aut auxiliandi dabatur. 3 Compluribus navibus fractis, reliquae cum essent, funibus, ancoris reliquisque armamentis amissis, ad navigandum inutiles, magna, id quod necesse erat accidere, totius exercitus perturbatio facta est. 4 Neque enim naves erant aliae, quibus reportari possent, et omnia deerant, quae ad reficiendas naves erant usui, et, quod omnibus constabat hiemari in Gallia oportere, frumentum in his locis in hiemem provisum non erat.

1 **eadem nocte:** the night of August 30, as determined by astronomical calculations. **accidit, ut:** *203.1.* **qui dies:** 'and this day,' i.e., the night of the full moon. **maritimos aestus maximos in Oceano:** 'the greatest sea-tides on the Ocean.' **aestus ... incognitum:** the rise and fall of the tide in the Mediterranean, as in America's Great Lakes, is hardly perceptible. Caesar's men had learned of the existence of tides in the Ocean the previous year (III.12); what they had failed to notice was the coincidence of the highest tides with the time of the full moon. At Dover, the highest tide rises about 19 feet; at Boulogne, 25 feet. **nostris:** this word choice seems to include Caesar himself (i.e., the coastal Gauls surely knew that the highest tides occurred at the full moon, yet they seem not to have warned Caesar), but its collective force has the effect of insulating Caesar from this failure of intelligence.

2 **uno tempore et longas naves ... et onerarias:** 'at one time both the galleys ... and the transports.' **exercitum transportandum curaverat:** 'had had the army brought over'; *229b.* **quasque:** the *–que* connects this *quas* to the previous *quibus*, meaning that both of these relative clauses describe *longas naves*. **subduxerat:** 'had hauled up.' **aut administrandi aut auxiliandi:** 'either of managing or of rendering aid' to the vessels, since the crews were on shore; objective genitives after *facultas*; *102; 235.*

3 **funibus ... amissis:** 'on account of the loss of the ropes,' etc.; *144b3.* **magna:** with *perturbatio*; emphatic; *245d.* **id quod necesse erat accidere:** 'as was bound to happen,' lit. 'a thing which was necessary to happen'; *160c.* **perturbatio:** 'commotion.' **facta est:** 'occurred.'

4 **Neque enim naves erant aliae:** 'For there were no other ships'; *90a.* **reportari:** 'be carried back.' **possent:** *194a.* **usui:** translate as if *utilia; 112a.* **quod omnibus constabat, hiemari in Gallia oportere:** 'because it was clear to all that they ought to winter in Gaul,' lit. 'that it ought to be wintered in Gaul.' **his locis:** in Britain. **in hiemem:** 'for the winter,' lit. 'against the winter'; *12a.* Since everyone expected to be back in Gaul for the winter, rations had been taken for only a limited stay in Britain.

The Britons, learning of the disaster, secretly plan a revolt.

30. 1 Quibus rebus cognitis, principes Britanniae, qui post proelium ad ea, quae iusserat Caesar, facienda convenerant, inter se collocuti, cum equites et naves et frumentum Romanis deesse intellegerent, et paucitatem militum ex castrorum exiguitate cognoscerent, quae hoc erant etiam angustiora, quod sine impedimentis Caesar legiones transportaverat, 2 optimum factu esse duxerunt, rebellione facta, frumento commeatuque nostros prohibere et rem in hiemem producere; quod, his superatis aut reditu interclusis, neminem postea belli inferendi causa in Britanniam transiturum confidebant. 3 Itaque, rursus coniuratione facta, paulatim ex castris discedere ac suos clam ex agris deducere coeperunt.

1 **inter se collocuti:** *159.* **intellegerent, cognoscerent:** *184a.* **quae erant hoc etiam angustiora, quod:** 'which (i.e., the camp) was even smaller (than usual for two legions) because of this thing, namely because.' **hoc:** *135a.* **impedimentis:** left in Gaul; *271.*
2 **optimum factu esse:** 'that the best thing to do (lit. 'in respect to doing') was'; *232.* **optimum:** in predicate, after *esse*; *148d.* **duxerunt:** 'considered'; the subject is *principes* in the first line of the chapter. **rebellione facta:** 'renewing hostilities'; how lit.? *144b2.* **frumento:** *127a.* **prohibere:** this infinitive (as well as *producere*) forms the subject of *optimum factu esse*: 'they considered that to cut off our men from grain was the best thing to do.' **rem:** i.e., their resistance to Caesar. **quod:** causal. **his superatis:** 'if these (invaders) should be overcome'; *144b4.* **reditu:** 'return'; *127a.*
3 **paulatim:** one or two at a time. That the British leaders were assembled in the Roman camp is clear from the beginning of this chapter.

Caesar, anticipating trouble, gathers supplies and hastens repairs on the ships.
31. 1 At Caesar, etsi nondum eorum consilia cognoverat, tamen et ex eventu navium suarum, et ex eo, quod obsides dare intermiserant, fore id, quod accidit, suspicabatur. 2 Itaque ad omnes casus subsidia comparabat. Nam et frumentum ex agris cotidie in castra conferebat et, quae gravissime afflictae erant naves, earum materia atque aere ad reliquas reficiendas utebatur et, quae ad eas res erant usui, ex continenti comportari iubebat. 3 Itaque, cum summo studio a militibus administraretur, XII navibus amissis, reliquis ut navigari commode posset, effecit.

1 **cognoverat:** 'was familiar with'; *176b.* **ex ... suarum:** 'from what had happened to his ships'; how lit.? **ex eo, quod:** 'from the fact that,' lit. 'from this, namely the fact that'; *198b.* **dare intermiserant:** 'had ceased to give.'
2 **ad omnes casus subsidia comparabat:** 'he was providing remedies for every misfortune.' **frumentum:** from the new harvest. **quae ... naves, earum:** = *earum navium, quae*; *165c.* **quae:** as antecedent sc. *ea,* subject-accusative with *comportari.* **ad eas res:** 'for that purpose.'
3 **cum ... administraretur:** impersonal passive, 'the work was carried on'; *184a; 73d.* **summo studio:** 'with the utmost enthusiasm'; *136b.* **XII navibus amissis:** *144b5.* **ut ... posset, effecit:** *203.3.* **reliquis ut navigari commode posset:** 'that the rest could be sailed reasonably well,' lit. 'that it was possible that there be a sailing by the rest in a suitable way.' **reliquis:** ablative of means with the impersonal passive infinitive *navigari*; *131a; 73d.*

The Britons undertake a surpise attack using war-chariots.
32. 1 Dum ea geruntur, legione ex consuetudine una frumentatum missa, quae appellabatur VII, neque ulla ad id tempus belli suspicione interposita, cum pars hominum in agris remaneret, pars etiam in castra ventitaret, ei, qui pro portis castrorum in statione erant, Caesari nuntiaverunt, pulverem maiorem, quam consuetudo ferret, in ea parte videri, quam in partem legio iter fecisset. 2 Caesar id, quod erat, suspicatus, aliquid novi a barbaris initum consilii, cohortes, quae in stationibus erant, secum in eam partem proficisci, ex reliquis duas in stationem cohortes succedere, reliquas armari et confestim sese subsequi iussit. 3 Cum paulo longius a castris processisset, suos ab hostibus premi atque aegre sustinere et, conferta legione, ex omnibus partibus tela conici animadvertit. 4 Nam quod, omni ex reliquis partibus demesso frumento, pars una erat reliqua, suspicati hostes, huc nostros esse venturos, noctu in silvis delituerant; 5 tum dispersos, depositis armis, in metendo occupatos subito adorti, paucis interfectis, reliquos, incertis ordinibus, perturbaverant, simul equitatu atque essedis circumdederant.

1 **geruntur:** *190a.* **legione ... una ... missa:** *144b2.* **frumentatum:** 'to get grain,' from the fields; *231a.* **VII:** *septima; 38a; 36.* **neque ulla ad id tempus belli suspicione interposita:** 'without any suspicion of war made manifest up to that time'; how lit.? *144b2.* Although Caesar suspected their intentions (IV.31.1), they had not yet revealed them. **hominum:** *Britannorum; 98a.* **ventitaret:** 'came frequently,' a frequentative from *venio; 78a.*

ei: *milites.* **portis castrorum:** *294a.* **in statione:** 'on guard.' **pulverem:** '(a cloud of) dust'; *13g.* **quam con-suetudo ferret:** 'than usual,' lit. 'than custom would bring'; a result clause following the comparative *maiorem*; *197c.* **parte:** 'direction.' **videri:** 'was being seen.' **quam in partem:** 'in which'; *165a.*

2 **quod erat:** 'which was (actually the case).' **suspicatus:** *226c.* **aliquid novi a barbaris initum consilii:** in apposition to *id*, 'namely that some new scheme had been worked up by the barbarians,' lit. 'that something of a new scheme had been gone into by the barbarians.' **aliquid:** *168; 49a.* **initum:** sc. *esse; 68b, c.* **consilii:** *97b.* **cohortes:** the object of *iussit* at the end of the sentence. Four cohorts were likely involved, one from each of the four gates of the camp. How many men? *267c.* **in stationibus:** 'on guard'; plural because each gate was thought of as a separate post. **ex reliquis duas . . . cohortes:** 'two cohorts of the remaining (six).' Of the ten cohorts of the 10th legion, the four on guard went with Caesar, two were ordered to stand guard in their place, and the last four to arm themselves and follow him. **armari:** 'to arm themselves'; *174.*

3 **paulo longius:** 'a little farther (than usual),' though the force of the comparative does not seem necessary, and the phrase may mean little more than 'some little distance'; *153a.* **suos:** the men of the 7th legion. **conferta legione:** 'since the legion was crowded together'; *144b3.* The more closely the men stood, the more effective were the missiles of the enemy surrounding them. **conici:** sc. *in legionem; 57b.*

4 **quod . . . pars una erat reliqua:** a causal clause that contains within it a causal ablative absolute (*omni . . . demesso frumento; 144b3*), the two clauses together explaining that all the nearby grain had been cut except for in one area. Because only that area remained, the enemy anticipated where the Romans foragers would go. **huc nostros esse venturos:** indirect statement after *suspicati.* **deliuerant:** 'had hidden.'

5 **dispersos, occupatos:** sc. *eos* (= *nostros* just above), object of *adorti.* **depositis armis:** 'having laid aside their weapons.' **in metendo:** 'in reaping' (grain); *230.4.* **adorti:** *226c.* **incertis ordinibus:** 'since their ranks were in disorder,' a proper formation being impossible under the circumstances. **simul:** 'as soon as.' **essedis:** 'with war chariots.' Scythed war chariots, with a long sharp blade projecting from each end of the axle, were in use in Eastern countries, but the British chariots to which Caesar refers were apparently without scythes. Remains of chariot wheels have been found in the graves of warriors.

The way the Britons use war chariots in battle.

33. 1 Genus hoc est ex essedis pugnae: primo per omnes partes perequitant et tela coniciunt, atque ipso terrore equorum et strepitu rotarum ordines plerumque perturbant; et cum se inter equitum turmas insinuaverunt, ex essedis desiliunt et pedibus proeliantur. 2 Aurigae interim paulum ex proelio excedunt, atque ita currus collocant, ut, si illi a multitudine hostium premantur, expeditum ad suos receptum habeant. 3 Ita mobilitatem equitum, stabilitatem peditum in proeliis praestant; ac tantum usu cotidiano et exercitatione efficiunt, uti in declivi ac praecipiti loco incitatos equos sustinere et brevi moderari ac flectere, et per temonem percurrere et in iugo insistere et se inde in currus citissime recipere consuerint.

1 **Genus hoc est:** 'this is (their) method.' **ex essedis:** with *pugnae; 150d.* **per . . . perequitant:** sc. *essedarii;* 'they (the chariot-fighters) ride everywhere.' Each chariot carried a driver and one fighter. As the drivers dashed against the enemy, the men in the chariots sprang out and fought on foot. The chariots meanwhile withdrew a little from the thick of the fight, so that the drivers could see how the battle was going. If they saw their warriors defeated in any part of the line they swiftly drove to that part, took on board those hard pressed, and escaped danger. **terrore equorum:** 'fright caused by the horses'; subjective genitive; *95.* **ordines:** 'the ranks' of the enemy. **se . . . insinuaverunt:** 'they have worked their way'; the British cavalry were deployed such that they left openings through which the chariots could be driven against the enemy. **pedibus:** 'on foot'; *131a.*

2 **Aurigae:** 'the drivers.' **ita . . . ut:** *197b.* **illi:** the chariot-fighters. **premantur:** *220.* **expeditum ad suos receptum:** 'an easy retreat to their own,' i.e., to their drivers and their chariots.

3 **stabilitatem:** 'steadiness.' **peditum:** *10d.* **praestant:** 'exhibit'; sc. *essedarii.* **tantum usu cotidiano et exercitatione efficiunt:** 'by daily practice and training they become so expert,' lit. 'by daily practice and training to so great an extent, they bring it about'; *118b;* **uti . . . consuerint:** *203.3.* **in declivi ac praecipiti loco:** 'on downward-sloping and even precipitous ground.' **incitatos equos sustinere:** 'to keep control of their horses at full gallop,' lit. 'horses having been spurred on.' **brevi:** for *brevi tempore,* 'in an instant.' **moderari:** 'to slow down' (their horses). **flectere:** 'to turn.' **per temonem percurrere:** 'to run along the tongue' of the chariot, i.e., the pole that connects the yoked horses to the chariot itself. **in iugo insistere:** 'to stand on the yoke' between the horses. **citissime:** *34b.*

Caesar brings aid; the Britons prepare to attack the camp.

34. 1 Quibus rebus perturbatis nostris, novitate pugnae, tempore opportunissimo Caesar auxilium tulit; namque eius adventu hostes constiterunt, nostri se ex timore receperunt. 2 Quo facto, ad lacessendum hostem et ad committendum proelium alienum esse tempus arbitratus, suo se loco continuit et, brevi tempore intermisso, in castra legiones reduxit. 3 Dum haec geruntur, nostris omnibus occupatis, qui erant in agris reliqui, discesserunt. 4 Secutae sunt continuos complures dies tempestates, quae et nostros in castris continerent et hostem a pugna prohiberent. 5 Interim barbari nuntios in omnes partes dimiserunt paucitatemque nostrorum militum suis praedicaverunt et, quanta praedae faciendae atque in perpetuum sui liberandi facultas daretur, si Romanos castris expulissent, demonstraverunt. 6 His rebus celeriter magna multitudine peditatus equitatusque coacta, ad castra venerunt.

1 **rebus:** ablative of means. **nostris:** dative after *tulit*. **novitate:** 'strangeness'; *135a.* **tempore opportunissimo:** *147a.* **nostri ex timore reciperent:** 'our men recovered (themselves) from their fear.'
2 **Quo facto:** 'though this had been accomplished,' referring to the effects of Caesar's arrival; *144b5.* **alienum:** 'unfavorable.'
3 **nostris omnibus occupatis:** while the Romans were busy repairing ships and strengthening their defenses, the Britons 'withdrew' from the open country, gathering for attack. **qui:** as antecedent, sc. *ei* as subject of *discesserunt.*
4 **continuos complures dies:** *118a.* **quae . . . continerent:** *194a.*
5 **quanta . . . facultas daretur:** *204.3.* **praedae faciendae:** 'of securing booty,' objective genitive after *facultas*; *230.1; 102.* **in perpetuum:** 'forever.' **sui:** 'themselves'; *154b.* **castris:** *127a.* **expulissent:** *218.1b.*
6 **His rebus:** 'by means of these circumstances.' **peditatus:** *98a.* **equitatus:** apparently including also the *essedarii*, whose close connection with the cavalry has already been noted.

Caesar repels the attack on the camp and pursues the Britons.

35. 1 Caesar, etsi idem, quod superioribus diebus acciderat, fore videbat, ut, si essent hostes pulsi, celeritate periculum effugerent, tamen nactus equites circiter XXX, quos Commius Atrebas, de quo ante dictum est, secum transportaverat, legiones in acie pro castris constituit. 2 Commisso proelio, diutius nostrorum militum impetum hostes ferre non potuerunt ac terga verterunt. 3 Quos tanto spatio secuti, quantum cursu et viribus efficere potuerunt, complures ex eis occiderunt; deinde, omnibus longe lateque aedificiis incensis, se in castra receperunt.

1 **idem:** 'the same thing'; subject of *fore*, explained by the appositive clause *ut . . . effugerent*; *203.4.* **celeritate:** *136b.* **effugerent:** 'they would escape.' Because Caesar's cavalry did not make the crossing as planned (see IV.28), he could not send them to run down the enemy as they retreated (see, e.g., IV.14.5). **nactus:** *61a3; 226c.* **XXX:** a squad (*turma*); *38b; 269c.* **ante:** see IV.21.7 and 27.2-4; how and why Commius arrived at this moment with a squad of cavalry is not clear. The 30 horsemen were too few to be of service except in scouting or in following up a fleeing enemy.
2 **diutius:** 'very long'; *153a.* **ac:** 'but'; *234b.*
3 **secuti:** sc. *nostri.* **tanto spatio, quantum cursu et viribus efficere potuerunt:** 'over as great a distance as their speed and strength allowed,' lit., 'for as great an interval (of space) as they were able to accomplish by means of their running and their strength'; *tanto* and *quantum* are correlatives. Their lack of cavalry limited how far they could pursue those retreating. **spatio:** *147c.* **complures:** sc. *hostes*, accusative. **ex eis:** *97d.*

The Britons seek peace; Caesar sails back to Gaul.

36. 1 Eodem die legati, ab hostibus missi, ad Caesarem de pace venerunt. 2 His Caesar numerum obsidum, quem ante imperaverat, duplicavit, eosque in continentem adduci iussit, quod, propinqua die aequinoctii, infirmis navibus, hiemi navigationem subiciendam non existimabat. 3 Ipse, idoneam tempestatem nactus, paulo post mediam noctem naves solvit; quae omnes incolumes ad continentem pervenerunt, 4 sed ex eis onerariae duae eosdem portus, quos reliquae, capere non potuerunt et paulo infra delatae sunt.

1 **Eodem die:** *147a.* **de pace:** this peace provides Caesar with adequate cover to return to Gaul honorably.
2 **His:** with *duplicavit*; what kind of dative? *109a* (note also that *imperaverat* would regularly be followed with

a dative, and *duplicavit*, in a sense, doubles *imperaverat*; *105*). **ante:** see IV.27.5-6. **duplicavit:** 'doubled.' **quod . . . non existimabat:** a causal clause, containing within it two causal ablative absolutes and an indirect statement. **propinqua die aequinoctii:** 'since the day of the equinox was near,' a period when storms are unusually prevalent; *144b3*. The equinox fell on September 26, and Caesar probably left Britain at least a week before that date. He had been on the island about three weeks, and had hardly been able to go out of sight of the seashore. **infirmis navibus:** 'since his ships were weakened.' **hiemi navigationem subiciendam:** *sc. esse*, 'that the voyage (back to Gaul) ought to be subjected to wintry weather.'

3 **quae:** *167*. **incolumes:** *151*.

4 **eosdem portus:** probably Boulogne and Ambleteuse. **quos reliquae:** *sc. naves ceperunt*, 'which the rest of the ships reached.' **capere non potuerunt:** 'could not reach.' **paulo infra:** i.e., to the southwest. Whether the two transports made some harbor, or were stranded on the beach, Caesar does not say.

Legionaries from two transports are attacked by the Morini.

37. 1 Quibus ex navibus cum essent expositi milites circiter CCC atque in castra contenderent, Morini, quos Caesar, in Britanniam proficiscens, pacatos reliquerat, spe praedae adducti primo non ita magno suorum numero circumsteterunt ac, si sese interfici nollent, arma ponere iusserunt. 2 Cum illi, orbe facto, sese defenderent, celeriter ad clamorem hominum circiter milia VI convenerunt. Qua re nuntiata, Caesar omnem ex castris equitatum suis auxilio misit. 3 Interim nostri milites impetum hostium sustinuerunt atque amplius horis quattuor fortissime pugnaverunt; et, paucis vulneribus acceptis, complures ex his occiderunt. 4 Postea vero quam equitatus noster in conspectum venit, hostes, abiectis armis, terga verterunt magnusque eorum numerus est occisus.

1 **Quibus navibus:** 'these vessels,' the two transports mentioned near the end of the preceding chapter. **essent expositi:** 'had been landed.' **CCC:** *trecenti*, averaging about 150 men to a ship. **castra:** probably constructed by Publius Sulpicius Rufus for the protection of the harbor at *portius Itius* (Boulogne); cf. IV.22.6. **Morini, quos . . . pacatos reliquerat:** see IV.22.1-2. **non ita magno suorum numero:** 'with (lit. 'by means of') a not very large number of their own men.' **circumsteterunt, iusserunt:** *sc. eos*, the three hundred of Caesar's men. **si . . . nollent, ponere:** in the direct form, *si . . . non vultis, ponite*. **ponere:** here = *deponere*, 'lay down.'

2 **orbe facto:** 'formed a circle and'; how lit.? *144b2*. The 'circle' formed by soldiers for defense was hollow; *298*. **ad clamorem:** 'on hearing the shouting,' lit. 'to the shouting,' of the attacking Morini. In Gaul news was transmitted quickly by shouting across the country (VII.3). **hominum:** i.e., *Morinorum*; dependent on *milia*, the subject of *convenerunt*; *98a*. **VI:** *sex*. The number is probably exaggerated; in any case it evidences a much denser population in this region than is implied for the regions penetrated in the expedition against the Morini and Menapii the previous year; cf. III.28-29. **omnem equitatum:** including probably the cavalry that had embarked in the 18 transports but had failed to reach Britain, as well as the contingent left with Sulpicius; the rest must have gone with Titurius Sabinus and Cotta (see IV.22.5). **suis auxilio:** *112b*.

3 **amplius horis quattuor:** *129a*. **complures:** accusative.

4 **Postea vero quam:** = *posteaquam* ('after') *vero*; *188a*. **vero:** *236a*.

Caesar inflicts punishment upon the Morini and Menapii; winter quarters in Belgium; thanksgiving decreed at Rome.

38. 1 Caesar postero die T. Labienum legatum cum eis legionibus, quas ex Britannia reduxerat, in Morinos, qui rebellionem fecerant, misit. 2 Qui cum propter siccitates paludum, quo se reciperent, non haberent, quo perfugio superiore anno erant usi, omnes fere in potestatem Labieni venerunt. 3 At Q. Titurius et L. Cotta legati, qui in Menapiorum fines legiones duxerant, omnibus eorum agris vastatis, frumentis succisis, aedificiis incensis, quod Menapii se omnes in densissimas silvas abdiderant, se ad Caesarem receperunt. 4 Caesar in Belgis omnium legionum hiberna constituit. Eo duae omnino civitates ex Britannia obsides miserunt, reliquae neglexerunt. 5 His rebus gestis, ex litteris Caesaris dierum XX supplicatio a senatu decreta est.

1 **T. Labienum:** he had probably accompanied Caesar to Britain.

2 **Qui cum:** 'and since they'; *184a*. **siccitates:** *92c*. **quo se reciperent, non haberent, quo perfugio superiore anno erant usi:** the primary difficulty here results from the fact that *perfugium*, the direct object of *haberent*, has been attracted into the relative clause to which it is the antecedent; *165b*. The secondary difficulty results

from the fact that the *quo* of *quo . . . erant usi* is a regular relative pronoun (in the ablative after *usi*) while the *quo* of *quo se reciperent* is the adverb meaning '(a place) to which' and introducing a relative clause of characteristic; *194a*. Translate as if: *non haberent perfugium, quo se reciperent, quo superiore anno erant usi*, 'did not have a refuge (which was the sort of place) to which they could retreat, (the sort of refuge) which they had (in fact) used in the previous year.' **superiore anno:** 56 BC; cf. III.28-29.

3 **Menapiorum:** cf. III.28. **quod . . . abdiderunt:** a causal clause explaining why the Romans laid waste the enemy's property but did not fight the enemy. **in densissimas silvas abdiderant:** see the note on *in proximas silvas abdiderunt* in I.12.3.

4 **legionum:** *102*. **hiberna constituit:** 'established the winter quarters.' **Eo:** adverb. **reliquae neglexerunt:** sc. *obsides mittere.*

5 **ex:** 'in consequence of.' **dierum XX supplicatio:** This 'thanksgiving of twenty days' was five days longer than the one decreed at the end of 57 BC, though that was the longest known up to that time (see II.35.4). The expedition to Britain, as that into Germany, was followed by no tangible results, but the daring that caused a Roman army to penetrate these hitherto unknown regions seems to have stimulated unprecedented excitement back in Rome.

BOOK V

V.1-23: Second Expedition into Britain

Caesar orders ships built, quiets disturbances in Illyricum.

1. 1 L. Domitio, Ap. Claudio consulibus, discedens ab hibernis Caesar in Italiam, ut quotannis facere consuerat, legatis imperat, quos legionibus praefecerat, uti, quam plurimas possent, hieme naves aedificandas veteresque reficiendas curarent. 2 Earum modum formamque demonstrat. Ad celeritatem onerandi subductionesque paulo facit humiliores quam quibus in nostro mari uti consuevimus, atque id eo magis, quod propter crebras commutationes aestuum minus magnos ibi fluctus fieri cognoverat; ad onera ac multitudinem iumentorum transportandam paulo latiores quam quibus in reliquis utimur maribus. 3 Has omnes actuarias imperat fieri, quam ad rem humilitas multum adiuvat. 4 Ea, quae sunt usui ad armandas naves, ex Hispania apportari iubet. 5 Ipse, conventibus Galliae citerioris peractis, in Illyricum proficiscitur, quod a Pirustis finitimam partem provinciae incursionibus vastari audiebat. 6 Eo cum venisset, civitatibus milites imperat certumque in locum convenire iubet. 7 Qua re nuntiata, Pirustae legatos ad eum mittunt, qui doceant, nihil earum rerum publico factum consilio, seseque paratos esse demonstrant omnibus rationibus de iniuriis satisfacere. 8 Percepta oratione eorum, Caesar obsides imperat eosque ad certam diem adduci iubet; nisi ita fecerint, sese bello civitatem persecuturum demonstrat. 9 Eis ad diem adductis, ut imperaverat, arbitros inter civitates dat, qui litem aestiment poenamque constituant.

1 **L. Domitio, Ap. Claudio consulibus:** 54 BC; *240a; 234a.* **hibernis:** in Belgium (IV.38.4). **Italiam:** *252b.* **consuerat:** *176b.* **legatis imperat . . . uti . . . curarent:** *199a1.* **quam plurimas:** *153c.* **reficiendas curarent:** *229b.*

2 **onerandi:** 'of loading.' **subductiones:** 'beaching'; *92a.* **humiliores:** 'shallower.' **quam quibus:** i.e., *quam eae* (*naves*) *sunt, quibus; 131c.* **in nostro mari:** 'our sea' describes, from the Roman point of view, the Mediterranean Sea. **id:** refers back to the idea of *facit humiliores*, '(he did) this.' **eo magis, quod:** 'all the more because,' lit. 'the more because of this, namely the fact that'; *135.* **commutationes aestuum:** cf. IV.29.1. **ad . . . transportandam:** *230.3.* **latiores:** predicative; sc. *eas facit.*

3 **actuarias:** predicative, '(as) swift vessels,' with the use of oars as well as sails. **humilitas:** the 'lowness' of the deck above the water.

4 **usui:** *112a.* **Hispania:** *266.* **apportari:** 'be brought.'

5 **conventibus:** the circuit of councils and courts over which a provincial governor adjudicated. **a Pirustis:** *126a.* **incursionibus:** 'raids'; *131a.* Note that this clause contains both an ablative of agent and an ablative of means.

6 **civitatibus milites imperat:** 'he levies soldiers on the cities,' i.e., he imposes a draft upon them that is to yield the number of soldiers he sets; *105; 106a.* **milites:** the object of *imperat* and *iubet.*

7 **qui doceant:** *193a.* **nihil . . . factum:** sc. *esse,* indirect discourse after *doceant.* **earum rerum:** the *incursiones* mentioned in V.1.5. **omnibus rationibus:** 'on all counts'; *136b.*

8 **ad:** 'up to,' i.e., before. **nisi ita fecerint, sese . . . persecuturum:** sc. *esse,* condition of fact in indirect discourse; *218.1a.*

9 **arbitros:** 'arbiters'; *7c; 80b.* **litem:** 'the (matter of) damages.' **aestiment:** *193a.*

Proceeding to Gaul he finds ships ready, visits the Treveri.

2. 1 His confectis rebus conventibusque peractis, in citeriorem Galliam revertitur atque inde ad exercitum proficiscitur. 2 Eo cum venisset, circumitis omnibus hibernis, singulari militum studio in summa omnium rerum inopia circiter DC eius generis, cuius supra demonstravimus, naves et longas XXVIII invenit instructas, neque multum abesse ab eo, quin paucis diebus deduci possint. 3 Collaudatis militibus atque eis, qui negotio praefuerant, quid fieri velit ostendit, atque omnes ad portum Itium convenire iubet, quo ex portu commodissimum in Britanniam traiectum esse cognoverat, circiter milium passuum XXX a continenti; huic rei, quod satis esse visum est militum, reliquit. 4 Ipse cum legionibus expeditis IIII et equitibus DCCC in fines Treverorum proficiscitur, quod hi neque ad concilia veniebant neque imperio parebant Germanosque Transrhenanos sollicitare dicebantur.

1 **revertitur:** from Illyricum (V.1.5-9).

2 **singulari:** 'extraordinary.' Caesar proudly recognizes the efforts of his men. **DC:** *sescentas*, with *naves*. **cuius:** *cuius generis naves*; translate *cuius* as if *quod*. **supra:** in V.1.2. **longas:** i.e., *naves duodetriginta*; *306a*. **invenit:** here taking accusative and infinitive: *naves instructas* (*esse*) and (impersonally) *neque multum abesse*. **neque multum abesse ab eo, quin paucis diebus deduci possint:** 'and that in a few days they would be about ready to launch,' lit. 'and that there was not much lacking from the situation that in a few days (the ships) would be able to be brought down (to the shore)'; *201b*.

3 **Collaudatis:** 'warmly commending'; how lit.? **quid fieri velit:** *204.2*. **convenire:** 'to assemble.' **traiectum:** a noun, the subject of *esse*, 'the crossing.' **circiter milium passuum XXX a continenti:** describing the *traiectum in Britanniam*. **huic rei:** 'for this purpose'; *112a*. **quod . . . militum:** 'as many soldiers as,' lit. 'what of soldiers'; *97b*.

4 **cum legionibus:** *137a*. **quod:** causal. **sollicitare dicebantur:** '(because) they (the Treveri) were said to be inciting'; this is the third reason why Caesar went against them. All three reasons reveal how he sought to take precautions so that a crisis did not develop on the mainland while he was invading Britain.

By means of hostages he binds Indutiomarus to keep the peace.

3. 1 Haec civitas longe plurimum totius Galliae equitatu valet magnasque habet copias peditum Rhenumque, ut supra demonstravimus, tangit. 2 In ea civitate duo de principatu inter se contendebant, Indutiomarus et Cingetorix; 3 e quibus alter, simul atque de Caesaris legionumque adventu cognitum est, ad eum venit, se suosque omnes in officio futuros neque ab amicitia populi Romani defecturos confirmavit, quaeque in Treveris gererentur, ostendit. 4 At Indutiomarus equitatum peditatumque cogere, eisque, qui per aetatem in armis esse non poterant, in silvam Arduennam abditis, quae, ingenti magnitudine, per medios fines Treverorum a flumine Rheno ad initium Remorum pertinet, bellum parare instituit. 5 Sed postea quam non nulli principes ex ea civitate, et auctoritate Cingetorigis adducti et adventu nostri exercitus perterriti, ad Caesarem venerunt et de suis privatim rebus ab eo petere coeperunt, quoniam civitati consulere non possent, veritus, ne ab omnibus desereretur, Indutiomarus legatos ad Caesarem mittit; 6 *sese idcirco ab suis discedere atque ad eum venire noluisse, quo facilius civitatem in officio contineret, ne omnis nobilitatis discessu plebs propter imprudentiam laberetur;* 7 *itaque civitatem in sua potestate esse, seque, si Caesar permitteret, ad eum in castra venturum, et suas civitatisque fortunas eius fidei permissurum.*

1 **plurimum:** *118b*. **equitatu:** *142a*. **supra:** see III.11.1. **tangit:** 'extends to,' lit. 'touches.'

2 **inter se:** *159*.

3 **alter:** 'the second' of those mentioned, i.e., Cingetorix. **in officio futuros** (*esse*): 'that they would be in allegiance' to Caesar, i.e., they would place themselves under his authority. **quae:** interrogative; *204.2*.

4 **cogere:** sc. *instituit*. **per aetatem:** 'by reason of age.' **in armis esse:** i.e., *arma ferre*. **ingenti magnitudine:** *143b*.

5 **postea quam:** 'after.' **ab eo petere:** 'to make requests of him (Caesar).' **quoniam:** 'since (as they said)'; *183a*. **ne ab omnibus desereretur:** *202*.

6 **sese,** etc.: '(saying) that he.' **idcirco:** 'on this account,' namely the purpose then given in *quo . . . contineret*. **quo:** *193b*. **contineret:** 'retain.' **ne . . . laberetur:** a second purpose clause, restating in the negative the idea of the first. **discessu:** *147b*. **propter imprudentiam:** 'in consequence of their lack of foresight.' **laberetur:** 'fall away,' i.e., go astray and become disloyal.

7 **in sua potestate:** predicative, to be taken after *esse*. **se:** to be taken with *venturum* (*esse*) and *permissurum* (*esse*). **permitteret, permissurum:** the first in the sense of 'allow,' the second in the sense of 'entrust.'

4. 1 Caesar, etsi intellegebat, qua de causa ea dicerentur, quaeque eum res ab instituto consilio deterreret, tamen, ne aestatem in Treveris consumere cogeretur, omnibus ad Britannicum bellum rebus comparatis, Indutiomarum ad se cum CC obsidibus venire iussit. 2 His adductis, in eis filio propinquisque eius omnibus, quos nominatim evocaverat, consolatus Indutiomarum hortatusque est uti in officio maneret; 3 nihilo tamen setius, principibus Treverorum ad se convocatis, hos singillatim Cingetorigi conciliavit; quod cum merito eius ab se fieri intellegebat, tum magni interesse arbitrabatur eius auctoritatem inter suos quam plurimum valere, cuius tam egregiam in se voluntatem perspexisset. 4 Id factum graviter tulit Indutiomarus, suam gratiam inter suos minui, et, qui iam ante inimico in nos animo fuisset, multo gravius hoc dolore exarsit.

1 **qua de causa:** 'why'; *204.3*. How lit.? **quae res:** *204.2*. **eum:** Indutiomarus. **ab instituto consilio:** 'from (carrying out) the plan (which he had) formed.' **ne . . . cogeretur:** *196a*.

2 **in eis filio:** '(his) son (being) among these,' the *eis* refers back to *his*. **evocaverat:** sc. *Caesar*.

3 **nihilo tamen setius:** 'yet none the less.' **quod cum merito eius ab se fieri intellegebat, tum magni interesse arbitrabatur eius auctoritatem inter suos plurimum valere:** 'and he (Caesar) not only judged that this was being done by him in accordance with his (Cingetorix') merit, but he also realized that it was of great importance that his (Cingetorix') authority be as great as possible among his (Cingetorix') own.' **quod:** connecting relative, functioning as the accusative subject of *fieri*, in indirect discourse after *intellegebat*. **cum . . . tum:** correlative, 'both . . . and' or 'not only . . . but also'; *186b*. **merito:** *136c*. **eius:** Cingetorigis; *19d*. **magni interesse:** the verb is impersonal, here with the genitive of value; *101*; *103d*. **eius auctoritatem inter suos:** 'his authority among his own,' where *suos* is reflexive from the perspective of Cingetorix. **quam plurimum:** *118b*; *153a*. **cuius tam egregiam in se voluntatem perspexisset:** *eius* is the antecedent of *cuius*, 'the authority of that man whose most (lit. 'so') outstanding goodwill toward himself (Caesar) had observed.'

4 **suam gratiam inter suos minui:** accusative and infinitive in apposition to *Id factum*: 'this action, namely the fact that . . . .' **qui:** 'although he'; *187*. **animo:** *143b*. **hoc dolore:** 'on account of this grievance.'

Caesar gathers his forces at portus Itius.

5. 1 His rebus constitutis, Caesar ad portum Itium cum legionibus pervenit. 2 Ibi cognoscit LX naves, quae in Meldis factae erant, tempestate reiectas cursum tenere non potuisse atque eodem, unde erant profectae, revertisse; reliquas paratas ad navigandum atque omnibus rebus instructas invenit. 3 Eodem equitatus totius Galliae convenit, numero milium quattuor, principesque ex omnibus civitatibus; 4 ex quibus perpaucos, quorum in se fidem perspexerat, relinquere in Gallia, reliquos obsidum loco secum ducere decreverat, quod, cum ipse abesset, motum Galliae verebatur.

1 **ad portum Itium:** see V.2.3.

2 **naves,** etc.: these vessels had to be taken down the Marne (on which the Meldi lived) and the Seine to the English Channel, then north to Boulogne (*portus Itius*); see Map 11. **eodem:** adv., 'to the same place.' **reliquas:** *171a*. **instructas:** 'equipped.'

3 **numero:** *142a*; *85*. **milium:** dependent on *equitatus*; *100a*; *269b*.

4 **relinquere, ducere:** complementary infinitives after *decreverat*; *221a*. **quod . . . verebatur:** *183a*. **cum ipse abesset:** *185c*.

Dumnorix attempts to elude Caesar.

6. 1 Erat una cum ceteris Dumnorix Aeduus, de quo ante a nobis dictum est. Hunc secum habere in primis constituerat, quod eum cupidum rerum novarum, cupidum imperii, magni animi, magnae inter Gallos auctoritatis cognoverat. 2 Accedebat huc, quod in concilio Aeduorum Dumnorix dixerat sibi a Caesare regnum civitatis deferri; quod dictum Aedui graviter ferebant, neque recusandi aut deprecandi causa legatos ad Caesarem mittere audebant. 3 Id factum ex suis hospitibus Caesar cognoverat. Ille omnibus primo precibus petere contendit, ut in Gallia relinqueretur, partim quod, insuetus navigandi, mare timeret, partim quod religionibus impediri sese diceret. 4 Postea quam id obstinate sibi negari vidit, omni spe impetrandi adempta, principes Galliae sollicitare, sevocare singulos hortarique coepit, uti in continenti remanerent; metu territare: 5 *non sine causa fieri, ut Gallia omni nobilitate spoliaretur; id esse consilium Caesaris, ut, quos in conspectu Galliae interficere vereretur, hos omnes in Britanniam traductos necaret;* 6 fidem reliquis interponere, ius iurandum poscere, ut, quod esse ex usu Galliae intellexissent, communi consilio administrarent. Haec a compluribus ad Caesarem deferebantur.

1 **Erat una cum ceteris:** 'There was, together with the rest'; *90a*; *171a*. **ante:** Dumnorix had always opposed Caesar; see I.16-20. **in primis:** 'especially.' **constituerat:** sc. *Caesar*. **eum:** sc. *esse*; *258c*. **rerum novarum, imperii:** *102*. **magni animi, magnae auctoritatis:** not the same type of genitive as *rerum novarum* and *imperii*; *100b*.

2 **Accedebat huc, quod:** 'There was the additional consideration that,' lit. 'There was added to this the fact that'; in this idiom, *accedebat* is best translated in English as passive; *198b*. **quod dictum:** *167*. **neque:** with *audebant*, lit. 'and . . . not,' but here in the sense 'but . . . not.'

3 **primo:** in relation to *postea quam* in V.6.4. **precibus:** *131a.* **ut ... relinqueretur:** 'that he be left behind'; *199a4.* **insuetus navigandi:** 'unused to sailing'; *230.1.* **diceret:** *183b.*

4 **obstinate:** 'steadfastly.' **sevocare:** 'to call aside,' for secret conference; *79d.* **uti ... remanerent:** *199a2.* **metu territare:** sc. *eos*; historical infinitive; 'he worked upon their fears, (saying),' lit. 'he was terrifying (them) with the fear'; *182; 213b.*

5 **ut ... spoliaretur:** the subject of *fieri*; *203.1.* **spoliaretur:** 'was being stripped,' by taking the leading men to Britain. **quos:** the antecedent is the *hos* that follows the relative clause.

6 **interponere, poscere:** also historical infinitives, which are often best translated as if imperfect indicatives, 'was pledging,' 'was demanding'; *182.* **ut ... administrarent:** *199a4.* **quod ... intellexissent:** *194a.* **ex usu Galliae:** 'to the advantage of Gaul.'

7. 1 Qua re cognita Caesar, quod tantum civitati Aeduae dignitatis tribuerat, coercendum atque deterrendum, quibuscumque rebus posset, Dumnorigem statuebat; 2 quod longius eius amentiam progredi videbat, prospiciendum, ne quid sibi ac rei publicae nocere posset. 3 Itaque dies circiter XXV in eo loco commoratus, quod Corus ventus navigationem impediebat, qui magnam partem omnis temporis in his locis flare consuevit, dabat operam, ut in officio Dumnorigem contineret, nihilo tamen setius omnia eius consilia cognosceret; 4 tandem idoneam nactus tempestatem milites equitesque conscendere naves iubet. 5 At, omnium impeditis animis, Dumnorix cum equitibus Aeduorum a castris, insciente Caesare, domum discedere coepit. 6 Qua re nuntiata, Caesar, intermissa profectione atque omnibus rebus postpositis, magnam partem equitatus ad eum insequendum mittit retrahique imperat; 7 si vim faciat neque pareat, interfici iubet, nihil hunc, se absente, pro sano facturum arbitratus, qui praesentis imperium neglexisset. 8 Ille autem revocatus resistere ac se manu defendere suorumque fidem implorare coepit, saepe clamitans, liberum se liberaeque esse civitatis. 9 Illi, ut erat imperatum, circumsistunt hominem atque interficiunt; at equites Aedui ad Caesarem omnes revertuntur.

1 **civitati Aeduae:** *104a.* **dignitatis:** *97b.* **quibuscumque rebus:** *127a.* **posset:** sc. *eum coercere et deterrere*; *214a.*
2 **quod:** causal. **longius:** 'too far'; *153a.* **prospiciendum:** sc. *esse statuebat.* **ne ... posset:** *199b.* **quid:** *118b.* **sibi ac rei publicae:** *105.* **posset:** sc. *Dumnorix*, to whom *sibi* also refers.
3 **dies:** *118a.* **eo loco:** *portus Itius* (Boulogne). **commoratus:** 'while waiting'; *226c.* **Corus:** 'from the northwest.' **contineret, cognosceret:** *199a8.*
4 **tempestatem:** 'weather'; cf. IV.23.1.
5 **impeditis:** 'occupied.' **insciente Caesare:** *144b2.*
6 **retrahi:** sc. *eum*, 'that he be brought back.'
7 **si vim faciat neque pareat, interfici:** sc. *eum*, a condition of possible realization in indirect discourse; *218.2.* **nihil hunc, se absente, pro sano facturum arbitratus, qui praesentis imperium neglexisset:** translate as if *arbitratus hunc, qui praesentis sui imperium neglexisset, facturum esse nihil pro sano, se absente.* **pro sano:** 'like a man in his senses'; how lit.? **praesentis:** sc. *sui*, i.e., *Caesaris.*
8 **clamitans:** 'crying out'; *78a.* **liberae civitatis:** *100b.*
9 **ut erat imperatum:** impersonal passive, 'as it had been ordered'; *73d.*

Caesar sails to Britain, lands, and captures a stronghold.

8. 1 His rebus gestis, Labieno in continenti cum III legionibus et equitum milibus duobus relicto, ut portus tueretur et rei frumentariae provideret quaeque in Gallia gererentur cognosceret consiliumque pro tempore et pro re caperet, 2 ipse cum V legionibus et pari numero equitum, quem in continenti relinquebat, solis occasu naves solvit. Et leni Africo provectus, media circiter nocte vento intermisso, cursum non tenuit, et longius delatus aestu, orta luce, sub sinistra Britanniam relictam conspexit. 3 Tum, rursus aestus commutationem secutus, remis contendit, ut eam partem insulae caperet, qua optimum esse egressum superiore aestate cognoverat. 4 Qua in re admodum fuit militum virtus laudanda, qui vectoriis gravibusque navigiis, non intermisso remigandi labore, longarum navium cursum adaequarunt. 5 Accessum est ad Britanniam omnibus navibus meridiano fere tempore, neque in eo loco hostis est visus; 6 sed, ut postea Caesar ex captivis cognovit, cum magnae manus eo convenissent, multitudine navium perterritae, quae cum annotinis privatisque, quas sui quisque commodi causa fecerat, amplius DCCC uno erant visae tempore, a litore discesserant ac se in superiora loca abdiderant.

1 **quaeque:** the *–que* links *provideret* and *cognosceret*, the *quae* is interrogative. **quae in Gallia gererentur:** *204.2.* **pro tempore et pro re:** 'as conditions at the time might require'; how lit.?

2 **pari:** translate as if *eodem.* **solis occasu:** 'at sunset.' **Africo:** 'southwest wind.' Caesar probably sailed about July 6. **longius:** *153a.* **sub sinistra:** 'on the left.' **relictam:** 'left behind,' i.e., behind him as the tide turned him eastward, back toward Gaul.

3 **aestus commutationem:** as the tide turned again, it drew Caesar south and west toward Britain; the change of course is shown on Map 11, A. **caperet:** 'reach.' **qua:** 'where.' **aestate:** *147a.*

4 **Qua in re:** i.e., the rowing. **vectoriis gravibusque navigiis:** 'heavy transport ships'; dative after the compound verb *adaequarunt*; *107b.* **remigandi:** 'of rowing'; the transports were provided with oars in addition to sails.

5 **Accessum est ad Britanniam:** impersonal passive, lit. 'it was arrived to Britain'; *73d.* **meridiano fere tempore:** 'around midday.'

6 **convenissent:** *187.* **annotinis:** sc. *navibus*, 'ships of the previous year.' **sui commodi causa:** 'for the sake of his own advantage.' **quae . . . amplius DCCC:** *octingentae*; 'of which more than 800'; *97c; 129b.*

9. 1 Caesar, exposito exercitu et loco castris idoneo capto, ubi ex captivis cognovit quo in loco hostium copiae consedissent, cohortibus X ad mare relictis et equitibus CCC, qui praesidio navibus essent, de tertia vigilia ad hostes contendit, eo minus veritus navibus, quod in litore molli atque aperto deligatas ad ancoras relinquebat; ei praesidio navibusque Q. Atrium praefecit. 2 Ipse, noctu progressus milia passuum circiter XII, hostium copias conspicatus est. 3 Illi, equitatu atque essedis ad flumen progressi, ex loco superiore nostros prohibere et proelium committere coeperunt. 4 Repulsi ab equitatu se in silvas abdiderunt, locum nacti egregie et natura et opere munitum, quem domestici belli, ut videbatur, causa iam ante praeparaverant; 5 nam crebris arboribus succisis omnes introitus erant praeclusi. 6 Ipsi ex silvis rari propugnabant, nostrosque intra munitiones ingredi prohibebant. 7 At milites legionis septimae, testudine facta et aggere ad munitiones adiecto, locum ceperunt eosque ex silvis expulerunt, paucis vulneribus acceptis. 8 Sed eos fugientes longius Caesar prosequi vetuit, et quod loci naturam ignorabat, et quod, magna parte diei consumpta, munitioni castrorum tempus relinqui volebat.

1 **quo in loco . . . consedissent:** *204.3.* **qui . . . essent:** 'to guard the ships'; how lit.? *193a; 112b.* **eo . . . quod:** 'because of this (reason), namely that.' **veritus navibus:** *109a.* **ei praesidio navibusque:** *107a.*

2 **milia:** *118a.*

3 **equitatu:** *136b.* **essedis:** see IV.33. **flumen:** the Great Stour; see Map 11.

4 **nacti:** 'having secured.' **domestici belli, ut videbatur, causa:** they did not anticipate, in other words, a foreign invasion such as Caesar's, but simply took advantage of their standing fortifications. The British stronghold was perhaps near Canterbury.

5 **crebris arboribus succisis:** *144b6.*

6 **rari propugnabant:** 'in small bodies'; *151.* **nostros . . . ingredi:** *223a3.* **prohibebant:** 'were trying to prevent'; *175e.*

7 **testudine:** *305.* **aggere:** probably made of tree trunks; *301.*

8 **eos fugientes:** *eos* is the subject, *fugientes* the object, of *prosequi.* **munitioni:** *112a.* **tempus:** the subject of *relinqui.*

A storm shatters the fleet; Caesar orders repairs, returns inland.

10. 1 Postridie eius diei mane tripertito milites equitesque in expeditionem misit, ut eos, qui fugerant, persequerentur. 2 His aliquantum itineris progressis, cum iam extremi essent in prospectu, equites a Q. Atrio ad Caesarem venerunt, qui nuntiarent, superiore nocte maxima coorta tempestate, prope omnes naves afflictas atque in litus eiectas esse, quod neque ancorae funesque subsisterent, neque nautae gubernatoresque vim tempestatis pati possent; 3 itaque ex eo concursu navium magnum esse incommodum acceptum.

1 **tripertito:** adv., 'in three columns.' **in expeditionem:** 'for a rapid march,' with light equipment.

2 **aliquantum itineris:** 'some distance'; how lit.? *97b.* **extremi:** 'the rear' of the departing Roman force was just visible to those in camp, hence not too much time had elapsed since they had set out. **nuntiarent:** *193a.* **quod neque . . . subsisterent, neque . . . possent:** these two reasons for the disaster are reported in indirect discourse; *214a.*

3 **concursu:** 'wreckage,' lit. 'dashing together.'

11. 1 His rebus cognitis, Caesar legiones equitatumque revocari atque in itinere resistere iubet, ipse ad naves revertitur; 2 eadem fere, quae ex nuntiis litterisque cognoverat, coram perspicit sic ut, amissis circiter XL navibus, reliquae tamen refici posse magno negotio viderentur. 3 Itaque ex legionibus fabros deligit et ex continenti alios arcessi iubet; 4 Labieno scribit ut, quam plurimas possit, eis legionibus, quae sint apud eum, naves instituat. 5 Ipse, etsi res erat multae operae ac laboris, tamen commodissimum esse statuit, omnes naves subduci et cum castris una munitione coniungi. 6 In his rebus circiter dies X consumit, ne nocturnis quidem temporibus ad laborem militum intermissis. 7 Subductis navibus castrisque egregie munitis, easdem copias, quas ante, praesidio navibus relinquit, ipse eodem, unde redierat, proficiscitur. 8 Eo cum venisset, maiores iam undique in eum locum copiae Britannorum convenerant, summa imperii bellique administrandi communi consilio permissa Cassivellauno; cuius fines a maritimis civitatibus flumen dividit, quod appellatur Tamesis, a mari circiter milia passuum LXXX. 9 Huic superiore tempore cum reliquis civitatibus continentia bella intercesserant; sed, nostro adventu permoti, Britanni hunc toti bello imperioque praefecerant.

1 **in itinere resistere:** 'to resist (the enemy while) on the march'; i.e., to hold off the enemy without halting for a pitched battle.

2 **eadem:** direct object of *perspicit* and the antecedent of *quae*. **nuntiis litterisque:** from Quintus Atrius; see V.10.2. **amissis . . . navibus:** *144b5*. **sic ut . . . viderentur:** *197b*.

3 **fabros:** 'builders,' workmen supervised by engineers; *7c; 270b*.

4 **eis legionibus:** 'with (the help of) those legions,' at *portus Itius*. **ut . . . instituat:** *199a1*. **quae sint:** *220*.

5 **res erat multae operae ac laboris:** 'it was a very wearisome and laborious undertaking'; how lit.? *100b*. **omnes naves subduci et . . . coniungi:** an accusative and infinitive clause that itself forms the subject of *commodissimum esse*; *222b*.

6 **ne . . . quidem:** *237c*.

7 **quas ante:** *reliquit*. **praesidio navibus:** *112b*. **eodem:** the British stronghold, near modern Canterbury (see V.9.4-8).

8 **summa . . . permissa:** *144b2*. **summa imperii belli administrandi:** 'the supreme responsibility for command and for administering the war.' **Tamesis:** only the upper Thames formed the boundary of the territories ruled by Cassivellaunus; *14c*. **mari:** at the point where Caesar landed, near Deal.

9 **Huic . . . cum reliquis civitatibus continentia bella intercesserant:** 'continuous wars had happened between him and (lit. 'with') the other (British) states.' **Huic:** *107a*. **toti:** dative; *23a*.

The Britons and their island.

12. 1 Britanniae pars interior ab eis incolitur, quos natos in insula ipsa memoria proditum dicunt; 2 maritima pars ab eis, qui praedae ac belli inferendi causa ex Belgio transierunt (qui omnes fere eis nominibus civitatum appellantur, quibus orti ex civitatibus eo pervenerunt), et, bello illato, ibi permanserunt atque agros colere coeperunt. 3 Hominum est infinita multitudo creberrimaque aedificia fere Gallicis consimilia, pecorum magnus numerus. 4 Utuntur aut aere aut nummo aureo, aut taleis ferreis ad certum pondus examinatis pro nummo. 5 Nascitur ibi plumbum album in mediterraneis regionibus, in maritimis ferrum, sed eius exigua est copia; aere utuntur importato. Materia cuiusque generis, ut in Gallia, est, praeter fagum atque abietem. 6 Leporem et gallinam et anserem gustare fas non putant; haec tamen alunt animi voluptatisque causa. Loca sunt temperatiora quam in Gallia, remissioribus frigoribus.

1 **Britanniae:** *263*. **quos natos in insula ipsa memoria proditum dicunt:** translate as if *dicunt memoria proditum esse illos natos esse in insula ipsa*, lit. 'they say that it has been handed down in memory that they were born on the island itself,' but more naturally rendered as 'who, they say, according to tradition, originated in the island itself.' *Quos natos (esse)* is thus the subject of *memoria proditum (esse)*, which is somewhat redundant with *dicunt*, especially since *dicunt* has a generic 'they' as subject; *172c*. Several ancient peoples (e.g., the Athenians) considered themselves "autochthonous," i.e., sprung from the soil in the region in which they dwelt.

2 **appellantur:** there was, for example, a British tribe called *Atrebates*. **quibus orti ex civitatibus:** since the antecedent of *quibus* is *civitatum* (not, as it might first appear, *eis nominibus*), the *civitatibus* is redundant (*165a*), though this word order does add emphasis to *orti*, which is appropriate, since the argument here is that their names in their place of origin are the source of their names in Britain.

3 **Hominum est infinita multitudo:** 'the population is beyond number'; how lit.? **aedificia:** sc. *sunt.* **Gallicis** (aedificiis): large round huts of timbers and wickerwork, with conical thatched roofs.

4 **aut aere aut nummo aureo:** 'either bronze or gold coinage'; *nummus* is properly one coin, i.e., one piece of money, but the word comes to mean currency in general. **taleis ferreis ad certum pondus examinatis:** 'iron bars measured (lit. 'weighed') to a certain standard.' The iron currency bars that have been found represent several different weights, the heaviest being twice as heavy as the second, and so on.

5 **Nascitur:** 'is found.' **plumbum album:** 'tin,' lit. 'white lead,' which began to be exported from Cornwall as early as the ninth century BC. **mediterraneis:** 'inland.' The Cornish tin mines were in reality near the sea, but they were a long distance from Caesar's landing-place. **ferrum:** iron mines were worked in Sussex from the prehistoric period to the nineteenth century. **aere:** some bronze seems to have been imported into Britain, but most of the bronze objects found in Britain were made there out of native mixtures of the component metals. **Materia cuiusque generis . . . est:** 'There is wood (i.e., timber) of every type.' **fagum:** 'beech'; *5b.* Caesar seems to have been mistaken in saying that the beech was not found in Britain, but his opportunities for direct observation were limited. **abietem:** 'fir'; *10e.*

6 **Leporem et gallinam et anserem:** 'hare, chicken, and goose'; *13g; 11c; 234a.* **gustare fas non putant:** 'they think it not right to taste'; *fas* implies that the restriction was sacred. **haec alunt:** 'they rear these' (animals). **animi voluptatisque causa:** 'for pleasure and amusement.' **Loca:** 'the region'; *6c.* **sunt temperatiora:** 'has a milder climate'; how lit.? **remissioribus frigoribus:** 'the cold being less severe'; how lit.? *92c; 13f.*

13. 1 Insula natura triquetra, cuius unum latus est contra Galliam. Huius lateris alter angulus, qui est ad Cantium, quo fere omnes ex Gallia naves appelluntur, ad orientem solem, inferior ad meridiem spectat. Hoc latus pertinet circiter milia passuum D. 2 Alterum vergit ad Hispaniam atque occidentem solem; qua ex parte est Hibernia insula, dimidio minor, ut existimatur, quam Britannia, sed pari spatio transmissus atque ex Gallia est in Britanniam. 3 In hoc medio cursu est insula, quae appellatur Mona; complures praeterea minores obiectae insulae existimantur; de quibus insulis non nulli scripserunt dies continuos XXX sub brumam esse noctem. 4 Nos nihil de eo percontationibus reperiebamus, nisi certis ex aqua mensuris breviores esse quam in continenti noctes videbamus. 5 Huius est longitudo lateris, ut fert illorum opinio, DCC milium. 6 Tertium est contra septentriones; cui parti nulla est obiecta terra, sed eius angulus lateris maxime ad Germaniam spectat. Hoc milia passuum DCCC in longitudinem esse existimatur. 7 Ita omnis insula est in circuitu vicies centum milium passuum.

1 **natura:** 'in shape'; lit. 'by nature.' **triquetra:** sc. *est*, 'is triangular.' **contra:** 'opposite,' in the sense of 'facing.' **alter angulus:** 'one corner,' contrasted with the *inferior* (*angulus*) mentioned next. **ad Cantium:** 'by Kent' (Map 12, A); the boundaries of Kent in Caesar's time are not known with exactness. **quo:** refers to *angulus.* **appelluntur:** 'come to land,' lit. 'are driven in.' **ad orientem solem:** 'toward the east'; how lit.? **inferior** (*angulus*): see Map 12, B. **ad meridiem:** 'toward the south.' **D:** *quingenta*; how many English miles in 500 Roman miles? *243a, b.*

2 **Alterum** (latus) **vergit ad Hispaniam atque occidentem solem:** 'The second side has a westerly trend, toward Spain'; how lit.? Caesar's erroneous belief that Spain extended north nearly to Britain was shared by his contemporaries, and even by some writers after his time. See Map 12. **qua ex parte:** 'and on this side.' **dimidio minor:** 'a half smaller'; how lit.? *140.* **Britannia:** sc. *est.* **pari spatio transmissus atque ex Gallia est in Britanniam:** 'with an equal space of passage as is (the passage) from Gaul to Britain,' i.e., Ireland is as far from Britain as Britain is from Gaul. **pari spatio:** descriptive ablative, taking the place of an adjective, and coordinated with *minor* by *sed.* **transmissus:** genitive, depending on *spatio.* **pari . . . atque:** *233c.*

3 **In . . . cursu:** 'halfway across,' between Britain and Ireland; how lit.? *152a.* **Mona:** see Map 12. **obiectae** (esse) **insulae existimantur:** 'islands are thought to lie opposite (lit. 'be placed opposite') (the coast on this side)'; probably the Hebrides are referred to. **non nulli scripserunt:** perhaps now lost Greek writers are meant. **sub brumam:** 'around the winter solstice.' A period of thirty days without the sun does not occur on the Hebrides or on the other islands near Scotland.

4 **Nos:** *156.* **percontationibus:** 'through inquiries.' **certis ex aqua mensuris:** 'by exact measurements (made) with a water-clock'; a water-clock, *clepsydra*, was used in a Roman camp, especially to mark the watches; *242e.* **ex aqua:** with *mensuris*; *150d.* **breviores:** Caesar's observations were made in summer; in winter the nights would correspondingly have been longer.

5 **ut fert illorum opinio:** 'as their opinion says,' which might mean 'according to the Britons' or 'according to the unnamed writers just mentioned.' **DCC:** *septingentorum.* **milium:** *100b.*

6 **Tertium** (latus): cf. *unum* in V.13.1 and *alterum* in V.13.2. **cui parti:** *107a.* **nulla est obiecta terra:** i.e., there is

only open water on that side. **eius angulus lateris maxime ad Germaniam spectat:** see Map 12, C. **Hoc:** *hoc latus.* **DCCC:** *octingenta.*

7 **vicies centum:** 'two thousand,' lit. 'twenty hundred.' Caesar's estimate is nearer the truth than might have been expected; no Roman is known to have sailed around the island until more than a century after Caesar's time (in 84 AD).

14. 1 Ex his omnibus longe sunt humanissimi, qui Cantium incolunt, quae regio est maritima omnis, neque multum a Gallica differunt consuetudine. 2 Interiores plerique frumenta non serunt, sed lacte et carne vivunt pellibusque sunt vestiti. Omnes vero se Britanni vitro inficiunt, quod caeruleum efficit colorem, atque hoc horridiores sunt in pugna aspectu; 3 capilloque sunt promisso atque omni parte corporis rasa praeter caput et labrum superius. 4 Uxores habent deni duodenique inter se communes, et maxime fratres cum fratribus parentesque cum liberis; 5 sed, qui sunt ex eis nati, eorum habentur liberi, quo primum virgo quaeque deducta est.

1 **his omnibus:** the Britons; *97d.* **humanissimi:** 'most civilized.' **omnis:** 'wholly'; *151.* **neque:** 'and . . . not.'
2 **Interiores plerique:** 'those living in the interior, for the most part.' **serunt:** 'sow.' **lacte:** cf. IV.1.8; *131a.*
carne: 'meat'; *18a.* **sunt vestiti:** 'clothe themselves'; *174.* Caesar was misinformed about the life of the inland tribes of Britain; some did raise crops and wore clothes of wool or linen. **se vitro inficiunt:** 'stain themselves with woad,' a plant from the leaves of which is made a bluish dye. **caeruleum colorem:** 'a bluish color.' **hoc:** 'on this account'; *135.* **horridiores aspectu:** 'rather wild-looking'; how lit.? *142a.*
3 **capillo sunt promisso atque omni parte corporis rasa:** 'they let their hair grow long and they shave their whole body,' lit. 'they are with hair grown long and with every part of their body shaved'; *capillo* and *parte* are ablatives of description; *143b.*
4 **Uxores habent deni duodenique inter se communes:** 'each group of ten or twelve men regard their wives as shared among themselves,' i.e., groups of men (e.g., brothers, or fathers and their sons) regarded groups of women as their wives, collectively. **deni duodenique:** distributives, 'ten or (lit. 'and') twelve each,' i.e., in each group; *36.* **maxime:** adv., 'especially.'
5 **qui sunt ex eis nati, eorum habentur liberi:** the relative clause is the subject of *habentur*, and *liberi* is predicative: 'those who were born from these (wives) are regarded as the children of those.' **quo primum virgo quaeque deducta est:** 'by whom each (wife) was first led (home in marriage) as a virgin.' **quo:** the antecedent is the plural *eorum*, but *quo* is here singular because of the distributive sense of the following *quaeque.*

The Britons fight fiercely, but Caesar defeats them.
15. 1 Equites hostium essedariique acriter proelio cum equitatu nostro in itinere conflixerunt, ita tamen ut nostri omnibus partibus superiores fuerint atque eos in silvas collesque compulerint; 2 sed, compluribus interfectis, cupidius insecuti non nullos ex suis amiserunt. 3 At illi, intermisso spatio, imprudentibus nostris atque occupatis in munitione castrorum, subito se ex silvis eiecerunt, impetuque in eos facto, qui erant in statione pro castris collocati, acriter pugnaverunt; 4 duabusque missis subsidio cohortibus a Caesare, atque his primis legionum duarum, cum hae perexiguo intermisso loci spatio inter se constitissent, novo genere pugnae perterritis nostris, per medios audacissime perruperunt seque inde incolumes receperunt. 5 Eo die Q. Laberius Durus, tribunus militum, interficitur. Illi, pluribus summissis cohortibus, repelluntur.

1 **Equites hostium essedariique:** cf. IV.33. The narrative, interrupted by the description of Britain, is here resumed from V.11. **ita tamen ut:** 'yet (they did so) in such a way that'; *197b.* **fuerint:** the perfect tense stresses the actuality of the result.
2 **cupidius:** *153a.*
3 **intermisso spatio:** 'after an interval,' lit. 'with a space (of time) having been left vacant.' **in statione:** 'on guard duty.'
4 **subsidio:** *112a.* **atque his primis legionum duarum:** 'and these (cohorts consisting of) the first men of two legions,' i.e., these were the first cohorts of their respective legions, led by *primipili*; *161c*; *275b.* **hae:** sc. *cohortes.*
perexiguo intermisso loci spatio inter se: 'with a very small interval of space left between themselves.' **per medios perruperunt:** 'they (the Britons) forced their way through the middle (of our men).'
5 **tribunus militum:** *274.* **summissis:** 'sent up as reinforcements.'

16. 1 Toto hoc in genere pugnae, cum sub oculis omnium ac pro castris dimicaretur, intellectum est nostros propter gravitatem armorum, quod neque insequi cedentes possent neque ab signis discedere auderent, minus aptos esse ad huius generis hostem; 2 equites autem magno cum periculo proelio dimicare, propterea quod illi etiam consulto plerumque cederent et, cum paulum ab legionibus nostros removissent, ex essedis desilirent et pedibus dispari proelio contenderent. 3 Equestris autem proelii ratio et cedentibus et insequentibus par atque idem periculum inferebat. 4 Accedebat huc ut numquam conferti, sed rari magnisque intervallis proeliarentur stationesque dispositas haberent atque alios alii deinceps exciperent integrique et recentes defatigatis succederent.

1 **Toto hoc in genere pugnae:** 'throughout the engagement, in fighting of this sort,' lit. 'in this whole type of battle.' **cum:** *184a.* **sub oculis omnium:** i.e., *in conspectu omnium.* **dimicaretur, intellectum est:** impersonal passives; *73d.* **cedentes:** the object of *insequi.* **ab signis discedere:** *284.*
2 **equites … dimicare:** still in indirect discourse after *intellectum est.* **illi etiam consulto plerumque cederent:** 'they (the Britons) would, for the most part, even fall back purposely.' **dispari proelio:** 'in unequal battle,' i.e., 'in battle with the advantage on their side,' because Caesar's Gallic cavalry were no match for warriors fighting on foot.
3 **ratio:** the general method of the Britons. **et cedentibus et insequentibus:** refers to the Romans, whether on attack or in retreat. **periculum:** reinforces *magno cum periculo* in the previous sentence.
4 **Accedebat huc ut:** 'there was the additional fact that,' lit. 'there was added to this that.' **conferti:** 'in close formation.' **rari:** 'in small bodies.' **stationes:** here 'reserves.' **dispositas:** 'set in various places.' **alios alii deinceps exciperent:** 'were relieving one another in turn'; *171b.* **defatigatis:** *227a4.*

17. 1 Postero die procul a castris hostes in collibus constiterunt, rarique se ostendere et lenius quam pridie nostros equites proelio lacessere coeperunt. 2 Sed meridie, cum Caesar pabulandi causa III legiones atque omnem equitatum cum C. Trebonio legato misisset, repente ex omnibus partibus ad pabulatores advolaverunt sic uti ab signis legionibusque non absisterent. 3 Nostri, acriter in eos impetu facto, reppulerunt neque finem sequendi fecerunt quoad, subsidio confisi, equites, cum post se legiones viderent, praecipites hostes egerunt; 4 magnoque eorum numero interfecto, neque sui colligendi neque consistendi aut ex essedis desiliendi facultatem dederunt. 5 Ex hac fuga protinus, quae undique convenerant, auxilia discesserunt, neque post id tempus umquam summis nobiscum copiis hostes contenderunt.

1 **a castris:** sc. *Romanis.* **constiterunt:** 'took up a position,' from *consisto.*
2 **pabulandi causa:** 'to forage'; *230.1.* Three legions and the cavalry made a foraging party of extraordinary size. **pabulatores:** 'foragers.' **advolaverunt:** 'rushed upon'; how lit.? **ab signis legionibusque non absisterent:** 'they did not hold back from the standards of (lit. 'and') the legions,' i.e., the Britons even charged upon the legionaries, formed in order of battle; *238d; 284b2.*
3 **quoad:** *190c.* **subsidio confisi:** 'trusting in the support (of the legions)'; *135a; 226c.* **cum:** *184a.* **praecipites:** 'headlong'; *151.*
4 **sui colligendi:** *154b.* **dederunt:** sc. *hostibus.*
5 **Ex:** 'after.' **auxilia:** *auxilia Britannorum,* which is the antecedent of *quae undique convenerant.* **summis copiis:** 'with their greatest forces,' i.e., 'with their full strength'; *136b.*

Caesar's men force the passage of the Thames.
18. 1 Caesar, cognito consilio eorum, ad flumen Tamesim in fines Cassivellauni exercitum duxit; quod flumen uno omnino loco pedibus, atque hoc aegre, transiri potest. 2 Eo cum venisset, animadvertit ad alteram fluminis ripam magnas esse copias hostium instructas. 3 Ripa autem erat acutis sudibus praefixis munita, eiusdemque generis sub aqua defixae sudes flumine tegebantur. 4 His rebus cognitis a captivis perfugisque, Caesar, praemisso equitatu, confestim legiones subsequi iussit. 5 Sed ea celeritate atque eo impetu milites ierunt, cum capite solo ex aqua exstarent, ut hostes impetum legionum atque equitum sustinere non possent ripasque dimitterent ac se fugae mandarent.

1 **consilio:** the 'plan' of the Britons, hinted at by their decision not to fight Caesar again with their full force (V.17.5), and fully realized in the next chapter (V.19). **loco:** *145c.* **hoc:** sc. *loco; 161c.*

₂ **alteram:** here 'opposite,' for *alter* designates 'the other (of two).'

₃ **acutis sudibus praefixis:** 'with sharp stakes driven in front,' at the water's edge.

₄ **praemisso:** 'sent ahead.' Given the defensive works just described, presumably Caesar here means that he sent his forces along the bank to find a more manageable crossing. If they were swift enough to retain the element of surprise, his troops could then cross unobstructed, reconstitute their lines once across, and attack the enemy position.

₅ **ea celeritate atque eo impetu:** 'with such speed and such force'; the demonstrative pronouns here set up the result clause that follows; *197*. **cum capite solo ex aqua exstarent:** 'though they were in water up to the chin,' lit. 'though they were projecting out of the water only by means of their head'; *187*. Caesar crossed the Thames from the south to the north side; precisely where he crossed is not known; see Map 11.

Cassivellaunus harasses Caesar's army on the march.

19. 1 Cassivellaunus, ut supra demonstravimus, omni deposita spe contentionis, dimissis amplioribus copiis, milibus circiter IIII essedariorum relictis, itinera nostra servabat paulumque ex via excedebat locisque impeditis ac silvestribus sese occultabat atque eis regionibus, quibus nos iter facturos cognoverat, pecora atque homines ex agris in silvas compellebat; 2 et, cum equitatus noster liberius praedandi vastandique causa se in agros effunderet, omnes viis notis semitisque essedarios ex silvis emittebat, et magno cum periculo nostrorum equitum cum eis confligebat atque hoc metu latius vagari prohibebat. 3 Relinquebatur ut neque longius ab agmine legionum discedi Caesar pateretur et tantum in agris vastandis incendiisque faciendis hostibus noceretur, quantum labore atque itinere legionarii milites efficere poterant.

₁ **supra:** see V.17.5. **contentionis:** i.e., a decisive engagement. **amplioribus copiis:** 'the greater part of his forces.' **IIII:** *quattuor*. It is unclear whether Caesar means that Cassivellaunus kept in the field 4000 chariot drivers, each having a chariot and accompanied by a warrior (see IV.33), making a force of 8000 men, or whether in *essedariorum* both drivers and warriors are included; in the latter case there would be 2000 chariots, each with two men, making a total of 4000 men.

₂ **se effunderet:** 'were dashing forth,' lit. 'were pouring themselves forth.' **viis notis semitisque:** 'by the roads and passageways well known (to them)'; *134a*. **equitum:** *102*. **hoc metu:** 'by their fear of this' danger. **vagari:** sc. *nostros*.

₃ **Relinquebatur ut neque longius ab agmine legionum discedi Caesar pateretur:** i.e., *equitibus*, lit. 'there was remaining that Caesar not allow that there be a withdrawing (to the cavalry) very far from the column of the legions'; the *ut*-clause is the subject of *relinquebatur* and *discedi* is impersonal passive. More smoothly rendered as: 'The only option left was for Caesar not to allow the cavalry to get very far from the legionary column.' **tantum . . . hostibus noceretur, quantum:** 'and to do as much harm to the enemy . . . as,' lit. 'and that harm be done to the enemy to so great an extent as great as'; *noceretur* is also impersonal passive. **labore atque itinere:** 'by toilsome marching,' hendiadys; *238d*.

The Trinovantes submit.

20. 1 Interim Trinovantes, prope firmissima earum regionum civitas, ex qua Mandubracius adulescens, Caesaris fidem secutus, ad eum in continentem venerat (cuius pater in ea civitate regnum obtinuerat interfectusque erat a Cassivellauno, ipse fuga mortem vitaverat), 2 legatos ad Caesarem mittunt pollicenturque sese ei dedituros atque imperata facturos; 3 petunt ut Mandubracium ab iniuria Cassivellauni defendat atque in civitatem mittat, qui praesit imperiumque obtineat. 4 His Caesar imperat obsides XL frumentumque exercitui Mandubraciumque ad eos mittit. Illi imperata celeriter fecerunt, obsides ad numerum frumentumque miserunt.

₁ **prope firmissima:** 'nearly the strongest.' **Caesaris fidem secutus:** 'pursuing Caesar's allegiance'; *226c*.

₂ **imperata:** 'as he commands,' lit. 'the things having been commanded.'

₃ **Cassivellauni:** 'at the hands of Cassivellaunus'; *95*. **mittat:** *Mandubracium* remains the direct object, and he is also the antecedent of *qui*. **qui:** *193a*.

₄ **His Caesar imperat:** 'Caesar gives the order to them to furnish.' **frumentumque exercitui:** 'and grain for the army.' **ad numerum:** 'at (lit. 'to') the number (levied).'

Caesar takes Cassivellaunus' stronghold.

21. 1 Trinovantibus defensis atque ab omni militum iniuria prohibitis, Cenimagni, Segontiaci, Ancalites, Bibroci, Cassi, legationibus missis, sese Caesari dedunt. 2 Ab his cognoscit non longe ex eo loco oppidum Cassivellauni abesse, silvis paludibusque munitum, quo satis magnus hominum pecorisque numerus convenerit. 3 Oppidum autem Britanni vocant, cum silvas impeditas vallo atque fossa munierunt, quo, incursionis hostium vitandae causa, convenire consuerunt. 4 Eo proficiscitur cum legionibus. Locum reperit egregie natura atque opere munitum; tamen hunc duabus ex partibus oppugnare contendit. 5 Hostes, paulisper morati, militum nostrorum impetum non tulerunt seseque alia ex parte oppidi eiecerunt. 6 Magnus ibi numerus pecoris repertus, multique in fuga sunt comprehensi atque interfecti.

1 **ab omni militum iniuria prohibitis:** 'protected from any injury at the hands of our soldiers'; 95. **Cenimagni, Segontiaci, Ancalites, Bibroci, Cassi:** almost nothing is known about these small states.
2 **eo loco:** where Caesar met the envoys. **oppidum:** 'the stronghold of Cassivellaunus' is thought to have been in the vicinity of St. Albans. **quo:** 'where,' lit. 'to where.' **satis magnus:** 'rather large.'
3 **Oppidum . . . vocant, cum:** 'call (a place) a stronghold when.' Several fortified enclosures of extreme antiquity, intended not for permanent habitation but for refuge and defense in times of danger, have been found in England.
4 **hunc:** sc. *locum.* **duabus ex partibus:** 'on two sides.'
5 **alia ex parte:** presumably the opposite side from that on which Caesar was attacking.
6 **repertus:** sc. *est.*

An attack on Caesar's naval camp is repulsed; Cassivellaunus yields.

22. 1 Dum haec in his locis geruntur, Cassivellaunus ad Cantium, quod esse ad mare supra demonstravimus, quibus regionibus IIII reges praeerant, Cingetorix, Carvilius, Taximagulus, Segovax, nuntios mittit atque his imperat, uti, coactis omnibus copiis, castra navalia de improviso adoriantur atque oppugnent. 2 Hi cum ad castra venissent, nostri, eruptione facta, multis eorum interfectis, capto etiam nobili duce Lugotorige, suos incolumes reduxerunt. 3 Cassivellaunus, hoc proelio nuntiato, tot detrimentis acceptis, vastatis finibus, maxime etiam permotus defectione civitatum, legatos per Atrebatem Commium de deditione ad Caesarem mittit. 4 Caesar, cum constituisset hiemare in continenti propter repentinos Galliae motus, neque multum aestatis superesset, atque id facile extrahi posse intellegeret, obsides imperat et, quid in annos singulos vectigalis populo Romano Britannia penderet, constituit; 5 interdicit atque imperat Cassivellauno, ne Mandubracio neu Trinovantibus noceat.

1 **in his locis:** in the region of St. Albans. **Cantium:** Kent. **supra:** in V.14.1. **quibus regionibus:** i.e., the regions of Kent; dative after *praeerant; 107a.* **uti . . . oppugnent:** *199a1.* **castra navalia:** see V.11.5-7. **de improviso:** 'suddenly,' i.e., as a surprise attack.
2 **Lugotorige:** nom. Lugotorix; *10c.* **incolumes:** predicative.
3 **tot detrimentis:** 'so many losses.' **per Atrebatem Commium:** 'through the agency of Commius, one of the Atrebates' (a people who were both in Belgium and in Britain); *123a.*
4 **cum constituisset:** *184a.* **neque multum aestatis superesset:** '(and because) there was not much of summer remaining.' **id facile extrahi posse:** 'that this (process) could easily be drawn out' in profitless negotiations. **quid . . . penderet:** *204.2.* **quid . . . vectigalis:** 'how much tribute,' lit. 'what of tribute,' i.e., tax; *97b.* **in annos singulos:** 'each year.'
5 **ne . . . noceat:** *199a1.* **Mandubracio:** *105.*

Caesar returns to the coast, finds ships ready, sails to Gaul.

23. 1 Obsidibus acceptis, exercitum reducit ad mare, naves invenit refectas. 2 His deductis, quod et captivorum magnum numerum habebat et non nullae tempestate deperierant naves, duobus commeatibus exercitum reportare instituit. 3 Ac sic accidit uti ex tanto navium numero tot navigationibus neque hoc neque superiore anno ulla omnino navis, quae milites portaret, desideraretur, 4 at ex eis, quae inanes ex continenti ad eum remitterentur (et prioris commeatus, expositis militibus, et quas postea Labienus faciendas curaverat, numero LX), perpaucae locum caperent, reliquae fere omnes reicerentur. 5 Quas cum aliquamdiu Caesar frustra exspectasset, ne anni tempore a navigatione excluderetur, quod aequinoctium suberat, necessario angustius milites collocavit 6 ac, summa tranquillitate consecuta, secunda inita cum solvisset vigilia, prima luce terram attigit omnesque incolumes naves perduxit.

1 **refectas:** 'repaired,' as ordered in V.11.1-6.
2 **deductis:** 'launched,' lit. 'drawn down' to the water, from the fortified enclosure in which they had been guarded and repaired. **quod:** causal. **duobus commeatibus:** 'in two trips'; *136b*.
3 **uti ... desideraretur, caperent, reicerentur:** *203.1.* **neque hoc neque superiore anno ulla omnino navis:** in translation, it is likely clearest to move the negative from *neque ... neque* to *ulla* and render as if *nulla omnino navis vel hoc vel superiore anno.* **quae milites portaret:** *194a.* **desideraretur:** 'was lost.'
4 **inanes:** predicative. **et** (naves) **prioris commeatus, expositis militibus, et** (naves) **quas:** 'both (the ships) of the first trip, (sent back) after the soldiers had been landed, and (other ships) which.' **postea:** i.e., after Caesar had departed Gaul for the campaign in Britain. **Labienus faciendas curaverat:** *229b.* **numero LX:** in apposition to *quas ... Labienus faciendas curaverat; 142a.* **locum caperent:** 'reached their destination,' Britain. **reicerentur:** 'were carried back,' i.e., pushed back to the coast of Gaul by wind and/or tide.
5 **Quas:** 'these' ships, sent from the continent; *167.* **ne ... excluderetur:** *196a.* **aequinoctium:** Caesar must have left Britain shortly after the middle of September, having been two months or more on the island. **necessario angustius:** 'of necessity rather closely'; *153a.*
6 **secunda inita ... vigilia:** *144b1.* **solvisset:** 'set sail.' **incolumes:** *151.*

V.24-58: Attacks of the Gauls upon Caesar's Winter Camps

Due to the scarcity of grain, Caesar divides his army for the winter more widely.
24. 1 Subductis navibus concilioque Gallorum Samarobrivae peracto, quod eo anno frumentum in Gallia propter siccitates angustius provenerat, coactus est aliter ac superioribus annis exercitum in hibernis collocare legionesque in plures civitates distribuere. 2 Ex quibus unam, in Morinos ducendam, C. Fabio legato dedit, alteram in Nervios Q. Ciceroni, tertiam in Esuvios L. Roscio; quartam in Remis cum T. Labieno in confinio Treverorum hiemare iussit; 3 tres in Bellovacis collocavit: his M. Crassum quaestorem et L. Munatium Plancum et C. Trebonium legatos praefecit. 4 Unam legionem, quam proxime trans Padum conscripserat, et cohortes V in Eburones, quorum pars maxima est inter Mosam ac Rhenum, qui sub imperio Ambiorigis et Catuvolci erant, misit. 5 His militibus Q. Titurium Sabinum et L. Aurunculeium Cottam legatos praeesse iussit. 6 Ad hunc modum distributis legionibus, facillime inopiae rei frumentariae sese mederi posse existimavit. 7 Atque harum tamen omnium legionum hiberna, praeter eam quam L. Roscio in pacatissimam et quietissimam partem ducendam dederat, milibus passuum C continebantur. 8 Ipse interea, quoad legiones collocatas munitaque hiberna cognovisset, in Gallia morari constituit.

1 **Subductis:** 'beached'; cf. V.1.2. **Samarobrivae:** *4a.* **siccitates:** *92c;* cf. IV.38.2. **aliter ac:** *233c.* **superioribus annis:** *147a.*
2 **Ex quibus unam:** sc. *ex quibus legionibus unam legionem.* **in Morinos ducendam:** 'to be led into the country of the Morini'; *229b.* **in confinio Treverorum:** 'on the Treveran frontier.' The site of Labienus' camp, as well as the further sites named in this chapter, are indicated on Map 11.
3 **M. Crassum quaestorem:** see Vocab. under *Crassus,* (3).
4 **trans Padum:** north of the Po, in Cisalpine Gaul; Caesar adopts the perspective of one in Rome.
5 **His militibus:** *107a.*
6 **Ad hunc modum:** 'in this way.' **inopiae:** dative after *mederi; 105.*
7 **hiberna:** the subject of *continebantur.* **praeter eam:** sc. *legionem.* **C:** *centum.* Caesar perhaps means that no two camps were more than 100 Roman miles apart, but the furthest two camps were somewhat more than 100 miles apart. Either Caesar is mistaken or the text is corrupt.
8 **quoad:** *190c.*

After Tasgetius is murdered, Caesar transfers Plancus to the country of the Carnutes.

25. 1 Erat in Carnutibus, summo loco natus, Tasgetius, cuius maiores in sua civitate regnum obtinuerant. 2 Huic Caesar pro eius virtute atque in se benevolentia, quod in omnibus bellis singulari
eius opera fuerat usus, maiorum locum restituerat. 3 Tertium iam hunc annum regnantem inimici
palam, multis ex civitate auctoribus, interfecerunt. Defertur ea res ad Caesarem. 4 Ille veritus, quod ad
plures pertinebat, ne civitas eorum impulsu deficeret, L. Plancum cum legione ex Belgio celeriter in
Carnutes proficisci iubet ibique hiemare, quorumque opera cognoverit Tasgetium interfectum, hos
comprehensos ad se mittere. 5 Interim ab omnibus legatis quaestoribusque, quibus legiones tradider-
at, certior factus est in hiberna perventum locumque esse munitum.

1 **summo loco natus:** *128a.*
2 **in se benevolentia:** 'loyalty to himself (Caesar)'; *150d.* **opera:** ablative after *usus fuerat*; *131a.*
3 **Tertium iam annum:** *118a.* **regnantem:** *227a5.* **multis ex civitate auctoribus:** *144b6.*
4 **quod ad plures pertinebat:** 'because a large number were implicated,' lit. 'because it was extending to a rather
large number.' **quorumque opera cognoverit Tasgetium interfectum** (esse): the *–que* of *quorumque* links
hiemare and *mittere*, while *quorum* defines the *hos* at the end of this clause: '(those) by whose effort he (Plancus)
learned that Tasgetius had been killed.' **hos comprehensos ad se mittere:** 'to apprehend and send to him,' lit.
'(he orderd Plancus) to send to him those having been apprehended'; *228a.*
5 **perventum:** sc. *esse*, impersonal passive, 'that they had arrived into . . . ,' lit. 'that there had been a coming
through into . . . '; *73d.*

V.26-37: Attack of the Eburones on the camp of Sabinus and Cotta

Ambiorix attacks the camp of Sabinus and Cotta, parleys.

26. 1 Diebus circiter XV, quibus in hiberna ventum est, initium repentini tumultus ac defectionis
ortum est ab Ambiorige et Catuvolco; 2 qui cum ad fines regni sui Sabino Cottaeque praesto fuissent
frumentumque in hiberna comportavissent, Indutiomari Treveri nuntiis impulsi, suos concitaverunt,
subitoque oppressis lignatoribus, magna manu ad castra oppugnanda venerunt. 3 Cum celeriter nostri
arma cepissent vallumque ascendissent, atque una ex parte, Hispanis equitibus emissis, equestri
proelio superiores fuissent, desperata re, hostes suos ab oppugnatione reduxerunt. 4 Tum suo more
conclamaverunt, uti aliqui ex nostris ad colloquium prodiret: *habere sese, quae de re communi dicere*
vellent, quibus rebus controversias minui posse sperarent.

1 **Diebus circiter XV, quibus:** 'about fifteen days after,' lit. 'within around 15 days, during which'; *147a.* **Ambiorige et Catuvolco:** see V.24.4-5; *19d; 10c.*
2 **qui:** connecting relative; *167.* **Sabino Cottaeque praesto fuissent:** lit. 'had been at hand for,' i.e., they had
to come meet Sabinus and Cotta when the Romans arrived at the frontier of the Eburones (*ad fines regni sui*).
praesto: adv. **Treveri:** genitive, in apposition to *Indutiomari*; see V.4 for Indutiomarus' motivation. **suos:** the
Eburones. **lignatoribus:** 'the wood foragers,' i.e., soldiers sent to collect wood. **manu:** *137b.*
3 **vallum:** the camp of Sabinus and Cotta was perhaps on the site of modern Limburg; see Map 11. **hostes suos:**
hostes is the subject, *suos* the object, of *reduxerunt.*
4 **suo more:** *136c.* **uti aliqui ex nostris ad colloquium prodiret:** 'in order that someone from our side come
forward for a conference.' **aliqui:** the adjective is here equivalent to the pronoun *aliquis*; *49a.* **habere sese,**
quae: 'that they had (things) which,' indirect statement representing what was said at the conference. **re communi:** the 'shared situation,' i.e., the situation in which each side found itself. **quibus rebus:** 'by means of which
(things).' **controversias:** 'the issues at hand.'

27. 1 Mittitur ad eos colloquendi causa C. Arpineius, eques Romanus, familiaris Q. Titurii, et Q.
Iunius ex Hispania quidam, qui iam ante, missu Caesaris, ad Ambiorigem ventitare consuerat; apud
quos Ambiorix ad hunc modum locutus est: 2 *sese pro Caesaris in se beneficiis plurimum ei confiteri*
debere, quod eius opera stipendio liberatus esset, quod Atuatucis, finitimis suis, pendere consuesset, quodque
*ei et filius et fratris filius a Caesare remissi essent, quos Atuatuci, obsidum numero missos, apud se in servi-
tute et catenis tenuissent; 3 neque id, quod fecerit de oppugnatione castrorum, aut iudicio aut voluntate sua*

fecisse, sed coactu civitatis, suaque esse eius modi imperia, ut non minus haberet iuris in se multitudo, quam ipse in multitudinem. 4 Civitati porro hanc fuisse belli causam, quod repentinae Gallorum coniurationi resistere non potuerit. Id se facile ex humilitate sua probare posse, quod non adeo sit imperitus rerum, ut suis copiis populum Romanum superari posse confidat. 5 Sed esse Galliae commune consilium; omnibus hibernis Caesaris oppugnandis hunc esse dictum diem, ne qua legio alteri legioni subsidio venire posset. 6 Non facile Gallos Gallis negare potuisse, praesertim cum de recuperanda communi libertate consilium initum videretur. 7 Quibus quoniam pro pietate satisfecerit, habere nunc se rationem officii pro beneficiis Caesaris; monere, orare Titurium pro hospitio, ut suae ac militum saluti consulat. 8 Magnam manum Germanorum conductam Rhenum transisse; hanc affore biduo. 9 Ipsorum esse consilium, velintne prius quam finitimi sentiant, eductos ex hibernis milites aut ad Ciceronem aut ad Labienum deducere, quorum alter milia passuum circiter L, alter paulo amplius ab eis absit. 10 Illud se polliceri et iure iurando confirmare, tutum se iter per suos fines daturum. 11 Quod cum faciat, et civitati sese consulere, quod hibernis levetur, et Caesari pro eius meritis gratiam referre. Hac oratione habita, discedit Ambiorix.

1 **Q. Titurii:** Q. Titurius Sabinus, referred to as Sabinus in V.26.2 (cf. V.24.5); *19, a-c.* **ex Hispania quidam:** 'a certain man from Spain,' whose choice is explained in the following relative clause. **missu Caesaris:** 'sent by Caesar,' lit. 'by the sending of Caesar.' **apud quos:** 'before whom,' i.e., Arpineius and Iunius.

2 **sese pro Caesaris in se beneficiis plurimum ei confiteri debere:** i.e., *sese confiteri, pro Caesaris beneficiis in se, (se) ei plurimum debere; 213b.* **ei:** Caesar. **quod, quod, quodque:** the first and third of these are causal conjunctions, while the second is a relative pronoun (*stipendio* is its antecedent). **quos:** *et filius et fratris filius* are the antecedents. **obsidum numero missos:** participial phrase in agreement with *quos.*

3 **neque id, quod fecerit . . . fecisse:** 'and that (he) had not done that which he did.' **iudicio:** *138.* **coactu civitatis:** 'forced by (lit. 'by the compulsion of') his state.' **suaque esse eius modi imperia:** 'and that the conditions of his authority were such,' lit. 'and that his commands were of such a sort'; *eius modi* thus prompts a result clause. **iuris in se:** '(of a) jurisdiction over him.'

4 **Civitati porro hanc fuisse belli causam, quod:** '(that), moreover, the state had this reason for going to war, the fact that,' lit. 'that this, moreover, was the cause of the war for the state, namely that.' **Civitati:** *111.* **quod:** *198b.* **Id:** '(that) this thing (was the cause of the war).' **ex sua humilitate:** 'by reason of his own insignificance.' **probare:** 'to prove.' **quod non sit:** causal, explaining his awareness of his *humilitas.* **confidat:** 'believed.'

5 **Sed esse:** 'rather, (it) was.' **Galliae:** *95.* **omnibus hibernis Caesaris oppugnandis:** *112a; 230.2.* **esse dictum:** 'had been set.' **ne . . . posset:** *196a.* **alteri:** *23a.* **legioni subsidio:** *112b.*

6 **negare:** 'to say no to,' i.e., 'to refuse.' **consilium initum videretur:** sc. *esse,* 'a plan seemed to have been formed,' lit. 'to have been entered into.'

7 **Quibus quoniam pro pietate satisfecerit, habere nunc se rationem officii pro beneficiis Caesaris:** 'since he had given satisfaction to them (i.e., the Gauls) in accordance with his obligation, he was now taking account of his duty in accordance with the kindnesses of Caesar.' Note how the speech shifts to historic present (*175b; 177b*) with *habere* (and *satisfecerit*), thus adding emphasis to Ambiorix' seemingly candid assessment of his competing obligations. *Pietas* toward his countrymen required that he take part in the larger plan, but his debt to Caesar meant that he was limiting his involvement to the initial assault that had already been countered. **monere, orare:** sc. *se,* i.e., Ambiorix. **pro hospitio:** 'in view of their relationship as host and guest.' **ut . . . consulat:** *199a4.* **suae ac militum saluti:** *157*

8 **conductam:** i.e., *conductam mercede;* lit. 'having been brought together (by means of pay),' i.e., a band of mercenaries. **hanc:** sc. *manum.*

9 **Ipsorum esse consilium:** 'the decision was their own,' i.e., it was up to the Romans to decide; *94d.* **velintne:** 'whether they wished'; *204.1.* **prius quam finitimi sentiant:** *189b.* Ambiorix' offer thus urges the Romans to act in quiet secrecy. **eductos ex hibernis milites . . . deducere:** 'to lead the soldiers out of winter quarters and away,' lit. 'to lead away the soldiers having been led out'; *227a4.*

10 **Illud:** the object of both *polliceri* and *confirmare,* then expanded (with accusative subject and infinitive verb) into *tutum se iter per suos fines daturum,* 'this: (namely) that he . . . .'

11 **Quod cum faciat:** 'in doing this,' lit. 'when (and because) he was doing this'; *185c.* **civitati:** *105.* **quod hibernis levetur:** 'because it (his *civitas*) was being relieved of the winter encampment'; *127a.* **gratiam referre:** 'was showing his gratitude.'

Cotta refuses to receive advice from Ambiorix, an enemy; Sabinus trusts him.

28. 1 Arpineius et Iunius, quae audierunt, ad legatos deferunt. Illi, repentina re perturbati, etsi ab hoste ea dicebantur, tamen non neglegenda existimabant, maximeque hac re permovebantur, quod civitatem ignobilem atque humilem Eburonum sua sponte populo Romano bellum facere ausam vix erat credendum. 2 Itaque ad consilium rem deferunt, magnaque inter eos exsistit controversia. 3 L. Aurunculeius compluresque tribuni militum et primorum ordinum centuriones nihil temere agendum, neque ex hibernis iniussu Caesaris discedendum existimabant; 4 *quantasvis Gallorum, magnas etiam copias Germanorum sustineri posse, munitis hibernis, docebant: rem esse testimonio, quod primum hostium impetum, multis ultro vulneribus illatis, fortissime sustinuerint; 5 re frumentaria non premi; interea et ex proximis hibernis et a Caesare conventura subsidia; 6 postremo, quid esse levius aut turpius quam, auctore hoste, de summis rebus capere consilium?*

1 **quae audierunt:** sc. *ea* as antecedent, the object of *deferunt*. **repentina:** 'unexpected.' **hac re . . . quod:** 'by this consideration, namely that.' **civitatem . . . ausam:** sc. *esse*, indirect statement after *erat credendum*; *62.* **ignobilem:** 'obscure.' **vix erat credendum:** lit. 'it was scarcely to be believed.'
2 **exsistit:** 'arose'; *175b.*
3 **primorum ordinum centuriones:** cf. I.41. **discedendum:** sc. *esse*, impersonal, lit. 'that it should be departed.'
4 **quantasvis Gallorum:** sc. *copias*, the subject of *sustineri posse*; 'any force of Gauls,' no matter how great. **magnas etiam copias Germanorum:** 'and great forces of Germans, too,' i.e., on top of the Gallic forces. **munitis hibernis:** *144b4.* **rem . . . quod:** 'this thing, (namely) that.' **testimonio:** *112a.* **ultro:** 'besides.'
5 **re frumentaria non premi:** 'that there was no difficulty about supplies,' lit. 'that (they) were not being pressed in respect to the grain supply.' **conventura:** sc. *esse*; *178.*
6 **quid esse levius atque turpius:** a rhetorical question; *217c.* **auctore hoste:** 'on the advice of an enemy'; *144b2.*

29. 1 Contra ea Titurius *sero facturos* clamitabat, *cum maiores manus hostium, adiunctis Germanis, convenissent, aut cum aliquid calamitatis in proximis hibernis esset acceptum. Brevem consulendi esse occasionem. 2 Caesarem, se arbitrari, profectum in Italiam; neque aliter Carnutes interficiendi Tasgetii consilium fuisse capturos, neque Eburones, si ille adesset, tanta contemptione nostri ad castra venturos esse. 3 Sese non hostem auctorem, sed rem spectare: subesse Rhenum; magno esse Germanis dolori Ariovisti mortem et superiores nostras victorias; 4 ardere Galliam, tot contumeliis acceptis, sub populi Romani imperium redactam, superiore gloria rei militaris exstincta. 5 Postremo, quis hoc sibi persuaderet, sine certa spe Ambiorigem ad eius modi consilium descendisse? 6 Suam sententiam in utramque partem esse tutam: si nihil esset durius, nullo cum periculo ad proximam legionem perventuros; si Gallia omnis cum Germanis consentiret, unam esse in celeritate positam salutem. 7 Cottae quidem atque eorum, qui dissentirent, consilium quem haberet exitum? in quo si non praesens periculum, at certe longinqua obsidione fames esset timenda.*

1 **sero:** 'too late.' **facturos:** *se facturos esse*. **clamitabat:** 'kept protesting loudly'; *78a.* **cum . . . convenissent:** 'when (and because)'; *185c.* **Brevem:** predicative, placed first for emphasis; English word order, in direct speech, would be *occasio consulendi est brevis*.
2 **Caesarem . . . profectum:** sc. *esse*, indirect statement after *se arbitrari*. **Italiam:** *252b.* **neque aliter Carnutes . . . consilium fuisse capturos:** 'otherwise (i.e., if Caesar had not departed to Italy), neither would the Carnutes have taken up their plan.' The clause functions as the apodosis of a contrafactual condition, with *aliter* functioning as the protasis. **interficiendi Tasgetii:** see V.25; *102.* **neque Eburones, si ille adesset, . . . venturos esse:** another contrary to fact condition in indirect discourse, 'nor, if he (Caesar) were present, would the Eburones have come'; *218.3.* **contemptione:** *136b.* **nostri:** *155.* **ad castra venturos esse:** i.e., *castra oppugnaturos esse*.
3 **Sese non hostem auctorem, sed rem spectare:** *hostem* and *rem* are both direct objects of *spectare*, with *auctorem* an object complement to *hostem*, 'that he had regard not for the enemy as adviser, but for (the facts of) the situation.' **Germanis, dolori:** *112b.* **mortem, victorias:** subjects of *esse*. **Ariovisti mortem:** nothing is known about the death of Ariovistus, who was last mentioned in I.53. **victorias:** over Ariovistus (I.30-54), the Usipetes and Tencteri (IV.1-15), and the expedition into Germany in the previous year (IV.16-19).
4 **tot contumeliis acceptis:** *144b3.* **redactam:** in agreement with *Galliam*, but with similar causal force to the ablative absolutes before and after this participial phrase.
5 **quis hoc sibi persuaderet:** 'who was persuading him (of) this'; an indirect question (i.e., a direct question reported in indirect discourse); *217a.* **hoc:** introducing the accusative and infinitive phrase that follows: 'this, namely that Ambiorix . . .'; *117a.* **ad . . . descendisse:** 'had resorted to.'
6 **in utramque partem:** 'for either alternative.' **si . . . durius:** 'if nothing serious should happen,' lit. 'if there was nothing more serious'; *218.1a.* **unam . . . salutem:** 'their only safety'; *245d.*

7 **dissentirent:** i.e., with him (Sabinus). **consilium quem haberet exitum:** an indirect question, as above in V.29.5; *quem exitum* is the object, *consilium* the subject, of *haberet*. **in quo:** i.e., *in eorum consilio*. **at:** 'at least.'

After heated argument Sabinus persuades Cotta to leave the camp.
30. 1 Hac in utramque partem disputatione habita, cum a Cotta primisque ordinibus acriter resisteretur, 'Vincite,' inquit, 'si ita vultis,' Sabinus, et id clariore voce, ut magna pars militum exaudiret; 2 'neque is sum,' inquit, 'qui gravissime ex vobis mortis periculo terrear. Hi sapient; si gravius quid acciderit, abs te rationem reposcunt; 3 qui, si per te liceat, perendino die, cum proximis hibernis coniuncti, communem cum reliquis belli casum sustineant, non, reiecti et relegati longe a ceteris, aut ferro aut fame intereant.'

1 **in utramque partem:** 'on both sides.' **ordinibus:** = *centurionibus*; see V.28.3. '**Vincite':** the shift to direct discourse heightens the dramatic tension. **et id:** *161c.*
2 **qui gravissime ex vobis . . . terrear:** relative clause of characteristic, 'who, of any of you, is (the sort of man who is) the most seriously terrified'; *194a*. **ex vobis:** *97d*. **Hi sapient:** 'These,' the soldiers, spoken with a gesture, 'will understand.' **si gravius quid acciderit, abs te rationem reposcunt:** future condition of fact; *206.3*.
3 **qui:** the *hi* of the previous sentence, the soldiers ringing the discussion. **qui, si per te liceat, . . . sustineant:** condition of possible realization; *207.1*. **si per te liceat:** 'if you would consent'; lit. 'if it should be permitted through you.' **per te:** as with *abs te*, Sabinus now focuses on Cotta in particular. **perendino die:** 'on the day after tomorrow'; *147a*. **cum:** the preposition. **coniuncti:** *227a1*. **non . . . intereant:** '(and who thus) would not perish.' **reiecti et relegati:** 'flung aside and cast away.'

31. 1 Consurgitur ex consilio; comprehendunt utrumque et orant ne sua dissensione et pertinacia rem in summum periculum deducant; 2 *facilem esse rem, seu maneant, seu proficiscantur, si modo unum omnes sentiant ac probent; contra in dissensione nullam se salutem perspicere.* 3 Res disputatione ad mediam noctem perducitur. Tandem dat Cotta, permotus, manus; superat sententia Sabini. 4 Pronuntiatur prima luce ituros. Consumitur vigiliis reliqua pars noctis, cum sua quisque miles circumspiceret, quid secum portare posset, quid ex instrumento hibernorum relinquere cogeretur. 5 Omnia excogitantur, quare nec sine periculo maneatur et languore militum et vigiliis periculum augeatur. 6 Prima luce sic ex castris proficiscuntur, ut quibus esset persuasum, non ab hoste, sed ab homine amicissimo consilium datum, longissimo agmine maximisque impedimentis.

1 **Consurgitur:** 'all stood up,' lit. 'there is an arising together.' **comprehendunt:** by the hand. **utrumque:** Sabinus and Cotta.
2 **facilem esse rem, seu maneant, seu proficiscantur:** the *seu* clauses are the subject of *esse*, 'whether they stay or whether they depart was an easy matter,' i.e., whichever option was chosen could be easily undertaken. **si modo:** 'if only.' **contra in dissensione:** 'in disagreement, on the other hand.'
3 **dat . . . manus:** 'yielded,' lit. 'he gives (up) his hands,' i.e., raising them in surrender; Sabinus was the senior officer. **sententia:** nominative.
4 **vigiliis:** 'in wakefulness'; *92a*. **cum:** *185c*. **quid:** '(to see) what'; *204.2*. **instrumento:** 'stock,' supplies had been laid up for the duration of the winter.
5 **Omnia excogitantur, quare nec sine periculo maneatur et languore militum et vigiliis periculum augeatur:** 'All things (i.e., all possible reasons) were thought of why remaining would not be without danger, and (why) the danger (of departing) would be increased by the exhaustion of the soldiers and their watches.' Both arguments hint at cowardice and laziness: enduring a siege would be dangerous, and assigning regular guard duty through the night would be exhausting. **quare:** *204.3*. **maneatur:** impersonal passive, lit. 'there would be a remaining.' **languore militum et vigiliis:** hendiadys, 'by the exhaustion of the soldiers' watches'; *238d*. [For my argument that the conventional understanding of this sentence, as presented here, is faulty and that the Latin text should be emended from *et languore* to *nec languore*, see *Classical Quarterly* 67 (2017): 307-10.]
6 **ut quibus esset persuasum:** 'like men convinced,' lit. 'as (men) to whom it had been persuaded,' i.e., *ut* ('as') *ei, quibus persuasum esset*; subjunctive in a relative clause of characteristic; *194a*; *106b*. **non . . . consilium datum:** sc. *esse*, indirect statement after *esset persuasum*. **longissimo agmine:** i.e., in a long and loose formation; *136b*.

The Roman force, enticed into a defile, is attacked.

32. 1 At hostes, postea quam ex nocturno fremitu vigiliisque de profectione eorum senserunt, col-locatis insidiis bipertito in silvis opportuno atque occulto loco a milibus passuum circiter duobus, Romanorum adventum exspectabant; 2 et cum se maior pars agminis in magnam convallem demis-isset, ex utraque parte eius vallis subito se ostenderunt novissimosque premere et primos prohibere ascensu atque, iniquissimo nostris loco, proelium committere coeperunt.

1 **postea quam:** 'after.' **eorum:** the Romans. **bipertito:** 'at two points,' on opposite sides of a valley through which the road ran. **loco:** *145c.* **a milibus passuum circiter duobus:** 'at (a distance of) about two miles'; *126c.* This phrase likely describes the distance between the two points (*bipertito*) of the ambush, since Caesar next describes how the enemy attacked both the front and the rear of the column simultaneously. Another possibil-ity is that the site of the ambush was two miles from the Roman camp.
2 **se . . . demisisset:** 'had descended,' lit. 'had marched itself down.' **ex utraque parte eius vallis:** 'from both sides of this valley.' **ostenderunt:** sc. *hostes* as subject. **novissimos premere et primos prohibere ascensu:** i.e., the enemy crowded toward those in the rear and checked the advance of those in front. **ascensu:** *127a.*

33. 1 Tum demum Titurius, qui nihil ante providisset, trepidare et concursare cohortesque disponere, haec tamen ipsa timide atque ut eum omnia deficere viderentur; quod plerumque eis accidere con-suevit, qui in ipso negotio consilium capere coguntur. 2 At Cotta, qui cogitasset haec posse in itinere accidere, atque ob eam causam profectionis auctor non fuisset, nulla in re communi saluti deerat; et in appellandis cohortandisque militibus imperatoris et in pugna militis officia praestabat. 3 Cum propter longitudinem agminis non facile per se omnia obire et, quid quoque loco faciendum esset, providere possent, iusserunt pronuntiari, ut impedimenta relinquerent atque in orbem consisterent. 4 Quod consilium, etsi in eius modi casu reprehendendum non est, tamen incommode accidit; 5 nam et nostris militibus spem minuit et hostes ad pugnam alacriores effecit, quod non sine summo timore et desperatione id factum videbatur. 6 Praeterea accidit, quod fieri necesse erat, ut vulgo milites ab signis discederent, quaeque quisque eorum carissima haberet, ab impedimentis petere atque arripere properaret, clamore et fletu omnia complerentur.

1 **qui:** 'since he'; *194c.* **trepidare, concursare, disponere:** historical infinitives; *182.* **haec tamen ipsa:** 'yet (he was doing) these very things,' in apposition to the historical infinitives. **ut eum omnia deficere viderentur:** '(in such a way) that all (his resources) seemed to fail him.' **quod:** *id, quod,* 'a thing which,' introducing a gener-alizing claim. **coguntur:** a universal present; *175c.*
2 **qui cogitasset . . . atque . . . non fuisset:** *194c.* **auctor:** 'instigator.' **haec:** subject of *posse accidere* after *cogi-tasset.* **communi saluti:** *109b.* **et in appellandis cohortandisque militibus imperatoris et in pugna militis officia praestabat:** 'he fulfilled both the duties of a commander, in calling upon the soldiers by name and ex-horting them, and (the duties) of a soldier, in the battle,' the duties appropriate to the genitives *imperatoris* and *miltis* are further defined through a prepositional phrase (*in* + abl.).
3 **Cum . . . possent:** *184a.* **per se omnia obire:** 'to attend to everything in person.' **quid:** after *providere; 204.2.* **quoque loco:** 'at each point.' **possent:** the plural subject ('they') presumably includes both Sabinus and Cotta. **iusserunt pronuntiari:** *pronuntiari* is impersonal passive, 'they gave orders that the word be passed.' **relinquer-ent:** 'that (the men) should abandon.' **orbem:** *298.*
4 **Quod:** *167.* **reprehendendum non est:** 'is not to be criticized.' **incommode accidit:** 'turned out unfortunately.'
5 **militibus:** *109a.* **quod:** causal. **non sine:** *239g.* **id factum** (esse) **videbatur:** 'this seemed to have been done.'
6 **quod fieri necesse erat:** in apposition to the subject of *accidit,* 'as was inevitable,' lit. 'that which was inevitable to happen.' **ut . . . discederent, properaret, complerentur:** *203.1.* **quaeque:** the *–que* connects *discederent* and *properarent.* **carissima:** 'most dear,' predicative; *petere ab impedimentis* (*ea*) *eorum quae quisque carissima haberet.* **haberet:** *220.* **arripere:** 'carry off,' before the enemy looted the abandoned baggage. **properaret:** supply *quis-que* as subject.

34. 1 At barbaris consilium non defuit. Nam duces eorum tota acie pronuntiari iusserunt, ne quis ab loco discederet: *illorum esse praedam atque illis reservari, quaecumque Romani reliquissent; proinde omnia in victoria posita existimarent.* 2 Erant et numero et virtute pugnandi pares. Nostri, tametsi ab duce et a fortuna deserebantur, tamen omnem spem salutis in virtute ponebant, et quotiens quaeque cohors procurrerat, ab ea parte magnus numerus hostium cadebat. 3 Qua re animadversa Ambiorix pronuntiari iubet, ut procul tela coniciant neu propius accedant et, quam in partem Romani impetum fecerint, cedant 4 (levitate armorum et cotidiana exercitatione nihil eis noceri posse), rursus se ad signa recipientes insequantur.

1 **consilium:** '(good) judgment,' contrasted with the confusion and panic on the Roman side. **illorum esse praedam atque illis reservari:** '(saying) that the booty was theirs and (it) was reserved for them,' indirect statement inherent to *pronuntiari*. **omnia in victoria posita:** sc. *esse*, indirect statement after *existimarent*. **existimarent:** imperative in direct discourse, thus subjunctive (as an indirect command) in indirect discourse, 'they should consider'; *216*.
2 **pugnandi:** *102*. **duce:** the singular targets Sabinus. **ab ea parte:** *126c*.
3 **coniciant:** 'that (his men) hurl.' **quam in partem:** 'wherever,' lit. 'into which direction'; *204.3*.
4 **nihil eis noceri posse:** '(saying that) no harm could be done to them,' *noceri* is impersonal passive, lit. 'that there could in no way be a harming to them'; a parenthetical indirect statement within a series of indirect commands. **eis:** *106b*. **rursus se ad signa recipientes insequantur:** '(and that his men) pursue (the Romans) again (as they are) returning themselves to their standards,' i.e., that they yield only as long as the Romans were attacking, but then pursue again once the Romans began to fall back to the place from which they had made their charge. **se:** reflexive with *recipientes*.

35. 1 Quo praecepto ab eis diligentissime observato, cum quaepiam cohors ex orbe excesserat atque impetum fecerat, hostes velocissime refugiebant. 2 Interim eam partem nudari necesse erat et ab latere aperto tela recipere. 3 Rursus cum in eum locum, unde erant egressi, reverti coeperant, et ab eis, qui cesserant, et ab eis, qui proximi steterant, circumveniebantur; 4 sin autem locum tenere vellent, nec virtuti locus relinquebatur, neque ab tanta multitudine coniecta tela conferti vitare poterant. 5 Tamen, tot incommodis conflictati, multis vulneribus acceptis, resistebant, et magna parte diei consumpta, cum a prima luce ad horam octavam pugnaretur, nihil, quod ipsis esset indignum, committebant. 6 Tum T. Balventio, qui superiore anno primum pilum duxerat, viro forti et magnae auctoritatis, utrumque femur tragula traicitur; 7 Q. Lucanius, eiusdem ordinis, fortissime pugnans, dum circumvento filio subvenit, interficitur; 8 L. Cotta legatus, omnes cohortes ordinesque adhortans, in adversum os funda vulneratur.

1 **eis:** the enemy. **quaepiam:** 'any'; *49a*. **refugiebant:** 'would rush back in flight'; *175d*.
2 **eam partem:** the charging cohort; the subject of both *nudari* and *recipere*. **ab latere aperto:** 'on the exposed side,' the right side, unprotected by a shield; *126c*.
3 **eum locum:** in the circle. **coeperant:** the formerly advancing Roman cohort is the subject.
4 **locum tenere:** in the circle, without charging. **nec virtuti locus relinquebatur:** 'and no place was left to virtue,' i.e., there was no opportunity to display their valor if they remained where they were being barraged by missiles. **vellent, reliquebatur:** a contrary to fact condition; the indicative is used in the apodosis in situations where propriety and possibility are emphasized; *208b*. **vitare poterant:** *conferti* (describing the Romans soldiers) is the subject, *tela* the object.
5 **conflictati:** 'although harassed'; *227a3*. **horam octavam:** *242a*. **pugnaretur:** *73d*. **quod ipsis esset indignum:** 'that was unworthy of them'; *142b*; *194a*.
6 **T. Balventio:** *109a*. **qui superiore anno primum pilum duxerat:** i.e., Balventius had been the first centurion of the legion the year before; he was now serving probably as a veteran volunteer (*evocatus*); *276*. **auctoritatis:** 'influence'; *100a*. **utrumque femur:** 'each thigh,' i.e., both of them; *18d*. **tragula:** a javelin hurled with torque from a sling.
7 **eiusdem ordinis:** 'of the same rank,' a first centurion. **dum:** *190a*. **circumvento:** 'who had been surrounded'; *227a4*.
8 **ordines:** here 'centuries.' **in adversum os:** 'full in the face.' **funda:** 'by a slingshot.'

Sabinus prepares to surrender to Ambiorix.

36. 1 His rebus permotus, Q. Titurius, cum procul Ambiorigem suos cohortantem conspexisset, interpretem suum, Cn. Pompeium, ad eum mittit rogatum ut sibi militibusque parcat. 2 Ille appellatus respondet *si velit secum colloqui, licere; sperare a multitudine impetrari posse, quod ad militum salutem* *pertineat; ipsi vero nihil nocitum iri, inque eam rem se suam fidem interponere.* 3 Ille cum Cotta saucio communicat, si videatur pugna ut excedant et cum Ambiorige una colloquantur; *sperare ab eo de sua ac militum salute impetrari posse.* Cotta se ad armatum hostem iturum negat atque in eo perseverat.

1 **cohortantem:** *228c.* **interpretem:** *10e.* **Cn. Pompeium:** presumably a provincial awarded Roman citizenship by Gnaeus Pompeius Magnus, whose name he thus adopted as his Roman name. **rogatum:** *231b.* **parcat:** 'to spare'; *199a4; 105.*
2 **si velit:** condition of fact in indirect discourse; *218.1a.* **sperare:** sc. *se* (Ambiorix) as subject. **impetrari posse, quod ad militum salutem pertineat:** 'that the request, so far as the safety of the soldiers was concerned, might be granted.' **quod:** a restrictive relative clause of characteristic, the antecedent of which is implied in the impersonal passive *impetrari; 194f.* **ipsi:** Titurius Sabinus. **vero:** *236a.* **nihil nocitum iri:** future passive infinitive; 'that no harm at all would be done'; *54; 73d.* **in eam rem se suam fidem interponere:** 'that he pledges his honor on behalf of this thing (i.e., these terms).'
3 **Ille:** Titurius Sabinus. **si videatur:** '(to see) whether it seemed (good to him)'; *204.4.* **pugna:** after *excedant; 127a.* **ut excedant:** this clause forms the subject of *videatur; 203.1.* **sperare:** sc. *se* (Sabinus) as subject. **ab eo:** from Ambiorix. **de sua ac militum salute:** 'regarding their own safety and that of the soldiers'; *157d.* **se . . . iturum negat:** = *se . . . non iturum esse dicere.* **in eo:** 'in this (refusal).'

Sabinus is betrayed by Ambiorix, Cotta dies heroically fighting; those spared by the day's slaughter end their own lives that night.

37. 1 Sabinus, quos in praesentia tribunos militum circum se habebat, et primorum ordinum centuriones, se sequi iubet et, cum propius Ambiorigem accessisset, iussus arma abicere, imperatum facit suisque, ut idem faciant, imperat. 2 Interim, dum de condicionibus inter se agunt longiorque consulto ab Ambiorige instituitur sermo, paulatim circumventus interficitur. 3 Tum vero suo more 'Victoriam' conclamant atque ululatum tollunt impetuque in nostros facto ordines perturbant. 4 Ibi L. Cotta pugnans interficitur cum maxima parte militum. Reliqui se in castra recipiunt, unde erant egressi. 5 Ex quibus L. Petrosidius aquilifer, cum magna multitudine hostium premeretur, aquilam intra vallum proiecit; ipse pro castris fortissime pugnans occiditur. 6 Illi aegre ad noctem oppugnationem sustinent; noctu ad unum omnes, desperata salute, se ipsi interficiunt. 7 Pauci, ex proelio elapsi, incertis itineribus per silvas ad T. Labienum legatum in hiberna perveniunt atque eum de rebus gestis certiorem faciunt.

1 **quos tribunos militum:** = *eos tribunos militum, quos;* both *tribunos* and *centuriones* are objects of *iubet.* **in praesentia:** 'at the time,' lit. 'in the present time.' **Ambiorigem:** *123b.* **imperatum facit:** 'obeys the command,' lit. 'does the thing having been commanded.' **ut idem faciant:** *199a1.*
2 **dum:** *190a.* **consulto:** adv., 'by design.' **circumventus:** *228a.* **interficitur:** the singular applies to Sabinus in particular, but presumably all the men with him were treated in the same way.
3 **suo more:** *136c.* **ululatum:** 'yell,' a kind of war whoop, likely an onomatopoeic word. **impetuque:** the *–que* links *tollunt* and *perturbant; impetu* should be taken with *facto* in an ablative absolute.
4 **pugnans:** *227b.*
5 **aquilifer:** 'eagle-bearer'; *284b1.* **cum:** *185c.*
6 **ad unum:** 'to a man.' **se ipsi:** i.e., they killed one another; *162c.* The number of Roman soldiers who died in this battle was probably above 5000.
7 **incertis itineribus:** *134a.*

V.38-45: Attack of the Nervii and Atuatuci on the camp of Quintus Cicero

A fierce attack, inspired by Ambiorix, is made on Cicero's camp.
38. 1 Hac victoria sublatus, Ambiorix statim cum equitatu in Atuatucos, qui erant eius regno finitimi, proficiscitur; neque noctem neque diem iter intermittit peditatumque sese subsequi iubet. 2 Re demonstrata Atuatucisque concitatis, postero die in Nervios pervenit hortaturque ne sui in perpetuum liberandi atque ulciscendi Romanos pro eis, quas acceperint, iniuriis occasionem dimittant; 3 *interfectos esse legatos duos magnamque partem exercitus interisse* demonstrat; 4 *nihil esse negotii, subito*

oppressam legionem, quae cum Cicerone hiemet, interfici; se ad eam rem profitetur adiutorem. Facile hac oratione Nerviis persuadet.

1 **neque noctem neque diem:** *118a.*
2 **Re:** i.e., the destruction of the forces under Sabinus and Cotta. **ne sui in perpetuum liberandi atque ulciscendi Romanos pro eis, quas acceperint, iniuriis occasionem dimittant:** in English word order: *ne dimittant occasionem liberandi sui in perpetuum atque (occasionem) ulciscendi Romanos pro eis iniuriis quas acceperint; 199a2.* **sui:** *154b.*
3 **legatos duos:** Sabinus and Cotta. **magnam partem:** in reality about one-fifth of Caesar's legionaries.
4 **nihil esse negotii, subito oppressam legionem . . . interfici:** the accusative and infinitive *legionem . . . interfici* functions as the subject of *esse,* itself an infinitive in indirect discourse after *demonstrat;* lit. 'that it was no trouble that the legion . . . , suddenly overwhelmed, be destroyed.' **nihil negotii:** *97a.* **oppressam:** *228a.* **hiemet:** *214a.* **adiutorem:** *115a.*

39. 1 Itaque confestim dimissis nuntiis ad Ceutrones, Grudios, Levacos, Pleumoxios, Geidumnos, qui omnes sub eorum imperio sunt, quam maximas possunt manus cogunt, et de improviso ad Ciceronis hiberna advolant, nondum ad eum fama de Titurii morte perlata. 2 Hic quoque accidit, quod fuit necesse, ut non nulli milites, qui lignationis munitionisque causa in silvas discessissent, repentino equitum adventu interciperentur. 3 His circumventis, magna manu Eburones, Nervii, Atuatuci atque horum omnium socii et clientes legionem oppugnare incipiunt. Nostri celeriter ad arma concurrunt, vallum conscendunt. 4 Aegre is dies sustentatur, quod omnem spem hostes in celeritate ponebant atque, hanc adepti victoriam, in perpetuum se fore victores confidebant.

1 **Ceutrones,** etc.: lesser Belgic peoples, clients of the Nervii. **eorum:** *Nerviorum.* **quam maximas possunt:** *153c.* **de improviso:** 'suddenly' or 'unexpectedly.'
2 **Hic:** 'Here,' i.e., the camp of Cicero, the probable location of which is indicated on Map 11. **quod fuit necesse:** lit. '(a circumstance) which was inevitable.' **ut . . . interciperentur:** *203.1.* **lignationis munitionisque causa:** 'to get timber for the fortification' of the camp, lit. 'for the sake of the wood-gathering and the fortification-building'; *238d.* **discessissent:** *220.*
3 **vallum conscendunt:** they stood on the rampart, behind the palisades (*valli*); *293.*
4 **is dies sustentatur:** '(the attack that filled out) this day was endured,' i.e., without yielding; *dies* is the subject, although it was the events of the day that had to be endured. **quod:** causal. **hanc adepti victoriam:** = *si hanc victoriam adepti essent; 227a2.* As written, *adepti* modifies *se,* the subject of *fore* in indirect statement after *confidebant.*

40. 1 Mittuntur ad Caesarem confestim a Cicerone litterae, magnis propositis praemiis, si pertulissent; obsessis omnibus viis, missi intercipiuntur. 2 Noctu ex ea materia, quam munitionis causa comportaverant, turres admodum CXX excitantur; incredibili celeritate, quae deesse operi videbantur, perficiuntur. 3 Hostes postero die, multo maioribus coactis copiis, castra oppugnant, fossam complent. 4 Eadem ratione, qua pridie, a nostris resistitur. Hoc idem reliquis deinceps fit diebus. 5 Nulla pars nocturni temporis ad laborem intermittitur; non aegris, non vulneratis facultas quietis datur. 6 Quaecumque ad proximi diei oppugnationem opus sunt, noctu comparantur; multae praeustae sudes, magnus muralium pilorum numerus instituitur; turres contabulantur, pinnae loricaeque ex cratibus attexuntur. 7 Ipse Cicero, cum tenuissima valetudine esset, ne nocturnum quidem sibi tempus ad quietem relinquebat, ut ultro militum concursu ac vocibus sibi parcere cogeretur.

1 **Mittuntur:** emphatic position; *245a.* **ad Caesarem:** at Samarobriva. **litterae:** in the plural when describing a letter or a dispatch. **si pertulissent:** *si nuntii eas litteras pertulissent;* implied indirect statement, i.e., when Cicero sent the messengers he told them that they would receive great rewards *if they had brought the letters through* to Caesar (in direct speech, a future perfect indicative); *218b.* **obsessis omnibus viis:** *144b3.* **missi:** 'those who had been sent'; *227a4.*
2 **admodum:** 'fully.' **CXX:** *centum viginti.* Unless the camp were larger than would seem to have been required for a single legion, the 120 towers must have been about 40 feet apart; if so, men on the towers could defend the short spaces between with any kind of missile. Ordinarily such towers were about 80 feet apart. **excitantur:** 'were erected.' **quae deesse operi videbantur, perficiuntur:** '(those things) are completed which seemed to

be lacking to the work (of fortification).' **quae:** sc. *ea* as antecedent, the subject of *perficiuntur*. **operi:** here the 'work' represents 'the line of works,' i.e., the fortifications being constructed.

3 **fossam:** *293*.

4 **qua pridie:** sc. *resistebatur*, impersonal passive. **hoc idem:** 'this same thing.' **reliquis . . . diebus:** 'on the rest of the days,' i.e., the days after the first two already described; *147a*.

5 **ad laborem:** 'with regard to the work.' **quietis:** *10e; 102*.

6 **Quaecumque . . . opus sunt:** 'whatever things are necessary'; *50a; 132b*. **praeustae sudes:** 'stakes hardened at the ends by burning'; the stock of ordinary weapons had given out. **muralium pilorum:** 'of wall-pikes'; heavy pikes, to be hurled from the towers. **contabulantur:** 'were provided with floors,' i.e., they had multiple levels or stories. **pinnae:** 'battlements.' **loricae ex cratibus:** 'breastworks of wickerwork,' made by interweaving branches, and put up as screens to protect the soldiers in the towers; *98b; 150d*. **attexuntur:** 'were attached (lit. 'woven') to the towers.'

7 **cum:** *187*. **tenuissima valetudine:** 'in very delicate health'; *143a*. **ne . . . quidem:** *237c*. **ut . . . cogeretur:** *197a*. **ultro:** 'on their own accord.' **militum concursu et vocibus:** 'by the crowding around and the protests of the soldiers,' i.e., by their repeated physical and vocal instruction. **sibi:** *105*.

Ambiorix's attempt at persuasion has no effect on Cicero.

41. 1 Tum duces principesque Nerviorum, qui aliquem sermonis aditum causamque amicitiae cum Cicerone habebant, colloqui sese velle dicunt. 2 Facta potestate, eadem, quae Ambiorix cum Titurio egerat, commemorant: 3 *omnem Galliam esse in armis; Germanos Rhenum transisse; Caesaris reliquorumque hiberna oppugnari.* 4 Addunt etiam de Sabini morte; Ambiorigem ostentant fidei faciundae causa. 5 *Errare eos* dicunt, *si quicquam ab his praesidii sperent, qui suis rebus diffidant; sese tamen hoc esse in Ciceronem populumque Romanum animo, ut nihil nisi hiberna recusent, atque hanc inveterascere consuetudinem nolint;* 6 *licere illis per se incolumibus ex hibernis discedere et, quascumque in partes velint, sine metu proficisci.* 7 Cicero ad haec unum modo respondit: *non esse consuetudinem populi Romani accipere ab hoste armato condicionem;* 8 *si ab armis discedere velint, se adiutore utantur legatosque ad Caesarem mittant; sperare, pro eius iustitia, quae petierint, impetraturos.*

1 **sermonis aditum:** 'pretext for an interview,' lit. '(means of) approach for a conversation.' **causamque amicitiae:** 'and (some) basis for friendship.'

2 **Facta potestate:** 'after permission was granted'; *144b2*.

3 **reliquorumque:** i.e., the rest of the forces that Caesar had stationed in the various winter camps.

4 **Addunt:** 'they make additional claims.' **Ambiorigem ostentant fidei faciundae causa:** 'they point to Ambiorix in order to inspire credence.' **faciundae:** *64b*.

5 **Errare eos:** 'that they (Cicero and his men) are deluding themselves.' **quicquam praesidii:** 'any help at all'; *49a; 97b*. **ab his:** the Romans in the other camps. **suis rebus:** *105*. **hoc esse in Ciceronem . . . animo:** 'had this feeling toward Cicero,' lit. 'were with this mind'; *143b*. **ut . . . recusent:** substantive clause explaining *hoc animo*; *203.4*. **consuetudinem:** 'custom' of imposing winter camps upon them; the subject of *inveterascere*.

6 **per se:** 'so far as they (the Nervii) were concerned,' to be understood with *incolumibus*. **quascumque in partes velint:** *204.3*.

7 **unum modo respondit:** 'made only one remark in response.' **armato:** 'in arms.'

8 **ab armis discedere:** in English idiom, 'to lay down their arms.' **se adiutore utantur:** 'let them utilize him as mediator'; *131f; 216*. **sperare:** sc. *se*, i.e., Cicero. **eius:** *Caesaris*. **impetraturos:** sc. *esse*; the Nervians are the subject, (*ea*) *quae petierunt* the object.

The Nervians besiege the camp of Cicero.

42. 1 Ab hac spe repulsi, Nervii vallo pedum X et fossa pedum XV hiberna cingunt. 2 Haec et superiorum annorum consuetudine a nobis cognoverant et, quosdam de exercitu nacti captivos, ab his docebantur; 3 sed nulla ferramentorum copia, quae sunt ad hunc usum idonea, gladiis caespites circumcidere, manibus sagulisque terram exhaurire cogebantur. 4 Qua quidem ex re hominum multitudo cognosci potuit; nam minus horis tribus milium passuum III in circuitu munitionem perfecerunt. 5 Reliquis diebus turres ad altitudinem valli, falces testudinesque, quas idem captivi docuerant, parare ac facere coeperunt.

1 **spe:** 'hope' of deceitfully coaxing Cicero. **pedem X:** in height. **pedum XV:** in width, at the top; *100a.*

2 **superiorum annorum consuetudine:** 'in the practice of earlier years.' **quosdam de exercitu nacti captivos:** 'having taken some men from our army as prisoners.' **ab his:** the prisoners.

3 **nulla ferramentorum copia:** *144b3.* **quae:** *ferramentorum* is the antecedent. **caespites:** 'chunks of sod.' **circumcidere:** 'cut'; lit. 'cut around.' **sagulis:** 'in their cloaks'; *131a; 308.* **exhaurire:** 'to take out.'

4 **Qua quidem ex re:** 'from which action, in fact.' **hominum multitudo:** i.e., their aggregate number; Caesar does not report a number, but he wishes to emphasize that a task of this magnitude could only be completed as quickly as it was with very large forces.

5 **Reliquis diebus:** 'in the remaining days,' i.e., in the days after the first one, in which they constructed the *vallum* and *fossa.* **turres:** movable 'towers.' **ad altitudinem valli:** 'in proportion to the height of the (Roman) rampart'; the towers would need to be higher than the rampart in order to be effective. **falces:** large 'hooks' for pulling down the palisade atop the rampart. **testudines:** 'turtle-shell sheds'; *302a.* **idem:** modifies *captivi.*

43. 1 Septimo oppugnationis die, maximo coorto vento, ferventes fusili ex argilla glandes fundis et fervefacta iacula in casas, quae more Gallico stramentis erant tectae, iacere coeperunt. 2 Hae celeriter ignem comprehenderunt et venti magnitudine in omnem locum castrorum distulerunt. 3 Hostes maximo clamore, sicuti parta iam atque explorata victoria, turres testudinesque agere et scalis vallum ascendere coeperunt. 4 At tanta militum virtus atque ea praesentia animi fuit ut, cum undique flamma torrerentur maximaque telorum multitudine premerentur, suaque omnia impedimenta atque omnes fortunas conflagrare intellegerent, non modo demigrandi causa de vallo decederet nemo, sed paene ne respiceret quidem quisquam, ac tum omnes acerrime fortissimeque pugnarent. 5 Hic dies nostris longe gravissimus fuit; sed tamen hunc habuit eventum, ut eo die maximus numerus hostium vulneraretur atque interficeretur, ut se sub ipso vallo constipaverant recessumque primis ultimi non dabant. 6 Paulum quidem intermissa flamma, et quodam loco turri adacta et contingente vallum, tertiae cohortis centuriones ex eo, quo stabant, loco recesserunt suosque omnes removerunt; nutu vocibusque hostes, si introire vellent, vocare coeperunt; quorum progredi ausus est nemo. 7 Tum ex omni parte lapidibus coniectis deturbati, turrisque succensa est.

1 **ferventes fusili ex argilla glandes:** 'red-hot balls of kneaded clay,' which would not crack to pieces when heated; red-hot balls of clay the size of one's fist when thrown will retain their heat long enough to ignite straw; *98b.* **fundis:** abl. of means after *iacere.* **fervefacta iacula:** 'burning javelins.' **casas:** 'huts'; *295b.* **stramentis:** 'with thatch.'

2 **ignem comprehenderunt:** 'caught fire.' **venti magnitudine:** 'because of the force of the wind.' **distulerunt:** *hae casae ignem distulerunt,* the huts being looked upon as agents, though it was really the wind that carried bits of burning thatch all over the camp.

3 **sicuti:** 'just as if.' **parta iam atque explorata victoria:** *144b4.* **explorata:** 'secured.' **agere:** 'to move up.' The Gauls were using Roman methods of attack; *302a, b.* **scalis:** 'with scaling-ladders'; *302d.*

4 **At:** *236a.* **ea praesentia animi fuit:** 'such was their presence of mind.' **ut ... decederet, respiceret, pugnarent:** *197.* **cum:** *187.* **flamma torrerentur:** 'they were being scorched by the flames'; *92b.* **fortunas:** 'their (personal) possessions.' **conflagrare:** 'were on fire.' **demigrandi causa:** 'in order to withdraw' temporarily to rescue his valuables or get a brief respite. **paene ne respiceret quidem quisquam:** 'but hardly anyone even looked behind (him).' **tum:** emphatic, 'then,' above all other times.

5 **ut ... constipaverant:** 'since they had crowded together.' **recessum primis ultimi non dabant:** 'those furthest back would not give those in front a chance to draw back.'

6 **Paulum quidem:** 'a little, at any rate.' **intermissa flamma:** the Gauls dared not risk moving forward the wooden towers while the flames were at their height. **quodam loco:** *145c.* **turri adacta et contingente:** note how this ablative absolute contains both a perfect and a present participle, emphasizing the temporal development. **recesserunt:** 'drew back.' **suos omnes:** i.e., all the soldiers of the third cohort serving under them. **si:** *204.4.*

7 **lapidibus:** the supply of ordinary weapons had given out; practice in hurling the pike enabled Roman soldiers to throw stones effectively. **deturbati:** sc. *sunt;* 'they (the enemy) were forced back in disorder.'

The deeds of two rival centurions, Pullo and Vorenus.

44. 1 Erant in ea legione fortissimi viri, centuriones, qui primis ordinibus appropinquarent, T. Pullo et L. Vorenus. 2 Hi perpetuas inter se controversias habebant, uter alteri anteferretur, omnibusque annis de loco summis simultatibus contendebant. 3 Ex his Pullo, cum acerrime ad munitiones pugnaretur, 'Quid dubitas,' inquit, 'Vorene? aut quem locum tuae probandae virtutis exspectas? hic dies de nostris controversiis iudicabit.' 4 Haec cum dixisset, procedit extra munitiones, quaeque pars hostium confertissima est visa, in eam irrumpit. 5 Ne Vorenus quidem sese tum vallo continet, sed, omnium veritus existimationem, subsequitur. 6 Mediocri spatio relicto, Pullo pilum in hostes immittit atque unum ex multitudine procurrentem traicit; quo percusso et exanimato, hunc scutis protegunt hostes, in illum universi tela coniciunt neque dant regrediendi facultatem. 7 Transfigitur scutum Pulloni et verutum in balteo defigitur. 8 Avertit hic casus vaginam et gladium educere conanti dextram moratur manum, impeditumque hostes circumsistunt. 9 Succurrit inimicus illi Vorenus et laboranti subvenit. 10 Ad hunc se confestim a Pullone omnis multitudo convertit; illum veruto transfixum arbitrantur. 11 Vorenus gladio rem comminus gerit atque, uno interfecto, reliquos paulum propellit; 12 dum cupidius instat, in locum deiectus inferiorem concidit. 13 Huic rursus circumvento subsidium fert Pullo, atque ambo incolumes, compluribus interfectis, summa cum laude sese intra munitiones recipiunt. 14 Sic fortuna in contentione et certamine utrumque versavit, ut alter alteri inimicus auxilio salutique esset, neque diiudicari posset, uter utri virtute anteferendus videretur.

1 **Erant:** *90a.* **qui primis ordinibus appropinquarent:** 'who were nearing the first rank,' i.e., the position of centurion of first rank; *194a; 275a.*

2 **uter alteri anteferretur:** *204.3.* **omnibus annis:** 'year in, year out.' **de loco:** i.e., regarding their status and their positioning for promotion to centurion of the first rank. **summis simultatibus:** *136b.*

3 **Quid:** 'Why'; *118e.* **quem:** interrogative adjective. **locum:** 'opportunity.'

4 **quaeque pars hostium confertissima est visa, in eam irrumpit:** *pars hostium* has been attracted into the relative clause, for the sense is *irrumpit in eam partem hostium quae confertissima visa est; 165c.* **quaeque:** the *–que* connects *procedit* and *irrumpit.*

5 **Ne Vorenus quidem:** 'Vorenus for sure was not'; *ne . . . quidem* as 'not even' does not fit here. **veritus:** *226c.*

6 **Mediocri spatio relicto:** i.e., when he was a moderate distance from the enemy. **quo:** connecting relative, = *et hoc,* referring to the wounded Gaul, who, as *protegunt* implies, was not killed; *167.* **hunc:** also referring to the Gaul, the *quo* of the ablative absolute. **illum:** Pullo.

7 **Pulloni:** *109a.* **verutum:** the same 'javelin' that pierced Pullo's shield. **balteo:** 'sword-belt'; *282e.*

8 **Avertit:** 'turned aside,' perhaps flipped over, or moved into an inconvenient position behind his back. **vaginam:** 'scabbard.' **et:** connects *avertit* and *moratur.* **conanti dextram manum:** 'his right hand as he was attempting,' lit. 'the right hand to him attempting'; *109a.* **impeditum:** sc. *eum.*

9 **inimicus:** marks a personal adversary, while *hostis* marks a public one.

10 **illum veruto transfixum arbitrantur:** i.e., they judge him to be dying or at least too weakened to be a threat.

11 **rem comminus gerit:** 'he fought at close quarters,' i.e., with the *gladius,* not with the *pilum;* a regular idiom.

12 **instat:** 'pressed forward.' **in locum deiectus inferiorem:** 'stumbling (lit. 'thrown down') into a dip in the ground.'

13 **rursus:** 'in turn.' **ambo:** 'both'; *37c.*

14 **in contentione et certamine:** 'in contest and combat.' **utrumque versavit:** 'shifted (the positions of) both.' **ut . . . esset, posset:** *197b.* **alter alteri:** *171b.* **alteri, auxilio:** *112b.* **posset:** the subject is the indirect question that follows. **uter utri virtute anteferendus videretur:** 'which seemed worthy of being preferred to the other in terms of valor'; cf. *uter alteri anteferretur* above in V.44.2. **utri:** *23a; 107a.* **virtute:** *142a.*

Word of Cicero's desperate plight finally reaches Caesar.

45. 1 Quanto erat in dies gravior atque asperior oppugnatio, et maxime quod, magna parte militum confecta vulneribus, res ad paucitatem defensorum pervenerat, tanto crebriores litterae nuntiique ad Caesarem mittebantur; quorum pars, deprehensa, in conspectu nostrorum militum cum cruciatu necabatur. 2 Erat unus intus Nervius, nomine Vertico, loco natus honesto, qui a prima obsidione ad Ciceronem perfugerat suamque ei fidem praestiterat. 3 Hic servo spe libertatis magnisque persuadet praemiis, ut litteras ad Caesarem deferat. 4 Has ille in iaculo illigatas effert et, Gallus inter Gallos sine ulla suspicione versatus, ad Caesarem pervenit. 5 Ab eo de periculis Ciceronis legionisque cognoscitur.

1 **Quanto erat . . . gravior atque asperior oppugnatio, . . . tanto crebriores litterae:** 'The heavier and rougher the assault . . . , the more frequently dispatches . . . ,' lit. 'by how much heavier was the assault . . . , by so much were the dispatches more frequent,' *tanto* and *quanto* are correlative ablatives of degree of difference; *140.* **in**

dies: 'day by day.' **et maxime quod:** 'and in particular (the assault was heavier and rougher) because.' **res ad paucitatem defensorum pervenerat:** 'the job had fallen to a small number of defenders.'

2 **unus:** 'one,' the only Nervian. **intus:** in the camp. **loco natus honesto:** 'of good family'; *128a*. **a prima obsidione:** 'soon after the beginning of the siege'; lit. 'at the first part of the siege'; *152a*. **praestiterat:** 'had displayed.'

3 **servo:** after *persuadet*; *105*. **spe, magnis praemiis:** *131a*.

4 **ille:** the slave of Vertico. **in iaculo illigatas:** 'tied in a javelin.' The javelin may have been split, the dispatch, written on papyrus, put between the parts and the javelin then tied with cords as if accidentally split and repaired. **Gallus inter Gallos . . . versatus:** 'moving about (as) a Gaul among Gauls'; *226c*.

5 **Ab eo . . . cognoscitur:** i.e., *Caesar ab eo cognoscit.*

V.46-52: Caesar relieves Cicero

Caesar makes hurried preparations, and proceeds by forced marches to relieve Cicero.

46. 1 Caesar, acceptis litteris hora circiter undecima diei, statim nuntium in Bellovacos ad M. Crassum quaestorem mittit, cuius hiberna aberant ab eo milia passuum XXV; 2 iubet media nocte legionem proficisci celeriterque ad se venire. 3 Exit cum nuntio Crassus. Alterum ad C. Fabium legatum mittit, ut in Atrebatium fines legionem adducat, qua sibi iter faciendum sciebat. 4 Scribit Labieno, si rei publicae commodo facere possit, cum legione ad fines Nerviorum veniat. Reliquam partem exercitus, quod paulo aberat longius, non putat exspectandam; equites circiter CCCC ex proximis hibernis cogit.

1 **Caesar:** at Samarobriva. **hora undecima:** about 5 p.m.; it was now early autumn; *242a, b.*

2 **media nocte:** *152a.*

3 **Exit cum nuntio Crassus:** i.e., he sets out as soon as the messenger himself set out after delivering the message. **Alterum:** sc. *nuntium.* **C. Fabium:** see V.24.2. **ut:** '(directing him) to'; *199a.* **qua sibi iter faciendum sciebat:** i.e., Caesar knew that he would have to march through the country of the Atrebatians in order to reach Cicero's camp in the country of the Nervians (see Map 11); *110.*

4 **rei publicae commodo:** 'with advantage to (lit. 'of') the state'; the same phrase is also used at I.35.4; *138; 102.* Caesar's condition acknowledges the danger of further local uprising if Labienus should leave the region around his winter camp unguarded. **veniat:** *216.* **Reliquam partem exercitus:** for its disposition, see V.24.

47. 1 Hora circiter tertia ab antecursoribus de Crassi adventu certior factus, eo die milia passuum XX procedit. 2 Crassum Samarobrivae praeficit legionemque ei attribuit, quod ibi impedimenta exercitus, obsides civitatum, litteras publicas frumentumque omne, quod eo tolerandae hiemis causa devexerat, relinquebat. 3 Fabius, ut imperatum erat, non ita multum moratus, in itinere cum legione occurrit. 4 Labienus, interitu Sabini et caede cohortium cognita, cum omnes ad eum Treverorum copiae venissent, veritus ne, si ex hibernis fugae similem profectionem fecisset, hostium impetum sustinere non posset, praesertim quos recenti victoria efferri sciret, 5 litteras Caesari remittit, quanto cum periculo legionem ex hibernis educturus esset; rem gestam in Eburonibus perscribit; docet omnes equitatus peditatusque copias Treverorum III milia passuum longe ab suis castris consedisse.

1 **antecursoribus:** 'the advance guard,' lit. 'the forerunners,' of Crassus.

2 **Crassum Samarobrivae praefecit:** Caesar left Samarobriva before Crassus arrived. **impedimenta:** *271.* **litteras publicas:** 'state documents,' such as dispatches and accounts.

3 **non ita multum:** 'only a short time,' lit. 'not very much.' **occurrit:** sc. *Caesari.*

4 **cum:** causal, which explains the following fear clause; *184a.* **veritus ne . . . non posset:** *202.* **fugae similem:** *108b.* **praesertim quos . . . efferri sciret:** *hostium* is the antecedent of *quos*, 'especially since he knew that they were elated'; *184b.*

5 **remittit:** Caesar had written to him at V.46.4. **quanto cum periculo . . . educturus esset:** sc., e.g., *docens*: '(explaining) how dangerous it would be for him to withdraw,' lit. 'with how much danger he would withdraw'; *204.3.* **rem gestam:** 'what had taken place,' lit. 'the thing having taken place,' referring to the destruction of the force under Sabinus and Cotta. Labienus would have wished to provide Caesar with any additional details (note the force of *per-* in *perscribit*) he had learned. **equitatus peditatusque:** genitive after *copias.*

48. 1 Caesar, consilio eius probato, etsi opinione trium legionum deiectus ad duas redierat, tamen unum communis salutis auxilium in celeritate ponebat. 2 Venit magnis itineribus in Nerviorum fines. Ibi ex captivis cognoscit, quae apud Ciceronem gerantur quantoque in periculo res sit. 3 Tum cuidam ex equitibus Gallis magnis praemiis persuadet uti ad Ciceronem epistulam deferat. 4 Hanc Graecis conscriptam litteris mittit ne, intercepta epistula, nostra ab hostibus consilia cognoscantur. 5 Si adire non possit, monet ut tragulam cum epistula ad ammentum deligata intra munitionem castrorum abiciat. 6 In litteris scribit se cum legionibus profectum celeriter affore; hortatur ut pristinam virtutem retineat. 7 Gallus, periculum veritus, ut erat praeceptum, tragulam mittit. 8 Haec casu ad turrim adhaesit, neque a nostris biduo animadversa, tertio die a quodam milite conspicitur, dempta ad Ciceronem defertur. 9 Ille perlectam in conventu militum recitat maximaque omnes laetitia afficit. 10 Tum fumi incendiorum procul videbantur; quae res omnem dubitationem adventus legionum expulit.

1 **opinione trium legionum deiectus ad duas redierat:** 'disappointed in his expectation of (having) three legions he had been reduced to two,' the legion which he had had at Samarobriva, and the one under Fabius that had joined him.

2 **magnis itineribus:** *289.* **quae:** *204.2.* **quanto:** *204.3.*

3 **cuidam ex equitibus Gallis:** *97d; 105.*

4 **Graecis litteris:** in Greek characters; some Nervians apparently could read Latin. **intercepta epistula:** *144b4.*

5 **Si adire non possit:** the subjunctive verb reveals that this clause should be understood as part of the *ut*-clause that follows *monet*. **adire:** 'to reach' the camp. **ut . . . abiciat:** *199a3.* **ammentum:** the 'thong' attached to a javelin and used in throwing. **abiciat:** 'hurl,' lit. 'throw away.'

6 **profectum:** a participle in agreement with *se.*

7 **Gallus:** the messenger. **veritus:** *226c.* **ut erat praeceptum:** 'as it had been instructed,' i.e., he threw the javelin into the camp without making verbal contact.

8 **turrim:** *14b.* **adhaesit:** 'stuck.' **neque:** 'and not.' **animadversa:** nominative, in agreement with *Haec* (*tragula*). **dempta:** 'was taken down and'; *228a.*

9 **perlectam . . . recitat:** sc. *eam;* 'after he had read it through he read it aloud,' lit. 'he reads aloud (the letter) having been read through'; *227a4.* **afficit:** 'filled.'

10 **fumi incendiorum:** of burning villages, set on fire as Caesar's relieving force passed through; the plural implies more than one fire. **videbantur:** passive, 'were seen.' **quae res:** referring to the sighting of the smoke, thus singular.

As Caesar approaches, the Gauls turn from Cicero's camp to attack him.

49. 1 Galli, re cognita per exploratores, obsidionem relinquunt, ad Caesarem omnibus copiis contendunt. 2 Haec erant armata circiter milia LX. Cicero, data facultate, Gallum ab eodem Verticone, quem supra demonstravimus, repetit, qui litteras ad Caesarem deferat; hunc admonet, iter caute diligenterque faciat; 3 perscribit in litteris hostes ab se discessisse omnemque ad eum multitudinem convertisse. 4 Quibus litteris circiter media nocte Caesar allatis suos facit certiores eosque ad dimicandum animo confirmat. 5 Postero die, luce prima, movet castra; et circiter milia passuum IIII progressus, trans vallem magnam et rivum multitudinem hostium conspicatur. 6 Erat magni periculi res tantulis copiis iniquo loco dimicare; tum, quoniam obsidione liberatum Ciceronem sciebat, aequo animo remittendum de celeritate existimabat. 7 Consedit et, quam aequissimo potest loco, castra communit, atque haec, etsi erant exigua per se, vix hominum milium VII, praesertim nullis cum impedimentis, tamen angustiis viarum, quam maxime potest, contrahit, eo consilio, ut in summam contemptionem hostibus veniat. 8 Interim, speculatoribus in omnes partes dimissis, explorat, quo commodissime itinere vallem transire possit.

1 **re:** 'the fact' of Caesar's approach. **per:** *123a.*

2 **Haec erant armata circiter milia LX:** 'these were about 60,000 under arms'; the neuter *milia* here influences the gender of *haec* and *armata*, both of which should logically be masculine (armed men), or perhaps feminine if understood to be in agreement with *omnibus copiis.* **data facultate:** *144b2.* **Gallum ab eodem Verticone . . . repetit:** 'asked the same Vertico . . . for another Gaul,' lit. 'sought again a Gaul from the same Vertico'; *116b.* **quem supra demonstravimus:** see V.45.2-3. **qui . . . deferat:** *193a.* **hunc admonet iter caute diligenterque faciat:** '(Cicero) warned him (Caesar) to proceed cautiously and diligently'; *200a.*

3 **ab se . . . ad eum:** = *ab Cicerone ad Caesarem.*

4 **animo:** *142a.*

5 **trans vallem magnam et rivum:** 'across a wide valley and (on the other side of) a brook.'

6 **Erat magni periculi res ... dimicare:** 'it was extremely hazardous to fight,' lit. 'To fight ... was a thing of great danger'; *100b; 222a.* **tantulis copiis iniquo loco:** i.e., given the small size of Caesar's force relative to the Gallic one, he could not afford to fight from an unfavorable position. **liberatum:** sc. *esse.* **aequo animo remittendum de celeritate:** sc. *esse;* 'that without anxiety he could slacken his pace,' lit. 'that with an equal mind it was to be diminished regarding speed'; *73e; 136b.*

7 **quam aequissimo potest loco:** *153c.* **haec, etsi erant exigua per se:** sc. *castra* after *haec,* the object of *contrahit;* 'this (camp), although it was small in itself.' **vix hominum milium VII:** '(consisting of) barely 7000 men'; the two legions with Caesar averaged a little over 3500 men each; *100b; 267b.* **tamen angustiis viarum, quam maxime potest, contrahit:** 'he nevertheless contracts by making the passages as narrow as possible'; *294b.* **eo consilio:** *138.* **ut ... faciat:** explains *eo consilio; 203.4.* **hostibus:** translate as if *hostium; 109a.*

8 **quo itinere:** 'by what route'; *134a; 204.2.*

Caesar, encamped, pretends fear, lures the Gauls on, routs them.

50. 1 Eo die, parvulis equestribus proeliis ad aquam factis, utrique sese suo loco continent: 2 Galli, quod ampliores copias, quae nondum convenerant, exspectabant; 3 Caesar, si forte timoris simulatione hostes in suum locum elicere posset, ut citra vallem pro castris proelio contenderet; si id efficere non posset, ut, exploratis itineribus, minore cum periculo vallem rivumque transiret. 4 Prima luce hostium equitatus ad castra accedit proeliumque cum nostris equitibus committit. 5 Caesar consulto equites cedere seque in castra recipere iubet; simul ex omnibus partibus castra altiore vallo muniri portasque obstrui atque in his administrandis rebus quam maxime concursari et cum simulatione agi timoris iubet.

1 **ad aquam:** 'by the water,' the brook mentioned in V.49.5. **utrique:** nominative. **suo loco:** *145c.*

2 **quod:** causal. **quae:** refers to *copiae.*

3 **Caesar, si ... posset, ut ... contenderet:** = *Caesar (se continet suo loco) ut, si ... posset, ... contenderet.* **suum locum:** 'his own location,' a position favorable to himself. **elicere:** 'to entice.' **proelio:** *131a.* **si ... non posset, ut ... transiret:** Caesar's backup plan; as above, these two clauses are to be understood as (*Caesar se continet suo loco*) *ut, si ... non posset, ... transiret.*

4 **equitatus ad castra accedit:** presumably the troops for which the Gauls were waiting had arrived in the interim.

5 **consulto:** adv. **ex omnibus partibus:** *126c.* **obstrui:** 'be blocked up.' **in his administrandis rebus:** 'in the execution of these tasks'; *230.4.* **quam maxime concursari:** 'that the men rush about as much as possible,' lit. 'that there be a rushing about'; *73d.* **agi:** 'act,' lit. 'there be an acting.'

51. 1 Quibus omnibus rebus hostes invitati copias traducunt aciemque iniquo loco constituunt; 2 nostris vero etiam de vallo deductis, propius accedunt et tela intra munitionem ex omnibus partibus coniciunt 3 praeconibusque circummissis pronuntiari iubent: *seu quis Gallus seu Romanus velit ante horam tertiam ad se transire, sine periculo licere; post id tempus non fore potestatem.* 4 Ac sic nostros contempserunt, ut, obstructis in speciem portis singulis ordinibus caespitum, quod ea non posse introrumpere videbantur, alii vallum manu scindere, alii fossas complere inciperent. 5 Tum Caesar, omnibus portis eruptione facta equitatuque emisso, celeriter hostes in fugam dat, sic uti omnino pugnandi causa resisteret nemo, magnumque ex eis numerum occidit atque omnes armis exuit.

1 **copias traducunt:** = *copias vallem rivumque traducunt; 114a.*

2 **etiam de vallo deductis:** 'withdrawn even from the rampart,' thus making it seem that the Roman camp could be attacked without difficulty. **propius:** 'nearer,' i.e., to the Roman camp.

3 **pronuntiari iubent:** 'they order that it be announced,' i.e., by their heralds to the Romans inside their camp. **seu quis Gallus seu Romanus velit:** *seu,* also written *sive,* introduces a disjunctive condition, 'or if.' When paired, *seu ... seu* indicates 'whether if ... or if.' Here the pairing underscores the two ethnic adjectives: 'whether if any Gaul or if any Roman should wish,' but it is smoother in English to separate out the conditional and translate 'if anyone, whether Gaul or Roman, should wish.' **velit:** *218.2.*

4 **ut ... alii ... alii ... inciperent:** *197b; 171b.* **in speciem:** 'for show.' The barriers in the gates, of turf and only the breadth of a sod in thickness, seemed solid but were easily pushed over from the inside. **singulis ordinibus:** ablative of means to be taken with the ablative absolute *obstructis portis.* **quod:** causal. **ea non posse introrumpere videbantur:** sc. *via* with *ea,* 'they seemed not to be able to break into (camp) in that way,' i.e., through the gates; *134a.*

5 **omnibus portis:** *134a.* **omnino ... nemo:** 'no one at all.' **armis:** *127a.*

Caesar, joining Cicero, praises him and his men.

52. 1 Longius prosequi veritus, quod silvae paludesque intercedebant – neque enim parvulo detrimento illorum locum relinqui videbat – omnibus suis incolumibus eodem die ad Ciceronem pervenit. 2 Institutas turres, testudines munitionesque hostium admiratur; producta legione, cognoscit non decimum quemque esse reliquum militem sine vulnere; 3 ex his omnibus iudicat rebus, quanto cum periculo et quanta cum virtute res sint administratae. Ciceronem pro eius merito legionemque collaudat; 4 centuriones singillatim tribunosque militum appellat, quorum egregiam fuisse virtutem testimonio Ciceronis cognoverat. De casu Sabini et Cottae certius ex captivis cognoscit. 5 Postero die, contione habita, rem gestam proponit, milites consolatur et confirmat; 6 quod detrimentum culpa et temeritate legati sit acceptum, hoc aequiore animo ferundum docet, quod, beneficio deorum immortalium et virtute eorum expiato incommodo, neque hostibus diutina laetitia neque ipsis longior dolor relinquatur.

1 **neque enim parvulo detrimento illorum locum relinqui videbat:** 'for he saw that no opportunity (lit. 'place') was left for (for the purpose of causing) even a slight loss upon (lit. 'for') them.' **parvulo:** *parvulus* is the diminutive of *parvus*, used to qualify the potential damage as smaller even than small. **detrimento:** *112a.* **illorum:** *102.*

2 **turres, testudines munitionesque:** see V.42.4-5. **producta:** 'drawn up' for review. **non decimum quemque esse reliquum militem sine vulnere:** 'that not one soldier in ten had escaped unwounded,' lit. 'that not each tenth soldier was left without a wound,' i.e., more than 90% of the men were wounded; *170a.*

3 **res:** the operations during the siege in defense of the camp.

4 **appellat:** 'he addressed and called by name' in complimentary terms. **quorum egregiam fuisse virtutem . . . cognoverat:** 'whose valor he knew had been outstanding.' **certius:** an earlier report had come from Labienus (see V.37.7 and V.47.4-5).

5 **contione:** 'an assembly.' **rem gestam proponit:** 'set forth what had happened,' lit. 'the thing accomplished.'

6 **quod detrimentum:** i.e., *id detrimentum, quod . . .* , with *detrimentum* being the subject of *ferundum (esse)* in indirect discourse after *docet.* **culpa et temeritate:** 'through the culpable rashness'; *238d.* **hoc . . . quod:** 'on this account, namely that.' **aequiore animo:** 'with greater tranquility.' **beneficio, virtute:** ablatives of means to be taken with the ablative absolute *expiato incommodo.* **expiato:** 'atoned for.' **neque . . . diutina laetitia neque . . . longior dolor:** 'neither a more lasting happiness . . . nor a longer grief . . . ' **relinquatur:** *183a.*

V.53-58: Attack of the Treveri on the camp of Labienus

A proposed attack on Labienus is abandoned, but almost all Gaul is stirred up.

53. 1 Interim ad Labienum per Remos incredibili celeritate de victoria Caesaris fama perfertur, ut, cum ab hibernis Ciceronis milia passuum abesset circiter LX eoque post horam nonam diei Caesar pervenisset, ante mediam noctem ad portas castrorum clamor oriretur, quo clamore significatio victoriae gratulatioque ab Remis Labieno fieret. 2 Hac fama ad Treveros perlata, Indutiomarus, qui postero die castra Labieni oppugnare decreverat, noctu profugit copiasque omnes in Treveros reducit. 3 Caesar Fabium cum sua legione remittit in hiberna, ipse cum tribus legionibus circum Samarobrivam trinis hibernis hiemare constituit et, quod tanti motus Galliae exstiterant, totam hiemem ipse ad exercitum manere decrevit. 4 Nam, illo incommodo de Sabini morte perlato, omnes fere Galliae civitates de bello consultabant, nuntios legationesque in omnes partes dimittebant et, quid reliqui consilii caperent atque unde initium belli fieret, explorabant nocturnaque in locis desertis concilia habebant. 5 Neque ullum fere totius hiemis tempus sine sollicitudine Caesaris intercessit, quin aliquem de consiliis ac motu Gallorum nuntium acciperet. 6 In his ab L. Roscio, quem legioni tertiae decimae praefecerat, certior factus est *magnas Gallorum copias earum civitatum, quae Aremoricae appellantur, oppugnandi sui causa convenisse* 7 *neque longius milia passuum VIII ab hibernis suis afuisse, sed nuntio allato de victoria Caesaris discessisse, adeo ut fugae similis discessus videretur.*

1 **per Remos:** 'through the (country of the) Remi,' on the border of which the camp of Labienus was situated. **fama:** nominative. **ut . . . oriretur:** *197a.* **cum . . . abesset, pervenisset:** *187.* **abesset:** sc. *Labienus; 187.* **eo:** to Cicero's camp. **ante mediam noctem:** from the ninth hour (about 2:00 p.m., for it was now autumn) to midnight would be about ten hours. **quo clamore significatio victoriae gratulatioque ab Remis Labieno fieret:**

'by which clamor the indication of the victory, and congratulations (for it), were made by the Remi to Labienus'; *193a*. **clamore:** *165a*.

2 **Indutiomarus:** he had prompted the attack on Titurius Sabinus and Cotta; see V.26.2. **reducit:** force of *re-*?

3 **Fabium:** he had left his winter-quarters among the Morini (V.24.2) to go with Caesar to the relief of Cicero (V.47.3). **tribus legionibus:** Caesar now had the legion of Cicero with him, in addition to the two legions mentioned in V.48.1. **trinis:** why is the distributive numeral used instead of the cardinal? *37e*.

4 **quid reliqui consilii caperent:** *204.2*. **reliqui:** sc. *Galli*; nominative. **consilii:** *97b*. **explorabant:** 'were trying to find out.'

5 **sine sollicitudine Caesaris:** 'without anxiety (on the part) of Caesar.' **intercessit:** 'passed.' **quin ... acciperet:** 'without his receiving'; the *quin* clause, which explains the reason for Caesar's *sollicitudo*, is employed because the main sentence describes a general expression of negation ('not any moment of that whole winter'); *201b*.

6 **In his:** sc. *nuntiis*, English idiom would say 'among others.' **L. Roscio:** see V.24.2. **copias:** the subject of *convenisse, afuisse*, and *discessisse*. **Aremoricae:** these are the states of the northwestern coast. **sui:** refers not to the subject, but to the agent, *L. Roscio*. **appellantur:** *214c*.

7 **milia:** *129b*.

54. 1 At Caesar, principibus cuiusque civitatis ad se evocatis, alias territando, cum se scire, quae fierent, denuntiaret, alias cohortando magnam partem Galliae in officio tenuit. 2 Tamen Senones, quae est civitas in primis firma et magnae inter Gallos auctoritatis, Cavarinum, quem Caesar apud eos regem constituerat, cuius frater Moritasgus adventu in Galliam Caesaris, cuiusque maiores regnum obtinuerant, interficere publico consilio conati, cum ille praesensisset ac profugisset, usque ad fines insecuti regno domoque expulerunt 3 et, missis ad Caesarem satisfaciendi causa legatis, cum is omnem ad se senatum venire iussisset, dicto audientes non fuerunt. 4 Tantum apud homines barbaros valuit, esse aliquos repertos principes belli inferendi, tantamque omnibus voluntatis commutationem attulit, ut praeter Aeduos et Remos, quos praecipuo semper honore Caesar habuit, alteros pro vetere ac perpetua erga populum Romanum fide, alteros pro recentibus Gallici belli officiis, nulla fere civitas fuerit non suspecta nobis. 5 Idque adeo haud scio mirandumne sit, cum compluribus aliis de causis, tum maxime quod ei, qui virtute belli omnibus gentibus praeferebantur, tantum se eius opinionis deperdidisse, ut a populo Romano imperia perferrent, gravissime dolebant.

1 **alias, alias:** 'sometimes ... sometimes,' lit. 'at one time, at another.' **cum ... denuntiaret:** *denuntio* is used of an important, solemn, or threatening announcement; *184a*. **quae fierent:** sc. *ea, quae fierent*, with *ea* being the object of *scire*; *194a*. **in officio:** 'in allegiance.'

2 **in primis firma:** 'especially strong.' **magnae ... auctoritatis:** *100b*. **Cavarinum:** the object of *conati*, which agrees with *Senones*. **regem:** *115a*. **frater Moritasgus:** sc. *regnum obtinuerat*. **adventu:** *147b*. **publico consilio:** through the decision of some tribunal that tried those guilty of crimes against the state. **insecuti:** sc. *eum* (*Cavarinum*). **regno domoque:** *127a*.

3 **missis ... legatis:** *144b5*. **omnem:** 'as a body.' **senatum:** a council consisting of the chief men of the state, to whom Caesar applies the name of the corresponding body at Rome. **dicto audientes:** 'obedient,' lit. 'listeners to the things said'; cf. I.39.7.

4 **Tantum ... valuit:** 'it had so much influence, (namely the fact that),' the subject of *valuit* is the following accusative and infinitive clause. **esse aliquos repertos principes belli inferendi:** '(the fact that) some leaders in (lit. 'for') making war had been found'; *222; 102*. **voluntatis:** 'loyalty.' **attulit:** has the same subject as *valuit*. **ut:** *197b*. **alteros, alteros:** in apposition to *quos*; 'the one people (i.e., the Aedui), the other (i.e., the Remi)'; *171b*. **Gallici belli:** 'in the Gallic war.' **non suspecta nobis:** 'beyond suspicion in our view,' lit. 'not suspected (with respect) to us'; *109a*.

5 **Idque adeo haud scio mirandumne sit:** lit. 'and I do not at all know whether this thing ought to be wondered at to such a degree,' i.e., I doubt whether this situation is all that surprising; *id ... mirandumne sit* is an indirect question (note the *-ne* of *mirandumne*) that forms the object of *scio*. The phrase *haud scio ... -ne* is idiomatic and, in practice, suggests affirmation rather than doubt, thus an effective translation into English would be 'I do not think it surprising,' or even an impersonal rendering: 'This is perhaps not all that remarkable.' **cum compluribus aliis de causis, tum maxime quod:** 'not only with regard to many other causes, but also especially because'; i.e., *cum* and *tum* are conjunctions. **qui ... omnibus gentibus praeferebantur:** 'who used to be ranked above all races'; *107a*. **virtute:** *142a*. **tantum se eius opinionis deperdidisse:** 'that they had lost so much of that reputation,' indirect discourse after *dolebant*.

55. 1 Treveri vero atque Indutiomarus totius hiemis nullum tempus intermiserunt, quin trans Rhenum legatos mitterent, civitates sollicitarent, pecunias pollicerentur, magna parte exercitus nostri interfecta multo minorem superesse dicerent partem. 2 Neque tamen ulli civitati Germanorum persuaderi potuit, ut Rhenum transiret, cum se bis expertos dicerent, Ariovisti bello et Tencterorum transitu; non esse amplius fortunam temptaturos. 3 Hac spe lapsus Indutiomarus nihilo minus copias cogere, exercere, a finitimis equos parare, exsules damnatosque tota Gallia magnis praemiis ad se allicere coepit. 4 Ac tantam sibi iam his rebus in Gallia auctoritatem comparaverat, ut undique ad eum legationes concurrerent, gratiam atque amicitiam publice privatimque peterent.

1 **nullum tempus intermiserunt, quin . . . mitterent:** 'they let pass no time without sending'; cf. V.53.5; *201b.* **mitterent, sollicitarent, pollicerentur, dicerent:** all with *quin.* **magna parte exercitus nostri interfecta:** causal ablative absolute to be understood in indirect discourse after *dicerent,* i.e., the reason why *multo minorem superesse partem; 144b3.*
2 **Neque tamen ulli civitati Germanorum persuaderi potuit:** 'but no German state could be persuaded'; *106b.* **ut Rhenum transiret:** *199a5.* **cum se bis expertos dicerent:** 'since, as they (the Germans) said, they had tried it twice'; *184a.* **Ariovisti bello:** see I.30-54. **Tencterorum transitu:** see IV.1-15.
3 **Hac spe lapsus:** 'disappointed in this hope,' lit. 'having slipped from this hope.' **tota Gallia:** 'throughout Gaul'; *145c.*
4 **publice, privatim:** i.e., for their states and for themselves as individuals.

Indutiomarus attacks the camp of Labienus and is killed; Gallic forces disperse.
56. 1 Ubi intellexit ultro ad se veniri, altera ex parte Senones Carnutesque conscientia facinoris instigari, altera Nervios Atuatucosque bellum Romanis parare, neque sibi voluntariorum copias defore, si ex finibus suis progredi coepisset, armatum concilium indicit. 2 Hoc more Gallorum est initium belli; quo lege communi omnes puberes armati convenire coguntur; qui ex eis novissimus venit, in conspectu multitudinis omnibus cruciatibus affectus necatur. 3 In eo concilio Cingetorigem, alterius principem factionis, generum suum, quem supra demonstravimus Caesaris secutum fidem ab eo non discessisse, hostem iudicat bonaque eius publicat. 4 His rebus confectis in concilio pronuntiat arcessitum se a Senonibus et Carnutibus aliisque compluribus Galliae civitatibus; 5 huc iturum per fines Remorum eorumque agros populaturum ac, prius quam id faciat, castra Labieni oppugnaturum. Quae fieri velit, praecipit.

1 **intellexit:** sc. *Indutiomarus.* **ultro:** 'of their own accord.' **veniri:** 'that (delegations) were coming,' lit. 'that there was a coming,' impersonal passive. **altera ex parte, altera:** 'on the one hand (lit. 'side'), on the other.' **conscientia facinoris:** 'by the knowledge of their deed,' suggestive of a guilty conscience (from Caesar's perspective, at least). For the deeds in question, see V.54.2-3 regarding the Senones and V.25.1-4 regarding the Carnutes. **sibi:** *109b.* **si . . . coepisset:** *218.1b.*
2 **Hoc:** nominative, i.e., *armatum concilium indicere.* **more Gallorum:** *136c.* **quo:** 'to which,' i.e., *ad quod (concilium),* 'to which (council).' **lege communi:** 'by a common law,' i.e., a law shared in common among all the peoples involved. **ex eis novissimus:** 'last of these,' i.e., last of all; *97d.* **omnibus cruciatibus:** 'all forms of torture.'
3 **Cingetorigem . . . hostem iudicat:** Indutiomarus is the subject, *Cingetorigem,* and the phrases that follow in apposition, is a predicate accusative; *115a.* **generum suum:** i.e., Indutiomarus' son-in-law. **quem supra demonstravimus Caesaris secutum fidem ab eo non discessisse:** *quem . . . discessisse* is in indirect statement after *demonstravimus,* while *Caesaris secutum fidem* is a participial phrase in agreement with *quem,* 'whom, as we showed above, having pursued the *fides* of Caesar, had not departed from him.' **supra:** see V.3-4 for the earlier events in the rivalry between Cingetorix and Indutiomarus. **ab eo non discessisse:** = *in eius fide mansisse.*
4 **arcessitum se:** sc. *esse* (after *pronuntiat*), 'that he had been summoned,' i.e., to come to their defense.
5 **huc:** = *ad eas civitates.* On the way to the Senones he would need to pass through the territory of the Remi. **iturum, populaturum, oppugnaturum:** sc. *esse.* **prius quam id faciat:** *189a; 214a.* **Quae fieri velit:** *204.2.*

57. 1 Labienus, cum et loci natura et manu munitissimis castris sese teneret, de suo ac legionis periculo nihil timebat, ne quam occasionem rei bene gerendae dimitteret cogitabat. 2 Itaque a Cingetorige atque eius propinquis oratione Indutiomari cognita, quam in concilio habuerat, nuntios mittit ad finitimas civitates equitesque undique evocat; his certam diem conveniendi dicit. 3 Interim prope cotidie cum omni equitatu Indutiomarus sub castris eius vagabatur, alias ut situm castrorum cognosceret, alias colloquendi aut territandi causa; equites plerumque omnes tela intra vallum coniciebant. 4 Labienus suos intra munitionem continebat timorisque opinionem, quibuscumque poterat rebus, augebat.

1 **cum:** *187.* **et loci natura et manu:** to be understood with *munitissimis*. **suo et legionis:** *157d.* **ne . . . dimitteret:** 'that he should not let slip'; *199a7.* **quam occasionem rei bene gerendae:** 'any opportunity for fighting a successful battle,' lit. 'for conducting the thing well'; *102; 230.1.* **quam:** after *ne = aliquam.*
2 **a Cingetorige:** 'from Cingetorix.' **Indutiomari:** *95.* **his:** *109a.* **dicit:** 'he sets.'
3 **prope cotidie:** 'nearly daily,' i.e., almost every day. **alias ut . . . , alias . . . causa:** 'sometimes so that . . . , sometimes for the sake of . . .'; varied expressions of purpose after correlative *alias; 247.*
4 **timoris opinionem:** 'the impression of fear.' Labienus was trying the same tactic that Caesar had recently employed to great success (see V.50), and Sabinus two years before (see III.17). **quibuscumque poterat rebus:** 'by whatever means he was able.'

58. 1 Cum maiore in dies contemptione Indutiomarus ad castra accederet, nocte una intromissis equitibus omnium finitimarum civitatum, quos arcessendos curaverat, tanta diligentia omnes suos custodiis intra castra continuit, ut nulla ratione ea res enuntiari aut ad Treveros perferri posset. 2 Interim ex consuetudine cotidiana Indutiomarus ad castra accedit atque ibi magnam partem diei consumit; equites tela coniciunt et magna cum contumelia verborum nostros ad pugnam evocant. 3 Nullo ab nostris dato responso, ubi visum est, sub vesperum dispersi ac dissipati discedunt. 4 Subito Labienus duabus portis omnem equitatum emittit; praecipit atque interdicit, perterritis hostibus atque in fugam coniectis (quod fore, sicut accidit, videbat), unum omnes petant Indutiomarum, neu quis quem prius vulneret quam illum interfectum viderit, quod mora reliquorum spatium nactum illum effugere nolebat; 5 magna proponit eis, qui occiderint, praemia; summittit cohortes equitibus subsidio. 6 Comprobat hominis consilium fortuna, et cum unum omnes peterent, in ipso fluminis vado deprehensus Indutiomarus interficitur caputque eius refertur in castra; redeuntes equites, quos possunt, consectantur atque occidunt. 7 Hac re cognita, omnes Eburonum et Nerviorum, quae convenerant, copiae discedunt, pauloque habuit post id factum Caesar quietiorem Galliam.

1 **in dies:** 'day by day,' or 'every day.' **nocte una:** *147a.* **intromissis:** 'introduced' into the camp. Labienus had no cavalry of his own with which to carry out his design against the Treveri. **quos . . . curaverat:** 'that he had caused to be collected' (see V.57.2); *229b.* **tanta diligentia:** *136b.* **custodiis:** 'by keeping guard,' lit. 'by means of guards.' Once he had conveyed into his camp the cavalry that he had recruited, Labienus took care that the fact should not become known to the enemy.
2 **magna cum contumelia verborum:** = *cum verbis magnae contumeliae; 137c.*
3 **ubi visum est:** 'when it seemed (good to them),' sc. *discedere,* 'to depart.' **dispersi ac dissipati discedunt:** alliterative synonyms.
4 **praecipit:** applies to *unum omnes petant Indutiomarum.* **interdicit:** applies to *neu quis quem prius vulneret quam illum interfectum viderit.* **perterritis hostibus:** *144b2.* **quod fore, sicut accidit, videbat:** 'which he saw would happen, just as it did.' **neu:** *199d.* **neu quis quem prius vulneret quam:** 'and that not anyone wound anyone before'; *quis* and *quem,* after *neu,* = *aliquis* and *aliquem; 49b.* **prius . . . quam . . . viderit:** *189b.* **illum interfectum:** sc. *esse,* after *viderit;* *illum = Indutiomarum.* **quod . . . nolebat:** the subject is Labienus; *183a.* **mora reliquorum spatium nactum:** 'having obtained a space (of time) because of the delay (caused by the pursuit) of the rest'; *nactum* agrees with *illum.*
5 **occiderint:** sc. *eum; 194a.* **equitibus subsidio:** *112b.*
6 **Comprobat hominis consilium fortuna:** 'fortune fully approves the plan of this man,' i.e., Labienus. **unum:** sc. *illum,* 'him alone.' **quos:** = *eos, quos;* the object of *consectantur atque occidunt.* **possunt:** sc. *consectari et occidere.* **consectantur:** from *consectari,* the frequentative of *consequi.*
7 **pauloque . . . quietorem:** a modest ending to the events of a dramatic year, suggesting Caesar's recognition that his conquest of Gaul was far from complete.

BOOK VI

VI.11-24: The Customs of the Gauls and Germans

Political conditions in Gaul, factions, motives for leadership.

11. 1 Quoniam ad hunc locum perventum est, non alienum esse videtur, de Galliae Germaniaeque moribus et, quo differant hae nationes inter sese, proponere. 2 In Gallia non solum in omnibus civitatibus atque in omnibus pagis partibusque, sed paene etiam in singulis domibus factiones sunt, 3 earumque factionum principes sunt, qui summam auctoritatem eorum iudicio habere existimantur, quorum ad arbitrium iudiciumque summa omnium rerum consiliorumque redeat. 4 Idque eius rei causa antiquitus institutum videtur, ne quis ex plebe contra potentiorem auxilii egeret; suos enim quisque opprimi et circumveniri non patitur, neque, aliter si faciat, ullam inter suos habet auctoritatem. 5 Haec eadem ratio est in summa totius Galliae; namque omnes civitates divisae sunt in duas partes.

1 **Quoniam ad hunc locum perventum est:** 'since we have reached this point' in the narrative, lit. 'since it has been come through to this point,' impersonal passive; *73d.* **non alienum:** 'not out of place,' lit. 'not belonging to another'; *239g.* **de . . . proponere:** 'to give an account of,' lit. 'to set forth (information) about.' **quo:** 'in what respect,' introducing an indirect question; *204.2; 142a.*
2 **pagis:** 'clans' and thus also 'villages.' **partibus:** 'districts.' **domibus:** *20.* **factiones:** *258c.*
3 **sunt, qui:** 'are (those) who.' **eorum:** *Gallorum.* **iudicio:** *138.* **quorum ad arbitrium iudiciumque:** '(and) to whose authority and judgment'; the *quorum* refers back to *qui . . . existimantur* and introduces a relative clause of characteristic; *194a.* **summa:** lit. 'the highest thing,' i.e., 'control.' **redeat:** lit. 'comes back,' i.e., 'is referred.'
4 **Id . . . institutum** (esse) **videtur:** *institutum* (*esse*) is perfect passive infinitive; 'this (practice) seems to have become established.' **eius rei causa:** lit. 'for the sake of this thing,' i.e., 'for the following reason,' which is then explained by the substantive clause *ne . . . egeret; 161a; 203.4.* **antiquitus:** adverb. **quis:** = *aliquis.* **potentiorem:** note the comparative form. **auxilii:** *127d.* **egeret:** 'lack.' **quisque:** 'each (leader).' **neque, aliter si faciat, . . . habet:** potential condition with an emphatic indicative in the apodosis; *207.*
5 **Haec eadem ratio est in summa totius Galliae:** 'this same principle applies generally to the whole of Gaul,' lit. 'this same principle is, in general, of the whole of Gaul.' **in summa:** idiomatic, referring to the topic in question in overall terms (i.e., 'in sum'). **divisae:** *148c.*

12. 1 Cum Caesar in Galliam venit, alterius factionis principes erant Aedui, alterius Sequani. 2 Hi cum per se minus valerent, quod summa auctoritas antiquitus erat in Aeduis magnaeque eorum erant clientelae, Germanos atque Ariovistum sibi adiunxerant eosque ad se magnis iacturis pollicitationibusque perduxerant. 3 Proeliis vero compluribus factis secundis, atque omni nobilitate Aeduorum interfecta, tantum potentia antecesserant, 4 ut magnam partem clientium ab Aeduis ad se traducerent obsidesque ab eis principum filios acciperent, et publice iurare cogerent, nihil se contra Sequanos consilii inituros, et partem finitimi agri per vim occupatam possiderent Galliaeque totius principatum obtinerent. 5 Qua necessitate adductus, Diviciacus, auxilii petendi causa, Romam ad senatum profectus, infecta re redierat. 6 Adventu Caesaris facta commutatione rerum, obsidibus Aeduis redditis, veteribus clientelis restitutis, novis per Caesarem comparatis, quod ei, qui se ad eorum amicitiam aggregaverant, meliore condicione atque aequiore imperio se uti videbant, reliquis rebus eorum gratia dignitateque amplificata, Sequani principatum dimiserant. 7 In eorum locum Remi successerant; quos quod adaequare apud Caesarem gratia intellegebatur, ei, qui propter veteres inimicitias nullo modo cum Aeduis coniungi poterant, se Remis in clientelam dicabant. 8 Hos illi diligenter tuebantur; ita et novam et repente collectam auctoritatem tenebant. 9 Eo tum statu res erat, ut longe principes haberentur Aedui, secundum locum dignitatis Remi obtinerent.

1 **Cum:** '(at the time) when'; *185b.* **alterius, alterius:** 'of the one, of the other'; *23b; 171b.*
2 **Hi:** 'The latter'; *161b.* Previously the Arvernians had held a position of leadership; see I.31. **cum:** *185c.* **per se minus valerent:** 'were less powerful in themselves,' i.e., when regarded only by themselves, as compared to the aggregate of the Aedui and their client states. **quod:** causal, introducing the explanation for why the Sequani were less powerful. **antiquitus erat in Aeduis:** 'was of old in the Aedui,' i.e., had long been awarded to them. **magnaeque eorum erant clientelae:** 'and their client states were large,' i.e., extensive. **eorum:** *Aeduorum.*

clientelae: 'client states' or 'dependent states,' i.e., states acknowledging the sovereignty of the Aeduans and thereby subordinating and allying themselves to the stronger power. **sibi:** *107a.* **eos ad se ... perduxerant:** 'had won them over (to themselves).' **iacturis:** 'sacrifices' of their financial reserves or their territory; *131a.*

3 **secundis:** 'favorable,' i.e., to the Sequani, the subject of *antecesserant*. **omni nobilitate:** see I.31.6-7. **tantum .. . ut:** 'to so great an extent that'; *118b; 197b.*

4 **obsides:** 'as hostages,' predicate accusative after the direct object *filios; 115a.* **iurare:** as subject sc. *eos*, i.e., *Aeduorum principes*. **cogerent:** 'compelled,' followed by accusative and infinitive. **nihil se contra Sequanos consilii inituros:** indirect statement after *iurare*; in English word order: *se inituros esse nihil consilii contra Sequanos*. **nihil ... consilii:** *97a.* **per vim occupatam possiderent:** 'forcefully seized ... and retained in their possession,' lit. 'they possessed (that land which had been) seized through force'; *228a.* **possiderent:** resuming the series of result clauses after *tantum* (i.e., *traducerent, acciperent, cogerent*). **obtinerent:** 'obtained.'

5 **Diviciacus:** Caesar summarizes the statement of Diviciacus at I.31. **auxilii petendi causa:** *230.1.* **infecta re:** 'without accomplishing his purpose'; how lit.? *144b2.*

6 **Adventu:** ablative of time and cause; *147b; 135a.* **facta, redditis, restitutis, comparatis:** the ablatives absolute are best translated into English as independent clauses; *144b2, 3.* **Aeduis:** dative. **novis:** sc. *clientelis.* **comparatis:** for the Aeduans. **quod:** causal, explaining why new client states attached themselves to the Aeduans. **ad eorum amicitiam:** 'to the friendship of them,' i.e., of the Aeduans. **condicione:** 'terms'; *131c.* **se uti:** 'that they enjoyed,' indirect statement after *videbant.* **reliquis rebus:** 'in other respects' also; *142a.* **gratia ... amplificata:** *144b3.* **Sequani:** not nominative.

7 **quos quod adaequare apud Caesarem gratia intellegebatur:** in English word order, *quod intellegebatur quos* (= *Remos; 167*) *adaequare gratia apud Caesarem.* **quod:** causal. **quos ... adaequare:** indirect statement after the impersonal *intellegebatur.* **adaequare:** 'equal,' i.e., with the Aedui. **gratia:** 'in influence'; *142a.* **nullo modo:** *136b.* **coniungi:** *174.* **dicabant:** from *dicare*, not *dicere.*

8 **illi:** *Remi.* **repente collectam:** 'suddenly acquired,' in the period since the defeat of Ariovistus five years before.

9 **Eo tum statu res erat:** 'In this arrangement, then, was the state (of Gaul),' a summary sentence to this chapter, with a bipartite substantive clause explaining *eo statu; 203.4.* **secundum:** 'the second.'

The two ruling classes and the common people in Gaul; the Druids: their power as priests and judges, their organization, their teachings about the soul.

13. 1 In omni Gallia eorum hominum, qui aliquo sunt numero atque honore, genera sunt duo; nam plebes paene servorum habetur loco, quae nihil audet per se, nulli adhibetur consilio. 2 Plerique, cum aut aere alieno aut magnitudine tributorum aut iniuria potentiorum premuntur, sese in servitutem dicant; nobilibus in hos eadem omnia sunt iura, quae dominis in servos. 3 Sed de his duobus generibus alterum est druidum, alterum equitum. 4 Illi rebus divinis intersunt, sacrificia publica ac privata procurant, religiones interpretantur; ad hos magnus adulescentium numerus disciplinae causa concurrit, magnoque hi sunt apud eos honore. 5 Nam fere de omnibus controversiis publicis privatisque constituunt et, si quod est facinus admissum, si caedes facta, si de hereditate, de finibus controversia est, idem decernunt, praemia poenasque constituunt; 6 si qui, aut privatus aut populus, eorum decreto non stetit, sacrificiis interdicunt. Haec poena apud eos est gravissima. 7 Quibus ita est interdictum, hi numero impiorum ac sceleratorum habentur, his omnes decedunt, aditum eorum sermonemque defugiunt, ne quid ex contagione incommodi accipiant, neque his petentibus ius redditur neque honos ullus communicatur. 8 His autem omnibus druidibus praeest unus, qui summam inter eos habet auctoritatem. 9 Hoc mortuo aut, si qui ex reliquis excellit dignitate, succedit, aut, si sunt plures pares, suffragio druidum, non numquam etiam armis, de principatu contendunt. 10 Hi certo anni tempore in finibus Carnutum, quae regio totius Galliae media habetur, considunt in loco consecrato. Huc omnes undique, qui controversias habent, conveniunt eorumque decretis iudiciisque parent. 11 Disciplina in Britannia reperta atque inde in Galliam translata esse existimatur, et nunc, qui diligentius eam rem cognoscere volunt, plerumque illo discendi causa proficiscuntur.

1 **hominum:** after *genera.* **aliquo sunt numero atque honore:** 'hold some status and honor,' lit. 'are with some account and honor,' ablative of description; *143b.* **genera sunt duo:** 'there are two classes.' **plebes:** = *plebs*, nominative singular. **paene servorum loco:** 'almost as (lit. 'in the place of') slaves.' **quae:** *plebes* is the antecedent. **adhibetur:** 'are brought in to,' i.e., 'included in.' **nulli consilio:** *23a; 107a.*

2 **Plerique:** 'the majority.' **cum:** *185a.* **aere alieno:** 'by debt,' lit. 'by the bronze of another,' i.e., bronze that they have borrowed from another. **tributorum:** 'of the taxes.' **iniuria potentiorum:** 'by unjust treatment (at the

hands) of the more powerful'; note that *potentiorum* is comparative and subjective genitive; *95.* **dicant:** from *dicare*, not *dicere*; cf. VI.12.7. **nobilibus in hos eadem omnia sunt iura:** 'and the nobles have all the same rights over (lit. 'onto') those men,' lit. 'and there are to the nobles,' dative of possession; *111.* **quae dominis in servos:** i.e., *quae* (*iura sunt*) *dominis in servos, dominis* also being dative of possession; 'as masters (have) over slaves.'

3 **de:** 'of.' **alterum est druidum, alterum equitum:** sc. *genus*, 'the one (class) is (that) of the Druids, the other (class is that) of the knights,' *171b.* Very little is known of the Druids in Caesar's time beyond what he tells us here.

4 **Illi:** 'the former,' i.e., the Druids. **intersunt:** 'take part in'; *107a.* **sacrificia ... procurant:** 'regulate the sacrifices.' **religiones interpretantur:** 'settle religious questions'; *238a.* **disciplinae causa:** 'for the sake of instruction.' **hi:** the Druids. **apud eos:** the young men. **honore:** *143b.*

5 **quod:** = the adjective *aliquod*; *49a; 168.* **admissum:** 'committed.' **facta:** sc. *est.* **hereditate:** 'an inheritance.' **finibus:** here 'boundaries' (of property). **idem decernunt:** 'these same men render judgment,' *idem* is masculine nominative plural; *45.*

6 **qui:** substantive form (= *aliqui*); 'any (party)' to a controversy; *49a.* **aut privatus aut populus:** 'whether an individual citizen or a people.' **eorum decreto non stetit:** 'has not stood by their decision,' i.e., obeyed it; *138.* **sacrificiis interdicunt:** 'they exclude (the offender) from the sacrifices'; *127a.*

7 **Quibus ita est interdictum:** 'who have been thus excluded,' lit. 'for whom there has been an exclusion'; *quibus* is dative after the impersonal passive *interdictum est; 109c; 73d.* **hi:** the antecedent of the *quibus* at the beginning of the sentence. **numero:** 'in the number of,' i.e., 'among.' **his:** 'from these (excluded men)'; dative after *decedunt; 109b.* **defugiunt:** 'shun.' **ne ... accipiant:** *196a.* **quid ... incommodi:** 'any harm,' lit. 'some(thing of) disadvantage'; *97b.* **ex contagione:** 'from contact' with the excommunicated. **his petentibus:** 'though they may seek (it, i.e., *ius*),' lit. 'to those seeking'; *227b.* **honos:** *13a, b.* **communicatur:** 'imparted.'

8 **druidibus:** *107a.* **unus:** i.e., an arch-Druid.

9 **Hoc:** *160b.* **Hoc mortuo:** 'when he (the arch-Druid) dies,' lit. 'with him having died'; *144b2.* **ex reliquis:** *97d.* **excellit:** 'is preeminent'; *205.1.* **dignitate:** 'in standing'; *142a.* **succedit:** the subject is the (*ali*)*qui* of the protasis. **pares:** i.e., *pares dignitate.* **suffragio, armis:** *131a.*

10 **tempore:** *147a.* **quae regio:** 'a region which'; *165b.* **totius Galliae media:** *media* is predicative nominative, 'the middle (part) of the whole of Gaul'; *152a.* **habetur:** sc. *esse*, 'is considered (to be).' **considunt:** 'hold a meeting,' lit. 'sit down.' **loco consecrato:** the 'hallowed spot' was probably a sacred grove; *145a.* **decretis:** *105.*

11 **Disciplina:** 'training' in Druidic lore. **reperta ... existimatur:** sc. *esse* after *reperta*, 'is thought to have been discovered'; *221b.* **diligentius:** comparative adverb. **eam rem:** *160d.* **illo:** adv., 'to that place.' **discendi causa:** *230.1.*

---

14. 1 Druides a bello abesse consuerunt neque tributa una cum reliquis pendunt, militiae vacationem omniumque rerum habent immunitatem. 2 Tantis excitati praemiis, et sua sponte multi in disciplinam conveniunt et a parentibus propinquisque mittuntur. 3 Magnum ibi numerum versuum ediscere dicuntur. Itaque annos non nulli vicenos in disciplina permanent. Neque fas esse existimant ea litteris mandare, cum in reliquis fere rebus, publicis privatisque rationibus, Graecis litteris utantur. 4 Id mihi duabus de causis instituisse videntur, quod neque in vulgus disciplinam efferri velint, neque eos, qui discunt, litteris confisos, minus memoriae studere; quod fere plerisque accidit, ut praesidio litterarum diligentiam in perdiscendo ac memoriam remittant. 5 In primis hoc volunt persuadere, non interire animas, sed ab aliis post mortem transire ad alios; atque hoc maxime ad virtutem excitari putant, metu mortis neglecto. 6 Multa praeterea de sideribus atque eorum motu, de mundi ac terrarum magnitudine, de rerum natura, de deorum immortalium vi ac potestate disputant et iuventuti tradunt.

1 **consuerunt:** *176b.* **una cum reliquis:** 'together with the rest'; i.e., the Druids paid taxes at a lower rate than others, or were not legally bound to pay taxes at all. **pendunt:** see note on I.36.5. **militiae vacationem:** 'exemption from (lit. 'of') military service'; *102.* **omnium:** 'all' taxes, presumably, and any other public responsibilities.

2 **et ... et:** joins *sua sponte ... conveniunt* and *a parentibus ... mittuntur.* **in disciplinam:** 'to receive instruction,' from the Druids, lit. 'into training.' **mittuntur:** sc. *multi.*

3 **versuum:** 'of verses,' i.e., lines of writing; a metrical form was probably adopted to facilitate memorizing. **annos:** *118a.* **non nulli:** 'some,' lit. 'not none.' **vicenos:** *36.* **Neque fas esse existimant ea litteris mandare:** in English word order, *Neque existimant esse fas mandare ea litteris.* **ea:** the teachings set forth in verse. **litteris:** 'to writing,' lit. 'to letters.' **cum:** 'although'; *187.* **rationibus:** 'accounts,' included within *rebus* but added as a concrete example. **Graecis litteris:** 'Greek characters,' used in writing the Gallic languages (cf. I.29.1); *131c.*

4 **Id mihi duabus de causis instituisse videntur:** in English word order, *videntur mihi instituisse id de duabus*

causis. **mihi:** a striking use of the first person singular; Caesar more often employs first person plural when he refers to himself as author. **quod . . . velint:** 'because (as it has been suggested; *183a*) they do not wish that their instruction be spread abroad among the common people,' who would remain in subjection to the druidical priesthood only so long as they should be kept in ignorance. **vulgus:** *6b.* **discunt:** vivid use of the indicative (i.e., not attracted into the subjunctive; *220*). **confisos:** in agreement with *eos,* which is the subject of *studere; 226c.* **litteris:** *135a.* **minus . . . studere:** 'pay too little heed.' **memoriae:** *105.* **studere:** sc. *velint.* **quod:** 'a thing which.' **ut . . . remittant:** *197a.* **praesidio litterarum:** 'through reliance upon written records,' lit. 'because of the protection of (written) letters.' **in perdiscendo:** 'in learning by heart'; *230.4.* The truth of this statement is unquestioned. **remittant:** 'relax.'

5 **in primis:** 'especially.' **hoc . . . persuadere:** *hoc* is direct object; 'to convince (the larger population around them) of this (idea), namely that' which is described in the subsequent accusative and infinitive (*animas non interire*); *117a; 160c.* **animas:** 'souls'; this is the doctrine of transmigration of souls, or metempsychosis. **aliis, alios:** *171b; 154a.* **hoc:** 'by this (belief),' i.e., the transmigration of souls; *135a.* **ad virtutem excitari:** 'men are spurred to virtue,' lit. 'there is a spurring to virtue,' impersonal passive. **metu mortis neglecto:** *144b3.*

6 **Multa . . . disputant:** 'They debate many (subjects, such as).' **mundi:** 'the universe.' **terrarum:** for *orbis terrarum,* 'the earth.'

The knights and their retainers.

15. 1 Alterum genus est equitum. Hi, cum est usus atque aliquod bellum incidit (quod fere ante Caesaris adventum quotannis accidere solebat, uti aut ipsi iniurias inferrent aut illatas propulsarent), omnes in bello versantur, 2 atque eorum ut quisque est genere copiisque amplissimus, ita plurimos circum se ambactos clientesque habet. Hanc unam gratiam potentiamque noverunt.

1 **Alterum:** see VI.13.3; the class of knights is the second important class to be discussed, after the Druids. **cum est usus:** 'whenever there is need'; *186a.* **aliquod:** nominative; *49a.* **incidit:** 'breaks out.' **quod:** '(a thing) which.' **uti . . . propulsarent:** *197a.* **inferrent:** here 'inflict.' **illatas:** sc. *iniurias.* **omnes:** resumes from *Hi.*
2 **eorum ut quisque est . . . , ita . . . habet:** 'as each of them is . . . , so he has,' correlative clauses (the correlation extends to *amplissimus* and *plurimos*). **genere:** 'in birth,' i.e., the social rank and resources of one's family; *142a.* **plurimos circum se ambactos clientesque:** a notable example is Orgetorix (I.4.2). **Hanc unam gratiam potentiamque noverunt:** 'They recognize only this (i.e., size of retinue) (as a sign of) influence and power'; *176b.*

Religious beliefs of the Gauls; their human sacrifices.

16. 1 Natio est omnis Gallorum admodum dedita religionibus, 2 atque ob eam causam, qui sunt affecti gravioribus morbis quique in proeliis periculisque versantur, aut pro victimis homines immolant aut se immolaturos vovent, administrisque ad ea sacrificia druidibus utuntur, 3 quod, pro vita hominis nisi hominis vita reddatur, non posse deorum immortalium numen placari arbitrantur; publiceque eiusdem generis habent instituta sacrificia. 4 Alii immani magnitudine simulacra habent, quorum contexta viminibus membra vivis hominibus complent; quibus succensis, circumventi flamma exanimantur homines. 5 Supplicia eorum, qui in furto aut latrocinio aut aliqua noxia sint comprehensi, gratiora dis immortalibus esse arbitrantur; sed cum eius generis copia deficit, etiam ad innocentium supplicia descendunt.

1 **omnis:** 'the whole.' **admodum:** 'entirely.' **dedita:** 'devoted'; *148c.* **religionibus:** 'religious observances.'
2 **quique:** the –*que* connects *qui sunt affecti* to *qui . . . versantur,* and both relative clauses form the subjects of *immolant, vovent,* and *utuntur.* **versantur:** 'are engaged.' **pro victimis:** 'as victims.' **homines:** 'human beings' of either gender. **se immolaturos:** sc. *esse pro victimis homines.* **administris:** 'as the officiants,' a predicate complement to *druidibus.* **druidibus:** *131c.*
3 **quod:** causal. **nisi . . . reddatur, non posse . . . numen:** a condition of fact in indirect speech after *arbitrantur; 218.1a.* **reddatur:** 'is rendered.' **numen:** 'divine majesty;' lit. 'nod.' **placari:** 'be appeased.' **habent instituta sacrificia:** 'they have instituted sacrifices,' lit. 'they have sacrifices having been instituted'; *229a.* **sacrificia:** human sacrifices were offered at times in Eastern lands (cf., e.g., 2 Kings 3.27) and in ancient Mexico; at Rome human sacrifice is reported as late as 216 BC.
4 **immani magnitudine:** *143a.* **simulacra:** 'images,' perhaps something like statues of wickerwork, having some resemblance to the human form. **quorum contexta viminibus membra:** 'the limbs of which, having been woven together with pliant branches.' **vivis:** 'living.' **hominibus:** *131a.* **quibus:** *et eis* (*simulacris*); *167.* **quibus succensis:** *144b2.* **circumventi flamma:** *227a1.*

5 **Supplicia:** 'punishments,' and here = 'capital punishments.' **in furto:** 'in (an act of) theft.' **latrocinio:** 'banditry.' **noxia:** 'crime.' **sint comprehensi:** relative clause of characteristic; *194a.* **gratiora:** 'more acceptable.' **cum:** *186a.* **eius generis copia:** 'a supply of this sort (of victim).' **descendunt:** 'resort.'

The gods worshipped by the Gauls.

17. 1 Deorum maxime Mercurium colunt. Huius sunt plurima simulacra; hunc omnium inventorem artium ferunt, hunc viarum atque itinerum ducem, hunc ad quaestus pecuniae mercaturasque habere vim maximam arbitrantur; 2 post hunc, Apollinem et Martem et Iovem et Minervam. De his eandem fere, quam reliquae gentes, habent opinionem: Apollinem morbos depellere, Minervam operum atque artificiorum initia tradere, Iovem imperium caelestium tenere, Martem bella regere. 3 Huic, cum proelio dimicare constituerunt, ea, quae bello ceperint, plerumque devovent; cum superaverunt, animalia capta immolant reliquasque res in unum locum conferunt. 4 Multis in civitatibus harum rerum exstructos tumulos locis consecratis conspicari licet; 5 neque saepe accidit, ut neglecta quispiam religione aut capta apud se occultare aut posita tollere auderet, gravissimumque ei rei supplicium cum cruciatu constitutum est.

1 **Deorum:** dependent on *maxime*; *97e.* **Mercurium:** in the case of Mercury and the other gods mentioned, Caesar gives the name of the Roman divinity whose attributes and functions seemed to him to correspond most nearly with those of the Gallic divinity; the Gallic names were of course not known to Roman readers. **simulacra:** since the Gauls began making statues only after the Roman conquest, it is possible that the 'images' of Mercury referred to here were the huge upright stones (menhirs) which Caesar must have seen in Gaul; pillars of a certain type were sacred to Hermes, the Greek god corresponding with Mercury. **hunc:** sc. *esse*, accusative and infinitive after *ferunt*. **artium:** 'arts.' **ferunt:** 'they say'; *172c.* **hunc:** sc. *esse*, accusative and infinitive after *arbitrantur*. **viarum atque itinerum:** Mercury is 'guide for roads' in that he points out the road, and 'for journeys' because he accompanies the traveler on the way. **quaestus:** 'acquisition,' accusative plural after *ad*; *92a.* **mercaturas:** also after *ad*; 'commercial transactions.'

2 **Minervam:** sc. *colunt*, as at the beginning of VI.17.1. **Apollinem morbos depellere:** the infinitive clause (and the three that follow) is in apposition to *eandem opinionem*, '(namely) that Apollo wards off diseases.' **operum atque artificiorum:** 'of the trades and crafts.' **initia:** 'the first things,' i.e., the foundational skills. **caelestium:** 'over (lit. 'of') the heavenly things,' i.e., 'the gods,' dwellers in the sky (*caelum*); *102.*

3 **Huic:** *Marti.* **proelio:** *131a.* **ceperint:** relative clause of characteristic; *194a.* **cum superaverunt:** 'when they have survived' the battle, i.e., 'those who are victorious'; *186a.* **animalia:** *16b.*

4 **harum rerum exstructos tumulos:** such heaped up piles of booty would slowly rot down and be covered with vegetation, presenting the appearance of a mound. **locis consecratis:** *145c.* **conspicari licet:** 'one can observe,' lit. 'it is permitted to catch sight of'; *73.*

5 **neque saepe:** 'only rarely,' lit. 'not often'; *239g.* **ut ... auderet:** *203.1.* **neglecta ... religione:** *144b2.* **quispiam:** 'anyone'; *49a.* **capta, posita:** neuter plural accusative; *227a4.* **apud se:** 'in his house.' **posita tollere:** 'to take away what had been deposited' as an offering to the gods. **ei rei:** 'for that crime (lit. 'thing').' **cum cruciatu:** *137c.*

Other customs of the Gauls.

18. 1 Galli se omnes ab Dite patre prognatos praedicant idque ab druidibus proditum dicunt. 2 Ob eam causam spatia omnis temporis non numero dierum, sed noctium finiunt; dies natales et mensium et annorum initia sic observant, ut noctem dies subsequatur. 3 In reliquis vitae institutis hoc fere ab reliquis differunt, quod suos liberos, nisi cum adoleverunt, ut munus militiae sustinere possint, palam ad se adire non patiuntur, filiumque puerili aetate in publico in conspectu patris assistere turpe ducunt.

1 **se omnes ... prognatos:** sc. *esse*, after *praedicant.* **Dite patre:** Caesar identifies the Gallic divinity with a Roman god of the Underworld known in earlier times as 'Father Dis' (*Dis pater*), later generally called Pluto; *128b.*

2 **Ob eam causam:** because sprung from the god of the Underworld, the realm of darkness and night. **spatia omnis temporis:** lit. 'the intervals of all (their) time,' but in English we would shift the sense of the *omnis* to *spatia*, 'all their intervals of time.' **finiunt:** lit. 'limit,' here in the sense of 'measure' or 'reckon.' The ancient Germans also reckoned time by the number of nights; a trace of this reckoning remains in the English word "fortnight" (= fourteen nights). **dies natales:** 'birthdays.' **initia:** 'the beginnings.' **sic ... ut:** *197b.* **ut noctem dies subsequatur:** 'that the day follows after the night,' i.e., the day was thought to begin at sunset. Therefore,

instead of saying 'the first day of the month,' as we do, the Gauls said 'the first night of the month,' 'the first night of the year,' 'birthnight,' etc. It is more difficult to keep track of time by days than by nights because it is easier to note the changes of the moon than of the sun.

3 **institutis:** here a noun, 'customs.' **hoc ... quod:** 'in this respect, namely that'; *142a.* **ab reliquis:** 'from all other people'; *171a.* **nisi cum adoleverunt:** 'unless when they have grown up,' i.e., 'until they have grown up.' **ut ... possint:** *197a.* **munus militiae:** 'the duty of military service.' **se:** only the fathers are referred to, as shown by what follows. **filium ... assistere turpe ducunt:** 'they consider (that it is) disgraceful that a son appear.' On public occasions the Gauls would appear armed; it was thought in bad form for an armed man to have with him, in a public place, a son who was not also armed. **puerili aetate:** *143a.* **turpe:** sc. *esse,* indirect statement after *ducunt; turpe* is predicative, for the subject of the supplied *esse* is the accusative and infinitive phrase *filium ... assistere.*

19. 1 Viri, quantas pecunias ab uxoribus dotis nomine acceperunt, tantas ex suis bonis, aestimatione facta, cum dotibus communicant. 2 Huius omnis pecuniae coniunctim ratio habetur fructusque servantur; uter eorum vita superavit, ad eum pars utriusque cum fructibus superiorum temporum pervenit. 3 Viri in uxores, sicuti in liberos, vitae necisque habent potestatem; et cum pater familiae, illustriore loco natus, decessit, eius propinqui conveniunt et, de morte si res in suspicionem venit, de uxoribus in servilem modum quaestionem habent et, si compertum est, igni atque omnibus tormentis excruciatas interficiunt. 4 Funera sunt pro cultu Gallorum magnifica et sumptuosa; omniaque, quae vivis cordi fuisse arbitrantur, in ignem inferunt, etiam animalia, ac, paulo supra hanc memoriam, servi et clientes, quos ab eis dilectos esse constabat, iustis funebribus confectis, una cremabantur.

1 **Viri, quantas pecunias ab uxoribus dotis nomine acceperunt, tantas ex suis bonis, aestimatione facta, cum dotibus communicant:** in English word order, *aestimatione facta, viri communicant cum dotibus tantas pecunias ex suis bonis quantas acceperunt ab uxoribus nomine dotis.* **Viri:** here = 'husbands.' **quantas pecunias .. ., tantas:** 'as much wealth ... , as'; correlative clauses; *pecunia* is literally 'money' but here likely indicates 'net worth' in whatever form was most appropriate. **dotis nomine:** 'as dowry,' lit. 'in the name of a dowry'; *17c.* **bonis:** 'possessions,' lit. 'goods.' **aestimatione facta:** 'making an estimate (of value)'; *144b2.* **cum dotis communicant:** 'add to the dowries,' lit. 'share with the dowries.' From his own property the husband set aside an amount equal to the dowry received with the wife. The income from this common fund, or estate, was saved up and added to the principal; when the husband or wife died the whole went to the survivor.

2 **coniunctim ratio habetur:** 'an account is kept jointly.' **fructus:** 'its income,' lit. 'its gains.' **uter eorum:** 'whichever of them,' either husband or wife. **vita superavit:** 'has survived in (respect to) life'; *142a.* **ad eum pars utriusque ... pervenit:** 'to that one (who survived) the part from (lit. 'of') both went.' **utriusque:** *51.* **cum fructibus superiorum temporum:** '(together) with the income of the earlier times,' i.e., any income earned since the initial capital was set aside until the death of one spouse. The custom could have prevailed only among the higher classes, on account of the abject poverty of the common folk (VI.13.1-2).

3 **in:** 'over.' **vitae necisque habent potestatem:** among the early Romans also the father had 'the power of life and death' over his household. **cum ... decessit:** *186a.* **pater familiae:** 'the head of a family.' **illustriore loco natus:** 'of higher rank,' lit. 'born from more illustrious stock'; *128a.* **de morte si res in suspicionem venit:** 'if suspicion has arisen regarding (the cause of) death,' lit. 'if the thing has come into suspicion.' **de uxoribus:** the plural implies the existence of polygamy among the higher classes in Gaul. **in servilem modum:** lit. 'in the servile way,' i.e., in the manner of an investigation regarding slaves; Roman law and custom sanctioned the torture of slaves on the death of a master under suspicious circumstances. **compertum est:** impersonal, 'there is a discovering,' i.e., about their guilt. **igni, tormentis:** ablatives of means after *excruciatas; 131a.* **excruciatas interficiunt:** = *eas excruciant et interficiunt; 228a; 205.3.*

4 **Funera:** 'funerals'; *13e.* **pro cultu Gallorum:** 'in proportion to the civilization of the Gauls,' i.e., for their comparatively limited wealth as a people, they lavish a lot of it upon their funerals. **magnifica:** 'splendid'; *31.* **sumptuosa:** 'costly'; *75f.* **vivis cordi fuisse:** double dative; 'to have been dear (lit. 'for their heart') to (them while) living'; *10g; 112b.* **in ignem:** i.e., onto the funeral pyre. **paulo supra hanc memoriam:** 'a little before our time,' lit. 'a little beyond this memory (of ours).' **quos ab eis dilectos esse constabat:** 'whom it was clear were loved by them'; *quos ... delectos esse* is accusative and infinitive after *constabat.* **iustis funebris confectis:** 'on the completion of the regular funeral rites,' how lit.? *144b2.* **una:** 'at the same time' with the body of the master. The burning of favorite dependents on their master's funeral pyre was probably intended to continue their service for him in the other world.

Their precautions in dealing with rumors affecting public safety.

20. 1 Quae civitates commodius suam rem publicam administrare existimantur, habent legibus sanctum, si quis quid de re publica a finitimis rumore aut fama acceperit, uti ad magistratum deferat neve cum quo alio communicet, 2 quod saepe homines temerarios atque imperitos falsis rumoribus terreri et ad facinus impelli et de summis rebus consilium capere cognitum est. 3 Magistratus, quae visa sunt, occultant, quaeque esse ex usu iudicaverunt, multitudini produnt. De re publica nisi per concilium loqui non conceditur.

1 **Quae civitates:** i.e., *eae civitates, quae*; this clause forms the subject of *habent*. **rem publicam:** 'public affairs.' **habent legibus sanctum:** 'have sanctioned by law'; *92a; 229a.* **si quis quid . . . acceperit:** 'if anyone has heard anything'; *49a.* **de re publica:** 'concerning public affairs.' **uti ad magistratum deferat:** substantive clause after *habent legibus sanctum*, with the subject and object of *deferat* being the (*ali*)*quis* and (*ali*)*quid* of the preceding clause (the protasis; *219*); *199a1.* **neve:** 'and not'; *235a.* **cum quo alio:** 'with anyone else'; *49a.*
2 **quod saepe . . . cognitum est:** an impersonal causal clause, 'because it has often been recognized.' **homines:** the subject of the following three infinitives. **falsis:** 'baseless'; note Caesar's further remarks about Gallic rumors at IV.5. **facinus:** lit. 'action' or 'deed,' but often 'crime.' **de summis rebus:** e.g., matters of life and death, of liberty and revolution.
3 **quae visa sunt:** '(those things) which seemed good (to them to conceal),' a not uncommon sense of *videor*. **quaeque:** *et* (*ea*) *quae*; this clause forms the direct object of *produnt*. **esse ex usu:** 'to be useful,' i.e., 'of advantage.' **De re publica nisi per concilium loqui non conceditur:** in English word order, *loqui de re publica non conceditur nisi per concilium*. **per concilium:** 'at an assembly' duly convoked, lit. 'through (the medium of) an assembly.' **loqui:** this infinitive is the subject of *conceditur*; *199c.*

Altogether different are the beliefs and customs of the Germans.

21. 1 Germani multum ab hac consuetudine differunt. Nam neque druides habent, qui rebus divinis praesint, neque sacrificiis student. 2 Deorum numero eos solos ducunt, quos cernunt et quorum aperte opibus iuvantur, Solem et Vulcanum et Lunam; reliquos ne fama quidem acceperunt. 3 Vita omnis in venationibus atque in studiis rei militaris consistit; a parvis labori ac duritiae student. 4 Qui diutissime impuberes permanserunt, maximam inter suos ferunt laudem; hoc alii staturam, alii vires nervosque confirmari putant. 5 Intra annum vero vicesimum feminae notitiam habuisse in turpissimis habent rebus; cuius rei nulla est occultatio, quod et promiscue in fluminibus perluuntur et pellibus aut parvis renonum tegimentis utuntur, magna corporis parte nuda.

1 **multum:** *118b.* **ab hac consuetudine:** i.e., from the Gallic way of life. **druides:** there were priests among the Germans, but they did not form a dominant class, as the Druids did in Gaul (cf., e.g., VI.13.4). **qui . . . praesint:** *193a.*
2 **eos solos . . . quos:** 'only those whom.' **opibus:** *131a.* **Vulcanum:** god of fire. **Lunam:** the army of Ariovistus dared not fight before the new moon (I.50). **reliquos:** sc. *deos.* **reliquos ne fama quidem acceperunt:** 'they have heard of the rest (of the gods) not even by rumor,' i.e., they have no awareness of them at all. **ne . . . quidem:** *237c.*
3 **venationibus:** 'hunting'; *92a.* **in studiis rei militaris:** 'in warlike pursuits.' **a parvis:** 'from childhood.' **duritiae:** 'hardship'; *105.*
4 **Qui . . . permanserunt:** forms the subject of *ferunt.* **impuberes:** lit. 'prepubescent,' in the sense of being younger than puberty, but the term comes to mean 'unmarried,' in the sense of remaining sexually chaste. **ferunt:** here 'receive.' **hoc:** 'by this,' i.e., by remaining asexual; *135a.*
5 **Intra:** lit. 'within,' i.e., 'before.' **feminae notitiam habuisse in turpissimis habent rebus:** 'they hold that to have had (carnal) knowledge of a woman (is) among the most shameful things.' **feminae notitiam habuisse:** this infinitive phrase forms the subject of an indirect statement (an *esse* is to be supplied) after *habent.* **cuius rei nulla est occultatio:** 'there is no concealment of this thing (sex),' because they have very little privacy in their manner of living, given how they bathe and sleep in the presence of others. **promiscue:** 'in common,' i.e., as a group. **perluuntur:** a passive verb used reflexively, 'they wash (themselves),' i.e., 'they bathe.' **renonum:** 'of deerskins'; cf. IV.1.10.

The Germans have little interest in farming, and have no private land.

22. 1 Agri culturae non student, maiorque pars eorum victus in lacte, caseo, carne consistit. 2 Neque quisquam agri modum certum aut fines habet proprios; sed magistratus ac principes in annos singulos gentibus cognationibusque hominum, quique una coierunt, quantum et quo loco visum est agri, attribuunt, atque anno post alio transire cogunt. 3 Eius rei multas afferunt causas: ne, assidua consuetudine capti, studium belli gerendi agri cultura commutent; ne latos fines parare studeant, potentioresque humiliores possessionibus expellant; ne accuratius ad frigora atque aestus vitandos aedificent; ne qua oriatur pecuniae cupiditas, qua ex re factiones dissensionesque nascuntur; 4 ut animi aequitate plebem contineant, cum suas quisque opes cum potentissimis aequari videat.

1 **culturae:** *105.* **victus:** genitive after *pars.* **lacte:** *10g.* **caseo:** 'cheese.' **carne:** *18a.* **consistit:** 'consists.'
2 **modum:** 'measure' or 'amount.' **fines proprios:** 'lands of his own,' i.e., there was no private ownership of land (also explained at IV.1.2-7). **in annos singulos:** 'each year.' **gentibus:** 'clans,' indirect object after *attribuunt.* **cognationibus hominum:** lit. 'to blood relations of men,' i.e., groups of families connected by bloodlines. **quique una coierunt:** *quique* = *et* (*eis*) *qui,* 'and (to those) who have joined together,' i.e., in order to be assigned a plot of land; this phrase is thus the third in the series after *gentibus* and *cognationibus.* **quantum et quo loco visum est agri:** 'as much land, and in what place, as seemed good (to them),' indirect questions that function as direct objects of *attribuunt; 204.3.* **visum est:** sc. *eis* (*magistratibus ac principibus*); cf. *visa sunt* in VI.20.3. **agri:** *97b.* **anno post:** 'the next year,' lit. 'after by a year,' *anno* is ablative of degree of difference; *140.* **alio:** adverb, 'to another place.'
3 **Eius rei causas:** 'explanations of this practice,' defined by the *ne*-clauses and *ut*-clause that comprise the remainder of this chapter. **assidua consuetudine capti:** 'captivated by a constant way of life,' i.e., the regularity of the agricultural year in an established location. **belli gerendi:** *102; 230.1.* **cultura:** *139.* **commutent:** *203.4.* **latos:** 'extensive.' **parare:** 'obtain.' **potentioresque:** *potentiores* is the subject of *expellant,* while *–que* links *studeant* and *expellant.* **humiliores:** the object of *expellant.* **possessionibus:** *109b.* **accuratius:** 'rather carefully,' which would be 'too carefully' from the German point of view. **ad frigora atque aestus vitandos:** *92c; 150a.* **qua:** = *aliqua* and modifies *cupiditas.* **qua ex re:** 'from which thing,' i.e., *cupiditas.* **nascuntur:** indicative as expressing the view of the writer (contrast the subjunctive by attraction; *220*).
4 **animi aequitate:** 'in a state of contentment,' lit. 'by means of an evenness of mind,' i.e., the plebs are content enough that they do not challenge the magistrates. **cum ... quisque ... videat:** 'since each one sees'; *184a.* **cum potentissimis:** *cum opibus potentissimorum; 238b.* **aequari:** passive, 'made equal.'

Their ambitions are military; but they protect a guest.

23. 1 Civitatibus maxima laus est, quam latissime circum se, vastatis finibus, solitudines habere. 2 Hoc proprium virtutis existimant, expulsos agris finitimos cedere, neque quemquam prope audere consistere; 3 simul hoc se fore tutiores arbitrantur, repentinae incursionis timore sublato. 4 Cum bellum civitas aut illatum defendit aut infert, magistratus, qui ei bello praesint et vitae necisque habeant potestatem, deliguntur. 5 In pace nullus est communis magistratus, sed principes regionum atque pagorum inter suos ius dicunt controversiasque minuunt. 6 Latrocinia nullam habent infamiam, quae extra fines cuiusque civitatis fiunt, atque ea iuventutis exercendae ac desidiae minuendae causa fieri praedicant. 7 Atque ubi quis ex principibus in concilio dixit, *se ducem fore; qui sequi velint, profiteantur,* consurgunt ei, qui et causam et hominem probant, suumque auxilium pollicentur atque a multitudine collaudantur; 8 qui ex his secuti non sunt, in desertorum ac proditorum numero ducuntur, omniumque his rerum postea fides derogatur. 9 Hospitem violare fas non putant; qui quacumque de causa ad eos venerunt, ab iniuria prohibent sanctosque habent hisque omnium domus patent victusque communicatur.

1 **Civitatibus:** *109a.* **Civitatibus maxima laus est ... solitudines habere:** 'the highest distinction for (German) states is ... to have wastelands'; *habere* is the subject of *est.* **quam:** *153c.* **vastatis finibus:** *144b2.*
2 **Hoc proprium virtutis:** sc. *esse,* accusative and infinitive after *existimant,* 'that this (is) characteristic of valor'; *hoc* ('this') is then explained through two accusative and infinitive clauses ('namely that ... '). **expulsos agris finitimos cedere:** *finitimos,* modified by *expulsos agris,* is the subject of *cedere; 228a.* **agris:** *109b.* **cedere:** 'withdraw.' **neque quemquam:** 'and that no one'; *168; 49a.* **consistere:** 'to settle'; *221a.* Cf. IV.3.1-2.
3 **hoc:** 'because of this,' i.e., 'for the following reason,' which is then explained in the causal ablative absolute that follows ('namely because ...'). **fore:** = *futuros esse; 52.* **incursionis:** *102.* **timore sublato:** *144b3.*
4 **Cum bellum civitas aut illatum defendit aut infert:** in English word order, *cum civitas aut defendit bellum illatum aut infert* (*bellum*); *186a.* **qui ei bello praesint:** *193a; 107a.*
5 **communis:** 'common' to a whole people or tribe. **principes regionum atque pagorum:** 'the head men of

divisions and districts.' Nothing is known about the details of the German civil administration in Caesar's time; these probably varied somewhat among the different peoples. **ius dicunt:** 'administer justice,' lit. 'speak the law.' 6 **Latrocinia:** 'brigandage,' i.e., 'marauding expeditions' outside their own borders. **nullam habent infamiam:** 'involve no disgrace,' lit. 'have no infamy.' **cuiusque:** *49a.* **ea . . . fieri:** indirect statement after *praedicant.* **iuventutis:** genitive after *causa.* **praedicant:** 'they (the Germans) declare.'
7 **quis:** *49b.* **ducem:** 'leader' of an expedition or raid. **qui:** as antecedent supply *ei,* subject of *profiteantur.* **velint:** subjunctive in a subordinate clause in indirect speech, likely also a relative clause of characteristic; *214a; 194a.* **profiteantur:** 'that they . . . are to declare (their interest),' indirect command (i.e., this verb was expressed in the imperative mood in direct speech); *216.* **auxilium:** 'assistance.'
8 **qui ex his:** *ei ex his qui.* **qui ex his secuti non sunt:** '(any) of those (who volunteered) who did not follow through (on his promised support)'; *ex his* looks back to the previous sentence, while *qui non secuti sunt* forms the subject of the subsequent *ducuntur.* **non:** emphatic word order. **in desertorum ac proditorum numero:** 'as (lit. 'in the number of') deserters and traitors.' **omnium rerum fides:** 'confidence in all matters,' lit. 'good faith for all things,' not merely in respect to warlike prowess; *102.* **his:** dative; *109b.* **derogatur:** 'is withdrawn.'
9 **Hospitem violare:** 'to maltreat a guest.' **fas:** sc. *esse,* of which *hospitem violare* is the subject. **qui:** as antecedent supply *eos,* object of *prohibent,* and modified by *sanctos.* **quacumque de causa:** 'for whatever reason'; *50a.* **ab iniuria:** *127b.* **domus:** nominative plural. **victus:** nominative singular.

The Gauls, once superior to the Germans, are now inferior.

24. 1 Ac fuit antea tempus, cum Germanos Galli virtute superarent, ultro bella inferrent, propter hominum multitudinem agrique inopiam trans Rhenum colonias mitterent. 2 Itaque ea, quae fertilissima Germaniae sunt, loca circum Hercyniam silvam, quam Eratostheni et quibusdam Graecis fama notam esse video, quam illi Orcyniam appellant, Volcae Tectosages occupaverunt atque ibi consederunt; 3 quae gens ad hoc tempus his sedibus sese continet summamque habet iustitiae et bellicae laudis opinionem. 4 Nunc, quod in eadem inopia, egestate, patientia, qua Germani, permanent, eodem victu et cultu corporis utuntur. 5 Gallis autem provinciarum propinquitas et transmarinarum rerum notitia multa ad copiam atque usus largitur, 6 paulatim assuefacti superari multisque victi proeliis, ne se quidem ipsi cum illis virtute comparant.

1 **Ac fuit antea tempus:** 'and there was even a time in the past (lit. 'before').' **Ac:** *233a.* **superarent:** 'surpass.' **superarent, inferrent, mitterent:** *238a.* **agrique:** the *–que* connects *multitudinem* and *inopiam* after *propter.* **trans Rhenum:** the Gauls in earlier times had not only held extensive regions east of the Rhine, but had pressed far down into Italy, giving Cisalpine Gaul its name.
2 **ea . . . loca:** accusative, the object of *occupaverunt; 6c.* **Hercyniam silvam:** the Hercynian forest followed the Danube River through what is now southern Germany and Austria. **quam . . . fama notam esse video:** 'which (forest) I see was known by report.' **Eratostheni:** Eratosthenes was a famed Greek writer and geographer of the 3rd century BC. **quibusdam:** *168.* **video:** Caesar evidently had before him the works of the unnamed Greek writers referred to. For his use of the 1st person singular, cf. VI.14.4. **Volcae Tectosages:** a people that developed from a colony of the Volcae, who dwelled in the Roman province.
3 **quae gens:** 'and that people'; *167.* **ad hoc tempus his sedibus sese continet:** 'to this day maintains itself in these settlements'; a Gallic outpost, as it were, on German soil. **his sedibus:** *145c.* **summam:** *245d.* **summamque habet iustitiae et bellicae laudis opinionem:** 'has the greatest reputation for justice and prowess in war.' **bellicae laudis:** lit. 'for martial distinction'; *102.*
4 **quod:** causal. **in eadem inopia, egestate, patientia:** 'in the same (condition of) lack, want, (and) endurance'; *234a.* **qua Germani:** sc. *sunt,* 'in which the Germans (are).' **permanent:** the subject remains the Volcae Tectosages. **cultu corporis:** 'care for their body.'
5 **Gallis autem:** 'As for the Gauls, however,' i.e., not the Volcae Tectosages, but the rest of the Gauls in Gaul itself; *109a.* **provinciarum:** the two provinces, Cisalpine Gaul and Transalpine Gaul, the latter of which Caesar usually refers to as "the Province." **transmarinarum rerum notitia:** 'knowledge of things from across the sea,' which entered Gaul chiefly through the port of Massilia; *262a.* **multa . . . largitur:** 'supplies many things'; *172b.* **ad copiam atque usus:** 'to (the point of) abundance and (regular) use.' Compare I.1.3.
6 **paulatim assuefacti superari:** 'having gradually become accustomed to being surpassed.' **proeliis:** *145c.* **ne se quidem . . . comparant:** 'they do not even compare themselves,' lit. 'they compare not even themselves'; *237c.* **ipsi:** *Galli.* **illis:** *Germanis.* **virtute:** *142a.*

A COMPANION TO CAESAR

GRAMMAR FOR THE STUDY OF CAESAR

References to AG are to Allen and Greenough's *New Latin Grammar*.
References to B are to Bennett's *New Latin Grammar*.

LATIN MORPHOLOGY

NOUNS

1. The Latin language has no article. When translating into English, the definite article *the* or the indefinite article *a/an* should be supplied with nouns as the sense requires.

FIRST DECLENSION

2. *a.* The nominative singular of nouns of the first declension ends in -ă.

b. Nouns of the first declension are nearly all feminine in gender; a few nouns referring to males are masculine, as **nauta**, *sailor* (III.9); **Cotta**, a man's name (II.11).

3. An example of a first declension noun is: **via**, **viae**, f., *way, road* (I.9):

SINGULAR

CASE		MEANING	ENDINGS
Nom.	via	*a road*	-ă
Gen.	viae	*of a road*	-ae
Dat.	viae	*to/for a road*	-ae
Acc.	viam	*a road*	-am
Abl.	viā	*from/by/in a road*	-ā
Voc.	via	*O road!*	-ă

PLURAL

Nom.	viae	*roads*	-ae
Gen.	viārum	*of roads*	-ārum
Dat.	viīs	*to/for roads*	-īs
Acc.	viās	*roads*	-ās
Abl.	viīs	*from/by/in roads*	-īs
Voc.	viae	*O roads!*	-ae

4. Besides the six cases of the first declension there is a rare locative case, of which the singular is exactly like the genitive, as **Samarobrīvae**, *at Samarobriva* (V.24).

SECOND DECLENSION

5. *a.* The nominative singular of the second declension ends in **-um** for neuter nouns and **-us, -er, -ir** for all others.

b. Nouns of the second declension in **-us, -er,** and **-ir** are generally masculine in gender. Feminine in gender are most names of trees and plants, as **fāgus**, *beech* (V.12), and most names of countries, islands, and cities.

6. *a.* Examples of nouns of the second declension in **-us** and **-um** are **lēgātus, lēgātī**, m., *envoy, lieutenant* (I.7), and **bellum, bellī**, n., *war* (I.1):

SINGULAR

CASE		ENDINGS		ENDINGS
Nom.	lēgātus	-us	bellum	-um
Gen.	lēgātī	-ī	bellī	-ī
Dat.	lēgātō	-ō	bellō	-ō
Acc.	lēgātum	-um	bellum	-um
Abl.	lēgātō	-ō	bellō	-ō
Voc.	lēgāte	-e	bellum	-um

PLURAL

Nom.	lēgātī	-ī	bella	-a
Gen.	lēgātōrum	-ōrum	bellōrum	-ōrum
Dat.	lēgātīs	-īs	bellīs	-īs
Acc.	lēgātōs	-ōs	bella	-a
Abl.	lēgātīs	-īs	bellīs	-īs
Voc.	lēgātī	-ī	bella	-a

b. Caesar uses the neuter noun **vulgus** in the nominative (IV.5), the genitive (**vulgī**, I.20), and the accusative (**vulgus**, I.46).

c. Caesar uses **locus, -ī**, m., *place*, with a neuter plural declined thus: *Nom.* **loca**, *Gen.* **locōrum**, *Dat.* **locīs**, *Acc.* **loca**, *Abl.* **locīs**.

d. The second declension has a rare locative case, of which the singular is like the genitive.

7. *a.* Examples of nouns of the second declension in **-er** and **-ir** are **puer, puerī**, m., *boy* (I.29), **ager, agrī**, m., *field* (I.4), and **vir, virī**, m., *man* (II.25):

SINGULAR

Nom.	puer	ager	vir	
Gen.	puerī	agrī	virī	-ī
Dat.	puerō	agrō	virō	-ō
Acc.	puerum	agrum	virum	-um
Abl.	puerō	agrō	virō	-ō
Voc.	puer	ager	vir	

PLURAL

Nom.	puerī	agrī	virī	-ī
Gen.	puerōrum	agrōrum	virōrum	-ōrum
Dat.	puerīs	agrīs	virīs	-īs
Acc.	puerōs	agrōs	virōs	-ōs
Abl.	puerīs	agrīs	virīs	-īs
Voc.	puerī	agrī	virī	-ī

b. Declined like **puer** are **socer**, m., *father-in-law* (I.12), **gener**, m., *son-in-law* (V.56), **vesper**, m., *evening* (I.26), **līberī**, m., plural only, *children* (I.11), and compounds of -**fer** and -**ger**, as **signifer**, *standard-bearer* (II.25).

c. Like **ager** is **arbiter**, -**trī**, m., *referee* (V.1); also **faber**, -**brī**, m., *builder*, genitive plural generally **fabrum** (V.11), **administer**, -**trī**, m., *helper* (VI.16).

8. *a.* In Caesar's time nouns of the second declension in -**ius** and -**ium** formed the genitive singular in -**ī** (not -**iī**), retaining the accent on the penult of words of more than two syllables even when this was short; thus, **fīlī**, **Vale'rī**, **negō'tī**, **impe'rī**. Afterwards common nouns in -**ius**, and many proper names in -**ius**, were written with the genitive in -**iī**, and for the sake of consistency such genitives are frequently printed with -**iī** today, as **cōnsiliī** (I.21), **Valeriī** (I.47).

b. The genitive of **Pompeius** is written with -**ī**, **Pompe'ī**, as are also the genitives of some other proper names in -**ius**.

c. The vocative of **fīlius** and of proper names in -**ius** ends in -**ī** (not -**ie**), the accent remaining on the penult of vocatives containing more than two syllables; thus: **Pompe'ī**.

d. The declension of **deus**, m., *god* (I.12), is irregular:

	SINGULAR	PLURAL
Nom.	deus	dī, deī, diī
Gen.	deī	deōrum, deum
Dat.	deō	dīs, deīs, diīs
Acc.	deum	deōs
Abl.	deō	dīs, deīs, diīs
Voc.	deus	dī, deī, diī

THIRD DECLENSION

9. The third declension includes nouns with stems ending in a consonant (mute stems, liquid stems, nasal stems, and -**s** stems), nouns with stems ending in -**i**, nouns with mixed stems, and nouns of irregular declension. The stem occasionally appears unchanged in the nominative, but is usually recognized in the genitive.

10. *a.* Mute stems may end in a labial, **p, b**; in a guttural, **c, g**; or in a dental, **t, d**. In guttural stems the -**s** of the case ending in the Nominative unites with the **c** or **g** of the stem, producing **x**; thus **dux** for **duc-s** and **rēx** for **rēg-s**.

b. Examples of nouns with mute stems are **prīnceps, prīncipis**, m., *leader* (I.13), **rēx, rēgis**, m., *king* (I.31), and **pēs, pedis**, m., *foot* (I.8); also **mīles, mīlitis**, m., *soldier* (I.7), **virtūs, virtūtis**, f., *valor, virtue* (I.1) and **caput, capitis**, n., *head* (I.29):

SINGULAR

Nom.	prīnceps	rēx	pēs	-s
Gen.	prīncipis	rēgis	pedis	-is
Dat.	prīncipī	rēgī	pedī	-ī
Acc.	prīncipem	rēgem	pedem	-em
Abl.	prīncipe	rēge	pede	-e
Voc.	prīnceps	rēx	pēs	-s

PLURAL

Nom.	prīncipēs	rēgēs	pedēs	-ēs
Gen.	prīncipum	rēgum	pedum	-um
Dat.	prīncipibus	rēgibus	pedibus	-ibus
Acc.	prīncipēs	rēgēs	pedēs	-ēs
Abl.	prīncipibus	rēgibus	pedibus	-ibus
Voc.	prīncipēs	rēgēs	pedēs	-ēs

SINGULAR

Nom.	mīles	virtūs	caput
Gen.	mīlitis	virtūtis	capitis
Dat.	mīlitī	virtūtī	capitī
Acc.	mīlitem	virtūtem	caput
Abl.	mīlite	virtūte	capite
Voc.	mīles	virtūs	caput

PLURAL

Nom.	mīlitēs	virtūtēs	capita
Gen.	mīlitum	virtūtum	capitum
Dat.	mīlitibus	virtūtibus	capitibus
Acc.	mīlitēs	virtūtēs	capita
Abl.	mīlitibus	virtūtibus	capitibus
Voc.	mīlitēs	virtūtēs	capita

c. Like **rēx** are declined Gallic proper names in **-rīx**, as (in singular only) **Orgetorīx**, *Gen.* **Orgetorīgis** (I.2), and **Dumnorīx, -rīgis** (I.3), and (in plural only) **Biturīgēs, Biturīgum** (I.18); also **dux, ducis,** m., *leader* (I.13), **pāx, pācis,** f., *peace* (I.3), and **vōx, vōcis,** f., *voice* (I.32).

d. Like **mīles** in declension are **eques, equitis,** m., *horseman* (I.15), **pedes, peditis,** m., *foot-soldier* (I.42); and **caespes,** m., *sod* (III.25), **comes,** m., *companion* (VI.30), **hospes,** m., *guest-friend* (I.53).

e. **Quiēs,** f., *repose* (V.40) is declined **quiēs, quiētis, quiētī,** *etc.*; but **ariēs,** m., *battering-ram* (II.32), **abiēs,** f., *fir-tree* (V.12), **interpres,** m., *interpreter* (I.19), have **-ĕtis** in the genitive and are declined **ariēs, arietis, arietī,** *etc.*

f. Like **virtūs** are **salūs, salūtis,** f., in singular only, *safety* (I.27), **servitūs, servitūtis,** f., *slavery* (I.11); here also belong the feminine nouns whose nominative ends in **-tās,** as **cīvitās, cīvitātis,** *state* (I.2), **aestās, aestātis,** *summer* (I.54).

g. The neuters lack a dental in the nominative: **cor, cordis,** *heart* (VI.19), and **lac, lactis,** *milk* (IV.1).

11. *a.* Liquid stems end in **-l** or **-r**.

b. Examples of nouns with liquid stems are **cōnsul, cōnsulis** m., *consul* (I.2), **victor, victōris** m., *victor* (I.31) and **pater, patris,** m., *father* (I.3):

SINGULAR

Nom.	cōnsul	victor	pater
Gen.	cōnsulis	victōris	patris
Dat.	cōnsulī	victōrī	patrī
Acc.	cōnsulem	victōrem	patrem
Abl.	cōnsule	victōre	patre
Voc.	cōnsul	victor	pater

PLURAL

Nom.	cōnsulēs	victōrēs	patrēs
Gen.	cōnsulum	victōrum	patrum

Dat.	cōnsulibus	victōribus	patribus
Acc.	cōnsulēs	victōrēs	patrēs
Abl.	cōnsulibus	victōribus	patribus
Voc.	cōnsulēs	victōrēs	patrēs

c. Like **cōnsul** are **sōl, sōlis**, m., *sun* (I.1), **exsul, exsulis**, m., *exile* (V.55); also some **-r** stems, as **Caesar, Caesaris**, m., *Caesar* (**19c**); **agger, aggeris**, m., *mound* (II.20), **ānser, -eris**, m., *goose* (V.12), **mulier, mulieris**, f., *woman* (I.29), **arbor, arboris**, f., *tree* (II.17).

d. Like **victor** are declined masculine nouns of agency in **-tor**, as **mercātor, -ōris**, *trader* (I.1), **dēprecātor, -ōris**, *intercessor* (I.9); and abstract nouns in **-or**, as **timor, -ōris**, m., *fear* (I.22).

e. Like **pater** are declined **frāter, frātris**, m., *brother* (I.3), and **māter, mātris**, f., *mother* (I.18).

12. *a.* Nasal stems end in **-n**, except **hiems, hiemis**, f., *winter* (IV.1), which ends in **-m**.

b. Examples are **sermō, sermōnis**, m., *conversation* (V.37), **homō, hominis**, m., *man* (I.2) and **nōmen, nōminis**, n., *name* (I.13):

SINGULAR

Nom.	sermō	homō	nōmen
Gen.	sermōnis	hominis	nōminis
Dat.	sermōnī	hominī	nōminī
Acc.	sermōnem	hominem	nōmen
Abl.	sermōne	homine	nōmine
Voc.	sermō	homō	nōmen

PLURAL

Nom.	sermōnēs	hominēs	nōmina
Gen.	sermōnum	hominum	nōminum
Dat.	sermōnibus	hominibus	nōminibus
Acc.	sermōnēs	hominēs	nōmina
Abl.	sermōnibus	hominibus	nōminibus
Voc.	sermōnēs	hominēs	nōmina

c. Like **sermō** are declined **latrō, latrōnis**, m., *bandit* (III.17); **Dīvicō, Dīvicōnis**, m., (I.13; in singular only); and nouns in **-iō**, as **suspīciō, suspīciōnis**, f., *suspicion* (I.4), **coniūrātiō, -ōnis**, f., *league* (I.2).

d. Like **homō** are declined **ōrdō, ōrdinis**, m., *rank* (I.40); **necessitūdō, -inis**, f., *close relationship* (I.43); **testūdō, testūdinis**, f., *testudo* (II.6; **305**); **nēmō**, *Dat.* **nēminī**, *Acc.* **nēminem** (the place of the *Gen.* and *Abl.*, and sometimes the *Dat.*, being supplied by *Gen.* **nūllīus**, *Abl.* **nūllō**, *Dat.* **nūllī**, from **nūllus**), m., *no one*; **Apollo, Apollinis**, m., (VI.17, in singular only); **sōlitūdō, sōlitūdinis**, f., *wilderness* (IV.18); and **virgō, -inis**, f., *maiden*.

e. Like **nōmen** are declined other neuters in **-men**, as **flūmen, flūminis**, *river* (I.1), **agmen, agminis**, *column* (I.15), and **certāmen, certāminis**, *contest* (III.14).

13. *a.* The **-s-** of **-s** stems becomes **r** between vowels in the oblique cases (i.e., not in the nominative case). In **honōs, -r** generally appears also in the nominative; **-r** is always found in the nominative of **rūmor** and many other nouns of this class.

b. Examples of nouns with **-s** stems are **mōs, mōris**, m., *custom* (I.4), **honōs** or **honor, honōris**, m., *honor* (VI.13), and **genus, generis**, n., *race* (I.48):

SINGULAR

Nom.	mōs	honōs *or* honor	genus
Gen.	mōris	honōris	generis
Dat.	mōrī	honōrī	generī

Acc.	mōrem	honōrem	genus
Abl.	mōre	honōre	genere
Voc.	mōs	honor	genus

PLURAL

Nom.	mōrēs	honōrēs	genera
Gen.	mōrum	honōrum	generum
Dat.	mōribus	honōribus	generibus
Acc.	mōrēs	honōrēs	genera
Abl.	mōribus	honōribus	generibus
Voc.	mōrēs	honōrēs	genera

c. Like **mōs** is declined **flōs**, m., *flower.*

d. Like **honor** are **soror, sorōris**, f., *sister* (I.18), **uxor, uxōris**, f., *wife* (I.18).

e. Like **genus** are declined the neuters **fūnus, fūneris**, *funeral* (VI.19); **latus, lateris**, *side* (I.25); **mūnus, mūneris**, *gift* (I.43); **onus, oneris**, *burden, load* (II.30); **opus, operis**, *work* (I.8); **scelus, sceleris**, *crime* (I.14); **vulnus, vulneris**, *wound* (I.25), etc.

f. Similar in declension to **genus**, but having a different vowel before the endings of the oblique cases, are the neuters **corpus, corporis**, *body* (I.25); **dēdecus, dēdecoris**, *disgrace* (IV.25); **facinus, facinoris**, *evil deed* (I.40); **frīgus, frīgoris**, *cold* (I.10); **lītus, lītoris**, *shore* (IV.23); **pecus, pecoris**, *cattle* (III.29); **tempus, temporis**, *time* (I.16); and **rōbur, rōboris**, *oak* (III.13).

g. Among other nouns of the third declension with nominative in -s and genitive in -ris are the masculine **pulvis, pulveris**, *dust* (*Acc.* **pulverem**, IV.32), **lepus, leporis**, *hare* (*Acc.* **leporem**, V.12), **mās, maris**, *male* (*Gen.* VI.26); and the neuters **iūs, iūris**, *right, law* (I.4; *Nom.* plural **iūra**, VI.13), **aes, aeris**, *copper* (IV.31), **crūs, crūris**, *leg* (VI.27), and **ōs, ōris**, *mouth, face* (V.35; *Acc.* plural **ōra**, VI.39).

h. **Iūs iūrandum**, n., *oath* (I.3), in the singular, is declined thus: *Nom.* **iūs iūrandum**, *Gen.* **iūris iūrandī**, *Dat.* **iūrī iūrandō**, *Acc.* **iūs iūrandum**, *Abl.* **iūre iūrandō**.

14. *a.* The nominative singular of masculine and feminine nouns with -i stems ends ordinarily in -**is**, the genitive plural always in -**ium**.

b. Examples of masculine and feminine -**i** stems with nominative singular in -**is** are **turris**, f., *tower* (II.30), **īgnis**, m., *fire* (I.4) and **hostis**, m. & f., *enemy* (I.21):

SINGULAR

Nom.	turris	īgnis	hostis	-is
Gen.	turris	īgnis	hostis	-is
Dat.	turrī	īgnī	hostī	-ī
Acc.	turrim *or* -em	īgnem	hostem	-im, -em
Abl.	turrī *or* -e	īgnī *or* -e	hoste	-e, -ī
Voc.	turris	īgnis	hostis	-is

PLURAL

Nom.	turrēs	īgnēs	hostēs	-ēs
Gen.	turrium	īgnium	hostium	-ium
Dat.	turribus	īgnibus	hostibus	-ibus
Acc.	turrīs *or* -ēs	īgnīs *or* -ēs	hostīs *or* -ēs	-īs, -ēs
Abl.	turribus	īgnibus	hostibus	-ibus
Voc.	turrēs	īgnēs	hostēs	-ēs

c. Like **turris**, but in the singular only, is **Sabis, -is**, *Acc.* -**im**, m., *the Sambre* (II.16); also **Tamesis, -is**, *Acc.* -**im**, m., *the Thames* (V.11, 18).

15. a. The nominative singular of some nouns with **-i** stems ends in **-ēs**, of a few others in **-er**. Examples are **caedēs, caedis**, f., *slaughter* (V.47) and **linter, lintris**, f., *skiff* (I.12):

	SINGULAR	PLURAL	SINGULAR	PLURAL
Nom.	caedēs	caedēs	linter	lintrēs
Gen.	caedis	caedium	lintris	lintrium
Dat.	caedī	caedibus	lintrī	lintribus
Acc.	caedem	caedēs *or* -īs	lintrem	lintrēs, -īs
Abl.	caede	caedibus	lintrī *or* -e	lintribus
Voc.	caedēs	caedēs	linter	lintrēs

b. Like **caedēs** are declined the feminine nouns **cautēs, cautis**, *jagged rock* (III.13), **mōlēs, mōlis**, *dike* (III.12), **rūpēs, -is**, *cliff* (II.29), **sēdēs, -is**, *abode* (I.31), **saepēs, -is**, *hedge* (II.17), **alcēs, -is**, *moose* (VI.27); also **famēs, -is**, *hunger* (I.28), which, however, has **famē** in the ablative singular.

c. Like **linter** is **imber, imbris**, m., *rainstorm* (III.29).

16. a. The nominative singular of neuter nouns with **-i** stems ends in **-e**, **-al**, and **-ar**; the ablative singular ends in **-ī**, the genitive plural in **-ium.**

b. Examples of neuter nouns with **-i** stems are **mare, maris**, n., *sea* (III.7) and **animal, animālis**, n., *animal* (VI.17):

	SINGULAR	PLURAL	SINGULAR	PLURAL	SINGULAR (ENDINGS)	PLURAL (ENDINGS)
Nom.	mare	maria	animal	animālia	-e, -al, -ar	-ia
Gen.	maris	marium	animālis	animālium	-ī	-ium
Dat.	marī	maribus	animālī	animālibus	-ī	-ibus
Acc.	mare	maria	animal	animālia	-e, -al, -ar	-ia
Abl.	marī	maribus	animālī	animālibus	-ī	-ibus
Voc.	mare	maria	animal	animālia	-e, -al, -a	-ia

c. The capital city of the Aeduans, **Bibracte**, n., in the singular, is declined thus: *Nom.* **Bibracte**, *Gen.* **Bibractis**, *Dat.* **Bibractī**, *Acc.* **Bibracte**, *Abl.* **Bibracte**.

d. Like **animal** is **vectīgal, -ālis** (I.18).

17. a. The declension of nouns with mixed stems conforms to that of mute stems in the singular, but to that of **-i** stems in the plural.

b. Examples of nouns with mixed stems are **mōns, montis**, m., *height* (I.1), **pars, partis**, f., *part* (I.1), **nox, noctis**, f., *night* (I.26) and **urbs, urbis**, f., *city* (I.39):

SINGULAR

Nom.	mōns	pars	nox	urbs
Gen.	montis	partis	noctis	urbis
Dat.	montī	partī	noctī	urbī
Acc.	montem	partem	noctem	urbem
Abl.	monte	parte	nocte	urbe
Voc.	mōns	pars	nox	urbs

PLURAL

Nom.	montēs	partēs	noctēs	urbēs
Gen.	montium	partium	noctium	urbium
Dat.	montibus	partibus	noctibus	urbibus
Acc.	montēs, -īs	partēs, -īs	noctēs, -īs	urbēs, -īs
Abl.	montibus	partibus	noctibus	urbibus
Voc.	montēs	partēs	noctēs	urbēs

c. Among nouns with mixed stems used by Caesar are **pōns, pontis**, m., *bridge* (I.6); **cliēns, clientis**, m., *retainer* (I.4); **parēns, -entis**, m. & f., *parent* (V.14); **falx, falcis**, f., *sickle, hook* (III.14); **glāns, glandis**, f., *acorn, slingshot* (V.43); **dōs, dōtis**, f., *dowry* (VI.19); **frōns, frontis**, f., *front* (II.8); **laus, laudis**, f., *praise* (I.40); **līs, lītis**, f., *damages* (V.1); **mors, mortis**, f., *death* (I.5); **plēbs, plēbis**, f., *people* (I.3); **trabs, trabis**, f., *beam* (II.29); **sors, sortis**, f., *lot* (I.50); **stirps, stirpis**, f., *stock* (VI.34).

d. Defective is the noun with the stem **spont-**, which has only a genitive, **spontis**, and an ablative, **sponte** (I.9).

18. *a.* The declension of the nouns **vīs**, f., *force* (I.6), **bōs, bovis**, m. & f., *ox, cow* (VI.26), **carō, carnis**, f., *flesh, meat* (V.14), and **Iuppiter, Iovis**, *Jupiter* (VI.17), is exceptional, not conforming to any of the types which have been given:

SINGULAR

Nom.	vīs	bōs	carō	Iuppiter
Gen.	—	bovis	carnis	Iovis
Dat.	—	bovī	carnī	Iovī
Acc.	vim	bovem	carnem	Iovem
Abl.	vī	bove	carne	Iove
Voc.	vis	bōs	carō	Iuppiter

PLURAL

Nom.	vīrēs	bovēs	carnēs
Gen.	vīrium	boum *or* bovum	carnium
Dat.	vīribus	bōbus *or* būbus	carnibus
Acc.	vīrēs	bovēs	carnēs
Abl.	vīribus	bōbus *or* būbus	carnibus
Voc.	vīrēs	bovēs	carnēs

b. **Senex**, m., *old man* (I.29), is declined thus: **senex, senis, senī, senem, sene, senex; senēs, senum, senibus, senēs, senibus, senēs.**

c. **Iter**, n., *journey, route* (I.3), has a stem **itiner-** in the oblique cases: **iter, itineris, itinerī, iter, itinere, iter; itinera, itinerum, itineribus, itinera, itineribus, itinera.**

d. **Femur**, n., *thigh*, in the oblique cases has two stems, **femor-** and **femin-**, thus: *Nom.* **femur**, *Gen.* **femoris** or **feminis**, *etc.*

e. **Arar**, m., *the Arar River* (I.12, 13, 16), is declined thus: **Arar, Araris, Ararī, Ararim, Ararī, Arar**; similar is **Liger, Ligeris**, m., *the Liger River* (III.9).

f. **Phalanx**, f., *mass formation, mass*, is declined thus: *Nom.* **phalanx**, *Gen.* **phalangis**, *Dat.* **phalangī**, *Acc.* **phalangem** or **phalanga**, *Abl.* **phalange**.

NAMES OF THE FIRST, SECOND, AND THIRD DECLENSIONS

19. *a.* Of the second declension are all Roman first names (**praenōmina**) used by Caesar, and in reading the text the name should be supplied, in the proper case form, from the abbreviation. The First Names are **Aulus**, *Gen.* **Aulī** (abbreviation **A.**), **Appius** (**Ap.**), **Gāius** (abbreviation **C.**, an old form of **G.**), **Decimus** (**D.**), **Gnaeus** (**Cn.**), **Lūcius** (**L.**), **Mārcus** (**M.**), **Pūblius** (**P.**), **Quīntus** (**Q.**), **Servius** (**Ser.**), and **Titus** (**T.**).

b. The clan names (**nōmina**), ending in **-ius** (as **Iūlius, Tullius**), are of the second declension.

c. The family names or surnames (**cognōmina**) are partly of the first declension, as **Galba** (**Servius Sulpicius Galba**); of the Second, as **Baculus** (**Pūblius Sextius Baculus**); and of the Third, as **Caesar** (see also **11c**), the full name being declined thus: *Nom.* **Gāius Iūlius Caesar**, *Gen.* **Gāī Iūlī Caesaris** or **Gāiī Iūliī Caesaris** (see also **8a**), *Dat.* **Gāiō Iūliō Caesarī**, *Acc.* **Gāium Iūlium Caesarem**, *Abl.* **Gāiō Iūliō Caesare**.

d. The names of Gauls or Germans are generally of the second declension, as **Dīviciācus, -ī**, or of the third, as **Dumnorīx**, *Gen.* **Dumnorīgis**; of the first declension are **Galba** (II.4, 13) and **Nasua** (I.37).

e. The names of foreign peoples are ordinarily declined in the plural only. A few are of the first declension, as **Belgae, -ārum** (I.1); the rest are of the second declension, as **Helvetiī, -ōrum** (I.1), or of the third, as **Allobrogēs, -um** (I.6).

f. In the accusative plural of names of foreign peoples Caesar sometimes has the Greek ending **-as** instead of **-ēs**; as **Allobrogas** (I.14), **Crētas** (II.7), **Coriosolitas** (II.34).

FOURTH DECLENSION

20. *a.* Nouns of the fourth declension ending in **-us** are generally masculine in gender, nouns ending in **-ū** are neuter; **domus, manus**, and **Īdūs** (plural) are feminine.

b. Examples of nouns of the fourth declension are **frūctus, frūctūs**, m., *fruit* (VI.19) and **cornū, cornūs**, n., *horn* (I.52):

	SINGULAR	PLURAL	SINGULAR	PLURAL
Nom.	frūctus	frūctūs	cornū	cornua
Gen.	frūctūs	frūctuum	cornūs	cornuum
Dat.	frūctuī	frūctibus	cornū	cornibus
Acc.	frūctum	frūctūs	cornū	cornua
Abl.	frūctū	frūctibus	cornū	cornibus
Voc.	frūctus	frūctūs	cornū	cornua

c. **Domus** (stem **domu-**), f., *house*, has also a stem **domo-** of the second declension, from which are formed a locative singular, **domī**, *at home* (I.18, 20, *etc.*), an ablative singular, **domō**, *from home*, (I.5, 6, *etc.*), an accusative plural, **domōs** (I.30), and some forms not used by Caesar.

d. Many nouns of the fourth declension are defective, being used only in the ablative singular, such as **iniussū** (I.19) and **nātū** (II.13).

FIFTH DECLENSION

21. *a.* Nouns of the fifth declension end in **-ēs**, and are feminine except **diēs**, *day*, and **merīdiēs**, *midday* (I.50), which are masculine; but **diēs** is usually feminine when referring to a certain day (as I.4, 8, 30), or to time in general.

b. Examples of nouns of the fifth declension are: **diēs, diēī**, *day*, and **rēs, reī**, f., *thing*:

	SINGULAR	PLURAL	SINGULAR	PLURAL
Nom.	diēs	diēs	rēs	rēs
Gen.	diēī	diērum	reī	rērum
Dat.	diēī	diēbus	reī	rēbus
Acc.	diem	diēs	rem	rēs
Abl.	diē	diēbus	rē	rēbus
Voc.	diēs	diēs	rēs	rēs

c. In the genitive and dative singular **-ēī** becomes **-eī** when a consonant precedes, as in **reī** (I.21).

ADJECTIVES

22. *a.* In adjectives of the first and second declensions the masculine is declined like **lēgātus** (6a), **puer** (7a), or **ager** (7a), the Feminine like **via** (3), and the Neuter like **bellum** (6a).

b. Many adjectives, such as **bonus, bona, bonum**, *good*, are declined like **lēgātus, via, bellum**:

	SINGULAR			PLURAL		
	MASCULINE	FEMININE	NEUTER	MASCULINE	FEMININE	NEUTER
Nom.	bonus	bona	bonum	bonī	bonae	bona
Gen.	bonī	bonae	bonī	bonōrum	bonārum	bonōrum

Dat.	bonō	bonae	bonō	bonīs	bonīs	bonīs
Acc.	bonum	bonam	bonum	bonōs	bonās	bona
Abl.	bonō	bonā	bonō	bonīs	bonīs	bonīs
Voc.	bone	bona	bonum	bonī	bonae	bona

c. Distributive adjectives are declined like **bonus** except that in the genitive plural they have **-um** instead of **-ōrum**, as **quadrāgēnum** (IV.17).

d. A few adjectives, such as **miser, misera, miserum,** *wretched* (I.32), are declined like **puer, via, bellum:**

	SINGULAR			PLURAL		
	MASCULINE	FEMININE	NEUTER	MASCULINE	FEMININE	NEUTER
Nom.	miser	misera	miserum	miserī	miserae	misera
Gen.	miserī	miserae	miserī	miserōrum	miserārum	miserōrum
Dat.	miserō	miserae	miserō	miserīs	miserīs	miserīs
Acc.	miserum	miseram	miserum	miserōs	miserās	misera
Abl.	miserō	miserā	miserō	miserīs	miserīs	miserīs
Voc.	miser	misera	miserum	miserī	miserae	misera

e. **Asper** (V.45), **līber** (I.44), and **tener** (II.17) are declined like **miser**.

f. Most adjectives in **-er,** like **aeger, aegra, aegrum,** *sick* (V.40) and **integer,** *whole* (III.4), are declined like **ager, via, bellum:**

	SINGULAR			PLURAL		
	MASCULINE	FEMININE	NEUTER	MASCULINE	FEMININE	NEUTER
Nom.	aeger	aegra	aegrum	aegrī	aegrae	aegra
Gen.	aegrī	aegrae	aegrī	aegrōrum	aegrārum	aegrōrum
Dat.	aegrō	aegrae	aegrō	aegrīs	aegrīs	aegrīs
Acc.	aegrum	aegram	aegrum	aegrōs	aegrās	aegra
Abl.	aegrō	aegrā	aegrō	aegrīs	aegrīs	aegrīs
Voc.	aeger	aegra	aegrum	aegrī	aegrae	aegra

23. *a.* Six adjectives in **-us** (**ūnus,** *one;* **sōlus,** *alone;* **tōtus,** *whole;* **alius,** *other;* **ūllus,** *any;* **nūllus,** *none*) and three in **-er** (**alter,** *the other;* **ūter,** *which* [*of two*]; and **neuter,** *neither*) have **-īus** (or **-ius**) in the genitive and **-ī** in the dative singular of all genders, and lack the vocative; the plural is regular. In the singular they are declined thus:

	SINGULAR			SINGULAR		
	MASCULINE	FEMININE	NEUTER	MASCULINE	FEMININE	NEUTER
Nom.	alius	alia	aliud	alter	altera	alterum
Gen.	[alīus	alīus	alīus]	alterius	alterius	alterius
Dat.	aliī	aliī	aliī	alterī	alterī	alterī
Acc.	alium	aliam	aliud	alterum	alteram	alterum
Abl.	aliō	aliā	aliō	alterō	alterā	alterō

Nom.	tōtus	tōta	tōtum	uter	utra	utrum
Gen.	tōtius	tōtīus	tōtīus	utrīus	utrīus	utrīus
Dat.	tōtī	tōtī	tōtī	utrī	utrī	utrī
Acc.	tōtum	tōtam	tōtum	utrum	utram	utrum
Abl.	tōtō	tōtā	tōtō	utrō	utrā	utrō

b. The genitive singular of **alter** is generally **alterius**, instead of **alterīus**; and **alterius** is ordinarily used in place of the genitive **alīus**.

24. Some adjectives of the third declension have three endings in the nominative singular, others two, and others only one. Adjectives with three endings are declined like **ācer, ācris, ācre,** *sharp*:

	SINGULAR			PLURAL		
	MASCULINE	FEMININE	NEUTER	MASCULINE	FEMININE	NEUTER
Nom.	ācer	ācris	ācre	ācrēs	ācrēs	ācria
Gen.	ācris	ācris	ācris	ācrium	ācrium	ācrium
Dat.	ācrī	ācrī	ācrī	ācribus	ācribus	ācribus
Acc.	ācrem	ācrem	ācre	ācrēs, -īs	ācrēs, -īs	ācria
Abl.	ācrī	ācrī	ācrī	ācribus	ācribus	ācribus
Voc.	ācer	ācris	ācre	ācrēs	ācrēs	ācria

25. *a.* Adjectives of the third declension with two endings are declined like **-i** stem nouns, as **fortis, forte,** *strong* (II.33):

	SINGULAR		PLURAL	
	MASC. AND FEM.	NEUTER	MASC. AND FEM.	NEUTER
Nom.	fortis	forte	fortēs	fortia
Gen.	fortis	fortis	fortium	fortium
Dat.	fortī	fortī	fortibus	fortibus
Acc.	fortem	forte	fortēs *or* -īs	fortia
Abl.	fortī	fortī	fortibus	fortibus
Voc.	fortis	forte	fortēs	fortia

Adjectives of the third declension in the comparative degree are formed on **-s** stems (**13a**) and are declined like **fortior, fortius,** *stronger* (III.14), and **melior, melius,** *better* (VI.12):

	SINGULAR		PLURAL	
	MASC. AND FEM.	NEUTER	MASC. AND FEM.	NEUTER
Nom.	melior	melius	meliōrēs	meliōra
Gen.	meliōris	meliōris	meliōrum	meliōrum
Dat.	meliōrī	meliōrī	meliōribus	meliōribus
Acc.	meliōrem	melius	meliōrēs *or* -īs	meliōra
Abl.	meliōre	meliōre	meliōribus	meliōribus
Voc.	melior	melius	meliōrēs	meliōra

b. **Plūs,** *more,* is defective, having only the neuter forms in the singular: *Nom.* **plūs,** *Gen.* **plūris,** *Acc.* **plūs,** *Abl.* **plūre;** the plural is declined *Nom.* **plūrēs** (m. & f.), **plūra** (n.), *Gen.* **plūrium, plūrium,** *Dat.* **plūribus, pluribus,** *Acc.* **plūrēs** or **plūrīs, plūra,** *Abl.* **plūribus, plūribus.**

26. *a.* Included with adjectives of the third declension that have only one ending in the nominative singular are present participles. Examples are **duplex,** *double* (II.29), **regēns,** *ruling,* and **vetus,** *old* (I.13):

	SINGULAR		PLURAL	
	MASC. AND FEM.	NEUTER	MASC. AND FEM.	NEUTER
Nom.	duplex	duplex	duplicēs	duplicia
Gen.	duplicis	duplicis	duplicium	duplicium
Dat.	duplicī	duplicī	duplicibus	duplicibus
Acc.	duplicem	duplex	duplicēs *or* -īs	duplicia
Abl.	duplicī	duplicī	duplicibus	duplicibus
Voc.	duplex	duplex	duplicēs	duplicia

	SINGULAR		PLURAL	
	MASC. AND FEM.	NEUTER	MASC. AND FEM.	NEUTER
Nom.	regēns	regēns	regentēs	regentia
Gen.	regentis	regentis	regentium	regentium

Dat.	regentī	regentī	regentibus	regentibus
Acc.	regentem	regēns	regentēs *or* -īs	regentia
Abl.	regente *(participle)*	regente *(participle)*		
	regentī *(adjective)*	regentī *(adjective)*	regentibus	regentibus
Voc.	regēns	regēns	regentēs	regentia

	SINGULAR		PLURAL	
	MASC. AND FEM.	NEUTER	MASC. AND FEM.	NEUTER
Nom.	vetus	vetus	veterēs	vetera
Gen.	veteris	veteris	veterum	veterum
Dat.	veterī	veterī	veteribus	veteribus
Acc.	veterem	vetus	veterēs	vetera
Abl.	vetere	vetere	veteribus	veteribus
Voc.	vetus	vetus	veterēs	vetera

b. The adjective **prīnceps, -cipis** (I.7) is declined like the noun (**10b**); the adjectives **anceps, ancipitis** (I.26), and **praeceps, -cipitis** (II.24), have additional syllables in the oblique cases.

COMPARISON OF ADJECTIVES

27. a. Examples of the regular comparison of adjectives, and of participles used as adjectives, are:

POSITIVE	COMPARATIVE	SUPERLATIVE
altus, -a, -um, *high*	altior, altius, *higher*	altissima, -a, -um, *highest*
antīquus, -a, -um, *ancient*	antīquior, -ius	antīquissimus
fortis, -e, *brave*	fortior, fortius	fortissimus
nōbilis, -e, *noble*	nōbilior, nobilius	nōbilissimus
ferāx, *fertile*	ferācior, feracius	ferācissimus
potēns, *able*	potentior, potentius	potentissimus
apertus, *open, exposed*	apertior, apertius	apertissimus

b. Novus, *new*, lacks the comparative, but has a superlative, **novissimus**, *last* (I.15).

28. a. Examples of adjectives in **-er**, with comparative in **-ior** and superlative in **-rimus**, are:

asper, -ra, -rum, *rough*	asperior, -ius	asperrimus, -a, -um
celer, -eris, -ere, *swift*	celerior, -ius	celerrimus
crēber, -bra, -brum, *frequent*	crēbrior, crebrius	crēberrimus
pulcher, -chra, -chrum, *beautiful*	pulchrior, -ius	pulcherrimus

b. Vetus, *Gen.* **veteris**, *old*, lacks the comparative, but has the superlative **viterrimus**.

29. Six adjectives in **-ilis** have **-limus** in the superlative: **facilis, difficilis, gracilis, humilis, similis, dissimilis:**

facilis, -e, *easy*	facilior, facilius	facillimus, -a, -um
difficilis, -e, *difficult*	difficilior, -ius	difficillimus
humilis, -e, *low*	humilior, -ius	humillimus
similis, -e, *like*	similior, -ius	simillimus

30. Some adjectives form the comparative and the superlative by prefixing **magis**, *more*, and **maximē**, *most*, as **magis dērēctum**, *straighter* (VI.26), and **maximē acceptus**, *very acceptable* (I.3), **maximē frūmentāriīs**, *exceedingly fertile* (I.10), **maximē ferī**, *most barbarous* (II.4).

31. The adjectives **dīves** or **dīs**, *rich* (I.2), **honōrificus**, *complimentary* (I.43), and **magnificus**, *splendid* (VI.19) are thus compared:

dīves *or* dīs	dīvitior *or* dītior	dīvitissimus *or* dītissimus
honōrificus	honōrificentior	honōrificentissimus
magnificus	magnificentior	magnificentissimus

32. Several common adjectives are irregular in comparison:

bonus, -a, -um, *good*	melior, melius, *better*	optimus, -a, -um, *best*
malus, *bad*	peior, peius, *worse*	pessimus, *worst*
parvus, *small*	minor, minus, *less*	minimus, *least*
magnus, *great*	maior, maius, *greater*	maximus, *greatest*
multus, *much*	plūs, *gen.* plūris (**25b**)	plūrimus, *most*

33. Several adjectives lack the positive, though the stem appears in prepositions and adverbs; others have a positive only in a limited or special use. Examples are:

(citrā, *on this side*)	citerior, citerius, *on this side, hither*	citimus, -a, -um, *nearest*
(ultrā, *beyond*)	ulterior, ulterius, *farther*	ultimus, *farthest*
(intrā, *within*)	interior, interius, *inner*	intimus, *inmost*
(prope, *near*)	propior, propius, *nearer*	proximus, *nearest*
(dē, *down*)	dēterior, dēterius, *inferior*	dēterrimus, *worst*
(prae, prō, *before*)	prior, prius, *former*	prīmus, *first*
posterus, *following*	posterior, *later*	postrēmus, *latest, last*
īnferus, *below*	inferior, inferius, *lower*	īnfimus, *lowest*
		īmus, *lowest*
superus, *above*	superior, superius, *higher*	suprēmus, *last*
		summus, *highest*
exterus, *foreign*	exterior, *outer*	extrēmus, *outermost*

ADVERBS

34. *a.* Adverbs regularly formed from adjectives have the positive in -ē (-ĕ in **facile**) or **-ter**, the comparative in **-ius**, and the superlative in **-ē**:

POSITIVE	COMPARATIVE	SUPERLATIVE
amplē (amplus), *fully*	amplius, *more fully*	amplissimē, *most fully*
aegrē (aeger), *ill*	aegrius	aegerrimē
mātūrē (mātūrus), *early*	mātūrius	mātūrrimē
facile (facilis), *easily*	facilius	facillimē
fortiter (fortis), *bravely*	fortius	fortissimē
audācter (audāx), *boldly*	audācius	audācissimē
ācriter (ācer), *fiercely*	ācrius	ācerrimē

b. Some adverbs formed from adjectives end in -ō (-ŏ in **cito**), as **continuō, subitō, prīmō**; such adverbs, with comparative and superlative, are:

crēbrō (crēber), *frequently*	crēbrius	crēberrimē
tūtō (tūtus), *safely*	tūtius	tūtissimē
cito (citus), *quickly*	citius	citissimē

c. A few adverbs formed from adjectives end in **-um** (accusative singular neuter), as **multum** (**multus**), *much* (III.9); in **-tim**, as **prīvātim** (**prīvātus**), *privately* (I.17); and in **-tus**, as **antīquitus** (**antīquus**), *in ancient times* (II.4).

35. The following adverbs have irregularities in formation or in comparison:

bene, *well*	melius, *better*	optimē, *best*
male, *ill*	peius, *worse*	pessimē, *worst*
magnopere, *greatly*	magis, *more*	maximē, *most*
multum, *much*	plūs, *more*	plūrimum, *most*
parum, *little*	minus, *less*	minimē, *least*
nūper, *recently*		nūperrimē, *most recently*
diū, *for a long time*	diūtius, *for a longer time*	diūtissimē, *for the longest time*
saepe, *often*	saepius, *more often*	saepissimē, *most often*
prope, *near*	propius, *nearer*	proximē, *nearest, next*
	potius, *rather*	potissimum, *especially*
satis, *enough*	satius, *better*	
	prius, *before*	prīmum, *first*

NUMERALS

36. The Roman notation, as well as cardinal, ordinal, and distributive adjectives are presented in the following list:

ROMAN NOTATION	CARDINALS	ORDINALS	DISTRIBUTIVES
I.	ūnus, ūna, ūnum, *one*	prīmus, *first*	singulī, *one by one*
II.	duo, duae, duo, *two*	secundus, *second*	bīnī, *two each*
III.	trēs, tria, *three*	tertius, *third*	ternī, trīnī, *three by three, three each*
IIII., or IV.	quattuor, *four*	quārtus, *fourth*	quaternī, *four by four, four each*
V.	quīnque, *five*	quīntus, *fifth*	quīnī, *five by five, five each*
VI.	sex, *six*	sextus, *sixth*	sēnī, *six by six, six each*
VII.	septem, *seven*	septimus, *seventh*	septēnī, *by sevens, seven each*
VIII.	octō, *eight*	octāvus, *eighth*	octōnī, *by eights, eight apiece*
IX.	novem, *nine*	nōnus, *ninth*	novēnī, *nine each*
X.	decem, *ten*	decimus, *tenth*	dēnī, *ten each*
XI.	ūndecim, *eleven*	ūndecimus, *eleventh*	ūndēnī, *eleven each*
XII.	duodecim, *twelve*	duodecimus, *twelfth*	duodēnī, *twelve each*
XIII.	tredecim, *thirteen*	tertius decimus, *thirteenth*	ternī dēnī, *thirteen each*
XIIII., or XIV.	quattuordecim, *fourteen*	quārtus decimus, *fourteenth*	quaternī dēnī, *fourteen each*
XV.	quīndecim, *fifteen*	quīntus decimus, *fifteenth*	quīnī dēnī, *fifteen each*
XVI.	sēdecim, *sixteen*	sextus decimus, *sixteenth*	sēnī dēnī, *sixteen each*

XVII.	septendecim, *seventeen*	septimus decimus, *seventeenth*	septēnī dēnī, *seventeen each*
XVIII.	duodēvīgintī, *eighteen*	duodēvīcēsimus, *eighteenth*	duodēvīcēnī, *eighteen each*
XVIIII., or XIX.	ūndēvīgintī, *nineteen*	ūndēvīcēsimus, *nineteenth*	ūndēvīcēnī, *nineteen each*
XX.	vīgintī, *twenty*	vīcēsimus, *twentieth*	vīcēnī, *twenty each*
XXI.	vīgintī ūnus, ūnus et vīgintī, *twenty-one*	vīcēsimus prīmus, ūnus et vīcēsimus, *twenty-first*	vīcēnī singulī, singulī et vīcēnī, *twenty-one each*
XXII.	vīgintī duo, duo et vīgintī, *twenty-two*	vīcēsimus secundus, alter et vīcēsimus, *twenty-second*	vīcēnī bīnī, bīnī et vīcēnī, *twenty-two each*
XXX.	trīgintā, *thirty*	trīcēsimus, *thirtieth*	trīcēnī, *thirty each*
XXXX., or XL.	quadrāgintā, *forty*	quadrāgēsimus, *fortieth*	quadrāgēnī, *forty each*
L.	quīnquāgintā, *fifty*	quīnquāgēsimus, *fiftieth*	quīnquāgēnī, *fifty each*
LX.	sexāgintā, *sixty*	sexāgēsimus, *sixtieth*	sexāgēnī, *sixty each*
LXX.	septuāgintā, *seventy*	septuāgēsimus, *seventieth*	septuāgēnī, *seventy each*
LXXX.	octōgintā, *eighty*	octōgēsimus, *eightieth*	octōgēnī, *eighty each*
LXXXX., or XC.	nōnāgintā, *ninety*	nōnāgēsimus, *ninetieth*	nōnāgēnī, *ninety each*
C.	centum, *one hundred*	centēsimus, *one hundredth*	centēnī, *one hundred each*
CI.	centum ūnus, centum et ūnus, *one hundred and one*	centēsimus prīmus, centēsimus et prīmus, *hundred and first*	centēnī singulī, *one hundred and one each*
CC.	ducentī, -ae, -a, *two hundred*	ducentēsimus, *two hundredth*	ducēnī, *two hundred each*
CCC.	trecentī, -ae, -a, *three hundred*	trecentēsimus, *three hundredth*	trecēnī, *three hundred each*
CCCC.	quadringentī, *four hundred*	quadringentēsimus, *four hundredth*	quadringēnī, *four hundred each*
D.	quīngentī, *five hundred*	quīngentēsimus, *five hundredth*	quīngēnī, *five hundred each*
DC.	sescentī, *six hundred*	sescentēsimus, *six hundredth*	sescēnī, *six hundred each*
DCC.	septingentī, *seven hundred*	septingentēsimus, *seven hundredth*	septingēnī, *seven hundred each*
DCCC.	octingentī, *eight hundred*	octingentēsimus, *eight hundredth*	octingēnī, *eight hundred each*
DCCCC.	nōngentī, *nine hundred*	nōngentēsimus, *nine hundredth*	nōngēnī, *nine hundred each*
M.	mīlle, *thousand*	mīllēsimus, *thousandth*	singula mīlia, *a thousand each*
MM.	duo mīlia, *two thousand*	bis mīllēsimus, *two thousandth*	bīna mīlia, *two thousand each*

37. *a*. Ūnus is declined like **tōtus** (**23a**).

***b*.** **Duo** (I.48) and **trēs** (I.1) are declined thus:

	Masc.	*Fem.*	*Neut.*	*Masc. & Fem.*	*Neut.*
Nom.	duo	duae	duo	trēs	tria
Gen.	duōrum	duārum	duōrum	trium	trium

Dat.	duōbus	duābus	duōbus	tribus	tribus
Acc.	duōs, duo	duās	duo	trēs, trīs	tria
Abl.	duōbus	duābus	duōbus	tribus	tribus

c. Like **duo** is declined **ambō** (V.44), except for **-ō** instead of **-o**.

d. **Ducentī, -ae, -a** (I.43) and the other words for hundreds are declined like the plural of **bonus**, but the genitive plural generally ends in **-um**.

e. When plural nouns that generally have a singular meaning are used with a plural meaning, a numeral in agreement must be distributive; with such nouns, e.g., **trīnī** is always used instead of **ternī**: **trīnīs catēnīs**, *with three chains* (I.53). (AG 137, B 81.4).

38. *a.* **Mīlle** (I.22) in the singular is used as an indeclinable adjective. In the plural it is used as a substantive and declined thus: *Nom.* **mīlia**, *Gen.* **mīlium**, *Dat.* **mīlibus**, *Acc.* **mīlia**, *Abl.* **mīlibus**.

b. The Roman numerical symbols are frequently used in place of ordinal as well as cardinal adjectives. In reading Latin aloud the proper form of the adjective should be supplied; thus **ducenta quadrāgintā** should be read for **CCXL** in **mīlia passuum CCXL** (I.2); **decimā** for **X** in **legiōne X**.

PRONOUNS

39. *a.* The personal pronouns of the first and the second person are declined as follows:

	SINGULAR	PLURAL	SINGULAR	PLURAL
Nom.	ego, *I*	nōs, *we*	tū, *you*	vōs, *you*
Gen.	meī	nostrum, nostrī	tuī	vestrum, vestrī
Dat.	mihi	nōbīs	tibi	vōbīs
Acc.	mē	nōs	tē	vōs
Abl.	mē	nōbīs	tē	vōbīs
Voc.	—	—	tū	vōs

b. The place of a personal pronoun of the third person is taken by the demonstratives (**160a, b**).

40. *a.* In the oblique cases, the pronouns of the first and second person may be used in a reflexive sense, as **vōs recipite**, lit. *take yourselves back, retreat;* **meī**, may mean *of myself,* **tibi**, *to* or *for yourself, etc.*

b. The reflexive pronoun of the third person has no separate forms for the three genders, and is declined the same in singular and plural, as follows:

Gen.	**suī**, of himself, of herself, of itself, of themselves
Dat.	**sibi**, to or for himself, herself, itself, themselves
Acc.	**sē** or **sēsē**, himself, herself, itself, themselves
Abl.	**sē** or **sēsē**, with, or by, himself, herself, itself, themselves

41. The possessive pronouns are declined like adjectives. They are: **meus, mea, meum**, *my;* **noster, nostra, nostrum**, *our;* **tuus, tua, tuum**, *your* (singular); **vester, vestra, vestrum**, *your* (plural); and **suus, sua, suum**, *his, her, its, their.* **Suus** is used only in a reflexive sense.

42. *a.* The demonstrative pronouns are **hīc**, *this, such;* **iste**, *that of yours, that:* **ille**, *that, such;* **is**, *that, he, such,* and **īdem**, *the same.*

b. **Hīc**, *this, such,* is declined thus:

	SINGULAR			PLURAL		
	MASCULINE	FEMININE	NEUTER	MASCULINE	FEMININE	NEUTER
Nom.	hīc	haec	hōc	hī	hae	haec
Gen.	huius	huius	huius	hōrum	hārum	hōrum
Dat.	huic	huic	huic	hīs	hīs	hīs
Acc.	hunc	hanc	hōc	hōs	hās	haec
Abl.	hōc	hāc	hōc	hīs	hīs	hīs

43. *a.* The demonstrative pronoun **ille**, *that, such,* is declined as follows:

	SINGULAR			PLURAL		
	MASCULINE	FEMININE	NEUTER	MASCULINE	FEMININE	NEUTER
Nom.	ille	illa	illud	illī	illae	illa
Gen.	illīus	illīus	illīus	illōrum	illārum	illōrum
Dat.	illī	illī	illī	illīs	illīs	illīs
Acc.	illum	illam	illud	illōs	illās	illa
Abl.	illō	illā	illō	illīs	illīs	illīs

b. The demonstrative pronoun **iste, ista, istud,** *that of yours, that,* is declined like **ille**.

44. The demonstrative pronoun **is**, *that, he, such,* is thus declined:

	SINGULAR			PLURAL		
	MASCULINE	FEMININE	NEUTER	MASCULINE	FEMININE	NEUTER
Nom.	is	ea	id	eī, iī	eae	ea
Gen.	eius	eius	eius	eōrum	eārum	eōrum
Dat.	eī	eī	eī	eīs, iīs	eīs, iīs	eīs, iīs
Acc.	eum	eam	id	eōs	eās	ea
Abl.	eō	eā	eō	eīs, iīs	eīs, iīs	eīs, iīs

45. The demonstrative pronoun **īdem**, *the same,* is declined as follows:

	SINGULAR			PLURAL		
	MASCULINE	FEMININE	NEUTER	MASCULINE	FEMININE	NEUTER
Nom.	īdem	eadem	idem	eīdem, iīdem, *or* īdem	eaedem	eadem
Gen.	eiusdem	eiusdem	eiusdem	eōrundem	eārundem	eōrundem
Dat.	eīdem	eīdem	eīdem	eīsdem	eīsdem	eīsdem
Acc.	eundem	eandem	idem	eōsdem	eāsdem	eadem
Abl.	eōdem	eādem	eōdem	eīsdem	eīsdem	eīsdem

b. The dative and ablative plurals may be **eīsdem, iīsdem,** or **īsdem**.

46. The intensive pronoun **ipse**, *self,* is declined thus:

	SINGULAR			PLURAL		
	MASCULINE	FEMININE	NEUTER	MASCULINE	FEMININE	NEUTER
Nom.	ipse	ipsa	ipsum	ipsī	ipsae	ipsa
Gen.	ipsīus	ipsīus	ipsīus	ipsōrum	ipsārum	ipsōrum
Dat.	ipsī	ipsī	ipsī	ipsīs	ipsīs	ipsīs
Acc.	ipsum	ipsam	ipsum	ipsōs	ipsās	ipsa
Abl.	ipsō	ipsā	ipsō	ipsīs	ipsīs	ipsīs

47. The relative pronoun **quī**, *who, which,* is declined thus:

	SINGULAR			PLURAL		
	MASCULINE	FEMININE	NEUTER	MASCULINE	FEMININE	NEUTER
Nom.	quī	quae	quod	quī	quae	quae
Gen.	cuius	cuius	cuius	quōrum	quārum	quōrum
Dat.	cui	cui	cui	quibus	quibus	quibus
Acc.	quem	quam	quod	quōs	quās	quae
Abl.	quō	quā	quō	quibus	quibus	quibus

48. *a.* The interrogative pronoun is **quis, quid,** *who? what?* It is declined thus:

	SINGULAR		PLURAL		
	MASC. & FEM.	NEUTER	MASCULINE	FEMININE	NEUTER
Nom.	quis	quid	quī	quae	quae
Gen.	cuius	cuius	quōrum	quārum	quōrum

Dat.	cui	cui	quibus	quibus	quibus
Acc.	quem	quid	quōs	quās	quae
Abl.	quō	quō	quibus	quibus	quibus

b. The adjectival interrogative is **quī, quae, quod**, *which, what?* For example: **quī numerus**, *what number?* (I.29). It is declined like the relative pronoun (**47**).

c. Interrogative **quis** and **quī** may be strengthened by **-nam**, as **quibusnam manibus**, *by what hands, indeed?* (II.30).

49. *a.* The indefinite pronouns follow the declension of the relative and interrogative pronouns, but only the pronominal part of the compound is declined. The following indefinite pronouns are used by Caesar, in both substantive and adjective forms:

SUBSTANTIVE FORMS				ADJECTIVE FORMS		
MASC.	FEM.	NEUT.		MASC.	FEM.	NEUT.
quis *or* quī		quid	*anyone, anything*	quī *or* quis	quae *or* qua	quod
aliquis, aliquī		aliquid	*someone, something*	aliquī	aliqua	aliquod
quispiam		quidpiam	*someone, something*	quispiam	quaepiam	quodpiam
quisquam		quicquam	*anyone, any thing at all*	quisquam		quicquam
quisque		quidque	*each one, each thing*	quisque	quaeque	quodque
quīvīs	quaevīs	quidvīs	*any you please*	quīvīs	quaevīs	quodvīs
quīdam	quaedam	quiddam	*a certain one*	quīdam	quaedam	quoddam

b. The indefinite pronoun **quis, quī**, is used by Caesar only after **sī, nisī, seu, nē, neu**, and **ubi.**

50. *a.* The indefinite relative **quīcumque, quaecumque, quodcumque**, *whoever, whatever*, the first part **quī-** being declined like the relative **quī**, is used both as an adjective and as a substantive; as **quaecumque bella**, *whatever wars* (I.44), **quīcumque bellum īnferant**, *whoever should wage war* (IV.7).

b. The parts of the indefinite relative **quisquis, quidquid** or **quicquid**, *whoever, whatever*, are both declined like **quis** (**48**), but only **quisquis, quicquid** (II.17), and **quōquō** are in common use.

51. Caesar uses two compounds of **uter** (**23a**) with the force of indefinite pronouns, **uterque, utraque, utrumque** (**utrīusque**, *etc.*), *each of two*, plural *both, the two*; and **alteruter, alterutra, alterutrum**, *one or the other*, as **alterutrō exercitū**, *the one or the other army.*

VERBS

Since the principal parts of all the Latin verbs in this book are given in the Vocabulary, neither a list of verbs nor a discussion of their stems has been included here.

52. The verb **sum** is inflected as follows. Principal parts:

PRESENT INDICATIVE	PRESENT INFINITIVE	PERFECT INDICATIVE	FUTURE PARTICIPLE (perf. particip. lacking)
sum	esse	fuī	futūrus

INDICATIVE MOOD		*SUBJUNCTIVE MOOD*	
PRESENT TENSE			
SINGULAR	*PLURAL*	*SINGULAR*	*PLURAL*
sum, *I am*	sumus, *we are*	sim	sīmus
es, *you are*	estis, *you are*	sīs	sītis
est, *he (she, it) is*	sunt, *they are*	sit	sint

IMPERFECT TENSE			
eram, *I was*	erāmus, *we were*	essem	essēmus
erās, *you were*	erātis, *you were*	essēs	essētis
erat, *he was*	erant, *they were*	esset	essent

FUTURE TENSE			
erō, *I shall be*	erimus, *we shall be*		
eris, *you will be*	eritis, *you will be*		
erit, *he will be*	erunt, *they will be*		

PERFECT TENSE			
fuī, *I have been, I was*	fuimus, *we have been, we were*	fuerim	fuerīmus
fuistī, *you have been, you were*	fuistis, *you have been, you were*	fuerīs	fuerītis
fuit, *he has been, he was*	fuērunt, fuēre, *they have been, they were*	fuerit	fuerint

PLUPERFECT TENSE			
fueram, *I had been*	fuerāmus, *we had been*	fuissem	fuissēmus
fuerās, *you had been*	fuerātis, *you had been*	fuissēs	fuissētis
fuerat, *he had been*	fuerant, *they had been*	fuisset	fuissent

FUTURE PERFECT TENSE			
fuerō, *I shall have been*	fuerimus, *we shall have been*		
fueris, *you will have been*	fueritis, *you will have been*		
fuerit, *he will have been*	fuerint, *they will have been*		

	IMPERATIVE		
Pres.	es, *be you*	este, *be you*
Fut.	estō, *you shall be*	estōte, *you shall be*
	estō, *he shall be*	suntō, *they shall be*
	INFINITIVE	
Pres.	esse, *to be*	
Perf.	fuisse, *to have been*	
Fut.	futūrus esse, *or* fore, *to be about to be*	
	PARTICIPLE	
Fut.	futūrus, *about to be*	

FIRST CONJUGATION

53. Verbs of the first conjugation are inflected like **amō**, *I love*. Principal parts:

PRESENT INDICATIVE	PRESENT INFINITIVE	PERFECT INDICATIVE	PERFECT PASSIVE PARTICIPLE
amō	amāre	amāvī	amātus

INDICATIVE MOOD
PRESENT TENSE

ACTIVE		PASSIVE	
SINGULAR	PLURAL	SINGULAR	PLURAL
amō, *I love*	amāmus, *we love*	amor, *I am loved*	amāmur, *we are loved*
amās, *you love*	amātis, *you love*	amāris or –re, *you are loved*	amāminī, *you are loved*
amat, *he loves*	amant, *they love*	amātur, *he is loved*	amantur, *they are loved*

IMPERFECT TENSE

ACTIVE		PASSIVE	
amābam, *I was loving, I used to love*	amābāmus, *we were loving*	amābar, *I was (being) loved*	amābāmur, *we were loved*
amābās, *you were loving*	amābātis, *you were loving*	amābāris, or –re, *you were loved*	amābāminī, *you were loved*
amābat, *he was loving*	amābant, *they were loving*	amābātur, *he was loved*	amābantur, *they were loved*

FUTURE TENSE

ACTIVE		PASSIVE	
amābō, *I shall love*	amābimus, *we shall love*	amābor, *I shall be loved*	amābimur, *we shall be loved*
amābis, *you will love*	amābitis, *you will love*	amāberis, or –re, *you will be loved*	amābiminī, *you will be loved*
amābit, *he will love*	amābunt, *they will love*	amābitur, *he will be loved*	amābuntur, *they will be loved*

PERFECT TENSE

ACTIVE		PASSIVE	
amāvī, *I have loved, I loved*	amāvimus, *we have loved, we loved*	amātus (-a, -um) sum, *I have been loved*	amātī (-ae, -a) sumus, *we have been loved*
amāvistī, *you have loved, you loved*	amāvistis, *you have loved, you loved*	amātus es, *you have been loved*	amātī estis, *you have been loved*
amāvit, *he has loved, he loved*	amāvērunt, -ēre, *they have loved, etc.*	amātus est, *he has been loved*	amātī sunt, *they have been loved*

PLUPERFECT TENSE

<table>
<tr><td colspan="2" align="center">ACTIVE</td><td colspan="2" align="center">PASSIVE</td></tr>
<tr>
<td>amāveram,</td><td>amāverāmus,</td><td>amātus eram,</td><td>amātī erāmus,</td>
</tr>
<tr>
<td>*I had loved*</td><td>*we had loved*</td><td>*I had been loved*</td><td>*we had been loved*</td>
</tr>
<tr>
<td>amāverās,</td><td>amāverātis,</td><td>amātus eras,</td><td>amātī erātis,</td>
</tr>
<tr>
<td>*you had loved*</td><td>*you had loved*</td><td>*you had been loved*</td><td>*you had been loved*</td>
</tr>
<tr>
<td>amāverat,</td><td>amāverant,</td><td>amātus erat,</td><td>amātī erant,</td>
</tr>
<tr>
<td>*he had loved*</td><td>*they had loved*</td><td>*he had been loved*</td><td>*they had been loved*</td>
</tr>
</table>

FUTURE PERFECT TENSE

<table>
<tr><td colspan="2" align="center">ACTIVE</td><td colspan="2" align="center">PASSIVE</td></tr>
<tr>
<td>amāverō,</td><td>amāverimus,</td><td>amātus erō, *I shall*</td><td>amātī erimus,</td>
</tr>
<tr>
<td>*I shall have loved*</td><td>*we shall have loved*</td><td>*have been loved*</td><td>*we shall have been loved*</td>
</tr>
<tr>
<td>amāveris,</td><td>amāveritis,</td><td>amātus eris,</td><td>amātī eritis,</td>
</tr>
<tr>
<td>*you will have loved*</td><td>*you will have loved*</td><td>*you will have been loved*</td><td>*you will have been loved*</td>
</tr>
<tr>
<td>amāverit,</td><td>amāverint,</td><td>amātus erit,</td><td>amātī erunt,</td>
</tr>
<tr>
<td>*he will have loved*</td><td>*they will have loved*</td><td>*he will have been loved*</td><td>*they will have been loved*</td>
</tr>
</table>

SUBJUNCTIVE MOOD
PRESENT TENSE

<table>
<tr><td colspan="2" align="center">ACTIVE</td><td colspan="2" align="center">PASSIVE</td></tr>
<tr><td colspan="2">*I may love, let us love, etc.*</td><td colspan="2">*I may be loved, etc.*</td></tr>
<tr><td>amem</td><td>amēmus</td><td>amer</td><td>amēmur</td></tr>
<tr><td>amēs</td><td>amētis</td><td>amēris, *or* -re</td><td>amēminī</td></tr>
<tr><td>amet</td><td>ament</td><td>amētur</td><td>amentur</td></tr>
</table>

IMPERFECT TENSE

<table>
<tr><td colspan="2" align="center">ACTIVE</td><td colspan="2" align="center">PASSIVE</td></tr>
<tr><td colspan="2">*I might love*</td><td colspan="2">*I might be loved*</td></tr>
<tr><td>amārem</td><td>amārēmus</td><td>amārer</td><td>amārēmur</td></tr>
<tr><td>amārēs</td><td>amārētis</td><td>amārēris, *or* -re</td><td>amārēminī</td></tr>
<tr><td>amāret</td><td>amārent</td><td>amārētur</td><td>amārentur</td></tr>
</table>

PERFECT TENSE

<table>
<tr><td colspan="2" align="center">ACTIVE</td><td colspan="2" align="center">PASSIVE</td></tr>
<tr><td colspan="2">*I may have loved*</td><td colspan="2">*I may have been loved*</td></tr>
<tr><td>amāverim</td><td>amāverīmus</td><td>amātus sim</td><td>amatī sīmus</td></tr>
<tr><td>amāverīs</td><td>amāverītis</td><td>amātus sīs</td><td>amātī sītis</td></tr>
<tr><td>amāverit</td><td>amāverint</td><td>amātus sit</td><td>amatī sint</td></tr>
</table>

PLUPERFECT TENSE

<table>
<tr><td colspan="2" align="center">ACTIVE</td><td colspan="2" align="center">PASSIVE</td></tr>
<tr><td colspan="2">*I might have loved*</td><td colspan="2">*I might have been loved*</td></tr>
<tr><td>amāvissem</td><td>amāvissēmus</td><td>amātus essem</td><td>amātī essēmus</td></tr>
<tr><td>amāvissēs</td><td>amāvissētis</td><td>amātus essēs</td><td>amātī essētis</td></tr>
<tr><td>amāvisset</td><td>amāvissent</td><td>amātus esset</td><td>amātī essent</td></tr>
</table>

IMPERATIVE
PRESENT TENSE

	ACTIVE			PASSIVE	
SINGULAR	PLURAL		SINGULAR	PLURAL	
amā, *love*	amāte, *love*		amāre, *be loved*	amāminī, *be loved*	

INFINITIVE

	ACTIVE			PASSIVE
Pres.	amāre, *to love*	Pres.	amārī, *to be loved*	
Perf.	amāvisse, *to have loved*	Perf.	amātus esse, *to have been loved*	
Fut.	amātūrus esse, *to be about to love*	Fut.	amātum īrī, *to be about to be loved*	

PARTICIPLES

	ACTIVE			PASSIVE
Pres.	amāns, *loving* (Gen. amantis)	Perf.	amātus, *loved, having been loved*	
Fut.	amātūrus, *about to love*	Ger.	amandus, *to be loved, worthy to be loved*	

GERUND

Gen.	amandī,	*of loving*
Dat.	amandō,	*for loving*
Acc.	amandum,	*loving*
Abl.	amandō,	*by loving*

SUPINE

Acc.	amātum,	*to love*
Abl.	amātū,	*to love*

In the perfect indicative passive the perfect forms of **sum** (**fuī, fuistī, fuit,** *etc.*) are sometimes used in place of the present forms (**sum, es, est,** *etc.*), with no change in meaning. In the pluperfect indicative passive, likewise, the pluperfect forms of **sum** (**fueram,** *etc.*) are sometimes used in place of the imperfect forms (**eram,** *etc.*), and, in the future perfect indicative passive, **fuerō,** *etc.*, in place of **erō,** *etc.* In the perfect subjunctive passive, **fuerim,** *etc.*, is sometimes used in place of **sim,** *etc.*; and in the pluperfect subjunctive passive, **fuissem,** *etc.*, is sometimes used in place of **essem,** *etc.*, all with no change in meaning.

SECOND CONJUGATION

54. Verbs of the second conjugation are conjugated like **moneō,** *I advise.* Principal parts:

PRES. INDICATIVE	PRES. INFINITIVE	PERF. INDICATIVE	PERF. PASS. PARTICIPLE
moneō	monēre	monuī	monitus

INDICATIVE MOOD
PRESENT TENSE

ACTIVE		PASSIVE	
I advise, etc.		*I am advised,* etc.	
moneō	monēmus	moneor	monēmur
monēs	monētis	monēris *or* -re	monēminī
monet	monent	monētur	monentur

IMPERFECT TENSE

ACTIVE		PASSIVE	
I was advising, or *I advised,* etc.		*I was advised,* etc.	
monēbam	monēbāmus	monēbar	monēbāmur
monēbās	monēbātis	monēbāris, *or* -re	monēbāminī
monēbat	monēbant	monēbātur	monēbantur

FUTURE TENSE

ACTIVE		PASSIVE	
I shall advise		*I shall be advised*	
monēbō	monēbimus	monēbor	monēbimur
monēbis	monēbitis	monēberis, *or* -re	monēbiminī
monēbit	monēbunt	monēbitur	monēbuntur

PERFECT TENSE

ACTIVE		PASSIVE	
I have advised, or *I advised*		*I have been advised, I was advised*	
monuī	monuimus	monitus sum	monitī sumus
monuistī	monuistis	monitus es	monitī estis
monuit	monuērunt, *or* -ēre	monitus est	monitī sunt

PLUPERFECT TENSE

ACTIVE		PASSIVE	
I had advised		*I had been advised*	
monueram	monuerāmus	monitus eram	monitī erāmus
monuerās	monuerātis	monitus erās	monitī erātis
monuerat	monuerant	monitus erat	monitī erant

FUTURE PERFECT TENSE

ACTIVE		PASSIVE	
I shall have advised		*I shall have been advised*	
monuerō	monuerimus	monitus erō	monitī erimus
monueris	monueritis	monitus eris	monitī eritis
monuerit	monuerint	monitus erit	monitī erunt

SUBJUNCTIVE MOOD
PRESENT TENSE

ACTIVE		PASSIVE	
I may advise, let us advise		*I may be advised,* etc.	
moneam	moneāmus	monear	moneāmur
moneās	moneātis	moneāris, *or* -re	moneāminī
moneat	moneant	moneātur	moneantur

IMPERFECT TENSE

ACTIVE		PASSIVE	
I might advise, etc.		*I might be advised*	
monērem	monērēmus	monērer	monērēmur

monērēs	monērētis	monērēris, *or* -re	monērēminī
monēret	monērent	monērētur	monērentur

PERFECT TENSE

ACTIVE		PASSIVE	
I may have advised, etc.		*I may have been advised, etc.*	
monuerim	monuerīmus	monitus sim	monitī sīmus
monuerīs	monuerītis	monitus sīs	monitī sītis
monuerit	monuerint	monitus sit	monitī sint

PLUPERFECT TENSE

ACTIVE		PASSIVE	
I might have advised, you would have advised, etc.		*I might have been advised*	
monuissem	monuissēmus	monitus essem	monitī essēmus
monuissēs	monuissētis	monitus essēs	monitī essētis
monuisset	monuissent	monitus esset	monitī essent

IMPERATIVE
PRESENT TENSE

ACTIVE		PASSIVE	
SINGULAR	PLURAL	SINGULAR	PLURAL
monē, *advise*	monēte, *advise*	monēre, *be advised*	monēminī, *be advised*

INFINITIVE

	ACTIVE	PASSIVE
Pres.	monēre, *to advise*	monērī, *to be advised*
Perf.	monuisse, *to have advised*	monitus esse, *to have been advised*
Fut.	monitūrus esse, *to be about to advise*	monitum īrī, *to be about to be advised*

PARTICIPLE

	ACTIVE		PASSIVE
Pres.	monēns, *advising* (Gen. *monentis*)	Perf.	monitus, *advised, having been advised*
Fut.	monitūrus, *about to advise*	Ger.	monendus, *to be advised*

GERUND

Gen.	monendī, *of advising*
Dat.	monendō, *for advising*
Acc.	monendum, *advising*
Abl.	monendō, *by advising*

SUPINE

Acc.	monitum, *to advise*
Abl.	monitū, *to advise, to be advised*

THIRD CONJUGATION

55. Verbs of the third conjugation are inflected like **regō**, *I rule.* Principal parts:

PRES. INDICATIVE	PRES. INFINITIVE	PERF. INDICATIVE	PERF. PASS. PARTICIPLE
regō	regere	rēxī	rēctus

INDICATIVE MOOD
PRESENT TENSE

ACTIVE		PASSIVE	
I rule, etc.		*I am ruled, etc.*	
SINGULAR	PLURAL	SINGULAR	PLURAL
regō	regimus	regor	regimur
regis	regitis	regeris *or* -re	regiminī
regit	regunt	regitur	reguntur

IMPERFECT TENSE

ACTIVE		PASSIVE	
I was ruling, or *I ruled*		*I was ruled*	
regēbam	regēbāmus	regēbar	regēbāmur
regēbās	regēbātis	regēbāris, *or* -re	regēbāminī
regēbat	regēbant	regēbātur	regēbantur

FUTURE TENSE

ACTIVE		PASSIVE	
I shall rule		*I shall be ruled*	
regam	regēmus	regar	regēmur
regēs	regētis	regēris, *or* -re	regēminī
reget	regent	regētur	regentur

PERFECT TENSE

ACTIVE		PASSIVE	
I have ruled, or *I ruled*		*I have been ruled,* or *I was ruled*	
rēxī	rēximus	rēctus sum	rēctī sumus
rēxistī	rēxistis	rēctus es	rēctī estis
rēxit	rēxērunt, *or* -ēre	rēctus est	rēctī sunt

PLUPERFECT TENSE

ACTIVE		PASSIVE	
I had ruled		*I had been ruled*	
rēxeram	rēxerāmus	rēctus eram	rēctī erāmus
rēxerās	rēxerātis	rēctus erās	rēctī erātis
rēxerat	rēxerant	rēctus erat	rēctī erant

FUTURE PERFECT TENSE

ACTIVE		PASSIVE	
I shall have ruled		*I shall have been ruled*	
rēxerō	rēxerimus	rēctus erō	rēctī erimus
rēxeris	rēxeritis	rēctus eris	rēctī eritis
rēxerit	rēxerint	rēctus erit	rēctī erunt

Subjunctive Mood
Present Tense

	ACTIVE		PASSIVE
I may rule, let us rule, etc.		*I may be ruled, etc.*	
SINGULAR	PLURAL	SINGULAR	PLURAL
regam	regāmus	regar	regāmur
regās	regātis	regāris, *or* -re	regāminī
regat	regant	regātur	regantur

Imperfect Tense

	ACTIVE		PASSIVE
I might rule, you would rule, etc.		*I might be ruled, you would be ruled*	
regerem	regerēmus	regerer	regerēmur
regerēs	regerētis	regerēris, *or* -re	regerēminī
regeret	regerent	regerētur	regerentur

Perfect Tense

	ACTIVE		PASSIVE
I may have ruled		*I may have been ruled*	
rēxerim	rēxerīmus	rēctus sim	rēctī sīmus
rēxerīs	rēxerītis	rēctus sīs	rēctī sītis
rēxerit	rēxerint	rēctus sit	rēctī sint

Pluperfect Tense

	ACTIVE		PASSIVE
I might have ruled, you would have ruled		*I might have been ruled, you would have been ruled*	
rēxissem	rēxissēmus	rēctus essem	rēctī essēmus
rēxissēs	rēxissētis	rēctus essēs	rēctī essētis
rēxisset	rēxissent	rēctus esset	rēctī essent

Imperative
Present Tense

	ACTIVE		PASSIVE
rege, *rule*	regite, *rule*	regere, *be ruled*	regiminī, *be ruled*

Infinitive

	ACTIVE	PASSIVE
Pres.	regere, *to rule*	regī, *to be ruled*
Perf.	rēxisse, *to have ruled*	rēctus esse, *to have been ruled*
Fut.	rēctūrus esse, *to be about to rule*	rēctum īrī, *to be about to be ruled*

Participles

	ACTIVE		PASSIVE
Pres.	regēns, *ruling* (Gen. regentis)	Perf.	rēctus, *ruled, having been ruled*
Fut.	rēctūrus, *about to rule*	Ger.	regendus, *to be ruled*

GERUND
Gen.   regendī, *of ruling*
Dat.   regendō, *for ruling*
Acc.   regendum, *ruling*
Abl.   regendō, *by ruling*

SUPINE
Acc.   rēctum, *to rule*
Abl.   rēctū, *to rule, to be ruled*

56. Verbs in **-iō** of the third conjugation have, in the present system, forms in which **-i-** is followed by a vowel; these forms are like the corresponding forms of the fourth conjugation. An example is **capiō**, *I take.* Principal parts:

PRES. INDICATIVE	PRES. INFINITIVE	PERF. INDICATIVE	PERF. PASS. PARTICIPLE
capiō	capere	cēpī	captus

INDICATIVE MOOD
PRESENT TENSE

	ACTIVE		PASSIVE
SINGULAR	PLURAL	SINGULAR	PLURAL
capiō	capimus	capior	capimur
capis	capitis	caperis, *or* -re	capiminī
capit	capiunt	capitur	capiuntur

IMPERFECT TENSE

	ACTIVE		PASSIVE
capiēbam	capiēbāmus	capiēbar	capiēbāmur
capiēbās	capiēbātis	capiēbāris	capiēbāminī
capiēbat	capiēbant	capiēbātur	capiēbantur

FUTURE TENSE

	ACTIVE		PASSIVE
capiam	capiēmus	capiar	capiēmur
capiēs	capiētis	capiēris	capiēminī
capiet	capient	capiētur	capientur

PERFECT TENSE

	ACTIVE		PASSIVE
cēpī	cēpimus	captus sum	captī sumus
cēpistī	cēpistis	captus es	captī estis
cēpit	cēpērunt *or* -ēre	captus est	captī sunt

PLUPERFECT TENSE

	ACTIVE		PASSIVE
cēperam	cēperāmus	captus eram	captī erāmus
cēperās	cēperātis	captus erās	captī erātis
cēperat	cēperant	captus erat	captī erant

FUTURE PERFECT TENSE

ACTIVE			*PASSIVE*
cēperō	cēperimus	captus erō	captī erimus
cēperis	cēperitis	captus eris	captī eritis
cēperit	cēperint	captus erit	captī erunt

SUBJUNCTIVE MOOD
PRESENT TENSE

ACTIVE		*PASSIVE*	
SINGULAR	*PLURAL*	*SINGULAR*	*PLURAL*
capiam	capiāmus	capiar	capiāmur
capiās	capiātis	capiāris *or* -re	capiāminī
capiat	capiant	capiātur	capiantur

IMPERFECT TENSE

ACTIVE			*PASSIVE*
caperem	caperēmus	caperer	caperēmur
caperēs	caperētis	caperēris	caperēminī
caperet	caperent	caperētur	caperentur

PERFECT TENSE

ACTIVE			*PASSIVE*
cēperim	cēperīmus	captus sim	captī sīmus
cēperis	cēperitis	captus sīs	captī sītis
cēperit	cēperint	captus sit	captī sint

PLUPERFECT TENSE

ACTIVE			*PASSIVE*
cēpissem	cēpissēmus	captus essem	captī essēmus
cēpissēs	cēpissētis	captus essēs	captī essētis
cēpisset	cēpissent	captus esset	captī essent

IMPERATIVE
PRESENT TENSE

ACTIVE		*PASSIVE*	
cape	capite	capere	capiminī

INFINITIVE

	ACTIVE	*PASSIVE*
Pres.	capere	capī
Perf.	cēpisse	captus esse
Fut.	captūrus esse	captum īrī

PARTICIPLES

	ACTIVE		*PASSIVE*
Pres.	capiēns	Perf.	captus
Fut.	captūrus	Ger.	capiendus

GERUND

Gen.	capiendī
Dat.	capiendō
Acc.	capiendum
Abl.	capiendō

SUPINE

Acc.	captum
Abl.	captū

57. *a.* Inflected like **capiō** are its compounds **accipiō, concipiō, dēcipiō, excipiō, incipiō, percipiō, praecipiō, recipiō,** and **suscipiō.**

b. The following verbs in **-iō**, inflected like **capiō**, are used by Caesar: **cupiō,** *ardently desire, wish well to* (I.18, *etc.*); **faciō,** *do, make,* and its compounds **afficiō, cōnficiō, dēficiō, efficiō, īnficiō, perficiō, praeficiō, prōficiō, reficiō** and **sufficiō**; **ēliciō,** *entice* (V.50), **fodiō,** *dig,* and its compound **subfodiō** (IV.12); **fugiō,** *run away,* and its compounds **cōnfugiō, dēfugiō, effugiō, perfugiō, prōfugiō,** and **refugiō**; **iaciō,** *throw,* and its compounds **abiciō, coniciō, dēiciō, disiciō, ēiciō, iniciō, obiciō, prōiciō, reiciō,** and **subiciō**; **quatiō,** *shake,* and its compound **percutiō** (V.44); five compounds of **rapiō,** *seize*: **arripiō** (V.33), **corripiō, dīripiō, ēripiō** and **praeripiō**; **sapiō,** *have sense* (V.30); **alliciō,** *attract* (V.55); and compounds of **speciō,** *look,* **cōnspiciō, dēspiciō, perspiciō, prōspiciō,** and **respiciō.**

c. Similar in inflection to the passive of **capiō** are the following deponent verbs in **-ior** used by Caesar: **patior,** *suffer* (conjugated below, **60**); **morior,** *die* (I.4, *etc.*); and the following compounds of **gradior,** *step*: **aggredior, congredior, dēgredior, dīgredior, ēgredior, ingredior, praegredior, prōgredior,** and **regredior.**

FOURTH CONJUGATION

58. Verbs of the fourth conjugation are inflected like **audiō,** *I hear.* Principal parts:

PRES. INDICATIVE	PRES. INFINITIVE	PRES. INDICATIVE	PERF. PASS. PARTICIPLE
audiō	audīre	audīvī	audītus

INDICATIVE MOOD
PRESENT TENSE

ACTIVE		PASSIVE	
I hear, etc.		*I am heard, etc.*	
SINGULAR	PLURAL	SINGULAR	PLURAL
audiō	audīmus	audior	audīmur
audīs	audītis	audīris, *or* -re	audīminī
audit	audiunt	audītur	audiuntur

IMPERFECT TENSE

ACTIVE		PASSIVE	
I was hearing, or I heard		*I was heard*	
audiēbam	audiēbāmus	audiēbar	audiēbāmur
audiēbās	audiēbātis	audiēbāris, *or* -re	audiēbāminī
audiēbat	audiēbant	audiēbātur	audiēbantur

FUTURE TENSE

ACTIVE		PASSIVE	
I shall hear		*I shall be heard*	
audiam	audiēmus	audiar	audiēmur
audiēs	audiētis	audiēris, *or* -re	audiēminī
audiet	audient	audiētur	audientur

PERFECT TENSE

ACTIVE		PASSIVE	
I have heard, or *I heard*		*I have been heard,* or *I was heard*	
audīvī	audīvimus	audītus sum	audītī sumus
audīvistī	audīvistis	audītus es	audītī estis
audīvit	audīvērunt, *or* -ēre	audītus est	audītī sunt

PLUPERFECT TENSE

ACTIVE		PASSIVE	
I had heard		*I had been heard*	
audīveram	audīverāmus	audītus eram	audītī erāmus
audīverās	audīverātis	audītus erās	audītī erātis
audīverat	audīverant	audītus erat	audītī erant

FUTURE PERFECT TENSE

ACTIVE		PASSIVE	
I shall have heard		*I shall have been heard*	
audīverō	audīverimus	audītus erō	audītī erimus
audīveris	audīveritis	audītus eris	audītī eritis
audīverit	audīverint	audītus erit	audītī erunt

SUBJUNCTIVE MOOD
PRESENT TENSE, ACTIVE

I may hear, let us hear, etc.

SINGULAR	PLURAL	SINGULAR	PLURAL
audiam	audiāmus	audiar	audiāmur
audiās	audiātis	audiāris, *or* -re	audiāminī
audiat	audiant	audiātur	audiantur

PRESENT TENSE, PASSIVE

I may be heard, let us be heard, etc.

IMPERFECT TENSE

ACTIVE		PASSIVE	
I might hear, you would hear		*I might be heard, you would be heard*	
audīrem	audīrēmus	audīrer	audīrēmur
audīrēs	audīrētis	audīrēris, *or* -re	audīrēminī
audīret	audīrent	audīrētur	audīrentur

PERFECT TENSE

ACTIVE		PASSIVE	
I may have heard		*I may have been heard*	
audīverim	audīverīmus	audītus sim	audītī sīmus
audīverīs	audīverītis	audītus sīs	audītī sītis
audīverit	audīverint	audītus sit	audītī sint

PLUPERFECT TENSE

	ACTIVE			PASSIVE	
	I might have heard			*I might have been heard*	
audīvissem		audīvissēmus	audītus essem		audītī essēmus
audīvissēs		audīvissētis	audītus essēs		audītī essētis
audīvisset		audīvissent	audītus esset		audītī essent

IMPERATIVE
PRESENT TENSE

	ACTIVE			PASSIVE	
audī, *hear*		audīte, *hear*	audīre, *be heard*		audīminī, *be heard*

INFINITIVE

	ACTIVE	PASSIVE
Pres.	audīre, *to hear*	audīrī, *to be heard*
Perf.	audīvisse, *to have heard*	audītus esse, *to have been heard*
Fut.	audītūrus esse, *to be about to hear*	audītum īrī, *to be about to be heard*

PARTICIPLES

Pres.	audiēns, *hearing*	Perf.	audītus, *heard, having been heard*
Fut.	audītūrus, *about to hear*	Ger.	audiendus, *to be heard*

GERUND

Gen.	audiendī, *of hearing*
Dat.	audiendō, *for hearing*
Acc.	audiendum, *hearing*
Abl.	audiendō, *by hearing*

SUPINE

Acc.	audītum, *to hear*
Abl.	audītū, *to hear, to be heard*

DEPONENT VERBS

59. *a.* Deponent verbs, generally, are passive in form yet active in meaning.

b. But in the gerundive, and sometimes in the Perfect Participle, deponent verbs can be both passive in form and in meaning; as **dīmēnsō,** *measured off* (II.19); **dēpopulātīs,** *having been ravaged* (I.11). (AG 190b, B 112b).

c. In the future infinitive, the present and future participles, the gerund, and the supine, deponent verbs are active in form and in meaning.

60. Deponent verbs in the four conjugations are inflected thus: **hortor,** *urge* (I.19); **vereor,** *fear* (I.19); **sequor,** *follow* (I.22), and **patior,** *suffer, allow* (I.6, 9); **largior,** *give freely* (I.18):

INDICATIVE

	FIRST CONJ.	SECOND	THIRD	THIRD –IO(R)	FOURTH
Pres.	hortor	vereor	sequor	patior	largior
	hortāris, -re	verēris, -re	sequeris, -re	pateris, -re	largīris, -re

	hortātur	verētur	sequitur	patitur	largītur
	hortāmur	verēmur	sequimur	patimur	largīmur
	hortāminī	verēminī	sequiminī	patiminī	largīminī
	hortantur	verentur	sequuntur	patiuntur	largiuntur
Imp.	hortābar, *etc.*	verēbar, etc.	sequēbar, *etc.*	patiēbar, *etc.*	largiēbar, *etc.*
Fut.	hortābor	verēbor	sequar	patiar	largiar
Perf.	hortātus sum	veritus sum	secūtus sum	passus sum	largītus sum
Plup.	hortātus eram	veritus eram	secūtus eram	passus eram	largītus eram
F.Pf.	hortātus erō	veritus erō	secūtus erō	passus erō	largītus erō

SUBJUNCTIVE

	horter	verear	sequar	patiar	largiar
Pres.	horter	verear	sequar	patiar	largiar
Imp.	hortārer	verērer	sequerer	paterer	largīrer
Perf.	hortātus sim	veritus sim	secūtus sim	passus sim	largītus sim
Plup.	hortātus essem	veritus essem	secūtus essem	passus essem	largītus essem

IMPERATIVE

Sing.	hortāre	verēre	sequere	patere	largīre
Pl.	hortāmini	verēmini	sequimini	patimini	largīmini

INFINITIVE

Pres.	hortārī	verērī	sequī	patī	largīrī
Perf.	hortātus esse	veritus esse	secūtus esse	passus esse	largītus esse
Fut.	hortātūrus esse	veritūrus esse	secūtūrus esse	passūrus esse	largītūrus esse

PARTICIPLES

Pres.	hortāns	verēns	sequēns	patiēns	largiēns
Fut.	hortātūrus	veritūrus	secūtūrus	passūrus	largītūrus
Perf.	hortātus	veritus	secūtus	passus	largītus
Ger.	hortandus	verendus	sequendus	patiendus	largiendus

GERUND

Gen.	hortandī	verendī	sequendī	patiendī	largiendī
Dat.	hortandō	verendō	sequendō	patiendō	largiendō
Acc.	hortandum	verendum	sequendum	patiendum	largiendum
Abl.	hortandō	verendō	sequendō	patiendō	largiendō

SUPINE

Acc.	hortātum	veritum	secūtum	passum	largītum
Abl.	hortātū	veritū	secūtū	passū	largītū

61. *a.* Besides those mentioned above, the most important deponent verbs used by Caesar are:

(1) First conjugation: **arbitror,** *think* (I.4); **cohortor,** *urge on* (I.25); **cōnor,** *attempt* (I.3); **cōnsector,** *pursue* (III.19); **cōnsōlor,** *reassure* (I.20); **cōnspicor,** *catch sight of* (I.25); **cunctor,** *delay* (III.23); **dominor,** *hold sway* (II.31); **frūmentor,** *get supplies* (IV.9); **glōrior,** *boast* (I.14); **grātulor,** *congratulate* (I.30); **interpretor,** *expound* (VI.13); **mīror,** *wonder* (I.32) and **admīror** (I.14); **miseror,** *lament* (I.39); **moror,** *delay* (I.39), and **dēmoror** (III.6); **pābulor,** *get fodder* (V.17); **populor,** *lay waste* (I.11); and **dēpopulor,** *completely lay waste* (II.7); **remūneror,** *compensate* (I.44); and **speculor,** *spy out* (I.47).

(2) Second conjugation: **fateor,** *acknowledge,* and its compounds **cōnfiteor** (V.27) and **profiteor** (VI.23); **liceor,** *bid* (I.18), and **polliceor,** *promise* (I.14); **mereor,** *earn* (I.40); **tueor,** *protect* (IV.8), and **intueor,** *look upon* (I.32); **vereor,** *be afraid* (I.19).

(3) Third conjugation: **complector,** *embrace* (I.20); **fruor,** *enjoy* (III.22); **lābor,** *slip, fall away* (V.3), and **ēlābor,** *escape* (V.37); **loquor,** *speak* (I.20); **nāscor,** *be born, rise* (II.18), and **ēnāscor,** *grow out,* (II.17); **nancīscor,** *obtain* (I.53); **nītor,** *strive, rely on* (I.13), and **innītor,** *lean upon* (II.27); **oblīvīscor,** *forget* (I.14); **proficīscor,** *set out* (I.3); **queror,** *complain* (I.16); the compounds of **sequor: cōnsequor, exsequor, īnsequor, persequor, prōsequor, subsequor; reminīscor,** *remember* (I.13); **ulcīscor,** *avenge* (I.12); and **ūtor,** *use, adopt* (I.5).

(4) Fourth conjugation: **experior,** *try* (I.31); **largior,** *give freely, bribe* (I.18); **mētior,** *measure* (I.16), and **dīmētior,** *measure off* (II.19, IV.17); **partior,** *divide* (III.10); and **potior,** *become master of* (I.3).

b. To the fourth conjugation also belongs the deponent **orior,** *rise,* with its compounds **adorior,** *attack* (I.13) and **coorior,** *arise* (III.7); but Caesar uses certain forms of **orior** which are like those of deponents in **-ior** of the Third Conjugation, as **oritur** (VI.25) and **orerētur** (imperfect subjunctive; VI.9).

62. Semi-deponent verbs have a perfect system that is passive in form but active in meaning; they are **audeō** (I.18), **fīdō** with its compounds **cōnfīdō** (I.23) and **diffīdō** (V.41), **gaudeō** (IV.13), and **soleō** (VI.15):

> audeō, audēre, ausus sum, *dare*
>
> fīdō, fīdere, fīsus sum, *trust*
>
> gaudeō, gaudēre, gāvīsus sum, *rejoice*
>
> soleō, solēre, solitus sum, *be accustomed*

PERIPHRASTIC CONJUGATION

63. The periphrastic conjugation has an active and a passive form, made up by combining the future active participle and the future passive participle (the gerundive), with the verb **sum,** thus:

ACTIVE PERIPHRASTIC CONJUGATION

INDICATIVE MOOD		*SUBJUNCTIVE MOOD*	
Pres.	amātūrus (-a, -um) sum, *I am about to love*	Pres.	amātūrus sim, *I may be about to love*
Imp.	amātūrus eram, *I was about to love*	Imp.	amātūrus essem, *I might be about to love*
Fut.	amātūrus erō, *I shall be about to love*		
Perf.	amātūrus fuī, *I have been, was, about to love*	Perf.	amātūrus fuerim, *I may have been about to love*
Plup.	amātūrus fueram, *I had been about to love*	Plup.	amātūrus fuissem, *I might have been about to love*
Fut. Perf.	amātūrus fuerō, *I shall have been about to love*		

INFINITIVE

Pres.   amātūrus esse, *to be about to love*

Perf.   amātūrus fuisse, *to have been about to love*

PASSIVE PERIPHRASTIC CONJUGATION

INDICATIVE		*SUBJUNCTIVE*	
Pres.	amandus (a, -um) sum, *I am to be loved, I must be loved*	Pres.	amandus sim, *I may have to be loved*
Imp.	amandus eram, *I had to be loved*	Imp.	amandus essem, *I might have to be loved*
Fut.	amandus erō, *I shall have to be loved*		
Perf.	amandus fuī, *I have had to be loved*	Perf.	amandus fuerim, *I may have had to be loved*
Plup.	amandus fueram, *I had had to be loved*	Plup.	amandus fuissem, *I might have had to be loved*
Fut. Perf.	amandus fuerō, *I shall have had to be loved*		

INFINITIVE

Pres.   amandus esse, *to have to be loved*

Perf.   amandus fuisse, *to have had to be loved*

64. *a*. Perfects in **-āvī**, **-ēvī**, and **-īvī**, and other tenses formed from the same stems, are sometimes contracted by the loss of **-vi-** or **-ve-** before **-s-** or **-r-**; perfects in **-īvī** lose the **-v-** before **-r-** but retain the vowel. (AG 181, B 116.1). Examples are:

(**1**) **oppugnārant** (I.5) for **oppugnāverant**; **adamāssent** (I.31) for **adamāvissent**; **commemorāssent** (I.14) for **commemorāvissent**; **superārint**, perfect subjunctive (I.40) for **superāverint**; **superāssent** (I.40) for **superāvissent**.

(**2**) **cōnsuērunt** (III.8, *etc.*) for **cōnsuēvērunt**; **cōnsuērint** (I.44, *etc.*) for **cōnsuēverint**; **cōnsuēsse** (I.14) for **cōnsuēvisse**.

(**3**) **audiērunt** (V.28) for **audīvērunt**; **audierit** (IV.5) for **audīverit**; **audierant** (II.12, VI.37) for **audīverant**.

***b*.** The future passive participle, or gerundive, sometimes has the ending **-undus** instead of **-endus**, as **faciundī** (I.7), **potiundī** (II.7).

IRREGULAR VERBS

65. The irregular verbs Caesar uses most frequently are **sum, dō, eō, ferō, fiō,** and **volō** (and compound forms of these verbs).

66. *a*. Of the compounds of **sum** Caesar uses **absum, adsum, dēsum, intersum, praesum, prōsum, subsum,** and **supersum.** These are inflected like **sum** (**53**).

***b*.** **Possum,** *I am able,* is inflected as follows. Principal parts:

possum   posse   potuī

INDICATIVE MOOD			*SUBJUNCTIVE MOOD*		
	SINGULAR	*PLURAL*		*SINGULAR*	*PLURAL*
Pres.	possum	possumus	Pres.	possim	possīmus
	potes	potestis		possīs	possītis
	potest	possunt		possit	possint

Imp.	poteram	poterāmus	Imp.	possem	possēmus
	poterās	poterātis		possēs	possētis
	poterat	poterant		posset	possent
Fut.	poterō	poterimus			
	poteris	poteritis			
	poterit	poterunt			
Perf.	potuī	potuimus	Perf.	potuerim	potuerīmus
	potuistī	potuistis		potuerīs	potuerītis
	potuit	potuērunt		potuerit	potuerint
Plup.	potueram	potuerāmus	Plup.	potuissem	potuissēmus
	potuerās	potuerātis		potuissēs	potuissētis
	potuerat	potuerant		potuisset	potuissent
Fut.	potuerō	potuerimus			
Perf.	potueris	potueritis			
	potuerit	potuerint			

INFINITIVE

Pres.   posse

Perf.   potuisse

67. *a*. Dō, dare, *give,* has -a- instead of -ā- in the present system except in the second person of the present indicative and the present imperative. The inflection of the perfect system (**dedī**, *etc.*), is regular. Principal parts:

dō   dare   dedī   datus

	INDICATIVE MOOD			SUBJUNCTIVE MOOD	
ACTIVE					
Pres.	dō	damus	Pres.	dem	dēmus
	dās	datis		dēs	dētis
	dat	dant		det	dent
Imp.	dabam, *etc.*	dabāmus	Imp.	darem	darēmus
Fut.	dabō, *etc.*	dabimus		darēs	darētis
Perf.	dedī, *etc.*	dedimus		daret	darent
Plup	dederam, *etc.*	dederāmus	Perf.	dederim, *etc.*	dederīmus, *etc.*
Fut. Perf.	dederō, *etc.*	dederimus	Plup.	dedissem, *etc.*	dedissēmus, *etc.*

	IMPERATIVE		INFINITIVE		PARTICIPLE	
Pres.	dā	date	Pres.	dare	Pres.	dāns

GERUND	SUPINE
dandī, *etc.*	datum, datū

b. The Passive of **dō** has -a- instead of -ā-, as **darī, datur, dabar, dabor, darer, datus,** *etc.*; the first person of the present indicative passive is not in use.

c. The compounds of **dō** are of the third conjugation, except **circumdō**, which is inflected like **dō**.

68. *a*. Eō, īre, *go,* is thus inflected. Principal parts:

eō   īre   iī (īvī)   itum (est)

INDICATIVE MOOD

			SUBJUNCTIVE MOOD			
Pres.	eō	īmus	Pres.	eam	eāmus
	īs	ītis		eās	eātis
	it	eunt		eat	eant
Imp.	ībam, *etc.*	ībāmus	Imp.	īrem	īrēmus
Fut.	ībō, *etc.*	ībimus		īrēs	īrētis
Perf.	iī	iimus		īret	īrent
	īstī *or* iistī	īstis *or* iistis	Perf.	ierim	ierīmus
	iit	iērunt *or* iēre		ierīs	ierītis
Plup.	ieram, *etc.*	ierāmus		ierit	ierint
Fut. Perf.	ierō, *etc.*	ierimus	Plup.	īssem, *etc.*	īssēmus, *etc.*

IMPERATIVE			INFINITIVE		PARTICIPLE	
Pres.	ī	īte	Pres.	īre	Pres.	iēns (euntis)
Fut.	ītō	ītōte	Perf.	īsse	Fut.	itūrus
			Fut.	itūrus esse		
			Pass.	īrī		

GERUND	SUPINE
eundī, eundō, *etc.*	itum, itū

b. Caesar uses the compounds **abeō, adeō, coeō, exeō, ineō, obeō, prōdeō, redeō, subeō,** and **trānseō,** inflected like **eō.**

c. Transitive compounds of **eō** are used also in the passive, such as **initā aestāte,** *at the beginning of summer* (II.2); **trānsītur,** *is crossed* (I.6).

d. Impersonal passive forms of **eō** are **īrī** (III.18), **īrētur** (III.24).

69. *a.* **Ferō, ferre,** *bear, carry,* is inflected as follows. Principal parts:

ferō	ferre	tulī	lātus

INDICATIVE MOOD

	ACTIVE			PASSIVE	
	SINGULAR	PLURAL		SINGULAR	PLURAL
Pres.	ferō	ferimus	Pres.	feror	ferimur
	fers	fertis		ferris	feriminī
	fert	ferunt		fertur	feruntur
Imp.	ferēbam	ferebāmus	Imp.	ferēbar	ferēbāmur
Fut.	feram	ferēmus	Fut.	ferar	ferēmur
Perf.	tulī	tulimus	Perf.	lātus sum	lātī sumus
Plup.	tuleram	tulerāmus	Plup.	lātus eram	lātī erāmus
Fut. Perf.	tulerō	tulerimus	Fut. Perf.	lātus erō	lātī erimus

SUBJUNCTIVE MOOD

	ACTIVE			PASSIVE	
Pres.	feram	ferāmus	Pres.	ferar	ferāmur
	ferās	ferātis		ferāris, *or* -re	ferāminī
	ferat	ferant		ferātur	ferantur
Imp.	ferrem	ferrēmus	Imp.	ferrer	ferrēmur
	ferrēs	ferrētis		ferrēris	ferrēminī
	ferret	ferrent		ferrētur	ferrentur
Perf.	tulerim	tulerīmus	Perf.	lātus sim	lātī sīmus
Plup.	tulissem	tulissēmus	Plup.	lātus essem	lātī essēmus

IMPERATIVE
PRESENT TENSE

	ACTIVE			PASSIVE
	fer	ferte	ferre	feriminī

INFINITIVE

	ACTIVE	PASSIVE
Pres.	ferre	ferrī
Perf.	tulisse	lātus esse
Fut.	lātūrus esse	lātum īrī

PARTICIPLES

	ACTIVE		PASSIVE		
Pres.	ferēns (ferentis)		Perf.	lātus	
Fut.	lātūrus		Ger.	ferendus *or* ferundus	

GERUND

Gen.	ferendī
Dat.	ferendō
Acc.	ferendum
Abl.	ferendō

SUPINE

Acc.	lātum
Abl.	lātū

b. Caesar uses the compounds, **afferō, anteferō, conferō, dēferō, differō, efferō, īnferō, offerō, perferō, praeferō, prōferō** and **referō**, which are inflected like **ferō**.

70. *a.* Fiō, *become* (with -ī- except in **fit** and before **-e-**), is used as the passive of **faciō**, with the meaning *be made, be done*. It is inflected as follows. Principal parts:

fīō	fierī	factus sum

INDICATIVE MOOD			SUBJUNCTIVE MOOD		
	SINGULAR	PLURAL		SINGULAR	PLURAL
Pres.	fīō	fīmus	Pres.	fīam	fīāmus
	fīs	fītis		fīās	fīātis
	fit	fīunt		fīat	fīant
Imp.	fīēbam, *etc.*	fīēbāmus	Imp.	fierem	fierēmus
Fut.	fīam	fīēmus		fierēs	ficrētis
Perf.	factus sum	factī sumus		fieret	fierent
Plup.	factus eram	factī erāmus	Perf.	factus sim	factī simus
Fut. P.	factus erō	factī erimus	Plup.	factus essem	factī essēmus

IMPERATIVE
Pres.	fī	fīte

213

INFINITIVE		PARTICIPLE	
Pres.	fierī		
Perf.	factus esse	Perf.	factus
Fut.	factum īrī		

b. Compounds of **faciō** with prepositions have their own passive forms; so **cōnfecta erat,** *had been made* (I.29); **patefierī,** *be kept open* (III.1).

71. Volō, *I wish,* and its compounds **nōlō,** *I am unwilling,* and **mālō,** *I prefer,* are inflected as follows: Principal parts:

volō, velle, voluī   nōlō, nōlle, nōluī   mālō, mālle, māluī

	INDIC.	SUBJ.	INDIC.	SUBJ.	INDIC.	SUBJ.
Pres.	volō	velim	nōlō	nōlim	mālō	mālim
	vīs	velīs	nōn vīs	nōlīs	māvīs	mālīs
	vult	velit	nōn vult	nōlit	māvult	mālit
	volumus	velīmus	nōlumus	nōlīmus	mālumus	mālīmus
	vultis	velītis	nōn vultis	nōlītis	māvultis	mālītis
	volunt	velint	nōlunt	nōlint	mālunt	mālint
Imp.	volēbam	vellem	nōlēbam	nōllem	mālēbam	māllem
Fut.	volam		nōlam		mālam	
Perf.	voluī	voluerim	nōluī	nōluerim	māluī	māluerim
Plup.	volueram	voluissem	nōlueram	nōluissem	mālueram	māluissem
Fut. Perf.	voluerō		nōluerō		māluerō	

IMPERATIVE		
Pres.	nōlī	nōlīte

INFINITIVE			
Pres.	velle	nōlle	mālle
Perf.	voluisse	nōluisse	māluisse

PARTICIPLE		
Pres.	volēns	nōlēns

DEFECTIVE VERBS

72. a. Caesar uses one or more forms of each of the following defective verbs: **inquam,** *I say,* which he uses in the third person singular indicative present only in direct quotations, **inquit,** *he says;* **coepī,** *I have begun, I began,* which belongs chiefly to the perfect system; **meminī,** *I remember,* and **ōdī,** *I hate,* which are perfect in form, but present in meaning.

b. Coepī, meminī, and **ōdī** are inflected as follows:

INDICATIVE MOOD				SUBJUNCTIVE MOOD		
Perf.	coepī	meminī	ōdī	coeperim	meminerim	ōderim
Plup.	coeperam	memineram	ōderam	coepissem	meminissem	ōdissem
Fut. Perf.	coeperō	meminerō	ōderō			

	IMPERATIVE		INFINITIVE		
Sing.	mementō	Perf.	coepisse	meminisse	ōdisse
Plur.	mementōte	Fut.	coeptūrus esse		

PARTICIPLE
Perf.   coeptus, *begun*
  .   Fut   coeptūrus

c. The passive forms of **coepī** are used with the passive infinitive, as **lapidēs iacī coeptī sunt**, *stones began to be thrown* (II.6).

IMPERSONAL VERBS

73. a. Of the impersonal verbs Caesar most often uses **licet**, *it is permitted* (I.7) and **oportet**, *it is necessary, it behooves* (I.4); he also uses **paenitet**, *it makes sorry* (IV.5).

b. The impersonal **licet** is inflected as follows:

	INDICATIVE		SUBJUNCTIVE
Pres.	licet, *it is permitted*	Pres.	liceat, *it may be permitted*
Imp.	licēbat, *it was permitted*	Imp.	licēret, *it might be permitted*
Fut.	licēbit, *it will be permitted*		
Perf.	licuit, *it has been permitted*	Perf.	licuerit, *it may have been permitted*
Plup.	licuerat, *it had been permited*	Plup.	licuisset, *it might have been permitted*
Fut. P.	licuerit, *it will have been permitted*		

INFINITIVE
Pres. licēre, *to be permitted*   Perf. licuisse, *to have been permitted*

c. Caesar uses impersonally the third person singular of a number of verbs, among which are **accēdit**, *it is added, there is the further fact that* (III.13); **accidit**, *it happens, it turns out* (I.31); **cōnstat**, *it is certain* (III.6); **interest,** *it is important* (II.5); **placet,** *it pleases* (I.34); and **praestat,** *it is better* (I.17).

d. Caesar uses impersonally the passive of several intransitive verbs, making prominent the action rather than the doer; as **pugnātum est**, *fighting went on* (I.26); **ubi eō ventum est**, *when (they) had come to that place,* lit. *when it was come to that place,* the *coming* being made prominent (I.43).

e. Verbs are often used impersonally in the passive periphrastic conjugation, denoting obligation or necessity (**229c**); as, [**sibi**] **reī frūmentāriae prōspiciendum** [**esse**], *that he should provide for supplies,* lit. *that it ought to be provided for supplies by him* (I.23).

WORD FORMATION

74. The following classes of words are derived from verbs:

a. Nouns with the suffix **-tor** denoting the agent, as **vic-tor,** (I.31), *victor,* from **vincō**; **dēfēn-sor** (II.6; for **defend-tor,** as **dēfēn-sus** for **defend-tus**), *defender,* from **dēfendō.**

b. Nouns with the suffixes **-tiō** (**-siō**), **-tus, -tūra, -ium,** denoting an action or the result of an action, as **coniūrā-tiō** (I.2), *a swearing together, league* (**coniūrō**); **mūnī-tiō** (I.10), *a fortifying, a fortification* conceived as a result of fortifying (**mūniō**); **adven-tus** (I.22), *arrival* (**adveniō**); **exerci-tus** (I.13), *army,* conceived as a product of training (**exerceō**); **armā-tūra** (II.10), *equipment* (**armō**); **imperium** (I.3), *command, sovereignty* (**imperō**); **iūdic-ium** (I.4), *judgment, trial* (**iūdicō**).

c. Nouns with the suffix **-or**, denoting a condition or state, as **tim-or** (I.22), *fear* (**timeō**).

d. Nouns with the suffixes **-men** or **-mentum, -ulum, -bulum, -crum,** denoting process, means, or result, as **flū-men** (I.12), *stream, river,* conceived as a flowing or current (**fluō**); **impedī-mentum**

(I.25), *hindrance* (**impediō**), pl. **impedīmenta** (I.24), *baggage,* conceived as an aggregation of hindrances; **vinc-ulum** (I.4), *bond, chain,* conceived as a means of binding (**vinciō**); **pā-bulum** (I.16), *fodder,* conceived as a means of feeding (**pāscō**): **simulā-crum** (VI.16), *image,* conceived as something made like something else (**simulō,** *make like*).

e. Adjectives with the suffix -**āx,** denoting a quality or tendency, as **ferāx** (II.4), *productive, fertile* (**ferō,** *bear*).

f. Adjectives with the suffixes -**ilis** and -**bilis,** denoting passive qualities, or capacity, as **fac-ilis** (I.6), *easy,* i.e. capable of being done or made (**faciō**); **mō-bilis** (IV.5), *easily moved, changeable* (**moveō**); **incrēdibilis** (I.12), *incredible* (negative **in-** + **crēdibilis,** *capable of being believed,* from **crēdō**).

g. A few adjectives in -**tīvus,** as **cap-tīvus** (I.50), *captive* (**capiō**), **fugi-tīvus** (I.23), *fugitive* (**fugiō**).

75. The following classes of words are derived from nouns:

a. Diminutive nouns, ending in -**lus** (Fem. -**la,** Neut. -**lum**), and in -**ulus, -olus, -culus,** *etc.,* as **articulus** (VI.27), *joint* (**artus**).

b. Nouns with the suffix -**ātus,** denoting an official position or body, as **cōnsul-ātus** (I.35), *consulship* (**cōnsul**); **magistrātus** (I.4), *magistracy, magistrate* (**magister**); **senātus** (I.3), *senate* (**senex**).

c. A few abstract nouns in -**tās** and -**tūs,** as **cīvi-tās** (I.2), *citizenship, state* (**cīvis**); **vir-tūs** (I.1), *valor* (**vir**).

d. Adjectives with the suffix -**eus,** denoting material, as **aureus** (V.12), *of gold* (**aurum**); **ferreus** (III.13), *of iron* (**ferrum**).

e. Adjectives with the suffixes -**ius, -icus, -cus, -ānus, -īnus, -nus, -ālis, -īlis, -ārius, -āris, -īvus,** meaning *connected with, belonging to, from, etc.,* as **patr-ius** (II.15), *of a father, ancestral* (**pater**); **bell-icus** (VI.24), *of war* (**bellum**); **Gall-icus** (I.31), *Gallic;* **Germān-icus** (IV.16), *Germanic;* **Rōm-ānus,** *of Rome,* (**Rōma**); **Lat-īnus,** *of Latium, Latin;* **nāv-ālis** (III.19), *naval* (**nāvis**); **legiōn-ārius** (I.51), *of a legion, legionary* (**legiō**).

f. Adjectives with the suffix -**ōsus,** denoting fullness, as **perīculōsus** (I.33), *full of danger* (**perīculum**); **bellic-ōsus** (I.10), *warlike* (**bellic-us, bellum**).

g. Denominative verbs, of the different conjugations, as **cūrō, -āre** (I.19), *care for, take care* (**cūra**); **tribuō, -ere** (I.13), *assign* (**tribus**); **fīniō, -īre** (IV.16), *limit* (**fīnis**); **partior, -īrī** (III.10), *divide* (**pars, partis**).

76. *a.* Derived from adjectives are abstract nouns with the suffixes -**tia, -ia, -tās,** and -**tūdō,** denoting quality or condition, as **dūri-tia** (VI.21), *hardness* (**dūrus**); **audāc-ia** (I.18), *boldness* (**audāx**); **grāt-ia** (I.9), *favor* (**grātus**); **cupidi-tās** (I.2), *desire* (**cupidus**); **forti-tūdō** (I.2), *bravery* (**fortis**).

b. Derived from adverbs are several adjectives in -**urnus, -turnus, -tinus,** referring to time, as **diū-turnus** (I.14), *long-continued* (**diū**), and **diū-tinus** (V.52), *protracted* (**diū**).

c. A few adjectives have a diminutive in -**ulus;** as **tantulus,** *so small,* from **tantus** (IV.22).

77. Adverbs (see also **34, 35**) are sometimes formed from the stem of the perfect passive participle with the suffix -**im,** as **stat-im** (I.53), *immediately,* (**status, stō**); and from nouns, with the ending -**tim** (or -**im**), as **part-im** (II.1), *partly,* which was originally an accusative of **pars.**

78. Verbs derived from verbs are:

a. Frequentatives, expressing repeated or intensive action; frequentatives derived from verbs of the first conjugation end in -**itō,** as **clāmitō** (V.7), *cry out loudly, shout* (**clāmō**); others end in -**tō** or -**sō,** as **iactō** (I.25), *toss about, cast* (**iaciō**), **concursō** (V.33), *rush hither and yon, rush about* (**concurrō**).

b. Inchoatives, or inceptives, expressing the beginning of an action or state, a becoming; they end in -**scō,** preceded by -**ā-, -ē-,** or -**ī-,** as **mātūrēscō** (VI.29), *become ripe* (**mātūrō**).

79. *a.* In the first part of a compound word the final vowel of the stem of a noun or adjective is dropped before a vowel, and becomes -**i-** before a consonant, while in the case of consonant stems -**i-** is often inserted; in the second part vowel changes frequently appear. Thus **signi-fer** (II.25), *standard-bearer* (for **signo-fer, signum** + **fer-** in **ferō**); **prīn-ceps** (I.30), *leader,* i.e. *taking foremost place* (for **prīmo-cap-s, prīmus** + **cap-** in **capiō**); **ampli-ficō** (II.14), *enlarge* (for **amplo-fac-ō, amplus** + **fac-** in **faciō**).

b. The first part of a compound is often a preposition or other indeclinable word, as **perficiō** (I.3), *carry through* (**per + faciō**); **in-iussū** (I.19), *without orders* (negative **in-** + **iussū**); **bi-enn-ium** (I.3), (*period of*) *two years* (for **bi-anno-ium**, **bis** + **annus** + suffix **-ium**); **quotannīs** (I.36), *annually* (**quot** + ablative of **annus**).

c. Compounds originating in phrases are sometimes declinable, as **prō-cōnsul**, *proconsul*; sometimes indeclinable, as **ob-viam**, *in the way*.

d. The following indeclinable prefixes are found only in compound words:

com-, co- (old form of **cum**, *with*), *with, together*; see under **cum** in the Vocabulary.

dis-, appearing also as **dir-, dī-**, *apart*, as in **dis-cēdō** (I.16), *go apart*; **dir-īmō** (I.46), *take apart, break off*; **dī-mittō** (I.18), *send about, send off*.

in-, = *un-, not*, as in **incertus** (IV.5); to be carefully distinguished from the preposition **in**.

por-, *forth, forward*, as in **por-rigō** (II.19), *extend*.

re-, red-, *back*, as in **re-maneō** (I.39), *stay behind*; **red-eō** (I.29), *return*.

sē-, sēd-, *apart*, as in **sē-vocō** (III.17), *call aside*.

THE DERIVATION OF ENGLISH WORDS FROM LATIN

80. *a.* Many words in common use in the English language are derived, indirectly or directly, from Latin. The percentage of classical Latin words that have been taken over into English directly, however, is exceedingly small; the people whose name survives in the word "English" reached Britain too late for any direct contact with classical Latin. But in the Middle Ages a modified Latin was spoken and written by educated people all over Europe; and classical Latin authors continued to be read, less in the Middle Ages, but extensively after the onset of the Renaissance. Meanwhile the Latin spoken by the common people in Italy, France, Spain, and other countries conquered by the Romans, had developed into the Romance languages, French, Italian, Spanish, and kindred tongues; and after the Norman Conquest, in the eleventh century, French was both spoken and written in England. Thus it happens that words of Latin origin have come down into the English of today in various ways, some through the writings and speech of those who read classical Latin, a great many through medieval Latin, but far the greatest number through the Romance languages, particularly French.

b. Some Latin words appear in English in their Latin forms, though they may have passed through other forms and may now have a different meaning; as "arbor" (II.17), "census" (I.29), "color" (V.14), "duplex" (II.29), "senator" (II.28), "victor" (I.31), and "omnibus," meaning originally *for all*, from the dative plural masculine of **omnis** (I.1).

81. Many Latin words appear in English with slight change of spelling, as "cent" from **centum** (I.37), "condition" from **condiciō** (I.28) through a late spelling **conditiō**; "difficulty" from **difficultās** (II.20), "fort" from **fortis** (I.48), "future" from **futūrus** (I.10), the future participle associated with **sum**; "office" from **officium** (I.40), "senate" from **senātus** (I.3), and "victory" from **victōria** (I.53); "false" from **falsus** (VI.20), and "pedal" from **pedālis** (III.13), which goes back to **pēs**, *Gen.* **pedis**, *foot* (I.25); "admire" from **admīror** (I.14), "ascend" from **ascendō** (I.21), "accept'" from **accipiō** (I.14) through the frequentative **acceptō**, *accept*, which is formed from **acceptus** (I.48), participle of **accipiō**.

82. *a.* Some English words have been formed from Latin words by analogy to Latin or French words already in the language. Examples are "magistracy" and "classical."

b. "Magistracy" goes back to **magistrātus** (I.4). From **magistrātus** came "magistrate," to which the suffix "-cy" was added by analogy to the English nouns of Latin origin ending in "-cy"; this suffix represents the Latin termination **-tia**, as in "clemency," from **clēmentia** (II.14). With the addition of the suffix "-cy" the last two letters of "magistrate" disappeared; hence "magistracy."

c. "Classical" comes from the adjective **classicus**, *first class*, which goes back to **classis**, *a class*, though in Caesar **classis** (III.14, *etc.*) has only the meaning *fleet*, as a class or division of military forces. From **classicus** comes "classic"; the suffix "-al" was added by analogy to the English words which are derived from Latin adjectives ending in -**ālis**, as "social" from **sociālis** (ultimately from **socius**, *fellow, ally,* I.5), "hospital" from **hospitālis** (ultimately from **hospes**, *Gen.* **hospitis**, *guest-friend,* I.53), and "legal" from **lēgālis** (ultimately from **lēx, lēgis**, *law,* I.1). Similarly, "aural" is derived from **auris**, *ear* (VI.26), "continual" from **continuus** (I.48), and "senatorial" from **senātōrius**, the suffix "-al" replacing the Latin terminations.

83. *a.* Some English words are formed from words of ultimate Latin origin by the addition of a suffix of English origin. Thus "falsehood" comes from "false" (Latin **falsus**, VI.20) with the suffix "-hood" denoting quality; "citizenship" from "citizen," which goes back ultimately to Latin **cīvis**, with the suffix "-ship" denoting state or office; "instantly" from " instant " (Latin **īnstāns**, *Gen.* **īnstantis**, present participle of **īnstō**, I.16), and "nobly" from "noble" (Latin **nōbilis**, I.2), by addition of the suffix "-ly," which has the same origin as the English word "like."

b. A few English words are formed from Latin words by the addition of an English suffix of Greek origin; as "jurist" from **iūs**, *Gen.* **iūris** (I.4) with the suffix "-ist," which represents a Greek termination denoting the agent; "Caesarism," "nihilism," "terrorism" from **Caesar** (I.7), **nihil** (I.11), and **terror** (II.12) with the suffix "-ism," also of Greek origin, implying doctrine or practice.

84. Many Latin words, especially those that have come into English through the French, have undergone such great changes that their Latin origin is not at once perceived, though it can always be traced through intermediate forms. Such are "captaincy," from "captain," which is ultimately derived from **caput** (I.29), *head,* with the suffix "-cy" (**82b**); "city," from **cīvitās** (I.2); "lieutenant," from **locum tenēns** (present participle of **teneō**, *hold*), one holding another's office or place; "madam," "Madonna," from **mea domina**; "governor" from **gubernātor** (III.9); "peril" from **perīculum** (I.17), and "perilous" from **perīculōsus** (I.33), "preach" from **praedicō** (I.44), and "receive" from **recipiō** (I.5).

85. A few common abbreviations represent Latin words; as "no." in "no. 9," where "no." stands not for "number" but for **numerō** (I.5), the ablative of **numerus**. Also, the symbols for English money, £ s. d., now read as "pounds, shillings, pence," are derived from Latin words: £ = **lībra**, a *pound* in weight, whence **lībrīlis**, *weighing a pound* ("lb"); s. = **solidus**, a Roman gold coin; and d. = **dēnārius**, a Roman silver coin, translated *penny*, though its value as silver was much higher. **Solidus**, the name of the coin, came from the adjective **solidus**, from which our word "solid" is derived; it survives in our word "soldier" as "one having pay" for military service. **Dēnārius** came from **dēnī**, *ten each* (I.43) because it originally contained ten of the monetary units called **as**, and **as** survives in our word "ace." Our abbreviation "Mr." is for "Master," but "Master" is of Latin origin, being derived from **magister.**

86. The value of the contribution which the English language has received from the Latin cannot be measured in percentages of words. The words of English origin which we use are largely concrete, and well fitted to express fundamental ideas; but we are indebted to Latin for a very large proportion of the words employed in the arts, science, and education, which fit the English language to be the vehicle of expression for a constantly developing civilization.

LATIN SYNTAX

NOUNS

87. *a.* A noun or pronoun, or an adjective taking the place of a noun, when used as the subject of a finite verb is in the nominative case; as, **lēgātī revertērunt**, *the envoys returned* (I.3).

b. A personal pronoun used as a subject is expressed only when there is emphasis or contrast; as, **Dēsilīte, commīlitōnēs, nisi vultis aquilam hostibus prōdere; ego certē meum . . . officium**

praestiterō, *Leap down, comrades, unless you want to abandon your eagle to the enemy; I at any rate shall have done my duty.* Here **ego** is emphatic, but the subject of the plural verbs is not emphatic, and hence is not expressed (IV.25).

c. Instead of a noun or other substantive word an infinitive or a clause may be used as the subject of a verb; as, **Commodissimum vīsum est Gāium Valerium Procillum . . . mittere,** *It seemed most expedient to send Gaius Valerius Procillus,* where **mittere** is the subject of **vīsum est** (I.47).

88. *a.* A predicate noun, in the same case as the subject, is used with **sum** and the passives of verbs of calling, choosing, making, esteeming, and the like; as, **Dīvicō prīnceps fuit,** *Divico was the leading man* (I.13); **quī . . . Gallī appellantur,** *who are called Gauls* (I.1); **ducēs eī dēliguntur,** *those are chosen (as) leaders* (III.23). (AG 284, B 168.2b).

b. A predicate noun after passive participles is similarly used; as, **obsidibus acceptīs prīmīs cīvitātis,** *having received the foremost men of the state as hostages,* lit. *the foremost men of the state having been received as hostages* (II.13).

89. *a.* A verb is sometimes omitted when it can easily be supplied from the context; as, **aciēs** (I.25), where **intulit** is to be supplied.

b. Forms of **sum** are often omitted in the compound tenses: as, **occīsa** (I.53) for **occīsa est,** *was killed.*

c. In the future active and perfect passive infinitive, and also in the present passive infinitive of the periphrastic conjugation, **esse** is frequently omitted; as, **conciliātūrum** (I.3) for **conciliātūrum esse**; **itūrōs atque futūrōs** (I.13) for **itūrōs esse atque futūrōs esse**; **lātūrī** for **lātūrī esse** (I.40); **occīsum . . . pulsum . . . missum** (I.7) for **occīsum esse . . . pulsum esse . . . missum esse**; **exspectandum** (I.11) for **exspectandum esse.**

90. *a.* In certain connections **est, erat,** *etc.,* may best be translated *there is, there was, etc.,* with the subject following; as, **Flūmen est Arar,** *There is a river, the Arar* (I.12); **Erant itinera duo,** *There were two routes* (I.6).

b. Occasionally *there* may be used in a similar way when translating other verbs than **sum**; as, **Relinquēbātur ūna via,** *There remained only the route* (I.9).

91. *a.* Nouns used as appositives, whether in the nominative or in the oblique cases, agree in case with the nouns to which they belong; as, **Ariovistus, rēx Germānōrum,** *Ariovistus, king of the Germans* (I.31); **ā Bibracte, oppidō** (ablative) **Aeduōrum,** *from Bibracte, a town of the Aeduans* (I.23). (AG 282, B 169.2).

b. Nouns in predicate apposition sometimes agree with an unexpressed subject, which is implied in the verb; as, **hominēs . . . (eī) afficiēbantur,** *(being) men . . . they were sorely troubled* (I.2).

c. A noun referring to a part may be in apposition to a noun expressing the whole (partitive apposition); as, **itinera duo: ūnum (iter), alterum (iter),** *two routes: the one (route) . . . , the other . . .* (I.6). (AG 282a, B 169.5).

92. *a.* A plural noun is often used in Latin where English usage prefers the singular; as, **ad effēminandōs animōs,** *to weaken the courage* (I.1).

b. An abstract noun is sometimes used in Latin where English usage expects a concrete plural noun; as, **coniūrātiōnem nōbilitātis,** *a conspiracy of the nobles,* lit. *of the nobility* (I.2).

c. Abstract nouns are sometimes used in the plural to denote instances of the quality; as, **ad frīgora atque aestūs vītandōs,** *to avoid heat and cold* (VI.22).

THE VOCATIVE CASE

93. The vocative case is used only in direct address; as, **Quid dubitās, Vorēne?** *Vorenus, why do you hesitate?* (V.44).

THE GENITIVE CASE

94. *a.* In the possessive genitive the idea of possession or of close connection is generally prominent: as, **fīnēs Sēquanōrum,** *the territory of the Sequanians, the Sequanians' country* (I.8); **ā hūmānitāte prōvinciae,** *from the refinement of the [Roman] province* (I.1).

b. The possessive genitive is used idiomatically with **causā, grātiā,** and **īnstar**; as, **auxiliī causā,** *as an auxiliary force,* lit. *for the sake of support* (II.24); **īnstar mūrī mūnīmentum,** *a barrier like a wall,* lit. *the image of a wall* (II.17).

c. A genitive, perhaps possessive in origin, is used with **prīdiē** and **postrīdiē**; as, **prīdiē eius diēī,** *the day before that day, on the previous day* (I.47); **postrīdiē eius diēī,** *the next day* (II.12). (AG 359b.n2, B 201.3a).

d. With **sum** and **fīō** the possessive genitive is used predicatively with the meaning (*in the circumstance*) *of belonging to, etc.*; as, **neque sē iūdicāre Galliam potius esse Ariovistī quam populī Rōmānī,** *and he judged that Gaul did not belong to Ariovistus* (lit. *was not Ariovistus'*) *any more than to the Roman people* (I.45). (AG 343b, B 198.2).

95. The subjective genitive designates the person or agent whose act or feeling is expressed in the noun on which the genitive depends; as, **ab Ariovistī iniūriā,** *from the wrongdoing of Ariovistus* (I.31); **terrōre equōrum,** *the fright caused by the horses,* lit. *of the horses* (IV.33).

96. The appositional genitive defines or explains the noun on which it depends; as, **iniūria retentōrum equitum,** *the wrong (committed by) detaining the knights,* the detaining of the knights being the wrong expressed in **iniūria** (III.10).

97. *a.* The partitive genitive, or genitive of the whole, designates the whole of which a part is expressed in the noun, pronoun, adjective, or numeral on which it depends; as, **quārum ūnam (partem),** *of which (i.e. three parts) one (part)* (I.1); **mīlia passuum CCXL,** *two hundred and forty miles,* lit. *two hundred and forty thousands of paces* (I.2); **prīmōs cīvitātis,** *the first (men) of the state* (II.3); **nihil reliquī . . . fēcērunt,** *they spared no effort,* lit. *nothing of the rest* (II.26). (AG 346a1, B 201.1).

b. The part on which the partitive genitive depends may be indefinitely expressed by the singular neuter of a pronoun or of an adjective, used substantively, or by the adverb **satis** used substantively; as, **quid negōtiī,** *what business,* lit. *what of business* (I.34); **quid suī cōnsiliī sit,** *what his plan was* (I.21); **aliquid novī cōnsiliī,** *some new scheme or other* (IV.32); **quantum bonī,** *how great good* (I.40); **plūs dolōris,** *more suffering* (I.20); **tōtīus Galliae plurimum possent,** *were the most powerful of all Gaul* (I.3); **satis causae,** *sufficient ground,* lit. *enough of cause* (I.19). (AG 346a3, B 201.2).

c. In the English phrase *all of these* there is no partitive idea, because *these* and *all* refer to the same whole. Such phrases are not expressed in Latin by the partitive genitive but by words agreeing in case; as, **Hī omnēs,** *all these* (I.1); **complūrēs nostrī,** *a large number of our men* (I.52); **omnium vestrum,** *of all of you, of you all.* (AG 346e, B 201.1b).

d. Caesar sometimes uses **dē** or **ex** with the ablative instead of the genitive of the whole; so regularly with **quīdam** and words referring to number. Thus, **quīdam ex hīs,** *some of these* (II.17); **paucī dē nostrīs,** *a few of our men* (I.15). (AG 346c, B 201.1a).

e. A genitive of the whole may be used with an adverb in the superlative degree; as **deōrum maximē Mercurium colunt,** *of the gods they worship Mercury above all others* (VI.17).

98. *a.* A variety of the genitive of the whole is the genitive of material, which is used to designate the material or units included in the noun on which it depends; as, **multitūdinem hominum,** *a force of men,* lit. *a multitude (made up) of men* (I.4); **aciem legiōnum quattuor,** *a line (consisting) of four legions* (I.24).

b. The material of which anything is made is expressed by the ablative with **ex**; as, **scūtīs ex cortice factīs,** *with shields made of bark* (II.33).

99. The genitive is used to express origin; as, **Catamantāloedis fīliō,** *son of Catamantaloedes* (I.3).

100. *a.* The genitive of quality (or description) and the genitive of measure are modified by adjectives or numerals; as, **hominēs magnae virtūtis**, *men of great valor* (II.15); **mūrum in altitūdinem pedum sēdecim**, *a rampart sixteen feet high*, lit. *to the height of sixteen feet* (I.8). (AG 345b, B 203.2).

b. The genitive of quality and genitive of measure may be used predicatively; as, **erant eius modī sitūs oppidōrum**, *The strongholds were so situated*, lit. *the locations of the strongholds were of such a character* (III.12). (AG 345, B 203).

101. The neuter genitives **magnī, tantī**, and some others are used predicatively, without a noun, to express indefinite value; as, **magnī habēbātur**, *was considered of great weight* (IV.21); **tantī**, *of so great account* (I.20). (AG 417, B 203.3).

102. The objective genitive is used with nouns to denote the object toward which action or feeling is directed, and with adjectives to limit their application: as, **reī pūblicae iniūriam**, *the wrong done to the state* (I.20); **rēgnī cupiditāte inductus**, *led by desire of kingly power* (I.2); **imperītum rērum**, *unversed in affairs* (I.44); **alicuius iniūriae cōnscius**, *conscious of any wrongdoing* (I.14). (AG 349a, B 204.1).

103. *a.* Caesar uses **reminīscor** and **oblīvīscor** with a genitive of the thing remembered or forgotten; as, **reminīscerētur incommodī**, *he should recall the disaster* (I.13); **contumēliae oblīvīscī**, *to be forgetful of an affront* (I.14). (AG 350, B 206.2).

b. A genitive of the charge is used with verbs of accusing and condemning; as, **prōditiōnis īnsimulātus**, *accused of treachery*; **capitis damnārent**, *should condemn (to loss) of civil rights*, lit. *of head*.

c. Caesar uses the impersonal **paenitet** with the accusative of the person repenting and the genitive of the object of repentance; as, **quōrum eōs paenitēre necesse est**, *of which they of necessity repent*, lit. *of which it is necessary that it repent them* (IV.5). (AG 354b, B 209.1).

d. Caesar uses **interest** with a genitive neuter to express the degree of concern; as, **magnī interesse arbitrābātur**, *he thought that it was of great importance* (V.4).

e. With **interest** Caesar uses a genitive of the interest concerned; as, **reī pūblicae commūnisque salūtis intersit** (historical present), *it concerned the state and their mutual welfare* (II.5). (AG 355, B 211.1).

THE DATIVE CASE

104. *a.* The dative of the indirect object is used with transitive verbs which have a direct object in the accusative, or an infinitive clause as object, and also with the passive of such verbs; as, **dat** (historical present) **negōtium Senonibus**, *he assigned the task to the Senones* (II.2); **nostrīs . . . dabātur**, *was given to our men* (IV.29). (AG 362, B 187.1).

b. With such verbs the place of the direct object may be taken by an adverb or a clause; as, **nē suae magnopere virtūtī tribueret**, *that he should not attribute too much to his own valor* (I.13).

105. The dative of the indirect object is used with many intransitive verbs meaning *persuade, trust, distrust; command, obey, serve, resist; pardon, spare; please, displease, favor, indulge; approach; envy, threaten, rebuke*, and some others; as, **persuādet Castīcō**, *he persuades Casticus* (I.3), that is, *he prevails upon Casticus*. The Roman point of view in these verbs is somewhat different from that of the English, which with corresponding verbs generally uses a direct object. The following are among the intransitive verbs thus used with the dative by Caesar: **accidit**, *happens to* (I.18); **appropinquō**, *approach* (II.10); **cēdō**, *yield to*; **concēdō**, *acknowledge inferiority to* (IV.7); **cōnfīdō**, *trust* (I.42); **contingit**, *it falls to the lot of* (I.43); **cupiō**, *wish well to* (I.18); **dēspērō**, *despair of* (III.12); **ēvenit**, *it turns out* (IV.25); **faveō**, *favor* (I.18); **ignōscō**, *pardon* (I.45); **imperō**, *command* (I.28); **indulgeō**, *treat with favor* (I.40); **invideō**, *envy, be jealous of* (II.31); **licet**, *it is permitted* (I.30); **medeor**, *remedy* (V.24); **noceō**, *do injury to* (III.13); **obtemperō**, *submit to* (IV.21); **parcō**, *spare* (VI.28); **pāreō**, *obey* (VI.13); **persuādeō**, *persuade* (I.2); **placet**, *it pleases* (I.34); **prōspiciō**, *arrange for* (I.23); **prōsum**, *be of benefit to* (VI.40); **repugnō**, *contend against* (I.19); **resistō**, *oppose* (I.25); **satisfaciō**, *make restitution* (I.14); **serviō**, *be* *the slave of* (IV.5); **studeō**, *be eager for* (I.9), *give attention to* (II.17); **temperō**, *restrain* (I.33). (AG 367, B 187.II.a).

106. *a.* A few of these intransitive verbs are also used transitively by Caesar, and govern the accusative: examples are, **impūnitātem concēdere**, *grant escape from punishment* (I.14); **mīlitēs, quōs imperāverat**, *the soldiers whom he had levied* (I.7). (AG 369, B 187.I).

b. If verbs that take the dative are used in the passive, they can only be used impersonally (since they are intransitive); as, **sibi persuādērī**, *that the conviction was forced upon him, that he was persuaded* (I.40).

107. *a.* The dative of the indirect object is used after many verbs compounded with the prepositions **ad, ante, com-** (for **cum**), **in, inter, ob, prae, sub,** and **super**; as, **omnibus praestārent**, *they excelled all* (I.2). (AG 370, B 187.III).

b. Transitive verbs compounded with these prepositions may have both a direct and an indirect object, the dative depending not on the preposition but on the compound; as, **fīnitimīs bellum īnferre**, *to wage war on their neighbors* (I.2).

108. *a.* The dative is used after adjectives meaning *agreeable, friendly, hurtful, hostile, like, unlike, near, subject, obedient, suitable, appropriate,* and many others; as, **plēbī acceptus**, *acceptable to the people* (I.3); **proximī Germānīs**, *next to the Germans* (I.1); **locum idōneum castrīs**, *a place suitable for a camp* (II.17). (AG 384, B 192.1).

***b.* Similis** is used with the genitive when referring to an inner or complete resemblance, as, **vērī simile**, *probable*, lit. *having the likeness of truth* (III.13); otherwise with the dative; as, **fugae similis**, *like a rout.* (V.53).

109. *a.* The dative of reference designates the person or interest affected by the action or state expressed in a verb, or in a clause as a whole; it should be translated with *to, for, of, from, in,* or left untranslated, according to the meaning of the clause in which it appears and English idiom. Thus, **iniūriae sibi cōnscius fuisset**, *had been conscious of wrongdoing*, lit. *had been conscious, to itself, of wrongdoing* (I.14); **sī sibi pūrgātī esse vellent**, *if they wanted to clear themselves in his sight*, lit. *to clear themselves with reference to himself* (I.28); **sēsē Caesarī ad pedēs prōiēcērunt**, *prostrated themselves at Caesar's feet*, lit. *in relation to Caesar* (I.31). (AG 376, B 188.1n).

b. A dative of reference is used with verbs of *taking away*, especially those compounded with **ab, dē,** and **ex** (sometimes called dative of separation); thus, **Aeduīs lībertātem sint ēreptūrī**, *that they were going to take away liberty from the Aeduans*, lit. *that as regards the Aeduans, they were, etc.* (I.17); **scūtō ūnī mīlitī dētrāctō**, *with a shield snatched from a soldier*, lit. *to a soldier*, the dative expressing the point of view of the soldier (II.25); **longē eīs āfutūrum**, *would be far from benefiting them*, lit. *would be far away with reference to them* (I.36). (AG 381, B 188.2d).

c. A dative of reference is used with **interdīcō**, which may take also the ablative of the thing; as, **Galliā Rōmānīs interdīxisset**, *had denied to the Romans any rights in Gaul*, lit. *from Gaul* (I.46).

110. The dative is used with the passive periphrastic conjugation to express agency; as, **omnibus Gallīs idem esse faciendum**, *that all the Gauls would have to do the same thing*; lit. *that the same thing had to be done by all the Gauls* (I.31); **Caesarī omnia erant agenda**, *Caesar had to see to everything*; lit. *all things had to be done by Caesar* (II.20). (AG 374, B 189.1).

111. The dative is used with the verb **sum** to denote possession; as, **mercātōribus est aditus**, *traders have access*; lit. *There is access for traders* (IV.2); **quid . . . Caesarī . . . negōtiī esset**, *what business Caesar . . . had*; lit. *what business was to Caesar* (I.34). (AG 373, B 190).

112. *a.* The dative is used with verbs to denote the purpose or tendency of an action; as, **locum domiciliō dēligerent**, *might select a place for a permanent habitation* (I.30); **locum castrīs dēligit**, *selects a place for a camp*; **diēs colloquiō dictus est**, *a day was appointed for a conference* (I.42). (AG 382.1, B 191).

***b.* Sum** and several other verbs may take a double dative, a dative of purpose or tendency and a dative of reference; as, **sibi eam rem cūrae futūram**, *that this matter should have his attention*, lit. *should be* to him for a care (I.33); **cum auxiliō Nerviīs venīrent,** *when they were coming to the assistance of the Nervians,* lit. *for an aid to the Nervians* (II.29). (AG 382.1.n1, B 191.2a).

The Accusative Case

113. a. The direct object of a transitive verb is in the accusative case; as, **frūmentum combūrunt** (historical present), *they burned the grain* (I.5).

b. Caesar uses as transitive verbs several intransitives compounded with **ad, ante, circum, com-, in, ob, prae, praeter, sub,** and **trāns;** as, **sī īnsulam adīsset,** *if he should have visited the island* (IV.20); **reliquōs antecēdunt,** *surpass the rest* (III.8); **eum convēnissent,** *had met him* (I.27); **initā hieme,** *at the beginning of winter,* lit. *winter having been begun* (III.7); **tēctum nōn subīssent,** *had not found shelter under a roof,* lit. *had not passed under a roof* (I.36); **tantam virtūtem praestitērunt,** *displayed such great valor* (II.27).

c. Caesar uses both **animadvertō** and **animum advertō** with the accusative of the direct object conceived as the object of the mental action expressed by the compound; thus, **id animum advertit,** *he noticed that* (I.24); **haec animadvertisset,** *had noticed this* (I.40).

114. a. Transitive verbs compounded with **trāns** or **circum** may have two accusatives, one dependent on the verb, the other on the preposition; as, **trēs partēs cōpiārum Helvētiōs id flūmen trādūxisse,** *that the Helvetians had taken three-fourths of their forces across the river* (I.12), **partēs** being the object of **dūcere,** while **flūmen** is governed by **trāns.** (AG 395.n1, B 179.1).

b. In the passive the object of the verb used with two accusatives becomes a subject, while the accusative governed by the preposition remains; as, **nē maior multitūdō Rhēnum trādūcātur,** *that no greater host be brought across the Rhine* (I.31). (AG 395n2, B 179.3).

115. a. Verbs of *making, choosing, regarding, giving, sending, having, calling, showing,* and some others, may have a double accusative, one a direct object, the other a predicate accusative; as, **quem rēgem constituerat,** *whom he had made king* (IV.21); **quem 'vergobretum' appellant Aeduī,** *which the Aeduans call Vergobret* (I.16).

b. In the construction of verbs of *making, choosing, calling,* etc., with double accusatives, the predicate accusative may be an adjective; as, **utī . . . cīvitātēs stīpendiāriās habērent,** *that they might have states tributary to them* (I.30).

c. In the passive of verbs of *making, choosing, calling,* etc., the direct object of the active is made the subject and the predicate accusative becomes a predicate nominative; as, **quī Celtae appellantur,** *who are called Celts* (I.1); **Helvētiī certiōrēs factī sunt,** *the Helvetians were informed,* where **certiōrēs,** an adjective in the comparative degree, is predicative (I.7).

116. a. Verbs of *asking, demanding, teaching* may have a double accusative, one of the person, the other of the thing; as, **Aeduōs frūmentum flāgitāre,** *kept pressing the Aeduans for the grain* (I.10). (AG 396, B 178.1a, b).

b. With verbs of *asking* and *demanding,* the person may be expressed by the ablative with a preposition, the thing asked by an accusative or by a clause; as, **abs tē ratiōnem reposcent,** *they will demand an accounting from you* (V.30); **cum ab eīs quaereret quae cīvitātēs . . . essent,** *when he was inquiring of them what states were . . .* (II.4).

c. With **quaerō** the person may be expressed by the ablative with **ab** or **ex**; as, **quaerit ex sōlō ea,** *asks* (*him*) *alone about those things* (I.18); the accusative of the thing may be replaced by an ablative with **dē;** as, **quōrum dē nātūrā cum quaereret,** *when he was inquiring about the character of whom* (II.15).

d. **Volō** is sometimes used like a verb of *asking,* with a double accusative; as, **sī quid ille sē velit,** *if he* (*Caesar*) *wished anything of him* (I.34).

117. a. With both intransitive and transitive verbs Caesar sometimes uses a neuter pronoun as an accusative of result produced, to carry forward or qualify the meaning: as, **Id eīs persuāsit,** *he persuaded them* (*to adopt*) *that* (*course*), lit. *he persuaded that to them* (I.2); **hōc facere,** *to do this* (III.27).

b. The accusative of result may be a noun of kindred meaning with the verb (cognate accusative); thus, **tūtam vītam vīvere,** *to live a safe life.*

118. *a.* The accusative is used to express extent and duration; as, **mīlia passuum XVIIII** (for **undēvīgintī**), *nineteen miles* (I.8); **multōs annōs,** *many years* (I.3); **magnam partem aestātis,** *during a great part of the summer* (III.12); **trīduī viam prōcessisset,** *had advanced a three days' march* (I.38). (AG 425, B 181).

b. Indefinite extent or degree may be expressed with certain verbs by the neuter accusative of pronouns, or of adjectives used substantively; as, **quicquid possunt,** *whatever strength they have,* lit. *to whatever degree they are able* (II.17); **quid Germānī virtūte possent,** *what mettle the Germans had,* lit. *to what degree the Germans were able in respect to bravery* (I.36); **quōrum auctōritās plūrimum valeat** (historical present), *whose influence carried very great weight,* lit. *is strong to the highest degree* (I.17); **sī quid opus esset,** *if there should be any need,* lit. *need to any extent* (I.42). (AG 390c, B 176.3).

c. Extent is expressed by the accusative of **nihil,** and also by **partem** (accusative of **pars**) used indefinitely, a construction often called adverbial accusative; as, **nihil Caesaris imperium exspectābant,** *were not waiting at all for Caesar's orders,* lit. *to extent of nothing, to no extent* (II.20); **maximam partem lacte atque pecore vīvunt,** *they live mostly on milk and meat,* where **partem** is used indefinitely, not being limited to a definite idea, as it is when a genitive is dependent upon it (IV.1). (AG 390d.n2, B 176.2b).

d. Caesar uses **quod,** singular neuter of the relative **quī,** as an adverbial accusative before **sī, nisi,** and **ubi,** where it may be translated *now, moreover, but, and,* or *even,* lit. *as to which;* as, **quod sī . . . vellet,** *even if he were willing* (I.14); **quod sī quid . . . ,** *now if anything* (I.20).

e. Caesar uses **quid,** singular neuter of the interrogative **quis,** as an adverbial accusative with the meaning *why?* lit. *as to what thing?* Thus: **quid dubitās,** *why do you hesitate?* (V.44).

119. *a.* Names of towns or small islands are put in the accusative to express the place to which; as, **Bibracte īre contendit,** *he made haste to go to Bibracte* (I.23). (AG 427.2, B 182.1a).

b. In like manner **domum,** the accusative of **domus,** is used to express place to which; as, **quī domum rediērunt,** *who returned home* (I.29). (AG 427.2, B 182.1b).

120. *a.* The accusative of names of towns is used with **ad** to express *to the vicinity of, in the neighborhood of;* as, **ad Genavam pervenit,** *he proceeded to the vicinity of Geneva* (I.7).

b. In such phrases as **ad oppidum Noviodūnum** (II.12) the name of the town is in the accusative, not because expressing place to which, but as an appositive of **oppidum.**

121. The subject of the infinitive is in the accusative; as, **diem īnstāre,** *that the day was at hand* (I.16).

122. *a.* Caesar uses the following prepositions with the accusative only: **ad,** *to;* **adversus,** *against;* **ante,** *before;* **apud,** *near, with, among;* **circiter,** *about;* **circum,** *around;* **cis,** *on this side of;* **citrā,** *on this side of;* **contrā,** *against;* **ergā,** *towards;* **extrā,** *outside of;* **īnfrā,** *below;* **inter,** *between;* **intrā,** *within;* **iuxtā,** *near;* **ob,** *on account of;* **penes,** *in the possession of;* **per,** *through;* **post,** *after;* **praeter,** *excepting;* **prope,** *near;* **propter,** *on account of;* **secundum,** *along, after, besides, according to;* **suprā,** *above;* **trāns,** *across, on the other side of;* **ultrā,** *beyond;* **versus,** *toward.*

b. Several of these prepositions are used by Caesar also as adverbs; as, **contrā,** *in opposition* (I.18); **suprā,** *above* (II.18).

123. *a.* With nouns referring to persons Caesar often uses **per** with the accusative to express the means through which something is done, as distinguished from direct agency, which is expressed by the ablative with **ab;** as, **per eōs,** *with their help,* lit. *by means of them* (I.4).

b. Caesar uses also **propius,** *nearer,* the comparative of **prope,** and **proximus,** *next,* the superlative of **propior,** with the accusative; as, **propius sē,** *nearer to themselves* (IV.9); **quī proximī Rhēnum incolunt,** *who dwell next to the Rhine* (I.54). (AG 432a, B 141.3).

124. *a.* The prepositions **in** and **sub** are used with the accusative to denote motion, with the ablative to denote rest; as, **in partēs trēs**, *into three parts* (I.1); **in eōrum fīnibus**, *in their country* (I.1); **sub iugum missum**, *sent under the yoke* (I.7); **sub aquā**, *under water* (V.18).

b. **Super** is used ordinarily with the accusative, but occasionally with the ablative.

The Ablative Case

125. *a.* Caesar uses the following prepositions with the ablative: **ā**, or **ab**, **abs**, *away from, by*; **cum**, *with*; **dē**, *down from, concerning*; **ex** or **ē**, *out from, out of*; **prae**, *before*; **prō**, *in front of, for, considering, as*; **sine**, *without*.

b. The form **abs** appears only in **abs tē** (V.30). **Ab** and **ex** are regularly used before vowels and **h**; **ā** and **ē**, before consonants, but before consonants **ab** and **ex** are also used.

c. With the ablative of the personal, reflexive, and relative Pronouns **cum** is ordinarily joined; thus **nōbīscum**, *with us* (V.17); **sēcum**, *with him* (I.8), *with himself* (I.36); **quibuscum**, *with whom* (I.1).

126. *a.* Direct agency with the passive is expressed by **ā, ab**, with the ablative; as, **ab Helvētiīs pulsum**, *routed by the Helvetians* (I.7).

b. Caesar sometimes uses an abstract or collective noun with **ā, ab**, to express agency; as, **ā multitūdine**, *by a host* (III.2).

c. Caesar often uses **ā, ab**, and sometimes **ex**, to indicate a location, where we use *on, in*, or *at*; as, **ā dextrō cornū**, *on the right wing*, lit. *from (the point of view of) the right wing* (I.52); **ā novissimō agmine**, *on the rear* (I.23); **ā fronte**, *in front* (II.23).

127. *a.* An ablative of separation without a preposition is regularly used by Caesar with many verbs meaning *keep from, refrain from; withdraw from; strip, deprive of; free from; lack, be without*; as, **proeliō abstinēbat**, *was refraining from battle* (I.22); **eā spē dēiectī**, *deprived of this hope* (I.8). (AG 401, B 214).

The most important of the verbs thus used by Caesar are: **abstineō**, *refrain from*; **careō**, *be without*; **dēiciō**, *cast down from*; **dēsistō**, *desist from, leave off* (I.8); **egeō**, *lack*; **emittō**, *let go from* (I.25); **excēdō**, *withdraw from, leave* (II.25); **exuō**, *strip* (III.6); **interclūdō**, *cut off* (I.23); **levō**, *relieve from* (V.27); **līberō**, *free from* (IV.19); **nūdō**, *clear* (II.6); **prohibeō**, *keep from* (I.1); and **spoliō**, *rob of, despoil* (V.6).

b. With several of these verbs the idea of separation may be expressed by a preposition; as, **ab oppidīs vim hostium prohibēre**, *to defend the towns against the violence of the enemy*, lit. *to hold back the violence of the enemy from the towns* (I.11).

c. With other verbs the ablative of separation is regularly accompanied by a preposition; as, **exercitum dēdūcat ex hīs regiōnibus**, *leads his army out of these regions* (I.44).

d. Caesar uses **egeō** with the genitive also: **nē quis . . . auxiliī egēret**, *that not anyone be without help* (VI.11).

128. *a.* A variety of the ablative of separation is the ablative of source, or origin, which Caesar uses with **nātus**, participle of **nāscor**, and **ortus**, participle of **orior**; as, **amplissimō genere nātus**, *sprung from most illustrious stock* (IV.12). (AG 403, B 215).

b. Origin is more broadly stated with prepositions; as, **quibus ortī ex cīvitātibus**, *tribes from which they (were) descended* (V.12); **ortōs ā Germānīs**, *descendants (lit. descended) from the Germans* (II.4); **ab Dīte patre prōgnātōs**, *descendants from Father Dis* (VI.18).

129. *a.* The ablative of comparison is used by Caesar after comparative adjectives and adverbs; as, **paulō cēterīs hūmāniōrēs**, **cēterīs** being used instead of **quam cēterī (sunt)**, *a little more civilized than the rest* (IV.3); **nōn amplius quīnīs aut sēnīs mīlibus passuum**, *not more than five or six miles each day* (I.15); **celerius omnī opīniōne**, *more quickly than anyone had anticipated*, lit. *than every expectation* (II.3). (AG 407, B 217.1).

b. In a few instances Caesar uses **amplius, longius**, and **minus** as if in place of **amplius quam, longius quam, minus quam**, without influence upon the construction of the noun following; as, **nōn**

amplius pedum sescentōrum (genitive of measure), *not more than six hundred feet* (I.38); **neque longius mīlia** (accusative of extent) **passuum VIII**, *and not further than eight miles* (V.53). (AG 407c, B 217.2).

130. a. The place from which is regularly expressed by the ablative with a preposition, generally **ex** or **dē**; as, **ex agrīs**, *from the country* (I.4).

b. Domō, ablative of **domus**, is used in the ablative of the place from which without a preposition; as, **domō exīre**, *to go out from home* (I.6). (AG 427.1, B 229.1b).

131. a. The ablative is used to denote means or instrument; as, **gladiīs partem eōrum interfēcērunt**, *killed a part of them with swords* (II.23); **proeliīs contendunt**, *they contend in battle*, lit. *by means of battles* (I.1); **memoriā tenēbat**, *he remembered*, lit. *held by means of memory* (I.7). (AG 409, B 218).

b. The ablative of means may denote persons as well as things; as, **quīngentīs equitibus**, *with five hundred horsemen* (I.15).

c. Caesar uses the ablative of means with **ūtor, abūtor, fruor, fungor, nītor, innītor**, and ordinarily with **potior**; thus **ephippiīs ūtī**, *to use saddle-cloths*, lit. *to assist themselves by means of saddle-cloths* (IV.2); **impedīmentīs potītī sunt**, *obtained possession of the baggage*, that is *made themselves masters by means of the baggage* (I.26). (AG 410, B 218.1).

d. Caesar uses **potior** also with the genitive; as, **tōtīus Galliae potīrī**, *to become masters of the whole (of) Gaul* (I.3). (AG 410a, B 212.2).

e. Caesar uses an ablative of means with **frētus**, *relying on*, lit. *supported by*; as, **victōriīs frētī**, *relying on their victories* (III.21). (AG 431a, B 218.3).

f. The ablative with **ūtor** is sometimes accompanied by a predicate ablative, the construction resembling that of a double accusative after verbs of *having* (**115a**); thus **īsdem ducibus ūsus**, *employing the same men as guides* (II.7).

132. a. Opus est, *there is need*, is used with the ablative of the thing needed, which may be expressed by a perfect passive participle; thus, **sī quid opus factō esset**, *if anything should require action*, lit. *if there should be need of (something) done, to any extent* (I.42). (AG 411a, B 218.2).

b. With **opus est** the thing needed may be expressed by a neuter pronoun in the nominative; as, **sī quid ipsī ā Caesare opus esset**, *if he himself had wanted anything of Caesar*, lit. *if anything were necessary to himself from Caesar* (I.34); **quid . . . opus esset**, *what was necessary* (II.22); **quaecumque opus sunt**, *whatever things are necessary* (V.40).

133. The ablative of means is used with a few adjectives; as, **nāvēs . . . omnī genere armōrum ōrnātissimae**, *ships completely fitted out with every kind of equipment* (III.14).

134. a. Caesar uses the ablative of the way by which (route) with several words referring to natural features and military operations; as, **adversō colle**, *up the hill*, lit. *by the hill facing them* (II.19); **quod flūmine subvexerat**, *which he had brought up the river*, lit. *by means of the river* (I.16); **duābus portīs ēruptiōnem fierī**, *that a sally be made from* (lit. *by*) *two gates* (III.19). (AG 429a, B 218.9).

The words thus used are: **collis, flūmen, iter**, especially in **magnīs itineribus**, *by forced marches* (I.37); **porta, vadum** (I.6, 8), and **via** (V.19).

b. The ablative of the way by which (route) is sometimes used indefinitely with words referring to distance; as, **tantō spatiō secūtī quantum efficere potuērunt**, *following at as great a distance* (lit. *by so great a space*) *as they were able to bring about* (IV.35).

135. a. An ablative denoting cause is used with many verbs and adjectives, particularly those which express *pleasure, pain, trust, distrust, boastfulness*, and the like; as, **annī tempore cōnfīsae**, *trusting in the time of year*, lit. *confident because of the time of year* (III.27); **quod sua victōriā glōriārentur**, *the fact that they were boasting of* (lit. *by reason of*) *their victory* (I.14). (AG 431, B 219.1).

b. In some phrases the force of the ablative of cause has become obscured, as in **causā** and **grātiā**, *for the sake of*, with the genitive (which precedes), and in **iussū, iniussū**, and the like; as, **auxiliī causā**, *as an auxiliary force*, lit. *for the sake of support* (III.18; II.24); **iussū Caesaris**, *by (reason of) Caesar's* *orders*; **iniussū suō et cīvitātis,** *without his own authorization and (that) of the state,* i.e. because of unauthorization (I.19).

136. *a.* The ablative of manner (answering the question "how?") is used by Caesar with **cum,** especially when the noun is modified by an adjective; as, **cum cruciātū necābātur,** *was put to death with torture* (V.45); **multīs cum lacrimīs,** *with many tears* (I.20).

b. The ablative of manner is also used without a preposition; as, **cum omnibus cōpiīs venīrent,** *when they were coming with all their forces* (II.29). (AG 412, B 220).

c. In certain circumstances Caesar uses an ablative with the meaning *in accordance with*; as, **mōribus suīs,** *in accordance with their customs* (I.4); **cōnsuētūdine populī Rōmānī,** *in accordance with the practice of the Roman people* (III.23). (AG 418a, B 220.3).

137. *a.* The ablative is used with **cum** to express accompaniment; as, **cum suīs omnibus cōpiīs,** *with all his forces* (I.38).

b. An ablative of accompaniment referring to military operations, when qualified by an adjective, may be used without **cum;** but if the modifier is a numeral, **cum** must be used. Thus, **omnibus cōpiīs contendērunt,** *they hastened with all their forces* (II.7); **cum duābus legiōnibus,** *with two legions* (I.21).

c. The use of **cum** with the ablative of accompaniment is much broader than the meaning *together with.* Examples are: **cōnstituerat cum lēgātīs,** *had appointed with the envoys* (I.8); **cōnsiliō cum lēgātīs commūnicātō,** *having imparted his determination to his lieutenants* (IV.13); **cum Caesare ēgit,** *conferred with Caesar* (I.13); **cum illā (cōnsuētūdine) comparandam,** *to be compared with that manner of life* (I.31).

138. An ablative of attendant circumstance is used by Caesar with an adjective, pronominal adjective, or genitive as modifying word, and without a preposition; as, **paribus intervāllīs,** *at equal intervals* (I.51); **imperiō nostrō,** *under our sovereignty* (II.1); **commodō reī pūblicae,** *with advantage to* (lit. *of*) *the State* (I.35); **Caesaris voluntāte,** *with Caesar's approval* (I.30). (B 221).

139. The ablative is used with certain verbs meaning *exchange, mix,* and *accustom*; thus, **nē studium bellī gerendī agrī cultūrā commūtent,** *that they may not exchange their devotion to aggressive warfare for farming* (VI.22); **nūllō officiō aut disciplīnā assuēfactī,** *habituated to* (lit. *familiarized with*) *no obligation or training* (IV.1). (AG 417b).

140. The ablative of degree of difference is used with comparatives, and with adverbs or phrases implying comparison; as, **paulō longius,** *a little further,* lit. *further by a little* (II.20); **paucīs ante diēbus,** *a few days before* (I.18); **mīlibus passuum duōbus ultrā eum,** *two miles beyond him,* lit. *beyond him by two miles* (I.48). (AG 414, B 223).

141. The ablative of price is used by Caesar only in indefinite expressions; thus, **parvō pretiō redēmpta,** *purchased at a low price* (I.18); **impēnsō pretiō,** *at a high price* (IV.2).

142. *a.* The ablative of specification (answering the question "in respect to what?") is used with verbs and adjectives and the adverb **saepe;** as, **cum virtūte omnibus praestārent,** *since they surpassed all in valor* (I.2); **Suēba nātiōne,** *a Sueban by birth* (I.53); **numerō ad duodecim,** *about twelve in number,* lit. *in number about twelve* (I.5); **saepe numerō,** *frequently,* lit. *often in respect to number* (I.33). (AG 418, B 226).

b. The ablative of specification is used with **dignus** and **indignus;** as, **nihil, quod ipsīs esset indignum, committēbant,** *they did nothing that was unworthy of them,* lit. *in respect to themselves* (V.35).

143. *a.* The ablative of description, or ablative of quality, is modified by an adjective (or, more rarely, by a noun in the genitive); as, **hominēs inimīcō animō,** *men of unfriendly (attitude of) mind* (I.7). (AG 415, B 224).

b. The ablative of description may be used predicatively; as, **ingentī magnitūdine Germānōs esse,** *that the Germans were of huge size* (I.39); **sunt speciē … taurī,** *they have* (lit. *are of*) *the appearance of a bull* (VI.28). (AG 415, B 224.1).

144. *a.* The ablative absolute consists of a noun or pronoun in the ablative with a participle, adjective, or noun in the same case, and is loosely related with the rest of the sentence; as, **rēgnō occupātō,**

having seized the governing power, lit. *the governing power having been seized* (I.3). (AG 420, B 227.2).

b. The ablative absolute may express time, attendant circumstance, cause, condition, concession, means, or manner, and may often be translated by a clause; thus:

(**1**) Time: **M. Messālā, M. Pisōne cōnsulibus,** *in the consulship of Marcus Messala and Marcus Piso,* lit. *Marcus Messala, Marcus Piso (being) consuls* (I.2). (AG 419a, B 227.1).

(**2**) Attendant circumstance: **convocātīs eōrum prīncipibus,** *having called together their leading men;* lit. *with their leading men having been called together* (I.16); **captō monte et succēdentibus nostrīs,** *after they had reached the height and our men were coming up* (I.25).

(**3**) Cause: **omnibus frūgibus āmissīs,** *since all the produce of the fields was gone,* lit. *all . . . having been lost* (I.28).

(**4**) Condition: **datā facultāte,** *if opportunity should have been granted* (I.7). (AG 420.4, B 227.2b).

(**5**) Concession or opposition: **superiōribus locīs occupātīs,** *though the higher positions had been seized* (I.23). (AG 420.3, B 227.2c).

(**6**) Means: **eō dēprecātōre,** *through his intercession,* lit. *he (being) intercessor* (I.9).

(**7**) Manner: **equō admissō,** *with (his) horse at top speed,* lit. *his horse having been let go* (I.22).

145. *a.* The place where is regularly expressed by the ablative with a preposition; as, **in eōrum fīnibus,** *in their territories* (I.1).

b. Names of towns, excepting those in the singular of the first and second declensions, are put in the ablative of place where, without a preposition; as, **Bibracte,** *at Bibracte.*

c. The noun **locus,** singular and plural, is often used in the ablative of the place where without a preposition, as are also several other nouns when modified by an adjective, particularly **tōtus;** thus, **aliēnō locō,** *on unfavorable ground,* lit. *in an unfavorable place* (I.15); **tōtīs castrīs,** *throughout the camp,* lit. *in the whole camp* (I.39); **eōdem vēstīgiō,** *in the same spot* (IV.2).

146. With names of towns of the first and second declensions, in the singular, place where is expressed by the locative; as, **Cēnabī,** *at Cenabum;* also **domī,** locative of **domus,** *at home* (I.18).

147. *a.* The time when, and time within which anything happens, may be denoted by the ablative without a preposition; as, **diē quārtō,** *on the fourth day* (I.26); **paucīs annīs,** *within a few years* (I.31). (AG 423, B 230).

b. Words that have only an indirect reference to time are sometimes put in the ablative of time when or within which; as, **patrum nostrōrum memoriā,** *within the memory of our fathers* (I.12); **initiō ōrātiōnis,** *at the beginning of his statement* (I.43). (AG 423, B 231).

c. Intervals of space and duration of time are sometimes expressed by the ablative, especially when modified by an adjective or genitive; as, **mīlibus passuum sex,** *six miles (distant),* lit. *by six thousands of paces* (I.48); **tōtā nocte iērunt,** *all night long they went on* (I.26). (AG 424b, B 231.1).

ADJECTIVES

148. *a.* Adjectives and participles, whether attributive or predicative, agree in gender, number, and case with the noun or pronoun to which they belong.

b. Attributive adjectives and participles stand in direct relation with a noun or pronoun; as, **fortissimō virō** (abl.), *a very brave man* (II.25); **is, rēgnī cupiditāte inductus,** *he, led on by a desire of kingly power* (I.2).

c. Predicate adjectives, and participles in predicate used as adjectives, are connected with a noun or pronoun through a verb or participle; as, **fortissimī sunt Belgae,** *the Belgians are the bravest* (I.1); **quī perītissimus habēbātur,** *who was considered highly skilled* (I.21); **Gallia est dīvīsa,** *Gaul is divided,* the perfect passive participle of **dīvidō** being used as an adjective; if **est dīvīsa** were here a perfect passive tense, it would have to be translated *has been divided* or *was divided* (I.1). (AG 495, B 337.2).

d. A predicate adjective or participle modifying an infinitive or clause is neuter; as, **perfacile esse .**

.. **potīrī**, *that it was exceedingly easy* (or, *a very easy thing*) *to obtain possession of*, **perfacile** being the predicate after **esse**, to which **potīrī** stands as subject (I.2).

e. A participle forming part of an infinitive may agree with the subject of the principal verb; as, **meritus [esse] vidēbātur**, *was seen to have earned* (I.40).

149. Demonstrative and other pronouns used like adjectives agree with the word to which they belong; as, **eō tempore**, *at that time* (I.8); **quā arrogantiā**, *with what presumption* (I.40); **id ipsum**, *that very thing*.

150. *a.* An attributive adjective used with two or more nouns regularly agrees with the nearest; as, **eādem alacritāte ac studiō**, *with the same eagerness and enthusiasm* (IV.24).

b. A predicate adjective used with two or more nouns is regularly plural; when the nouns are of different genders, the adjective is generally masculine if persons are referred to, neuter if only things or abstract qualities are denoted, though even in this case the agreement may be with the nearer substantive; as, **frāter et soror eōrum bonī sunt**, *their brother and sister are good*; **et mūrus et porta alta erant**, *both the wall and the gate were high.*

c. An adjective or participle may agree with a noun in sense, without regard to grammatical gender or number; as, **hominum mīlia** (neuter) **VI, perterritī** (masculine), *six thousand (of) men, thoroughly frightened* (I.27).

d. A noun, particularly a noun with verbal force, is sometimes modified by a prepositional phrase; as, **lēgātiōnem ad cīvitātēs**, *the office of envoy to the states* (I.3). (B 353.5n).

151. Adjectives are sometimes used in Latin where in English an adverb or a phrase is required; as, **laetī . . . ad castra pergunt**, *joyfully . . . they advance against the camp* (III.13); **viātōrēs etiam invītōs cōnsistere cōgant**, *they oblige travelers, even against their will, to stop* (IV.5). (AG 290, B 239).

152. *a.* Certain adjectives often designate a part of that to which they refer; as, **in colle mediō**, *halfway up the hill* (I.24); **prīmā nocte**, *in the first part of the night* (I.27); **summus mōns**, *the top of the height* (I.22). The adjectives thus used by Caesar are **extrēmus** (as II.5); **īnfimus** (II.18); **medius; multus** (I.22); **novissimus**, in **novissimum agmen** (I.15 and often), *the rear of a marching column* as the *latest part* of a column to pass a given point; **prīmus**; and **summus**. (AG 293, B 241.1).

b. The adjectives **prīnceps, prior, prīmus** are sometimes used by Caesar to designate the first to do or experience something; as, **prīnceps poenās persolvit**, *was the first to pay the penalty* (I.12); **neque priōrēs bellum īnferre**, *did not take the lead in waging war*, where **prior** is used because only two peoples, the Germans and the Romans, are referred to (IV.7).

c. The adjective **multus** and another adjective agreeing with the same noun are joined by **et** or **-que**; as, **multīs gravibusque vulneribus**, *many severe wounds* (II.25).

153. *a.* The comparative and superlative of both adjectives and adverbs sometimes have shades of meaning best expressed in English by *too, rather, very, exceedingly*, or *highly*, and the like, with the positive; as, **cupidius**, *too eagerly* (I.15); **lātissimō atque altissimō**, *very wide and very deep* (I.2).

b. A superlative is sometimes modified by an adverb; as, **longē nōbilissimus**, *far the highest in rank* (I.2).

c. The highest possible degree is expressed by **quam** with the superlative, as **quam maximum numerum**, *as great a number as possible, the greatest possible number* (I.3); **quam celerrimē potuit**, *as quickly as possible* (I.37); **quam prīmum**, *as soon as possible* (I.40). (B 240.3).

154. *a.* Adjectives and participles are used as substantives, frequently in the plural, less often in the singular; as, **vērī simile**, *probable*, lit. *like truth* (III.13); **nostrī**, *our men* (I.52); **novissimīs**, *for the rear*, lit. *for those last* (I.25); **sua**, *their possessions* (I.11); **prō vīsō**, *as seen*, lit. *for (that which was) seen* (I.22). (AG 288, B 236).

b. Caesar uses the genitive singular neuter **suī** with a collective force in the gerundive construction, and in such cases it should be translated as if plural; as, **suī colligendī facultātem**, *opportunity of collecting their forces*, lit. *of collecting themselves* (III.6). (AG 504c, B 339.5).

PRONOUNS

155. The genitives **meī, nostrī, tuī,** and **vestrī** (see also **39a**) are regularly objective, **nostrum** and **vestrum** being used in other circumstances; as, **tantā contemptiōne nostrī,** *with so great contempt for us* (V.29).

156. The plural is often used for the singular of the pronoun of the first person, just as in our "editorial we"; likewise, when referring to himself as writer, Caesar often uses a plural verb, as, **ut ante dēmōnstrāvimus,** *as we have previously shown* (II.22); **dē quō ante ā nōbis dictum est,** *of whom it has been spoken by us* (V.6). (AG 143a, B 242.3).

157. *a.* The possessive pronouns are expressed only when required for the sake of clearness, emphasis, or contrast; in translating they must be supplied in accordance with English idiom: as, **Cōnsidius, equō admissō,** *Considius with* (*his*) *horse at top speed* (see **144b7**; I.22).

b. When expressed for clearness, and unemphatic, the possessive pronoun follows its noun, as, **in cīvitāte suā,** *in his state* (I.3); when used for emphasis or contrast, the possessive pronoun precedes its noun, as, **meum officium,** _my_ *duty* (IV.25).

c. Caesar often uses **noster** to designate that which is Roman; as, **nostram amīcitiam,** *our friendship* (I.43).

d. A possessive pronoun and a genitive are sometimes coordinated in construction; as, **suō populīque Rōmānī beneficiō,** *with his own kindness and that of the Roman people,* that is, *kindness of himself and of the Roman people* (I.35).

e. **Suus** may mean *his characteristic, his well-known;* as **suā clēmentiā,** *his well-known clemency* (II.14).

158. *a.* The reflexive pronoun of the third person, **sē,** and the corresponding possessive **suus,** refer to the subject of the verb; in a subordinate clause they may refer to the subject of the principal clause (indirect reflexive). Thus, **sē ēripuit,** *he rescued himself* (I.4); **legiō . . . eī grātiās ēgit, quod dē sē optimum iūdicium fēcisset,** *the legion . . . conveyed thanks to him because he had passed an extremely favorable opinion on it* (I.41).

b. In the pronouns of the first and second persons the regular forms are sometimes reflexive.

c. In translating into Latin the English possessives "his," "hers," "its," and "theirs" when referring to the subject of the verb, must be rendered by forms of the reflexive **suus.**

159. Reciprocal relationships are expressed by **inter sē** (lit. *among themselves*), the translation of which must be determined by context; as, **inter sē dant,** *they give to one another* (I.3); **inter sē differunt,** *they differ from one another* (I.1); **inter sē collocūtī,** *having conferred with one another* (IV.30); **cohortātī inter sē,** *urging one another on* (IV.25); **inter sē contenderent,** *they strove together* (I.31); **inter sē,** referring to two persons, *with each other* (V.44). (AG 301f, B 245.1).

160. *a.* The demonstrative pronoun **hīc,** *this,* refers to something near the speaker or the subject of thought; **iste,** *that of yours,* to something near the person addressed; **ille,** *that,* to something more remote; and **is,** *that,* to something thought of in a less definite relation.

b. Caesar frequently uses the demonstrative **is,** less frequently **hīc** and **ille,** where English would use a personal pronoun of the third person; as, **ad eōs,** *to them* (I.1); **cur hunc quisquam discessūrum iūdicāret,** *why should anyone suppose that he* (*Ariovistus*) *would withdraw* (I.40); **illum ūnō diē fēcisse . . .** , *that he* (*Caesar*) *had in one day accomplished* (I.13).

c. Caesar frequently uses the neuter singular and neuter plural of **hīc, ille,** and **is** with the meaning *this* (*thing*), *that* (*thing*), *it, these things, those things;* a noun may sometimes be supplied in translation. Thus, **id quod,** *that* (*course of action*) *which* (I.5); **id eīs persuāsit,** *he persuaded them* (*to*) *that course* (I.2); **illa esse vēra,** *that those statements were true* (I.20).

d. A demonstrative pronoun is sometimes used in Latin where English prefers an article; thus, **ea rēs,** *the matter,* lit. *that thing* (I.4); **eum locum,** *a place* (II.16).

e. A demonstrative pronoun used as subject can be attracted into agreement with a noun in the predicate.

161. *a.* The demonstratives **hīc** and **ille** sometimes refer to what follows; as, **hōc facilius . . . quod,** *the more easily on this* (*account*) *because* (I.2); **multīs dē causīs . . . quārum illa fuit iūstissima . . . quod,** *for many reasons, of which this was the most weighty, that* (IV.16).

b. Caesar sometimes uses **hīc** and **ille** in contrast, with the meaning *the latter* (that last mentioned) and *the former* (that previously mentioned); as, **reliquī . . . sē atque illōs alunt; hī rūrsus annō post in armīs sunt, illī domī remanent,** *the rest support themselves and those in the field; the latter after one year are again in arms, the former remain at home* (IV.I).

c. A conjunction followed by **is** or **hīc** may express an emphatic characterization; as, **legiōnem, neque eam plēnissimam** (sc. **legiōnem**), *the legion, and that lacking its full strength,* lit. *and that not most full* (III.2).

162. *a.* The intensive pronoun **ipse** with nouns and pronouns has the meaning *self, very*; as, **ipsī magistrātūs,** *the magistrates themselves* (I.17); **ipsum esse Dumnorīgem,** *that Dumnorix was the very man* (I.18); **in ipsīs rīpīs,** *on the very banks* (II.23).

b. In subordinate clauses **ipse** may be used as an indirect reflexive referring to the principal subject, or to avoid ambiguity; as, **Ariovistus respondit, sī quid ipsī ā Caesare opus esset,** *Ariovistus answered that if he himself had wanted anything from Caesar,* lit. *if anything were necessary to himself from Caesar* (I.34).

c. Contrasted pronouns are often placed in proximity; as, **sē ipsī interficiunt,** *they all killed one another,* lit. *they themselves slay themselves* (V.37).

163. *a.* A relative pronoun agrees with its antecedent in gender and number, but its case depends upon its construction in the clause to which it belongs; as, **trēs** (**legiōnēs,** fem., pl., acc.), **quae** (fem., pl., nom.) **. . . hiemābant,** *three legions which were wintering* (I.10).

b. A relative referring to two or more antecedents of the same gender and number agrees with them in gender, but in number may agree with the nearest antecedent, or be plural; as, **prō suā clēmentiā ac mānsuētūdine, quam audīrent,** *in accordance with his forbearance and graciousness, of which they were hearing* (II.31); **fīlius et frātris fīlius, . . . quōs . . . ,** *his son and his brother's son, whom . . .* (V.27).

c. A relative referring to two or more antecedents of different gender or number may agree with the nearest antecedent, or be masculine plural in case one antecedent denotes a man, feminine plural in case one antecedent denotes a woman and the other denotes things, or neuter plural in case only things are denoted; thus, **frūmentō** (neut.) **commeātūque, quī** (masc., sing.), *grain and* (*other*) *supplies which . . .* (I.48); **ūsus ac disciplīna, quae** (neut. pl.) **. . . ,** *experience and training, which . . .* (I.40). (AG 305a, B 250.2).

164. *a.* The antecedent of a relative pronoun is sometimes omitted; as, (**eī incolunt**) **quī,** *those inhabit who* (I.1).

b. Caesar sometimes uses a relative referring to an implied antecedent; as, **servīlī tumultū, quōs . . . ,** as if he had said **tumultū servōrum, quōs . . . ,** *in the uprising of the slaves, whom . . .* (I.40). (AG 306b, B 251.2).

c. A noun in predicate attracts a relative pronoun standing as subject into agreement with it; as, **Belgās, quam** (for **quōs**) **tertiam esse Galliae partem dīxerāmus,** *the Belgians who, we had said, form* (lit. *are*) *a third of Gaul* (II.1). (AG 306, B 250.3).

d. A plural relative may refer for its antecedent to a singular collective noun which suggests plurality; as, **equitātum . . . quī videant,** *cavalry . . . to see,* lit. *who should see* (I.15).

165. *a.* An antecedent is sometimes repeated in a relative clause, and need be translated only once; as, **itinera duo, quibus itineribus,** *two routes by which* (I.6). (AG 307a, B 251.3).

b. An appositional antecedent is sometimes incorporated into a relative clause, and should be translated; as, **quod tempus convēnerat,** *the time which had been agreed on* (II.19).

c. An antecedent is often incorporated into a relative clause; as, **cui ratiōnī, . . . hāc,** *by the cunning, . . . for which* (I.40). (AG 307b, B 251.4a).

166. Caesar uses the neuter of a relative or demonstrative pronoun, sometimes both a demonstrative and a relative, referring to a clause or thought as a whole; as, **supplicātiō dēcrēta est, quod . . . ,** *a thanksgiving was decreed, (a distinction) which . . .* (II.35); **magna, id quod necesse erat accidere, perturbātiō facta est,** *a great commotion, as was bound to be the case, ensued* (IV.29).

167. A relative is often used in Latin at the beginning of a clause or sentence where English idiom requires a demonstrative, with or without a connective; as, **quā dē causā,** *and for this reason,* or *for this reason* (I.1); **quī . . . proelium committunt,** *they* (or *and they*) *. . . join battle* (I.15). (AG 308f, B 251.6).

168. Of the indefinite pronouns, Caesar uses **quīdam,** *a certain,* in respect to persons or things distinctly thought of but not described; **aliquis,** *some, any, somebody,* of persons or things referred to in a general way; **quis** and **quī,** *any, some,* after **sī, nisi, seu, nē,** and **ubi;** and **quisquam,** *any at all,* in interrogative or negative clauses or in a clause following a comparative; as, **quāsdam rēs,** *certain things* (I.30); **quīdam ex mīlitibus,** *a certain one* (or *one*) *of the soldiers* (I.42); **alicuius iniūriae,** *of any wrongdoing* (I.14); **sī quid vellent,** *if they wanted anything* (I.7); **cur quisquam iūdicāret,** *why should anyone suppose* (I.40); **prius quam quicquam cōnārētur,** *before taking any measures,* lit. *before he should attempt anything at all* (I.19).

169. Caesar uses the indefinite distributive pronoun **uterque,** *each of two,* in the plural as well as the singular; as, **utrīsque castrīs,** *for each camp* (I.51); **ab utrīsque,** *by those on each side* (IV.26).

170. *a.* Caesar sometimes uses the indefinite distributive pronoun **quisque,** *each,* with a superlative to designate a class, or with a numeral ordinal to indicate a proportion; thus, **nōbilissimī cuiusque līberōs,** *the children of every man of high rank* (I.31); **decimum quemque mīlitem,** *one soldier in ten,* lit. *each tenth soldier* (V.52). (AG 313b, B 252.5).

b. Caesar uses **quisque,** *each,* in close connection with **sē** and **suus;** as, **cum sibi quisque . . . peteret,** *when each one was seeking for himself* (II.11); **utī eōs testēs suae quisque virtūtis habēret,** *that each might have them as witnesses of his own valor* (I.52).

171. *a.* Of the pronominal adjectives, **cēterī** (plural) means *the other, the rest besides those mentioned;* **reliquī,** *the rest* in the sense *those remaining* after some are taken; as, **Aeduōs cēterōsque amīcōs populī Rōmānī,** *the Aeduans and the other friends of the Roman people* (I.35); **reliquōs Gallōs,** *the rest of the Gauls,* after the Helvetians have been singled out (I.1).

b. Caesar repeats **alter** and **alius** in a correlative relation; as, **hārum altera occīsa, altera capta est,** *of these* (*daughters*) *one was killed, the other captured* (I.53); **aliae** (**nāvēs**) *. . .* **aliae** *. . . , some* (*ships*) *. . . others* (IV.28).

c. Caesar repeats **alius** with the sense *one . . . one, another . . . another;* as, **legiōnēs aliae aliā in parte resisterent,** *legions were offering resistance, one at one point, another at another* (II.22).

VERBS

AGREEMENT, MOODS AND TENSES, QUESTIONS

172. *a.* A finite verb agrees with its subject in number and person; in compound forms of the verb the participle must agree with the subject also in gender. Thus, **Orgetorīx dēligitur,** *Orgetorix is chosen* (I.3); **ea rēs est ēnūntiāta,** *that matter* (lit. *thing*) *was made known* (I.4).

b. When a verb is used with more than one subject, it may agree with the nearest subject, or be plural; as, **fīlia et ūnus ē fīliīs captus est,** *a daughter and one of the sons were taken captive* (I.26); **Nammeius et Verucloetius . . . obtinēbant,** *Nammeius and Verucloetius held* (I.7).

c. Verbs are sometimes used in the third person plural with an implied indefinite subject, as, **dīcunt**, *they say* (V.12).

d. A verb in Latin is sometimes used with a personal subject where the English prefers the impersonal construction with "it"; as, **Quod nōn fore dictō audientēs . . . dīcantur**, *As to the fact that it was said that they would not be obedient*, lit. *that they are said not to be about to be obedient.* (I.40).

173. *a.* When two subjects express a single idea, the verb may be singular; as, **Matrona et Sēquana dīvidit**, *the Marne and the Seine separate . . .* , the two rivers being thought of as forming one boundary (I.1). (AG 317b, B 255.3).

b. A plural verb may be used with a singular noun, or with an unexpressed subject representing a singular noun, where the sense suggests plurality; as, **cum tanta multitūdō lapidēs conicerent**, *when so great a multitude were hurling stones* (II.6). (AG 317d, B 254.4).

174. Caesar occasionally uses a passive verb or participle in a reflexive sense; as, **sublevātī**, *supporting themselves* (I.48); **armārī**, *to arm themselves* (IV.32). (B 256.1).

175. *a.* The present, imperfect, and future tenses represent an action as going on in present, past, or future time; as, **eōrumque agrōs populābantur**, *and were laying waste their country* (I.11). (AG 470, B 260.2).

b. In vivid narration Caesar often thinks of past events as in progress and uses the present indicative (historical present). In translating the historical present, one can retain the present tense for its vividness or restore the past time to the narration, since the deeds described did in fact happen in the past; as, **dīcit līberius**, *he spoke* (or, lit., *speaks*) *more freely* (I.18).

c. The present is used in statements true at all times (universal present), and statements about customs; as, **hominēs id, quod [crēdere] volunt, crēdunt**, *men readily believe what they wish to believe* (III.18).

d. The imperfect may be used of repeated or customary action; as, **perīclitābātur**, *he kept trying* (II.8); **adoriēbantur . . . circumsistēbant . . . coniciēbant**, *would attack . . . would surround . . . would hurl* (IV.26). (AG 470, B 260.2).

e. The imperfect is sometimes used of attempted action (conative imperfect); as, **nostrōs intrā mūnītiōnēs ingredī prohibēbant**, *were trying to prevent our men from getting inside the fortification* (V.9).

f. The imperfect with **iam**, used of an action already in progress for a considerable period, should be translated with a progressive pluperfect; as, **Cum iam amplius hōrīs sex pugnārētur**, *when fighting had now been going on more than six hours* (III.5).

176. *a.* Caesar generally uses the historical perfect, as **discessit**, *he withdrew* (I.14); occasionally he uses the perfect in the sense of the English present perfect, as **nōn vēnērunt**, *they have not come*.

b. The perfect and pluperfect of **nōscō, cognōscō, cōnsuēscō** express a state resulting from action, and are generally best translated by the present and imperfect; as, **nōvērunt**, *they are familiar with*, lit. *have come to know* (VI.15); **īre cōnsuērant**, *were accustomed (had become accustomed) to go* (III.1). The perfect and pluperfect of **meminī** and **ōdī** also are translated by the present and imperfect.

c. The Latin future perfect is used with great precision where frequently in English a future or present tense might be used: as, **meum officium praestiterō**, *I shall have done my duty*, where an English speaker would likely say, *I shall do my duty* (IV.25).

177. *a.* In the sequence of tenses a primary tense (present, future, or future perfect) in the principal clause is ordinarily followed by a primary tense in the subordinate clause (present or perfect subjunctive); and a secondary tense (imperfect, perfect, or pluperfect) of the principal clause by a past tense in the subordinate clause (imperfect or pluperfect subjunctive). Thus, **mercātōribus est aditus ut, quae bellō cēperint, quibus vēndant, habeant**, *traders have access (to them) . . . that they may have purchasers for the things that they have captured in war*, lit. *that they may have (those) to whom they may sell (those things) which they have taken in war* (IV.2); **equitātumque, quī sustinēret impetum, mīsit**, *and he sent his cavalry to sustain the attack* (I.24).

b. A historical present in the principal clause is sometimes followed by a primary tense, sometimes by a secondary tense, in the subordinate clause; as, **diem dīcunt, quā diē ... conveniant,** *they set a day on which they were* (lit. *are*) *to come together* (I.6); **pontem, quī erat ad Genavam, iubet rescindī,** *he gave* (lit. *gives*) *orders that the bridge, which was near Geneva, be cut down* (I.7). (AG 485e, B 268.3).

c. A verb in a subordinate clause containing a statement of fact or a general truth may be in the present tense even though the verb of the principal clause is in a past tense; as, **eīs persuāsit, quod Helvetiī .. . continentur,** *he persuaded them, because the Helvetians are hemmed in* (I.2).

178. The tenses of the infinitive in indirect discourse express time relative to that of the verbs on which they depend, the present infinitive expressing the same time as the governing verb; the perfect infinitive, time earlier than that of the governing verb; and the future infinitive, time later than that of the governing verb. Thus, **nōn sē hostem verērī ... dīcēbant,** *were saying that they did not fear the enemy* (I.39); **illum fēcisse intellegerent,** *they understood that he had done* (I.13); **Caesar ... sēsē eōs ... cōnservātūrum** [**esse**] **dīxit,** *Caesar said that he would spare their lives* (II.15).

179. *a.* Direct questions in Latin are introduced by question words and are of two kinds:

(1) Single questions, introduced by interrogative pronouns and adverbs, or by the enclitic **-ne** attached to the emphatic word of the question and asking for information, by **nōnne** implying the answer "Yes," or **num** implying the answer "No." Thus: **quem locum ... exspectās?** *what* (*kind of a*) *chance are you waiting for* (V.44)? **Audīsne?** *Do you hear?* **Nōnne audīs?** *Do you not hear?* **Num audīs?** *You don't hear, do you?*

(2) Double questions, which ordinarily have **utrum** or the enclitic **-ne** in the first member, and **an,** *or,* or **annōn,** *or not,* in the second; as, **utrum officium, an timor, plūs valet,** *is sense of duty, or cowardice, stronger?* The first member of a double question may be omitted, **an** alone introducing the second; as, **an ... dubitātis?** *do you have* (*any*) *doubt?*

b. In indirect discourse Caesar uses rhetorical questions, implying a negative answer, doubt, or perplexity; these in the direct form would have had the indicative, or the deliberative subjunctive. Thus:

(1) Indicative in the direct form: **num ... memoriam dēpōnere posse?** *could he lay aside the recollection?* As a direct question: **num ... memoriam dēpōnere possum,** *can I put aside the recollection?* implying the answer "No"; as when we say "How can I do that?" meaning, emphatically, "I cannot do that" (I.14).

(2) Deliberative subjunctive in the direct form: **cūr quisquam ... iūdicāret,** *why should anyone infer?* in the direct form, **cūr iūdicet?** (I.40); **neque satīs Brūtō ... centuriōnibusque ... cōnstābat, quid agerent,** *and Brutus and the centurions ... did not quite know what to do,* lit. *and it was not quite clear to Brutus and the centurions ... what they should do*; as a direct question, **Quid agāmus?** *What are we to do?* (III.14).

180. *a.* Caesar occasionally uses the subjunctive in the first person to express an exhortation (hortatory subjunctive).

b. Caesar occasionally uses the subjunctive in the third person to express a command (jussive subjunctive).

c. A wish capable of realization is expressed by the present subjunctive, often with **utinam**; as, **utinam redeant,** *may they return!*

d. A wish incapable of realization is expressed in present time by **utinam** with the imperfect subjunctive and in past time by **utinam** with the pluperfect subjunctive; as, **utinam adessent,** *if only they were here* (but they are not); **utinam redīssent,** *if only they had come back* (but they did not).

181. *a.* Caesar occasionally uses the imperative in direct quotations, as, **Dēsilīte,** *Jump down* (IV.25).

b. Caesar uses the imperatives **nōlī, nōlīte** with the infinitive to express prohibition; as, **nōlīte hōs vestrō auxiliō exspoliāre,** *do not* (lit. *be unwilling to*) *rob them of your assistance.*

182. Caesar occasionally uses an infinitive in a principal clause in the place of an imperfect or perfect indicative (historical infinitive), the subject being in the nominative; as, **Caesar Aeduōs frūmentum**

flāgitāre, *Caesar kept pressing the Aeduans for the grain* (I.16); **hostēs . . . signō datō dēcurrere**, *the enemy at a given signal rushed down* (III.4). (AG 463, B 335).

CLAUSES
CAUSAL AND TEMPORAL, RELATIVE, AND PURPOSE AND RESULT

183. *a.* In causal clauses introduced by quod and quoniam Caesar uses the indicative when the reason is stated as that of Caesar the writer, the subjunctive when the reason is presented as someone else's. Thus, in Dumnorīx . . . Helvētiīs erat amīcus, quod . . . dūxerat, Dumnorix was friendly to the Helvetians, because he had taken . . . , the quod-clause contains Caesar's explanation of the reason why Dumnorix favored the Helvetians (I.9); in eī grātiās ēgit, quod optimum iūdicium fēcisset, thanked him because (as the delegation said) he had passed a most favorable judgment, the quod-clause here has the subjunctive because it presents the reason given by the delegation for the expression of thanks (I.41). (AG 540, B 286.1).

b. In causal clauses Caesar sometimes uses the subjunctive of a verb of saying or thinking to introduce a statement of a reason ascribed to someone else.

c. The subjunctive introduced by **nōn quod**, *not because*, or **quam quō** (= **quam eō quod**), *than because*, may be used to express an alleged or assumed reason; as, **quam quō . . . dēsīderent**, *than because they desire* (IV.2).

184. *a.* A causal clause introduced by **cum**, *since*, has its verb in the subjunctive; as, **cum . . . persuādēre nōn possent**, *since they were not able to persuade* (I.9). (AG 549, B 286.2).

b. Caesar sometimes uses the adverb **praesertim**, *especially*, to make prominent the causal idea in a clause introduced by **cum**; as, **praesertim cum eōrum precibus adductus bellum suscēperit**, *especially since he, prevailed upon by their entreaties, had undertaken the campaign* (I.16).

185. *a.* Cum temporal, *when*, referring to the present or future is used with the indicative; as, **cum . . . premuntur**, *when they are overwhelmed* (VI.13).

b. With **cum** temporal, *when*, and **cum prīmum**, *as soon as*, referring to past time, Caesar uses the indicative when the force of **cum** is purely temporal; as, **cum prīmum potuit**, *as soon as he could* (III.9).

c. With **cum** temporal, *when*, and **cum prīmum**, *as soon as*, referring to past time, Caesar uses the subjunctive when an idea of circumstance, condition, or cause is involved; as, **cum ferrum sē īnflexisset**, *when (i.e. when and because) the iron had become bent*, lit. *had bent itself* (I.25); **cum prīmum pābulī cōpia esse inciperet**, *as soon as (and because) there began to be plenty of forage* (II.2). (AG 546, B 288.1).

186. *a.* Caesar sometimes uses **cum** temporal or **ubi** with the indicative to denote recurrent action; as, **cum ūsus est**, *whenever it is necessary* (IV.2). (B 288.b3).

b. Caesar sometimes uses **cum** temporal correlatively with the adverb **tum** in the sense *not only . . . but also, but, both . . . and*; as, **cum omnis iuventūs . . . convēnerant, tum nāvium quod ubīque fuerat**, *not only* (lit. *when*) *had all the youth . . . assembled but* (lit. *then*) *all the ships they had* (III.16). (B 290.2).

187. Caesar sometimes uses **cum** adversative, *although, while*, with the subjunctive; as, **cum ea ita sint**, *although those things are true* (I.14). (AG 549, B 309). (B 283.3b).

188. *a.* Caesar uses the temporal conjunctions **ubi, ut**, *when*, **postquam**, *after*, **posteā quam** (written as two words) *after that, after*, and **simul atque, simul**, *as soon as*, with the indicative, usually in the perfect tense. Thus, **quod ubi Caesar resciit**, *when Caesar found this out* (I.28); **postquam Caesar pervēnit**, *after Caesar arrived* (I.27); **simul atque sē recēpērunt**, *as soon as they rallied* (IV.27). (AG 543).

b. The conjunction **ut**, *as*, introducing a comparison, is used with the indicative; as, **ut . . . nōluerant, ita**, *as they had been unwilling, so . . .* (II.1).

c. **Ubi prīmum,** *as soon as* (lit. *when first*), is used with the perfect indicative; as, **ubi prīmum nostrōs equitēs cōnspexērunt,** *as soon as they saw our horsemen* (IV.12).

d. The pluperfect indicative with **ubi** may denote a repeated action; as, **ubi . . . cōnspexerant,** *whenever they saw,* lit. *when they had seen* (IV.26).

189. *a.* Caesar uses **prius quam,** *until, before,* with the indicative to denote an actual occurrence or a fact; as, **neque prius fugere dēstitērunt quam ad flūmen Rhēnum . . . pervēnērunt,** *and they did not stop their flight until they reached the river Rhine* (I.53).

b. Caesar uses **prius quam** and **ante quam,** *sooner than, before,* with the subjunctive, implying expectancy or purpose in an action; as, **prius quam sē hostēs reciperent,** *before the enemy could rally* (II.12). (AG 551b, B 292).

190. *a.* Caesar uses **dum** temporal in the sense of *while* with the indicative historical present; in the sense of *so long as, while,* with the indicative present, imperfect, and perfect. Thus, **dum ea conquīruntur,** *while those things were* (lit. *are*) *being sought out* (I.27). (AG 556, B 293.1).

b. Caesar uses **dum,** *until,* with the subjunctive to denote intention or expectancy; as, **dum . . . Helvētiī pervenīrent,** *until the Helvetians should reach* (I.11). (AG 553, B 293.III.2).

c. Caesar uses **quoad** in the temporal sense of *so long as, until,* with the indicative; in the sense of *until* denoting intention or expectancy, with the subjunctive. Thus, **quoad potuit,** *so long as he could* (IV.12); **quoad ipse propius . . . accessisset,** *until he himself should have come up nearer* (IV.11). (AG 553, B 293.III.2).

191. *a.* Caesar uses the adversative conjunctions **etsī, tametsī,** *although,* with the indicative; as, **etsī . . . vidēbat,** *although he saw* (I.46).

b. Concessive **ut,** meaning *granted that, although,* is followed by the subjunctive; as, **ut omnia contrā opīniōnem accidant,** *granted that everything turn out contrary to expectation* (in indirect form, III.9). (AG 527a, B 308).

192. Relative clauses introduced by a relative or general relative pronoun have their verb in the indicative unless an idea of purpose, characteristic, cause, result, or condition is involved; as, **Allobrogum, quī nūper pācātī erant,** *of the Allobroges, who had lately been subdued* (I.6); **quaecumque pars castrōrum . . . premī vidēbātur,** *whenever any part* (lit. *whatever part*) *of the camp seemed to be hard pressed* (III.4).

193. *a.* A relative clause of purpose may be introduced by **quī** (= **ut is,** *in order that he*), or by the relative adverbs **quō** (= **ut eō**), **quā** (= **ut eā**), and has its verb in the subjunctive; as, **lēgātōs mittunt** (historical present) **nōbilissimōs cīvitātis . . . quī dīcerent,** *they sent as envoys the citizens of highest rank to say,* lit. *who should say* (I.7); **quō gravius hominēs . . . doleant,** *in order that men may more bitterly suffer* (I.14); see also **247.** (AG 531.2, B 282.2).

b. In relative clauses of purpose **quō** is generally used with a comparative; as, **quō facilius . . . possit,** *that he might* (lit. *may*) *be more easily able* (I.8). (AG 531.2a, B 282.1a).

194. *a.* A relative clause with the subjunctive, introduced by a relative pronoun or relative adverb, may characterize an indefinite antecedent (clause of characteristic); as, **itinera duo, quibus itineribus . . . exīre possent,** *two routes by which they could go out,* i.e. *two routes of such a character that by them they could go out* (I.6); **nihil [eīs] erat quō famem tolerārent,** *they had nothing with which they could satisfy their hunger* (I.28). (AG 535, B 283).

b. A clause of characteristic may be used after a comparative; as **nōn longius aberant quam quō tēlum adigī posset,** *were already within range,* lit. *not further away than* (the distance) *to which a spear could be thrown* (II.21). (AG 571a, B 283.2a).

c. A relative clause with the subjunctive may have causal force; as, **Catuvolcus . . . dētestātus Ambiorīgem, quī eius cōnsiliī auctor fuisset, . . . sē exanimāvit,** *having cursed Ambiorix, since he* (lit. *who*) *had been the originator of that scheme, Catuvolcus killed himself* (VI.31). (AG 535e, B 283.3a).

d. A relative clause with the subjunctive may have adversative force; as, **Cicerō, quī . . . mīlitēs in**

castrīs continuisset, *Cicero, although he had kept the soldiers in camp* (VI.36).

e. A relative clause with the subjunctive may have conditional force.

f. A restrictive clause may be introduced by the relative **quod** and have the subjunctive; as, **quod . . . posset,** *so far as he might be able,* (lit. *that*) *which,* etc. (I.35). (AG 535d, B 283.5).

195. A relative clause of result may be introduced by **quī** (= **ut is,** *so that he*), or **quīn** (= **quī nōn, quae nōn, quod nōn**), and have its verb in the subjunctive; as, **nēmō est tam fortis, quīn reī novitāte perturbētur,** *no one (of them) was so strong that he was not upset by the unexpectedness of the occurrence* (VI.39).

196. *a.* Clauses of purpose in Caesar are most often introduced by **ut, utī,** *in order that, that,* or **nē,** *in order that not, lest,* and have their verb in the subjunctive; as, **ut spatium intercēdere posset,** *in order that a period of time might be able to intervene* (I.7); **id nē accideret,** *in order that this might not happen* (I.38). (AG 530, 531; B 282).

b. In clauses of purpose Caesar uses **nē . . . nēve (neu)** in the sense of *that not . . . nor,* and **ut (utī) . . . nēve (neu)** in the sense of *that . . . and that not,* with the subjunctive; as, **ut . . . eārum rērum vīs minuerētur, neu pontī nocērent,** *that the force of these things might be lessened and that they might not damage the bridge* (IV.17).

197. *a.* Clauses of result are most often introduced by **ut** or **utī,** *so that, that* (negative **nōn**), and have their verb in the subjunctive; as, **ut perpaucī prohibēre possent,** *so that a very few (men) could stop them* (I.6); **ut . . . iūdicārī nōn possit,** *that it cannot be determined* (I.12). (AG 537.1, B 284.1).

b. Clauses of result are often preceded by a word of measure or quality, **tam, tantus, ita, sīc,** etc.; as, **tanta rērum commūtātiō est facta, ut nostrī . . . proelium redintegrārent,** *so great a change was brought about that our (men) renewed the fight* (II.27); **sīc mūniēbātur, ut magnam . . . daret facultātem,** *was so fortified that it afforded a great resource* (I.38).

c. A clause of result with the subjunctive may be introduced by **quam** after a comparative, with or without **ut**; as, **pulverem maiōrem, quam cōnsuētūdō ferret,** *a cloud of dust greater than usual,* lit. *greater than (so that) an ordinary condition would bring it* (IV.32).

SUBSTANTIVE (NOUN) CLAUSES

198. *a.* Substantive clauses are used as subject of a verb, as object of a verb, and in other relations similar to those in which nouns are used.

b. A substantive clause introduced by **quod,** meaning *the fact that, that,* has its verb in the indicative, and may stand as subject, or predicate, or object of a verb, or in apposition. Thus, **magnō erat impedīmentō, quod . . . neque . . . poterant,** *A great hindrance . . . was the fact that they were able neither to . . . ,* the **quod**-clause being the subject of **erat** (I.25); **causa mittendī fuit quod . . . volēbat,** *the reason for sending was the fact that he wanted . . . ,* the **quod**-clause being in predicate, explaining *causa* (III.1); **multae rēs in prīmīs quod . . . vidēbat,** *many circumstances, first of all the fact that he saw . . . ,* the **quod**-clause being in apposition with **rēs** (I.33). (AG 572, B 299.1a).

c. A substantive clause introduced by **quod,** meaning *as to the fact that, as regards the fact that,* may have the force of an accusative or ablative of specification. Thus, **quod . . . ēnūntiārit,** *as to the fact that he had reported*; in the direct form, **quod ēnūntiāvī,** *as to the fact that I have reported* (I.17). (B 299.2).

199. *a.* Substantive clauses with the subjunctive introduced by **ut,** or **utī,** *that,* and **nē,** *that not,* are used after verbs of *commanding, urging, reminding, asking, persuading, conceding* and *permitting, deciding, striving*; the subjunctive may often best be translated by an infinitive. Thus, **Allobrogibus imperāvit, ut . . . cōpiam facerent,** *ordered the Allobroges to furnish* (lit. *that they should furnish*) *a supply* (I.28); **persuādet Casticō . . . ut rēgnum . . . occupāret,** *persuades Casticus to seize the kingly power* (I.3). (AG 563, B 295.1).

Such verbs and phrases used by Caesar are:

(1) Commanding: **imperō**, *order*; **mandō**, *command* (I.47); **negōtium dō**, *assign the task* (II.2); **praecipiō**, *enjoin, direct* (I.22).

(2) Urging: **cohortor**, *encourage* (II.21); **hortor**, *urge* (I.19); **sollicitō**, *press* (III.8).

(3) Reminding: **admoneō**, *admonish* (V.49); **moneō**, *warn* (I.20).

(4) Asking: **dēprecor**, *beg to escape* (II.31); **ōrō**, *beg* (IV.16); **obsecrō**, *beseech* (I.20); **obtestor**, *pray* (IV.25); **petō**, *ask earnestly* (I.28); **postulō**, *demand* (I.34); **rogō**, *ask* (I.7).

(5) Persuading: **addūcō**, *prevail upon* (I.31); **persuādeō**, *persuade*; **impellō**, *incite* (IV.16).

(6) Conceding and permitting: **concēdō**, *grant* (III.18); **patior**, *suffer, allow* (I.45); **permittō**, *permit* (I.35).

(7) Deciding: **cēnseō**, *decree* (I.35); **cōnstituō**, *determine* (II.10); **placuit**, *it pleased* (I.34); **sanciō**, *bind* (I.30).

(8) Striving: **agō**, *arrange* (I.41); **contendō**, *strive* (I.31); **dō operam**, *take pains* (V.7); **impetrō**, *obtain one's request* (I.9); **labōrō**, *put forth effort* (I.31).

b. Such verbs are sometimes used impersonally in the passive, the substantive clause taking the place of a subject; as **erat eī praeceptum, nē proelium committeret**, *he had been ordered not to join battle*, lit. *it had been ordered to him that he should not join battle* (I.22). (AG 566).

c. With such verbs the substantive clause is sometimes replaced by the infinitive, with or without a subject accusative; as, **loquī concēditur**, *permission is given to speak* (VI.20); **hās [nāvēs] āctuāriās imperat fierī**, *he orders that these (ships) be built for fast movement* (V.1).

d. As a negative connective between substantive subjunctive clauses Caesar uses **nēve** (before vowels and **h**) and **neu** (before consonants), with the meaning *and that . . . not*, or *that . . . not*.

200. *a.* In substantive clauses with **ut** after **admoneō, cohortor, cōnstituō, imperō, mandō, nūntiō,** *order*, **postulō**, *demand*, and **rogō**, *ask*, and a few phrases, the **ut** is sometimes omitted; as, **rogat fīnem ōrandī faciat**, *asks him to make an end of his pleading* (I.20).

b. **Iubeō**, *order, bid*, and **vetō**, *forbid*, are regularly used by Caesar with the infinitive and subject accusative; **cōnor**, *attempt*, with the infinitive; as, **quemque efferre iubent**, *they order that each person carry away* (I.5); **exsequī cōnārētur**, *attempted to enforce* (I.4).

201. *a.* Substantive clauses with the subjunctive introduced by **nē**, *that not*, **quō minus**, *that not* (lit. *by which the less*), and **quīn**, *that not,* are used after verbs of *hindering, preventing*, and *refusing*; the conjunction often may best be rendered by *from* with a gerund. Thus, **hōs . . . dēterrēre nē frūmentum cōnferant**, *these through fear were holding back (the people) from furnishing the grain* (I.17); **retinērī nōn potuerant quīn . . . tēla conicerent**, *could not be restrained from hurling spears* (I.47). Such verbs used by Caesar are: **dēterreō**, *hold back through fear*; **recūsō**, *refuse* (I.31); **retineō**, *restrain*; **temperō**, *restrain one's self* (I.33); **teneō**, *hold back* (IV.22). (AG 558b, B 295.3).

b. Substantive clauses with the subjunctive introduced by **quīn** are used also after general expressions of doubt and negation, **quīn** being translated *that*. Thus, **nōn esse dubium, quīn . . .**, *that there was no doubt that* (I.3); **neque abest suspīciō . . . quīn**, *and there is ground for suspecting that*, lit. *and there is not lacking suspicion that* (I.4). (AG 558, B 298).

c. After **dubitō**, meaning *doubt*, Caesar uses a substantive clause with **quīn** and the subjunctive; after **dubitō**, *hesitate*, generally the infinitive, occasionally a clause with **quīn**. Thus, **nōn dubitāre quīn . . . sūmat**, *he did not doubt that he (Ariovistus) would inflict* (I.31); **trānsīre flūmen nōn dubitāvērunt**, *did not hesitate to cross the river* (II.23); **dubitandum nōn exīstimāvit quīn . . . proficīscerētur**, *thought that he ought not to hesitate to set out* (II.2). (AG 558a, B 298).

202. Substantive clauses with the subjunctive introduced by **ut** and **nē** are used after verbs of *fearing*; after such verbs **ut** is to be translated *that not*, and **nē**, *that*, or *lest*. Thus, **nē . . . offenderet verēbātur**, *was afraid that he might offend* (I.19); **ut . . . supportārī posset, timēre dīcēbant**, *were saying that they feared that (the supply of grain) could not be brought up* (I.39).

203. Clauses of result introduced by **ut** or **utī** and **ut nōn** are used as substantive clauses in four ways:

(**1**) As the subject of impersonal verbs; thus, **fīēbat ut . . . vagārentur**, *it came about that they wandered* (I.2); **accēdēbat ut . . . tempestātem ferrent**, *there was the additional fact that they weathered the storm* (III.13). The more important impersonal forms thus used by Caesar are **accēdēbat; accidit,** *it happened* (IV.29); **fīēbat; factum est** (III.19); **factum esse** (I.31), **fierī** (II.4); **relinquēbātur,** *the result was,* lit. *it was left* (V.19); and the future infinitive of **sum** in both forms, **futūrum esse** (I.10, 20, 31), and **fore** (I.42). (AG 569.2, B 297.2).

(**2**) As predicate or appositive with **cōnsuētūdō est** and **iūs est**; thus, **ea cōnsuētūdō esset, ut mātrēs familiae . . . dēclārārent**, *there was the custom that the matrons should declare* (I.50).

(**3**) As the object after verbs of action and accomplishment; thus, **committeret ut is locus . . . nōmen caperet,** lit. *bring it about that the place . . . should assume a name* (I.13); **commeātūs ut . . . portārī possent, efficiēbat,** *made it possible for supplies to be brought,* lit. *was accomplishing that supplies could be brought* (II.5). The verbs thus used by Caesar are **committō, efficiō, perficiō** (I.9). (AG 568, B 297.1).

(**4**) As appositive of a noun or neuter pronoun whose meaning the **ut**-clause defines; thus, **poenam, ut īgnī cremārētur,** *the penalty of being burned by fire,* lit. *that he should be burned by fire* (I.4); **id, quod cōnstituerant . . . ut ē fīnibus suīs exeant,** *that which they had resolved upon, a migration from their country,* lit. *that they should go out from their territories* (I.5). (AG 561a, 570; B 297).

204. Indirect questions are used as substantive clauses after expressions of inquiry, narration, deliberation, and uncertainty, and have the subjunctive. The following types of indirect questions are used by Caesar:

(**1**) Introduced by the interrogative particle **-ne** (V.27) or **num** (I.14) in single questions; in double questions, by the correlative particles **utrum . . . an,** *whether . . . or* (I.40); **utrum . . . necne,** *whether . . . or not,* **necne** representing **annōn** of the direct form (I.50); **-ne . . . an,** *whether . . . or;* **-ne . . . an . . . an,** *whether . . . or . . . or* (IV.14); **-ne . . . -ne,** *whether . . . or;* and **an** alone, **utrum** being omitted, *or.* Thus, **cōnsultum [esse], utrum īgnī statim necārētur an . . . reservārētur,** *that counsel was taken whether he should at once be put to death by fire, or saved for another occasion* (I.53). (AG 335, B 300.4).

(**2**) Introduced by an interrogative pronoun or adjective; as, **Dumnorīgī cūstōdēs pōnit, ut, quae agat, quibuscum loquātur, scīre possit,** (*Caesar*) *set guards over Dumnorix in order to be able to know what things he did, with whom he talked* (I.20). (AG 574, B 300.1).

(**3**) Introduced by pronominal adjectives, and adverbs used interrogatively; as, **in utram partem fluat,** *in which direction it flows* (I.12). Adjectives and adverbs thus used by Caesar are **quālis,** *of what sort* (I.21); **quam** with an adjective, *how* (I.43); **quantus,** *how great* (I.17); **quem ad modum,** *in what way* (I.36); **uter,** *which;* **cūr,** *why* (I.40); **quārē,** *wherefore, why* (I.45); **quō,** *to where* (III.16); **quot,** *how many;* **quotiēns,** *how often* (I.43); **unde,** *from where* (V.53); **ut,** *how* (I.43). (AG 574, B 300.1).

(**4**) Introduced by **sī,** *if, whether,* after verbs of effort and expectation; as, **sī perrumpere possent, cōnātī,** *having attempted (to see) whether they could break through* (I.8). (AG 576a, B 300.3).

CONDITIONAL SENTENCES

There are three types of conditions in Caesar: conditions of fact (general and specific), conditions of possible realization, and conditions contrary to fact. Conditions contain a protasis (the if-clause) and an apodosis (the then-clause).

205. General conditions of fact are introduced by **sī,** *if,* with the indicative in both protasis and apodosis, the protasis implying customary or repeated action; **sī** is almost equivalent to *whenever.* Thus:

(**1**) Present tense in both protasis and apodosis: **sī quī ex reliquīs excellit, succēdit,** *if anyone of the rest is preeminent, he becomes the successor* of the arch-druid (VI.13).

(**2**) Imperfect tense in both protasis and apodosis: **sī quid erat dūrius, concurrēbant,** *if there was* *unusually serious difficulty* (lit. *if there was anything rather hard*), *they would rush to the rescue* (I.48).

(**3**) Perfect tense in the protasis, present in the apodosis: **sī compertum est, interficiunt,** *if the fact* (*of crime*) *has been established, they kill* (VI.19).

(**4**) Pluperfect tense in the protasis, imperfect in the apodosis: **sī quī . . . equō dēciderat, circumsistēbant,** *if anyone had fallen from his horse, they would gather around him* (I.48).

206. Specific conditions of fact are introduced by **sī,** *if,* or **nisi,** *unless,* with the indicative in the protasis, and the indicative or imperative in the apodosis. Thus:

(**1**) Present indicative in both protasis and apodosis.

(**2**) Present indicative in the protasis, present imperative in the apodosis: **dēsilīte . . . nisi vultis aquilam hostibus prōdere,** *jump down, unless you wish to abandon your eagle to the enemy* (IV.25).

(**3**) Future perfect indicative in the protasis, future indicative in the apodosis: **sī gravius quid acciderit, ratiōnem reposcent,** *if any disaster shall befall them* (lit. *anything rather heavy shall have happened*), *they will demand an accounting* (V.30).

207. Conditions of possible realization are introduced by **sī,** *if,* **nisi,** *unless,* or **sīn,** *but if,* with the subjunctive in the protasis, and the potential subjunctive (or the indicative, emphasizing the situation as an actual one) in the apodosis; thus:

(**1**) Present subjunctive in both protasis and apodosis: **quī, sī per tē liceat, . . . cum reliquīs bellī cāsum sustineant,** *if they should have your permission, they would share the fortune of war with the rest* (V.30).

(**2**) Present subjunctive in the protasis, present indicative in the apodosis: **neque, aliter sī faciat, ūllam habet auctōritātem,** *and if* (*a leading man*) *should do otherwise, he has no influence at all* (VI.11).

208. *a.* Conditions contrary to fact are introduced by **sī,** *if,* or **nisi,** *unless,* with the subjunctive in both protasis and apodosis, the imperfect referring to present time, the pluperfect to past time.

b. The indicative is used in the apodosis of conditions contrary to fact when an idea of necessity, propriety, or possibility is present; as, **sī populus Rōmānus alicuius iniūriae sibi cōnscius fuisset, nōn fuit difficile cavēre,** *if the Roman people had been conscious of any wrongdoing, it would not have been* (lit. *was not*) *difficult* (*for them*) *to take precautions* (from the indirect form in I.14). (AG 437a, 517c; B 304.3a).

c. The imperfect subjunctive, referring to past time, may be used in conditions contrary to fact, if a lasting state of affairs is implied; as, **sī quid mihi ā Caesare opus esset, ad eum vēnissem,** *If I had wanted* (*or now wanted*) *anything from Caesar, I should have come to him* (from the indirect form in I.34).

209. In the protasis of a conditional sentence, an ablative absolute, a participle, or another form of expression implying a condition, may be used in place of the clause with **sī;** as, **datā facultāte,** taking the place of **sī facultās data esset,** *if an opportunity should have been granted,* in the direct form, **sī facultās data erit** (I.7); **damnātum** (**eum**), *him, if condemned,* **damnātum** taking the place of **sī damnātus esset** (I.4). (AG 496, B 337.2b).

210. Caesar has conditional clauses of comparison with the subjunctive introduced by **velut sī, quasi,** and **proinde ac sī.** Thus: **quod . . . absentis Ariovistī crūdēlitātem velut sī cōram adesset, horrērent,** that is . . . **velut horrērent, sī cōram adesset, horrērent,** *because they dreaded Ariovistus's cruelty when he was away just as* (*they would dread it*) *if he were present* (I.32). (AG 524, B 307).

DIRECT AND INDIRECT QUOTATION
INDIRECT DISCOURSE

211. *a.* Caesar presents the language of another person in two ways, in direct quotation or in indirect quotation, with the latter being a form of indirect discourse.

b. In direct quotation Caesar quotes words spoken directly to him, as well as:

(1) Words reported to him, presumably by his officers, such as the exhortation of the unnamed standard-bearer of the Tenth Legion when landing on the British shore, if this was spoken outside of Caesar's hearing (IV.25), and the challenge of Pullo to Vorenus (V.44).

(2) Words or speeches, sometimes in dialects foreign to Caesar, which he presents in his own language, but throws into the form of direct quotation in order to enhance the effect.

212. *a.* In indirect quotation, or indirect discourse in the narrower sense, Caesar in most cases aims to present not a word-for-word reproduction of what was said or written, but a summary, as brief as possible, of the main points. For example, in order to move to action the other prominent Helvetians, and carry through the negotiations with Casticus and Dumnorix, Orgetorix must have had many conferences, extending over a considerable period of time; yet the gist of the argument by which, according to Caesar, he persuaded the whole Helvetian nation to migrate, is given in ten words of indirect discourse (I.2), while the gist of the argument by which Casticus and Dumnorix were induced to join him in forming a triumvirate of usurpation is summarized in thirty-one words (I.3).

b. The kind of summary found in the longer passages of Caesar's indirect discourse has a parallel in the condensed reports of addresses in newspapers. A reporter, sent to prepare a synopsis of a lecture on the moon an hour in length, might return to the office to find his space reduced to sixty words; he might nevertheless summarize the main points thus: "The lecturer said *that the moon is nearly two hundred and thirty-nine thousand miles from the earth; that under the telescope it has the appearance of a dead planet; that most careful observations have failed to detect the presence of air or water; and that, notwithstanding the moon's brightness, due to reflection, its surface must be as cold as ice.*"

c. In a manner somewhat similar, but with marvelous clearness and cogency in view of the amount of material condensed, Caesar in indirect discourse presents summarizing statements, or outlines, including:

(1) Conferences with Gallic and German leaders, conducted no doubt haltingly through interpreters; such as with Divico (I.13, 14), Liscus and other Aeduans (I.17, 18), the Gallic delegation (I.30-33), and Ariovistus (I.43-45).

(2) His own addresses; such as the speech with which he quelled an incipient mutiny (I.40).

(3) Reports made to him; such as by Labienus (II.1) and the envoys of the Remi (II.3-4).

(4) Requests and replies, messages and instructions; such as the request of the Helvetian envoys and Caesar's answer (I.7), the plea of the Aeduans (I.11), Caesar's message to the Lingones (I.26), messages to and from Ariovistus (I.34-36, 47).

(5) Arguments; such as the arguments of Orgetorix (I.2-3) and of disloyal natives (II.17).

(6) Brief reports, explanations or speeches, presented in some cases with little or no condensation; such as the hurried report of Considius (I.22), the apology of the soldiers (I.41), the joke by the soldier of the Tenth Legion (I.42), and the taunt of the Atuatuci as translated into Latin (II.30).

d. Indirect discourse in a broader sense includes all statements in the indirect form after words of thought as well as speech; as, **biennium satis esse dūxērunt**, *they reckoned that two years would be sufficient* (I.3).

e. In the Latin text of this book, the more important indirect quotations and summaries are printed in italics.

213. *a.* Indirect discourse is introduced by a verb or other expression of *saying, perceiving, ascertaining, thinking, knowing,* or *remembering*; as, **sē ... condōnāre dīcit**, *he says that he would pardon* (I.20).

Such verbs and expressions used by Caesar are: **agō**, *present a case* (I.13); **animadvertō**, *notice* (I.32); **arbitror**, *think* (I.2); **audiō**, *hear* (IV.7); **certiōrem faciō**, *inform* (I.11); **certior fit**, *is informed* (I.12); **clāmitō**, *cry out* (V.7); **cogitō**, *think* (V.33); **cognōscō**, *learn* (I.22); **commemorō**, *relate* (IV.16); **comperiō**, *ascertain* (IV.19); **conclāmō**, *shout* (III.18); **cōnfīdō**, *be confident, trust* (III.9); **cōnfirmō**, *assure* (I.3); **cōnspiciō**, *see* (II.24); **cōnstat**, *it is agreed* (III.6); **cōnstituō**, *resolve* (II.10); **crēdō**, *believe* (II.33); **dēmōnstrō**, *show, prove* (I.11); **dēnūntiō**, *threaten* (I.36); **dīcō**, *say*; **doceō**, *explain* (I.43);

dūcō, *reckon* (I.3); **exīstimō**, *reckon, think* (I.6); **faciō verba**, *make a plea* (II.14); **intellegō**, *understand* (I.16); **inveniō**, *find out* (II.16); **iūdicō**, *judge* (I.45); **iūrō**, *swear* (VI.12); **loquor**, *speak, say* (II.31); **meminī**, *remember* (III.6); **memoriā teneō**, *hold in memory, remember* (I.7); **mihi persuāsum habeō**, *am convinced* (III.2); **negō**, *declare that ... not* (I.8); **nūntiō**, *announce* (II.2); **nūntium mittō**, *send word* (II.6); **ostendō**, *make plain* (I.8); **perscrībō**, *write fully* (V.49); **perspiciō**, *perceive* (III.9); **polliceor**, *promise* (I.33); **praedicō**, *declare* (I.39); **probō**, *show, prove* (I.3); **prōnūntiō**, *announce* (V.56); **putō**, *think* (IV.3); **referō**, *report* (VI.10); **renūntiō**, *bring (back) report* (I.10); **reperiō**, *find out, ascertain* (I.18); **respondeō**, *answer* (I.14); **sciō**, *know* (I.20); **scrībō**, *write* (V.13); **sentiō**, *perceive* (I.18); **spem habeō**, *have hope that* (I.33); **significō**, *give intimation* (II.13); **simulō**, *pretend* (IV.4); **spērō**, *hope* (I.3); **statuō**, *determine* (I.42); **suspicor**, *suspect* (I.44); **videō**, *see* (I.33); **voveō**, *vow* (VI.16).

b. The verb of saying, on which indirect discourse depends, is sometimes not expressed, but implied in the context; as, **obsecrāre coepit ... scīre sē**, *he began to beseech (Caesar, saying) that he knew* (I.20). (AG 579, 580; B 314.2).

Rules for Indirect Discourse

214. *a.* In indirect discourse the principal statements, corresponding with the principal clauses of direct discourse, are expressed by the subject accusative and the infinitive; subordinate clauses have the subjunctive. Thus, **cōnsuēsse deōs immortālēs ... , quōs prō scelere eōrum ulcīscī velint, hīs secundiōrēs interdum rēs et diūturniōrem impūnitātem concēdere**, *the immortal gods are accustomed to grant, for a time, more favorable circumstances and longer freedom from punishment to those whom they desire to punish for their wickedness*; in the direct form **cōnsuēsse deōs** would become **cōnsuērunt dī**, and **velint** in the subordinate clause would be **volunt**, the other words remaining unchanged, and the sentence would read **cōnsuērunt dī immortālēs ... , quōs prō scelere eōrum ulcīscī volunt, hīs secundiōrēs interdum rēs et diūturniōrem impūnitātem concēdere** (I.14).

b. A subordinate clause containing an implied quotation may have the subjunctive; as, **frūmentum, quod essent pollicitī**, *the grain which (as he said) they had promised* (I.16).

c. In indirect discourse a subordinate or parenthetical clause, presenting a statement of fact which is not necessarily a part of the indirect discourse, may have the indicative; as, **Condrūsōs ... Paemānōs, quī Germānī appellantur**, *that the Condrusi ... and the Paemani, who are called Germans* (II.4).

215. The subject accusative in indirect discourse is sometimes omitted when it is easily understood from the context, especially when it refers to the same person as the subject of the verb on which the indirect discourse depends; as, **scīre**, for **sē scīre**, *that he knew* (I. 40); **prohibitūrum ostendit**, for **sē prohibitūrum esse ostendit** (historical present), *he showed that he would prevent them* (I.8).

216. Commands expressed in direct quotation by the imperative, or by the jussive subjunctive, in indirect discourse have the subjunctive, the negative being **nē**. Thus, **reminīscerētur**, *let him remember*, which in the direct form would be imperative, **reminīscere**, *remember* (I.13); **nē ... tribueret**, *that he should not presume*, the direct form being **nōlī tribuere** (I.13). (AG 588, B 316).

217. *a* Ordinary questions in indirect discourse have the subjunctive; as, **cūr in suās possessiōnēs venīret**, *why did he (Caesar) come into his possessions?* in the direct form this would be, **cūr in meās possessiōnēs venīs?** *why do you come into my possessions* (I.44)? (AG 586, B 315.1).

b. Deliberative questions in indirect discourse retain the subjunctive, but the tense is governed by that of the verb on which the indirect discourse depends (**177a, b**); thus, **quid agāmus?** *what are we to do?* after a past tense in indirect discourse becomes **quid agerent**; as, **neque satis ... cōnstābat, quid agerent**, *and it was not quite clear ... what they should do* (III.14). (AG 587, B 315.3).

c. Rhetorical questions in indirect discourse (**179b**) have the infinitive; as, **quid esse levius**, *what is more capricious*, implying that nothing could be more capricious (V.28).

218. An apodosis of a conditional sentence containing a statement is expressed in indirect discourse by the accusative and infinitive, containing a command, by the subjunctive; the protasis, containing the condition, has the subjunctive, as follows:

(1) *a.* In conditions of fact, the tense of the infinitive in indirect discourse corresponds with the tense of the apodosis in the direct form, while the tense of the protasis, introduced by **sī** or **sīn**, is governed by that of the verb on which the indirect discourse depends (**177a, b**). Thus, **is ita cum Caesare ēgit: sī pācem populus Rōmānus cum Helvētiīs faceret, in eam partem itūrōs** [**esse**] **atque ibi futūrōs** [**esse**] **Helvētiōs, ubi eōs Caesar cōnstituisset atque esse voluisset,** *he took up* (*the matter*) *with Caesar thus: if the Roman people would make peace with the Helvetians, they would go wherever Caesar should have appointed and wished them to be, and would there remain*; in the direct form, **Sī pācem populus Rōmānus cum Helvētiīs faciet, in eam partem ībunt atque ibi erunt Helvētiī, ubi eōs tū cōnstitueris** (future perfect indicative) **atque esse volueris** (I.13). (AG 580, B 314.1).

b. In the protasis of conditions of fact a perfect or pluperfect subjunctive in indirect discourse may represent a future perfect indicative in the direct form; as, **quod sī fēcerit** (perfect subjunctive), **Aeduōrum auctōritātem amplificātūrum** [**esse**], *if he should do this, he would increase the prestige of the Aeduans*; in the direct form, **quod sī fēceris** (future perfect indicative) **Aeduōrum auctōritātem amplificābis,** *if you will have done this, you will increase the prestige of the Aeduans* (II.14).

(2) In conditions of possible realization the infinitive in indirect discourse represents the subjunctive of the direct form; the tense of the present subjunctive in the protasis is present after a present tense, but imperfect in case the indirect discourse follows a past tense. Thus, after a present tense, **sī quid accidat Rōmānīs, summam in spem . . . venīre,** *if any* (*disaster*) *should befall the Romans, he would entertain the highest expectation*, lit. *would come into the highest hope*; in the direct form, **sī quid accidat Rōmānīs, summam in spem veniat** (I.18).

(3) In conditions contrary to fact in indirect discourse the perfect infinitive of the active periphrastic conjugation corresponds to the active pluperfect subjunctive in the apodosis of the direct form, the protasis being in the subjunctive; as, **neque Eburōnēs, sī ille adesset,** (**fuisse**) **ventūrōs,** *nor would the Eburones have come if he* (*had been and*) *were at hand* (V.29; see also **208c**).

219. The apodosis of a conditional sentence is sometimes incorporated in a substantive clause introduced by **ut, nē,** or **quīn.** Thus, **ut, sī vellet Ariovistus proeliō contendere, eī potestās non deesset,** *in order that, if Ariovistus wished to contend in battle, opportunity might not be lacking to him,* in the direct form, **sī . . . volet . . . nōn deerit** (I.48); **neque dubitāre dēbēre quīn, sī Helvētiōs superāverint** (perfect subjunctive) **Rōmānī . . . Aeduīs lībertātem sint ēreptūrī,** *and that they ought not to doubt that, if the Romans should have overpowered the Helvetians, they were going to take away liberty from the Aeduans,* in the direct form, **sī Helvētiōs superāverint** (future perfect indicative) **Rōmānī . . . ēreptūrī sunt** (I.17).

220. The verb of a clause subordinate to a clause having its verb in the subjunctive, or in the infinitive, is ordinarily put in the subjunctive (subjunctive by attraction); as, **utī frūmentō commeātūque, quī . . . supportārētur, Caesarem interclūderet,** *that he might cut Caesar off from the grain and other supplies that were being brought up* (I.48). (AG 593, B 324).

THE INFINITIVE

221. *a.* Caesar uses the infinitive after many verbs to complete the meaning (complementary infinitive); as, **. . . exīre possent,** *they were able to go out,* **exīre** filling out the sense which with **possent** alone would be incomplete (I.6). (AG 457, B 328.1).

b. A participle, adjective, or noun in predicate with a complementary infinitive is attracted to the case of the subject of the verb on which the infinitive depends; as, **pūrgātī esse vellent,** *they should wish to be guiltless* (I.28).

c. Caesar has the infinitive after certain participles used as adjectives; as, **parātum** (accusative) **dēcertāre,** *ready to fight it out* (I.44). (AG 460b).

222. *a.* An infinitive may be the subject of an impersonal verb, or of other verbs used impersonally; as, **maiōrī partī placuit ... dēfendere**, *the majority decided* (lit. *to the greater part it was pleasing*) *to defend* ... (III.3); **commodissimum vīsum est ... mittere**, *it seemed most expedient to send*, **mittere** being the subject of **vīsum est** (I.47). (AG 454, B 327.1).

b. An infinitive is sometimes used as the subject of an infinitive, especially in indirect discourse; as, **commodissimum esse statuit ... impōnere**, *he decided that the most expedient* (*thing*) *was to place ... on*, **impōnere** being the subject of **esse** used impersonally (I.42).

c. An infinitive used as subject may have a subject accusative; as, **intersit manūs distinērī**, *it is important that the forces be kept apart* (II.5).

223. *a.* Caesar uses the accusative with the infinitive not only after words of speech and thought (indirect discourse, **212d**), but also after words expressing *will* or *desire, feeling, permission* and *prevention, persuasion, command, training* and *compulsion*; as, **eās rēs iactārī nōlēbat**, *he was unwilling that those matters should be discussed* (I.18); **eōs īre paterentur**, *would allow them to go* (I.6).

Such words used by Caesar are:

(**1**) Expressing will or desire: **dēsīderō**, *desire* (IV.2); **nōlō**, *be unwilling*; **vōlō**, *wish* (I.13).

(**2**) Expressing feeling: **admīror**, *be surprised* (I.14); **doleō**, *grieve* (III.2); **gaudeō**, *rejoice* (IV.13); **molestē ferō**, *feel irritation* (II.1).

(**3**) Expressing permission or prevention: **patior**, *suffer, allow* (sometimes followed by an **ut**-clause); **prohibeō**, *prevent ... from* (II.4).

(**4**) Expressing command, training, or compulsion: **iubeō**, *order* (I.5); **vetō**, *forbid* (II.20); **assuēfaciō**, *train* (IV.2); **cōgō**, *force* (I.4).

b. **Cupiō, mālō, nōlō, studeō,** and **volō** frequently have the infinitive without a subject accusative (complementary infinitive); as, **ulcīscī velint**, *may wish to punish* (I.14).

224. *a.* When verbs which, in the active voice, have the accusative and infinitive, are used in the passive, a subject nominative may take the place of the accusative, the infinitive remaining the same; in translating, the English impersonal construction should often be used. Thus, **nōn fore dictō audientēs ... dīcantur**, *that it is said they will not be obedient to the command*, lit. *that they are said not to be about to be obedient* (I.40).

b. The accusative and the infinitive may stand as the subject of an impersonal verb, or of other verbs used impersonally; as, **poenam sequī oportēbat**, *the penalty would inevitably follow*, lit. *that the penalty follow, was inevitable* (I.4); **nōn esse fās Germānōs superāre**, *that it was not right for the Germans to conquer*, **Germānōs superāre** being the subject of **esse** used impersonally (I.50).

225. The place of the future infinitive may be taken by **fore** or **futūrum esse** and a clause with **ut** and the subjunctive; as, **fore, utī pertināciā dēsisteret**, *that he would desist from his obstinate course*, lit. *that it would be that he would desist* (I.42).

PARTICIPLES

226. *a.* The time denoted by a present participle is the same as that of the principal verb; as, **flēns peteret**, *with tears* (lit. *weeping*) *he was entreating* (I.20).

b. The time denoted by a perfect participle is prior to that of the principal verb; as, **cupiditāte inductus**, *having been led on by a desire* (I.2).

c. Caesar sometimes uses perfect participles of deponent or semi-deponent verbs where English usage prefers a present participle; as, **Caesarem complexus**, *embracing Caesar*, lit. *having embraced* (I.20). Other examples are: **arbitrātus**, *thinking* (III.28); **commorātus**, *delaying* (V.7); **cōnfīsus**, *trusting* (I.53); **cōnsōlātus**, *comforting* (I.20); **gāvīsus**, *rejoicing* (IV.13); **mīrātus**, *wondering* (I.32); **secūtus**, *following* (I.24); **ūsus**, *using* (II.7); **veritus**, *fearing* (II.11).

227. *a.* A participle is often used to express concisely an idea that might have been expanded into a clause, particularly an idea of *cause, condition, opposition, characterization,* or *description.* Thus:

(1) Expressing cause: **sē, Biturīgum perfidiam veritōs, revertisse,** *that they, fearing the treachery of the Bituriges, had come back,* that is, *that they had come back because they feared the treachery of the Bituriges* (VII.5). (AG 496, B 337.2f).

(2) Expressing condition: **hanc adeptī victōriam, in perpetuum sē fore victōrēs cōnfīdēbant,** *having won this victory, they were confident that they would be victorious for all time,* **adeptī** being equivalent to **sī adeptī essent** (V.39).

(3) Expressing opposition: **in colloquium venīre invītātus,** *although invited to come to a conference* (I.35).

(4) Expressing characterization or description: **victīs, venientēs,** *those beaten, those coming up,* meaning *those who had been beaten, those who were coming up* (I.25).

(5) Expressing time: **cōnantēs,** *when they were attempting* (I.47).

b. A participle may express manner or circumstance; as, **flēns peteret,** *with tears* (lit. *weeping*) *he was entreating* (I.20); **pugnāns interficitur,** *is killed while fighting* (V.37).

228. *a.* Caesar sometimes uses a perfect participle in agreement with the subject or the object of a verb where English prefers a coordinate clause. Thus, **persuādent Rauracīs . . . ūtī, eōdem ūsī cōnsiliō, . . . cum eīs proficīscantur,** *persuade the Rauraci . . . to adopt the same plan, and set out with them,* lit. *that, having used the same plan, they should set out* (I.5); **Boiōs . . . receptōs ad sē sociōs sibi ascīscunt,** *they received and associated with themselves the Boians,* lit. *the Boians, having been received . . . they associated* (I.5). (AG 496.n2, B 337).

b. Caesar sometimes uses a perfect passive participle in agreement with a noun where the participle has the main idea and is best translated by a noun; as, **ante prīmam cōnfectam vigiliam,** *before the end of the first watch,* lit. *before the first watch having been completed* (VII.3).

c. Caesar sometimes uses a participle in agreement with the object of a verb to depict an action or a situation more vividly. Thus, **aliquōs ex nāvī ēgredientēs cōnspexerant,** *had seen some (soldiers) disembarking,* is more vivid than **aliquōs . . . ēgredī,** *that some (soldiers) were disembarking* (IV.26).

229. *a.* Habeō with a perfect passive participle in agreement with its object may have almost the force of a perfect or pluperfect tense; as, **quem . . . coāctum habēbat,** *which he had collected,* lit. *which, having been collected, he was having* (I.15). (AG 497b, B 337.7).

b. Caesar uses the future passive participle (the gerundive) in agreement with the object of certain verbs to express purpose or accomplishment; as, **pontem faciendum cūrat,** *he has a bridge built, he attends to the building of a bridge,* lit. *provides for a bridge to be built* (I.13). The verbs thus used are **cūrō,** *arrange, provide,* and **dō,** *give* (IV.22). (AG 500.4, B 337.8b2).

c. The future passive participle combined with the forms of **sum** in the passive periphrastic conjugation (**63**) is often used to express *obligation, necessity,* or *propriety;* as, **revocandī [erant] mīlitēs,** *the soldiers had to be called back* (II.20); see also **249a, b.**

GERUNDIVES AND SUPINES

230. In place of the gerund, Caesar more often uses the gerundive construction, with the noun in the case in which the gerund might have been put, and the gerundive agreeing with it. His use of the gerund and of the gerundive construction is as follows:

(1) Genitive after nouns and adjectives, and with **causā** and **grātiā** expressing purpose: **bellandī cupidī,** *desirous of waging war* (I.2); **Galliae impugnandae causā,** *in order to attack Gaul* (I.44); see also **247.** (AG 349a, B 204.1).

(2) Dative after verbs (gerundive construction only): **vix ut eīs rēbus . . . collocandīs . . . tempus darētur**, *barely time (enough) was given for making those arrangements*, lit. *for those things to be arranged* (III.4).

(3) Accusative after **ad** to express purpose: **ad dēlīberandum**, *for consideration* (I.7); **ad eās rēs cōnficiendās,** *to complete these preparations*, lit. *for these things to be accomplished* (I.3); see also **247**. (AG 503, 506; B 339.2).

(4) Ablative of means without a preposition, and ablative with the prepositions **in** or **dē: fallendō,** *by practicing deception* (IV.13); **in quaerendō,** *on making inquiry* (I.18); **dē expugnandō oppidō,** *in regard to storming the stronghold* (II.10).

231. *a.* The supine in **-um** is used, chiefly after verbs of motion, to express purpose; as, **ad Caesarem grātulātum convēnērunt,** *came to Caesar to offer congratulations* (I.30); see also **247**. (AG 509, B 340).

b. The supine in **-um** may be followed by a direct object, or by a clause; as, **lēgātōs mittunt rogātum auxilium,** *send envoys to ask for help* (I.11); **questum, quod Harūdēs . . . fīnēs eōrum populārentur,** *to complain because the Harudes were laying waste their country* (I.37).

232. Caesar uses the supine in **-ū** after a few adjectives to denote in what respect their meaning is to be taken; as, **perfacile factū,** *very easy to do*, lit. *very easy in respect to the doing* (I.3). The adjectives thus used by Caesar are **horridus** (V.14), **optimus** (IV.30), and **perfacilis**. (AG 510.n2, B 340.2).

CONJUNCTIONS

233. *a.* Of the copulative conjunctions Caesar uses **et,** *and,* **et . . . et,** *both . . . and, on the one hand . . . on the other,* to express simple connection; **-que,** *and,* **-que . . . -que,** *both . . . and,* to express a closer connection; **atque** or **ac,** *and also, and indeed, and,* to express a close connection and also make that which follows slightly more prominent; and **neque** or **nec,** *and . . . not,* **neque** (or **nec**) **. . . neque** (or **nec**), *neither . . . nor, not . . . and not;* **et . . . neque,** *both . . . and not;* **neque** or **nec . . . et,** *and not . . . and,* to express a connection with a negative idea.

b. The enclitic conjunction **-que,** *and,* is attached to the word introduced by it, or to the first word of a phrase or clause which it introduces, excepting a prepositional phrase; **-que** introducing a prepositional phrase may be attached to the first word after the preposition. Thus, **ob eāsque rēs,** *and on account of these things* (II.35).

c. After words expressing similarity, or the opposite, **atque** or **ac** has the force of *than, as;* as, **in parem . . . condiciōnem atque ipsī erant,** *into the same condition . . . as themselves,* lit. *as (and) they themselves were* (I.28). (AG 324c, B 341.1c).

d. Caesar uses the conjunctions **et, -que, atque, ac,** and **neque** in various combinations, sometimes joining more than two members; as, **et . . . que** (III.11), **-que . . . et** (II.22), **et . . . atque** (I.15), **atque . . . et** (II.8), **atque . . . -que** (VI.11), **neque . . . atque** (II.10), **neque . . . et** (II.25), **-que . . . -que . . . -que** (I.30), **ac . . . atque . . . -que** (III.5), **et . . . atque . . . et . . . et . . . et** (IV.33).

234. *a.* When more than two words stand in the same relation, the copulative conjunction may be expressed with all, or omitted with all, or the last two words may be joined by **-que;** in each case English generally prefers "and" between the last two words. Thus, **Rauracīs et Tulingīs et Latobrīgīs,** *the Rauraci, Tulingi, and Latobrigi* (I.5); **linguā, īnstitūtīs, lēgibus,** *in respect to language, institutions, and laws* (I.1); **puerī, senēs mulierēsque,** *children, old men, and women* (I.29).

b. Sometimes, especially after a negative expression, Caesar uses **et, -que,** and **atque** or **ac,** where English prefers *but;* as, **portūs . . . capere nōn potuērunt, et paulō īnfrā dēlātae sunt,** *could not make the harbors but were carried a short distance below* (IV.36).

235. *a.* Of the disjunctive conjunctions Caesar uses **aut,** *or,* to connect alternatives that cannot, in most cases, both be true at the same time; **vel,** *or,* negative **nēve** or **neu,** *or not, and not,* to connect alternatives between which there might be a choice; and **sīve** or **seu**, *or if*, to connect alternatives involving a condition. Thus, **quīnīs aut sēnīs mīlibus passuum**, *five or six miles each day* (1.15); **Brūtō . . . vel tribūnīs**, *to Brutus or the tribunes* (III.14).

b. The disjunctive conjunctions are often used in pairs, as **aut . . . aut**, *either . . . or* (I.1), **vel . . . vel**, *either . . . or* (I.6), **sīve . . . sīve**, *whether . . . or, either . . . or* (I.12).

236. *a.* Of the adversative conjunctions Caesar uses **at**, *but, at any rate*, to express contrast or restriction; **autem**, *however, on the other hand, moreover*, to express contrast or addition; **sed**, *but*, to correct or limit a preceding statement; **tamen**, *nevertheless, yet*, to emphasize the importance of something that follows in opposition to a preceding statement; and **vērō**, *in fact, but in truth*, to emphasize a contrast with a preceding statement.

b. The adversative conjunctions **autem** and **vērō** are regularly placed after the first word of a clause.

c. The adversative conjunction **tamen** sometimes stands after the first word of a clause.

d. Caesar uses correlatively **nōn sōlum . . . sed etiam**, *not only. . . but also*; **nōn modo . . . sed etiam**, *not only . . . but also*; **nōn modo . . . sed**, *not only . . . but*; **nōn modo nōn . . . sed nē . . . quidem**, *not only not . . . but not even*.

e. In **nōn modo . . . nē . . . quidem** Caesar uses **nōn modo** as equivalent to **nōn modo nōn**, when a verb appears only in the second member; as **nōn modo defessō . . . sed nē sauciō quidem**, *not only not to one (who was) exhausted . . . but even to a wounded man* (III.4).

237. *a.* Of the conjunctions denoting logical relations Caesar uses chiefly **itaque**, *accordingly* (lit. *and so*), to introduce a statement of a fact or situation naturally resulting from what preceded; **proinde**, *hence*, to introduce a command; **nam** or **enim**, *for*, to introduce an explanation of a preceding statement; and **quārē**, *wherefore, and therefore*, to introduce a logical consequence, or a command.

b. In presenting a succession of points Caesar often uses **prīmum**, *first*, and **deinde**, *then, in the second place*; sometimes, also, **dēnique**, *finally*, to introduce the conclusion of an argument.

c. In the adverbial phrase **nē . . . quidem**, *not even*, the word or phrase emphasized is placed between the two words; as, **nē pabulī quidem**, *not even of fodder* (I.16). (B 347).

FIGURES OF SPEECH

238. Caesar uses the following grammatical figures:

a. Asyndeton (a-sin'de-ton), the omission of a conjunction where a connective might have been used; as, **loca, portūs, aditūs cognōvisset**, *should have become acquainted with the natural features, the harbors, (and) the approaches* (IV.20); **L. Pīsōne, A. Gabīniō cōnsulibus**, *in the consulship of Lucius Piso (and) Aulus Gabinius* (I.6).

b. Brachylogy (bra-kil'o̧-ji), a condensed form of expression; as, **cōnsimilis caprīs figūra**, *shape like (that of) goats*, that is, **figūra cōnsimilis figūrae** (dative) **caprārum** (VI.27).

c. Ellipsis (e-lip'sis), the omission of words essential to the meaning; as, **duae fīliae**, for **duae fīliae fuērunt**, *there were two daughters* (I.53).

d. Hendiadys (hen-dī'a-dis), the use of two nouns with a connective where a noun with a modifying genitive or adjective might have been expected; as, **fidem et iūs iūrandum**, *a pledge of good faith bound by an oath*, lit. *good faith and oath* (I.3). (AG 640, B 374.4).

e. Parenthesis (pa-ren'the-sis), the insertion of an independent sentence or phrase, interrupting the construction; as, **quam maximum potest mīlitum numerum imperat (erat . . . legiō ūna), pontem . . . iubet, rescindī**, *he levies as many soldiers as possible (there was only one legion, altogether, in further Gaul) and gave orders that the bridge be cut down* (I.7).

f. Polysyndeton (pol-i-sin'de-ton), the use of more conjunctions than the sense requires; as, **Ceutronēs et Graiocelī et Caturīgēs**, *the Ceutrones, the Graioceli, and the Caturiges* (I.10).

g. Prolepsis (prō-lep'sis), or *anticipation*, the use of a noun as object in a clause preceding that in which it naturally belongs as subject; as, **rem frūmentāriam, ut supportārī posset, timēre,** *that they feared that the supply of grain could not be brought up*, lit. *they feared the supply of grain, that it could not be brought up* (I.39). (B 374.5).

h. Synesis (sin'ẹ-sis), construction according to the sense, without regard to the grammatical form; as, **cīvitātī persuāsit, ut . . . exīrent,** *persuaded the (people of his) state to go out*, lit. *persuaded his state that they should go out* (I.2). (B 254.4a).

239. Caesar uses the following rhetorical figures:

a. Anaphora (an-af'o-ra), the repetition of the same word at the beginning of successive phrases or clauses; as, **nōn aetāte cōnfectīs, nōn mulieribus, nōn īnfantibus pepercērunt,** *they spared not the aged, not the women, not the children* (VII.28).

b. Antithesis (an-tith'e-sis), the juxtaposition of contrasted expressions in like order; as, **nōn sēsē Gallīs, sed Gallōs sibi, bellum intulisse,** *he did not make war on the Gauls, but the Gauls on him* (I.44).

c. Chiasmus (kī-as'mus), an arrangement of contrasted words in inverse order; as, **fāmā nōbilēs potentēsque bellō,** *in reputation notable, and powerful in war* (VII.77).

d. Climax (klī'max), an arrangement of words, phrases, or clauses with gradual increase of interest or vigor of expression to the end; as, **cōnferre, comportārī, adesse,** *that it was being collected, was on the way, was at hand* (I.16).

e. Euphemism (ū'fe-mizm), the use of a mild expression in order to avoid a word of bad omen; as, **sī quid accidat Rōmānīs,** *if anything should happen to the Romans*, meaning *if any disaster should befall the Romans* (I.18).

f. Hyperbaton (hī-per'ba-ton), the arrangement of words in unusual order, as the separation of words that belong together, such as the insertion of one or more words between the parts of an ablative absolute; thus, **simulātā Caesarem amīcitiā,** *that Caesar under the pretense of friendship*, the usual order being **Caesarem, simulātā amīcitiā** (I.44).

g. Litotes (lit'ọ-tēz), the affirmation of an idea through the negation of its opposite; as, **neque tam imperītum esse rērum ut nōn scīret,** *and he was not so unversed in affairs as not to know*, meaning *that he was so worldly wise that he very well knew* (I.44).

EXPRESSIONS RELATING TO TIME

240. *a.* The Roman year (**annus**) is usually dated by the consuls in office, their names being given (most often as an ablative absolute) with **cōnsulibus;** as, **Cn. Pompeiō, M. Crassō cōnsulibus,** *in the consulship of Gnaeus Pompey and Marcus Crassus*, 55 BC (IV.1).

b. In Caesar's time the year commenced on January 1, and the months were named (**mēnsis**) **Iānuārius, Februārius, Mārtius** (originally the first month of the year), **Aprīlis, Maius, Iūnius, Quīnctīlis** (from **quīnque;** named the *fifth* month when the year began with March), **Sextīlis** (**sex**), **September, Octōber, November, December** (the *tenth* month, reckoning March as the first). Afterwards **Quīnctīlis** was changed to **Iūlius** (our *July*) in honor of Julius Caesar, and **Sextīlis** to **Augustus** (our *August*) in honor of the Emperor Augustus.

241. *a.* Dates in the month were reckoned backward from three points. These points, designated by feminine plural nouns, are *the Kalends*, **Kalendae,** the *first* day of the month; *the Nones*, **Nōnae** (ninth before the Ides), the *seventh* day of March, May, July, and October, the *fifth* day of other months; and *the Ides* (**Īdūs**), the *fifteenth* day of March, May, July, and October, the *thirteenth* of other months. (AG 631, B 371).

b. In giving dates the days at the beginning and end of a given period were both included, and abbreviations were employed. Thus, **a. d. v. Kal. Apr.** (I.6), in full would be **ante diem quīntum**

Kalendās Aprīlēs, which is translated as if it were (**diēs**) **quīntus ante Kalendās Aprīlēs**, *the fifth* (*day*) *before the Kalends of April*; we start from April 1 and count back:

Day I	Day II	Day III	Day IV	Day V
'1 April'	'31 March'	'30 March'	'29 March'	'28 March'

and so we find the fifth day, which is March 28 according to our method of writing dates.

242. *a.* The day from sunrise to sunset was divided into twelve hours, **hōrae,** which varied in length according to the season of the year, and were numbered 1-12; thus, **hōrā septimā**, *the seventh hour* (I.26). Since the sixth hour ended at noon, the seventh hour at the equinoxes would correspond exactly with the hour between twelve and one o'clock according to our reckoning; at other times the seventh hour would end after, or before, one o'clock.

b. The method of reducing the Roman hours to our system of reckoning may be illustrated by the following problem: *Question.* "What, approximately, is our equivalent of the fourth Roman hour in the last week of August in the region of Dover, England?" *Answer.* In the region of Dover in the last week of August the sun rises about 5 o'clock and sets about 7. The length of the day is therefore about 14 hours by our reckoning. Since the Romans divided the full day into 12 equal hours, we divide 14 by 12 and have 1.167, that is, the Roman hour in this problem = 1.167 of our hours. At the beginning of the fourth Roman hour 3 Roman hours have passed; 3 x 1.167 = 3.5, that is, at the beginning of the fourth Roman hour 3.5 of our hours have passed since sunrise. As sunrise is reckoned about 5 o'clock by our time, we add 3.5 to 5, making 8:30; that is, 8:30 a.m., by our reckoning from midnight, will approximately represent the beginning of the fourth hour of the day by Roman reckoning under the conditions of the problem.

c. In military usage the night was divided into four watches of three hours each: **prīma vigilia,** *first watch*, commencing at sunset by Roman reckoning (= 6–9 p.m.); **secunda vigilia** (II.11), 9 p.m.–midnight; **tertia vigilia** (II.33), midnight–3 a.m.; **quārta vigilia** (I.21), 3–6 a.m., ending at sunrise by Roman reckoning.

d. Caesar uses the Preposition **dē** in certain expressions of time with the meaning *just after, in the course of*; as **dē mediā nocte**, *just after midnight* (II.7); **dē tertiā vigiliā**, *soon after the beginning of the third watch* (I.12), which lasted from midnight to 3:00 a.m.

e. When the sun was not visible, recourse might be had to water clocks, **ex aquā mensūrae** (V.13), for the measurement of time.

EXPRESSIONS OF LENGTH AND DISTANCE

243. *a.* Of the terms denoting measurement Caesar uses **digitus**, *finger-breadth*; **pēs**, *foot*, which measured approximately 0.97 of the English foot; **passus**, *pace*; and **mīlle passūs**, *mile*, plural **mīlia passuum,** *miles*. The **passus** contained two ordinary steps (**gradus**), and measured the distance between the points where the same heel is lifted and touches the ground again.

b. The relations of the units of measurement, and their modern equivalents, are as follows:

		ENGLISH FEET	METERS
	1 digitus	= 0.728 inch	= 0.0185 m
16 digiti	= 1 pes	= 11.65 inches	= 0.296 m
2.5 pedes	= 1 gradus	= 2 feet 5.125 inches	= 0.74 m
2 gradus	= 1 passus	= 4 feet 10.25 inches	= 1.48 m
1000 passus	= mille passus	= 4854 feet	= 1480 m

Since the Roman foot was approximately 0.97 of the English foot in length, the Roman mile, 4854 English feet in length, was 426 feet shorter than the English mile of 5280 feet; 12 English miles are a little more than the equivalent of 13 Roman miles.

c. Long distances may be loosely expressed by **iter** (accusative) with the genitive; as, **novem diērum iter**, *a nine days' journey* (VI.25).

WORD ORDER, COMPOSITION

244. Normal word order:

a. When the emphasis is evenly distributed in a Latin sentence, the subject comes first, the predicate last, and the modifiers of the predicate precede the verb in this order: indirect object, direct object, adverb or adverbial phrase; as, **is sibi lēgātiōnem ad cīvitātēs suscēpit**, *he took upon himself the misson of envoy to the states* (I.3).

b. Genitives, adjectives, possessive pronouns, and ordinal numerals when unemphatic follow their nouns; as **glōriā bellī**, *reputation for war* (I.2); **cupiditāte rēgnī**, *by desire of kingly power* (I.9); **locīs patentibus maximēque frūmentāriīs**, *open and exceedingly productive places* (I.10); **fīliam suam**, *his daughter* (I.3); **diē quārtō**, *on the fourth day* (I.26).

c. The demonstrative pronouns **hīc, iste, ille, is,** the intensive **ipse,** and adjectives indicating quantity or position precede their nouns when unemphatic; as, **hīs rēbus**, *by these conditions* (I.3); **ipse imperātor**, *the general himself* (I.40); **trēs populōs**, *three peoples* (I.3); **magnum numerum**, *a great number* (I.4); **extrēmum oppidum**, *the furthest town* (I.6); **superiōre aciē**, *the upper line* (I.24).

245. Emphatic word order:

a. For the sake of emphasis the normal order of words in the sentence may be reversed, the subject being placed last; as, **apud Helvētiōs longē nōbilissimus fuit et dītissimus Orgetorīx**, *among the Helvetians Orgetorix was by far the highest in rank, and wealthiest* (I.2).

b. Genitives, adjectives, possessive pronouns, and ordinal numerals precede their nouns when emphatic; as, **rēgnī cupiditāte**, *by desire of kingly power* (I.2); **inimīcō animō**, *of hostile disposition* (I.7); **decima legiō**, *the tenth legion* (I.41).

c. When emphatic, the demonstratives **hīc, iste, ille, is,** the intensive **ipse** and adjectives indicating quantity or position follow their nouns; as, **in īnsulā ipsā**, *in the island itself* (V.12); **Galliae tōtīus**, *of entire Gaul* (I.31); **partēs trēs**, *three parts* (I.1); **locīs superiōribus**, *the higher places* (I.10).

d. For the sake of emphasis words belonging together in construction are often separated; as, **aliud iter habērent nūllum**, *they had no other way* (I.7); **magnō ad pugnam erat impedīmentō**, *was a great hindrance for battle* (I.25).

e. An important word in a clause may be made emphatic by placing it before the conjunction introducing the clause; as **diū cum esset pugnātum**, *when the fighting had continued a long time* (I.26).

246. The sequence of tenses should be particularly noted when a subjunctive is required in a dependent clause. For convenience, the statement of the grammar (**177a**) is here supplemented by tabular outlines:

	MAIN VERB	*SUBJUNCTIVE VERB*	
		SAME OR LATER TIME	*PREVIOUS TIME*
PRIMARY TENSES	Present Future Future Perfect	Present	Perfect
SECONDARY TENSES	Imperfect Perfect Pluperfect	Imperfect	Pluperfect

PRIMARY SEQUENCE

rogat	quid faciam	*He asks, is asking*	*what I am doing*
rogābit	*(incomplete action)*	*He will ask*	
rogāverit		*He will have asked*	
rogat	quid fēcerim	*He asks, is asking*	*what I did* or *have done*
rogābit	*(completed action)*	*He will ask*	
rogāverit		*He will have asked*	

SECONDARY SEQUENCE

rogābat	quid facerem	*He asked, was asking*	*what I was doing*
rogāvit	*(incomplete action)*	*He asked*	
rogāverat		*He had asked*	
rogābat	quid fēcissem	*He asked, was asking*	*what I had done*
rogāvit	*(completed action)*	*He asked*	
rogāverat		*He had asked*	

247. Purpose in Latin may be expressed in five ways:

By the use of **ut** with the subjunctive (**196a**);

By the use of a relative with the subjunctive (**193a**);

By **ad** with the accusative of the gerund or the gerundive construction (**230.3**);

By **causā** with the genitive of the gerund or the gerundive construction (**230.1**);

By the supine in -**um** (**231**).

248. *a.* "May" and "might" often appear in clauses expressing purpose, which are translated into Latin by **ut** with the subjunctive; as, **ut parātiōrēs essent**, *in order that they might be more ready* (I.5); see **196a**.

b. "May" and "might" may also express permission and be best translated by **licet** with the dative of the person and the infinitive; as, **nōbīs cum eō agere licet**, *we may discuss with him*, lit. *it is permitted to us*; see **73b**; **222a**.

249. *a.* "Must" implies necessity, and is translated by the passive periphrastic conjugation (see **73e**; **229c**), or by **necesse est** with the infinitive or infinitive with subject-accusative, the infinitive with **necesse est** being the subject of **est**; as, **quod necesse erat accidere**, *as was bound to happen*, lit. *which was necessary to happen*, **quod accidere** being the subject of **erat** (IV.29).

b. "Ought," implying obligation or propriety, is translated either by the passive periphrastic conjugation (see **73e**; **229c**), by **oportet** and the present infinitive with subject accusative (**73a**), or by **dēbeō** with a present infinitive; since "ought" is a defective verb in English, past time is expressed in English by the past infinitive with "ought," while in Latin past time is expressed by the principal verb and only the present infinitive is used. The idea "they ought to fight bravely" (in present time) is expressed thus in Latin: **fortiter pugnāre dēbent** or **eōs fortiter pugnāre oportet** or **eīs fortiter pugnandum est**. The phrase "he ought to have sent hostages" (in past time) is expressed thus: **obsidēs mittere dēbuit** or **eum obsidēs mittere oportuit** or **obsidēs eī mittendī erant**.

THE GEOGRAPHY OF CAESAR'S COMMENTARIES

250. The geography of Caesar's commentaries on the Gallic War touches Italy, Cisalpine Gaul, Transalpine Gaul, Britain, Germany, and Spain.

251. Caesar frequently uses the name of a people for that of the country inhabited by them, where English usage expects the word "country" or "land" or an equivalent; as **quī agrum Helvētium ā Germānīs dīvidit**, *which separates the Helvetian territory from that of the Germans*, lit. *from the Germans* (I.2); **ūnum per Sēquanōs**, *one (route) through the country of the Sequanians*, lit. *through the Sequanians* (I.6).

252. Caesar uses **Italia**, *Italy*, in two senses:

a. Italy in the narrower sense as a political unit, Italy proper, having as its northern boundary on the east side the small river Rubicon, on the west the lower course of the river Auser, and between the two rivers a line running a short distance south of Luca (modern Lucca).

b. Italy in the geographical sense (I.10), designating the entire peninsula as far as the Alps, and including Cisalpine Gaul in addition to Italy proper.

253. Cisalpine Gaul is designated by Caesar as **Cisalpīna Gallia** (VI.1), **Gallia citerior**, *Nearer Gaul* (I.24), and **citerior prōvincia**, *the nearer province* (I.10). It comprised the great drainage area of the **Padus**, *Po* (V.24), extending from Italy proper to the Alps. The entire region was brought under Roman domination in the second century BC, but Cisalpine Gaul was not joined with Italy politically until the reign of Augustus.

254. Of the cities of Cisalpine Gaul Caesar mentions two, **Aquileia** (I.10), at the head of the Adriatic Sea, chief city of the Cisalpine Veneti, who gave their name to modern Venice; and **Ocelum** (I.10), in the extreme western part.

255. Transalpine Gaul is designated by Caesar as **Trānsalpīna Gallia, Gallia Trānsalpīna, Gallia ulterior** (I.7), and **ulterior Gallia** (I.10), *Further Gaul*; or simply **Gallia**, *Gaul* (I.1). It extended from the Alps and the Rhine to the Atlantic Ocean, comprising the countries now known as France and Belgium, the German possessions west of the Rhine, and the greater part of Switzerland and Holland. In this book, where "Gaul" stands alone, *Transalpine Gaul* is meant.

256. On account of differences in speech and other characteristics, Caesar describes Transalpine Gaul as divided into three parts:

a. The land of the Belgians, Belgium, in the northeast, extending from the rivers **Sēquana**, *Seine*, and **Matrona**, *Marne*, to the river **Rhēnus**, *Rhine*. The Belgium described by Caesar was much larger than the modern country. The ancient Belgian stock survives in the Walloons. The language was mostly Celtic.

b. The land of the Galli, the Celtic country, Celtic Gaul, extending from the *Seine* and *Marne* to the river **Garumna**, *Garonne*. This part is often called **Gallia** (I.1, 30). The numerous dialects of Celtic Gaul belonged to the great Celtic family, which has modern representatives in Armoric, spoken in Brittany, and the Welsh language.

c. The land of the Aquitanians, Aquitania, extending from the Garonne River to the Pyrenées. The language of the Aquitanians seems to have been related to the Basque.

257. *a.* The three divisions of Gaul were made up of many small *states*, **cīvitātēs**, each of which had its own political organization. A number of the states had their own coinage in gold and other metals; but the coins were mostly imitations of those struck by Greek states and Rome.

b. In Celtic Gaul the governing power was in the hands of two classes, the knights and the Druid priests; the condition of the common people was not much above slavery (VI.13).

258. *a.* Government in Gaul was administered by *magistrates*, **magistrātūs**, such as the Vergobrets (I.16), who were chosen by the dominant classes; a few states had *kings*, **rēgēs**, such as Galba, king of the Suessiones (II.4), and Commius, king of the Atrebates (IV.21).

b. In some states there was a *council of elders*, **senātus** (II.5).

c. Politically, Gaul in Caesar's time was in a condition of unrest. Usurpations of power and changes of rulers were frequent (II.1). Not only in the different states but in the subdivisions of states, and even in powerful families, there were party divisions (VI.11), from which conflicts of great bitterness arose. A conspicuous example is the antagonism between the brothers Diviciacus and Dumnorix (I.18), of whom the former did everything possible to advance Caesar's interests (II.5, 10), while the latter, as leader of an anti-Roman party among the Aeduans, sought to thwart Caesar, until finally he was killed, while resisting capture, by Caesar's cavalry (V.7).

259. The southeastern part of Gaul, not specified in Caesar's threefold division, had been conquered by the Romans and organized into a province in 121 BC. This was the only part of Transalpine Gaul that properly came under Caesar's jurisdiction when he went out as governor in 58 BC. It is designated by Caesar as **Gallia prōvincia** (I.19) or **prōvincia Gallia** (I.53), *the Gallic province,* **ulterior prōvincia,** *the Further province* (I.10), **prōvincia nostra,** *our province* (I.2), or simply **prōvincia,** *the province* (I.1).

260. Of the mountains of Gaul the most important are: **Alpēs,** *the Alps* (I.10), of which the western and southern portion, the French and the Swiss Alps, were known to Caesar; **mons Cebenna,** *the Cévennes* (VII.8), in Southern Gaul; **mōns Iūra,** *the Jura Mountains* (I.2), extending from the Rhone below Geneva northeast to the Rhine; **mōns Vosegus,** *the Vosges* (IV.10), west of the Rhine and north of the Jura range; **Pȳrēnaeī mōntēs,** *the Pyrenees,* on the border toward Spain (I.1).

261. The more important rivers of Gaul mentioned by Caesar are: **Rhodanus,** *the Rhone* (I.2), which flows through **lacus Lemannus,** *Lake Geneva* (I.2), and empties into the Mediterranean; **Arar,** *Saône* (I.12), a tributary of the *Rhone,* which it enters from the north; **Sēquana,** *the Seine* (I.1); **Matrona,** *Marne* (I.1), a tributary of the *Seine,* which it enters from the east; **Axona,** *Aisne* (II.5), a tributary of the *Oise,* which in turn flows into the *Seine* from the northeast, below the confluence with the *Marne;* **Rhēnus,** *Rhine* (I.1); **Garumna,** *Garonne* (I.1); **Liger,** *Loire* (III.9), the largest river of Gaul, flowing into the Bay of Biscay; **Mosa,** *Meuse* (IV.9), in northeastern Gaul; **Sabis,** *Sambre,* a tributary of the *Meuse,* which it enters from the west (II.16).

262. The cities of Gaul in Caesar's time were situated on or near a coast, on a river, or on the top of a high mountain. The more noteworthy were:

a. In the Province: **Massilia,** *Marseilles,* founded by Greeks from Phocaea about 600 BC, a prosperous city, which retained its Greek character, carried on an extensive commerce, and became an important civilizing influence; **Narbo,** *Narbonne* (III.20), on the river Atax not far from the sea, colonized by the Romans in 118 BC; **Tolōsa,** *Toulouse* (III.20), on the Garonne river; **Genava,** *Geneva* (I.6), on **lacus Lemannus,** *Lake Geneva* (I.2).

b. In Celtic Gaul: **Agedincum,** *Sens* (VI.44); **Alesia,** *Alise-Sainte-Reine* (VII.68); **Avaricum,** *Bourges* (VII.13); **Bibracte,** on *Mt. Beuvray* (I.23); **Cēnabum,** *Orléans* (VII.3); **Decetia,** *Decize* (VII.33); **Gergovia** (VII.36); **Lutecia Parīsiōrum,** *Paris* (VI.3); **Vesontiō,** *Besançon* (I.38).

c. In Belgium: **Bibrax** (II.6), near the *Aisne;* **Dūrocortorum,** *Reims* (VI.44); **Noviodūnum** of the Suessiones, near *Soissons* (II.12); **Samarobrīva,** *Amiens* (V.24).

263. Caesar uses **Britannia,** *Britain* (II.4), to designate the island of Great Britain, including modern England, Scotland, and Wales. He was the first Roman general to invade the island, whose inhabitants he found similar to those of Celtic Gaul in language and institutions, but not so far advanced in other ways. His two expeditions, in 55 and 54 BC, had slight apparent effect, but they stimulated commerce and prepared the way for the introduction of Roman wares and customs. The subjugation of Britain by the Romans began in 43 AD.

264. Caesar uses **Germānia,** *Germany* (IV.4), to designate a country of indefinite extent east of the Rhine and north of the Danube. He came into contact only with the German peoples near the Rhine. His two expeditions across the Rhine, in 55 and 53 BC, produced slight effect; the Romans never conquered more of Germany than a narrow strip along the Rhine and the Danube.

265. Ancient *Spain,* **Hispānia,** included modern Spain and Portugal. After the Roman conquest, about 200 BC, it was divided into two provinces, **citerior Hispānia,** *Nearer Spain* (III.23), including the northern and eastern part of the peninsula, and **ulterior Hispānia,** *Further Spain,* on the south and west.

266. Caesar sometimes uses **Hispānia,** *Spain,* to designate the peninsula as a whole (V.1): sometimes the plural, **Hispāniae,** *the Spains,* referring to the two Spanish provinces.

THE ROMAN ART OF WAR IN CAESAR'S TIME

COMPOSITION OF THE ARMY

267. The legion. *a.* The *legion,* **legiō** (I.7), in Caesar's time was composed exclusively of Roman citizens. Probably Caesar's *legionary soldiers,* **legiōnāriī** or simply **mīlitēs** (I.7), were mainly volunteers who were willing to enlist for the regular term of twenty years on account of the certainty of the pay, and of provision for their old age in case they lived beyond the period of service. However, citizens between the ages of seventeen and forty-six were liable to be called out by a *levy,* **dīlectus**, at any time. Romans of the upper classes who wished to serve in the army, or found themselves unable to evade conscription, were employed as officers, or attached to the bodyguard of the commander.

b. The normal strength of a legion at the end of the Republic was 6000 men; but the average number of men in Caesar's legions probably did not exceed 3600 in the Gallic War.

c. The legion was divided into ten *cohorts,* **cohortēs** (III.1), averaging, in Caesar's army, about 360 men each; the cohort was divided into three *maniples,* **manipulī** (II.25), of 120 men; the maniples into two *centuries* or *companies,* **ōrdinēs** (I.40). In legions having a full complement of men each century would contain 100; in Caesar's army the number could hardly have averaged more than 60.

d. The legions that had seen long service, apparently not less than nine or ten years, were called *veteran,* **legiōnēs veterānae** (I.24); the rest, *last levied,* or *raw,* **legiōnēs proximē cōnscrīptae** (I.24). The legions were designated by number.

e. In the first year of the Gallic War Caesar had four veteran legions, numbered VII, VIII, IX (these three apparently brought from the vicinity of Aquileia (I.10)), and X; the Tenth Legion was in the province at the time of his arrival in Gaul (I.7). After Caesar learned that the Helvetians proposed to go through the country of the Sequanians and Aeduans he hastily raised two legions in Cisalpine Gaul (I.10), which were numbered XI and XII. With these six legions he gained his first two victories, over the Helvetians and over Ariovistus.

f. In the second year of the war Caesar raised two new legions in Cisalpine Gaul (II.2), numbered XIII and XIV, so that he now had four veteran and four raw legions, eight in all.

g. In the fifth year (54 BC) the XIVth legion and half of another were annihilated in the ambush set by Ambiorix (V.26-37). At the beginning of the next year Caesar raised two more legions in Cisalpine Gaul, one replacing the lost XIVth (VI.32), the other numbered XV, and he also obtained a legion from Pompey, which was numbered VI (VI.1, VIII.54). In the last two years of the war he had thus ten legions (VII.34), numbered VI to XV inclusive.

268. The infantry auxiliaries. In addition to the legions, a Roman army contained bodies of infantry and cavalry drawn from allied and subject peoples, or hired outright from independent nations, called *auxiliaries* or *auxiliary troops,* **auxilia** (I.24). These men retained their native dress, equipment, and mode of fighting in some cases, but in others were armed and trained after the Roman fashion. To the former class belong the *light-armed troops,* **levis armātūrae peditēs** (II.24), including as special classes the slingers and bowmen. In the Gallic War Caesar availed himself of the help of *slingers,* **funditōrēs**, from the Balearic Islands (II.7), *bowmen,* **sagitāriī**, from Crete and from Numidia (II.7), and light-armed German troops (VII.65). He utilized also contingents from the Gallic States that he subdued (III.18). Caesar, like other Roman writers, usually does not state the exact number of the auxiliary troops; they were regarded as relatively unimportant. The officers of the auxiliaries, both infantry and cavalry, were Romans. Auxiliary troops posted on the wing of an army might be called *wing-men,* **ālāriī** (I.51).

269. The cavalry. *a.* A troop of cavalry usually accompanied each legion. While the evidence is not conclusive, it is probable that in the latter part of the Gallic War, if not from the beginning, Caesar had contingents of cavalry in connection with his legions, averaging 200 to 300 men each. These horsemen were foreigners, serving for pay; they were drawn from Spain, from Germany, and from Gaul.

b. Apart from the legionary contingents, Caesar had a force of cavalry raised from the Gallic states subject or friendly to Rome, which was reckoned as a single body, numbering under ordinary circumstances about 4000 (I.15, V.5) or 5000 men (IV.12).

c. The cavalry was divided into *squadrons,* **turmae,** of about 30 horsemen; such a squad went with Commius to Britain (IV.35). Probably the squad contained three *decuries,* **decuriae,** of 10 men each, under the command of *decurions,* **decuriōnēs** (I.23). The higher officers were called *cavalry prefects,* **praefectī equitum** (III.26).

270. The non-combatants. *a.* There were two classes of non-combatants, slaves employed for menial services, and free men, or freedmen. In the former class were included the officers' servants and *camp servants,* **cālōnēs** (II.24), as well as the drivers and *muleteers* with the heavy baggage, **mūliōnēs;** in the latter class were citizens or others who were allowed to accompany the army but were obliged to find quarters outside of the camp, such as the *traders,* **mercātōrēs.**

b. The *builders,* **fabrī** (V.11), were not enrolled as a separate corps, but were drawn from the ranks of the legionary soldiers whenever needed.

271. The baggage train. Each legion had a separate baggage train. The heavy *baggage,* **impedīmenta** (II.19), comprised tents, hand-mills for grinding grain, artillery, extra weapons, and other military stores, as well as supplies of food. For better defense in the enemy's country the baggage trains of a number of legions might be formed into a single column (II.19). The baggage of the soldiers, carried in individual *packs,* **sarcinae,** is distinct from the baggage of the legion.

THE OFFICERS

272. The general was properly called *leader,* **dux,** until he had won a victory; after the first victory he had a right to the title **imperātor,** *commander* or *general* (I.40). Caesar used the title Imperator from the time that he defeated the Helvetians, in 58 BC, until his death (I.40, *etc.*).

273. *a.* Next in rank came the *lieutenant,* or *lieutenant-general,* **lēgātus** (I.10), who was frequently placed by Caesar in command of separate legions, or of corps containing more than one legion. When acting in the absence of the general the lieutenant became *lieutenant in the general's place,* **lēgātus prō praetōre** (I.21), and exercised unusual authority. The title "lieutenant general" would more accurately define the military position of Labienus, for example, than that of "lieutenant" as the word is used in the United States and England.

b. The *quaestor,* **quaestor** (I.52), was charged with the care of the military chest and the supplies, but sometimes was clothed with purely military authority and assumed the functions of a lieutenant. The quaestor and the lieutenants belonged to the staff of the general, and had, as he did, the distinction of a *bodyguard,* **cohors praetōria** (I.40), composed of picked soldiers and of young men of rank who wished to acquire military experience.

274. The *military tribunes,* **trībūnī mīlitum** (I.39), numbered six to a legion. In Caesar's army the tribunes appear to have received appointment for personal rather than military reasons; and they were entrusted with subordinate services, such as the leading of troops on the march, the command of detachments smaller than a legion, the securing of supplies (III.7), and the oversight of the watches. Only one military tribune, Gaius Volusenus (III.5), is mentioned by Caesar in terms of praise.

275. *a.* In marked contrast with the higher officers, who were of good social position, were the captains, or *centurions,* **centuriōnēs, ōrdinēs** (V.30). These were often of the humblest origin; they were promoted from the ranks for their bravery and efficiency. At the drill, on the march, and in battle, they were at the same time the models and the leaders of the soldiers.

b. As each century had a centurion, there were 2 centurions in each maniple (distinguished as *first,* **prior**, and *second,* **posterior**), 6 in each cohort, and 60 in the legion. The first in rank was the *first centurion* (of the first maniple) *of the first cohort,* **prīmipīlus** (II.25). The first centurion of the second maniple of a cohort was called **prīnceps prior**.

276. Below the centurions, but ranking above the common soldiers, were the privileged soldiers, who were relieved from picket duty as well as work on fortifications and other manual labor. Such were the *veteran volunteers,* **ēvocātī**, soldiers who had served their full time but had reenlisted at the general's request; the musicians; and the *standard-bearers,* **signiferī**.

PROVISIONING AND PAY OF THE SOLDIERS

277. Caesar was careful to have ample supplies always at hand. The care of the stores was in the hands of the quaestor, with his staff. Not bread or flour, but *grain,* **frūmentum** (I.16), usually wheat, was served out to the soldiers for rations. This they themselves ground with *hand-mills,* **molae manuālēs**, and prepared for food by boiling into a paste or by making into bread without yeast.

The grain was portioned out every fifteen days, and on the march each soldier carried his share in a sack. The amount furnished does not seem large when we reflect that the men lived almost exclusively on a vegetable diet. The allowance for the fifteen days was two Roman *pecks,* **modiī**, about half a bushel by our measure. As the weight of this was not far from thirty pounds, the soldier had about two pounds per day. On difficult or forced marches extra rations were served out.

If the soldier desired to do so he could trade off his grain for bread, or buy other articles of food from the numerous *traders,* **mercātōrēs** (I.39), who accompanied the army and had a flourishing business. When wheat was scarce, *barley,* **hordeum**, was substituted. Rations of barley were frequently served out also instead of wheat as a punishment for slight offenses. In traversing an enemy's country fresh meat was often secured.

278. The wages of the Roman soldier were very small, but in successful campaigns the men had a share of the *booty,* **praeda**, consisting largely of captives, who were sold as slaves. These were bought up on the spot by the traders, and thus readily turned into cash. Sometimes Caesar gave money realized from the sale of booty. As other *rewards,* **praemia** (V.58), the commander could make special *gifts,* **mīlitāria dōna**, such as disk-shaped *decorations* of metal, **phalerae**, clothing, and double pay.

When convicted of cowardly or disgraceful conduct the soldier was deprived of his weapons and driven from the camp, or in extreme cases put to death; officers and privileged soldiers might be reduced in rank.

279. At the close of his period of service, twenty years, or on reaching his fiftieth year of age, the soldier who had served well was entitled to an *honorable discharge,* **missiō honesta**, together with an allotment of land or a payment of money.

DRESS AND EQUIPMENT

280. The legionary soldier wore a thick woolen undergarment, *tunic,* **tunica**, reaching nearly to the knees. His *cloak,* **sagum**, which served also as a blanket, was likewise of undyed wool, and fastened by a *clasp,* **fibula**, on the right shoulder, so as not to impede the movement of the right arm. The soldier's *shoes,* **caligae**, were like a sandal, but had heavy soles which were fastened on by straps over the foot and instep.

281. The *cloak* of the commander, **palūdāmentum**, differed from that of the soldier only in being more ample, of finer quality, and ornamented; Caesar's was scarlet in color (VII.88).

282. The weapons of the legionary were part offensive, part defensive.

As defensive *weapons*, **arma**, he had:

a. A *helmet*, **galea**, ornamented with a *crest*, **crista**. On the march the helmet was hung on a cord that passed through the ring at the top and around the soldier's neck. The crest was fastened on before going into action.

b. A *cuirass*, or *coat of mail*, **lōrīca**, of leather, or of leather strengthened with strips of metal, or of metal.

c. A *shield*, ordinarily rectangular, **scūtum** (II.25), but in some cases oval, **clipeus**, made of two layers of boards fastened together, strengthened on the outside by layers of linen or of leather, and at the edges by a rim of metal. At the middle of the outside was an iron knob, **umbō**, used in striking. On the march the shield was protected from the wet by a leather *covering*, **tegimentum** (II.21). In battle it was held on the left arm.

The offensive weapons of the legionary were:

d. A *pike*, **pīlum** (I.25), a heavy and formidable javelin. It consisted of a shaft of wood about four feet long, into the end of which was fitted a small iron shaft, **ferrum** (I.25), with a pointed head, which projected two feet beyond the end of the wood. The weight of the whole was not far from ten or eleven pounds. Pikes could be thrown only about 75 feet, but they were hurled with such skill and force that the first hurling often decided the battle.

e. A *sword*, **gladius** (I.25), called *Spanish sword*, **gladius Hispānus**, because it was made according to a pattern brought from Spain after the Second Punic War. The Spanish sword was short, broad, two-edged, and pointed, better adapted for stabbing than for slashing, though used for both purposes. It was kept in a *scabbard*, **vāgīna** (V.44), fastened to a *belt*, **balteus** (V.44), which was passed over the left shoulder; this brought the sword on the right side, so that it was not in the way of the shield.

f. In the time of the Empire, and probably also in Caesar's day, officers carried a *dagger*, **pugiō**, which was attached to a belt running around the waist.

283. The dress and equipment of the light-armed soldiers varied greatly. They, as well as the cavalry, seem generally to have had a light round or oval *shield*, **parma**, about three feet in diameter. The cavalry had *helmets* of metal, **cassidēs**, light lances for hurling, and a longer sword than that used by the infantry.

THE STANDARDS

284. *a.* While the ancient battle lacked the noise and smoke of cannon and other devices of modern war, great clouds of dust were raised that obscured the movements of the combatants; the standards were consequently more numerous, and had a more important role than flags have today.

b. The standards of Caesar's army were:

(1) The *eagle* of the legion, **aquila** (IV.25), of silver, carried in battle on the end of a pole by the *eagle-bearer*, **aquilifer** (V.37). In camp it was kept in a little *shrine*, **sacellum**. It was the standard of the legion as a whole; the eagle with extended wings borne aloft seemed to signify that the bird sacred to Jupiter, god of victory, was ready to lead the legion to success; and the loss of the eagle was the deepest disgrace that could be incurred (IV.25, V.37).

(2) The *standards*, **signa** (II.21), one to each maniple, carried by *standard-bearers*, **signiferī** (II.25). These varied in appearance. There was no separate standard for the cohort.

(3) The *banners*, **vēxilla**, rectangular flags of different sizes used for a variety of purposes. A large red flag was the special sign of the commander (II.20). Smaller banners were used by special detachments not formed of regular maniples, or attached to the standards of the maniples.

285. On the march the standard was at the front, in battle some distance behind the front, of the maniple. From the immediate association of the manipular standards with military movements arose several idiomatic expressions used by Caesar, such as: **signa ferre**, *to go forward* (I.39), **signa īnferre**, *to advance* (II.26), and **signa convertere**, *to face about* (I.25).

The Musical Instruments

286. *a.* The musical instruments were:

(1) The *trumpet*, **tuba** (II.20), about three feet long, with a funnel-shaped opening; it had a deep tone, and was sounded by the *trumpeters*, **tubicinēs**.

(2) The *horn*, **cornū**, a large curved instrument, with a shriller note.

(3) The *shell trumpet*, **būcina**, was used especially in camp for giving the signals to change the watches.

b. As the maniple was the unit of military movement, musical signals were addressed to the standard-bearers, **signiferī**.

c. The order to advance or to fall back was conveyed by the general to the *trumpeters*, **tubicinēs**; their signal was taken up by the horn blowers, **cornicinēs**, of whom there was one to each maniple. The notes of the instruments could be heard above the din of battle much more clearly than the spoken words of the officers.

The Army on the March

287. When in an enemy's country Caesar maintained an exceedingly efficient information service. Parties of mounted *patrols*, **explōrātōrēs** (I.21), scoured the country; and their observation was supplemented by single *scouts* or *spies*, **speculātōrēs** (II.11), who gathered information wherever they could.

288. The army advanced ordinarily in three divisions. At the *front*, **prīmum agmen**, came the cavalry, with perhaps a division of light-armed troops, sent ahead to feel out the enemy (I.15), and in case of attack, to hold him at bay until the rest of the army could prepare for action (II.19). Next came the main force, each legion being accompanied by its baggage train; but when there was danger of attack the legions marched in single column, with the baggage of the whole army united (II.19). The *rear*, **novissimum agmen**, might in case of danger be formed from part of the legionary force, the baggage being between the rear and the main body (II.19).

289. The regular *day's march*, **iūstum iter**, was from six to seven hours long. The start was usually made at sunrise; but in emergencies the army got under way at midnight, or two or three o'clock in the morning. The distance ordinarily traversed was about 15 or 16 English miles; on a *forced march*, **iter magnum** (II.12), a much greater distance might be made, 25 or 30 English miles. Caesar's forced marches manifested astonishing powers of endurance on the part of his soldiers. Rivers were often crossed by fording; in such operations the ancient army had the advantage over the modern, because it carried no ammunition that would be spoiled by the water (V.18).

290. On the march the soldier carried his rations, his cooking utensils, his arms, blanket, and one or two *rampart stakes*, or *palisades*, **vallī**. The luggage was secured in tight *bundles* or *packs*, **sarcinae**, which were fastened to forked poles, and raised over the shoulder. The helmet was hung by a cord from the neck, the other weapons disposed of in the most convenient way. When it rained, the oblong *shields*, **scūta** (282c), could be put over the head like a roof.

The Army in Camp

291. *a.* A camp was fortified at the close of every day's march. When the army was still on the march, men were sent forward to choose a suitable location for a camp and measure it off.

b. Whenever possible, a site for the camp was selected on a slight elevation, with water and wood for fuel near at hand. The proximity of a dense forest or overhanging mountain was avoided, so that a favorable opportunity of attack might not be given to the enemy. Sometimes the rear or one side was placed parallel with a river (II.5).

292. The camp was usually rectangular; in a few cases there were camps of irregular shapes, adapted to the nature of the ground. The size of the camp varied according to the size of the force.

293. In fortifying a camp, first an embankment was thrown up on all four sides; for digging the soldiers used spades. Outside of this embankment was a trench, usually triangular (V-shaped), from which the earth for the embankment was taken. On the outer edge of the embankment a row of strong *rampart stakes* or *palisades*, **vallī** was driven firmly in, forming a *stockade*. The *rampart*, **vallum** (II.5), thus made was several feet high and wide enough so that the soldiers could stand on it behind the palisades. The *trench*, or *moat*, **fossa** (II.8), was from twelve to eighteen feet wide (II.5) and from seven to ten feet deep. When the army expected to remain in the same place for a long time, as in *winter quarters*, **hīberna** (I.54), or a *stationary camp*, **castra statīva**, sometimes *towers*, **turrēs** (V.40), were added at brief intervals, and the intervening spaces further protected by a roof. The labor of fortifying a camp was prodigious.

294. a. The camp had four gates. That in the direction of the advance, toward the enemy, was called the *general's gate*, **porta praetōria**, the one opposite to this, at the rear, *the decuman gate*, **porta decumāna** (II.24); the gates on the right and left side respectively, as one faced the front, were called the *main right gate*, **porta prīncipālis dextra**, and *main left gate*, **porta prīncipālis sinistra**. The last two were connected by the *main street*, **via prīncipālis**. The entrances were made more easily defensible by being constructed such that an enemy attempting to enter would be forced to expose the right, or unprotected side. (AG 429a, B 218.9).

b. Inside the rampart, between it and the tents, a vacant space two hundred feet wide was left on all sides. The remaining room in the enclosure was systematically divided, so that every maniple, decuria, and body of light-armed troops knew its place and could find its quarters at once. The *general's quarters*, **praetōrium**, was near the middle of the camp; near it was an open space where he could address his troops from a *platform*, **suggestus**. Access to all parts of the camp was made by means of *passageways*, **viae** (V.49).

295. a. The *tents*, **tabernācula** (I.39), were of leather; hence **sub pellibus**, lit. *under hides*, means *in tents* (III.29). Each was calculated to hold ten men; but a centurion seems generally to have had more room than the soldiers.

b. The *winter quarters*, **hīberna**, were made more comfortable by the substitution of straw-thatched *huts*, **casae** (V.43), for tents.

c. In a hostile country a strong guard was kept before the gates of the camp (IV.32). In earlier times, and probably in Caesar's army, the password that allowed admittance to the camp was different each night; it was written on slips of wood, which were given by the commander to the military tribunes, and passed by these to the men on duty.

296. Many Roman camps became the nucleus of permanent settlements that survive as cities today. A marked instance is the city of *Chester* in England, the name of which is derived from **castra**; so *Rochester* from **Rodolphī castra**.

The Army in Battle Array

297. a. When the Roman force was far outnumbered by the enemy, the legionary soldiers might be arranged in a *double line*, **duplex aciēs** (III.24), or even in a *single line*, **aciēs simplex**. But under ordinary circumstances Caesar drew up his legions in a *triple line*, **triplex aciēs**, as in the battles with the Helvetians, Ariovistus, and the Usipetes and Tencteri. This arrangement was probably as follows:

(1) Four cohorts of each legion stood in the first line; about 160 feet behind them stood three cohorts; and ordinarily the remaining three cohorts of the legion were posted still farther back as a reserve.

(2) In each cohort the three maniples stood side-by-side, one of the centuries in each maniple being

behind the other. The soldiers in each battle line stood about three feet apart each way; and in Caesar's cohorts the men seem to have stood 8 ranks deep. The standard-bearers did not stand in the front rank, but were protected by soldiers selected for their agility and strength.

b. As the first line went into action the second followed closely behind; as the men of the first fell or withdrew exhausted, those of the second pressed forward and took their places; if needed, the third line advanced and in like manner relieved the combined first and second. In the battle with the Helvetians the whole third line faced about and repelled an attack on the rear.

298. When circumstances required it, soldiers were massed in serried ranks, as in a wedge-shaped column, *wedge*, **cuneus**, or under a *turtle-shell*, **testūdō**. For defense a force was sometimes formed into a *circle*, **orbis**, corresponding to a hollow square (IV.37).

299. The place of the light-armed troops and cavalry was ordinarily at first in front of the triple line, or on the wings. They opened the engagement by skirmishing, prevented flank movements of the enemy, drew the brunt of the attack if the legions wished to take another position, and were employed in various other ways as occasion demanded. The cavalry were especially utilized to cut down the fleeing.

OPERATIONS AGAINST FORTIFIED PLACES

300. The taking of walled towns was accomplished either by *sudden storming* without long preparation, (**repentīna**) **oppugnātiō**; by *siege blockade*, **obsidiō** or **obsessiō**, which aimed to repel all attempts of the enemy to escape or secure supplies and so reduce him by starvation; or by *siege and storming*, **longinqua oppugnātiō**, with the help of engineering deployed to break down the enemy's fortifications and gain admission to the city. When storming a city, the forces rushed forward, tried to batter down the gates, fill up the moat, and mount the walls with ladders.

301. The siege was begun by extending a line of works, if the nature of the site allowed, entirely around the place to be reduced. Then a *siege embankment*, or *mole*, **agger**, a wide roadway of timber and earth, was begun outside the reach of the enemy's weapons; it was gradually advanced toward the city wall, and raised until at the front the top was on a level with the wall, or even higher. Where the ground allowed, tunnels were run under the town and the city walls undermined.

302. ***a.*** The workmen at the front were protected by movable *breastworks*, **pluteī**, or by *arbor-sheds*, or *sappers' huts*, **vīneae** (II.12), made of timber or of thick wickerwork, with rawhides stretched over the outside as a protection against fire. Rows of arbor-sheds were placed along the sides of the mole to afford passageways to the front; a long arbor-shed was called a *mousie*, **mūsculus**. A sappers' shed with a sloping roof of strong boards specially adapted for use in undermining a wall was called a *turtle-shell shed*, **testūdō**.

b. *Movable towers*, **turrēs ambulātōriae** (II.12, 31), to be filled with soldiers, were built out of range of the enemy's missiles and brought up near the walls, usually on the siege embankment, which sloped gently from the rear up to the wall.

c. In the lowest story of the movable tower, or under a separate roof, was the *battering ram*, **ariēs** (II.32), an enormous beam with a metallic head which was swung against the walls with terrific force. The attacking force tried also to pry stones out of the walls with *wall hooks*, **falcēs** (**mūrālēs**), light poles with a strong iron hook at the end.

d. Walls and ramparts were mounted by means of *scaling ladders*, **scālae** (V.43).

303. For throwing heavy missiles the Romans had *torsioners*, **tormenta**, so named from the method of developing the force required for hurling; **tormentum** is derived from **torqueō**, *twist*. This was obtained by twisting with great tension strong ropes, which were suddenly released by means of a trigger; the force was utilized for the shooting of three principal types of missiles:

a. The *catapult*, **catapulta**, for shooting large arrows or darts. A small catapult is called a *scorpion*, **scorpiō**.

b. The *ballista*, **ballista**, which cast stones; the trough was sharply inclined, while that of the catapult was nearly horizontal. The ballista is not mentioned by Caesar.

c. The *wild ass*, **onager**, which hurled stones, but was probably not used in Caesar's time.

304. The besieged responded to tunneling under their defenses with counter-tunnels of their own. Above ground, they tried to catch the head of the battering ram with great hooks and hold it, or let down masses of wood or wickerwork along the side of the wall to deaden the force of the blow, or they drew the wall hooks over into the city with windlasses. By frequent *sallies*, **ēruptiōnēs**, they endeavored to destroy the works of the besiegers, drive the workmen from their posts, and hurl firebrands into the sheds and towers. Owing to the amount of wood used in siege works, the danger from fire was great.

305. When a breach had been made in the wall, or a gate battered down, an attack was begun wherever it was thought possible to force an entrance. The siege embankment and towers were connected with the top of the wall by means of planks, and beams were thrown across. Detachments of soldiers, holding their oblong shields close together above their heads, formed a *turtle-shell*, **testūdō**, under which they marched up close to the walls and tried to scale them, or they entered the breach.

The Roman Battleships

306. *a.* The *battleships* or *galleys*, **nāvēs longae** (III.9), of Caesar's time were propelled mainly by oars; they had only one mast, and generally one large sail. There were usually three rows or banks of oars, hence the name *trireme*, **(nāvis) trirēmis**, but sometimes vessels with two banks of oars were used, *bireme*, **birēmis**, and even five banks, *quinquereme*, **quīnquerēmis**. The rowers kept time to the sound of a horn or click of a hammer.

b. The *rudders*, **gubernācula**, were not like those of today, but consisted of two large paddles thrust down into the sea, one on each side of the stern; they were controlled by the *steersman*, **gubernātor** (III.9). The anchor was like those of our own time.

c. At the prow, near the water line, was the ship's *beak*, **rōstrum** (III.13), consisting of one or more sharp metal-pointed beams projecting in front, for use in ramming a hostile ship. When the galleys were not in use they might be drawn up on the shore (IV.29).

d. Before the galley went into action the sail was rolled up and the mast taken down; a *tower*, **turris** (III.14), was raised on the front part of the ship, from which missiles could be hurled over into a vessel near at hand; *grappling hooks*, **ferreae manūs** (lit. *iron hands*), were provided, by which the opposing ship might be seized, as well as a movable bridge that could be thrown across in boarding.

e. For the carrying of his troops Caesar used *transports*, **onerāriae nāvēs** (IV.22), which were broader and slower than the galleys; these were accompanied by galleys as escort (V.8).

f. The admiral's ship, or flagship, was distinguished by a red *banner*, **vēxillum**, resembling that used by the general on land (**284b**).

307. The naval tactics of the Romans consisted mainly in either propelling a vessel with great force against a rival and crushing the side by ramming, or in catching hold of the hostile craft with grappling hooks, pulling alongside, springing over onto it, and settling the conflict with a hand-to-hand fight. In the sea-fight with the Venetans, who had only sailing vessels, the Roman sailors crippled the enemy's ships by cutting down the sail yards; the legionaries on the galleys then boarded the Venetan ships and dispatched the crews (III.13-15).

Dress and Equipment of the Gauls and Germans

308. The Gauls wore trousers, **brācae**, which the Romans considered barbaric. The Gallic military *cloak*, **sagulum** (V.42), was apparently smaller than that of the Roman soldiers.

309. The Gallic infantry were protected by large oblong or oval shields, of wood or metal (called by Caesar, **scūta**, I.25), and by helmets of metal. The offensive weapons of the Gauls were a long sword and several types of missile for throwing, such as *javelins*, **gaesa** (III.4), *spears*, **matarae** (I.26), and *darts*, **trāgulae** (I.26) or **verūta** (V.44).

310. The Gallic standard, in some cases at least, was an image of a boar mounted on a pole. Signals in Gallic armies were given on a curved *war-trumpet*, **carnyx**.

311. The clothing of the Germans was largely of skins (IV.1), but some wore trousers, like the Gauls, and confined their long hair in a kind of knot. The principal weapons of the Germans were a shield and spear, and a long sword with a single edge.

VOCABULARY

ABBREVIATIONS

References to the *Gallic War* are noted thus: I.7 (= Book I, chapter 7).

References to the *Companion to Caesar* (within this book) are noted in bold after the lexical entry but before the definition, thus: **meus, -a, -um**, adj., (**41**), *my, mine*.

English derivatives of Latin words are inserted at the end of the definitions, set off by a half-bracket, thus: [accuse.

* Implies that the form before which it stands is hypothetical.

abl.	ablative		intens.	intensive
abs.	absolute		inter.	interrogative
acc.	accusative		interj.	interjection
adj.	adjective		intr.	intransitive
adv.	adverb, adverbial		irr.	irregular
comp.	comparative		lit.	literally
conj.	conjunction		m.	masculine
dat.	dative		n., neut.	neuter
decl.	declension		nom.	nominative
def.	defective		num.	numeral
dem.	demonstrative		ord.	ordinal
dep.	deponent		part.	participle
dim.	diminutive		pass.	passive
distrib.	distributive		patr.	patronymic
e.g.	exempli gratia = for example		pers.	person, personal
et al.	et alibi = and elsewhere		pf.	perfect
et seq.	et sequentia = and what follows		pl.	plural
etc.	et cetera = and so forth		pos.	positive
excl.	exclamation		pred.	predicate
f.	feminine		prep.	preposition
freq.	frequentative		pres.	present
fut.	future		pron.	pronoun
gen.	genitive		reflex.	reflexive
i.e.	id est = that is		rel.	relative
imp.	imperative		semi-dep.	semi-deponent
impers.	impersonal		sing.	singular
impf.	imperfect		subj.	subjunctive
inch.	inchoative		sup.	superlative
indecl.	indeclinable		trans.	translate, or translation
indef.	indefinite		v.	verb
indic.	indicative		voc.	vocative
inf.	infinitive		1, 2, 3, 4	1st, 2nd, 3rd, 4th conjugation

A.

A., with proper names, = *Aulus.*

a. d. = **ante diem.**

ā, ab, abs, prep. with abl., *from, away from, out of; at, on;* of agency, with the passive voice, *by, on the part of;* of time, *from, since, after.* **ab utrōque latere,** *on both sides.* **ā parvīs,** *from childhood* (VI.21).

abditus, -a, -um, [part. of **ābdo**], adj., *concealed, secluded.*

abdō, -dere, -didī, -ditus, [**ab + dō**], 3, *put away, remove; conceal.* **sē abdere,** *to hide one's self.*

abdūcō, -dūcere, -dūxī, -ductus, [**ab + dūcō**], 3, *withdraw; lead away, take off* (I.11). [abduct.

abeō, -īre, -iī, -itūrus, [**ab + eō**], irr., *go away, depart.*

abesse, see **absum.**

abiciō, -icere, -iēcī, -iectus, [**ab + iaciō**], 3, *throw away, throw down; hurl* (V.48). [abject.

abiēs, -ietis, f., (**10e**), *fir tree, spruce* (V.12).

abscīdō, -cīdere, -cīdī, -cīsus, [**abs + caedō**], 3, *cut off* (III.14).

absēns, [part. of **absum**], adj., *absent.* **sē absente,** *in his absence.* [absent

absimilis, -e, [**ab + similis**], adj., *unlike.*

absistō, -sistere, -stitī, [**ab + sistō**], 3, *withdraw, go away.*

abstineō, -tinēre, -tinuī, -tentus, [**abs + teneō**], 2, *hold back; refrain from* (I.22). [abstain.

abstrahō, -trahere, -trāxī, -trāctus, [**abs + trahō**], 3, *drag away, drag off, take away by force.* [abstract.

absum, -esse, āfuī, āfutūrus, [**ab + sum**], irr., *be distant, be absent or away from; be wanting, be lacking.* **longē abesse,** *to be far away.* **ā bellō abesse,** *to be exempt from military service* (VI.14).

accēdō, -cēdere, -cessī, -cessūrus, [**ad + cēdō**], 3, *come to, draw near, approach; be added.*

acceptus, -a, -um, comp. **-ior,** sup. **-issimus,** [part. of **accipiō**], adj., *acceptable, welcome, dear* (I.3).

accidō, -cidere, -cidī, [**ad + cadō**], 3, *fall* (III.14, 25); *happen, occur, turn out; befall, fall to the lot of.* Impers., **accidit,** *it happens.* [accident.

accipiō, -cipere, -cēpī, -ceptus, [**ad + capiō**], 3, *take to one's self, receive, accept; hear of, learn.* [accept.

acclīvis, -e, [**ad,** cf. **clīvus**], adj., *sloping; uphill, rising.*

acclīvitās, -tātis, [**acclīvis**], f., *upward slope, ascent* (II.18).

Accō, -ōnis, m., a leader of the Senones.

accommodātus, -a, -um, comp. **-ior,** sup. **-issimus,** [part. of **accommodō**], adj., *suited, adapted* (III.13). [accommodate.

accommodō, -āre, -āvī, -ātus, [**ad + commodō,** from **commodus**], 1, *adjust, put on.* (II.21).

accūrātē, comp. **-ius,** sup. **-issimē,** [**accūrātus**], adv., *carefully.*

accurrō, -currere, -cucurrī or **-currī, -cursum est,** [**ad + currō**], 3, *run to* (III.5), *hasten to* (I.22).

accūsō, -āre, -āvī, -ātus, [**ad + causa**], 1, *call to account, find fault with; reproach, accuse.* [accuse.

acerbē, comp. **acerbius,** sup. **acerbissimē,** [**acerbus**], adv., *bitterly.*

acerbus, -a, -um, comp. **-ior,** sup. **-issimus,** [**ācer**], adj., *bitter, harsh.*

ācerrimē, see **ācriter.**

acervus, -ī, m., *heap, pile* (II.32).

aciēs, -ēī, f., *edge;* of the eye, *keen look* (I.39); of an army, *line of battle, army in battle array, battle.*

ācriter, comp. **ācrius,** sup. **ācerrimē,** [**ācer**], adv., *sharply, fiercely, with vigor, courageously.*

āctuārius, -a, -um, [**agō**], adj., *easily driven, swift.* **nāvis āctuāria,** *swift vessel,* driven by oars as well as sails (V.1).

āctus, see **agō.**

acūtus, -a, -um, comp. **-ior,** sup. **-issimus,** [part. of **acuō,** sharpen], adj., *sharpened, sharp.* [acute.

ad, prep. with acc., *to, towards, up to;* of place, *in the vicinity of, at, near to, by, in the presence of, among, on;* of time, *till, to, up to, until;* of purpose, especially with the gerundive constr., *for, in order to, for the purpose of, in;* of other relations, *with regard to, according to, in respect to, in consequence of, as to, in;* with words of number, with adverbial force, *about;* **ad hunc modum,** *after this manner.* **ad ūnum,** *to a man.* **ad exercitum manēre,** *to remain with the army* (V.53).

adāctus, see **adigō.**

adaequō, -āre, -āvī, -ātus, [**ad + aequō**], 1, *make equal to, bring up to a level with* (III.12); *be equal to, keep up with* (I.48), *keep abreast of* (V.8). [adequate.

adamō, -āre, -āvī, -ātus, [**ad + amō**], 1, *conceive a love for, covet* (I.31).

addō, -dere, -didī, -ditus, [**ad + dō**], 3, *add, join to.* [add.

addūcō, -dūcere, -dūxī, -ductus, [**ad + dūcō**], 3, *lead to, bring, bring up to a place; lead, draw; induce, prevail upon.* [adduce.

adēmptus, see **adimō.**

adeō, -īre, -iī, -itum est, [**ad + eō**], irr., *go to, come near, draw near, approach; reach, visit.*

adeō, [**ad + eō,** from **is**], adv., *so far, to such a degree; so, so much.*

adeptus, see **adipīscor.**

adequitō, -āre, -āvī, [**ad + equitō,** from **eques**], 1, *ride towards; ride up to* (I.46).

adhaerēscō, -haerēscere, -haesī, [**ad + haerēscō**], 3, *stick, adhere; remain clinging* (V.48).

adhibeō, -hibēre, -hibuī, -hibitus, [**ad + habeō**], 2, *hold toward; bring forward, bring in, call in, summon, admit; use, employ.*

adhortor, -ārī, -ātus, [**ad + hortor**], 1, dep., *encourage, rally, exhort, rouse, urge.*

adhūc, [**ad + hūc**], adv., *hitherto, until now, as yet* (III.22).

adiaceō, -iacēre, -iacuī, [**ad + iaceō**], 2, *lie near, border upon, be adjacent.* [adjacent.

Adiatunnus, -ī, m., a leader of the Sotiates (III.22).

adiciō, -icere, -iēcī, -iectus, [**ad + iaciō**], 3, *throw to, hurl; throw up; join to, add.*

adigō, -igere, -ēgī, -āctus, [**ad + agō**], 3, *drive* (*to*), *drive in;* of missiles, *cast, hurl* (*to*); of piles, *drive home* (IV.17); of a tower, *move up* (V.43).

adimō, -imere, -ēmī, -ēmptus, [**ad + emō**], 3, *take away* (V.6).

adipīscor, -ipīscī, -eptus, [**ad + apīscor,** *reach*], 3, dep., *gain, obtain, secure* (V.39). [adept.

aditus, -ūs, [**adeō**], m., *approach, access; way of approach, means of access;* pl. *landing-places* (IV.20).

adiungō, -iungere, -iūnxī, -iūnctus, [**ad + iungō**], 3, *join to, attach; add, unite with; annex.* [adjunct.

adiūtor, -ōris, [**adiuvō**], m., *helper, confederate* (V.38); *mediator* (V.41).

adiuvō, -iuvāre, -iūvī, adiūtus, [**ad + iuvō**], 1, *help, assist, support; render assistance, be of assistance.*

administer, -trī, [**ad + minister**], m., (**7c**), *assistant, helper; officiating priest* (VI.16).

administrō, -āre, -āvī, -ātus, [**ad + ministrō**], 1, *render assistance; manage, carry on; arrange for, get ready;* of orders, *execute, carry out.* [administer.

admīror, -ārī, -ātus, [**ad + mīror**], 1, dep., *wonder at, be surprised at; admire.*

admittō, -mittere, -mīsī, -missus, [**ad + mittō**], 3, *let go; admit, receive; become guilty of, commit; incur* (IV.25).

facinus admittere, *to commit a crime.* [admit.

admodum, [**ad +** acc. of **modus**], adv., lit. *up to the measure; quite, very;* with numbers, *fully, at least.*

admoneō, -ēre, -uī, -itus, [**ad + moneō**], 2, *warn.* [admonish.

adolēscō, -olēscere, -olēvī, -ultus, [**ad + olēscō,** *grow*], 3, *grow up, reach maturity* (VI.18). [adolescent.

adorior, -orīrī, -ortus, [**ad + orior**], 4, dep., *fall upon, attack, assail.*

adsum, -esse, affuī, [**ad + sum**], irr., *be at hand, be present.*

adulēscēns, -entis, [**adolēscō**], adj., *young.* As noun, m., *young man, youth.*

adulēscentia, -ae, [**adulēscēns**], f., (I.20). [adolescence.

adulēscentulus, -ī, [dim. of **adulēscēns**], m., *very young man* (III.21).

adventus, -ūs, [**adveniō**], m., *coming, approach, arrival.* [advent.

adversārius, -a, -um, [**adversor**], adj., *opposed.* As noun, **adversārius, -ī,** m., *opponent, enemy.* [adversary.

adversus, -a, -um, sup. **-issimus,** [part. of **advertō**], adj., *turned towards, fronting, in front, facing, opposite; unfavorable, adverse, unsuccessful.* **in adversum ōs,** *full in the face* (V.35). [adverse.

adversus, [**advertō**], prep. with acc. only, *opposite to; against* (IV.14).

advertō, -tere, -tī, -sus, [**ad + vertō**], 3, *turn to, direct.* **animum advertō,** *notice, observe.*

advolō, -āre, -āvī, [**ad + volō,** *fly*], 1, *fly to; hasten to, rush upon.*

aedificium, -ī, [**aedificō**], n., *building.* [edifice.

aedificō, -āre, -āvī, -ātus, [**aedēs,** *building,* + FAC, in **faciō**], 1, *build, construct.*

Aeduus, -a, -um, adj., *Aeduan.* As noun, **Aeduus, -ī,** m., *an Aeduan;* pl., *Aeduans, the Aedui,* a Gallic people, between the upper waters of the Sequana (*Seine*) and the Liger (*Loire*), in alliance with the Romans before Caesar's arrival in Gaul and prominent throughout the Gallic War.

aeger, -gra, -grum, adj., (**22f**), *sick.* As noun, **aegrī, -ōrum,** *the sick* (V.40).

aegerrimē, see **aegrē.**

aegrē, comp. **aegrius,** sup. **aegerrimē,** [**aeger**], adv., *with difficulty, scarcely, hardly.* **aegerrimē,** *with the greatest difficulty* (I.13).

Aemilius, -ī, m., *Lucius Aemilius,* a decurion in charge of a squad of Gallic cavalry (I.23).

aequāliter, [**aequālis,** *equal*], adv., *evenly, uniformly* (II.18).

aequinoctium, -ī, [**aequus + nox**], n., *equinox* (IV.36; V.23). [equinox.

aequitās, -tātis, [**aequus**], f., *evenness; justness, fairness.* **animī aequitās,** *contentment* (VI.22). [equity.

aequō, -āre, -āvī, -ātus, [**aequus**], 1, *equalize, make equal.* [equate.

aequus, -a, -um, comp. **aequior,** sup. **aequissimus,** adj., *level, even, flat; fair, just, equitable; like, equal; favorable, advantageous.* **aequō animō,** *with tranquil mind, without anxiety.*

aerāria, -ae, [**aerārius,** *of copper*], 1, *copper mine* (III.21).

aes, aeris, n., (**13g**), *copper; bronze,* an alloy of copper and tin; *money.* **aes aliēnum,** (lit., *another's money*), *debt* (VI.13).

aestās, -tātis, f., (**10f**), *warm season, summer.*

aestimātiō, -ōnis, [**aestimō**], f., *valuation, appraisement.* [estimation.

aestimō, -āre, -āvī, -ātus, [**aes**], 1, *value, appraise; regard, consider.* [estimate.

aestīvus, -a, -um, [**aestās**], adj., *of summer.*

aestuārium, -ī, [**aestus**], n., *place overflowed at high tide,* (*salt*) *marsh* (II.28; III.9). [estuary.

aestus, -ūs, m., *heat; tide.*

aetās, -tātis, f., *age, time of life; old age.* **aetāte cōnfectus,** *advanced in years.* **puerīlis aetās,** *age of childhood.* **per aetātem,** *by reason of age.*

afferō, -ferre, attulī, allātus, [**ad + ferō**], irr., *bring, convey, deliver; bring forward, allege; produce, cause, occasion.*

afficiō, -ficere, -fēcī, -fectus, [**ad + faciō**], 3, *do something to, treat, use; visit with, afflict, trouble, weaken, impair; treat with kindness, place under obligation* (I.35); *visit with punishment* (I.27); *fill with joy* (V.48). [affect.

affīgō, -figere, -fīxī, -fīxus, [**ad + figō**], 3, *fasten to* (III.14). [affix.

affīnitās, -tātis, [**affīnis,** from **ad + fīnis**], f., *relationship* by marriage, *kinship, connection.* [affinity.

affīxus, see **affīgō.**

afflīctō, -āre, -āvī, -ātus, [freq. of **afflīgō**], 1, *shatter, damage.*

afflīgō, -flīgere, -flīxī, -flīctus, [**ad + flīgō,** *strike*], 3, *dash against; throw down, knock down; shatter, damage.* [afflict.

affore (= **affutūrus esse**), future infinitive of **adsum.**

Āfricus, -a, -um, [**Āfrica**], adj., *of Africa.* As noun, **Āfricus, -ī,** m. (originally sc. **ventus**), *southwest wind* (V.8).

āfuisse, āfutūrus, see **absum.**

Agedincum, -ī, n., chief city of the Senones, now *Sens.*

ager, agrī, m., (**7**), *land under cultivation, field, territory, domain;* pl. *lands, territory, country, the country.*

agger, -geris, [**aggerō, ad + gerō**], m., (**11c**), *that which is brought to a place, material for an embankment, filling* of earth and timber; *earth; embankment, mound, dike; rampart.*

aggredior, -gredī, -gressus, [**ad + gradior,** *walk, go*], 3, dep., *approach; go against, attack, fall upon.* [aggressive.

aggregō, -āre, -āvī, -ātus, [**ad + gregō,** from **grex,** *flock*], 1, *bring together, join.* **sē aggregāre,** *to place one's self with* (IV.26), *to join one's self to* (VI.12). [aggregate.

agmen, -minis, [**agō**], n., (**12e**), *army on the march, marching column; line of march.* **agmen claudere,** *to bring up the rear* (I.25, II.19). **novissimum agmen,** *the rear.* **prīmum agmen,** *the van.* **in agmine,** *on the march* (III.24).

agō, agere, ēgī, āctus, 3, *set in motion, drive, move forward; direct, conduct, guide; incite, urge; press forward, chase, pursue; drive off as plunder, rob; do, act, transact, perform; manage, carry on, accomplish; treat, discuss, confer, plead with;* of time, *spend, pass, live;* of court, *hold;* of sheds and towers, *bring up.* **gratiās agere,** *to thank.* [act.

alacer, -cris, -cre, comp. **alacrior,** adj., *lively; eager, in high spirits.*

alacritās, -tātis, [**alacer**], f., *liveliness; enthusiasm.* [alacrity.

ālārius, -a, -um, [**āla,** *wing*], adj., *of the wing.* As noun, **alāriī, -ōrum,** m., pl., *auxiliary troops* posted on the wings, *wing-men.*

albus, -a, -um, adj., *white.* **plumbum album,** *tin* (V.12).

alcēs, -is, f., (**15b**), *moose,* European *elk.*

ali-, the form of **alius** in combination.

aliās, [**alius**], adv., *at another time.* **aliās ... aliās,** *at one time ... at another, sometimes ... sometimes, now ... now.* [alias.

aliēnus, -a, -um, [**alius**], adj., *belonging to another, another's; strange, foreign; unsuitable, unfavorable, disadvantageous.* As noun, **aliēnissimī, -ōrum,** sup., m., pl., *entire strangers.* [alien.

aliō, [**alius**], adv., *to another place, elsewhere* (VI.22).

aliquamdiū, [**aliquī, diū**], adv., *for some time, for a while.*

aliquantus, -a, -um, [**ali- + quantus**], adj., *some, considerable.* Neut., **aliquantum,** as noun, *a little, somewhat.* **aliquantum itineris,** *some distance* (V.10).

aliquī, aliqua, aliquod, [**ali + quī**], indefinite pronominal adj., (**49a, 168**), *some, any, some other.*

aliquis (occasionally **aliquī**), **aliqua, aliquid,** nom. and acc. pl., n., **aliqua,** [**ali- + quis**], indefinite pron., (**49a, 168**), *some one, any one, anybody;* pl., *some, any.* Neut., **aliquid,** *something, somewhat, anything.* **aliquid calamitātis,** *some disaster* (V.29).

aliquot [**ali- + quot**], num. adj., indecl., *some, several.*

aliter, [**alis, alius**], adv., *otherwise, differently.* **aliter ac,** *otherwise than, different from what.*

alius, -a, -ud, dat. **aliī,** adj., (**23**), *another, some other, other, different, else.* **alius ... alius,** *one ... another, the one ... the other;* pl., **aliī ... aliī,** *some ... other;* often as noun, **alius,** *another,* **aliī,** *others.* **longē alius atque,** *very different from.*

allātus, see **afferō.**

alliciō, -licere, -lexī, [**ad + laciō,** *entice*], 3, *attract, allure.*

Allobrogēs, -um, (acc. **Allobrogas,** I.14), m., pl., *a Gallic people in the northeastern part of the Province.*

alō, alere, aluī, altus, 3, *nourish, increase; maintain, keep; rear, foster, raise.*

Alpēs, -ium, 3, f., pl., *Alps,* general term for the mountains separating Cisalpine Gaul from Transalpine Gaul and Germany.

alter, -era, -erum, gen. **alterīus** or **alterius,** adj., often with the force of a noun, (**23**), *one of two, the other, another; second.* **alter ... alter,** *the one ... the other.* **alterī ... alterī,** *the one division, the one party ... the other.* [alter.

altitūdō, -inis, [**altus**], f., *height, depth;* of a beam, *thickness* (III.13). [altitude.

altus, -a, -um, comp. **-ior,** sup. **-issimus,** [part. of **alō**], adj., *high, deep.* As noun, **altum, -ī,** n., *the deep, the open sea.*

alūta, -ae, f., *soft leather* (III.13).

am-, see **ambi-.**

ambactus, -ī, m., *vassal, dependent* (VI.15).

Ambarrī, -ōrum, m., pl., *a people east of the Arar* (*Saône*) *near its junction with the Rhone* (I.11,14).

ambi-, amb-, am-, an-, prep. found only in combination, *round about, around.*

Ambiānī, -ōrum, m., pl., *a small state in Belgic Gaul.*

Ambiliatī, -ōrum, m., pl., *a small state in Central Gaul* (III.9).

Ambiorīx, -īgis, m., *a leader of the Eburones, who destroyed the Roman force under Sabinus and Cotta.*

Ambivaretī, -ōrum, m., pl., *a people in Central Gaul, clients of the Aeduans.*

Ambivaritī, -ōrum, m., pl., *a small state in Belgic Gaul* (IV.9).

ambō, -ae, -ō, [cf. **ambi-**], adj., often used as noun, (**37c**), *both* (V.44).

āmentia, -ae, [**āmēns,** from **ā + mēns**], f., *madness, folly.*

āmmentum, -ī, n., *thong, strap,* for hurling a javelin (V.48).

amīcitia, -ae, [**amīcus**], f., *friendship.*

amīcus, -a, -um, comp. **-ior,** sup. **-issimus,** [**amō**], adj., *friendly, faithful, well-disposed.* [amicable.

amīcus, -ī, [**amō**], m., *friend, ally.*

āmittō, -mittere, -mīsī, -missus, [**ā + mittō**], 3, *send away; let go, let slip, lose.*

amor, -ōris, [**amō**], m., *affection, love.*

amplificō, -āre, -āvī, -ātus, [**amplus + faciō**], 1, *make large, increase.* [amplify.

amplitūdō, -inis, [**amplus**], f., *breadth, size; greatness, dignity.* [amplitude.

amplius, [comp. of **amplē,** from **amplus**], sup. **amplissimē,** adv., *more, further.*

amplus, -a, -um, comp. **-ior,** sup. **-issimus,** adj., *large in extent, great, extensive; distinguished, noble, prominent.* As noun, **amplius,** comp., n., *more.* [ample.

an, inter. conj., *or, or rather, or indeed,* **-ne ... an,** or **utrum ... an,** *whether ... or.*

an-, see **ambi-.**

Anartēs, -ium, m., pl., a tribe on the Tibiscus (*Theiss*), in Dacia (*Hungary*).

Ancalitēs, -um, m., pl., a British tribe (V.21).

anceps, -cipitis, [an- + CAP in **caput**], adj., (**26b**), *two-headed, twofold, double.* **anceps proelium,** *battle on two fronts.*

ancora, -ae, f., *anchor.* **in ancorīs,** *at anchor.* [anchor.

Andecumborius, -ī, m., a leader among the Remi.

Andēs, -ium, or **Andī, -ōrum,** m., pl., a Gallic people north of the Liger (*Loire*).

angulus, -ī, m., *corner* (V.13). [angle.

angustē, comp. **-ius,** sup. **-issimē,** [**angustus**], adv., *closely, in close quarters; scantily, sparingly.*

angustiae, -ārum, [**angustus**], f., pl., *narrow place, narrow part, defile, narrowness; straits, difficulties, perplexity; scarcity.*

angustus, -a, -um, comp. **-ior,** sup. **-issimus,** [cf. **angō,** *squeeze*], adj., *contracted, narrow, close.* Neut. as noun, **angustum, -ī,** *crisis* (II.25).

anima, -ae, f., *breath; soul, life* (VI.14). [animate.

animadvertō, -tere, -tī, -sus, [**animus + advertō**], 3, *turn the mind to, attend to; notice, observe, perceive.* **in eum animadvertō,** *inflict punishment upon him* (I.19).

animal, -ālis, [**anima**], n., (**16b**), *living being, animal* (VI.17, 19). [animal.

animus, -ī, m., *soul, mind, consciousness; disposition, feelings; courage, spirit, temper, resolution.* **esse in animō,** *to intend.* [animus

annōtinus, -a, -um, [**annus**], adj., *of the year before, last year's* (V.8).

annus, -ī, m., *year.* [annual.

annuus, -a, -um, [**annus**], adj., *of a year, yearly, annual* (I.16). [annuity.

ānser, -eris, m., (**11c**), *goose* (V.12).

ante, adv. and prep.: (1) As adv., *in front; before, previously.* **ante quam,** (**189b**), *before.* **paulō ante,** *a little while before, a short time previously.* **paucīs ante diēbus,** *a few days before.* (2) As prep., with acc., *before, in front of, in advance of.*

anteā, [**ante + eā**], adv., *previously, before.*

antecēdō, -cēdere, -cessī, [**ante + cēdō**], 3, *go in advance, outstrip; surpass, excel.* [antecedent.

antecursor, -ōris, [**antecurrō**], m., lit., *fore-runner;* pl., *advance guard, vanguard.*

anteferō, -ferre, -tulī, -lātus, [**ante + ferō**], irr., *carry in front; place before, prefer.*

antemna, -ae, f., *sail-yard.* [antennae.

antepōnō, -pōnere, -posuī, -positus, [**ante + pōnō**], 3, *place before; prefer, value above* (IV.22).

antevertō, -tere, -tī, [**ante + vertō**], 3, *place before, take precedence.*

antīquitus [**antīquus**], adv., *in former times, long ago.*

antīquus, -a, -um, comp. **-ior,** sup. **-issimus,** [**ante**], adj., *old, former, old-time, ancient.* [antique.

Ap., with proper names, = *Appius.*

apertē, -ius, -issimē, [**apertus**], adv., *openly, clearly, manifestly.*

apertus, -a, -um, comp. **-ior,** sup. **-issimus,** [part. of **aperiō**], adj., *open, uncovered; exposed, unprotected.* **loca aperta,** *open country.* **latus apertum,** *open flank, exposed flank.*

Apollō, -inis, m., (**12d**), a deity worshipped by the Greeks and Romans, identified by Caesar with a Gallic deity (VI.17).

apparō, -āre, -āvī, -ātus, [**ad + parō**], 1, *prepare, get ready.* [apparatus.

appellō, -pellere, -pulī, -pulsus, [**ad + pellō**], 3, *drive to, bring in;* of ships, *make for, put in, land.*

appellō, -āre, -āvī, -ātus, 1, *address, accost, call to, appeal to; call by name, name.* [appellate.

appetō, -petere, -petīvī or **-iī, -petītus,** [**ad + petō**], 3, *strive after, seek; approach, draw near.* [appetite.

Appius, -ī, m., a Roman first name.

apportō, -āre, -āvī, -ātus, [**ad + portō**], 1, *carry to, bring* (V.1).

approbō, -āre, -āvī, -ātus, [**ad + probō**], 1, *approve, favor.* [approve.

appropinquō, -āre, -āvī, -ātum est, [**ad + propinquō**], 1, *approach, come near.*

appulsus, see **appellō.**

Aprilis, -e, adj., *of April.*

aptus, -a, -um, comp. **-ior,** sup. **-issimus,** adj., *fitted, adapted, suited; suitable, appropriate, ready.* [apt.

apud, prep. with acc. only, *at, with, near, close to, by; among, in the presence of.*

aqua, -ae, f., *water.* [aqueous.

aquātiō, -ōnis, [**aquor**], f., *obtaining water.*

aquila, -ae, f., *eagle;* as an eagle of silver or gold on the end of a pole formed the chief ensign of the legion, *eagle, standard.* [aquiline.

Aquileia, -ae, f., a city at the head of the Adriatic Sea (I.10).

aquilifer, -erī, [**aquila + ferō**], m., *bearer of the eagle, eagle-bearer.*

Aquītānia, -ae, f., one of the three main divisions of Gaul.

Aquītānus, -a, -um, adj., *of Aquitania.* As noun, **Aquītānus, -ī,** m., *Aquitanian* (IV.12); pl., *Aquitanians, Aquitani, inhabitants of Aquitania* (I.1; III.21).

Arar, -aris, acc. **-im,** m., (**18e**), *Arar River,* now *Saône.* It rises in the Vosges Mountains, and flows southward into the Rhone.

arbiter, -trī, m., (**7c**), *witness; referee, commissioner* (V.1). [arbiter.

arbitrium, -ī, [**arbiter**], n., *decision; authority.*

arbitror, -ārī, -ātus, [**arbiter**], 1, dep., *think, consider, believe.* [arbitrate.

arbor, -oris, f., (**11c**), *tree* [arboretum.

accessō, -sere, -sīvī, -sītus, 3, *cause to come, fetch; send for, summon, invite.*

ārdeō, -ēre, ārsī, arsūrus, 2, *be on fire; be ablaze, be aroused; be eager, desire ardently.* [ardent.

Arduenna, -ae, f., *the Ardennes,* a forest-covered range of hills in the northeastern part of France, extending also into Belgium.

arduus, -a, -um, adj., *steep, high; hard, difficult.* [arduous.

Arecomicī, -ōrum, m., pl., a division of the Volcae, in the Province.

Aremoricus, -a, -um, [Celtic, **arē = ad,** + **mori, = mare,** *'by the sea'*], adj., *Aremorican,* name applied to a group of small states along the northwest coast of Gaul (**Aremoricae cīvitātēs**).

argentum, -ī, n., *silver.*

argilla, -ae, f., *clay* (V.43).

āridus, -a, -um, sup. **-issimus,** [**āreō,** *be dry*], adj., *dry.* As noun, **āridum, -ī,** n., *dry land, shore.* [arid.

ariēs, -ietis, m., (**10e**), *ram; battering ram; prop, buttress* (IV.17). [Aries.

Ariovistus, -ī, m., a German king, defeated by Caesar, 58 BC.

arma, -ōrum, n., pl., *implements; implements of war, arms, armor, weapons;* of a ship, *equipment, tackle* (III.14). **ad arma concurrere,** *to rush to arms.* [arms.

armāmenta, -ōrum, [**armō**], n., pl., *equipment;* of a ship, *rigging.* [armament.

armātūra, -ae, [**armō**], f., *armor, equipment.* **levis armātūrae peditēs,** *light infantry.* **levis armātūrae Numidae,** *light-armed Numidians* (II.10). [armature.

armātus, -a, -um, sup. **armātissimus,** [part. of **armō**], adj., *armed, in arms, equipped.* As noun, **armātī, -ōrum,** m., pl., *armed men, warriors, soldiers.*

armō, -āre, -āvī, -ātus, [**arma**], 1, *provide with weapons, arm;* of a ship, *equip, fit out.* [arm.

Arpineius, -ī, m., *Gaius Arpineius,* a Roman knight, envoy to Ambiorix (V.27).

arripiō, -ripere, -ripuī, -reptus, [**ad + rapiō**], 3, *lay hold of, snatch* (V.33).

arroganter, comp. **-ius,** [**arrogāns**], adv., *presumptuously, arrogantly.*

arrogantia, -ae, [**arrogāns**], f., *presumption, insolence.* [arrogance.

ars, artis, f., *skill; art, science* (VI.17). [art.

artē, comp. **artius,** sup. **artissimē,** [**artus,** *close*], adv., *closely, tightly.*

artificium, -ī, [**artifex,** *artist*], n., *an art, trade; skill; craft, cunning.* [artifice.

Arvernus, -a, -um, adj., *of the Arverni, Arvernian.* As noun, **Arvernī, -ōrum,** m., pl., *Arvernians, the Arverni,* a powerful people about the upper part of the Elaver (*Allier*); their chief city was Gergovia.

arx, arcis, f., *citadel, stronghold.*

ascendō, -scendere, -scendī, -scēnsus, [**ad + scandō,** *climb*], 3, *ascend, climb up; mount.* [ascend.

ascēnsus, -ūs, [**ascendō**], m., *ascent, climbing; approach.*

ascīscō, ascīscere, ascīvī, ascītus, [**ad + scīscō,** *approve*], 3, *admit to association with one's self, accept.*

aspectus, -ūs, [**aspiciō,** *look at*], m., *appearance, sight, look.* [aspect.

asper, -era, -erum, comp. **-ior,** sup. **-rimus,** adj., (**22e**), *rough, uneven; fierce, violent.*

assiduus, -a, -um, [**ad** + SED, SID, in **sedeō,** *sit*], adj., *constant, incessant.* [assiduous.

assistō, -ere, astitī, [**ad** + **sistō**], 3, *stand near, stand by; appear* (VI.18). [assist.

assuēfaciō, -facere, -fēcī, -factus, [**assuētus** + **factō**], 3, *accustom, habituate, familiarize, train.*

at, conj., *but, yet, but yet, at least.*

atque, ac, [**ad** + **-que**], conj.: (1) Copulative, *and, and also, and even, and in particular.* 2) Comparative, after words of likeness or unlikeness, (**233c**), *as, than.* **idem atque, par atque,** *the same as.*

Atrebās, -ātis, m., *an Atrebatian;* pl., *Atrebatians, the Atrebates,* a Belgic people.

Ātrius, -ī, m., *Quintus Atrius,* an officer in Caesar's army (V.9).

attexō, -ere, -texuī, attextus, [**ad** + **texō**], 3, *weave to, join on* (V.40).

attingō, -tingere, -tigī, -tāctus, [**ad** + **tangō**], 3, *touch upon, touch; reach;* of territorial divisions, *border on, extend to.*

attribuō, -uere, -uī, -ūtus, [**ad** + **tribuō**], 3, *assign, allot.* [attribute.

attulī, see **afferō.**

Atuatucī, -ōrum, m., pl., *the Atuatuci,* a warlike people of Belgic Gaul descended from the Cimbrians and Teutons.

auctor, -ōris, [**augeō**], m., *originator, instigator; adviser; promoter.* [author.

auctōritās, -tātis, [**auctor**], f., *influence, weight; prestige, power.* [authority.

auctus, -a, -um, comp. **auctior,** [**augeō**], adj., *increased; rich* (I.43).

audācia, -ae, [**audax**], f., *boldness, daring, recklessness.* [audacity.

audācter, comp. **audācius,** sup. **audācissimē,** [**audāx**], adv., *boldly, courageously, fearlessly.*

audeō, audēre, ausus sum, 2, semi-dep., (**62**), *venture, dare, risk; attempt.*

audiō, -īre, -īvī or **-iī, -ītus,** 4, (**58**), *hear, listen to; hear of.* Present participle as Adj. in **dictō audiens esse,** *to be obedient to the word of command, to obey.* [audience.

audītiō, -ōnis, [**audiō**], f., *report, rumor, hearsay.* [audition.

augeō, augēre, auxī, auctus, 2, semi-dep., *increase, enlarge, augment, add to.*

Aulercus, -ī, m., *an Aulercan;* pl., *the Aulerci,* a people of Central Gaul.

Aulus, -ī, m., a Roman first name.

aureus, -a, -um, [**aurum**], adj., *of gold, golden* (V.12).

aurīga, -ae, [**aurea,** *bridle,* + **agō**], m., *charioteer, driver* (IV.33).

auris, -is, f., *ear.* [aural.

Aurunculeius, -i, m., *Lucius Aurunculeius Cotta,* a lieutenant of Caesar, killed by the Eburones.

Auscī, -ōrum, m., pl., a people in the eastern part of Aquitania (III.27).

ausus, see **audeō.**

aut, conj., *or.* **aut . . . aut,** *either . . . or.* **aut . . . aut . . . aut,** *either . . . or . . . or.*

autem, conj., *but, however, on the contrary; and now, moreover.*

autumnus, -ī, m., *autumn.* [autumn.

auxiliāris, -e, [**auxilium**], adj., *auxiliary.* As noun, **auxiliārēs, -ium,** m., pl., *auxiliary troops, auxiliaries* (III.25).

auxilior, -ārī, -ātus, [**auxilium**], 1, dep., *render aid, assist, help.*

auxilium, -ī, [cf. **augeō**], n., *help, aid, assistance; relief, remedy, resource.* Pl., **auxilia,** *auxiliary troops, auxiliaries, allied forces.*

avāritia, -ae, [**avārus,** *greedy*], f., *greed, covetousness.* [avarice.

āvehō, -vehere, -vexī, -vectus, [**ā** + **vehō**], 3, *carry off, carry away.*

āversus, -a, -um, sup. **āversissimus,** [part. of **āvertō**], adj., *turned away; behind, in the rear.* [averse.

āvertō, -tere, -tī, -sus, [**ā** + **vertō**], 3, *turn away, turn aside, avert; divert, alienate, estrange.* [avert.

avis, -is, f., *bird* (IV.10). [aviation.

avus, -ī, m., *grandfather.*

Axona, -ae, f., a river in the southern part of Belgic Gaul, now *Aisne.*

B.

Baculus, -ī, m., *Publius Sextius Baculus,* one of the bravest of Caesar's centurions. He distinguished himself in the battle with the Nervians (II.25) and when Galba was attacked in the Alps (III.5).

Baleārēs, -ium, m., pl., natives of the Balearic Islands, off the east coast of Spain; famous as slingers (II.7).

balteus, -ī, m., *belt, sword-belt.*

Balventius, -ī, m., *Titus Balventius,* a brave centurion (V.35).

barbarus, -a, -um, adj., *foreign, strange; rude, savage, uncivilized.* As noun, **barbarī, -ōrum,** m., pl., *strangers, foreigners; natives, barbarians.* [barbarous.

Basilus, -ī, m., *Lucius Minucius Basilus,* an officer of Caesar.

Batāvī, -ōrum, m., pl., *the Batavians, Batavi,* a people dwelling near the mouth of the Rhine (IV.10).

Belgae, -ārum, m., pl., *the Belgians, Belgae,* inhabitants of one of the three main divisions of Gaul, divided into many small states.

Belgium, -ī, n., *the land of the Belgians, Belgic Gaul, Belgium* (V.12, 25).

bellicōsus, -a, -um, comp. **-ior,** sup. **-issimus,** [**bellicus**], adj., *warlike, fond of war* (I.10). [bellicose.

bellicus, -a, -um, [**bellum**], adj., *of war, martial, military* (VI.24).

bellō, -āre, -āvī, -ātus, [**bellum**], 1, *wage war, carry on war, fight.*

Bellovacī, -ōrum, m., pl., a powerful Belgic people.

bellum, -ī, n., (**6**), *war, warfare.* **bellum gerere,** *to wage war.* **bellum īnferre,** *to make war.* **bellum parāre,** *to prepare for war.*

bene, comp. **melius,** sup. **optimē,** [**bonus**], adv., *well, ably, successfully.*

beneficium, -ī, [**bene + faciō**], n., *kindness, favor, service.*

benevolentia, -ae, [**benevolus**], f., *good will, friendly disposition, kindly feeling, friendship.* [benevolence.

Bibracte, -is, n., (**16c**), capital of the Aeduans, situated on a mountain now called *Mont Beuvray* (height, 2690 ft.).

Bibrax, -actis, f., a town of the Remi, north of the Axona (*Aisne*) (II.6).

Bibrocī, -ōrum, m., pl., a people in the southern part of Britain (V.21).

bīduum, -ī, [**bi- = bis,** cf. **diēs**], n., *space of two days, two days.*

biennium, -ī, [**bi-, = bis,** cf. **annus**], n., *period of two years, two years' time* (I.3). [biennial.

Bigerriōnēs, -ōnum, m., pl., a people in Aquitania (III.27).

bīnī, -ae, -a, [**bis**], distributive adj., *two by two, two each, by twos, two.*

bipedālis, -e, [**bi- = bis, + pedalis,** from **pēs**], adj., *two feet* in width, length, or height; *two feet thick* (IV.17).

bipertītō, [**bipartītus, bi- = bis, + partītus**], adv., *in two divisions* (I.25).

bis, [for **duis,** cf. **duo**], num. adv., *twice.*

Biturīgēs, -um, m., pl., a people in Central Gaul.

Boduognātus, -ī, m., a leader of the Nervians (II.23).

Boiī, -ōrum, m., pl., *Boians,* a Celtic people once widely diffused over Central Europe.

bonitās, -tātis, [**bonus**], f., *goodness, excellence;* of land, *fertility* (I.28).

bonus, -a, -um, comp. **melior,** sup. **optimus,** adj., (**22b**), *good, advantageous; pleasant, well-disposed, friendly.* As noun, **bonum,** n., *profit, advantage;* pl., **bona, -ōrum,** *goods, property, possessions.* [bonus; optimist.

bōs, bovis, gen. pl. **boum,** m. and f., (**18a**), *ox, bull, cow.* [bovine.

bracchium, -ī, n., *arm, forearm.*

Brātuspantium, -ī, n., a stronghold of the Bellovaci (II.13).

brevis, -e, comp. **-ior,** sup. **-issimus,** adj., *short, brief.*

brevitās, -tātis, [**brevis**], f., *shortness* (II.20); *smallness, small stature* (II.30). [brevity.

Britannī, -ōrum, m., pl., *natives of Britain, Britons.*

Britannia, -ae, f., *Britain.*

Britannicus, -a, -um, adj., *of Britain, British* (V.4).

brūma, -ae, [for *brevuma, sup. of **brevis,** sc. **diēs**], f., *winter solstice, shortest day; winter* (V.13).

Brūtus, -ī, m., *Decimus Junius Brutus Albinus,* an officer of Caesar.

C.

C, in expressions of number, = 100.

C., see **Gāius.**

Cabūrus, -ī, m., *Gaius Valerius Caburus,* a Gaul who received Roman citizenship.

cadāver, -eris, [cf. **cadō**], n., *corpse, dead body.* [cadaver.

cadō, cadere, cecidī, cāsūrus, 3, *fall; be slain, die.*

caedēs, -is, [**caedō**], f., (**15a**), *killing; slaughter, murder, massacre.*

caedō, caedere, cecīdī, caesus, 3, *cut, cut down; cut to pieces, slay.*

caelestis, -e, [**caelum**], adj., *heavenly.* As noun, **caelestēs, -ium,** m., pl., *the gods* (VI.17). [celestial.

Caerōsī, -ōrum, m., pl., a people in Belgic Gaul (II.4).

caeruleus, -a, -um, adj., *deep blue, dark blue* (V.14). [cerulean.

Caesar, -aris, m., (**19c**), *Gaius Julius Caesar,* author (and usually subject) of these *Commentaries on the Gallic War.*

caespes, -itis, m., (**10d**), *sod, turf.*

calamitās, -tātis, f., *loss, damage; disaster, defeat.* [calamity.

Caletī, -ōrum, also **Caletēs, -um,** m., pl., a people near the mouth of the Sequana (*Seine*).

callidus, -a, -um, comp. **-ior,** sup. **-issimus,** [**calleō,** *be skillful*], adj., *skillful; tactful, crafty* (III.18).

cālō, -ōnis, m., *soldier's servant, camp servant.*

campester, -tris, -tre, [**campus**], adj., *of level ground, flat, level.*

campus, -ī, m. *plain.* [campus.

canō, canere, cecinī, 3, *sing;* of a musical instrument, *sound, play.*

Cantabrī, -ōrum, m., pl., *Cantabrians, Cantabri,* a people in northern Spain.

Cantium, -ī, n., *Kent, Cantium,* a district in the southeast part of England.

capillus, -ī, [cf. **caput**], m., *hair of the head, hair.* [capillary.

capiō, capere, cēpī, captus, 3, (**56**), *take, get; seize, capture; occupy, take possession of; select, win over, captivate; receive;* of vessels, *reach, make; deceive* (I.40). **initium capere,** *to begin.* **cōnsilium capere,** *to form a plan.* **dolōrem capere,** *to be grieved.* [capture.

capra, -ae, [**caper**], f., *she-goat.*

captīvus, -a, -um, [cf. **capiō**], adj., *taken prisoner, captured.* As noun, **captīvus, -ī,** m., *captive, prisoner.* [captive.

captus, -a, -um, see **capiō.**

captus, -ūs, [**capiō**], m., *capacity; understanding, notion* (IV.3).

caput, -itis, n., (**10b**), *head;* by metonymy, *person, man, life, safety;* of a river, *mouth* (IV.10). **duo milia capitum,** *two thousand souls.* [capital.

Carcasō, -ōnis, f., a town in southern Gaul, now *Carcassonne* (III.20).

carīna, -ae, f., *keel of a ship.*

Carnutēs, -um, m., pl., a people in Central Gaul, north of the Liger (*Loire*); chief city, Cenabum.

carō, carnis, f., (**18a**), *flesh, meat.* [carnage.

carpō, -ere, -sī, -tus, 3, *pluck; censure, criticize* (III.17). [carp.

carrus, -ī, m., *cart, wagon.* [car.

cārus, -a, -um, comp. **-ior,** sup. **carissimus,** adj., *dear, precious.*

Carvilius, -ī, m., one of four British rulers in Kent (V.22).

casa, -ae, f., *hut, cottage, barrack.*

cāseus, -ī, m., *cheese* (VI.22).

Cassī, -ōrum, m., pl., a tribe in Britain (V.21).

Cassiānus, -a, -um, [**Cassius**], adj., *of Cassius* (I.13).

cassis, -idis, f., *helmet* of metal.

Cassius, -ī, m., *Lucius Cassius Longinus,* when consul in 107 BC he engaged in battle with the Tigurians in the territory of the Allobroges and was defeated (I.7, 12).

Cassivellaunus, -ī, m., *Cassivellaunus, Caswallon,* leader of the British army against Caesar in 54 BC.

castellum, -ī, [dim. of **castrum**], n., *redoubt, fortress, stronghold.* [castle.

Casticus, -i, m., a leading Sequanian (I.3).

castra, -ōrum, n., [pl. of **castrum,** *fortress*], *camp, encampment; military service* (I.39). **castra movēre,** *to break camp.* **castra pōnere,** *to encamp, camp.* [-chester in Ro-chester, etc.

cāsus, -ūs, [**cadō**], m., *fall; chance, occurrence, happening, fortune; opportunity, event; accident, mishap, evil plight, death.* **cāsū,** *by chance.* [case.

Catamantāloedis, -is, m., a leader among the Sequanians before Caesar's time (I.3).

catēnae, -ārum, f., pl., *chains; fetters.*

Caturīgēs, -um, m., pl., a Gallic people in the eastern part of the Province (I.10).

Catuvolcus, -ī, m., a ruler of the Eburones.

causa, -ae, f., *cause, ground, reason; pretext, excuse; condition, state, case.* **causā,** with preceding gen., *for the sake of, on account of.* [cause.

cautē, comp. **-ius,** sup. **-issimē,** [**cautus,** from **caveō**], adv., *cautiously, carefully.*

cautēs, -is, f., (**15b**), *jagged rock, cliff.*

Cavarīnus, -ī, m., a ruler among the Senones (V.54).

caveō, cavēre, cāvī, cautūrus, 2, *be on one's guard, beware of, take precaution; give security.* [cautious.

Cebenna, -ae, f., *Cebenna, the Cévennes,* a mountain range in southern Gaul, about 250 miles long.

cēdō, cēdere, cessī, cessūrus, 3, *go away, depart, withdraw, retreat; yield, give up to; abandon.* [cede.

celer, -eris, -ere, comp. **-ior,** sup. **celerrimus,** adj., *quick, speedy.*

celeritās, -tātis, [**celer**], f., *speed, quickness, swiftness, rapidity, dispatch.* [celerity.

celeriter, comp. **celerius,** sup. **celerrimē,** [**celer**], adv., *quickly, speedily, at once, immediately.*

cēlō, -āre, -āvī, -ātus, 1, *conceal, hide, keep secret* (II.32).

Celtae, -ārum, m., pl., *Celts,* inhabitants of central Gaul, divided into many states.

Cēnabēnsēs, -ium, [**Cēnabum**], m., pl., *the inhabitants of Cenabum.*

Cēnabum, -ī, n., chief city of the Carnutes, later called *Aurelianensis Urbs,* whence comes *Orleans,* name of the city on the site of Cenabum.

Cēnimagnī, -ōrum, m., pl., a British people (V.21).

cēnseō, -ēre, -uī, -us, 2, *estimate; think, hold, judge; decree, resolve upon, determine; vote for, favor.*

cēnsus, -ūs, [**cēnseō**], m., *count, enumeration* (I.29). [census.

centum, or **C,** indeclinable num., *hundred.* [-cent in percent.

centuriō, -ōnis, [**centuria**], m., *centurion.*

cernō, cernere, crēvī, 3, *separate; distinguish, discern, see, perceive.*

certāmen, -inis, [**certō**], n., (**12e**), *contest, rivalry* (V.44); *struggle, battle, engagement* (III.14).

certē, comp. **certius,** [**certus**], adv., affirmative, *certainly, surely;* restrictive, *at least, at any rate* (IV.25, V.29).

certus, -a, -um, comp. **-ior,** sup. **-issimus,** [part. of **cernō**], adj., *certain, fixed, definite; positive, undoubted, trustworthy, true.* **certiōrem facere,** *to inform.* **certior fierī,** *to be informed.* [certain.

cēterus, -a, -um, nom. sing. m. not in use, adj., *other, the other, the rest, remainder;* pl., *the rest, all the others, the other.* As noun, **cēterī, -ōrum,** m., pl., *the others, all the rest, everyone else;* **cētera, -ōrum,** n., pl., *the rest, everything else.*

Ceutronēs, -um, m., pl.: (1) A Belgic people, subject to the Nervians. (V.39). (2) A people in the eastern part of the Province (I.10).

cibāria, -ōrum, [**cibārius,** from **cibus**], n., pl., *provisions, rations.*

cibus, -ī, m., *food, nourishment.*

Cicerō, -ōnis, m., *Quintus Tullius Cicero,* brother of the orator Marcus Tullius Cicero; born about 102 BC, he became a lieutenant of Caesar in Gaul in 55, and made a heroic defense of his camp in 54.

Cimberius, -ī, m., a leader of the Suebi (I.37).

Cimbrī, -ōrum, m., pl., *Cimbrians, Cimbri,* a Germanic people that joined with the Teutones in the invasion of Gaul.

Cingetorīx, -īgis, m.: (1) Rival of Indutiomarus for the headship of the Treverans, and loyal to Caesar (V.3, 56). (2) A British ruler (V.22).

cingō, cingere, cīnxī, cīnctus, 3, *surround, encircle; invest.* [cincture.

circinus, -ī, m., *pair of compasses* (I.38).

circiter, [**circus,** *circle*], adv. and prep.: (1) As adv., *about, not far from, near.* (2) As prep., with acc. only, *about* (I.50).

circuitus, -ūs, [**circumeō**], m., *a going around; detour, circuit, winding path, way around.* [circuit.

circum, [acc. of **circus,** *circle*], adv. and prep.: (1) As adv., *about, around.* (2) As prep., with acc., *around, about; in the neighborhood of, near, near by.*

circumcīdō, -cīdere, -cīdī, -cīsus, [**circum** + **caedō**], 3, *cut around, cut* (V.42).

circumdō, -dare, -dedī, -datus, [**circum** + **dō,** *place*], 1, *place around, encompass, surround, encircle.*

circumdūcō, -dūcere, -dūxī, -ductus, [**circum** + **dūcō**], 3, *lead around; trace.*

circumeō, -īre, -iī, -itus, [**circum** + **eō**], irr., *go around, pass around; surround, encircle; go about and inspect* (V.2).

circumfundō, -fundere, -fūdī, -fūsus, [**circum** + **fundō**], 3, *pour around; surround, hem in;* pass. often used reflexively, *spread (themselves) around, crowd around.*

circumiciō, -icere, -iēcī, -iectus, [**circum + iaciō**], 3, *throw around, place around.*

circummittō, -mittere, -mīsī, -missus, [**circum + mittō**], 3, *send around* (V.51).

circummūniō, -īre, -īvī, -ītus, [**circum + mūniō**], 4, *surround with walls, fortify; hem in* (II.30).

circumsistō, -sistere, -stetī or **-stitī,** [**circum + sistō**], 3, *stand around, surround, take a position around.*

circumspiciō, -icere, -exī, -ectus, [**circum + speciō,** *look*], 3, *look about, survey; ponder, consider; look about for, look over* (V.31). [circumspect.

circumvāllō, -āre, -āvī, -ātus, [**circum + vāllō**], 1, *surround with a rampart, blockade.*

circumveniō, -venīre, -vēnī, -ventus, [**circum + veniō**], 4, *come around, go around; surround, encompass; ensnare, overreach, deceive.* [circumvent.

cis, prep. with acc., *on this side of.*

Cisalpīnus, -a, -um, [**cis + Alpīnus**], adj., *Cisalpine, on this* (the Italian) *side of the Alps.* [Cisalpine.

citātus, -a, -um, comp. **-ior,** sup. **-issimus,** [**citō**], adj., *rapid* (IV.10).

citerior, -us, [**citer,** from **cis**], comp. adj., *on this side, hither, nearer.*

cito, comp. **citius,** sup. **citissimē,** [**citus**], adv., *speedily.* **citissimē,** *with the utmost rapidity* (IV.33).

citrā, [**citer,** from **cis**], prep. with acc. only, *on this side of.*

citrō, [**citer,** from **cis**], adv., *to this side, hither.* **ultrō citrōque,** *to and fro, back and forth* (I.42).

cīvis, -is, m. and f., *citizen, fellow-citizen.* [civil.

cīvitās, -tātis, [**cīvis**], f., (**10f**), *body of citizens, state, nation; citizenship* (I.47).

clam, [cf. **cēlō**], adv., *secretly.*

clāmitō, -āre, -āvī, -ātus, [freq. of **clāmō**], 1, *cry out loudly, shout.*

clāmor, -ōris, [cf. **clāmō,** *cry out*], m., *outcry, shout, din.* [clamor.

clārus, -a, -um, comp. **-ior,** sup. **-issimus,** adj., *clear, distinct; of the voice, loud* (V.30); *famous.* [clear.

classis, -is, f., *a class; a fleet.* [class.

Claudius, -ī, m., *Appius Claudius Pulcher,* consul in 54 BC (V.1).

claudō, claudere, clausī, clausus, 3, *shut, close.* [close.

clāvus, -ī, m., *nail, spike* (III.13).

clēmentia, -ae, [**clēmēns**], f., *forbearance, mercifulness.* [clemency.

cliēns, -entis, m., (**17c**), *retainer, dependent, client, adherent.* [client.

clientēla, -ae, [**cliēns**], f., *relation of client to patron, clientship;* pl., *following of clients, dependencies* (VI.12). [clientele.

Cn. = **Gnaeus,** a Roman first name.

co-, see **com-.**

coacervō, -āre, -āvī, -ātus, [**co- + acervō**], 1, *heap up, pile up* (II.27).

coāctus, pf. pass. part. of **cōgō.**

coāctus, -ūs, [**cōgō**], m., only abl. sing. in use, *compulsion* (V.27).

Cocosātēs, -um, m., pl., *a people in Aquitania* (III. 27).

coëmō, -emere, -ēmī, -ēmptus, [**co- + emō**], 3, *buy up, purchase.*

coeō, -īre, -īvī or **-iī, -itum est,** [**co- + eō**], irr., *come together, join together* (VI.22).

coepī, -isse, coeptus, def., (present supplied by **incipiō**), (**72**), *have begun, began.*

coërceō, -ercēre, -ercuī, -ercitus, [**co- + arceō,** *shut up*], 2, *confine; restrain, check* (I.17; V.7). [coerce.

cōgitō, -āre, -āvī, -ātus, [**co- + agitō**], 1, *think about, think; intend, plan.* [cogitate.

cognātiō, -ōnis, [**cognātus**], f., *blood-relationship; blood-relations, kindred.*

cognōscō, -gnōscere, -gnōvī, cognitus, [**co- + (g)nōscō**], 3, *become acquainted with, learn, learn of, ascertain; be familiar with, know, recognize; spy out, examine; take cognizance of.* [cognizance.

cōgō, cōgere, coēgī, coāctus, [**co- + agō**], 3, *drive together, bring together, collect, gather, assemble; compel, force, oblige.* [cogent.

cohors, -hortis, f., *cohort, battalion,* the tenth part of a legion. [cohort.

cohortātiō, -ōnis, [**cohortor**], f., *encouraging, exhortation* (II.25).

cohortor, -ārī, -ātus, [**co- + hortor**], 1, dep., *encourage; urge, exhort; address* with encouraging words.

collātus, see **cōnferō.**

collaudō, -āre, -āvī, -ātus, [**com- + laudō**], 1, *praise warmly, commend.*

colligō, -āre, -āvī, -ātus, [**com- + ligō,** *bind*], 1, *bind together, fasten together.*

colligō, -ligere, -lēgī, -lēctus, [com- + legō, *gather*], 3, *gather together, collect, assemble; obtain, get.* **sē colligere,** *to gather themselves together; to form in battle order* (III.19); *to recover themselves, rally.* [collect.

collis, -is, m., *hill, height, elevation.*

collocō, -āre, -āvī, -ātus, [com- + locō, *place*], 1, *place, set, post, station; set in order, arrange;* with or without **nūptum,** *give in marriage* (I.18). [collocate.

colloquium, -ī, [colloquor], n., *conference, interview.*

colloquor, -loquī, -locūtus, [com- + loquor], 3, dep., *talk with, hold a conference, hold a parley.*

colō, colere, coluī, cultus, 3, *cultivate, till* (IV.1; V.12); *honor, worship* (VI.17).

colōnia, -ae, [colōnus], f., *colony, settlement* (VI.24). [colony.

color, -ōris, m., *color.*

com-, co-, prep., old form of **cum,** *with,* found only in combination; see **cum.**

combūrō, -ūrere, -ussī, -ūstus, [com- + *būrō, = ūrō, *burn*], 3, *burn up, consume* by fire (I.5). [combustion.

comes, -itis, [co- + eō], m. and f., (10d), *companion, comrade.*

commeātus, -ūs, [commeō], m., *passing to and fro, trip, voyage* (V.23); *supplies, provisions,* often including grain, **frūmentum.**

commemorō, -āre, -āvī, -ātus, [com- + memorō], 1, *call to mind, recount, relate.* [commemorate.

commendō, -āre, -āvī, -ātus, [com- + mandō], 1, *commit* to one *for protection, entrust; ask favor for, commend.*

commentārius, -ī, [commentor], m., *note-book, source-book.* [commentary.

commeō, -āre, -āvī, -ātus, [com- + meō, *go*], 1, *go to and fro, visit, resort to* (I.1).

commīlitō, -ōnis, [com- + mīlitō, from **mīles**], m., *fellow-soldier, comrade.*

comminus, [com- + manus], adv., *hand to hand, at close quarters.*

committō, -mittere, -mīsī, -missus, [com- + mittō], 3, *join, bring together, connect; entrust, commit; cause, do, perpetrate.* **committere proelium,** *to join battle, begin the engagement.* [commit.

Commius, -i, m., *Commius,* an Atrebatian, valuable in the British campaigns.

commodē, comp. **-ius,** sup. **-issimē,** [commodus], adv., *conveniently, opportunely, to advantage; readily, easily; fitly, suitably, properly.*

commodus, -a, -um, comp. **-ior,** sup. **-issimus,** [com- + modus, i.e. *having full measure*], adj., *convenient, advantageous, easy; good, favorable; suitable, fit.* As noun, **commodum, -ī,** n., *convenience, advantage, profit.* [commodious.

commonefaciō, -facere, -fēcī, -factus, [commoneō + faciō], 3, *remind; impress upon one* (I.19).

commoror, -ārī, -ātus, [com- + moror], 1, dep., *delay, linger.*

commoveō, -movēre, -mōvī, commōtus, [com- + moveō], 2, *disturb, disquiet, alarm; move, stir.* [commotion.

communicō, -āre, -āvī, -ātus, [commūnis], 1, *share together, share with; impart; consult with* (V.36). [communicate.

commūniō, -īre, -īvī or **-iī, -ītus,** [com- + mūniō], 4, *fortify on all sides, strongly fortify, entrench.*

commūnis, -e, [com- + mūnus], adj., *common, in common, general, public.* **commūnī cōnciliō,** *in accordance with the general plan, by common consent.* **in commūnī cōnciliō,** *at a general council* (II.4). [common.

commūtātiō, -ōnis, [commūtō], f., *complete change, alteration.*

commūtō, -āre, -āvī, -ātus, [com- + mūtō], 1, *change, wholly change, alter; exchange* (VI.22). [commute.

comparō, -āre, -āvī, -ātus, [com- + parō], 1, *prepare, make ready, get together; acquire, secure; amass* (I.18); *match, compare.*

compellō, -pellere, -pulī, -pulsus, [com- + pellō], 3, *drive together, collect; drive, force.* [compel.

comperiō, -perīre, -perī, -pertus, [com- + PER in **experior**], 4, *ascertain, learn, discover, find out.*

complector, -plectī, -plexus, [com- + plectō, *braid*], 3, dep., *embrace* (I.20); *surround.*

compleō, -plēre, -plēvī, -plētus, [com- + pleō, *fill*], 2, *fill up, fill; complete, cover;* of troops, *fully occupy, fill full.* [complete.

complexus, see **complector.**

complūrēs, -a, [com- + plūrēs, from **plūs**], adj., pl., *several, a number of; many.* As noun, **complūrēs, -ium,** m., pl., *a great many, quite a number, many.*

comportō, -āre, -āvī, -ātus, [com- + portō], 1, *bring in, carry, convey, bring over.*

comprehendō, -hendere, -hendī, -hēnsus, [com- + prehendō], 3, *grasp; seize; arrest, capture;* of fire, *catch* (V.43).

comprobō, -āre, -āvī, -ātus, [com- + **probō**], 1, *approve fully, justify.*

cōnātum, -ī, [n. of **cōnātus,** part. of **cōnor**], n., *attempt, undertaking.*

cōnātus, -ūs, [**cōnor**], m., *attempt.*

cōnātus, pf. part. of **cōnor.**

concēdō, -cēdere, -cessī, -cessūrus, [com- + **cēdō**], 3, *withdraw, depart; give up, yield, cede; submit; allow, grant; grant permission, permit.* [concede.

concessus, -ūs, [**concēdō**], m., used only in abl. sing., *permission, leave.*

concidō, -cīdere, -cīdī, [com- + **cadō**], 3, *fall down, fall; perish, be slain.*

concīdō, -cīdere, -cīdī, -cīsus, [com- + **caedō**], 3, *cut up, cut off; cut to pieces, kill, slay, destroy.*

conciliō, -āre, -āvī, -ātus, [**concilium**], 1, *win over, reconcile; win, gain, procure.* [conciliate.

concilium, -ī, n., *meeting, assembly.* [council.

concitō, -āre, -āvī, -ātus, [com- + **citō**], 1, *rouse, stir up.*

conclāmō, -āre, -āvī, -ātus, [com- + **clāmō,** shout], 1, *cry aloud together, shout, cry out.*

conclūsus, -a, -um, [**conclūdō**], adj., *confined, shut in* (III.9).

concurrō, -currere, -cucurrī or **-currī, -cursum est,** [com- + **currō**], 3, *run together, run up, rush; charge; gather; resort* (VI.13). [concur.

concursō, -āre, [freq. of **concurrō**], 1, *rush to and fro, run about.*

concursus, -ūs, [**concurrō**], m., *running together; dashing together, collision* (V.10). [concourse.

condiciō, -ōnis, [com- + DIC, declare], f., *condition, situation; terms, stipulation; arrangement, agreement.*

condōnō, -āre, -āvī, -ātus, [com- + **dōnō**], 1, *give up, overlook, disregard, pardon* (I.20). [condone.

Condrūsī, -ōrum, m., pl., a Belgic people on the right bank of the Mosa (*Meuse*).

condūcō, -dūcere, -dūxī, -ductus, [com- + **dūcō**], 3, *bring together, collect; hire.*

cōnfectus, see **cōnficiō.**

cōnferō, -ferre, -tulī, collātus, [com- + **ferō**], irr., *bring together, gather, collect, convey; compare* (I.31); *ascribe, refer* (I.40); *put off, postpone* (I.40). **sē cōnferre,** *to betake one's self, turn, proceed.* [confer.

cōnfertus, -a, -um, comp. **-ior,** sup. **-issimus,** [part. of **cōnferciō**], adj., *crowded together, close, dense.*

cōnfestim, adv., *immediately, at once, speedily.*

cōnficiō, -ficere, -fēcī, -fectus, [com- + **faciō**], 3, *do thoroughly, complete, finish, accomplish, do; bring to an end, wear out, exhaust, enfeeble;* of troops, *bring together, furnish* (II.4).

cōnfīdō, -fīdere, -fīsus sum, [com- + **fīdō,** trust], 3, semi-dep., **(62)**, *rely upon, have confidence in; believe* [confide.

cōnfīgō, -fīgere, -fīxī, -fīxus, [com- + **fīgō,** fasten], 3, *fasten together, join* (III.13).

cōnfīnium, -ī, [**cōnfīnis,** bordering], n., *boundary, frontier* (V.24). [confine.

cōnfīrmātiō, -ōnis, [**cōnfīrmō**], f., *assurance* (III.18). [confirmation.

cōnfīrmō, -āre, -āvī, -ātus, [com-, cf. **fīrmus**], 1, *strengthen, confirm; arrange for, establish; reassure, encourage; assert, declare; assure.* [confirm.

cōnfīsus, -a, -um, see **cōnfīdō.**

cōnfiteor, -fitērī, -fessus, [com- + **fateor,** confess], 2, dep., *confess, acknowledge* (V.27). [confess.

cōnfīxus, -a, -um, see **cōnfīgō.**

cōnflagrō, -āre, -āvī, -ātus, [com- + **flagrō,** blaze], 1, *be in flames, be on fire* (V.43). [conflagration.

cōnflīctō, -āre, -āvī, -ātus, [freq. of **cōnflīgō**], 1, dep., *harass, assail.* [conflict.

cōnflīgō, -flīgere, -flīxī, -flīctus, [com- + **flīgō,** strike], 3, *dash together; contend, fight.*

cōnfluēns, -entis, [**cōnfluō**], m., *flowing together* of two streams, *confluence* (IV.15).

congredior, -gredī, -gressus, [com- + **gradior,** step], 3, dep., *come together, meet, unite with; join battle, engage, contend.*

congressus, -a, -um, see **congredior.**

congressus, -ūs, [**congredior**], m., *meeting; encounter, engagement* (III.13). [congress.

coniciō, -icere, -iēcī, -iectus, [com- + **iaciō**], 3, *throw together, hurl, cast; throw up, throw; place, put.* **in fugam conicere,** *to put to flight.*

coniectūra, -ae, [**coniciō**], f., *inference.* [conjecture.

coniūnctim, [**coniungō**], adv., *jointly, in common.*

coniungō, -iungere, -iūnxī, -iūnctus, [com- + **iungō**], 3, *join together, unite, join.* [conjoin.

coniūrātiō, -ōnis, [**coniūrō**], f., (**12c**), *a union bound by oath, league; conspiracy, plot.*

coniūrō, -āre, -āvī, -ātus, [**com- + iūrō**], 1, *take oath together; form a league, conspire, plot.* [conjure.

cōnor, -ārī, -ātus, 1, dep., *endeavor, attempt, undertake, try.* [conative.

conquīrō, -quīrere, -quīsīvī, -quīsītus, [**com- + quaerō**], 3, *seek out, hunt up; bring together, collect.*

cōnsanguineus, -a, -um, [**com- + sanguineus,** from **sanguis**], adj., *of the same blood.* As noun, m., and f., *relative, kinsman;* pl., *kinsfolk, blood-relations.*

cōnscendō, -scendere, -scendī, -scēnsus, [**com- + scandō,** *climb*], 3, *mount, ascend.* **nāvēs cōnscendere,** *to embark.*

cōnscientia, -ae, [**cōnsciō**], f., *knowledge* (V.56). [conscience.

cōnscīscō, -scīscere, -scīvī, -scītus, [**com- + scīscō,** *approve*], 3, *decree; inflict, bring upon.* **sibi mortem cōnscīscere,** *to commit suicide* (I.4; III.22).

cōnscius, -a, -um, [**com-,** cf. **sciō**], adj., *conscious, aware (of).* [conscious.

cōnscrībō, -scrībere, -scrīpsī, -scrīptus, [**com- + scrībō**], 3, *write* (V.48); *enroll, levy, enlist.* [conscript.

cōnscrīptus, see **cōnscrībō.**

cōnsecrātus, -a, -um, [part. of **cōnsecrō**], adj., *holy, sacred.* [consecrate.

cōnsector, -ārī, -ātus, [**cōnsequor**], 1, dep., *follow up, pursue, hunt down* (IV.14).

cōnsecūtus, see **cōnsequor.**

cōnsēnsus, -ūs, [**cōnsentiō**], m., *common feeling, agreement, understanding.*

cōnsentiō, -sentīre, -sēnsī, -sēnsus, [**com- + sentiō**], 4, *agree; plot together, conspire.* [consent.

cōnsequor, -sequī, -secūtus, [**com- + sequor**], 3, dep., *follow after, follow; pursue, overtake; obtain, secure, gain.* [consequence.

cōnservō, -āre, -āvī, -ātus, [**com- + servō**], 1, *save, spare;* of laws or rights, *observe, maintain.* [conserve.

cōnsīderātē, [**cōnsīderātus,** from **cōnsīderō**], adv., *circumspectly.*

Cōnsidius, -ī, m., *Publius Considius,* an officer in Caesar's army.

cōnsīdō, -sīdere, -sēdī, -sessum, [**com- + sīdō,** *sit*], 3, *sit down, seat one's self; halt, encamp; establish one's self, settle.*

cōnsilium, -ī, [cf. **cōnsulō**], n., *consultation, deliberation, counsel; gathering for deliberation, council; advice; decision, plan, design, scheme; project, proposal; good judgment, prudence, discretion.* **cōnsilium inīre** or **habēre** or **capere,** *to form a plan.* [counsel.

cōnsimilis, -e, [**com- + similis**], adj., *very like, quite like.*

cōnsistō, -sistere, -stitī, [**com- + sistō,** *set, place*], 3, *stand, stop, halt; take a position, be posted, make a stand; stay, remain; sojourn, settle; consist (in), depend (on).* **in orbem cōnsistere,** *to form a circle* (V.33). [consist.

cōnsōlor, -ārī, -ātus, [**com- + sōlor,** *comfort*], 1, dep., *comfort, cheer, encourage.* [console.

cōnspectus, -ūs, [**cōnspiciō**], m., *sight, view, presence.* [conspectus.

cōnspiciō, -spicere, -spexī, -spectus, [**com- + speciō,** *look*], 3, *observe, see, perceive.*

cōnspicor, -ārī, -ātus, 1, dep., *catch sight of, see, observe.*

cōnspīrō, -āre, -āvī, -ātus, [**com- + spīrō,** *breathe*], 1, *agree; combine, form a league, conspire* (III.10). [conspire.

cōnstanter, comp. **-ius,** sup. **-issimē,** [**cōnstāns**], adv., *resolutely* (III.25); *uniformly, unanimously* (II.2).

cōnstantia, -ae, [**cōnstāns**], f., *firmness, resolution.* [constancy.

cōnsternō, -sternere, -strāvī, -strātus, [**com- + sternō**], 3, *cover.*

cōnstīpō, -āre, -āvī, -ātus, [**com- + stīpō,** *press*], 1, *crowd together, crowd closely.*

cōnstituō, -stituere, -stituī, -stitūtus, [**com- + statuō**], 3, *station, place, draw up; bring to a halt, stop;* of ships, *moor; appoint, establish; resolve upon, determine, decide, fix, settle.* [constitute.

cōnstō, -stāre, -stitī, -stātūrus, [**com- + stō**], 1, *stand together, stand firm.* **cōnstat,** impers., *it is certain, well-known, evident, it is clear.*

cōnsuēscō, -suēscere, -suēvī, -suētus, [**com- + suēscō,** *become used*], 3, *form a habit, become accustomed.*

cōnsuētūdō, -inis, [**cōnsuēscō**], f., *habit, practice, custom, usage; mode of life* (V.14, VI.21); *practice in speaking a language* (I.47). **cōnsuētūdō vīctūs,** *standard of living* (I.31). [custom.

cōnsuētus, see **cōnsuēscō.**

cōnsul, -ulis, m., (**11b**), *consul,* one of the two chief magistrates at Rome, elected annually.

cōnsulātus, -ūs, [**cōnsul**], m., *consulship* (I.35). [consulate.

cōnsulō, -sulere, -suluī, -sultus, 3, *consult, deliberate, take counsel of;* with dat., *have regard for, look out for.*

cōnsultō, [cōnsulō], adv., *on purpose, designedly, purposely.*

cōnsultō, -āre, -āvī, -ātus, [freq. of cōnsulō], 1, *deliberate, take counsel* (V.53). [consult.

cōnsultum, -ī, [cōnsultus, from cōnsulō], n., *deliberation; resolution, decree.*

cōnsūmō, -sūmere, -sūmpsī, -sūmptus, [com- + sūmō], 3, *use up, devour, eat up; waste, exhaust, destroy;* of time, *spend, pass.* [consume.

cōnsurgō, -surgere, -surrēxī, consurrēctum est, [com- + surgō, *rise*], 3, *rise together, arise, stand up.*

contabulō, -āre, -āvī, -ātus, [com-, cf. tabula, *board*], 1, *construct of boards; build up in stories.*

contāgiō, -ōnis, [cf. contingō], f., *contact* (VI.13). [contagion.

contemnō, -temnere, -tempsī, -temptus, [com- + temnō, *despise*], 1, *despise, hold in contempt.*

contemptiō, -ōnis, [cf. contemnō], f., *a despising, contempt, scorn.*

contemptus, -ūs, [contemnō], m., *scorn.* [contempt.

contendō, -tendere, -tendī, -tentus, [com- + tendō], 3, *put forth effort, strive for, make effort, strive; hasten, make haste, push forward; struggle, contend, vie; maintain, insist, protest.* [contend.

contentiō, -ōnis, [contendō], f., *effort; struggle, fight, contest; dispute, controversy.* [contention.

contexō, -texere, -texuī, -textus, [com- + texō, *weave*], 3, *weave together, weave; bind together, join, construct.* [context.

continēns, -entis, [part. of contineō], adj., *adjoining; continuous, unbroken, consecutive.* As noun (originally sc. terra), f., *mainland.* [continent.

continenter, [continēns], adv., *constantly, without interruption, continually.*

contineō, -tinēre, -tinuī, -tentus, [com- + teneō], 2, *hold together; hold; hold back, keep in hand; keep, retain, detain, shut in;* of places and regions, *hem in, bound, border;* of space, *fill* (I.38). [contain.

contingō, -tingere, -tigī, -tāctus, [com- + tangō], 3, *touch, extend to, border on, reach; happen, fall to the lot of* (I.43). [contact.

continuātiō, -ōnis, [verb continuō], f., *succession* (III.29). [continuation.

continuus, -a, -um, [com-, cf. teneō], adj., *successive, uninterrupted.* [continuous.

cōntiō, -ōnis, [for *coventiō, co-, cf. veniō], f., *assembly, meeting* (V.52).

contrā, [related to com-], adv. and prep.: (1) As adv., *opposite, in opposition, on the other side; on the other hand, on the contrary* (V.31). **contrā atque,** *otherwise than, contrary to what* (IV.13). (2) As prep., with acc. only, *opposite to, facing, over against, contrary to; against, in hostility to, to the disadvantage of, in spite of; in reply to* (V.29).

contrahō, -trahere, -trāxī, -trāctus, [com- + trahō], 3, *bring together, collect; draw in, contract, make smaller.* [contract.

contrārius, -a, -um, [contrā], adj., *opposite, contrary.* [contrary.

contrōversia, -ae, [contrōversus], f., *dispute, debate, controversy, quarrel.* **minuere contrōversiās,** *to settle the questions at issue* (V.26; VI.23).

contumēlia, -ae, f., *insult, indignity;* of waves, *buffeting* (III.13).

convallis, -is, [com- + vallis], f., *valley, ravine, defile.*

conveniō, -venīre, -vēnī, -ventum est, [com- + veniō], 4, *come together, gather, assemble, meet, come in a body; come to an assembly* (V.56); *be agreed upon* (I.36, II.19); *fall in with, meet* (I.27). [convene.

conventus, -ūs, [cf. conveniō], m., *assembly, meeting; court.* [convent.

convertō, -vertere, -vertī, -versus, [com- + vertō], 3, *turn, direct, turn about, wheel around; change* (I.41). **conversa signa īnferre,** *to face about and advance* (I.25; II.26). [convert.

convincō, -vincere, -vīcī, -victus, [com- + vincō], 3, *prove clearly, establish, prove* (I.40). [convict.

convocō, -āre, -āvī, -ātus, [com- + vocō], 1, *call together, summon, assemble.* [convoke.

coörior, -orīrī, -ortus, [co- + orior], 4, dep., *arise;* of storm and wind, *arise, rise, spring up;* of war, *break out* (III.7).

cōpia, -ae, [= co-opia, from co- + ops], f., *quantity, abundance, supply, plenty.* Pl., **cōpiae, -ārum,** *means, resources, wealth; forces, troops.*

cōpiōsus, -a, -um, comp. -ior, sup. -issimus, [cōpia], adj., *well-supplied, wealthy, rich* (I.23). [copious.

cōpula, -ae, [co- + AP in aptus], f., *band;* pl., *grappling-hooks* (III.13). [copula.

cor, cordis, n., (10g), *heart.* **cordī esse,** *to be dear* (VI.19). [cordial.

cōram, [co-, cf. ōs, *face*], adv., *face to face, in person.* **cōram perspicit** (V.11), *he sees with his own eyes.* As prep., with the ablative, *in the presence of.*

Coriosolitēs, -um, m., pl., a people along the northwestern coast of Gaul.

cornū, -ūs, n., (**20b**), *horn;* of a deer, *antler;* of an army, *wing.*

corōna, -ae, f., *crown, wreath* (III.16).

corpus, -oris, n., (**13f**), *body.* [corporal.

cortex, corticis, m. and f., *bark* of a tree.

Cōrus, -ī, m., *northwest wind* (V.7).

coss. = **cōnsulibus,** from **cōnsul.**

cotīdiānus, -a, -um, [**cotīdiē**], adj., *daily; ordinary, usual.*

cotīdiē, [**quot + diēs**], adv., *daily, every day.*

Cotta, -ae, m.: *L. Aurunculeius Cotta,* see **Aurunculeius.**

crassitūdō, -inis, [**crassus,** *thick*], f., *thickness* (III.13).

Crassus, -ī, m., (1) *Marcus Licinius Crassus,* member of the triumvirate with Caesar and Pompey, consul in 55 BC (I.21; IV.1). (2) *Publius Licinius Crassus,* younger son of the triumvir, lieutenant of Caesar in Gaul, 58-56 BC (I.52; II.34; III.7, 8, 9, 11, 20-27). (3) *Marcus Licinius Crassus,* elder son of the triumvir, quaestor in Caesar's army after his brother Publius left Gaul (V.24, 46, 47).

crātēs, -is, f., *wicker-work, wattle; hurdle.* [crate, grate.

crēber, -bra, -brum, comp. **crēbrior,** sup. **crēberrimus,** adj., *thick, numerous, frequent.*

crēdō, crēdere, crēdidī, crēditus, 3, *trust, believe, think, suppose.* [creed, credit.

cremō, -āre, -āvī, -ātus, 1, *burn; burn to death* (I.4). [cremate.

creō, -āre, -āvī, -ātus, 1, *create, make; choose, elect, appoint.* [create.

crēscō, crēscere, crēvī, crētus, 3, inch., *grow; become great, become powerful* (I.20). [crescent.

Crētēs, -um, accusative **Crētas,** m., pl., *Cretans,* inhabitants of Crete.

cruciātus,-ūs, [**cruciō,** *torture*], m., *torture, cruelty, torment, suffering.*

crūdēlitās, -tātis, [**crūdēlis**], f., *cruelty, barbarity.* [cruelty.

crūdēliter, comp. **crūdēlius,** sup. **crūdēlissimē,** [**crūdēlis**], adv., *cruelly, with cruelty* (I.31).

crūs, crūris, n., (**13g**), *leg.*

culmen, -inis, n., *height, summit, top* (III.2). [culminate.

culpa, -ae, f., *blame, fault, error* (IV.27; V.52). [culpable.

cultūra, -ae, [cf. **colō**], f., *tilling, cultivation.* [culture.

cultus, -ūs, [**colō**], m., *cultivation, care; mode of life, civilization.* [cult.

cum, prep., with ablative only, *with, along with, together with.* In combination the earlier form **com-** is used, which remains unchanged before **b, p, m,** but is changed to **col-** or **con-** before **l, cor-** or **con-** before **r, con-** before other consonants, and **co-** before vowels and **h;** implies doing anything *in concert with* others, or *thoroughly* and *completely.*

cum, conj., temporal, *when, while, as;* causal, *since;* adversative, *although.* **cum . . . tum,** *both . . . and, not only . . . but also.* **cum prīmum,** *as soon as.*

cunctātiō, -ōnis, [**cunctor**], f., *delay, hesitation* (III.18, 24).

cunctor, -ārī, -ātus, 1, dep., *delay, hesitate* (III.23; IV.25).

cūnctus, -a, -um, adj., *all together, all.*

cuneātim, [**cuneātus, cuneus**], adv., *in the form of a wedge; in wedge-shaped masses.*

cunīculus, -ī, m., *rabbit;* in military language, *underground passage, mine.*

cupidē, comp. **-ius,** sup. **-issimē,** [**cupidus**], adv., *eagerly, ardently.*

cupiditās, -tātis, [**cupidus**], f., *ardent desire, eagerness.* [cupidity.

cupidus, -a, -um, comp. **-ior,** sup. **-issimus,** [**cupiō**], adj., *desirous, eager for, fond of.*

cupiō, cupere, cupīvī, cupītus, 3, *desire; wish well to* (I.18).

cūr, adv., *why? wherefore?*

cūra, -ae, f., *care, attention, anxiety, trouble.* [cure (noun).

cūrō, -āre, -āvī, -ātus, [**cūra**], 1, *take care, provide for, arrange.* **nāvēs aedificandās cūrāre,** *to have ships built* (V.1). [cure.

currus, -ūs, [cf. **currō**], m., *chariot.*

cursus, -ūs, [cf. **currō**], m., *running; speed; course.* [course.

cūstōdia, -ae, [**cūstōs**], f., *a watching; guard, watch;* pl., *watch stations.* [custody.

cūstōs, -tōdis, m. and f., *guard, keeper.*

D.

D., with proper names, = **Decimus.**

D = **quīngentī**, *500.*

d., see **a. d.**

damnō, -āre, -āvī, -ātus, [**damnum**], 1, *condemn, sentence.* Part. as noun, **damnātī, -ōrum,** m., pl., *those condemned, criminals* (V.55).

dē, prep. with abl., denoting separation, *from, down from, away from; out of, of; from among; on account of, for, through, by; concerning, about, in respect to; after, during, in the course of, in.*

dēbeō, dēbēre, dēbuī, dēbitus, [**dē + habeō**], 2, *owe;* pass., *be due;* followed by infin., *ought, must, should.* [debit.

dēcēdō, -cēdere, -cessī, -cessūrus, [**dē + cēdō**], 3, *go away, retire, withdraw; avoid, shun; die* (VI.19).

decem, or **X,** indecl. num., *ten.*

dēceptus, see **dēcipiō.**

dēcernō, -cernere, -crēvī, -crētus, [**dē + cernō**], 3, *pass judgment, decide; resolve upon, resolve, determine; assign by vote.*

dēcertō, -āre, -āvī, -ātus, [**dē + certō,** contend], 1, *fight to a finish, fight a decisive battle.*

dēcessus, -ūs, [**dēcēdō**], m., *departure, withdrawal.* [decease.

dēcidō, -cidere, -cidī, [**dē + cadō**], 3, *fall down, fall off.* [deciduous.

decimus, -a, -um, or **X,** [**decem**], num. adj., *tenth.* [decimal.

Decimus, -ī, m., a Roman first name.

dēcipiō, -cipere, -cēpī, -ceptus, [**dē + capiō**], 3, *catch; deceive* (I.14). [deceive.

dēclārō, -āre, -āvī, -ātus, [**dē + clārō,** from **clārus**], 1, *make clear, announce* (I.50). [declare.

dēclīvis, -e, [**dē + clīvus**], adj., *sloping, descending.*

dēcrētum, -ī, [**dēcernō**], n., *decree, decision.* [decree.

decumānus, -a, -um, [**decimus**], adj., *of a tenth part, decuman.* **decumāna porta,** *rear gate* of the Roman camp, opposite the **porta praetōria.**

decuriō, -ōnis, [**decuria**], m., *decurion,* a cavalry officer in charge of a *decuria,* consisting of 10 horsemen.

dēcurrō, -currere, -cucurrī or **-currī, -cursūrus,** [**dē + currō**], 3, *run down, rush down, hasten.*

dēdecus, -oris, [**dē + decus,** honor], n., (**13f**), *disgrace, dishonor* (IV. 25).

dēditīcius, -ī, [**dēditus,** from **dēdō**], adj., *that has surrendered, subject.* As noun, **dēditīciī, -ōrum,** m., pl., *prisoners of war, captives.*

dēditiō, -ōnis, [**dēdō**], f., *surrender.* **accipere** or **recipere in dēditiōnem,** *to receive by capitulation.* **in dēditiōnem venīre,** *to surrender.*

dēditus, -a, -um, [part. of **dēdō**], adj., *devoted* (VI.16).

dēdō, -dere, -didī, -ditus, [**dē + dō**], 3, *give up, surrender; devote* (III. 22).

dēdūcō, -dūcere, -dūxī, -ductus, [**dē + dūcō**], 3, *lead down; lead away, lead off, withdraw; lead, induce; conduct, bring;* of ships, *draw down, launch* (V.2, 23); *bring home as a bride, marry* (V.14). [deduce.

dēfatīgātiō, -ōnis, [**dēfatīgō**], f., *weariness, exhaustion* (III.19).

dēfatīgō, -āre, -āvī, -ātus, [**dē + fatīgō,** weary], 1, *tire out, exhaust.*

dēfectiō, -ōnis, [**dēficiō**], f., *a failing; desertion, revolt.* [defection.

dēfendō, -fendere, -fendī, -fēnsus, 3, *ward off, repel; defend, guard, protect.* [defend.

dēfēnsiō, -ōnis, [**dēfendō**], f., *defense, protection.*

dēfēnsor, -ōris, [**dēfendō**], m., *defender, protector;* of piles protecting a bridge, *guards* (IV.17).

dēferō, -ferre, -tulī, -lātus, [**dē + ferō**], irr., *bring down; carry away, bear away; bring* (to), *carry* (to); *refer* (to), *confer upon, lay before; report, announce.* [defer.

dēfessus, -a, -um, [part. of **dēfetīscor**], adj., *worn out, exhausted.* As noun, **dēfessus, -ī,** m., *an exhausted person* (III.4).

dēficiō, -ficere, -fēcī, -fectus, [**dē + faciō**], 3, *fail, be lacking; fall away, revolt, rebel.* [deficit.

dēfīgō, -fīgere, -fīxī, fīxus, [**dē + fīgō,** fasten], 3, *make fast, fix, fasten; stick fast.*

dēfore, see **dēsum** (**52, 66a**).

dēfōrmis, -e, comp. **-ior,** [**dē + fōrma**], adj., *ill-shaped* (IV.2). [deform.

dēfugiō, -fugere, -fūgī, [**dē + fugiō**], 3, *flee from, shun, avoid.*

dēiciō, -icere, -iēcī, -iectus, [dē + iaciō], 3, *throw down, cast down, throw; dislodge, drive from, rout;* of a ship, pass., *be carried* (IV.28); *kill, destroy; disappoint.* [dejection.

dēiectus, see **dēiciō.**

dēiectus, -ūs, [dēiciō], m., *descent, slope, declivity* (II.8, 22, 29).

deinceps, [dein = deinde, + CAP in capiō], adv., *one after the other, in succession, in turn; without interruption* (III.29).

deinde, [dē + inde], adv., *thereafter, afterwards, then, next.*

dēlātus, see **dēferō.**

dēlectō, -āre, -āvī, -ātus, [freq. of dēliciō], 1, *please;* in pass., *have pleasure in* (IV.2). [delectation.

dēlēctus, see **dēligō.**

dēleō, -ēre, -ēvī, -ētus, 2, *destroy, annihilate;* of disgrace, *wipe out* (II.27). [delete.

dēlīberō, -āre, -āvī, -ātus, [dē, cf. lībra, *balance*], 1, *deliberate, ponder, consider.*

dēligō, -āre, -āvī, -ātus, [dē + ligō, *bind*], 1, *bind fast, make fast, tie, fasten.*

dēligō, -ligere, -lēgī, -lēctus, [dē + legō], 3, *choose, select, pick out.*

dēlitēscō, -litēscere, -lituī, [dē + latēscō, from lateō], 3, *conceal one's self* (IV.32).

dēmentia, -ae, [dēmēns], f., *madness, folly* (IV.13). [dementia.

dēmetō, -metere, -messuī, -messus, [dē + metō], 3, *reap* (IV.32).

dēmigrō, -āre, -āvī, -ātus, [dē + migrō, *depart*], 1, *move from, withdraw; depart, migrate.*

dēminuō, -minuere, -minuī, -minūtus, [dē + minuō], 3, *lessen, make smaller; impair.* [diminish.

dēmittō, -mittere, -mīsī, -missus, [dē + mittō], 3, *send down, let down;* of the head, *bow* (I.32). **sē dēmittere,** *to go down, come down, descend* (V.32).

dēmō, dēmere, dēmpsī, dēmptus, [dē + emō], 3, *take down* (V.48).

dēmōnstrō, -āre, -āvī, -ātus, [dē + mōnstrō, *show*], 1, *point out, state, mention; show, explain.* [demonstrate.

dēmoror, -ārī, -ātus, [dē + moror], 1, dep., *delay, retard, hinder.*

dēmptus, see **dēmō.**

dēmum, adv., *at length, finally.*

dēnegō, -āre, -āvī, -ātus, [dē + negō], 1, *refuse, deny* (I.42). [deny.

dēnī, -ae, -a, [decem], distrib. num. adj., *ten each, ten apiece.*

dēnique, adv., *at last, finally; in a word, in short; at any rate* (II.33).

dēnsus, -a, -um, comp. **-ior,** sup. **-issimus,** adj., *thick, closely packed, dense, crowded.* [dense.

dēnūntiō, -āre, -āvī, -ātus, [dē + nūntiō], 1, *announce, declare; threaten* (I.36); *order* (VI.10). [denounce.

dēpellō, -pellere, -pulī, -pulsus, [dē + pellō], 3, *drive away, dislodge;* of disease, *ward off* (VI.17).

dēperdō, -dere, -didī, -ditus, [dē + perdō, *destroy*], 3, *lose.*

dēpereō, -īre, -iī, -itūrus, [dē + pereō], irr., *be destroyed, lost* (V.23).

dēpōnō, -pōnere, -posuī, -positus, [dē + pōnō], 3, *lay aside, lay down, place; give up.* [deposit.

dēpopulor, -ārī, -ātus, [dē + populor], 1, dep., *lay waste, plunder;* part. **dēpopulātus,** pass., *laid waste, devastated* (I.11). [depopulate.

dēportō, -āre, -āvī, -ātus, [dē + portō], 1, *remove* (III.12). [deport.

dēposcō, -poscere, -poposcī, [dē + poscō], 3, *demand, earnestly desire.*

dēpositus, see **dēpōnō.**

dēprāvō, -āre, -āvī, -ātus, [dē + prāvus], 1, *distort, corrupt.* [deprave.

dēprecātor, -ōris, [dēprecor], m., (11d), *intercessor, mediator.* [deprecator.

dēprecor, -ārī, -ātus, [dē + precor, *pray*], 1, dep., *pray to be delivered from, beg to escape; ask for quarter, beg for mercy* (IV.7). [deprecate.

dēprehendō, -hendere, -hendī, -hēnsus, [dē + prehendō], 3, *catch, seize; surprise.*

dēpulsus, see **dēpellō.**

dērēctē, comp. **-ius,** [dērēctus], adv., *directly, straight up and down* (IV.17).

dērēctus, -a, -um, [part. of dērigō], adj., *laid straight, straight; straight up and down, perpendicular.* [direct.

dērigō, -rigere, -rēxī, -rēctus, [dē + regō], 3, *lay straight.*

dērogō, -āre, -āvī, -ātus, [dē + rogō], 1, *withdraw* (VI.23). [derogate.

dēscendō, -scendere, -scendī, dēscēnsum est, [dē + scandō, *climb*], 3, *come down, descend;* with **ad** and the acc., *resort to, stoop to.* [descend.

dēserō, -serere, -seruī, -sertus, [dē + serō, *join*], 3, *leave, abandon, desert.* [desert.

dēsertor, -ōris, [dēserō], m., *deserter, runaway* (VI.23).

dēsertus, -a, -um, comp. **-ior,** sup. **-issimus,** [part. of dēserō], adj., *deserted, solitary.*

dēsīderō, -āre, -āvī, -ātus, 1, *wish for, want, long for, miss; lack, lose;* pass. often, especially of soldiers, *be missing, be lost.* [desideratum.

dēsidia, -ae, [dēses, *idle,* cf. dēsideō], f., *indolence, idleness* (VI.23).

dēsignō, -āre, -āvī, -ātus, [dē + signō, *mark*], 1, *point out; designate* (I.18).

dēsiliō, -silīre, -siluī, -sultus, [dē + saliō, *leap*], 4, *leap down, jump down;* from horses, *dismount.*

dēsistō, -sistere, -stitī, -stitūrus, [dē + sistō], 3, *leave off, cease; desist from, stop, give up.* [desist.

dēspectus, see dēspiciō.

dēspectus, -ūs, [dēspiciō], m., *a looking down* from an elevation, *view.*

dēspērātiō, -ōnis, [dēspērō], f., *despair, hopelessness.* [desperation.

dēspērō, -āre, -āvī, -ātus, [dē + spērō], 1, *give up hope of, despair of, have no hope of.* [despair.

dēspiciō, -spicere, -spexī, -spectus, [dē + speciō, *look*], 3, *look down upon; despise, disdain.* [despise.

dēspoliō, -āre, -āvī, -ātus, [dē + spoliō], 1, *despoil, rob* (II.31). [despoil.

dēstinō, -āre, -āvī, -ātus, 1, *make fast, bind, stay.* [destine.

dēstituō, -stituere, -stituī, -stitūtus, [dē + statuō], 3, *desert, abandon, leave* (I.16). [destitute.

dēstringō, -stringere, -strīnxī, -strictus, [dē + stringō, *pluck off*], 3, *unsheathe, draw* (I.25).

dēsum, deesse, defuī, [dē + sum], irr., *be wanting, fail, lie lacking.*

dēsuper, [dē + super], adv., *from above.*

dēterior, comp. **-ius,** sup. **dēterrimus,** [dē], adj., *worse, poorer; of less value* (I.36). [deteriorate.

dēterreō, -terrēre, -terruī, -territus, [dē + terreō], 2, *frighten off, prevent, deter; repress* (V.7). **dēterrēre nē, quō minus,** or **quīn,** *to prevent from.* [deter.

dētestor, -ārī, -ātus, [dē + testor], 1, dep., *curse, execrate.* [detest.

dētineō, -tinēre, -tinuī, -tentus, [dē + teneō], 2, *hold back* (III.12). [detain.

dētrahō, -trahere, -trāxī, trāctus, [dē + trahō], 3, *draw off, take off; take away, remove.* [detract.

dētrīmentum, -ī, [dē, cf. terō, *wear away*], n., *loss, damage, injury; loss in war, repulse, reverse, defeat.* [detriment.

dēturbō, -āre, -āvī, -ātus, [dē + turbō, *disturb*], 1, *force back in disorder, dislodge* (V.43).

deus, -ī, m., (**8d**), *god.* [deity.

dēvehō, -vehere, -vexī, -vectus, [dē + vehō], 3, *carry away, remove, convey.*

dēveniō, -venīre, -vēnī, -ventūrus, [dē + veniō], 4, *come* (II.21).

dēvōtus, [part. of dēvoveō], adj., *bound by a vow.* As noun, **dēvōtī, -ōrum,** m., pl., *faithful followers* (III.22).

dēvoveō, -vovēre, -vōvī, -vōtus, [dē + voveō], 2, *vow, devote* (III.22); *offer to the gods, consecrate* (VI.17). [devote.

dexter, -tra, -trum, adj., *right.* [dexterous.

dextra, -ae, [dexter, sc. manus], f., *right hand* (I.20).

Diablintēs, -um, m., pl., a numerically small people in northwestern Gaul, probably a division of the Aulerci (III.9).

diciō, -ōnis, pl. and nom. sing. not in use, f., *sway, sovereignty, authority, lordship* (I.31, 33; II.34).

dicō, -āre, -āvī, -ātus, 1, *dedicate; devote, offer* (VI.12, 13).

dīcō, dīcere, dīxī, dictus, 3, *say, converse, speak; mention, tell, utter; appoint; of a case, plead; of a day, set.*

dictiō, -ōnis, [dīcō], f., *speaking; pleading* (I.4). [diction.

dictum, -ī, [dīcō], n., *saying, word; command, order.* **dictō audiēns, audientēs,** *obedient to (his) order.* [dictum.

dīdūcō, -dūcere, -dūxī, -ductus, [dis- + dūcō], 3, *lead in different directions; divide, separate* (III.23).

diēs, diēī, m. and f., (**21**), *day; time* (I.7). **in diēs,** *day by day, every day.* **diem dīcere,** *to set a day.*

differo, differre, distulī, dīlātus, [dis- + ferō], irr., *spread, scatter* (V.43); *put off, delay; differ, be different.* [differ.

difficilis, -e, comp. **difficilior,** sup. **difficillimus,** [dis- + facilis], adj., *difficult, hard.*

difficultās, -tātis, [difficilis], f., *difficulty, trouble.* [difficulty.

diffīdō, -fīdere, -fīsus sum, [dis- + fīdō], 3, semi-dep., *distrust, lose confidence in, despair of.* [diffident.

diffluō, -ere, difflūxī, [dis- + fluō], 3, *flow in different directions, divide* (IV.10).

digitus, -ī, m., *finger;* as a measure, *finger's breadth,* the 16th part of a Roman foot, .728 of an inch. **digitus pollex,** *thumb* as a measure (III.13). [digit.

dignitās, -tātis, [**dignus**], f., *worth, merit; greatness, rank, reputation.* [dignity.

dignus, -a, -um, comp. **-ior,** sup. **-issimus,** adj., *worthy, worth.*

dīiūdicō, -āre, -āvī, -ātus, [**dis-** + **iūdicō**], 1, *decide* (V.44).

dīlēctus, see **dīligō.**

dīlēctus, -ūs, [**dīligō**], m., *levy, draft, enlistment.*

dīligenter, comp. **dīligentius,** sup. **dīligentissimē,** [**dīligēns**], adv., *carefully, punctually.*

dīligentia, -ae, [**dīligēns**], f., *care, diligence.*

dīligō, -ligere, -lēxī, -lēctus, [**dis-** + **legō,** *choose*], 3, *love, prize* (VI.19).

dīmētior, -mētīrī, -mēnsus [**dis-** + **mētior**], 4, dep., passive in Caesar, *measure, measure off* (IV.17); of work, *lay out* (II.19). [dimension.

dīmicō, -āre, -āvī, -ātum est, [**dis-** + **micō**], 1, *fight, contend, struggle.*

dīmidius, -a, -um, [**dis-** + **medius**], adj., *half.* As noun, **dīmidium, -ī,** n., *half.*

dīmittō, -mittere, -mīsī, -missus, [**dis-** + **mittō**], 3, *send in different directions, send about; dismiss, send off; let go, let slip, lose; abandon; disband* (II.14). [dismiss.

dirimō, -imere, -ēmī, -ēmptus, [**dis-** + **emō,** *take*], 3, *take apart; break off, put an end to* (I.46).

dīripiō, -ripere, -ripuī, -reptus, [**dis-** + **rapiō,** *seize*], 3, *tear asunder; ravage, plunder, pillage.*

dis- (dī-), inseparable prep., used only as a prefix with other words, adding the force of *apart, asunder, in different directions, utterly, entirely; not, un-.* In combination **dis-** becomes **dif-** before **f, dir-** before vowels, **dī-** before **d, g, l, m, n, r,** and **v.**

Dīs, Dītis, m., with **pater,** *Dis pater, Father Dis,* god of the Underworld (VI.18).

discēdō, -cēdere, -cessī, -cessūrus, pf. pass. impers., **discessum est,** [**dis-** + **cēdō**], 3, *go apart, disperse, scatter; depart, withdraw, leave, go away, go off.* **ab armīs discēdere,** *to lay down one's arms.*

discessus, -ūs, [**discēdō**], m., *departure, going away.*

disciplīna, -ae, [**discipulus**], f., *instruction, training; doctrine.* [discipline.

disclūdō, -clūdere, -clūsī, -clūsus, [**dis-** + **claudō**], 3, *keep apart, hold apart* (IV.17).

discō, discere, didicī, 3, *learn.*

disiciō, -icere, -iēcī, -iectus, [**dis-** + **iaciō**], 3, *drive asunder; disperse, scatter, rout.*

dispār, -paris, [**dis-** + **pār**], adj., *unequal, unlike* (V.16).

disparō, -āre, -āvī, -ātus, [**dis-** + **parō**], 1, *divide, separate.* [disparate.

dispergō, -spergere, -spersī, -spersus, [**dis-** + **spargō,** *scatter*], 3, *scatter, scatter about, disperse.* [disperse.

dispōnō, -pōnere, -posuī, -positus, [**dis-** + **pōnō**], 3, *set in various places, distribute; station, post.* [dispose.

disputātiō, -ōnis, [**disputō**], f., *discussion, debate, dispute.* [disputation.

disputō, -āre, -āvī, -ātus, [**dis-** + **putō**], 1, *investigate, discuss* (VI.14). [dispute.

dissēnsiō, -ōnis, [**dissentiō**], f., *disagreement.* [dissension.

dissentiō, -sentīre, -sēnsī, -sēnsus, [**dis-** + **sentiō**], 4, *differ in opinion, disagree* (V.29). [dissent.

dissimulō, -āre, -āvī, -ātus, [**dis-** + **simulō**], 1, *make unlike; disguise, keep secret* (IV.6). [dissimulate.

dissipō, -āre, -āvī, -ātus, 1, *scatter, disperse.* [dissipate.

distineō, -tinēre, -tinuī, -tentus, [**dis-** + **teneō**], 2, *keep apart, hold apart, separate; hinder, delay.*

distō, -āre, [**dis-** + **stō**], 1, *stand apart, be separated, be distant.* [distant.

distribuō, -tribuere, -tribuī, -tribūtus, [**dis-** + **tribuō**], 3, *distribute, divide, assign, apportion.* [distribute.

dītissimus, see **dīves.**

diū, comp. **diūtius,** sup. **diūtissimē,** adv., *long, for a long time.* **quam diū,** *as long as* (I.17).

diurnus, -a, -um, [cf. **diēs**], adj., *of the day, by day.* [diurnal.

diūtinus, -a, -um, [**diū**], adj., *long continued, lasting* (V.52).

diūturnitās, -tātis, [**diūturnus**], f., *long duration* of time (I.40; III.4).

diūturnus, -a, -um, comp. **-ior,** [**diū**], adj., *long, prolonged* (I.14).

dīversus, -a, -um, [part. of **dīvertō**], adj., *opposite; separate, apart; different.*

dīvertō, -ere, -tī, -sus, [**dis-** + **vertō**], 3, *separate* (II.24). [divert.

dīves, -itis, comp. **dītior,** sup. **dītissimus,** adj., *rich, wealthy* (I.2).

Dīviciācus, -ī, m.: (1) An Aeduan of influence, loyal to Caesar, who at his intercession pardoned Dumnorix (I.18-20) and the Bellovaci (II.14, 15). (2) A ruler of the Suessiones (II.4).

Dīvicō, -ōnis, m., leader of the Helvetians in their war with Cassius, 107 BC, and head of an embassy to Caesar, 58 BC (I.13).

dīvidō, -videre, -vīsī, -vīsus, 3, *separate, divide.*

dīvīnus, -a, -um, comp. **-ior**, sup. **-issimus**, [**dīvus**], adj., *divine, sacred.*

dō, dare, dedī, datus, irr., (**67**), *give, give up, give over, grant; offer, furnish, allow.* **in fugam dare**, *to put to flight.* **operam dare**, *to take pains* (V.7).

doceō, docēre, docuī, doctus, 2, *teach; inform; point out, state.* [doctor.

doleō, dolēre, doluī, dolitūrus, 2, *suffer; be grieved, be annoyed.*

dolor, -ōris, [**doleō**], m., *pain, suffering; grief, distress.*

dolus, -ī, m., *cunning, fraud, deceit.*

domesticus, a, -um, [**domus**], adj., *home, native, internal; their own* (II.10). **domesticum bellum**, *civil war* (V.9).

domicilium, -ī, [**domus**], n., *dwelling, abode, habitation.* [domicile.

dominor, -ārī, -ātus, [**dominus**], 1, dep., *be master, have dominion* (II.31). [dominate.

dominus, -ī, [**domō**, *subdue*], m., *master, lord* (VI.13).

Domitius, -ī, m., *Lucius Domitius Ahenobarbus,* consul with Appius Claudius Pulcher, 54 BC (V.1).

domus, -ūs, f., (**20c**), *house, home.*

dōnō, -āre, -āvī, -ātus, [**dōnum**], 1, *give, grant, confer* (I.47). [donate.

dōnum, -ī, [**dō**], n., *gift, present.*

dorsum, -ī, n., *back.* [dorsal.

dōs, dōtis, [cf. **dō**], f., (**17c**), *dowry, marriage portion* (VI.19).

Druidēs, -um, m., pl., *Druids.*

Dubis, -is, m., a river in Gaul, tributary of the Arar (*Saône*); now the *Doubs* (I.38).

dubitātiō, -ōnis, [**dubitō**], f., *doubt, hesitation.* [dubitation.

dubitō, -āre, -āvī, -ātus, [**dubius**], 1, *be uncertain, doubt; hesitate, delay.*

dubius, -a, -um, adj., *doubtful, uncertain.* [dubious.

ducentī, -ae, -a, or **CC**, [**duo** + **centum**], adj., (**37d**), *two hundred.*

dūcō, dūcere, dūxī, ductus, 3, *lead, guide, conduct, bring, take; of a trench, make; protract, prolong, put off; think, consider, reckon.* **in mātrimōnium dūcere**, *to marry* (I.9, 53).

dum, conj., (**190**), *while; until.*

Dumnorīx, -īgis, m., an Aeduan, brother of Diviciacus, and son-in-law of Orgetorix; enemy of Caesar, and leader of an Aeduan anti-Roman party; slain by Caesar's orders while trying to escape from him, 54 BC.

duo, -ae, -o, or **II**, adj., (**37b**), *two.* [duet.

duodecim, or **XII**, [**duo** + **decem**], indecl. num. adjective, *twelve.* [duodecimal.

duodecimus, -a, -um, [**duodecim**], num. adj., *twelfth.*

duodēnī, -ae, -a, [**duodecim**], distributive num. adj., *twelve at a time, by twelves.*

duodēseptuāgintā, or **LXVIII**, [**duo** + **dē** + **septuāgintā**], indecl .num., *sixty-eight* (I.29).

duodētrīgintā, or **XXVIII**, [**duo** + **dē** + **trīgintā**], indecl. num., *twenty-eight* (V.2).

duodēvīgintī, -ae, -a, or **XVIII**, [**duo** + **dē** + **vīgintī**], num. adj., *eighteen.*

duplex, -icis, [**duo**, cf. **plicō**, *fold*], adj., (**26a**), *twofold, double.* [duplex.

duplicō, -āre, -āvī, -ātus, [**duplex**], 1, *make double, double.* [duplicate.

dūritia, -ae, [**dūrus**], f., *hardness; severe mode of life* (VI.21). [duress.

dūrus, -a, -um, comp. **-ior**, sup. **-issimus**, adj., *hard, severe, difficult.*

Dūrus, -ī, m., *Quintus Laberius Durus,* a military tribune (V.15).

dux, ducis, [**dūcō**, *lead*], m., (**10c**), *leader, guide; general, commander.* [duke.

E.

ē, see **ex.**

eā, [properly abl. of **is**, sc. **parte**], adv., *there, on that side* (V.51).

Eburōnēs, -um, m., pl., a Belgic people north of the Treverans. In 54 BC they destroyed a detachment of Caesar's army under Sabinus and Cotta.

Eburovīcēs, -um, m., pl., a division of the *Aulerci,* a people of Central Gaul.

ēdiscō, -discere, -didicī, [**ex** + **discō**], 3, *learn by heart* (VI.14).

ēditus, -a, -um, comp. **-ior**, [part. of **ēdō**], adj., *elevated; rising* (II.8).

ēdō, -dere, -didī, -ditus, [**ex + dō**], 3, *put forth; inflict* (I.31). [edit.

ēdoceō, -docēre, -docuī, -doctus, [**ex + doceō**], 2, *teach carefully, instruct, inform.*

ēdūcō, -dūcere, -dūxī, -ductus, [**ex + dūcō**], 3, *lead out, lead forth; of a sword, draw* (V.44).

effēminō, -āre, -āvī, -ātus, [**ex + fēmina**], 1, *make womanish, weaken, enervate* (I.1; IV.2). [effeminate.

efferō, -ferre, extulī, ēlātus, [**ex + ferō**], irr., *bring out, carry forth, carry away* (I.5; V.45); *spread abroad, publish* (I.46; VI.14); *elate* (V.47). [elate.

efficiō, -ficere, -fēcī, -fectus, [**ex + faciō**], 3, *bring about, accomplish, effect, produce; make, render; build, construct.* [effect.

effugiō, -fugere, -fūgī, [**ex + fugiō**], 3, *escape.*

effundō, -fundere, -fūdī, -fūsus, [**ex + fundō**], 3, *pour out.* **sē effundere,** of a crowd, *pour out;* of cavalry, *dash forth* (V.19). [effusive.

egeō, egēre, eguī, 2, *lack, be in want* (*of*).

egestās, -tātis, [**egēns**], f., *privation, destitution, want* (VI.24).

ego, meī, personal pron., (**39a**), *I;* pl. **nōs, nostrum,** *we.* [egotism.

ēgredior, -gredī, -gressus, [**ex + gradior,** *step*], 3, dep., *go out, go forth, come forth, leave;* from a ship, *land, disembark.*

ēgregiē, [**ēgregius**], adv., *remarkably well, admirably, splendidly.*

ēgregius, -a, -um, [**ex + grex,** *herd, crowd*], adj., *outstanding, marked, distinguished, excellent.* [egregious.

ēgressus, see **ēgredior.**

ēgressus, -ūs, [**ēgredior**], m., *departure; disembarking, landing* (V.8). [egress.

ēiciō, -icere, -iēcī, -iectus, [**ex + iaciō**], 3, *throw out, cast out, expel; cast up* (V.10). **sē ēicere,** *to rush, sally forth.* [eject.

eius modī, see **modus.**

ēlābor, -lābī, -lāpsus, [**ex + lābor**], 3, dep., *slip away; escape* (V.37). [elapse.

ēlātus, see **efferō.**

ēlēctus, -a, -um, comp. **-ior,** sup. **-issimus,** [part. of **ēligō**], adj., *chosen, picked.* [elect.

ēliciō, -licere, -licuī, [**ex + laciō,** *entice*], 3, *entice forth, lure forth; bring out, draw out.* [elicit.

Elusātēs, -ium, m., pl., a people in Central Aquitania (III.27).

ēmigrō, -āre, -āvī, [**ex + migrō,** *depart*], 1, *go forth, move, emigrate* (I.31).

ēminus [**ex + manus,** *hand*], adv., *at a distance, from afar.*

ēmittō, -mittere, -mīsī, -missus, [**ex + mittō**], 3, *send out; hurl, cast, shoot, discharge* (II.23); *throw away, let go* (I.25). [emit.

emō, emere, ēmī, ēmptus, 3, *buy, purchase* (I.16; II.33).

ēnāscor, -nāscī, -nātus, [**ex + nāscor**], 3, dep., *grow out;* of branches, *shoot out.*

enim [**nam**], conj., postpositive, *for, for in fact.* **neque enim,** *and* (*with good reason*) *for . . . not, for in fact . . . not.*

ēnūntiō, -āre, -āvī, -ātus [**ex + nūntiō**], 1, *report, reveal, disclose.*

eō, abl. of **is,** (**44**).

eō, [cf. **is**], adv., *thither, to that place, there.*

eō, īre, iī, itūrus, ītum est, irr., (**68**), *go, pass, march, advance.*

eōdem [**idem**], adv., *to the same place; to the same thing* (I.14), *to the same end* (IV.11).

ephippiātus, -a, -um, adj., *riding with saddle-cloths* (IV.2).

ephippium, -ī, n., *saddle-cloth* (IV.2).

epistula, -ae, f., *letter, dispatch* (V.48). [epistle.

eques, -itis, [**equus**], m., (**10d**), *horseman, cavalryman, trooper;* as a member of a social order, *knight.*

equester, -tris, -tre, [**eques**], adj., *of cavalry, cavalry.* [equestrian.

equitātus, -ūs, [**equitō,** *ride*], m., *cavalry; knighthood,* collectively *knights* (I.31).

equus, -ī, m., *horse.* [equine.

Eratosthenēs, -is, m., a Greek, lived 276 –196 BC; librarian of the great library at Alexandria in Egypt, and famous as a geographer, mathematician, historian, and grammarian (VI.24).

ērēctus, -a, -um, comp. **-ior,** [part. of **ērigō**], adj., *high, elevated* (III.13).

ēreptus, see **ēripiō.**

ergā, prep. with acc., *towards* (V.54).

ērigō, -rigere, -rēxī, -rēctus, [**ex + regō**], 3, *raise to a standing position; erect.*

ēripiō, -ripere, -ripuī, -reptus, [**ex + rapiō,** seize], 3, *take away, snatch away; rescue, save* (I.53). **sē ēripere,** *to rescue one's self, make one's escape.*

errō, -āre, -āvī, -ātus, 1, *wander; be mistaken, delude one's self.* [err.

ērumpō, -rumpere, -rūpī, -ruptus, [**ex + rumpō,** break], 3, *burst forth, sally forth* (III.5). [erupt.

ēruptiō, -ōnis, [**ērumpō**], f., *a bursting forth; sally, sortie.* [eruption.

essedārius, -ī, [**essedum**], m., *fighter from a chariot, chariot-fighter.*

essedum, -ī, n., two-wheeled *war-chariot* (IV.32, 33; V.9, 16, 17).

Esuviī, -ōrum, m., pl., a people in northwestern Gaul.

et, conj., *and.* **et . . . et,** *both . . . and.*

etiam [**et + iam**], conj., *also; even.* **nōn sōlum . . . sed etiam,** *not only . . . but also.*

etsī [**et + sī**], conj., (**191a**), *although, though, even if.*

ēvādō, -vādere, -vāsī, -vāsūrus, [**ex + vādō**], 3, *escape* (III.19). [evade.

ēvellō, -vellere, -vellī, -vulsus, [**ex + vellō,** pluck], 3, *pull out* (I.25).

ēveniō, -venīre, -vēnī, -ventūrus, [**ex + veniō**], 4, *turn out, happen* (IV.25).

eventus, -ūs, [cf. **ēveniō**], m., *outcome, result; chance, fortune; fate, accident* (IV.31). [event.

ēvocātus, -ī, [part. of **ēvocō**], m., *veteran volunteer,* a soldier serving voluntarily after the completion of his time of service.

ēvocō, -āre, -āvī, -ātus, [**ex + vocō**], 1, *call out, call forth, call, summon; invite* (V.58). [evoke.

ēvolō, -āre, -āvī, [**ex + volō,** fly], 1, *fly forth, rush out, dash out.*

ex, often before consonants **ē,** prep. with abl., *from, out of, down from; since; after; of; by reason of, by, because of, in consequence of; according to, with, in, on.* **ex ūnā parte,** *on one side.* In combination **ex** becomes **ef** before **f, ē** before **b, d, g, i** (when a consonant), **l, m, n,** and **v.**

exāctus, see **exigō.**

exagitō, -āre, -āvī, -ātus, [**ex + agitō,** freq. of **agō**], 1, *disturb, harass* (II.29; IV.1).

exāminō, -āre, -āvī, -ātus, [**exāmen,** tongue of a balance], 1, *weigh* (V.12). [examine.

exanimō, -āre, -āvī, -ātus, [**exanimus**], 1, *deprive of life, kill;* pass., *be out of breath, weakened, exhausted* (II.23, III.19).

exārdēscō, -ārdēscere, -ārsī, -ārsūrus, [**ex + ārdēscō**], 3, *take fire; be incensed* (V.4).

exaudiō, -dīre, -dīvī, -dītus, [**ex + audiō**], 4, *hear distinctly, hear plainly.*

excēdō, -cēdere, -cessī, -cessūrus, [**ex + cēdō**], 3, *go out, leave, withdraw, depart.*

excellō, -cellere, participial adj. **excelsus,** 3, *be eminent, surpass* (VI.13). [excel.

exceptus, see **excipiō.**

excipiō, -cipere, -cēpī, -ceptus, [**ex + capiō**], 3, *take out; take up; cut off, catch; receive, withstand* (I.52, III.5, IV.17); *cope with, encounter* (III.13); *take the place of, relieve, succeed, follow* (V.16). [except.

excitō, -āre, -āvī, -ātus, [**ex + citō,** move], 1, *erect, raise rapidly* (III.14; V.40); *stir up, rouse, spur on.* [excite.

exclūdō, -clūdere, -clūsī, -clūsus, [**ex + claudō**], 3, *shut out, shut off, cut off; hinder, prevent.* [exclude.

excōgitō, -āre, -āvī, -ātus, [**ex + cōgitō**], 1, *think out, think of* (V.31).

excruciō, -āre, -āvī, -ātus, [**ex + cruciō,** from **crux,** cross], 1, *torment, torture.* [excruciate.

excursiō, -ōnis, [**ex,** cf. **currō**], f., *a running out; sally, sortie* (II.30). [excursion.

excūsō, -āre, -āvī, -ātus, [**ex,** cf. **causa**], 1, *excuse, make excuse for* (IV.22). [excuse.

exemplum, -ī, [cf. **eximō**], n., *example, precedent;* as an example to warn others, *kind of punishment* (I.31). [example.

exeō, -īre, -iī, -itum est, [**ex + eō**], irr., *go forth, go out; withdraw, leave.*

exerceō, -ercēre, -ercuī, -ercitus, [**ex + arceō**], 2, *exercise, practice; train, discipline.* [exercise.

exercitātiō, -ōnis, [**exercitō,** freq. of **exerceō**], f., *practice, exercise, training.*

exercitātus, -a, -um, comp. **-ior,** sup. **-issimus,** [**exercitō,** freq. of **exerceō**], adj., *practiced, experienced, trained.*

exercitus, -ūs, [**exerceō**], m., *army,* as a trained and disciplined body.

exhauriō, -haurīre, -hausī, -haustus, [**ex + hauriō,** draw up], 4, *take out* (V.42). [exhaust.

exigō, -igere, -ēgī, -āctus, [**ex + agō**], 3, *drive out;* of time, *spend, complete, end* (III.28). [exact.

exiguitās, -ātis, [**exiguus**], f., *smallness* (IV.30); *scantness* (IV.1); *small number, fewness* (III.23); *shortness* (II.21, 33).

exiguus, -a, -um, sup. **-issimus,** [**exigō**], adj., *small, scanty, little.*

eximius, -a, -um, [cf. **eximō**], adj., *distinguished, excellent* (II.8).

exīstimātiō, -ōnis, [**exīstimō**], f., *opinion, judgment* (I.20; V.44).

exīstimō, -āre, -āvī, -ātus, [**ex + aestimō,** *compute*], 1, *reckon; think, consider, judge, suppose, believe.*

exitus, -ūs, [**exeō**], m., *a going out, egress; passage; conclusion, end; issue, event, outcome.* [exit.

expediō, -pedīre, -pedīvī, -pedītus, [**ex,** cf. **pēs**], 4, *disengage, set free; get ready, make ready.* [expedite.

expedītiō, -ōnis, [**expediō**], f., *rapid march,* (V.10). [expedition.

expedītus, -a, -um, comp. **-ior,** sup. **-issimus,** [part. of **expediō**], adj., *with light equipment, unencumbered, light-armed; convenient, easy.* **legiōnēs expedītae,** *legions in light marching order,* without baggage. As noun, **expedītus, -ī,** m., *lightly armed soldier.*

expellō, -pellere, -pulī, -pulsus, [**ex + pellō**], 3, *drive out, away; remove.* [expel.

experior, -perīrī, -pertus, 4, dep., *put to the test, try.* [expert.

expiō, -āre, -āvī, -ātus, [**ex + piō,** *appease*], 1, *atone for, make amends for.* [expiate.

expleō, -plēre, -plēvī, -plētus, [**ex + pleō,** *fill*], 2, *fill up; fill out, complete.*

explōrātor, -ōris, [**explōrō**], m., *scout, patrol.*

explorātus, -a, -um, comp. **-ior,** sup. **-issimus,** [part. of **explōrō**], adj., *established, certain, settled, sure.*

explōrō, -āre, -āvī, -ātus, 1, *search out, investigate, explore; spy out, reconnoiter; gain, secure.* [explore.

expōnō, -pōnere, -posuī, -positus, [**ex + pōnō**], 3, *set out, put out; place in full view, array* (IV.23); *from ships, set on shore, land; set forth, state, explain.* [expose.

exportō, -āre, -āvī, -ātus, [**ex + portō**], 1, *carry away* (IV.18). [export.

exprimō, -primere, -pressī, -pressus, [**ex + premō**], 3, *press out; force out.* [express.

expugnō, -āre, -āvī, -ātus, [**ex + pugno**], 1, *take by storm, take by assault, capture.*

expulsus, see **expellō.**

exquīrō, -quīrere, -quīsīvī, -quīsītus, [**ex + quaerō**], 3, *seek out, search out* (I.41); *ask for, inquire into* (III.3). [exquisite.

exsequor, -sequī, -secūtus, [**ex + sequor**], 3, dep., *follow up; maintain, enforce* (I.4). [execute.

exsistō, -sistere, -stitī, [**ex + sistō**], 3, *appear; spring up, arise, ensue.* [exist.

exspectō, -āre, -āvī, -ātus, [**ex + spectō**], 1, *look out for, wait for, await; look to see, expect.* [expect.

exstinguō, -stinguere, -stīnxī, -stīnctus, [**ex + stinguō**], 3, *quench completely* (V.29). [extinguish.

exstō, -stāre, [**ex + stō**], 1, *stand out, project* (V.18). [extant.

exstruō, -struere, -strūxī, -strūctus, [**ex + struō,** *pile*], 3, *pile up, heap up; rear, build, construct.*

exsul, -ulis, m. and f., (**11c**), *outlaw, exile.*

exter or **exterus, -a, -um,** comp. **exterior,** sup. **extrēmus,** [**ex**], adj., *outward, outer.* Sup. **extrēmus,** *last, extreme, at the end.* As noun, **extrēmī, -ōrum,** m., pl., *the rear* (V.10); neut. sing., in **ad extremum,** *at the end, finally* (IV.4). [extreme.

exterreō, -ēre, -uī, -itus, [**ex + terreō,** *scare*], 2, *greatly frighten, terrify.*

extimēscō, -timēscere, -timuī, [**ex + timēscō,** *fear*], 3, *fear greatly, dread.*

extrā [**exter**], prep. with acc., *outside of beyond, without.* [extra.

extrahō, -trahere, -trāxī, -trāctus, [**ex + trahō,** *draw*], 3, *draw out; draw out to no purpose, waste* (V.22). [extract.

extrūdō, -trūdere, -trūsī, -trūsus, [**ex + trūdō**], 3, *thrust out; shut out.* [extrude.

exuō, -uere, -uī, -ūtus, 3, *strip, strip off, despoil, deprive.*

exūrō, -ūrere, -ussī, -ūstus, [**ex + ūrō,** *burn*], 3, *burn up* (I.5).

F.

faber, fabrī, m., (**7c**), *skilled workman, builder.* [fabric.

Fabius, -ī, m.: (1) *Quintus Fabius Maximus,* called *Allobrogicus,* in honor of his victory over the Allobroges, Arvernians, and Ruteni in the year of his consulship, 121 BC. (I.45). (2) *Gaius Fabius,* a lieutenant of Caesar in the Gallic War.

facile, comp. **facilius,** sup. **facillimē,** [**facilis**], adv., *easily, readily.*

facilis, -e, comp. **facilior,** sup. **facillimus,** [cf. **faciō**], adj., *easy, not hard.* [facile.

facinus, -oris, [**faciō**], n., (**13f**), *action; wicked action, misdeed, crime.*

faciō, facere, fēcī, factus, 3, *do, make; act, perform, accomplish, form; bring about, cause; furnish, give.* For pass., **fīō, fierī, factus sum,** see **fīō. certiōrem facere,** *to inform.* **imperāta facere,** *to obey commands.* **iter facere,** *to march.* **vim facere,** *to use violence* (I.8, V.7). [factor.

factiō, -ōnis, [**faciō**], f., *party, political party; league.* [faction.

factū, supine of **faciō.**

factum, -ī, [**faciō**], n., *deed, action, achievement.* [fact.

facultās, -ātis, [**facilis**], f., *ability, capability; opportunity, chance; abundance; supply* (III.9). Pl., *resources, wealth.* [faculty.

fāgus, -ī, f., (**5b**), *beech-tree* (V.12).

fallō, fallere, fefellī, falsus, 3, *deceive, cheat; disappoint.*

falsus, -a,-um, [part. of **fallō**], adj., *false, ungrounded.* [false.

falx, falcis, f., (**17c**), *sickle;* sickle-shaped *hook.*

fāma, -ae, [cf. **fārī,** to speak], f., *report, rumor, common talk; reputation.* [fame.

famēs, -is, f., (**15b**), *hunger, starvation.* [famine.

familia, -ae, [**famulus,** *servant*], f., *household, family,* including the whole body of serfs and retainers under the authority of a nobleman (I.4). **pater familiae,** *head of a family, house-holder;* **patrēs familiae,** *heads of families.* **mātrēs familiae,** *matrons* (I.50). [family.

familiāris, -e, comp. **-ior,** sup. **-issimus,** [**familia**], adj., *belonging to a family, private.* **rēs familiāris,** *private property, estate, private fortune* (I.18). As noun, **familiāris, -is,** m., *close friend, companion.* [familiar.

familiāritās, -ātis, [**familiāris**], f., *intimacy, close friendship.* [familiarity.

fās, only nom. and acc. sing. in use, [cf. **fārī,** to speak], indecl., n., *right,* in accordance with the laws of nature, mankind, and the divine. **fās est,** *it is right, allowable, lawful.*

fastīgātē [**fastīgātus**], adv., *sloping; slanting* (IV.17).

fastīgātus, -a, -um, [cf. **fastīgium**], adj., *sloping, sloping down* (II.8).

fātum, -ī, [cf. **fārī,** to speak], n., *fate, destiny* (I.39). [fate.

faveō, favēre, fāvī, fautūrus, 2, *be favorable, inclined toward, favor.* [favor.

fēlīcitās, -ātis, [**felix,** *happy*], f., *good fortune* (I.40); *success.* [felicity.

fēliciter, comp. **fēlīcius,** sup. **fēlīcissimē,** [**felix**], adv., *with good fortune, luckily, happily* (IV.25).

fēmina, -ae, f., *woman; female.* [feminine.

femur, -oris and **-inis,** n., (**18d**), *thigh.*

ferāx, -ācis, comp. **ferācior,** sup. **ferācissimus,** [**ferō**], adj., *fertile, productive* (II.4).

ferē, adv., *almost, nearly;* with words denoting time, *about; for the most part, as a rule, usually, generally.*

ferō, ferre, tulī, latus, irr., (**69**), *bear, carry, bring; endure, support, suffer, hold out against; bear away; obtain, receive; report, say.* **signa ferre,** *to advance.*

ferrāmentum, -ī, [**ferrum**], n., *iron tool.*

ferreus, -a, -um, [**ferrum**], adj., *of iron, iron.* **ferreae manūs,** *grappling hooks.*

ferrum, -ī, n., *iron* (V.12); figuratively, *the iron,* with a barbed point, at the end of a pike (I.25), *sword* (V.30). [ferrous.

fertilis, -e, comp. **-ior,** sup. **-issimus,** [**ferō**], adj., *fertile, fruitful, productive.* [fertile.

fertilitās, -ātis, [**fertilis**], f., *productiveness* (II.4). [fertility.

ferus, -a, -um, adj., *wild; savage, fierce.*

fervefaciō, -facere, -fēcī, -factus, [**ferveō** + **faciō**], 3, *make hot, heat, heat red-hot.*

ferveō, -ēre, 2, *be boiling hot, be heated, glow.* Present participle as adj., **fervēns, -tis,** *red-hot* (V.43). [fervent.

fibula, -ae, [cf. **fīgō,** *fasten*], f., *clasp; brace, bolt* (IV.17).

fidēlis, -e, comp. **-ior,** sup. **-issimus,** [**fidēs**], adj., *faithful, trustworthy; true, loyal.*

fidēs, -eī, f., *good faith, fidelity, loyalty; pledge of good faith, promise; confidence, trust; protection, alliance.* [faith.

fidūcia, -ae, [**fidus**], f., *reliance, confidence, assurance.* [fiduciary.

figūra, -ae, [cf. **fingō**], f., *form, shape.* [figure.

fīlia, -ae, f., *daughter.*

fīlius, -ī, m., *son.* [filial.

fingō, fingere, finxī, fictus, 3, *form, shape; invent, devise* (IV.5); of the features, *change, control* (I.39). [feign.

fīniō, fīnīre, fīnīvī, fīnītus, [**fīnis**], 4, *bound, define* (IV.16); *measure, limit.* [finite.

fīnis, -is, m., *limit, border, boundary, end.* Pl. *borders,* hence *territory, country, land.*

fīnitimus, -a, -um, [**fīnis**], adj., *bordering on, neighboring, adjoining.* As noun, **fīnitimī, -ōrum,** m., pl., *neighbors, neighboring peoples.*

fīō, fierī, factus, irr., used as pass. of **faciō, (70),** *be made, be done; be performed* (II.5); *become, take place, happen; come about, come to pass.* **certior fierī,** *to be informed.*

fīrmiter, [**fīrmus**], adv., *steadily, firmly.*

fīrmitūdō, -inis, [**fīrmus**], f., *strength, solidity; rigidity* (III.13; IV.17).

fīrmus, -a, -um, comp. **-ior,** sup. **-issimus,** adj., *strong, firm; powerful.* [firm.

fistūca, -ae, f., *rammer, pile-driver* (IV.17).

Flaccus, -ī, see **Valerius** (2).

flāgitō, -āre, -āvī, -ātus, 1, *ask earnestly, importune, demand* (I.16).

flamma, -ae, f., *flame, fire.* [flame.

flectō, flectere, flexī, flexus, 3, *bend, turn, curve* (IV.33). [flex.

fleō, flēre, flēvī, flētus, 2, *weep, shed tears, cry.*

flētus, -ūs, [**fleō**], m., *weeping.*

flō, -āre, -āvī, -ātus, 1, *blow* (V.7).

flōrēns, -entis, comp. **-entior,** sup. **-entissimus,** [**flōreō,** *bloom*], adj., *flourishing, prosperous* (I.30, IV.3).

fluctus, -ūs, [cf. **fluō**], m., *wave.*

flūmen, -inis, [cf. **fluō**], n., **(12e),** *flowing water, current; stream, river.* **adversō flūmine,** *up the stream.*

fluō, fluere, flūxī, sup. **flūxum,** 3, *flow.* [flux.

fore = futūrum esse; see **sum (52).**

forem = essem; see **sum (52).**

fōrma, -ae, f., *shape, form.* [form.

fors, fortis, [cf. **ferō**], f., *chance, luck, accident* (II.21).

forte [abl. of **fors**], adv., *by chance, by accident; perchance, perhaps.*

fortis, -e, comp. **-ior,** sup. **-issimus,** adj., **(25a),** *strong; brave, courageous.*

fortiter, comp. **fortius,** sup. **fortissimē,** [**fortis**], adv., *bravely, courageously.*

fortitūdō, -inis, [**fortis**], f., *courage, bravery* (I.2). [fortitude.

fortuītō, [abl. of **fortuītus,** from **forte**], adv., *by chance.* [fortuitous.

fortūna, -ae, [**fors**], f., *luck, lot, fate, chance, fortune; good fortune; the goddess Fortune.* Pl., *fortunes* (III.12; V.3); *possessions, property* (I.11; V.43).

fossa, -ae, [cf. **fodiō**], f., *trench, ditch.*

frangō, frangere, frēgī, frāctus, 3, *break; dash to pieces, wreck* (IV.29); *crush, dishearten* (I.31). [fracture.

frāter, -tris, m., **(11e),** *brother;* pl. as a name of honor applied to allies, *brethren* (I.33, 44).

frāternus, -a, -um, [**frāter**], adj., *of a brother, brotherly.* [fraternal.

fremitus, -ūs, [cf. **fremō,** *roar*], m., *uproar, noise, din.*

frequēns, -entis, comp. **frequentior,** sup. **-issimus,** adj., *in large numbers, crowded.* [frequent.

frētus, -a, -um, adj., *relying on, depending on;* followed by abl.

frīgidus, -a, -um, comp. **-ior,** sup. **-issimus,** [**frīgeō,** *be cold*], adj., *cold* (IV.1). [frigid.

frīgus, frīgoris, n., **(13f),** *cold, cold weather.* Pl., *cold seasons, cold climate.*

frōns, frontis, f., **(17c),** *forehead; front.*

frūctuōsus, -a, -um, sup. **-issimus,** [**frūctus**], adj., *fruitful, fertile* (I.30).

frūctus, -ūs, m., **(20b),** *fruit, product; profit, gain, reward, income* (VI.19). [fruit.

frūgēs, -um, f., pl., *produce, crops, fruits,* (I.28). [frugal.

frūmentārius, -a, -um, [**frūmentum**], adj., *relating to grain* or *supplies* of grain; *productive* of grain (I.10). **rēs frūmentāria,** *supply of grain, supplies.*

frūmentor, -ārī, -ātus, [**frūmentum**], 1, dep., *get grain, forage.*

frūmentum, -ī, n., *grain;* pl. often *crops of grain, grain-crops.*

fruor, fruī, frūctus, 3, dep., **(131c),** *enjoy* (III.22).

frūstrā, adv., *in vain, without effect; for nothing, without reason.* [frustrate.

fuga, -ae, f., *flight.* **in fugam dare,** *to put to flight, rout.*

fugiō, fugere, fūgī, 3, *flee, run away, make off; avoid, shun; escape.*

fugitīvus, -a, -um, [**fugiō**], adj., *fleeing, runaway.* As noun, **fugitīvus, -ī,** m., *runaway slave* (I.23). [fugitive.

fūmus, -ī, m., *smoke* (II.7; V.48).

funda, -ae, f., *sling.*

funditor, -ōris, [**funda**], m., *slinger.*

fundō, fundere, fūdī, fūsus, 3, *pour; scatter, rout* (III.6).

fūnebris, -e [**fūnus**], adj., *funeral.* As noun, **fūnebria, -ium,** neut. plural, *funeral rites.*

fūnis, -is, m., *rope; rope cable* (III.13, IV.29, V.10); *halyards* (III.14).

fūnus, -eris, n., (**13e**), *funeral* (VI.19).

furor, -ōris, [**furō,** *rage*], m., *rage, madness, fury.* [furor.

fūrtum, -ī, [**fūr,** *thief*], n., *theft.*

fūsilis, -e, [cf. **fundō**], adj., *molten; of clay, kneaded, molded* (V.43).

futūrus, -a, -um, see **sum.**

G.

Gabīnius, -ī, m., *Aulus Gabinius,* consul with Lucius Calpurnius Piso, 58 BC. (I.6).

gaesum, -ī, n., *heavy javelin* used by the Gauls (III.4).

Gaius, -ī, abbreviation **C.,** m., *Gaius,* sometimes in English written *Caius,* a Roman first name.

Galba, -ae, m.: (1) *Servius Sulpicius Galba,* a lieutenant of Caesar in the earlier part of the Gallic War; praetor at Rome in 54 BC. (2) *Galba,* a ruler of the Suessiones (II.4).

galea, -ae, f., *helmet* (II.21).

Gallia, -ae, [**Gallus**], f., *Gaul,* used of Transalpine Gaul, and of the middle one of its three parts, Celtic Gaul (I.1); also of Cisalpine Gaul, and of the Province; once in the plural, **Galliae,** as referring to the several divisions (IV.20). After Caesar's conquest the plural was used of three provinces in Transalpine Gaul.

Gallicus, -a, -um, [**Gallus**], adj., *of Gaul, Gallic.*

gallīna, -ae, [**gallus,** *cock*], f., *hen.*

Gallus, -a, -um, adj., *Gallic.* As noun, m., *a Gaul;* pl., **Gallī, -ōrum,** *Celts,* used by Caesar as referring to the inhabitants of *Gallia Celtica,* the middle of the three main divisions of Gaul.

Gallus, -ī, m., see **Trebius.**

Garumna, -ae, f., the great river of southwestern France, which rises in the Pyrenees Mountains and flows in a northwesterly direction to the Atlantic Ocean, after a course of about 350 miles; now *Garonne* (I.1).

Garumnī, -ōrum, m., pl., a people in Aquitania, probably near the sources of the Garonne (III.27).

Gatēs, -ium, m., pl., a people in Aquitania (III.27).

gaudeō, gaudēre, gāvīsus sum, 2, semi-dep., (**62**), *rejoice, be glad* (IV.13).

Geidumnī, -ōrum, m., pl., a people of Belgic Gaul (V.39).

Genava, -ae, f., a city of the Allobroges, on the Lacus Lemannus; now *Geneva* (I.7).

gener, generī, m., (**7b**), *son-in-law* (V.56).

generātim [**genus**], adv., *by kind; by peoples, by tribes, nation by nation* (I.51).

gēns, gentis, f., *clan, family* (VI.22); *nation, people.* [gentile.

genus, generis, n., (**13b**), *birth, descent, family; race* (IV.3); *kind, species; class, rank; method, nature.* [genus.

Germānia, -ae, [**Germānus**], f., *Germany.*

Germānicus, -a, -um, [**Germānī**], adj., *German.*

Germānus, -a, -um, adj., *of or from Germany, German.* As noun, **Germānī, -ōrum,** m., pl., *Germans, the Germans.*

gerō, gerere, gessī, gestus, 3, *bear, carry; manage, transact, do, carry on; carry out, perform, accomplish;* of an office, *fill;* of war, *wage.* **rem gestam perscrībit,** *he wrote a full account of what had been done* (V.47). [jest.

gladius, -ī, m., *sword.* [gladiolus.

glāns, glandis, f., (**17c**), *acorn; slingshot, bullet* hurled by a sling (V.43). [gland.

glōria, -ae, f., *fame, renown.* [glory.

glōrior, -ārī, -ātus, [**gloria**], 1, dep., *boast, brag* (I.14).

Gnaeus, -ī, abbreviation **Cn.,** m., a Roman first name.

Graecus, -a, -um, adj., *Greek.* As noun, **Graecus, -ī,** m., *a Greek* (VI.24).

Graiocelī, -ōrum, m., a Gallic people in the Alps (I.10).

grandis, -e, comp. **-ior,** sup. **-issimus,** adj., *large, great.* [grand.

grātia, -ae, [**grātus**], f., *favor, gratitude; esteem, regard; recompense, requital* (I.35, V.27); *popularity; influence* (I.9, 18, 20, 43, etc.). Pl. **grātiae, -ārum,** *thanks.* **grātiās agere,** *to thank.* **grātiā,** *for the sake of.* [grace.

grātulātiō, -ōnis, [**grātulor**], f., *rejoicing, congratulation.*

grātulor, -ārī, -ātus, [**grātus**], 1, dep., *offer congratulations, congratulate* (I.30).

grātus, -a, -um, comp. **-ior,** sup. **-issimus,** adj., *acceptable, pleasing* (VI.16). Neut. as noun, **grātum, -ī,** *a kindness, a favor* (I.44). [grateful.

gravis, -e, comp. **-ior,** sup. **-issimus,** adj., *heavy* (IV.24); *heavily laden* (V.8); *severe, hard, serious, troublesome;* of age, *advanced* (III.16). [grave (adjective).

gravitās, -ātis, [**gravis**], f., *weight* (V.16); *importance* (IV.3). [gravity.

graviter, comp. **gravius,** sup. **gravissimē,** [**gravis**], adv., *heavily* (III.14); *severely, warmly, bitterly; seriously, with great displeasure.* **graviter ferre,** *to be annoyed, be disturbed.*

gravō, -āre, -āvī, -ātus, [**gravis**], 1, *weigh down.* Pass. as dep., *hesitate, be unwilling* (I.35).

Grudiī, -ōrum, m., pl., a Belgic people near the Nervians (V.39).

gubernātor, -ōris, [**gubernō,** *steer*], m., *helmsman, pilot.* [governor.

gustō, -āre, -āvī, -ātus, [**gustus,** *tasting*], 1, *taste, taste of.* [gustatory.

H.

habeō, habēre, habuī, habitus, 2, *have, hold, possess, keep; regard, think, consider; account, repute, reckon;* of a count, *make* (I.29). **ōrātiōnem habēre,** *to make a speech, deliver an address.* [habit.

Harūdēs, -um, m., pl., a German tribe between the Danube and the upper part of the Rhine.

haud, adv., *not at all, not* (V.54).

Helvētius, -a, -um, adj., *of the Helvetians, Helvetian.* **cīvitās Helvētia,** *the State of the Helvetians,* divided into four cantons, the names of two of which, **pāgus Tigurīnus, pāgus Verbigenus,** are known (I.12). As noun, **Helvētiī, -ōrum,** m., pl., *the Helvetians.*

Hercynius, -a, -um, adj., *Hercynian.* **Silva Hercynia,** a forest in southern Germany and Austria, which followed the course of the Danube from its source eastward beyond modern Vienna to the Carpathian Mountains.

hērēditās, -ātis, [**hērēs,** *heir*], f., *inheritance* (VI.13). [heredity.

Hibernia, -ae, f., *Hibernia, Ireland* (V.13).

hībernus, -a, -um, [**hiems**], adj., *of winter.* As noun, **hīberna, -ōrum** (sc. **castra**), n., pl., *winter-quarters.*

hīc, haec, hōc, gen. **huius,** dem. pron., (**42b**), *this, the following, he, she, it.*

hīc [pron. **hīc**], adv., *here, at this place;* of time, *at this point.*

hiemō, -āre, -āvī, -ātūrus, [**hiems**], 1, *pass the winter, winter.*

hiems, hiemis, f., (**12a**), *winter; wintry storm, stormy weather* (IV.36).

hinc [**hīc**], adv., *hence, from this place, from this point.*

Hispānia, -ae, f., *Spain.* Pl., **Hispāniae, -ārum,** *Spanish provinces,* referring to the division into the two parts. **Hispānia citerior,** *Nearer Spain,* and **ulterior,** *Further Spain.*

Hispānus, -a, -um, adj., *Spanish* (V.26).

homō, hominis, m. and f., (**12b**), *human being, man.*

honestus, -a, -um, comp. **-ior,** sup. **-issimus,** [**honōs**], adj., *honorable, noble; of good family.* **locō nātus honestō,** *of excellent family* (V.45). [honest.

honōrificus, -a, -um, comp. **honōrificentior,** sup. **-centissimus,** [**honōs,** cf. **faciō**], adj., *conferring honor, complimentary* (I.43). [honorific.

honōs, or **honor, -ōris,** m., (**13**), *honor, esteem, respect, dignity; public office.* [honor.

hōra, -ae, f., *hour,* a twelfth part of the day, from sunrise to sunset, the Roman hours varying in length with the season of the year.

horreō, horrēre, horruī, 2, *tremble at, shudder at, dread* (I.32).

horribilis, -e, comp. **-ior,** [**horreō**], adj., *dread-inspiring.* [horrible.

horridus, -a, -um, comp. **-ior,** [**horreō**], adj., *wild, frightful* (V.14). [horrid.

hortor, -ārī, -ātus, 1, dep., (**60**), *urge, encourage; exhort, incite, press.*

hospes, hospitis, m., (**10d**), *host; guest* (VI.23); *friend* bound by hospitality, *guest-friend* (I.53, V.6). [host.

hospitium, -ī, [**hospes**], n., *relation of guest and host, tie of hospitality, hospitality* [hospice.

hostis, -is, m., (**14b**), public *enemy, foe*; in this book both the sing. and the pl. — **hostēs, -ium** —in most cases = *the enemy.* Cf. **inimīcus.**

hūc, [**hīc**], adv., *hither, here, to this place.*

huius modī, see **modus.**

hūmānitās, -ātis, [**hūmānus**], f., *humanity; refinement, culture* (I.1, 47). [humanity.

hūmānus, -a, -um, comp. **-ior**, sup. **-issimus**, [**homō**], adj., *of man, human; refined, civilized* (IV.3; V.14). [human.

humilis, -e, comp. **-ior**, sup. **humillimus**, [**humus**, *ground*], adj., *low; shallow* (V.1); *humble, insignificant.* [humble.

humilitās, -ātis, [**humilis**], f., *lowness* (V.1); *humble position, insignificance* (V.27). [humility.

I.

iaceō, iacēre, iacuī, iacitūrus, 2, *lie, lie prostrate; lie dead.* Pres. part. as noun, **iacentēs, -ium**, m., pl., *the fallen* (II.27).

iaciō, iacere, iēcī, iactus, 3, *throw, cast, hurl; throw up, construct* (II.12); of an anchor, *drop* (IV.28).

iactō, -āre, -āvī, -ātus, [freq. of **iaciō**], 1, *throw, cast; throw about, jerk back and forth* (I. 25); *discuss, agitate* (I.18).

iactūra, -ae, [**iaciō**], f., *a throwing; loss, sacrifice, cost.*

iactus, see **iaciō.**

iaculum, -ī, [cf. **iaciō**], n., *javelin* (V.43).

iam, adv., *already, now; at once, immediately; at length* (I.42); *actually* (III.17); *in fact, indeed* (III.9).

ibi or **ibī**, adv., *in that place, there.*

Iccius, -ī, m., a leader of the Remi.

ictus, -ūs, [**īcō**, *strike*], m., *blow, stroke.*

Id., abbreviation for **Īdūs**, see below.

idcircō, [**id** + abl. of **circus**], adv., *on that account, therefore* (V.3).

īdem, eadem, idem, eiusdem, dem. pron., (**45**), *the same.*

identidem, [**idem et idem**], adv., *repeatedly, again and again* (II.19).

idōneus, -a, -um, adj., *suitable, convenient, fit, capable.*

Īdūs, -uum, f., pl., abbreviation **Īd.**, *the Ides*, the fifteenth day of March, May, July, and October; the thirteenth day of the other months (I.7).

īgnis, -is, m., (**14b**), *fire.* Pl. **īgnēs**, *fire signals, watch-fires* (II.33). [igneous.

ignōbilis, -e, [**in-** + (**g**)**nōbilis**], adj., *unknown; obscure* (V.28). [ignoble.

ignōminia, -ae, [**in-** + (**g**)**nōmen**], f., *disgrace, dishonor.* [ignominy.

ignōrō, -āre, -āvī, -ātus, [cf. **ignōscō**], 1, *be ignorant of, not to know, be unaware; overlook* (I.27). [ignore.

ignōscō, -gnōscere, -gnōvī, -gnōtus, [**in-** + (**g**)**nōscō**, *know*], 3, (**105**), *pardon, overlook; forgive, excuse.*

ignōtus, -a, -um, comp. **-ior**, sup. **-issimus**, [**in-** + (**g**)**nōtus**], adj., *unknown; unfamiliar* (IV.24).

illātus, see **īnferō.**

ille, illa, illud, gen. **illīus**, dem. pron., used with or without a noun, (**43a**), *that; he, she, it.*

illīc [loc. of **ille**], adv., *there, in that place, in that region* (I.18).

illigō, -āre, -āvī, -ātus, [**in** + **ligō**, *bind*], 1, *tie on; bind* (IV.17); *fasten* (V.45).

illō [**ille**], adv., *thither, to that place; to that end* (IV.11).

illūstris, -e, comp. **-ior**, sup. **-issimus**, [**in**, cf. **lūx**], adj., *prominent, distinguished; remarkable, noteworthy.* [illustrious.

Illyricum, -ī, n., a region along the east coast of the Adriatic Sea, now *Istria* and *Dalmatia* (II.35; III.7; V.1).

imbēcillitās, -ātis, [**imbēcillus**, *weak*], f., *weakness.*

imber, imbris, m., (**15c**), *rain, rainstorm.*

imitor, -ārī, -ātus, 1, dep., *copy, imitate.*

immānis, -e, comp. **-ior**, sup. **-issimus**, adj., *huge, enormous, immense.*

immineō, -minēre, [**in** + **mineō**, *overhang*], 2, *overhang; be near at hand, threaten.* [imminent.

immittō, -mittere, -mīsī, -missus, [**in** + **mittō**], 3, *send into; send against;* of pikes, *hurl, cast against* (V.44); of timbers, *let down into, let in between* (IV.17).

immolō, -āre, -āvī, -ātus, [**in**, cf. **mola**, *meal*], 1, lit. *sprinkle meal on* a victim for sacrifice; *sacrifice, offer up* (VI.16, 17). [immolate.

immortālis, -e, [**in-** + **mortālis,** from **mors**], adj., *immortal.*

immūnitās, -ātis, [**immūnis**], f., *freedom, exemption* (VI.14). [immunity.

impedīmentum, -i, [**impediō**], n., *hindrance, interference* (I.25; II.25). Pl. **impedīmenta, -ōrum,** *heavy baggage, baggage; pack-animals.* [impediment.

impediō, -pedīre, -pedīvī, -pedītus, [**in,** cf. **pēs**], 4, *hinder, obstruct, interfere with; prevent, disorder;* of the mind, *occupy, engage* (V.7). [impede.

impedītus, -a, -um, comp. **-ior,** sup. **-issimus,** [part. of **impediō**], adj., *encumbered* with baggage, *hindered, hampered, obstructed; difficult, hard* (II.28, III.9); of places, *hard, inaccessible.*

impellō, -pellere, -puli, -pulsus, [**in** + **pellō**), 3, *strike against; urge, urge on, drive on.* [impel.

impendeō, -pendēre, [**in** + **pendeō,** *hang*], 2, *hang over, overhang.* [impend.

impēnsus, -a, -um, comp. **-ior,** [part, of **impendō,** *expend*], adj., *ample, great;* of price, *dear, high* (IV.2).

imperātor, -ōris, [**imperō**], m., *commander, general.* [emperor.

imperātum, -ī, [**imperō**], n., *command, order.* **ad imperātum,** *in accordance with his command.*

imperītus, -a, -um, comp. **-ior,** sup. **-issimus,** [**in-** + **perītus**], adj., *unskilled, inexperienced, unacquainted with.*

imperium, -ī, [cf. **imperō**], n., *command, order; control, government, dominion; military authority.* **nova imperia,** *a revolution* (II.1). [empire.

imperō, -āre, -āvī, -ātus, 1, *command, order; exercise authority over, rule* (I.31, 36); *requisition, order to furnish, levy, draft, demand.* After **imperō, ut** is ordinarily to be translated by *to,* and **nē** by *not to,* with the infin. [imperative.

impetrō, -āre, -āvī, -ātus, [**in** + **patrō,** *execute*], 1, *obtain by request, procure, get; accomplish, bring to pass; gain one's request.* **rē impetrātā,** *the request having been granted, after the request had been granted.*

impetus, -ūs, [**in,** cf. **petō**], m., *attack, assault, charge; raid* (I. 44); *fury, impetuosity, force.* [impetus.

impius, -a, -um, [**in** + **pius**], adj., *wicked, impious.* As noun, **impiī, -ōrum,** m., pl., *the wicked* (VI.13). [impious.

implōrō, -āre, -āvī, -ātus, [**in** + **plōrō,** *cry out*], 1, *beseech, implore* (I.51); *invoke, appeal to* (V.7). **auxilium implōrāre,** *to solicit aid* (I.31). [implore.

impōnō, -ponere, -posuī, -positus, [**in** + **pōnō**], 3, *put on, place on, put; impose* (*upon*); *levy upon* (I.44); of horses, *mount* (I.42). [impose.

importō, -āre, -āvī, -ātus, [**in** + **portō**], 1, *bring in, import* (I.1; IV.2; V.12).

improbus, -a, -um, comp. **-ior,** sup. **-issimus,** [**in-** + **probus,** *good*], adj., *bad, shameless* (I.17).

imprōvīsō [**imprōvīsus**], adv., *unexpectedly, suddenly* (I.13).

imprōvīsus, -a, -um, comp. **-ior,** [**in-** + part. of **prōvideō**], adj., *unforeseen, unexpected.* Neut. as noun in **dē imprōvīsō,** *unexpectedly, suddenly.*

imprūdēns, -entis, [contr. from **imprōvidēns, in-** + part. of **prōvideō**], adj., *unawares, off one's guard* (III.29; V.15). [imprudent.

imprūdentia, -ae, [**imprūdēns**], f., *lack of foresight, indiscretion, ignorance.* [imprudence.

impūbēs, -eris, [**in-** + **pūbēs**], adj., *underage; unmarried* (VI.21).

impugnō, -āre, -āvī, -ātus, [**in** + **pugnō**], 1, *attack, make an attack on* (I.44); *fight* (III.26). [impugn.

impulsus, -ūs, [**impellō**], m., *push; instigation* (V.25). [impulse.

impulsus, see **impellō.**

impūne [**impūnis,** from **in-** + **poena**], adv., *without punishment, with impunity* (I.14).

impūnitās, -ātis, [**impūnis,** from **in-** + **poena**], f., *exemption from punishment, impunity* (I.14). [impunity.

īmus, see **īnferus.**

in, prep. with acc. and abl.: (1) With the acc: *into, to, up to, towards, against; until, till; for, with a view to; in, respecting, concerning, according to; after, over.* (2) With the abl.: *in, within, on, upon, among, over; in the course of, within, during, while; involved in, in case of, in relation to, respecting.* In combination **in** retains its form before the vowels and most consonants; is often changed to **il-** before **l, ir-** before **r;** usually becomes **im-** before **m, b, p.**

in-, inseparable prefix, = *un-, not,* as in **incertus,** *uncertain.*

inānis, -e, comp. **-ior,** sup. **-issimus,** adj., *empty* (V.23). [inane.

incendium, -ī, [cf. **incendō**], n., *fire, conflagration.* [incendiary.

incendō, -cendere, -cendī, -cēnsus, 3, *set on fire, burn; rouse, excite.* [incense.

inceptus, see **incipiō.**

incertus, -a, -um, comp. **-ior,** sup. **-issimus,** [**in- + certus**], adj., *uncertain, doubtful; of reports, unreliable, unauthenticated* (IV.5); *of a military formation, in disorder* (IV.32).

incidō, -cidere, -cidī, [**in + cadō**], 3, with **in** and the acc., *fall in with, come upon, fall in the way of* (I.53); *occur, happen; of war, break out* (II.14, VI.15). [incident.

incīdō, -cīdere, -cīdī, -cīsus, [**in + caedō**], 3, *cut into* (II.17). [incise.

incipiō, -cipere, -cēpī, -ceptus, [**in + capiō**], 3, *begin, commence, undertake.* [incipient.

incīsus, see **incīdō.**

incitō, -āre, -āvī, -ātus, [**in + citō,** *move rapidly*], 1, *urge, urge on, hurry; of vessels, drive forward* with oars, *drive* (III.14; IV.25); *of horses, urge on, spur; of water, with* **sē,** *rush against* (IV.17) *, run in* (III.12); *of men, rouse, stir up, excite; spur on* (III.10). [incite.

incognitus, -a, -um, [**in- +** part. of **cognōscō**], adj., *unknown, not known* (IV.20, 29). [incognito.

incolō, -colere, -coluī, [**in + colō**], 3, intrans., *live, dwell;* trans., *inhabit, dwell in, live in.*

incolumis, -e, adj., *safe, unharmed, unhurt.*

incommodē, comp. **-ius,** sup. **-issimē,** [**incommodus**], adv., *inconveniently; unfortunately* (V.33).

incommodum, -ī, [**incommodus**], n., *inconvenience, disadvantage; misfortune, disaster, injury, defeat.* **quid incommodī,** *any harm* (VI.13).

incrēdibilis, -e, [**in- + crēdibilis**], adj., *beyond belief, extraordinary, incredible.*

increpitō, -āre, [freq. of **increpō,** *chide*], 1, *reproach, rebuke* (II.15); *taunt* (II.30).

incursiō, -ōnis, [**incurrō**], f., *invasion, raid, inroad.* [incursion.

incursus, -ūs, [**incurrō**], m., *onrush* (II.20); *assault, attack.*

incūsō, -āre, -āvī, -ātus, [**in- + causa**], 1, *find fault with, accuse; chide, rebuke* (I.40; II.15).

inde, adv., *of place, from that place, thence; of time, after that, then.*

indicium, -ī, [cf. **indicō,** *reveal*], n., *information, disclosure.*

indīcō, -dīcere, -dīxī, -dictus, [**in + dīcō**], 3, *proclaim, declare; of a council, call, appoint.* [indict.

indignitās, -ātis, [**indignus**], f., *indignity, ill-treatment* (II.14).

indignus, -a, -um, comp. **-ior,** sup. **-issimus,** [**in- + dignus**], adj., *unworthy.*

indīligēns, -entis, comp. **-ior,** [**in- + dīligēns**], adj., *negligent, remiss.*

indīligenter, comp. **-ius,** [**indīligens**], adv., *negligently, carelessly* (II.33).

indūcō, -dūcere, -dūxī, -ductus, [**in + dūcō**], 3, *lead in; lead on, induce, influence* (I.2, 27); *cover* (II.33). [induce.

indulgeō, -dulgēre, -dulsī, 2, *be kind to, favor.* [indulge.

induō, -duere, -duī, -dūtus, 3, *put on.*

industria, -ae, [**industrius**], f., *activity, energy* (III.73). [industry.

indūtiae, -ārum, f., pl., *truce, armistice.*

Indutiomārus, -ī, m., *a Treveran, rival of Cingetorix and hostile to Caesar.*

ineō, -īre, -iī, -itus, [**in + eō**], irr., *enter, enter upon, begin; of a plan, form; of an account or enumeration, make.*

inermis, -e, [**in- + arma**], adj., *unarmed, without arms.*

iners, -ertis, comp. **inertior,** sup. **inertissimus,** [**in- + ars**], adj., *indolent; unmanly* (IV.2). [inert.

īnfāmia, -ae, [**īnfāmis,** from **in- + fāma**], f., *disgrace, dishonor.* [infamy.

infectus, -a, -um, [**in- + factus**], adj., *not done, unaccomplished.* **īnfectā rē,** *without accomplishing his purpose* (VI.12).

īnferō, -ferre, intulī, illātus, [**in + ferō**], irr., *bring in, import* (II.15); *throw upon, throw into* (VI.19); *of injuries, inflict; of hope and fear, inspire, infuse; of an excuse, offer, allege* (I.39); *of wounds, make, give.* **bellum īnferre,** *to make war.* **signa īnferre,** *to advance.* [infer.

īnferus, -a, -um, comp. **īnferior,** sup. **īnfimus** or **īmus,** adj., *below, underneath;* comp., *lower, inferior;* sup., *lowest, at the bottom.* Neut. as noun, **ab īmō,** *from the bottom* (III.19), *at the lower end* (IV.17). [inferior.

īnfestus, -a, -um, comp. **-ior,** sup. **-issimus,** adj., *hostile, threatening.*

īnficiō, -ficere, -fēcī, -fectus, [**in + faciō**], 3, *stain* (V.14). [infect.

īnfimus, see **īnferus.**

īnfīnītus, -a, -um, comp. **-ior,** [**in- + fīnītus,** from **finiō**], adj., *unlimited, boundless; vast, immense; numberless.* [infinite.

īnfirmitās, -ātis, [**īnfirmus**], f., *weakness, feebleness; fickleness* (IV.5). [infirmity.

īnfirmus, -a, -um, comp. **-ior,** sup. **-issimus,** [**in- + fīrmus**], adj., *not strong, weak; depressed, timid* (III. 24); comp., *less strong* (IV.3). [infirm.

īnflectō, flectere, -flexī, -flexus, [**in** + **flectō**], 3, *bend* (I.25; II.17). [inflect.

īnfluō, -fluere, -flūxī, [**in** + **fluō**], 3, *flow into, flow; drain into.* [influx.

īnfrā, [for **īnferā**, sc. **parte**], adv. and prep.: (1) As adv., *below* (IV.36). (2) As prep., with acc., *below.*

ingēns, -entis, comp. **ingentior**, adj., *large, vast, great; huge* (I.39).

ingrātus, -a, -um, comp. **-ior**, sup. **-issimus**, [**in-** + **grātus**], adj., *unacceptable, unwelcome.* [ingrate.

ingredior, -gredī, -gressus, [**in** + **gradior**, *step*], 3, dep., *advance; enter, go into* (II.4; V.9). [ingress.

iniciō, -icere, -iēcī, -iectus, [**in** + **iaciō**], 3, *throw in; lay on* (IV.17); *inspire, infuse* (I. 46); of fear, *strike into* (IV.19). [inject.

inimīcitia, -ae, [**inimīcus**], f., *enmity, hostility* (VI.12).

inimīcus, -a, -um, comp. **-ior**, sup. **-issimus**, [**in-** + **amīcus**], adj., *unfriendly, hostile.* As noun, **inimīcus, -ī.**, m., *enemy, personal enemy*, as distinguished from **hostis**, *a public enemy; adversary.* [inimical.

inīquitās, -ātis, [**inīquus**], f., *unevenness; unfairness, unreasonableness; disadvantage.* **inīquitās locī**, *unfavorableness of (the) position, disadvantageous position.* [iniquity.

inīquus, -a, -um, comp. **-ior**, sup. **-issimus**, [**in-** + **aequus**], adj., *uneven, sloping; unfavorable; unfair, unjust* (I.44).

initium, -ī, [cf. **ineō**], n., *beginning, commencement;* pl., *elements, first principles* (VI.17). [initial.

initūrus, see **ineō.**

initus, -a, -um, see **ineō.**

iniūria, -ae, [**iniūrius, in-** + **iūs**], f., *wrong, outrage, injustice, injury.*

iniussus, -ūs, [**in-** + **iussus**], m., only abl. in use, *without command, without orders* (I.19; V.28).

innāscor, -nāscī, -nātus, [**in** + **nāscor**], 3, dep., *be born in; arise in.* [innate.

innītor, -nītī, -nīxus or **-nīsus**, [**in** + **nītor**], 3, dep., (**131c**), *support one's self with, lean upon.*

innocēns, -entis, comp. **innocentior**, sup. **-issimus**, [**in-** + **nocēns**, from **noceō**], adj., *blameless, innocent.* As noun, **innocentēs, -ium**, m., pl., *the innocent* (VI.9, 16).

innocentia, -ae, [**innocēns**], f., *blamelessness, integrity* (I.40). [innocence.

inopia, -ae, [**inops**, *needy*], f., *want, lack, need, shortage, scarcity.*

inopīnāns, -antis, [**in-** + **opīnāns**, from **opīnor**], adj., *not expecting, unawares, off one's guard.*

inquam, inquis, inquit, present indicative, def., (**72**), *say, says.*

īnsciēns, -entis, [**in-** + **sciēns**, from **sciō**], adj., *not knowing, unaware.*

īnscientia, -ae, [**īnsciēns**], f., *ignorance, lack of knowledge.*

īnscius, -a, -um, [**in-**, cf. **sciō**]. adj., *not knowing, unaware, ignorant.*

īnsequor, -sequī, -secūtus, [**in** + **sequor**], 3, dep., *follow up, pursue, follow in pursuit.*

īnserō, -serere, -seruī, -sertus, [**in** + **serō**], 3, *fasten in* (III.14). [insert.

īnsidiae, -ārum, [cf. **īnsideō**], f., pl., *ambush, ambuscade; artifice, device, trap, pitfall.* **per īnsidiās**, *by stratagem* (I.42; IV.13). [insidious.

īnsigne, -is, [**īnsignis**], n., *sign, mark, signal; decoration.* [ensign.

īnsignis, -e, comp. **-ior**, [**in** + **signum**], adj., *noteworthy* (I.12).

īnsiliō, -silīre, -siluī, [**in** + **saliō**, *leap*], 4, *leap upon* (I.52).

īnsinuō, -āre, -āvī, -ātus, [**in** + **sinuō**, *curve*], 1, *push in;* with **sē**, *make one's way* (IV.33). [insinuate.

īnsistō, -sistere, -stitī, [**in** + **sistō**], 3, *stand, stand upon, keep one's footing; press on; follow, pursue* (III.14). [insist.

īnsolenter [**īnsolēns**], adv., *arrogantly, haughtily* (I.14).

īnstabilis, -e, [**in-** + **stabilis**, from **stō**], adj., *unsteady* (IV.23).

īnstāns, -antis, comp. **īnstantior**, [part. of **īnstō**], adj., *impending, pressing.* [instant.

īnstar, n., indecl., *likeness;* followed by gen., *like* (II.17).

īnstīgō, -āre, -āvī, -ātus, 1, *urge on, incite* (V.56). [instigate.

īnstituō, -stituere, -stituī, -stitūtus, [**in** + **statuō**], 3, of troops, *draw up, arrange; devise, build, construct; make; make ready, furnish; obtain* (III.9); *establish, institute* (VI.16); *undertake, commence, begin; resolve upon, determine; train, teach.* [institute (verb).

īnstitūtum, -ī, [**īnstituō**], n., *plan, practice* (I.50); *custom, usage* (IV.20; VI.18); *institution* (I.1). [institute (noun).

īnstō, -stāre, -stitī, -stātūrus, [**in** + **stō**], 1, *be near at hand, approach; press on, press forward.*

īnstrūmentum, -ī, [**īnstruō**], n., *tool;* singular with collective force, *stock, store, equipment.*

īnstruō, -struere, -strūxī, -strūctus, [**in** + **struō,** *build*], 3, *build, construct;* of troops, *draw up, form; fit out, equip, supply* (V.5). [instruct.

īnsuēfactus, -a, -um, [**īnsuēscō** + **faciō**], adj., *accustomed, trained* (IV.24).

īnsuētus, -a, -um, [part. of **īnsuēscō**], adj., *unaccustomed.*

īnsula, -ae, f., *island.* [insular.

īnsuper [**in** + **super**], adv., *above, on top.*

integer, -gra, -grum, comp. **integrior,** sup. **integerrimus,** [**in-** + TAG in **tangō**], adj., (**22f**), *untouched, whole, undamaged; fresh, vigorous.* As noun, **integrī, -ōrum,** m., pl., *fresh troops.* [integer.

intellegō, -legere, -lēxī, -lēctus, [**inter** + **legō**], 3, *understand, realize.* [intelligent.

intendō, -tendere, -tendī, -tentus, [**in-** + **tendō**], 3, *stretch, struggle, apply to.*

intentus, -a, -um, comp. **-ior,** sup. **-issimus,** [part. of **intendō**], adj., *attentive, eager.* [intent.

inter, prep. with acc., *between, among;* of time, *during, for* (I.36). **inter sē,** *among themselves, with one another.*

intercēdō, -cēdere, -cessī, -cessūrus, [**inter** + **cēdō**], 3, *go between, be placed between* (II.17); *lie between* (I.39; V.52); of time, *intervene, pass* (I.7; V.53); *take place, occur* (V.11). [intercede.

intercipiō, -cipere, -cēpī, -ceptus, [**inter** + **capiō**], 3, *cut off, intercept.*

interclūdō, -clūdere, -clūsī, -clūsus, [**inter** + **claudō**], 3, *shut off, cut off; block up, blockade, hinder.*

interdīcō, -dīcere, dīxī, -dictus, [**inter** + **dīcō**], 3, (**109c**), *forbid, prohibit, exclude;* followed by a prohibition, *enjoin* (V.58). [interdict.

interdiū, [**inter,** cf. **diēs**], adv., *in the daytime, by day.*

interdum, [**inter** + **dum**], adv., *for a time, for a season* (I.14); *sometimes* (I.39).

intereā, [**inter** + **eā**], adv., *in the meantime, meanwhile.*

intereō, -īre, -iī, -itūrus, [**inter** + **eō**], 4, *perish, be destroyed, die.*

interest, see **intersum.**

interficiō, -ficere, -fēcī, -fectus, [**inter** + **faciō**], 3, *slay, kill.*

intericiō, -icere, iēcī, iectus, [**inter** + **iaciō**], 3, *throw between, place between, put between;* pass. part., **interiec-tus,** *lying between, intervening.* [interject.

interim, [**inter** + **-im**], adv., *in the meantime, meanwhile.*

interior, -ius, gen. **-ōris,** sup. **intimus,** [**inter**], adj. in comp. degree, *inner, interior.* As noun, **interiōrēs, -um,** m., pl., *those* living *in the interior* (V.14), *those within.* [interior.

interitus, -ūs, [**intereō**], m., *destruction, death* (V.47).

intermittō, -mittere, -mīsī, -missus, [**inter** + **mittō**], 3, *leave an interval, leave vacant; leave off, leave; stop, break, cease, discontinue; interrupt, suspend;* pass., of fire, *abate* (V.43). [intermittent.

interneciō, -ōnis, [cf. **internecō,** *destroy*], f., *slaughter* (I.13); *utter destruction* (II.28). [internecine.

interpellō, -āre, -āvī, -ātus, 1, *interrupt; disturb, obstruct* (I.44).

interpōnō, -pōnere, -posuī, -positus, [**inter** + **pōnō**], 3, *place between, put between, interpose; put forward* (I.42); *present, manifest* (IV.32); of time, *suffer to elapse.* **fidem interpōnere,** *to pledge one's honor* (V.6, 36). [interpose.

interpres, -pretis, m., (**10e**), *interpreter.*

interpretor, -ārī, -ātus, [**interpres**], 1, dep., *explain, expound* (VI.13). [interpret.

interscindō, -scindere, -scidī, -scissus, [**inter** + **scindō**], 3, *cut down* (II.9), *cut off, demolish.*

intersum, -esse, -fuī, irr., *be between, lie between; be present at, take part in.* Impers., **interest,** (**103d-e**), *it concerns, is important.* **magnī interest,** *it is of great importance* (V.4). **neque interest,** *and it makes no difference* (VI.14). [interest.

intervāllum, -ī, [**inter** + **vāllum**], n., *interval, space, distance.* [interval.

interventus, -ūs, [**interveniō**], m., *intervention* (III.15).

intexō, -texere, -texuī, -textus, [**in** + **texō,** *weave*], 3, *weave in, interweave* (II.33).

intrā, [for **interā** sc. **parte**], prep. with acc., *inside of, within.*

intrō, adv., *within, inside.*

intrō, -āre, -āvī, -ātus, [**in** + ***trō,** cf. **trāns**], 1, *enter, go in.* [enter.

intrōdūcō, -dūcere, -dūxī, -ductus, [**intrō** + **dūcō**], 3, *lead into, bring into.* [introduce.

introeō, -īre, -īvī, [**intrō** + **eō**], irr., *go in; come in, enter* (V.43).

introitus, -ūs, [introeō], m., *an entering; entrance* (V.9). [introit.

intrōmittō, -mittere, -mīsī, -missus, [intrō + mittō], 3, *send in; let in* (V.58).

intrōrsus, [intrō + versus], adv., *within, inside.*

intrōrumpō, -rumpere, -rūpī, -ruptus, [intrō + rumpō, *break]*, 3, *burst into; break in* (V.51).

intueor, -tuērī, -tuitus, [in + tueor], 2, dep., *look upon* (I.32). [intuition.

intulī, see **īnferō.**

intus, adv., *within, on the inside.*

inūsitātus, -a, -um, comp. **-ior, [in- + part. of ūsitor,** freq. of **ūtor]**, adj., *unfamiliar, unprecedented.*

inūtilis, -e, comp. **-ior, [in- + utilis]**, adj., *useless, unserviceable, of no use.*

inveniō, -venīre, -vēnī, -ventus, [in + veniō], 4, *come upon, find, discover; find out, learn* (II.16). [invent.

inventor, -ōris, [inveniō], m., *originator, inventor* (VI.17).

inveterāscō, -ere, inveterāvī, [in + veterāscō, from **vetus]**, 3, *grow old; become established, become fixed* (V.41); *establish one's self* (II.1).

invictus, -a, -um, [in- + part. of vincō], adj., *unconquerable, invincible* (I.36).

invideō, -vidēre, -vīdī, -vīsus, [in + videō], 2, (**105**), *look askance at; envy* (II.31).

invidia, -ae, [invidus], f., *envy, jealousy.*

inviolātus, -a, -um, [in- + part. of violō], adj., *inviolable* (III.9). [inviolate.

invītō, -āre, -āvī, -ātus, 1, *invite, request* (I.35; IV.6); *entice, attract* (V.51). [invite.

invītus, -a, -um, sup. **-issimus,** adj., *unwilling, reluctant.* **sē invītō** (I.8; IV.16), **eō invītō** (I.14), *against his will.*

ipse, -a, -um, gen. **ipsīus,** dem. pron., (**46**), *self; himself, herself, itself, themselves; he, they* (emphatic); *very.*

īrācundus, -a,-um, comp. **-ior, [īra]**, adj., *passionate, quick-tempered* (I.31).

irrīdeō, -rīdere, -rīsī, -rīsus, [in + rīdeō, *laugh]*, 2, *laugh at, make fun of, ridicule.*

irridiculē, [in- + rīdiculē], adv., *without wit* (I.42).

irrumpō, -rumpere, -rūpī, -ruptus, [in + rumpō, *break]*, 3, *break into, burst into, rush in.*

is, ea, id, gen. **eius,** dem. pron., (**44**), *he, she, it; that, this, the, the one;* before **ut, is = tālis,** *such;* after **et,** *and that too;* after **neque,** *and that not* (III.2); with comparatives, abl. **eō** = *the, all the,* as **eō magis,** *all the more.*

ita, [cf. is], adv., *in this way, so, thus; in the following manner, in such a way, accordingly.* **nōn ita,** *not so very, not very* (IV.37; V.47).

Italia, -ae, f., *Italy.*

itaque, [ita + -que], adv., *and thus, accordingly, therefore, consequently;* = **et ita,** *and so* (I.52).

item, adv., *also, further; just so, in like manner.*

iter, itineris, [cf. eō, īre], n., (**18c**), *journey, line of march, march; road, route.* **magnum iter,** *forced march,* from 20 to 25 miles a day. **ex itinere,** *directly after marching, from the line of march;* used of a force which turns from marching at once, without encamping, to attack an enemy in the field (I.25), to storm a town (II.6, 12; III.21), or to retreat (II.29). [itinerary.

iterum, adv., *again, a second time.*

Itius, -ī, m., *portus Itius,* harbor from which Caesar sailed to Britain, probably *Boulogne.*

itūrus, see **eō.**

iuba, -ae, f., *mane* (I.48).

iubeō, iubēre, iussī, iussus, 2, *order, give orders, bid, command.* [jussive.

iūdicium, -ī, [iūdex, *judge]*, n., *judgment, decision, decree; place of judgment, trial* (I.4); *opinion.* [judicial.

iūdicō, -āre, -āvī, -ātus, [iūdex], 1, *judge, decide; think, be of the opinion; pronounce, declare* (V.56). [judge (verb).

iugum, -ī, [IUG, cf. **iungō]**, n., *yoke* (I.7, 12; IV.33); *of hills and mountains, ridge, summit, height.*

iūmentum, -ī, [for ***iugumentum,** root IUG in **iungō]**, n., *yoke-animal, beast of burden, draft-animal,* used of horses, mules, and asses.

iūnctūra, -ae, [iungō], f., *juncture, joint* (IV.17). [juncture.

iungō, -ere, iūnxī, iūnctus, 3, *join together, join, connect, unite.* [join.

Iūnius, -ī, m., *Quintus Junius,* a Roman of Spanish birth in Caesar's army (V.27).

Iuppiter, Iovis, m., (**18a**), *Jupiter.* [jovial.

Iūra, -ae, m., *Jura,* a range of mountains extending from the Rhine to the Rhone (about 170 miles), and forming the boundary between the Helvetians and the Sequanians (I.2, 6, 8).

iūrō, -āre, -āvī, -ātus, [iūs], 1, *take an oath, swear.* [jury.

iūs, iūris, n., (**13g**), *right, justice, authority.* **iūre bellī,** *by the laws of war* (I.44). **in suō iūre,** *in the exercise of his own rights* (I.36, 44). **iūs reddere,** *to render justice* (VI.13). **iūs dīcere,** *to administer justice* (VI.23). **iūra in hōs,** *rights over these* (VI.13).

iūs iūrandum, iūris iūrandī, [**iūs** + gerundive of **iūrō**], n., (**13h**), *oath.*

iūstitia, -ae, [**iūstus**], f., *justice, fairness.*

iūstus, -a, -um, comp. **-ior,** sup. **-issimus,** [**iūs**], adj., *just, rightful, fair; proper, suitable, due.* [just.

iuventūs, -ūtis, [**iuvenis**], f., *youth; young men.*

iuvō, -āre, iūvī, iūtus, 1, *help, aid, assist.*

iūxtā, adv., *near by, near.*

K.

Kalendae, -ārum, (= **Kal.**), f., pl., *Calends,* the first day of the month. [calendar.

L.

L., with proper names = **Lūcius.**

Laberius, -ī, m., see **Dūrus.**

Labiēnus, -ī, m., *Titus Labienus,* the most prominent of Caesar's lieutenants in the Gallic War.

lābor, lābī, lapsus, 3, dep., *slip; go astray* (V.3); *fail, be deceived, be disappointed* (V.55). [lapse.

labor, -ōris, m., *toil, work, exertion, labor; endurance* (IV.2). [labor.

labōrō, -āre, -āvī, -ātus, [**labor**], 1, *make effort, labor, strive* (I.31); *be hard pressed, be in distress, be in danger.* [labor (verb).

labrum, -ī, [LAB, cf. **lambō,** *lick*], n., *lip.*

lac, lactis, n., (**10g**), *milk.* [lacteal.

lacessō, -ere, -īvī, -ītus, [obsolete **laciō,** *entice*], 3, *arouse, provoke; harass, attack.*

lacrima, -ae, f., *tear.* [lacrimal.

lacus, -ūs, m., *lake.*

laetitia, -ae, [**laetus**], f., *rejoicing, joy, delight* (V.48, 52).

laetus, -a, -um, comp. **-ior,** sup. **-issimus,** adj., *joyful, glad* (III.18).

languidus, -a, -um, comp. **-ior,** [cf. **languor**], adj., *weak, exhausted.* [languid.

languor, -ōris, [**langueō,** *be faint*], m., *faintness; exhaustion, weariness.*

lapis, -idis, m., *stone.* [lapidary.

lāpsus, see **lābor.**

largior, largīrī, largītus, [**largus,** *abundant*], 4, dep., (**60**), *give freely, supply, bestow* (VI.24); *bribe* (I.18).

largiter, [**largus,** *abundant*], adv. *abundantly, much.*

largītiō, -ōnis, [**largior**], 1, *lavish giving, bribery* (I.9).

lassitūdō, -inis, [**lassus,** *weak*], f., *faintness, weariness.* [lassitude.

lātē, comp. **lātius,** sup. **lātissimē,** [**lātus**], adv., *widely, broadly, extensively.* **quam lātissimē,** *as far as possible.*

latebra, -ae, [cf. **lateō**], f., *hiding place.*

lateō, latēre, latuī, 2, *lie hid* (II.19); *be unnoticed* (III.14). [latent.

lātitūdō, -inis, [**lātus**], f., *width, breadth, extent.* [latitude.

Latobrīgī, -ōrum, m., pl., a people near the Helvetians.

latrō, -ōnis, m., (**12c**), *bandit, robber.*

latrōcinium, -ī, [**latrōcinor,** *plunder*], n., *brigandage, robbery.*

lātūrus, see **ferō.**

lātus, -a, -um, comp. **-ior,** sup. **-issimus,** adj., *broad, wide; of territory, extensive* (II.4; VI.22).

latus, -eris, n., (**13e**), *side; of an army, flank.* **latus apertum,** *exposed flank.* **ab latere,** *on the flank.* [lateral.

laudō, -āre, -āvī, -ātus, [**laus**], 1, *praise, commend, compliment.* [laud.

laus, laudis, f., (**17c**), *praise, glory, commendation, distinction.*

lavō, -āre, lāvī, lautus and **lōtus,** 1, *wash;* pass. **lavārī,** used reflexively, *bathe.*

laxō, -āre, -āvī, -ātus, 1, *make wide, spread out, extend.* [laxative.

lēgātiō, -ōnis, [**lēgō,** *dispatch*], f., *envoyship, mission* (I.3); referring to persons (= **lēgātī**), *deputation, embassy, envoys.* [legation.

lēgātus, -ī, [**legō,** *dispatch*], m., (**6**), *envoy;* of the army, *lieutenant, lieutenant-general.* [legate.

legiō, -ōnis, [cf. **legō,** *collect*], f., *legion.* [legion.

legiōnārius, -a, -um, [**legiō**], adj., *of a legion, legionary.* [legionary.

Lemannus, -ī, m., with **lacus,** *Lake Geneva.*

Lemovīcēs, -um, m., pl., a Gallic people west of the Arvernians.

lēnis, -e, comp. **-ior,** sup. **-issimus,** adj., *smooth, gentle.* [lenient.

lēnitās, -ātis, [**lēnis**], f., *smoothness* (I.12).

lēniter, comp. **lēnius,** sup. **-issimus,** [**lēnis**], adv., *mildly, gently, slightly.*

Lepontiī, -ōrum, m., pl., a people in the Alps (IV.10).

lepus, -oris, m., (**13g**), *hare* (V.12).

Leucī, -ōrum, m., pl., the people in a Gallic state south of the Mediomatrici (I.40).

Levācī, -ōrum, m., pl., a Belgic people, dependents of the Nervians (V.39).

levis, -e, comp. **-ior,** sup. **-issimus,** adj., *light, slight.* Comp., *more capricious, less serious.*

levitās, -ātis, [**levis**], f., *lightness* (V.34); *fickleness, instability* (II.1). [levity.

levō, -āre, -āvī, -ātus, [**levis**], 1, *lighten; relieve, free from* (V.27).

lēx, lēgis, f., *law, enactment.* [legal.

Lexoviī, -ōrum, m., pl., the people in a Gallic state on the coast west of the Sequana (*Seine*).

libenter, comp. **libentius,** sup. **libentissimē,** [**libēns,** *glad*], adv., *willingly, gladly.*

līber, -era, -erum, comp. **-ior,** sup. **līberrimus,** adj., (**22e**), *free, independent; unimpeded, unrestricted.* [liberal.

līberālitās, -ātis, [**līberālis**], f., *generosity* (I.18); *generous help* (I.43). [liberality.

līberāliter, comp. **līberālius,** sup. **-issimē,** [**līberālis**], adv., *graciously, generously.*

līberē, comp. **-ius,** [**līber**], adv., *freely; boldly* (V.19); *openly* (I.18).

līberī, -ōrum, m., pl., (**7b**), *children.*

līberō, -āre, -āvī, -ātus, [**līber**], 1, *set free, free; release, relieve.* [liberate.

lībertās, -ātis, [**līber**], f., *freedom, liberty, independence.* [liberty.

liceor, licērī, licitus, 2, dep., *bid, make a bid,* at an auction (I.18).

licet, licēre, licuit and **licitum est,** 2, impers., (**73**), *it is allowed, lawful, permitted.* **licet mihi,** I *am allowed, I may.* **petere ut liceat,** *to ask permission.* [licit.

Liger, -eris, m., (**18e**), the *Loire,* which rises in the Cévennes (*Cebenna*) mountains, flows northwest, receives as a tributary the Allier (*Elaver*), flows west, and empties into the Atlantic, after a course of more than 500 miles.

lignātiō, -ōnis, [**lignor,** from **lignum**], f., *getting wood.* (V.39).

lignātor, -ōris, [**lignor,** from **lignum**], m., *wood-cutter.* Pl., *men sent to get wood, wood foragers* (V.26).

Lingonēs, -um, m., pl., a Gallic people west of the Sequanians.

lingua, -ae, f., *tongue; language.* [language.

lingula, -ae, [dim. of **lingua**], f., *tongue of land* (III.12).

linter, -tris, f., (**15a**), *boat, skiff.*

līnum, -ī, n., *flax* (III.13).

līs, lītis, f., (**17c**), *strife; lawsuit; damages,* adjudged by legal process (V.I).

Liscus, -ī, m., chief magistrate (*vergobret*) of the Aeduans in 58 BC.

Litaviccus, -ī, m., a prominent Aeduan.

littera, -ae, f., *letter, character,* of the alphabet. Pl. **litterae, -ārum,** *writing* (VI.14); *letter, dispatch.* **litterae pūblicae,** *public records* (V.47). [letter.

lītus, -oris, n., (**13f**), *shore* of the sea, *strand, beach.* [littoral.

locus, -ī, m., pl. **loca, -ōrum,** n., (**6c**), *place, ground; position, situation; room; social position, rank, standing; opportunity;* pl. **loca** often *region, country.* [local.

locūtus, see **loquor.**

longē, comp. **longius,** sup. **longissimē,** [**longus**], adv., *at a distance, far, by far.* Comp., of space, *further;* of time, *further, longer.* **quam longissimē,** *as far as possible.*

longinquus, -a, -um, comp. **-ior,** [**longus**], adj., *far removed, remote, distant; long-continued, prolonged, lasting.*

longitūdō, -inis, [**longus**], f., *length.* [longitude.

longurius, -ī, [**longus**], m., *long pole.*

longus, -a, -um, comp. **-ior,** sup. **-issimus,** adj., *long, extended, distant;* used of either space or time. **nāvis longa,** *battleship, galley.*

loquor, loquī, locūtus, 3, dep., *speak, say.* [loquacious.

lōrīca, -ae, [cf. **lōrum,** *leather straps*], f., *cuirass* of leather; *breastwork* (V.40).

Lūcānius, -ī, m., *Quintus Lucanius,* a brave centurion (V.35).

Lūcius, -ī, m., a Roman first name; abbreviation, **L.**

Lugotorīx, -igis, m., a British chief (V.22).

lūna, -ae, f., *moon.* [lunar.

Lūna, -ae, f., *moon* as a divinity, *moon-goddess* (VI.21).

lūx, lūcis, f., *light, daylight.* **prīmā luce,** at daybreak.

lūxuria, -ae, [**lūxus,** *excess*], f., *high living, luxury* (II.15).

M.

M., with proper names = **Mārcus.**

M as a designation of number = *1000.*

māchinātiō, -ōnis, [**māchinor,** *contrive*], f., *mechanical appliance, machine.* [machination.

maestus, -a, -um, sup. **-issimus,** [cf. **maereō,** *be sad*], adj., *sad, dejected.*

Magetobriga, -ae, f., a place in Gaul (I.31).

magis, sup. **maximē,** [cf. **magnus**], adv. in comp. degree, *more, rather.* **eō magis,** *all the more.* Sup. **maximē,** *very greatly, exceedingly, chiefly, especially.* **quam maximē,** *as much as possible.*

magistrātus, -ūs, [**magister**], m., *magistracy, civil office;* one holding a magistracy, *magistrate.*

magnificus, -a, -um, comp. **magnificentior,** sup. **-issimus,** [**magnus,** cf. **faciō**], adj., *splendid, magnificent* (VI.19).

magnitūdō, -inis, [**magnus**], f., *greatness, extent; size, bulk;* of winds and waves, *violence.* [magnitude.

magnopere, [for **magnō opere,** abl. of **magnum + opus**], adv., *very much, greatly, specially, deeply, urgently.*

magnus, -a, -um, comp. **maior,** sup. **maximus,** adj., *great, large, powerful;* of wind, *violent;* of voices, *loud* (IV.25). Sup., *greatest, very great, largest, very large.* As noun, **maiōrēs, -um,** m., pl., *forefathers, ancestors;* **maiōrēs natū,** lit. *those older by birth, the old men, elders* (II.13, 28; IV.13). [maximum.

maiōrēs, -um, see **magnus.**

malacia, -ae, f., *calm, dead calm* (III.15).

male, comp. **peius,** sup. **pessimē,** [**malus,** *bad*], adv., *badly, ill, unsuccessfully.*

maleficium, -ī, [**maleficus**], n., *mischief, wrong-doing, outrage, harm.*

mālō, mālle, māluī, [**magis + volō**], irr., (**71**), *prefer.*

mālus, -ī, m., *upright pole, upright;* of a ship, *mast* (III.14).

mandātum, -ī, [part. of **mandō**], n., *commission, order; command; injunction, instruction.* [mandate.

mandō, -āre, -āvī, -ātus, [**manus + dō**], 1, *commit, entrust, commission; order, direct.* [mandatory.

Mandubracius, -ī, m., a British chieftain, loyal to Caesar (V.20, 22).

māne, adv., *in the morning.*

maneō, manēre, mānsī, mānsūrus, 2, *stay, remain; continue.*

manipulus, -ī, m., *company* of soldiers, *maniple,* one-third of a cohort.

Mānlius, -ī, m., *Lucius Manlius,* a proconsul in Gaul (III.20).

mānsuētūdō, -inis, [**mānsuētus,** *tame*], f., *gentleness, compassion.*

manus, -ūs, f., *hand;* of troops, *band, force.* [manicure.

Marcomanī, -ōrum, m., pl., a Germanic people.

Mārcus, -ī, m., a Roman first name, abbreviated **M.,** our *Mark.*

mare, -is, n., (**16b**), *the sea.* [marine.

maritimus, -a, -um, [**mare**], adj., *of the sea, by the sea, near the sea; maritime, sea-.* **maritimae rēs,** *naval operations* (IV.23).

Marius, -ī, m., *Gaius Marius,* a great Roman general; lived 157 - 86 BC; famous for his victories over Jugurtha and the Cimbrians and Teutons; seven times consul, popular hero but foe of the aristocracy (I.40).

Mārs, Mārtis, m., *Mars,* god of war (VI.17). [March.

mās, maris, m., (**13g**), *male* (VI.26).

matara, -ae, f., *javelin, spear* (I.26).

māter, -tris, f., (**11e**), *mother.* **mātrēs familiae,** *matrons.* [maternal.

māteria, -ae, and **māteriēs,** acc. **māteriem,** [**māter**], f., *material, stuff; timber, wood.*

māterior, -ārī, [**māteria**], 1, dep., *procure timber, get wood.*

mātrimōnium, -ī, [**māter**], n., *marriage.* [matrimony.

Matrona, -ae, f., the *Marne,* a tributary of the Sequana (*Seine*), into which it flows four miles above Paris, after a course of more than two hundred miles (I.1).

mātūrē, comp. **mātūrius,** sup. **mātūrrimē,** [**mātūrus**], adv., *early.* **quam mātūrrimē,** *as early as possible* (I.33).

mātūrō, -āre, -āvī, -ātus, [**mātūrus**], 1, *make haste, hasten.*

mātūrus, -a, -um, comp. **-ior,** sup. **mātūrrimus,** adj., *ripe; early* (IV.20). [mature.

maximē, [**maximus**], see **magis.**

maximus, see **magnus.**

Maximus, see **Fabius** (1).

medeor, -ērī, 2, dep., *heal; remedy, provide for* (V.24). [medicine.

mediocris, -cre, [**medius**], adj., *common, ordinary;* of distance, *moderate, short.* [mediocre.

mediocriter, comp. **mediocrius** [**mediocris**], adv., *moderately, in a slight degree.*

Mediomatricī, -ōrum, m., pl., a Gallic people near the Rhine.

mediterrāneus, -a, -um, [**medius + terra**], adj., *inland* (V.12). [Mediterranean.

medius, -a, -um, adj., *middle, in the midst, mid-.* **media nox,** *midnight.* **dē mediā nocte,** *just after midnight.* [medium.

Meldī, -ōrum, m., pl., a Gallic people on the Matrona (*Marne*), east of the Parisii (V.5).

melior, adj., (**25a**), see **bonus.**

melius, adv., see **bene.**

membrum, -ī, n., *limb.* [member.

meminī, -isse, def., (**72**), *remember, bear in mind.*

memoria, -ae, [**memor**], f., *memory, recollection, remembrance.* **memoriā tenēre,** *to recollect.* **memoriā prōditum,** *handed down by tradition* (V.12).

Menapiī, -ōrum, m., pl., a people in the northeast part of Belgic Gaul.

mendācium, -ī; [**mendāx,** *false*], n., *lie, falsehood.* [mendacious.

mēns, mentis, f., *mind; temper* (III.19); *attitude of mind, feeling* (I.41). **et mente et animō,** *heart and soul.* [mental.

mēnsis, -is, m., *month.*

mēnsūra, -ae, [**mētior**], f., *measuring, measure.* **ex aquā mēnsūra,** *water-clock* (V.13). [measure.

mercātor, -ōris, [**mercor,** *trade*], m., (**11d**), *trader, merchant.*

mercātūra, -ae, [**mercor,** *trade*], f., *traffic, trade;* pl., *commercial transactions.*

mercēs, -ēdis, f., *pay, hire* (I.31).

Mercurius, -ī, [cf. **merx,** *merchandise*], m., *Mercury,* messenger of the gods, patron of traders and thieves, promoter of eloquence, and conductor of souls to the lower world; also, patron divinity of athletes and athletics (VI.17).

mereō, -ēre, -uī, -itus, and **mereor, -ērī, -itus,** 2, dep., *deserve, merit.*

merīdiānus, -a, -um, [**merīdiēs**], adj., *of midday.* **merīdiānō ferē tempore,** *about noon* (V.8). [meridian.

merīdiēs, -ēī, [**medī-diē,** loc.], m., *midday; south* (V.13).

meritum, -ī, [part. of **mereō**], n., *desert, merit, service.* [merit.

Messāla, -ae, m., *Marcus Valerius Messala,* consul, 61 BC (I.2, 35).

-met, enclitic, *self;* see **egō.**

mētior, mētīrī, mēnsus, 4, dep., *measure, measure out, distribute.*

Metius, -ī, m., *Marcus Metius,* an envoy of Caesar to Ariovistus.

metō, metere, messuī, messus, 3, *reap.*

metus, -ūs, m., *fear, apprehension.*

meus, -a, -um, [**mē**], adj., (**41**), *my, mine.*

mīles, -itis, m., (**10b**), *soldier, foot soldier.*

mīlitāris, -e, [**mīles**], adj., *of a soldier, military.* **rēs mīlitāris,** *art of war.*

mīlitia, -ae, [**mīles**], f., *military service* (VI.14, 18). [militia.

mīlle or **M**, indecl. adj., (**38a**), *a thousand.* As noun, **mīlia, -um,** n., pl., *thousand, thousands.* [mile.

Minerva, -ae, f., goddess of wisdom and the arts; compared to a Gallic divinity (VI.17).

minimē, see **parum.**

minimus, -a, -um, see **parvus.**

minor, -us, see **parvus.**

Minucius, see **Basilus.**

minuō, -uere, -uī, -ūtus, 3, *lessen, diminish, reduce;* of the tide, *ebb* (III.12); of controversies, *settle, put an end to* (V.26; VI.23). [minute.

minus, see **parum.**

mīror, -ārī, -ātus, [**mīrus**], 1, dep., *wonder, wonder at* (I.32; V.54).

mīrus, -a, -um, [**mīror**], adj., *wonderful, remarkable, marvelous.*

miser, -era, -erum, comp. **-ior,** sup. **miserrimus,** adj., (**22d**), *wretched, unfortunate, pitiable, poor.* As noun, **miserī, -ōrum,** m., pl., *the wretched* (II.28). [miser.

misericordia, -ae, [**misericors**], f., *pity, compassion, mercy.*

miseror, -ārī, -ātus, [**miser**], 1, dep., *lament, deplore* (I.39).

missus, -ūs, [**mittō**], m., used only in abl. sing., *a sending, dispatching.* **missū Caesaris,** *being sent by Caesar* (V.27).

mittō, mittere, mīsī, missus, 3, *send, dispatch; release, let go;* of weapons, *throw, hurl, shoot.* [missile.

mōbilis, -e, comp. **-ior,** sup. **-issimus,** [cf. **moveō**], adj., *fickle, changeable* (IV.5). [mobile.

mōbilitās, -tātis, [**mōbilis**], f., *quickness of movement, speed* (IV.33); *instability, changeableness* (II.1). [mobility.

mōbiliter, [**mōbilis**], adv., *easily* (III.10).

moderor, -ārī, -ātus, [**modus**], 1, dep., *keep under control* (IV.33). [moderate.

modo, [**modus**], adv., *only, merely, even;* of time, *lately, just now.* **nōn modo . . . sed etiam,** *not only . . . but also.*

modus, -ī, m., *measure, amount* (VI.22); *plan* (V.1); *manner, fashion, style.* **ad hunc modum,** *after this manner, in this way.* **eius modī,** *of such a character, of that kind.* **quem ad modum,** *in what way, how; in whatever way, just as* (I.36). **modō,** abl., with a dependent genitive, *after the manner of, as* (IV.17, 27). **nūllō modō,** *by no means* (VI.12). [mode.

moenia, -ium, n., pl., *walls* of a city, *fortifications* as a whole.

mōlēs, -is, f., (**15b**), *mass, massive structure; dam, dike* (III.12). [mole.

molestē, comp. **-ius,** sup. **-issimē,** [**molestus,** *troublesome*], adv., *with annoyance.*

mōlīmentum, -ī, [cf. **mōlior,** from **mōlēs**], n., *great effort* (I.34).

molitus, see **molō.**

mollis, -e, comp. **-ior,** sup. **-issimus,** adj., *pliant, gentle; smooth* (V.9); *weak, yielding* (III.19); *effeminate.*

molō, -ere, -uī, -itus, 3, *grind.*

Mona, -ae, f., the *Isle of Man,* in the Irish Sea (V.13).

moneō, -ēre, -uī, -itus, 2, (**54**), *advise, warn, remind, admonish.*

mōns, montis, m., (**17b**), *mountain, mountain-range, elevation, height.* **summus mōns,** *top of the height* (I.22). **rādīcēs montis,** *foot of the mountain or height* (I.38).

mora, -ae, f., *delay.*

morātus, -a, -um, see **moror.**

morbus, -ī, [cf. **morior, mors**], m., *disease, sickness* (VI.16, 17). [morbid.

Morinī, -ōrum, m., pl., a Belgic people, on the seacoast opposite Kent.

morior, morī, mortuus, 3, dep., *die* (I.4; VI.13). [mortuary.

Moritasgus, -ī, m., a chief of the Senones (V.54).

moror, -ārī, -ātus, [**mora**], 1, dep., *delay, wait, stay; hinder, delay, check, impede.* [moratorium.

mors, mortis, f., (**17c**), *death.* [mortal.

mortuus, -a, -um, see **morior.**

mōs, mōris, m., (**13b**), *usage, custom, practice.* Pl., *customs, manners, character.* [moral.

Mosa, -ae, f., the *Meuse,* or *Maas,* which rises in the western spurs of the Vosges, pursues a northerly course till joined by the Waal, then flows westward into the North Sea.

mōtus, -ūs, [**moveō**], m., *movement, motion; disturbance, revolt, uprising.*

moveō, movēre, mōvī, mōtus, 2, *move, set in motion, remove;* of feelings, *disturb; stir.* **castra movēre,** *to break camp.*

mulier, -eris, f., (**11c**), *woman.*

multitūdō, -inis, [**multus**], f., *great number, host, large body; crowd.* [multitude.

multō, multum, comp. **plūs,** sup. **plūrimum,** [**multus**], adv., *much, by far, greatly.* **multum posse** or **valēre,** *to have great power, influence.*

multus, -a, -um, adj., comp. **plūs,** sup. **plūrimus,** *much;* pl., *many.* As noun, m., pl., **multī, -ōrum,** *many* (people); **plūrēs, -ium,** *more, quite a number, several;* neut., sing., **multum,** *much;* **plūs,** *more;* **plūrimum,** *very much;* neut., pl., **multa,** *many things, many considerations.* [plural.

Mūnātius, see **Plancus.**

mundus, -ī, m., *world, universe* (VI.14). [mundane.

mūnīmentum, -ī, [**mūniō**], n., *fortification, defense, barrier* (II.17).

mūniō, -īre, -īvī, -ītus, [**moenia**], 4, *fortify; protect, make secure.*

mūnītiō, -ōnis, [**mūniō**], f., *a fortifying, building of fortifications; works of fortification, fortification, entrenchment, defenses.* **mūnītiōnī castrōrum,** *for the fortifying of the camp* (V.9). [munition.

mūnītus, -a, -um, comp. **-ior,** sup. **-issimus,** [part. of **mūniō**], adj., *fortified, protected, secure.* **mūnītissima castra,** *a camp very strongly fortified* (V.57).

mūnus, -eris, n., (**13e**), *duty, service, function; present, gift* (I.43). **mūnus mīlitiae,** *military service* (VI.18).

mūrālis, -e, [**mūrus**], adj., *of a wall,* **mūrālis falx,** *wall-hook* (III.14). **mūrāle pīlum,** *wall-pike* (V.40). [mural.

mūrus, -ī, m., *wall; rampart, line of works.*

mutilus, -a, -um, adj., *maimed, broken.*

N.

nactus, -a, -um, see **nancīscor.**

nam, conj., introducing an explanation or reason, *for.*

-nam; enclitic, *possible;* see **quisnam.**

Nammeius, -ī, m., a Helvetian sent as envoy to Caesar (I.7).

Namnetēs, -um, m., pl., a Gallic state north of the mouth of the Liger (*Loire*); the name survives in *Nantes* (III.9).

namque [**nam** + **-que**], conj., *for indeed, for truly, and* (with good reason) *for.*

nancīscor, -cīscī, nactus and **nanctus,** 3, dep., *come upon, find, obtain; get, secure.*

Nantuātēs, -um, m., pl., a Gallic people southeast of Lake Geneva.

Narbō, -ōnis, m., capital of the Province, which was later named from it, *Gallia Narbonensis;* made a Roman colony in 118 BC; now *Narbonne* (III.20).

nāscor, nāscī, nātus, 3, dep., *be born, produced; is found* (V.12); *rise* (II.18); *arise* (VI.22). [nascent.

Nasua, -ae, m., a chieftain of the Suebi (I.37).

nātālis, -e, [**nātus**], adj., *of birth.* **diēs nātālis,** *birthday* (VI.18). [natal.

nātiō, -ōnis, [**nāscor**], f., *birth; people, tribe.* [nation.

nātīvus, -a, -um, [cf. **nātus**], adj., *natural, native* (VI.10). [native.

nātūra, -ae, [**nātus,** from **nāscor**], f., *nature, character; natural features; nature of things, Nature.* **nātūrā et opere,** *naturally and artificially* (V.9, 21).

nātus, -ūs, [cf. **nāscor**], m., used only in abl. sing., *birth.* **maiōrēs nātū,** see **magnus.**

nauta, -ae, [for *nāvita from **nāvis**], m., (**2**), *sailor, seaman* (III.9; V.10).

nauticus, -a, -um, adj., *naval, nautical.*

nāvālis, -e, [**nāvis**], adj., *naval.* As noun, **nāvālia, -ium,** n., pl., *shipyards.*

nāvicula, -ae, [dim. of **nāvis**], f., *boat, skiff* (I.53).

nāvigātiō, -ōnis, [**nāvigō**], f., *navigation, sailing; voyage.*

nāvigium, -ī, [**nāvigō**], n., *vessel, boat.*

nāvigō, -āre, -āvī, -ātus, [**nāvis,** cf. **agō**], 1, *sail, go by water.* [navigate.

nāvis, -is, f., *ship, vessel;* for river navigation, *barge.* **nāvis longa,** *battleship, galley.* **nāvis onerāria,** *a transport.* [navy.

nāvō, -āre, -āvī, -ātus, [(**g**)**nāvus,** *busy*], 1, *do with zeal.*

nē, adv., *not.* **nē . . . quidem**, *not . . . even.*

nē, conj., *that . . . not, lest, not to,* after words of fearing, *that;* after words of beseeching, ordering, commanding, *not to.* **nē quis**, *that no one.* **nē qua spēs . . .** *that no hope.* **dēterrēre nē . . .** *to frighten from.*

-ne, enclitic interrog. particle, *whether.* **-ne . . . an**, or **-ne . . . -ne**, *whether . . . or.*

nec, conj., see **neque**.

necessāriō, [**necessārius**], adv., *of necessity, unavoidably.*

necessārius, -a, -um, [**necesse**], adj., *needful, necessary; urgent, pressing.* As noun, **necessārius, -ī**, m., *relative, kinsman* (I.11). [necessary.

necesse, indecl. adj., *necessary, unavoidable, inevitable.*

necessitās, -tātis, [**necesse**], f., *necessity, need, urgency.*

necessitūdō, -inis, [**necesse**], f., (**12d**), *necessity, need; close relationship, friendship* (I.43).

necne, [**nec + -ne**], conj., *or not.* **utrum . . . necne**, *whether or not* (I.50).

necō, -āre, -āvī, -ātus, 1, *put to death, kill.*

neglegō, -legere, -lēxī, -lēctus, [**nec + legō**], 3, *disregard, leave out of consideration, be indifferent to; neglect* (III.27; IV.38); *overlook, leave unnoticed* (I.35, 36; III.10). [neglect.

negō, -āre, -āvī, -ātus, 1, *deny, say not, say no,* often = **dīcit nōn**; *refuse.* [negative.

negōtium, -ī, [**neg-**, = **nē**, **+ ōtium**], n., *business, enterprise, task; effort, trouble, difficulty.* **nihil negōtiī**, *no trouble* (V.38).

Nemetēs, -um, m., pl., a Germanic people, settled west of the Rhine.

nēmō, dat. **nēminī**, [**nē + *hemō = homō**], m., (**12d**), *no one, nobody.*

nēquāquam [**nē + quāquam**, *anywhere*], adv., *not at all, by no means.*

neque or **nec** [**ne**, = **nē**, **+ -que**], adv., *nor, and . . . not.* **neque . . . neque** or **nec**, *neither . . . nor.*

nē . . . quidem, *not . . . even.*

nēquīquam [**nē + quīquam**], adv., *in vain, to no purpose* (II.27).

Nervicus,-a,-um, adj., *of the Nervians.* **Nervicum proelium**, *battle with the Nervians* (III.5).

Nervius, -ī, m., *a Nervian* (V.45). Pl., **Nerviī, -ōrum**, *the Nervians,* a warlike people of Belgic Gaul.

nervus, -ī, m., *sinew, muscle* (VI.21); pl., *power, force* (I.20). [nerve.

neu, see **nēve**.

neuter, -tra, -trum, gen. **neutrīus**, [**nē + uter**], pron. adj., (**23**), *neither.* As noun, **neutrī, -ōrum**, m., pl., *neither side* (II.9). [neuter.

nēve or **neu**, [**nē + -ve**, *or*], conj., *or not, and not, and that not, nor.* **neu . . . -que**, *and not . . . but* (II.21). **neu . . . et**, *and not . . . but* (V.34).

nex, necis, f., *death by violence.*

nihil [**ne**, = **nē**, **+ hīlum**, *trifle*], n., indecl., *nothing;* as adverbial acc., = emphatic **nōn**, *not at all.* [nihilism.

nihilō sētius, see **sētius**.

nihilum, -ī, [**ne**, = **nē + hīlum**], n., *nothing.* **nihilō**, abl. of degree of difference, lit. *by nothing;* **nihilō minus**, *none the less.*

nisi [**ne**, = **nē**, **+ sī**], conj., *if not, unless, except.*

nītor, nītī, nīxus and **nīsus**, 3, dep., (**131c**), *strive, endeavor; rely upon, depend on* (I.13).

nōbilis, -e, comp. **-ior**, sup. **-issimus**, [cf. **nōscō**], adj., *noted, renowned; of high rank, noble* (I.2, 18; V.22). As noun, **nōbilēs, -ium**, m., pl., *nobles, men of rank* (I.44; VI.13); **nōbilissimus, -ī**, m., *man of highest rank;* pl., *men of highest rank* (I.7, 31). [noble.

nōbilitās, -tātis, [**nōbilis**], f., *nobility, rank* (II.6); collective (for **nōbilēs**), *nobility, nobles, men of rank.* [nobility.

nocēns, -entis, comp. **nocentior**, sup. **-issimus**, [part. of **noceō**], adj., *guilty.* As noun, **nocēntēs, -um**, m., pl., *the guilty* (VI.9).

noceō, -ēre, -uī, -itūrus, 2, (**105**), *hurt, do harm, injure.*

noctū, [cf. **nox**], adv., *by night, at night, in the night.*

nocturnus, -a, -um, [cf. **nox**], adj., *by night, of night.* **nocturnum tempus**, *night-time* (V.11, 40). [nocturnal.

nōlō, nōlle, nōluī, [**nē + volō**], irr., (**71**), *be unwilling, not wish, not want.* **nōlī, nōlīte**, with infin., *do not.*

nōmen, -inis, n., (**12b**), *name, appellation, title; reputation, renown; account.* **suō nōmine**, *on his own account* (I.18). [noun.

nōminātim [**nōminō**], adv., *by name.*

nōminō, -āre, -āvī, -ātus, [nōmen], 1, *name, call* by a name; *mention.* [nominate.

nōn, adv., *not, no.* **nōn nihil,** *to some extent, somewhat* (III.17). **nōn nūllus,** *some, several.* **nōn numquam,** *sometimes.*

nōnāgintā, or **XC,** indecl. num., *ninety.*

nōndum [nōn + dum], adv., *not yet.*

nōnus, -a, -um, [novem], numeral ord. adj., *ninth.* [noon.

Nōreia, -ae, f., chief city of the Norici, now *Neumarkt* (I.5).

Nōricus, -a, -um, adj., *of the Norici, Norican* (I.5). As noun, **Nōrica, -ae,** f., *Norican woman* (I.53).

nōs, see **ego.**

nōscō, nōscere, nōvī, nōtus, 3, *obtain a knowledge of, learn;* in tenses from the pf. stem, *know, be familiar with, be acquainted with.*

noster, -tra, -trum, [nōs], pron. adj., **(41),** *our, our own.* As noun, **nostrī, -ōrum,** m., pl., *our men, our side.*

nōtitia, -ae, [nōtus], f., *knowledge, acquaintance.* [notice.

nōtus, -a, -um, comp. **-ior,** sup. **-issimus,** [part. of **nōscō**], adj., *known, well-known, familiar.*

novem, or **VIIII,** indecl. num., *nine.*

Noviodūnum, -ī, [Celtic word = *Newtown*], n., a town of the Suessiones, on the Axona (*Aisne*) (II.12).

novitās, -tātis, [novus], f., *novelty, newness, strangeness.*

novus, -a, -um, adj., *new, fresh, strange.* Sup. **novissimus,** *last, at the rear.* As noun, **novissimī, -ōrum,** m., pl., *those at the rear, the rear.* **novissimum agmen,** *rear of the line of march, the rear.* [novice.

nox, noctis, f., **(17b),** *night.* **multā nocte,** *late at night, when much of the night was past.*

noxia, -ae, [**noxius, -a, -um,** *hurtful*], f., *hurt, offense, crime* (VI.16).

nūbō, nūbere, nūpsī, supine **nūptum,** 3, *veil one's self* for marriage, *marry, wed* (I.18). [nuptial.

nūdō, -āre, -āvī, -ātus, [nūdus], 1, *strip, make bare; clear* (II.6); *expose, leave unprotected.*

nūdus, -a, -um, adj., *naked, bare; unprotected* (I.25). [nude.

nūllus, -a, -um, gen. **nūllīus,** dat. **nūllī,** [**ne,** = **nē,** + **ūllus**], adj., **(23),** *none, no.* As noun, especially in the dat., m., *no one.*

num, interrogative particle, expecting the answer No.

nūmen, -inis, [cf. **nuō,** *nod*], n., *divine will; divine majesty* (VI.16).

numerus, -ī, m., *number, amount; estimation, account* (VI.13). [number.

Numidae, -ārum, m., pl., *Numidians,* a people in Northern Africa, in the country now called Algeria, famous as archers, and employed by Caesar as light-armed troops (II.7, 10, 24).

nummus, -ī, m., *piece of money, money.*

numquam [**ne,** = **nē,** + **umquam**], adv., *never, not at any time.*

nunc, adv., *now, at present.*

nūntiō, -āre, -āvī, -ātus, [nūntius], 1, *announce, report.* Impers. **nūntiātur,** *word is brought, it is reported.*

nūntius, -ī, m., *messenger, agent* (I.44); *message, tidings.*

nūper, sup. **nūperrimē,** adv., *lately, recently.*

nūtus, -ūs, [nuō, *nod*], m., *nod, nodding* (V.43); *bidding, command* (I.31; IV.23).

O.

ob, prep. with acc., *on account of, for.* **ob eam causam,** *for that reason.* **ob eam rem,** *on that account, therefore.* **quam ob rem,** *wherefore; for what reason.*

obaerātus, -a, -um, comp. **-ior,** [**ob,** cf. **aes**], adj., *in debt.* As noun, **obaerātus, -ī,** m., *debtor, serf* (I.4).

obdūcō, -dūcere, -dūxī, -ductus, [ob + dūcō], 3, *lead forward;* of a trench, *prolong, extend* (II.8).

obeō, -īre, -iī, -itus, [ob + eō], irr., *go to meet; attend to.* **omnia per se obīre,** *to see to everything in person* (V.33).

obiciō, -icere, -iēcī, -iectus, [ob + iaciō], 3, *throw before; place in front, place; put in the way.* [object.

obitus, -ūs, [cf. **obeō**], m., *destruction* (II.29). [obituary.

oblātus, see **offerō.**

oblīquē, [**obliquus,** *slanting*], adv., *obliquely, with a slant* (IV.17). [oblique.

oblīvīscor, -līvīscī, -lītus, 3, dep., **(103a),** *forget.* [oblivion.

obsecrō, -āre, -āvī, -atus, [**ob + sacrō,** from **sacer**], 1, *beseech* in the name of that which is sacred, *implore, beg.*

observō, -āre, -āvī, -ātus, [**ob + servō**], *watch, observe; keep track of* (VI.18); *heed, comply with* (I.45; V.35). [observe.

obses, -idis, [cf. **obsideō**], m. and f., *hostage.*

obsideō, -sidēre, -sēdī, -sessus, [**ob** + **sedeō**], 2, *besiege, blockade;* of roads, *seize upon, block.* [obsess.

obsidiō, -ōnis, [cf. **obsideō**], f., *siege, blockade; oppression* (IV.19).

obsignō, -āre, -āvī, -ātus, [**ob** + **signō**], 1, *seal up, seal.*

obstinātē [**obstinātus,** part. of **obstinō,** *persist*], adv., *firmly, steadfastly* (V.6).

obstringō, -stringere, -strīnxī, -strictus, [**ob** + **stringō,** *tie*], 3, *bind, place under obligation* (I.9, 31).

obstruō, -struere, -strūxī, -strūctus, [**ob** + **struō,** *pile*], 3, *block up, stop up.* [obstruct.

obtemperō, -āre, -āvī, -ātus, [**ob** + **temperō**], 1, *submit to, obey.*

obtentūrus, fut. act. part. of **obtineō.**

obtestor, -ārī, -ātus, [**ob** + **testor**], 1, dep., *appeal to, implore, call as witness.*

obtineō, -tinēre, -tinuī, -tentus, [**ob** + **teneō**], 2, *hold fast, maintain, keep, retain, hold* (I.3); *get possession of, obtain* (I.18; VI.12); *possess, occupy, inhabit* (I.1).

obveniō, -venīre, -vēnī, -ventūrus, [**ob** + **veniō**], 4, *fall in with, encounter* (II.23); *fall to the lot of, fall to.*

occāsiō, -ōnis, [cf. **occidō**], f., *opportunity, favorable moment; surprise.* [occasion.

occāsus, -ūs, [cf. **occidō**], m., *going down, setting.* **sōlis occāsus,** *sunset, the west.*

occidēns, -entis, [part. of **occidō**], adj., of the sun, *setting.* **occidēns sōl,** *the west* (V.13). [Occident.

occidō, -cidere, -cidī, [**ob** + **cadō**], 3, *fall.*

occīdō, -cīdere, -cīdī, -cīsus, [**ob** + **caedō**], 3, *kill, slay.*

occultātiō, -ōnis, [**occultō**], f., *concealment.*

occultē, comp. **-ius,** sup. **-issimē,** [**occultus**], adv., *secretly, in secret.*

occultō, -āre, -āvī, -ātus, [freq. of **occulō,** *cover*], 1, *hide, conceal; keep secret.*

occultus, -a, -um, comp. **-ior,** sup. **-issimus,** [part. of **occulō,** *cover*], adj., *hidden, secret, concealed.* As noun, **ex occultō,** *from ambush, in ambush;* **in occultō,** *in hiding, in concealment* (II.18), *in a secret place* (I.31, 32). [occult.

occupātiō, -ōnis, [**occupō**], f., *employment, engagement.* [occupation.

occupō, -āre, -āvī, -ātus, [**ob,** cf. **capiō**], 1, *seize upon, seize, take possession of; fill, occupy* (II.8); of the attention, *engage, occupy.* **occupātus, -a, -um,** as adj., *engaged; busied* (II.19). [occupy.

occurrō, -currere, -currī (occasionally –**cucurrī**), **-cursūrus,** [**ob** + **currō**], 3, *run to meet, come to meet, meet; meet with, fall in with, encounter.* [occur.

Ōceanus, -ī, m., *Ocean,* considered by Caesar as one body of water, including the Atlantic Ocean, the English Channel, and the North Sea; *the sea.*

Ocelum, -ī, n., a town of the Graioceli in the Alps, west of modern Turin (I.10).

octāvus, -a, -um, [**octō**], num. adj., *eighth.* [octave.

octingentī, -ae, -a, or **DCCC,** [**octō** + **centum**], num. adj., *eight hundred.*

octō, or **VIII,** indecl. num., *eight.* [October.

octōdecim, or **XVIII,** [**octō** + **decem**], indecl. num., *eighteen.*

Octodūrus, -ī, m., chief town of the Veragri, in the Rhone valley (III.1).

octōgēnī, -ae, -a, or **LXXX,** [**octō**], distrib. num. adj., *eighty in each case.*

octōgintā, or **LXXX,** [**octō**], indecl. num., *eighty.*

oculus, -ī, m., *eye.*

ōdī, ōdisse, ōsūrus, def., (**72**), *hate.*

odium, -ī, [**ōdī**], n., *hatred.* [odium.

offendō, -fendere, -fendī, -fēnsus, 3, *hit against; hurt, wound* (I.19). [offend.

offēnsiō, -ōnis, [**offendō**], f., *hurting, wounding.*

offerō, -ferre, obtulī, oblātus, [**ob** + **ferō**], irr., *bring before; offer, present; put in one's way, afford.* **sē offerre,** *to offer, expose one's self, rush against* (IV.12).

officium, -ī, [for ***opificium, ops** + FAC in **faciō**], n., *service, duty; allegiance; sense of duty* (I.40). [office.

omittō, -mittere, -mīsī, -missus, [**ob** + **mittō**], 3, *lay aside, neglect, disregard* (II.17). [omit.

omnīnō, [**omnis**], adv., *altogether;* after negatives, *at all;* with numerals, *in all, altogether, only.* **nihil omnīnō,** *nothing at all.*

omnis, -e, adj., *every, all; as a whole.* As noun, pl., **omnēs, -ium,** m., *all men, all;* **omnia, -ium,** n., *all things, everything.* [omnibus.

onerārius, -a, -um, [**onus**], adj., *of burden;* see **nāvis.**

onerō, -āre, -āvī, -ātus, [**onus**], 1, *load.*

onus, -eris, n., (**13e**), *load, burden, weight; cargo* (V.1). [onus.

opera, -ae, [**opus**], f., *effort, work, pains; service, aid, assistance.* **dare operam,** *to take pains.* [opera.

opīniō, -ōnis, [**opīnor,** *think*], f., *idea, notion; good opinion, reputation; expectation.* **opīniō timōris,** *impression of fear.* **iūstitiae opīniō,** *reputation for fair dealing* (VI.24). [opinion.

oportet, oportēre, oportuit, 2, impers., (**73**), *it behooves; one ought, should; it is proper.*

oppidānus, -a, -um, [**oppidum**], adj., *of the town.* As noun, **oppidānī, -ōrum,** m., pl., *townspeople, inhabitants of the town.*

oppidum, -ī, n., fortified *town, city;* fortified *enclosure, stronghold* (V.21).

oppōnō, -pōnere, -posuī, -positus, [**ob + pōnō**], 3, *place over against, set against, oppose.* [oppose.

opportūnē, sup. **-issimē,** [**opportūnus**], adv., *conveniently, seasonably, opportunely.*

opportūnitās, -ātis, [**opportūnus**], f., *fitness, favorableness; favorable situation, advantage.* [opportunity.

opportūnus, -a, -um, comp. **-ior,** sup. **-issimus,** adj., *fit, suitable, favorable, advantageous.* [opportune.

oppositus, -a, -um, [part. of **oppōnō**], adj., *placed opposite.* [opposite.

opprimō, -primere, -pressī, -pressus, [**ob + premō**], 3, *weigh down; overwhelm, crush; take by surprise.* [oppress.

oppugnātiō, -ōnis, [**oppugnō**], f., *storming* of a city or camp, *assault, attack.*

oppugnō, -āre, -āvī, -ātus, [**ob + pugnō**], 1, *attack, assault; storm, besiege; take by storming.*

ops, opis, nom. and dat. sing. not in use, f., *help, power, might.* Pl., **opēs, -um,** *help* (VI.21); *resources, means, wealth; influence; strength.* [opulent.

optimē, see **bene.**

optimus, see **bonus.**

opus, n., used only in nom. and acc., *necessity, need.* **opus est,** (**132**), *there is need, it is necessary.*

opus, operis, n., (**13e**), *work, labor; that produced by labor, structure, works; line of works, fortification.* [opus.

ōra, -ae, f., *coast, shore.* **ōra maritima,** *sea-coast* (IV.20); when the place stands in for the people: *inhabitants of the coast, people along the sea* (III.8, 16).

ōrātiō, -ōnis, [**ōrō**], f., *speech, words, remarks, plea.* [oration.

ōrātor, -ōris, [**ōrō**], m., *speaker; envoy* (IV.27). [orator.

orbis, -is, m., *circle.* **in orbem cōnsistere,** *to form a circle* (V.33). **orbis terrārum,** *the world.* [orb.

Orcynia, -ae, f., with **silva,** *the Hercynian forest* (VI.24).

ōrdō, -inis, m., (**12d**), *row, series; rank, order; century* (half a maniple), *company* (I.40, V.35); *officer commanding a century, centurion.* [order.

Orgetorīx, -īgis, m., a Helvetian nobleman who formed a plot to seize power.

oriēns, -entis, [part. of **orior**], adj., *rising.* **oriēns sōl,** *rising sun; the east.* [orient.

orior, orīrī, ortus, 4, dep., *rise, arise; begin, spring from; start from* (I.39). **oriente sōle,** *at sunrise.* **ortā lūce,** *at daybreak.*

ōrnāmentum, -ī, [**ōrnō**], n., *decoration; distinction, honor* (I.44). [ornament.

ōrnātus, -a, -um, comp. **-ior,** sup. **-issimus,** [part. of **ōrnō,** *furnish*], adj., *equipped.* [ornate.

ōrō, -āre, -āvī, -ātus, [**ōs,** *mouth*], 1, *plead, beg, entreat.* [orate.

ōs, ōris, n., (**13g**), *mouth; face* (V.35). [oral.

Osismī, -ōrum, m., pl., a small state in the northwest corner of Gaul.

ostendō, -tendere, -tendī, -tentus, [**obs,** for **ob, + tendō**], 3, *show, display; point out, set forth, declare.* [ostentation.

ostentō, -āre, -āvī, -ātus, [freq. of **ostendō**], 1, *display, show;* with **sē,** *show off.*

ōtium, -ī, n., *rest, quiet, peace, leisure.*

ōvum, -ī, n., *egg* (IV.10). [oval.

P.

P., with proper names = **Pūblius.**

pābulātiō, -ōnis, [**pābulor**], f., *foraging.*

pābulātor, -ōris, [**pābulor**], m., *forager.*

pābulor, -ārī, -ātus, [**pābulum**], 1, dep., *forage, obtain fodder.*

pābulum, -ī, n., *fodder, forage.* [pabulum.

pācātus, -a, -um, comp. **-ior,** sup. **-issimus,** [part. of **pācō**], adj., *peaceful, quiet.*

pācō, -āre, -āvī, -ātus, [**pāx**], 1, *pacify.*

Padus, -ī, m., *Po,* the great river of Northern Italy (V.24).

Paemānī, -ōrum, m., pl., a people in Belgic Gaul.

paene, adv., *almost, nearly.*

paenitet, -ēre, -uit, 2, impers., (**103c**), *it makes sorry, it causes regret.* [penitent.

pāgus, -ī, m., *district, canton,* generally referring to the inhabitants rather than to the country; *clan.*

palam, adv., *openly, publicly.*

palma, -ae, f., *palm of the hand; hand.*

palūs, -ūdis, f., *marsh, swamp, bog.*

pandō, pandere, pandī, passus, 3, *spread out;* of hair, *dishevel.* **passīs manibus,** *with hands outstretched.*

pār, paris, adj., *like, similar, same; equal.* **pār atque,** *same as.* [par.

parātus, -a, -um, comp. **-ior,** sup. **-issimus,** [part. of **parō**], adj., *ready, prepared; provided.*

parcō, parcere, pepercī and **parsī, parsūrus,** 3, (**105**), *spare, refrain from injuring.*

parēns, -entis, [**pariō**], m. and f., (**17c**), *parent.*

pāreō, pārēre, pāruī, 2, (**105**), *obey; submit to, be subject to.*

pariō, parere, peperī, partus, 3, *bring forth; obtain, get, acquire.*

parō, -āre, -āvī, -ātus, 1, *prepare, make ready, make ready for; obtain, secure.*

pars, partis, f., (**17b**), *part, portion, share, number; region, district, division; side, direction; party, faction* (VI.11, I.15). **pars maior,** *the majority.* **ūnā ex parte,** *on one side.* **quā ex parte,** *and on that account* (I.2). **in omnēs partēs,** *in every direction.* [part.

partim, [acc. of **pars**], adv., *partly, in part.*

partior, partīrī, partītus, [**pars**], 4, dep., *divide, divide up, share.* Part. **partītus** in a passive sense, *divided, shared.* [-partite.

partus, see **pariō.**

parum, comp. **minus,** sup. **minimē,** adv., *too little, not enough.* Comp., *less.* Sup., *least, very little; not at all, by no means.* [minus.

parvulus, -a, -um, [dim. of **parvus**], adj., *very small; very young; slight, trifling.*

parvus, -a, -um, comp. **minor,** sup. **minimus,** adj., *small, trifling, insignificant.* Comp., *smaller, less.* As noun, **minus,** n., *less;* **minimum,** n., *the least.* [minimum.

passim, [**passus,** from **pandō**], adv., *in all directions* (IV.14).

passus, -ūs, m., *step, pace;* as a measure of length, *pace* (reckoned as a double step, from the place where either foot is raised to the place where the same foot rests on ground again), = 5 Roman feet, or 4 feet, 10.25 inches by English measurement; **mīlle passūs,** *mile;* pl., **mīlia passuum,** *miles.* [pace.

passus, see **pandō.**

passus, see **patior.**

patefaciō, -facere, -fēcī, -factus, pass., **patefīō, -fierī, -factus,** [**pateō + faciō**], 3, *lay open, open.*

patēns, -entis, comp. **patentior,** [part. of **pateō**], adj., *open.* [patent.

pateō, patēre, patuī, 2, *be open, lie open, stand open; extend.*

pater, -tris, m., (**11b**), *father.* Pl. **patrēs, -um,** *fathers, forefathers.* [paternal.

patientia, -ae, [**patiēns**], f., *endurance* (VI.24); *forbearance.* [patience.

patior, patī, passus, 3, dep., (**60**), *suffer, bear, endure; permit, allow.* [passive.

patrius, -a, -um, [**pater**], adj., *of a father; ancestral, of* (their) *forefathers* (II.15).

paucitās, -ātis, [**paucus**], f., *fewness, small number.* [paucity.

paucus, -a, -um, comp. **-ior,** sup. **-issimus,** adj., *little;* pl., *few.* As noun, **paucī, -ōrum,** m., pl., *few, only a few;* n., pl., **pauca, -ōrum,** *a few words* (I.44).

paulātim, [**paulum**], adv., *little by little, by degrees; gradually; one by one* (IV.30).

paulisper, [**paulum, per**], adv., *for a short time, a little while.*

paulō, [abl. of **paulus**], adv., *by a little, just a little.*

paululum [**paulus**], adv., *a very little, only a little* (II.8).

paulum, [neut. acc. of **paulus**], adv., *a little, somewhat.*

pāx, pācis, f., (**10c**), *peace.*

peccō, -āre, -āvī, -ātus, 1, *do wrong.*

pectus, -oris, n., *breast.* [pectoral.

pecūnia, -ae, [cf. **pecus,** *cattle*], f., *property; money.* Pl., **pecūniae,** *contributions of money.*

pecus, -oris, n., (**13f**), *cattle,* general term for domestic animals; *flesh of cattle, meat.*

pedālis, -e, [**pēs**], adj., *measuring a foot, a foot thick* (III.13). [pedal.

pedes, -itis, [**pēs**], m., (**10d**), *foot-soldier.* Pl., **peditēs, -um,** *infantry.*

pedester, -tris, -tre, [**pēs**], adj., *on foot.* **pedestrēs cōpiae,** *infantry.* [pedestrian.

peditātus, -ūs, [**pedēs**], m., *infantry.*

Pedius, -ī, m., *Quintus Pedius,* nephew of Julius Caesar, under whom he served as lieutenant in the Gallic War (II.2, 11).

peior, see **malus.**

pellis, -is, f., *skin, hide.*

pellō, pellere, pepulī, pulsus, 3, *drive out, drive off; rout, defeat.*

pendō, pendere, pependī, pēnsus, 3, *weigh out; pay.* [pendent.

penitus, adv., *far within* (VI.10).

per, prep. with acc., *through; across, along, over, among; during, in the course of; by, by the hands of, by means of; by reason of.* In oaths, *in the name of, by.* In combination, **per** adds the force of *through, thoroughly, very much, very.*

peragō, -agere, -ēgī, -āctus, [**per + agō**], 3, *finish, complete, bring to an end.*

percipiō, -cipere, -cēpī, -ceptus [**per + capiō**], 3, *get, secure, gain; hear* (V.1); *learn.* [perceive.

percontātiō, -ōnis, [**percontor,** *inquire*], f., *questioning, inquiry.*

percurrō, -currere, -cucurrī or **-currī, -cursūrus,** [**per + currō**], 3, *run through; run along* (IV.33).

percutiō, -cutere, -cussī, -cussus, [**per + quatiō,** *shake*], 3, *thrust through* (V.44).

perdiscō, -discere, -didicī, [**per + discō**], 3, *learn thoroughly, learn by heart* (VI.14).

perditus, -a, -um, comp. **-ior,** sup. **-issimus,** [part. of **perdō,** *ruin*], adj., *abandoned, desperate* (III.17).

perdūcō, -dūcere, -dūxī, -ductus, [**per + dūcō**], 3, *lead through, bring, conduct, convey; bring over, win over* (VI.12); *draw out, prolong* (V.31); *extend, construct, make.*

perendinus, -a, -um, [**perendiē,** *day after tomorrow*], adj., *after tomorrow.* **perendinō diē,** *day after tomorrow.*

pereō, -īre, -iī, -itūrus, [**per + eō**], irr., *perish, be lost.*

perequitō, -āre, -āvī, [**per + equitō,** *ride*], 1, *ride through; ride about* (IV.33).

perexiguus, -a, -um, [**per + exiguus**], adj., *very small.*

perfacilis, -e, [**per + facilis**], adj., *very easy.*

perferō, -ferre, -tulī, -lātus, [**per + ferō**], irr., *carry through; carry, convey, bring, report; endure, suffer; bear; submit to.*

perficiō, -ficere, -fēcī, -fectus, [**per + faciō**], 3, *finish, complete; perform, accomplish, carry out; cause, effect; bring about, arrange.* [perfect.

perfidia, -ae, [**perfidus**], f., *faithlessness, bad faith, treachery.* [perfidy.

perfringō, -fringere, -frēgī, -frāctus, [**per + frangō**], 3, *break through.*

perfuga, -ae, [**perfugiō**], m., *deserter.*

perfugiō, -fugere, -fūgī, [**per + fugiō**], 3, *flee for refuge, flee.*

perfugium, -ī, [cf. **perfugiō**], n., *place of refuge, refuge* (IV.38).

pergō, pergere, perrēxī, perrēctus, [**per + regō**], 3, *proceed, advance.*

perīclitor, -ārī, -ātus, [**perīculum**], 1, dep., *try, prove, make trial of, test; risk danger.*

perīculōsus, -a, -um, comp. **-ior,** sup. **-issimus,** [**perīculum**], adj., *full of danger, dangerous* (I.33). [perilous.

perīculum, -ī, n., *risk, danger, hazard; trial, test* (I.40); *attempt* (IV.21). [peril.

perītus, -a, -um, comp. **-ior,** sup. **-issimus,** adj., *skilled, practiced; familiar with.*

perlātus, see **perferō.**

perlegō, -legere, -lēgī, -lēctus, [**per + legō**], 3, *read through, peruse* (V.48).

perluō, -luere, -luī, -lūtus, [**per + -luō,** *wash*], 3, *wash.* Pass. used reflexively, *bathe* (VI.21).

permaneō, -manēre, -mānsī, mānsūrus, [**per + maneō**], 2, *continue, stay, remain.* [permanent.

permittō, -mittere, -mīsī, -missus, [**per + mittō**], 3, *give over, entrust, commit; grant, allow.* [permit.

permoveō, -movēre, -mōvī, -mōtus, [**per + moveō**], 2, *deeply move, disturb, alarm; arouse, stir; influence, induce.*

permulceō, -ēre, -sī, -sus, [**per + mulceō,** *soothe*], 2, *calm, soothe* (IV.6).

perniciēs, -eī, [**per**, cf. **nex**], f., *ruin, destruction* (I.20, 36).

perpaucī, -ae, -a, [**per + paucus**], adj., *very few*. As noun, **perpaucī, -ōrum,** m., pl., *a very few*.

perpendiculum, -ī, [cf. **perpendō**], n., *plumb-line*. [perpendicular.

perpetuō [**perpetuus**], adv., *continually, constantly; always, forever* (I.31).

perpetuus, -a, -um, [**per**, cf. **petō**], adj., *continuous, unbroken, unceasing, entire, perpetual*. As noun, **in perpetuum,** *for ever, ever after*. [perpetual.

perrumpō, -rumpere, -rūpī, -ruptus, [**per + rumpō,** *break*], 3, *break through, burst through, force a passage*.

perscrībō, -scrībere, -scrīpsī, -scrīptus, [**per + scrībō**], 3, *write fully, report* in writing.

persequor, -sequī, -secūtus, [**per + sequor**], 3, dep., *follow up, pursue; assail, attack* (I.13; V.1); *avenge*. [persecute.

persevērō, -āre, -āvī, -ātus, [**persevērus,** *very strict*], 1, *continue steadfastly, persist*. [persevere.

persolvō, -solvere, -solvī, -solūtus, [**per + solvō**], 3, *pay in full, pay*.

perspiciō, -spicere, -spexī, -spectus, [**per + speciō,** *look*], 3, *see, look; inspect, survey; perceive, observe, ascertain*. [perspective.

persuādeō, -suādēre, -suāsī, -suāsum est, [**per + suādeō,** *persuade*], 2, (**105**), *convince, persuade, prevail upon, induce*. **mihi persuādētur,** *I am convinced*.

perterreō, -terrēre, -terruī, -territus, [**per + terreō**], 2, *greatly alarm, frighten, terrify, dismay*. Part., **perterritus, -a, -um,** often *panic-stricken*.

pertinācia, -ae, [**pertināx, per + tenāx,** from **teneō**], 1, *obstinacy, stubbornness*.

pertineō, -tinēre, -tinuī, [**per + teneō**], 2, *reach out, extend; pertain to, concern, belong to*. [pertain.

perturbātiō, -ōnis, [**perturbō**], f., *disturbance, confusion*.

perturbō, -āre, -āvī, -ātus, [**per + turbō,** *disturb*], 1, *disturb greatly, disorder, confuse*. [perturb.

perveniō, -venīre, -vēnī, -ventum est, [**per + veniō**], 4, *come* (*to*), *arrive* (*at*), *reach; of an inheritance, fall to* (VI.19).

pēs, pedis, m., (**10b**), *foot;* as a measure of length, = .9708 of the English foot, or 296 millimeters. **pedem referre,** *to retreat*. [pedestrian.

petō, petere, petīvī and **petiī, petītus,** 3, *make for, try to reach, seek; get, secure; beg, ask, request*. **petere ut liceat,** *to ask permission*.

Petrosidius, -ī, m., *Lucius Petrosidius,* a brave standard-bearer (V.37).

phalanx, -angis, Greek acc. sing., **phalanga** (I.52), f., (**18f**), *compact host, mass, phalanx*.

Pictonēs, -um, m., pl., a Gallic people bordering on the Atlantic south of the Liger (*Loire*).

pietās, -ātis, [**pius,** *dutiful*], f., *dutiful conduct, devotion,* to the gods, one's country, or one's kindred. [piety.

pīlum, -ī, n., *javelin, pike*.

pīlus, -ī, [**pīlum**], m., with **prīmus,** *maniple of the triarii,* a division in the army containing the most experienced soldiers. **prīmī pīlī centuriō,** *first centurion of the first maniple of the triarii, first centurion* of the legion in rank (III.5). **prīmum pīlum dūcere,** *to lead the first maniple of the triarii, to hold the rank of first centurion* (V.35).

pinna, -ae, f., *feather;* in military language, *battlement*. [pen.

Pīrustae, -ārum, m., pl., a people in Illyricum (V.1).

piscis, -is, m., *fish* (IV.10). [Pisces.

Pīsō, -ōnis, m.: (1) *Lucius Calpurnius Piso Caesoninus,* consul 112 BC (I.12). (2) *Lucius Calpurnius Piso Caesoninus,* consul with *Aulus Gabinius,* 58 BC; father-in-law of Caesar (I.6, 12). (3) *Marcus Pupius Piso Calpurnianus,* consul with *M. Valerius Messala,* 61 BC (I.2, 35). (4) *Piso,* a brave Aquitanian (IV.12).

placeō, placēre, placuī, placitum est, 2, *please, be agreeable, be welcome to*. Used impersonally, **placet,** *it pleases, it seems good; it is agreed, it is resolved*. **eī placuit,** *he resolved* (I.34). [please.

plācō, -āre, -āvī, -ātus, 1, *appease, conciliate* (VI.16). [placate.

Plancus, -ī, m., *Lucius Munatius Plancus,* a lieutenant in Caesar's army (V.24).

plānē, comp. **-ius,** sup. **-issimē,** [**plānus**], adv., *clearly, plainly; entirely*.

plānitiēs, -ēī, [**plānus**], f., *level ground, plain*.

plānus, -a, -um, comp. **-ior,** sup. **-issimus,** adj., *level, even* (IV.23); *flat* (III.13). [plain.

plēbs, plēbis, or **plēbēs, -eī,** f., (**17c**), *the common folk, the common people, the masses*. **apud plēbem,** *among the masses*. [plebeian.

plēnē, comp. **-ius,** [**plēnus**], adv., *fully, completely* (III.3).

plēnus, -a, -um, comp. **-ior,** sup. **-issimus,** adj., *full.*

plērumque, [n. acc. of **plērusque**], adv., *generally, usually, for the most part.*

plērusque, -aque, -umque, [**plērus**, *very many*], adj., *very many, most.* As noun, **plērīque, -ōrumque,** m., pl., *the most, the greater part, the majority, most.*

Pleumoxiī, -ōrum, m., pl., a Belgic people, subject to the Nervians (V.39).

plumbum, -ī, n., *lead.* **plumbum album,** *tin* (V.12). [plumber.

plūrēs, plūrīmus, see **multus.**

plūs, plūrimum, see **multum.**

poena, -ae, f., *compensation, fine* (V.1); *punishment, penalty.* **poenās pendere** (VI.9) or **persolvere** (I.12), *to pay the penalty.* [penal.

pollex, pollicis, m., *thumb.*

polliceor, -licērī, -licitus, [**por- + liceor**], 2, dep., *promise, offer.*

pollicitātiō, -ōnis, [**pollicitor,** freq. of **polliceor**], f., *promise, offer.*

Pompeius, -ī, m.: (1) *Gnaeus Pompeius Magnus, Pompey,* Caesar's father-in-law and rival. (2) *Gnaeus Pompeius,* an interpreter serving under *Titurius Sabinus* (V.36).

pondus, ponderis, [cf. **pendō**], n., *heaviness, weight* (II.29); *a weight* as a standard of value (V.12). [ponderous.

pōnō, pōnere, posuī, positus, 3, *place, put; lay down* (IV.37); *set aside* (VI.17); *station; pitch.* Pass. often *be situated, be dependent, depend on.* **castra pōnere,** *to pitch camp, encamp.*

pōns, pontis, m., (**17c**), *bridge.*

populātiō, -ōnis, [**populor**], f., *a laying waste, ravaging* (I.15).

populor, -ārī, -ātus, 1, dep., *lay waste, devastate* (I.11).

populus, -ī, m., *people* as a political whole, *nation.* [people.

por-, in combination, *forth, forward.*

porrigō, -rigere, -rēxī, -rēctus, [**por- + regō**], 3, *reach out, extend.*

porrō, adv., *moreover, furthermore* (V.27).

porta, -ae, f., *gate* of a city, *gateway;* of a camp, *gate, entrance, passage.*

portō, -āre, -āvī, -ātus, 1, *carry, bring, convey, take.* [portage.

portōrium, -ī, n., *toll, tax, customs duties* (I.18; III.1).

portus, -ūs, m., *harbor, haven.* [port.

poscō, poscere, poposcī, 3, *demand, ask for urgently.*

possessiō, -ōnis, [cf. **possīdō**], f., *possession.*

possideō, -sidēre, -sēdī, [**por- + sedeō**], 2, *hold, occupy, possess* (I.34; II.4; VI.12).

possīdō, -sīdere, -sēdī, -sessus, [**por- + sīdō**], 3, *take possession of* (IV.7).

possum, posse, potuī, [**potis,** *able,* + **sum**], irr., (**66b**), *be able, can; have power, have influence.* **multum posse,** *to have great influence;* **plūrimum posse,** *to have very great power, influence.* [posse.

post, adv., *afterwards, later, after;* with abl. of degree of difference, **annō post,** *a year later, the following year;* **paucīs post diēbus,** *a few days later.*

post, prep. with acc. only: (1) Of place, *behind.* **post tergum,** *in the rear.* (2) Of time, *after.* **post mediam noctem,** *after midnight.*

posteā [**post eā**], adv., *afterwards.* **posteā quam,** with the force of a conjunction, *after that, after.*

posterus, -a, -um, nom. sing. m. not in use, comp. **posterior,** sup. **postrēmus,** [**post**], adj., *the following, next.*

postpōnō, -pōnere, -posuī, -positus, [**post + pōnō**], 3, *put after, lay aside.* **omnibus rēbus postpositīs,** *laying everything else aside* (V.7). [postpone.

postquam [**post + quam**], conj., *after that, after, when;* **post** and **quam** are often separated by intervening words.

postrēmō [abl. of **postrēmus,** sc. **tempore**], adv., *at last, finally.*

postrīdiē, [locative from **posterus diēs**], adv., *the next day.* **postrīdiē eius diēī,** *the next day, the following day.*

postulātum, -ī, [part. of **postulō**], n., *demand, claim, request.*

postulō, -āre, -āvī, -ātus, 1, *claim, demand, ask, request.* [postulate.

potēns, -entis, comp. **potentior,** sup. **-issimus,** [part. of **possum**], adj., *powerful.* As noun, **potentior, -ōris,** m., *one more powerful;* pl., *the more powerful* (II.1; VI.13, 22). **potentissimī, -ōrum,** m., pl., *the most powerful* (VI.22). [potent.

potentātus, -ūs, [**potēns**], m., *power, leadership, supremacy* (I.31). [potentate.

potentia, -ae, [**potēns**], f., *might, power, influence.* [potency.

potestās, -ātis, [**potis**], f., *might, power, authority; possibility, opportunity.* **potestātem facere,** *to give opportunity; to grant permission* (IV.15).

potior, potīrī, potītus, [**potis,** *able*], 4, dep., (**131c-d**), *obtain possession of, become master of, acquire, obtain.*

potius, adv. in comp. degree, sup. **potissimum,** [**potis**], adv., *rather, more, preferably.* **potius quam,** *rather than.*

prae, prep. with abl., *in comparison with* (II.30), *on account of.*

praeacuō, -cuere, -cuī, -cūtus, 3, *sharpen at the end.*

praeacūtus, -a, -um, [part. of **praeacuō**], adj., *sharpened at the end, sharpened, pointed; very sharp.*

praebeō, -ēre, praebuī, praebitus, [**prae + habeō**], 2, *hold forth; exhibit, manifest; furnish, provide* (II.17); *produce* (III.17).

praecaveō, -cavēre, -cāvī, -cautus, [**prae + caveō**], 2, *take precautions* (I.38).

praecēdō, -cēdere, -cessī, -cessūrus, [**prae + cēdō**], 3, *go before; surpass, excel* (I.1). [precede.

praeceps, -cipitis, [**prae + CAP** in **caput**], adj., (**26b**), *headlong, with great speed, head over heels* (II.24; V.17); *steep, precipitous* (IV.33). [precipitous.

praeceptum, -ī, [part. of **praecipiō**], n., *order, command, instruction.* [precept.

praecipiō, -cipere, -cēpī, -ceptus, [**prae + capiō**], 3, *order, direct, instruct.*

praecipitō, -āre, -āvī, -ātus, [**praeceps**], 1, *hurl headlong, fling down.* [precipitate.

praecipuē, [**praecipuus**], adv., *especially, specially, particularly.*

praecipuus, -a, -um, [**prae + CAP** in **capiō**], adj., *special, particular.*

praeclūdō, -clūdere , -clūsī, -clūsus, [**prae + claudō**], 3, *close up, block.* [preclude.

praecō, -ōnis, m., *herald, crier.*

Praecōnīnus, see **Valerius** (I).

praeda, -ae, [cf. **praehendō**], f., *booty, spoil, plunder.* [prey.

praedicō, -āre, -āvī, -ātus, [**prae + dicō**], 1, *make known, declare, announce; boast* (I.44). [preach.

praedor, -ārī, -ātus, [**praeda**], 1, dep., *obtain booty, pillage, plunder.*

praefectus, see **praeficiō.**

praefectus, -ī, [**praeficiō**], m., *commander, prefect; subsidiary official* (I.39).

praeferō, -ferre, -tulī, -lātus, [**prae + ferō**], irr., *carry before; put before, prefer to* (V.54). **sē praeferre,** *to show one's self superior to* (II.27). [prefer.

praeficiō, -ficere, -fēcī, -fectus, [**prae + faciō**], 3, *place in command of, appoint to command.*

praefīgō, -fīgere, -fīxī, -fīxus, [**prae + fīgō,** *fasten*], 3, *fix in front.* **sudibus praefīxīs,** *by driving stakes in front* (V.18). [prefix.

praemittō, -mittere, -mīsī, -missus, [**prae + mittō**], 3, *send forward, send ahead, send in advance.* [premise.

praemium, -ī, [**prae,** cf. **emō**], n., *reward, distinction.* [premium.

praeoptō, -āre, -āvī, -ātus, [**prae + optō**], 1, *choose before, prefer* (I.25).

praeparō, -āre, -āvī, -ātus, [**prae + parō**], 1, *make ready beforehand, make ready, prepare.* [prepare.

praepōnō, -pōnere, -posuī, -positus, [**prae + pōnō**], 3, *set over, place in command of.*

praerumpō, -rumpere, -rūpī, -ruptus, [**prae + rumpō,** *break*], 3, *break off in front, break off* (III.14).

praeruptus, -a, -um, [part. of **praerumpō**], adj., *steep, precipitous.*

praescrībō, -scrībere, -scrīpsī, -scrīptus, [**prae + scrībō**], 3, *give directions, direct* (I.36, 40); *determine* (II.20). [prescribe.

praescrīptum, -ī, [part. of **praescrībō**], n., *direction, order, instructions* (I.36).

praesēns, -entis, comp. **-ior,** [part. of **praesum**], adj., *at hand, present.* [present.

praesentia, -ae, [**praesēns**], f., *presence* (V.43); *present time.* **in praesentiā,** *for the present.* [presence.

praesentiō, -sentīre, -sēnsī, -sēnsus, [**prae + sentiō**], 4, *perceive beforehand* (V.54).

praesertim [**prae,** cf. **serō,** *join*], adv., *especially, particularly.*

praesidium, -ī, [**praeses,** *guard*], n., *guard, detachment, garrison, protection; post, redoubt; safety* (II.11).

praestō, -stāre, -stitī, -stitus, [**prae + stō**], 1, *surpass, excel; exhibit, display, manifest; discharge, perform, do.* Impers. **praestat,** *it is preferable, it is better.*

praestō, adv., *at hand.* **praestō esse,** *to meet* (V.26).

praesum, -esse, -fuī, [**prae + sum**], irr., *preside over; be at the head of, have command of, have charge of.*

praeter, prep. with acc. only, *beyond* (I.48); *except, besides; contrary to.*

praetereā [**praeter** + **eā**], adv., *besides, further.*

praetereō, **-īre**, **-īvī** or **-iī**, **-itus**, [**praeter** + **eō**], irr., *pass over, go by.*

praetermittō, **-mittere**, **-mīsī**, **-missus**, [**praeter** + **mittō**], 3, *pass over, let pass, allow to go by.*

praeterquam [**praeter** + **quam**], adv. with comparative force, *other than, besides.*

praetor, **-ōris**, [****praeitor** from **praeëō**], m., *commander* (I.21); *praetor*, a Roman magistrate, next in rank to the consul.

praetōrius, **-a**, **-um**, [**praetor**], adj., *of the commander, general's* (I.40); *praetorian.*

praeūstus, **-a**, **-um**, [part. of **praeūrō**], adj., *burnt at the end, hardened at the end by burning.*

prāvus, **-a**, **-um**, comp. **-ior**, sup. **-issimus**, adj., *crooked, bad, wicked.*

precēs, see **prex**.

premō, **-ere**, **-pressī**, **-pressus**, 3, *press, harass, oppress*; pass., *be hard pressed, be beset, be burdened, be in need.* [press.

prēndō (for **prehendō**), **prēndere**, **prēndī**, **prēnsus**, 3, *take, grasp* (I.20).

pretium, **-ī**, n., *price, value.*

prex, **precis**, f., generally pl., nom. and gen. sing. not in use, *prayer, entreaty, supplication; curse, imprecation.*

prīdiē, adv., *the day before, the previous day.* **prīdiē eius diēī**, *the day before that day, on the previous day* (I.47).

prīmipīlus, **-ī**, [**prīmus** + **pīlus**], m., = **prīmus pīlus**, *first centurion; see* **pīlus** (II.25).

prīmō [abl. of **prīmus**], adv., *at first, in the first place.*

prīmum [acc. of **prīmus**], adv., *first, before everything else, in the first place.* **quam prīmum**, *as soon as possible.* **cum prīmum**, *as soon as.*

prīmus, see **prior**.

prīnceps, **-ipis**, [**prīmus** + CAP in **capiō**], adj., (**10b, 26b**), *first, chief, at the front.* As noun, m., *leading man, leader,* pl. often *leading men.* [prince.

prīncipātus, **-ūs**, [**prīnceps**], m., *first place, chief authority.* [principate.

prior, **-us**, gen. **priōris**, adj. in comp. degree, sup. **prīmus**, [cf. **prō**], *former, previous, first.* As noun, **priōrēs**, **-um**, m., pl., *those in front* (II.11). Sup. **prīmus**, *first, the first.* As noun, **prīmī**, **-ōrum**, m., pl., *the foremost men, the first.* **prīma**, **-ōrum**, n., pl., in the phrase **in prīmīs**, *especially.* [prior, prime.

prīstinus, **-a**, **-um**, [****prīs**, = **prius**, + **-tinus**], adj., *former, previous, earlier, old-time.* [pristine.

prius [**prior**], adv., *before, sooner, earlier.*

priusquam, **prius quam**, conj., (**189**), *before, sooner than;* **prius** and **quam** are often separated by intervening words.

prīvātim [**prīvātus**], adv., *privately, as individuals,* opposed in meaning to **pūblicē**. (I.17; V.55).

prīvātus, **-a**, **-um**, [part. of **prīvō**], adj., *private, personal.* As noun, **prīvātus**, **-ī**, m., *private individual* (VI.13). [private.

prō, prep. with abl. only, *in front of, before; for, in behalf of; instead of, as; on account of, in return for; in accordance with* (II.31); *in proportion to, considering* (I.2, 51; VI.19).

probō, **-āre**, **-āvī**, **-ātus**, [**probus**], 1, *approve; show to be worthy, display, demonstrate; prove* (V.27). [probe.

prōcēdō, **-cēdere**, **-cessī**, [**pro** + **cēdō**], 3, *advance, go forward.* [proceed.

Procillus, see **Valerius** (4).

prōcōnsul, **-ulis**, [**prō** + **cōnsul**], m., *proconsul,* an ex-consul appointed as governor of a province.

procul, adv., *at a distance, from afar, far off.*

prōcumbō, **-cumbere**, **-cubuī**, [**prō** + **cumbō**, for **cubō**, *lie down*], 3, *fall prostrate; sink down* (II.27); *be beaten down; lean forward* (IV.17).

prōcūrō, **-āre**, **-āvī**, **-ātus**, [**prō** + **cūrō**], 1, *look after, have charge of, regulate.*

prōcurrō, **-currere**, **-cucurrī** or **-currī**, [**prō** + **currō**], 3, *run forward, hasten forward, rush forward.*

prōdeō, **-īre**, **-iī**, **-itum est**, [**prōd-**, for **prō**, + **eō**], irr., *come out, come forth, advance.*

prōditiō, **-ōnis**, [**prōdō**], f., *treachery.*

prōditor, **-ōris**, [**prōdō**], m., *traitor.*

prōdō, **-dere**, **-didī**, **-ditus**, [**prō** + **dō**], 3, *give forth, make known; transmit, hand down; surrender, betray; give up* (IV.25).

prōdūcō, **-dūcere**, **-dūxī**, **-ductus**, [**prō** + **dūcō**], 3, *bring out, lead forth; prolong* (IV.30). [product.

proelior, -ārī, -ātus, [**proelium**], 1, dep., *fight.*

proelium, -ī, n., *battle, combat, engagement.*

profectiō, -ōnis, [**proficīscor**], f., *departure, setting out.*

prōfectus, see **prōficiō.**

profectus, see **proficīscor.**

prōferō, -ferre, -tulī, -lātus, [**prō + ferō**], irr., *bring out, bring forth.*

prōficiō, -ficere, -fēcī, -fectus, [**prō + faciō**], 3, *effect, gain, accomplish.* [profit.

proficīscor, -ficīscī, -fectus, [**prōficiō**], 3, dep., *set out, depart; set out (for), proceed.*

profiteor, -fitērī, -fessus, [**pro,** = **prō,** + **fateor,** *confess*], 2, dep., *declare openly, avow; offer, promise.* [profess.

prōflīgō, -āre, -āvī, -ātus, [**prō + flīgō,** *strike*], 1, *put to flight, rout* (II.23; VI.13). [profligate.

prōfluō, -fluere, -flūxī, [**prō + fluō**], 3, *flow forth.* (IV.10).

prōfugiō, -fugere, -fūgī, [**pro,** = **prō,** + **fugiō**], 3, *flee, escape.*

prōgnātus, -a, -um, [**prō + (g)nātus,** from **(g)nāscor**], adj., *sprung, descended.*

prōgredior, -gredī, -gressus, [**prō + gradior,** *step*], 3, dep., *advance, go forward, proceed.* [progress.

prohibeō, -hibēre, -hibuī, -hibitus, [**prō + habeō**], 2, *hold, restrain; prevent, hinder; cut off, shut off; protect, defend.* [prohibit.

prōiciō, -icere, -iēcī, -iectus, [**prō + iaciō**], 3, *throw forward, throw, fling, cast; of arms, throw down; abandon, lose* (II.15). **sē prōicere,** *to leap down* (IV.25), *to prostrate one's self* (I.27, 31). [project.

proinde [**prō + inde**], adv., *hence, therefore, and so.*

prōmiscuē [**prōmiscuus**], adv., *in common, promiscuously* (VI.21).

prōmissus, -a, -um, [part. of **prōmittō**], adj., *of hair, hanging down, flowing.*

prōmoveō, -movēre, -mōvī, -mōtus, [**prō + moveō**], 2, *move forward, push forward.* [promote.

prōmptus, -a, -um, comp. **-ior,** sup. **-issimus,** [part. of **prōmō,** *bring forward*], adj., *ready, quick.* [prompt.

prōmunturium, -ī, [cf. **prōmineō**], n., *headland* (III.12). [promontory.

prōnē [**prōnus**], adv., *bending forward, leaning forward.* (IV.17).

prōnūntiō, -āre, -āvī, -ātus, [**prō + nūntiō**], 1, *tell openly, declare; announce, give notice.* Impers., **prōnūntiātur,** *notice is given.* [pronounce.

prope, comp. **propius,** sup. **proximē,** adv., *near, nearly, almost;* followed by the acc., *near.* **proximē,** *nearest, next, very near; last, most recently.*

prōpellō, -pellere, -pulī, -pulsus, [**prō + pellō**], 3, *drive away, put to flight, rout; force back* (V.44). [propel.

properō, -āre, -āvī, -ātus, [**properus,** *quick*], 1, *hurry, make haste, hasten.*

propinquitās, -ātis, [**propinquus**], f., *nearness, proximity; relationship, kinship* (II.4). [propinquity.

propinquus, -a, -um, comp. **-ior,** [**prope**], adj., *near, neighboring.* As noun, **propinquus, -ī,** m., *relative, kinsman;* pl., **propinquī, -ōrum,** m., *relatives, kinsfolk;* **propinquae, -ārum,** f., *female relatives* (I.18).

propior, -us, gen. **propiōris,** adj. in comp. degree, sup. **proximus,** [cf. **prope**] (the positive is lacking), *nearer.*

proximus, -a, -um, *nearest, next, last,* of space or time. **proximā nocte,** *on the following night.* [proximate.

propius, see **prope.**

prōpōnō, -pōnere, -posuī, -positus, [**prō + pōnō**], 3, *set forth, put forward, present; declare, explain; propose, intend; raise, display* (II.20). [propose.

proprius, -a, -um, adj., *one's own, particular, characteristic* (VI.22). [proper.

propter, prep. with acc. only, *on account of, in consequence of.*

proptereā [**propter + eā**], adv., *for this reason, therefore.* **proptereā quod,** *because.*

prōpugnō, -āre, -āvī, -ātus, [**prō + pugnō**], 1, *come forth to fight* (V.9); *fight on the defensive* (II.7).

prōpulsō, -āre, -āvī, -ātus, [freq. of **prōpellō**], 1, *drive off, drive back* (I.49); *ward off, repel* (VI.15).

prōra, -ae, f., *prow.* [prow.

prōruō, -ere, -uī, -utus, 3, *throw down; tear down* (III.26).

prōsequor, -sequī, -secūtus, [**prō + sequor**], 3, dep., *follow after; follow up, pursue; attend to* (II.5). [prosecute.

prōspectus, -ūs, [cf. **prōspiciō**], m., *view, sight.* **in prōspectū,** *in sight, visible* (V.10). [prospect.

prōspiciō, -spicere, spexī, -spectus, [**prō + speciō,** *look*], 3, *look out, see to it* (V.7); *provide for, look out for* (I.23).

prōtegō, -tegere, -tēxī, -tēctus, [**prō + tegō**], 3, *cover, protect.*

prōtinus [**prō + tenus**], adv., *forthwith, at once, immediately.*

prōturbō, -āre, -āvī, -ātus, [**prō + turbō,** *disturb*], 1, *drive away, repulse* (II.19).

prōvehō, -vehere, -vexī, -vectus, [**prō + vehō**], 3, *carry forward* (V.8); pass., in a middle sense, *put out* to sea.

prōveniō, -venīre, -vēnī, -ventum est, [**prō + veniō**], 4, *come forth; grow* (V.24).

prōvideō, -vidēre, -vīdī, -vīsus, [**prō + videō**], 2, *foresee, perceive in advance; provide for, look out for.* [provide.

prōvincia, -ae, f., *province;* often the Province, the part of Transalpine Gaul subdued by the Romans before 58 BC.

prōvolō, -āre, -āvī, [**prō + volō,** *fly*], 1, *fly forward, dash forth* (II.19).

proximē, see **prope.**

proximus, -a, -um, see **propior.**

prūdentia, -ae, [**prūdēns,** for **prōvidēns,** *far-seeing*], f., *foresight, good judgment* (II.4). [prudence.

Ptiāniī, -ōrum, m., pl., a small state in Aquitania (III.27).

pūberēs, -um, [adj. **pūbēs** used as a noun], m., pl., *adults* (V.56).

pūblicē [**pūblicus**], adv., *in the name of the state, as a state, publicly.*

pūblicō, -āre, -āvī, -ātus, [**pūblicus**], 1, *make public; confiscate* (V.56). [publish.

pūblicus, -a, -um, adj., *of the state, public, common.* **litterae pūblicae,** *state documents* (V.47). **rēs pūblica,** *the state, public business, public interest.* As noun, **pūblicum, -ī,** n., *a public place.* **in pūblicō,** *in a public place* (VI.18).

Pūblius, -ī, m., a Roman first name, abbreviated **P.**

pudet, pudēre, puduit or **puditum est,** 2, impers. form of **pudeō,** *it shames; it makes ashamed.*

pudor, -ōris, [cf. **pudeō**], m., *shame, sense of shame.*

puer, puerī, m., (**7**), *child, boy.*

puerīlis, -e, comp. **-ior,** [**puer**], adj., *of a child.* [puerile.

pugna, -ae, f., *fight, combat, battle.*

pugnō, -āre, -āvī, -ātus, [**pugna**], 1, *fight, engage* in battle. **pugnātum est,** *the battle raged.*

Pullō, -ōnis, m., a brave centurion. (V.44).

pulsus, see **pellō.**

pulsus, -ūs, [**pellō**], m., *stroke;* of oars, *movement* (III.13). [pulse.

pulvis, pulveris, m., (**13g**), *dust.* [pulverize.

puppis, -is, i., *stern* of a ship. [poop.

purgō, -āre, -āvī, -ātus, [for **pūrigō;* **pūrus + agō**], 1, *make clean; free from blame, excuse, clear.* **suī pūrgandī causā,** *in order to excuse themselves.* [purge.

putō, -āre, -āvī, -ātus, 1, *think, consider, believe, judge.* [putative.

Pȳrēnaeus, -a, -um, adj., **Pȳrēnaeī montēs,** *the Pyrenees Mountains* (I.1).

Q.

Q., with proper names = **Quīntus.**

quā [abl. fem. of **quī,** originally sc. **viā** or **parte**], adv., *where.*

qua, nom. sing. fem., and neut. pl., of the indefinite pron. **quis,** or **quī.**

quadrāgēnī, -ae, -a, [**quadrāgintā**], num. distributive adj., (**22c**), *forty each, forty in each case* (IV.17).

quadrāgintā, or **XL,** [**quattuor**], indecl. num., *forty.*

quadringentī, -ae, -a, or **CCCC,** [**quattuor + centum**], numeral adj., *four hundred.*

quaerō, -ere, quaesīvī, quaesītus, 3, *look for, seek* (II.21); *ask, inquire.* [query.

quaestiō, -ōnis, [cf. **quaerō**], f., *inquiry; examination, investigation.* [question.

quaestor, -ōris, [cf. **quaerō**], m.: (1) *quaestor, state treasurer,* the lowest in rank of the great officers of state. (2) *quaestor, quartermaster,* an officer accompanying the army on campaigns, having charge of money and supplies, sometimes detailed for military service in charge of troops.

quaestus, -ūs, [cf. **quaerō**], m., *getting* of money, *gain* (VI.17).

quālis, -e, [cf. **quis**], inter. adj., *of what sort? what sort of?* (I.21).

quam [**quī**], adv. and conj., *how much, how;* with superlatives (with or without **possum**), *as possible;* after comparatives and comparative expressions, *than, as;* with expressions of time, *after.* **quam vetus,** *how old.* **quam diū,** *as long as.* **nāvēs quam plūrimās,** *as many ships as possible.* **quam celerrimē,** *as quickly as possible.* **post diem quārtum quam,** *the fourth day after.*

quamvīs [**quam + vīs,** from **volō**], adv., *however much; however* (IV.2).

quandō, adv., *ever, at any time.*

quantō opere, see **quantus.**

quantus, -a, -um, adj., *how great, how much, how large;* after **tantus,** *as;* **tantum . . . quantum,** *so much* or *so far . . . as.* As noun, with gen. of the whole, **quantum bonī,** *how much advantage* (I.40); **quantum agrī,** *as much land as* (VI.22). **quantō opere,** *how much, how greatly* (II.5). **quantō opere . . . tantō opere,** *as much as . . . so much.*

quantusvīs, quantavīs, quantumvīs, [**quantus** + **vīs,** from **volō**], adj., *however great, no matter how great.*

quārē [**quā** + **rē**], adv., *wherefore, on account of which, and for this reason.*

quārtus, -a, -um, [**quattuor**], adj., *fourth.* [quart.

quartus decimus, or **XIIII,** *fourteenth.*

quasi [**quam** + **sī**], conj., *as if.*

quattuor, or **IIII,** indecl. num. adj., *four.*

quattuordecim, or **XIIII,** [**quattuor** + **decem**], indecl. num. adj., *fourteen.*

-que, enclitic conj., *and,* appended to a word which in construction belongs after it.

quem ad modum, see **modus.**

queror, querī, questus, 3, dep., *complain, lament; complain of.* [querulous.

quī, quae, quod, gen. **cuius,** rel. and inter. pron.: (1) As rel. pron., (**47**), *who, which;* at the beginning of a clause often best rendered by a personal or demonstrative pron., with or without *and.* **īdem quī,** *the same as.* (2) As inter. adj. pron., (**48b**), *what? what kind of?*

quī, quae or **qua, quod,** indef. pron., (**49a, 168**), *any, any one,* or *anything,* used both as subst. and as adj. after **sī, nisi, num,** and **nē. sī quī,** *if anyone.*

quicquam, see **quisquam.**

quīcumque, quaecumque, quodcumque, indef. pron., (**50a**), *whoever, whatever, whichever.*

quid, see **quis.**

quīdam, quaedam, quiddam, indef. pron., (**49a, 168**), *a certain one, a certain thing.* As adj., **quīdam, quaedam, quoddam,** *a certain, some, certain.*

quidem, adv., *indeed, at least.* **nē . . . quidem,** *not even.*

quidnam, see **quisnam.**

quiēs, -ētis, f., (**10e**), *rest, repose.*

quiētus, -a, -um, [part. of **quiēscō,** from **quiēs**], adj., *at rest, calm, quiet; at peace.*

quīn, [old abl. **quī** + **ne**], conj., (**201**), *that not, but that, without;* after words expressing doubt or suspicion, *that;* after **dēterreō, retineō,** etc., trans. by *from* with a gerund. **quīn etiam,** *moreover.*

quīndecim, or **XV,** [**quīnque** + **decem**], indecl. num., *fifteen.*

quīngentī, -ae, -a, or **D,** [**quīnque** + **centum**], num., *five hundred.*

quīnī, -ae, -a, [**quīnque**], distrib. num. adj., *five each, five at a time.*

quīnquāgintā, or **L,** [**quīnque**], indecl. num., *fifty.*

quīnque, or **V,** indecl. num., *five.*

quīntus, -a, -um, [**quīnque**], adj., *fifth.*

Quīntus, -ī, m., a Roman first name, abbreviated **Q.**

quis, quid, inter. pron., (**48a**), *who? what?* Neut. **quid,** with gen. of the whole; **quid cōnsiliī,** *what plan?* neut. **quid,** as adverbial acc., *why?*

quis, quid, indef. pron., (**49, 168**), *any one, anything.* After **sī, nisi, num,** and **nē.** As adj., **quī, quae** or **qua, quod,** *any.* **sī quis,** *if anyone.* **nē quis,** *that not any one, that no one.* Neut. **quid,** with partitive gen., *any;* as, **sī quid cōnsiliī,** *if any plan.*

quisnam, quidnam, inter. pron., *who, indeed? what, indeed?* As adj., **quīnam, quaenam, quodnam,** *of what kind* (II.30).

quispiam, quidpiam, indef. pron., (**49a**), *anyone, anything* (VI.17). As adj., **quispiam, quaepiam, quodpiam,** *any* (V.35).

quisquam, quicquam, indef. pron., (**168**), *anyone, anything.* As adj., *any.*

quisque, quidque, indef. pron., (**49a**), *each one, each thing.* As adj., **quisque, quaeque, quodque,** *each.*

quisquis, quicquid, indef. rel. pron., (**50b**), *whoever, whatever.*

quīvīs, quaevīs, quidvīs, [**quī** + **vīs,** from **volō**], indef. pron., (**49a**), *anyone, anything you please.* As adj., **quīvīs, quaevīs, quodvīs,** *any whatever you please.*

quō, adv. and conj.: (1) **quō** [dat. or abl. of **quī**], 1, adv., relative and interrogative, *whither, to where;* indefinite, after **sī** and **nē,** *to any place, at any point, anywhere.* (2) **quō** [abl. of **quī**], conj., used especially with comparatives, followed by subj., *in order that, that, that thereby.* **quō minus,** *that not,* often best translated by *from* with a gerund.

quoad [**quō + ad**], conj., *as long as* (IV.12); *until, till* (IV.11; V.17, 24).

quod [acc. of **quī**], conj., *because, inasmuch as, since; as to the fact that, so far as.*

quod sī, conj., *but if, now if.*

quō minus, see **quō** (2).

quoniam [**quom,** old form of **cum,** + **iam**], conj., (**183**), *since, seeing that, because, inasmuch as.*

quoque, conj., following the emphatic word of a clause, *also, too.*

quōque, abl. of **quisque.**

quōque = **et quō.**

quōque versus, see **versus** (2).

quot, indecl. adj., *how many, as many as* (IV.22).

quotannīs [**quot** + abl. pl. of **annus**], adv., *yearly, every year.*

quotiēns [**quot**], adv., *as often as* (V.34); *how often* (I.43). [quotient.

R.

rādīx, -īcis, f., *root;* of an elevation, *foot, base.* **rādīcēs montis,** *the base of the height, the foot of the mountain.* [radish.

rādō, -ere, -rāsī, -rāsus, 3, *shave.* [razor.

raeda, -ae, f., *wagon* with four wheels.

rāmus, -ī, m., *branch, bough, limb.*

rapiditās, -ātis, [**rapidus,** *swift*], f., *swiftness* (IV.17). [rapidity.

rapīna, -ae, [cf. **rapiō,** *seize*], f., *pillaging, plundering* (I.15).

rārus, -a, -um, comp. **-ior,** sup. **rārissimus,** adj., *not thick;* pl., *few, scattered, in small parties.* [rare.

rāsus, see **rādō.**

ratiō, -ōnis, [**reor,** *reckon*], f., *reckoning, enumeration; account; method, means, way; plan, theory, system, science; reason, ground; condition, situation.* **ratiōnem habere,** *to keep an account* (VI.19), *take account of* (V.27). **abs tē ratiōnem reposcent,** *they will call you to account, will hold you responsible* (V.30). [ratio, rationale, reason.

ratis, -is, f., *raft.*

Rauracī, -ōrum, m., pl., a people along the upper Rhine, north of the Helvetians.

re-, red-, used only in combination, *again, back.*

rebelliō, -ōnis, [**rebellis,** from **re-** + **bellum**], f., *renewal of fighting, uprising.* **rebelliōnem facere,** *to enter into rebellion, rebel, revolt.* [rebellion.

recēdō, -cēdere, -cessī, -cessūrus, [**re-** + **cēdō**], 3, *withdraw.* [recede.

recēns, -entis, adj., *fresh; recent, late.* As noun, **recentēs, -ium,** m., pl., *those who were fresh, the unwearied* (V.16). [recent.

receptus, see **recipiō.**

receptus, -ūs, [**recipiō**], m., *retreat.*

recessus, -ūs, [**recēdō**], m., *a receding; opportunity to draw back* (V.43). [recess.

recipiō, -cipere, -cēpī, -ceptus, [**re-** + **capiō**], 3, *take back, get back, recover, win; receive, admit; take upon one's self.* **sē recipere,** *to retreat, withdraw; to recover one's self* (II.12; IV.27, 34). **recipere in dēditiōnem,** *receive into submission.* [receive.

recitō, -āre, -āvī, -ātus, [**re-** + **citō,** *quote*], 1, *read aloud, recite* (V.48). [recite.

rēctus, -a, -um, comp. **-ior,** sup. **rēctissimus,** [part. of **regō**], adj., *straight, direct.*

recuperō, -āre, -āvī, -ātus, [**re-,** cf. **capiō**], 3, *get back, recover.* [recuperate.

recūsō, -āre, -āvī, -ātus, [**re-,** cf. **causa**], 1, *refuse, make refusal, decline; raise objections* (V.6).

redāctus, see **redigō.**

reddō, -dere, -didī, -ditus, [**red-** + **dō**], 3, *give back, restore, return; render, make* (II.5). **iūs reddere,** *to dispense justice* (VI.13). **vītam prō vītā reddere,** *to give life for life* (VI.16). [rendition.

redēmptus, see **redimō.**

redeō, -īre, -iī, -itum est, [**red-** + **eō**], irr., *go back, come back, return; slope down* (II.8); *be reduced* (V.48); *be referred* (VI.11).

redigō, -igere, -ēgī, -āctus, [**red-** + **agō**], 3, *force back; reduce; render, make* (II.27; IV.3). [redact.

redimō, -imere, -ēmī, -ēmptus, [**red-** + **emō**], 3, *buy back, purchase;* of revenues, *buy up* (I.18). [redeem.

redintegrō, -āre, -āvī, -ātus, [**red-** + **integrō,** *make whole*], 1, *commence again, renew; revive.*

reditiō, -ōnis, [cf. **redeō**] f., *a going back, returning* (I.5).

reditus, -ūs, [cf. **redeō**] m., *returning, return* (IV.30).

Redonēs, -um, m., pl., a people in northwestern Gaul.

redūcō, -dūcere, -dūxī, -ductus, [**re-** + **dūcō**], 3, *lead back, bring* or *conduct back; carry back, put back.* [reduce.

refectus, see **reficiō.**

referō, -ferre, rettulī, -lātus, [**re-** + **ferō**], 3, *bring back, carry back* (IV.28); *bring, carry, convey* to a place or person; *report, announce.* **pedem referre,** *to retreat.* **grātiam referre,** *to make return, requite.* [refer.

reficiō, -ficere, -fēcī, -fectus, [**re-** + **faciō**], 3, *repair, refit, restore;* of troops, *refresh* (III.5). [refectory.

refringō, -fringere, -frēgī, -frāctus, [**re-** + **frangō**], 3, *burst in, break open, break down* (II.33). [refract.

refugiō, -fugere, -fūgī, [**re-** + **fugiō**], 3, *flee back* (V.35); *flee away, escape.* [refuge.

regiō, -ōnis, [cf. **regō,** *keep straight*], f., *direction, line; boundary; region, tract, territory.* **ē regiōne,** *directly opposite.*

rēgnō, -āre, -āvī, -ātus, [**rēgnum**], 1, *be king, reign* (V.25). [reign.

rēgnum, -ī, [cf. **regō**], n., *kingship, sovereignty, royal power; absolute authority; territory subject to a king or ruler, kingdom.*

regō, -ere, rēxī, rēctus, 3, (**55**), *keep straight; regulate; control, manage* (III.13); *conduct, carry on* (VI.17).

regredior, -gredī, -gressus, [**prō** + **gradior,** *step*], 3, dep., *go back, retreat.* [regress.

reiciō, -icere, -iēcī, -iectus, [**re-** + **iaciō**], 3, *throw back, hurl back* (I.46); of ships, *cast back, carry back* (V.5, 23); *drive back, repulse* (I.24; II.33); *cast away* (V.30); *throw away* (I.52). [reject.

relanguēscō, -ere, -uī, [**re-** + **languēscō**], 3, *become enfeebled, become enervated.*

relātus, see **referō.**

relēgō, -āre, -āvī, -ātus, [**re-** + **lēgō,** *depute*], 1, *banish, remove, treat as an outlaw.* [relegate.

religiō, -ōnis, f., *religious scruple, religious obligation, religious observance, superstition.* [religion.

relinquō, -linquere, -līquī, -lictus, [**re-** + **linquō,** *quit*], 3, *leave, leave behind; desert, abandon;* of a siege or attack, *leave off, give up.* [relinquish.

reliquus, -a, -um, [cf. **relinquō**], adj., *remaining, left, the rest.* As noun, **reliquī, -ōrum,** m., pl., *the rest;* **reliquī,** gen. sing. neut., in **nihil reliquī,** *nothing left* (I.11).

remaneō, -manēre, -mānsī, [**re-** + **maneō**], 2, *remain, stay behind.* [remain.

rēmex, -igis, [**rēmus,** cf. **agō**], m., *rower.*

Rēmī, -ōrum, m., pl., a Belgic people dwelling near the Axona (*Aisne*); chief city, Durocortorum, now *Reims.*

rēmigō, -āre, [**rēmex**], 1, *row* (V.8).

remigrō, -āre, -āvī, [**re-** + **migrō,** *remove*], 1, *move back, return* (IV.4, 27).

reminīscor, -minīscī, [**re-** + MEN in **mēns**], 3, dep., (**103a**), *remember, recollect.* [reminiscent.

remissus, -a, -um, comp. **-ior,** [part. of **remittō**], adj., *relaxed; mild.* **remissior,** *less severe* (V.12). [remiss.

remittō, -mittere, -mīsī, -missus, [**re-** + **mittō**], 3, *send back; give back, restore; relax, diminish* (II.15; V.49); *impair, lose* (VI.14); of a tax, *remit* (I.44). [remit.

remollēscō, -lēscere, [**re-** + **mollēscō,** *grow soft*], 3, *become weak* (IV.2).

remōtus, -a, -um, comp. **-ior,** sup. **-issimus,** [**removeō**], adj., *far off, remote* (I.31).

removeō, -movēre, -mōvī, -mōtus, [**re-** + **moveō**], 2, *move back, remove; dismiss.*

remūneror, -ārī, -ātus, [**re-,** cf. **mūnus**], 1, dep., *recompense, repay.* [remunerate.

rēmus, -ī, m., *oar.*

Rēmus, -ī, m., *one of the Remi, a Reman.*

rēnō, -ōnis, m., *reindeer skin, deerskin.*

renovō, -āre, -āvī, -ātus, [**re-** + **novō,** from **novus**], 1, *renew, begin again.* [renovate.

renūntiō, -āre, -āvī, -ātus, [**re-** + **nūntiō**], 1, *bring back word, announce.* [renounce.

repellō, -pellere, reppulī, repulsus, [**re-** + **pellō**], 3, *drive back, repulse.* [repel.

repente, [abl. of **repēns,** *sudden*], adv., *suddenly.*

repentīnus, -a, -um, [**repēns,** *sudden*], adj., *sudden, unexpected.*

reperiō, -perīre, repperī, repertus, 4, *find, find out; discover, ascertain, learn.*

repetō, -petere, -petīvī or **-petiī, -petītus,** [re- + petō], 3, *seek again, again try to obtain* (V.49); *demand* (I.31); *exact* (I.30). [repeat.

reportō, -āre, -āvī, -ātus, [re- + portō], 1, *carry back, convey back.* [report.

reposcō, -poscere, [re- + poscō], 3, *demand, require* (V.30).

repraesentō, -āre, -āvī, -ātus, [re- + praesentō, from **praesēns**], 1, *do at once, do forthwith* (I.40). [represent.

reprehendō, -hendere, -hendī, -hēnsus, [re- + prehendō], 3, *hold back; criticize, blame.* [reprehend.

reprimō, -primere, -pressī, -pressus, [re- + premō], 3, *restrain, check; repress.*

repudiō, -āre, -āvī, -ātus, 1, *reject, scorn* (I.40). [repudiate.

repugnō, -āre, -āvī, -ātus, [re- + pugnō], 1, *fight back, resist.* [repugnant.

repulsus, see **repellō.** [repulse.

rēs, reī, f., (**21**), *matter, affair; transaction, circumstance, fact; object, project, business.* **rēs mīlitāris,** *warfare, military science.* **rēs novae,** *a revolution.* [real.

rescindō, -scindere, -scidī, -scissus, [re- + scindō], 3, *cut down, break up, destroy.* [rescind.

rescīscō, -scīscere, -scīvī, or **-sciī, -scītus,** [re- + scīscō, inquire], 3, *discover, find out* (I.28).

rescrībō, -scrībere, -scrīpsī, -scrīptus, [re- + scrībō], 3, *write again; enroll anew, transfer* from one branch of the service to another (I.42).

reservō, -āre, -āvī, -ātus, [re- + servō], 1, *keep back, keep.* [reserve.

resideō, -sidēre, -sēdī, [re-+ sedeō, *sit*], *linger, remain.* [reside.

resistō, -sistere, -stitī, [re- + sistō, *set*], 3, *remain, stay; stand still; oppose, withstand, offer resistance.* [resist.

respiciō, -spicere, -spexī, -spectus, [re- + speciō, *look*], 3, *look back* (II.24; V.43); *look at; consider.* [respect.

respondeō, -spondēre, -spondī, -spōnsus, [re- + spondeō, *promise*], 2, *answer, reply.* [respond.

respōnsum, -ī, [part. of **respondeō**], n., *answer, reply.* [response.

res pūblica, see **pūblicus.**

respuō, -spuere, -spuī, [re- + spuō], 3, *spit out; reject* (I.42).

restituō, -uere, -uī, -ūtus, [re- + statuō], 3, *replace, restore; renew, revive; rebuild* (I.28). [restitution.

retineō, -tinēre, -tinuī, -tentus, [re- + teneō], 2, *restrain, detain, keep back; hold.* [retain.

retrahō, -trahere, -trāxī, -trāctus, [re- + trahō], 3, *bring back* by force (V.7). [retract.

revellō, -vellere, -vellī, -vulsus, [re- + vellō, *pull*], 3, *pull back* (I.52); *tear away.*

revertō, revertī, [re- + vertō], 3, only in tenses from pf. stem, and **revertor, -vertī, -versūrus,** 3, dep., *return, go back.* [revert.

revinciō, -vincīre, -vinxī, -vinctus, [re- + vinciō], 4, *bind back, fasten.*

revocō, -āre, -āvī, -ātus, [re- + vocō], 1, *call back, recall.* [revoke.

rēx, rēgis, [cf. regō, *rule*], m., (**10b**), *king, ruler, chieftain.*

Rhēnus, -ī, m., *the Rhine.*

Rhodanus, -ī, m., *the Rhone,* which rises in the Alps near the sources of the Rhine, and passing through Lake Geneva, follows at first a southwesterly direction, then flows south, reaching the Mediterranean after a course of about 500 miles.

rīpa, -ae, f., *bank* of a stream. [riparian.

rīvus, -ī, m., *stream, brook.*

rōbur, -oris, n., (**13f**), *oak* (II.13). [robust.

rogō, -āre, -āvī, -ātus, 1, *ask, request.*

Rōma, -ae, f., *Rome.*

Rōmānus, -a, -um, [**Rōma**], adj., *Roman.* As noun, **Rōmānus, -ī,** m., *a Roman;* usually pl., *the Romans, Romans.* [Roman.

Rōscius, -ī, m., *Lucius Roscius,* a lieutenant in Caesar's army.

rōstrum, -ī, [cf. **rōdō,** *gnaw*], n., *beak;* of a ship, *beak.* [rostrum.

rota, -ae, f., *wheel.* [rotary.

rubus, -ī, m., *briar, bramble* (II.17).

Rūfus, -ī, m., *P. Sulpicius Rufus,* see **Sulpicius.**

rūmor, -ōris, m., *rumor, report, gossip.*

rūpēs, -is, [cf. **rumpō**], f., (**15b**), *cliff* (II.29).

rūrsus, [for **revorsus,** from **revertō**], adv., *again, anew; in turn, on the contrary.*

Rutēnī, -ōrum, m., pl., a Gallic people, west of the Cebenna (*Cévennes*) Mountains; part of them were in the Province, and were called **Rutēnī prōvinciālēs.**

S.

Sabīnus, see **Titūrius.**

Sabis, -is, m., (**14c**), *the Sambre,* a river in the central part of Belgic Gaul flowing northeast into the Mosa (*Meuse*) (II.16).

sacrificium, -ī, [**sacrificus,** from **sacrum** + FAC in **faciō**], n., *sacrifice* (VI.13, 16, 21).

saepe, comp. **-ius,** sup. **-issimē,** adv. *often, frequently.* Comp., *too often* (III.6). **saepe numerō,** *oftentimes, repeatedly.*

saepēs, -is, f., (**15b**), *hedge* (II.17, 22).

saeviō, -īre, -iī, -ītus, [**saevus,** *fierce*], 4, *rage; be violent* (III.13).

sagitta, -ae, f., *arrow.*

sagittārius, -ī, [**sagitta**], m., *archer, bowman.* [Sagittarius.

sagulum, -ī, [dim. of **sagum,** *mantle*], n., *small cloak, cloak* (V.42).

salūs, -ūtis, [cf. **salvus,** *well*], f., (**10f**), *health, welfare; safety.* [salutary.

Samarobrīva, -ae, f., a city of the Ambiani on the Samara (*Somme*); now *Amiens.*

sanciō, sancīre, sānxī, sānctus, 4, *make sacred; make binding, ratify.* [sanction.

sānctus, -a, -um, comp. **-ior,** sup. **-issimus,** [**sanciō**], adj., *hallowed, sacred.* [saint.

sanguis, -inis, m., *blood.* [sanguine.

sānitās, -tātis, [**sānus**], f., *soundness* of mind, *good sense.* [sanity.

Santonēs, -um, or **Santonī, -ōrum,** m., pl., a Gallic people on the seacoast north of the Garumna (*Garonne*).

sānus, -a, -um, comp. **-ior,** sup. **sānissimus,** adj., *sound, healthy, rational.* As noun, **prō sanō,** *as a prudent man* (V.7). [sane.

sapiō, -ere, -īvī, 3, *taste; be sensible, understand* (V.30). [sapient.

sarcinae, -ārum, [**sarciō**], f., pl., *packs,* carried by the soldiers on their backs.

sarmentum, -ī, [**sarpō,** *prune*], n., *a branch;* pl., *brushwood* (III.18).

satis, adv., *enough, sufficiently, tolerably, rather;* often used as a noun, especially with a gen. of the whole, as **satis causae,** *sufficient reason.*

satisfaciō [**satis** + **faciō**], **-facere, -fēcī, -factus,** irr., *satisfy, give satisfaction; make restitution* (I.14, V.1); *appease, placate; make apology, apologize* (I.41, V.54).

satisfactiō, -ōnis, [**satisfaciō**], f., *apology, excuse.* [satisfaction.

satus, see **serō.**

saucius, -a, -um, adj., *wounded.* As noun, **saucius, -ī,** m., *a wounded man.*

saxum, -ī, n., *stone, rock.*

scālae, -ārum, [cf. **scandō,** *climb*], f., pl., *ladder, scaling-ladder.* [scale.

scapha, -ae, f., *skiff, small boat.*

scelerātus, -a, -um, comp. **-ior,** sup. **-issimus,** [part. of **scelerō,** from **scelus**], adj., *wicked, infamous.* As noun, **scelerātus, -ī,** m., *a crime-polluted man.*

scelus, sceleris, n., (**13e**), *crime, wickedness.*

scientia, -ae, [**sciēns**], f., *knowledge, skill.* [science.

scindō, -ere, scidī, scissus, 3, *tear, cut, split; tear down, break down* (III.5; V.51).

sciō, scīre, scīvī, scītus, 4, *know, understand.*

scrībō, scrībere, scrīpsī, scrīptus, 3, *write, write down.* [scribe.

scūtum, -ī, n., oblong *shield.*

sē, sēsē, see **suī.**

sē-, sēd-, in combination, *apart from, without.*

sēbum, -ī, n., *fat, tallow.* [sebaceous.

sēcrētō [**sēcrētus**], adv., *secretly, privately.*

sectiō, -ōnis, [**secō**], f., *the buying or selling of confiscated goods* (II.33).

sectūra, -ae, [**secō**], f., *a cutting* through earth, *digging, excavation* (III.21).

secundum, [**sequor**], prep. with acc. only, *along, next to, by the side of* (II.18); *according to* (IV.17); *besides* (I.33).

secundus, -a, -um, comp. **-ior,** sup. **-issimus,** [**sequor**], adj., *second, next; propitious, fortunate, favorable.* [second.

sed, conj., *but; yet, but yet.*

sēd-, see **sē-.**

sēdecim, or **XVI,** [**sex + decem**], indecl. num., *sixteen.*

sēdēs, -is, [cf. **sedeō,** *sit*], f., (**15b**), *seat; habitation, abode, settlement, home.*

sēditiōsus, -a, -um, sup. **-issimus,** [**sēditiō,** *mutiny*], adj., *mutinous.* [seditious.

Sedūnī, -ōrum, m., pl., a people in the Alps southeast of Lacus Lemannus (*Lake Geneva*).

Sedusiī, -ōrum, m., pl., a German tribe.

Segontiācī, -ōrum, m., pl., a people in the southern part of Britain (V.21).

Segovax, -actis, m., a British chieftain.

Segusiāvī, -ōrum, m., pl., a Gallic people, subject to the Aeduans.

semel, adv., *once.*

sēmentis, -is, [**sēmen,** *seed*], 1, *sowing, seeding* (I.3).

sēmita, -ae, f., *path, byway.*

semper, adv., *always, ever, constantly.*

senātor, -ōris, [cf. **senex**], m., member of the Roman Senate, *senator;* member of a Gallic state-council (II.28).

senātus, -ūs, [cf. **senex**], m., *council of elders, senate.* [senate.

senex, -is, comp. **senior,** adj., (**18b**), *old, aged.* As noun, m., *old man* (I.29). [senile.

sēnī, -ae, -a, [**sex**], distrib. num. adj., *six each, six* (I.15).

Senonēs, -um, m., pl., a Gallic people south of the Matrona (*Marne*); chief city Agedincum, now *Sens.*

sententia, -ae, [cf. **sentiō**], f., *opinion, view; decision, judgment.* **sententiam dīcere,** *to express an opinion.* [sentence.

sentiō, sentīre, sēnsī, sēnsus, 4, *perceive* through the senses, *become aware, learn; feel, think; know.* [sense.

sentis, -is, m., *thorn-bush* (II.17).

sēparātim [**sēparātus**], adv., *separately, apart.*

sēparātus, -a, -um, [part. of **sēparō**], adj., *separate, marked off.* [separate.

sēparō, -āre, -āvī, -ātus, [**sē- + parō**], 1, *part, separate.*

septem, or **VII,** indecl. num., *seven.* [September.

septentriō, -ōnis, [**septem + triō,** *plough-ox*], m., generally pl., **septentriōnēs, -um,** *the seven plough-oxen, the seven stars forming the constellation of the Great Bear; the North.*

septimus, -a, -um, [**septem**], num. adj., *the seventh.* [septimal.

septingentī, -ae, -a, or **DCC,** [**septem + centum**], num. adj., *seven hundred* (V.13).

septuāgintā, or **LXX,** indecl. num., *seventy.* [Septuagint.

sepultūra, -ae, [cf. **sepeliō,** *bury*], f., *burial.*

Sēquana, -ae, f., the *Seine,* the principal river of Northern France.

Sēquanī, -ōrum, m., pl., *the Sequanians,* a Gallic people west of the Jura; chief city Vesontio, now *Besançon.*

Sēquanus, -a, -um, adj., *Sequanian, of the Sequanians* (I.31). As noun, **Sēquanus, -ī,** m., *a Sequanian* (I.3).

sequor, -quī, -cūtus, 3, dep., (**60**), *follow, follow after; pursue; take advantage of* (V.8). **Caesaris fidem sequī,** *to attach one's self to Caesar* (V.20, 56). [sequence.

Ser., = Servius.

sermō, -ōnis, m., (**12b**), *talk, conversation.* [sermon.

sērō, comp. **sērius,** sup. **-issimē,** [**sērus,** *late*], adv., *late; too late* (V.29).

serō, serere, sēvī, satus, 3, *sow, plant.*

Sertōrius, -ī, m., *Quintus Sertorius,* a Roman general (III.23).

servīlis, -e, [**servus**], adj., *servile, of slaves.*

serviō, -īre, -iī, -ītus, [**servus**], 4, (**105**), *be the slave of, follow* (IV.5). [serve.

servitus, -tutis, [**servus**], f., (**10f**), *slavery, bondage, subjection.* [servitude.

Servius, -ī, m., a Roman first name.

servō, -āre, -āvī, -ātus, 1, *save; keep, maintain, preserve; save up* (VI.19); *keep watch of, watch* (V.19); *keep up the watch* (II.33).

servus, -ī, m., *slave.* [serf.

sescentī, -ae, -a, or **DC,** [**sex + centum**], num., *six hundred.*

sēsē, see **suī.**

sēsquipedālis, -e, [**sēsqui-,** *one half more,* + **pedālis; sēsqui- = sēmis,** *one half,* + **-que**], adj., *a foot and a half* in thickness (IV.17).

sēstertius, -a, -um, [for **sēmis tertius,** *three less one half*], num. adj., *two and a half.* As subst., **sēstertius, -ī,** (originally sc. **nummus**), gen. pl. **sēstertium,** m., *sesterce, a small silver coin.*

sētius, adv., comp. *less.* **nihilō sētius,** *none the less, nevertheless.*

seu, see **sīve.**

sēvocō, -āre, -āvī, -ātus, [**sē- + vocō**], 1, *call apart, call aside.*

sex, or **VI,** indecl. num., *six.* [sextet.

sexāgintā, or **LX,** indecl. num., *sixty.*

Sextius, -ī, m., see **Baculus.**

sī, conj., *if whether.* **quod sī,** *but if, now if.* **sī quidem,** *if indeed, in so far as.*

Sibusātēs, -um, m., pl., a people in Aquitania (III.27).

sīc, adv., *so, in this way, thus; as follows* (II.4). **ut ... sīc,** *as ... so.* **sīc ... ut,** *so ... that.*

siccitās, -tātis, [**siccus,** *dry*], f., *dryness.*

sīcut or **sīcutī,** [**sīc + utī**], adv., *just as, as.*

sīdus, -eris, n., *constellation;* pl., **sīdera,** *heavenly bodies, sun, moon, and stars* (VI.14). [sidereal.

signifer, -ferī, [**signum,** cf. **ferō**], m., (**7b**), *standard-bearer, ensign* (II.25).

significātiō, -ōnis, [**significō**], f., *sign, signal; demeanor.* **significātiōnem facere,** *to give notice, convey information.*

significō, -āre, -āvī, -ātus, [**signum,** + FAC in **faciō**], 1, *show by signs, show, intimate, indicate; transmit the news.* [significant.

signum, -ī, n., *signal; standard, ensign.* **signum dāre,** *to give the signal.* [sign.

silentium, -ī, [**silēns,** *silent*], n., *silence, stillness.*

Sīlius, -ī, m., *Titus Silius,* a military tribune.

silva, -ae, f., *wood, forest.* [sylvan.

silvestris, -e, [**silva**], adj., *covered with woods, wooded.*

similis, -e, comp. **similior,** sup. **simillimus,** adj., (**108b**), *like, similar.* [similar.

similitūdō, -inis, [**similis**], f., *likeness, similarity.* [similitude.

simul, adv., *at the same time, at once; as soon as* (IV.26). **simul ... simul,** *both ... and, partly ... partly.* **simul atque,** *as soon as.*

simulācrum, -ī, [cf. **simulō**], n., *image.*

simulātiō, -ōnis, [cf. **simulō**], f., *pretense, deceit.* [simulation.

simul atque, see **simul.**

simulō, -āre, -āvī, -ātus, [**similis**], 1, *make like; pretend, feign* (I.44; IV.4). [simulate.

simultās, -tātis, [**simul**], f., *rivalry, jealousy, bitterness* toward a rival (V.44).

sīn [**sī + ne**], conj., *if however, but if.*

sine, prep. with abl. only, *without.*

singillātim, [**singulī**], adv., *one by one, singly* (III.2; V.4, 52).

singulāris, -e, [**singulī**], adj., *one by one, one at a time* (IV.26); *singular, extraordinary.* [singular.

singulī, -ae, -a, distrib. num. adj., *one to each, one by one, one apiece; separate, single.* [single.

sinister, -tra, -trum, adj., *left.* [sinister.

sinistra, -ae, [sc. **manus**], f., *left hand* (I.25). **sub sinistrā,** *on the left* (V.8).

sī quidem, see **sī.**

situs, -ūs, [cf. **sinō**], m., *situation, location, site.* [site.

sīve or **seu** [**sī + ve**], conj., *or if.* **sīve (seu) ... sīve (seu),** *if ... or if, whether ... or, either ... or, it might be ... or.*

socer, -erī, m., (**7b**), *father-in-law* (I.12).

socius, -ī, m., *comrade, ally;* generally pl., **sociī,** *allies.* [social.

sōl, sōlis, m., (**11c**), *the sun.* **oriente sōle,** *at sunrise.* [solar.

Sōl, -is, m., *god of the sun, sun-god* (VI.21).

soldurius, -ī, m., *retainer, follower, vow-beholden* (III.22).

soleō, -ēre, -itus sum, 2, semi-dep., (**62**), *be wont, be accustomed.*

sōlitūdō, -inis, [**sōlus**], f., (**12d**), *wilderness, wasteland* (IV.18; VI.23). [solitude.

sollertia, -ae, [**sollers,** *skillful*], f., *skill, cleverness, ingenuity.*

sollicitō, -āre, -āvī, -ātus, [**sollicitus,** *agitated*], 1, *instigate, urge, incite; tamper with, tempt.* [solicit.

sollicitūdō, -inis, [**sollicitus**], f., *anxiety, apprehension.* [solicitude.

solum, -ī, n., *lowest part, ground; of a trench, bottom.* **agrī solum,** *the bare ground* (I.11).

sōlum [acc. of **sōlus**], adv., *only.* **nōn sōlum . . . sed etiam,** *not only . . . but also.*

sōlus, -a, -um, gen. **sōlius,** adj., (**23**), *only, alone.* [sole.

solvō, -ere, solvī, solūtus, [**se-, = sē-, + luō,** *loose*], 3, *loose; set sail* (IV.23). [solve.

soror, -ōris, f., (**13d**), *sister.* [sorority.

sors, sortis, f., (**17c**), *lot, chance.* [sort.

Sōtiātēs, -ium, m., pl., a people in northern Aquitania (III.20, 21).

spatium, -ī, n., *space, distance; interval, time, period, duration.* **nactus spatium,** *having gained time* (V.58). [space.

speciēs, -iēī, [cf. **speciō,** *look*], f., *sight, show, appearance; pretense.* **ad speciem,** *for show* (I.51). [species.

spectō, -āre, -āvī, -ātus, [freq. of **speciō,** *look*], 1, *look at, regard* (I.45; V.29); *lie* (I.1; V.13). [spectacle.

speculātor, -tōris, [**speculor**], m., *spy, scout.* [speculator.

speculātōrius, -a, -um, [**speculātor**], adj., *scouting, spying.* **speculātōrium nāvigium,** *spy-boat* (IV.26). [speculatory.

speculor, -ārī, -ātus, [cf. **specula,** *watch-tower*], 1, dep., *spy out, spy* (I.47). [speculate.

spērō, -āre, -āvī, -ātus, [cf. **spēs**], 1, *hope, expect.*

spēs, speī, f., *hope, expectation.*

spīritus, -ūs, [cf. **spīrō,** *breathe*], m., *breath, air;* pl., *haughtiness, pride* (I.33; II.4). [spirit.

spoliō, -āre, -āvī, -ātus, [**spolium,** *booty*], 1, *strip, despoil.*

sponte, abl., and **spontis,** gen., only forms in use of an obsolete nom. **spōns,** f., *of one's own accord, willingly.* **suā sponte,** *of their own accord, of their own initiative* (I.44, VI.14); *on their own account, unaided* (V.28); *by their own influence* (I.9). [spontaneous.

stabilitās, -tātis, [**stabilis**], f., *steadiness* (IV.33). [stability.

statim [**stō**], adv., *on the spot; immediately, at once, straightaway.*

statiō, -ōnis, [cf. **stō**], f., *outpost, picket, guard; reserves* (V.16). **in statiōne,** *on guard.* [station.

statuō, -uere, -uī, -ūtus, [**status**], 3, *set, place; determine, resolve; judge, think.* [statute.

statūra, -ae, [cf. **stō**], f., *height, stature.*

status, -ūs, [**stō**], m., *condition, position, situation.* [status.

stīpendiārius, -a, -um, [**stīpendium**], adj., *tributary, subject to payment of tribute* (I.30, 36). As noun, **stīpendiāriī, -ōrum,** m., pl., *tributaries, dependents.*

stīpendium, -ī, [**stips,** *coin,* cf. **pendō,** *weigh*], n., *tribute; of soldiers, pay.* [stipend.

stirps, -is, f., (**17c**), *stem; stock, race.*

stō, stāre, stetī, statūrus, 1, *stand; be posted, be placed* (V.35, 43); *abide by* (VI.13).

strāmentum, -ī, [cf. **sternō,** *strew*], n., *thatch of houses* (V.43).

strepitus, -ūs, [**strepō**], m., *noise, uproar.*

studeō, -ēre, -uī, 2, *be eager for, strive for; be devoted to, pay heed to; eagerly desire, strive.* [student.

studiōsē, comp. **-ius,** sup. **-issimē,** [**studiōsus,** *eager*], adv., *eagerly, diligently.*

studium, -ī, [cf. **studeō**], n., *eagerness, energy, enthusiasm; goodwill* (I.19); *pursuit.* **studia reī mīlitāris,** *pursuits of war, military pursuits* (VI.21). [study.

sub, prep.: (1) With acc., after verbs of motion, *under, towards, near to, just before.* (2) With abl., *under, at the foot of, close by; of time, on, in, during.*

subdūcō, -dūcere, -dūxī, -ductus, [**sub + dūcō**], 3, *lead up* from a lower to a higher position (I.22, 24); of ships, *draw up, haul on shore, beach* (IV.29; V.11, 24).

subductiō, -ōnis, [**subdūcō**], f., *hauling on shore, beaching* (V.1).

subeō, -īre, -iī, -itūrus, [**sub + eō**], irr., *go under* (I.36); *come up, approach, go up* (*to*), from a lower position (II.25, 27); *undergo, suffer.*

subfodiō, -fodere, -fōdī, -fossus, [**sub + fodiō**], 3, *stab underneath* (IV.12).

subiciō, -icere, -iēcī, -iectus, [**sub + iaciō**], 3, *throw under, place near; throw from beneath* (I.26); *expose* (IV.36).

subiectus, -a, -um, comp. **-ior,** [**subiciō**], adj., *lying near, adjacent* (V.13). [subject.

subitō, [abl. of **subitus**], adv., *suddenly, all of a sudden.*

subitus, -a, -um, [**subeō**], adj., *sudden, unexpected.*

sublātus, see **tollō.**

sublevō, -āre, -āvī, -ātus, [**sub + levō**], 1, *lift up, support, hold up* (I.48); *relieve, assist, aid, support* (I.16, 40); of labor, *lighten.*

sublica, -ae, f., *stake, pile.*

subruō, -ruere, -ruī, -rutus, [**sub + ruō,** *fall*], 3, *undermine.*

subsequor, -sequī, -secūtus, [**sub + sequor**], 3, dep., *follow close upon, follow after, follow up.* [subsequent.

subsidium, -ī, [cf. **subsīdō**], n., *reserve, reserve force, auxiliaries; support, relief, help, aid; relieving force; resource.* **mittere subsidiō,** *to send help.* [subsidy.

subsistō, -sistere, -stitī, [**sub + sistō,** *set*], 3, *halt, make a stand* (I.15); *hold out* (V.10). [subsist.

subsum, -esse, [**sub + sum**], irr., *be near* (I.25; V.29); of time, *be close at hand, not far off* (III.27; V.23).

subtrahō, -trahere, -trāxī, -trāctus, [**sub + trahō**], 3, *carry off, draw off underneath; withdraw, take away* (I.44). [subtract.

subvehō, -vehere, -vexī, -vectus, [**sub + vehō**], 3, *bring up* (I.16).

subveniō, -venīre, -vēnī, subventum est, [**sub + veniō**], 4, *come to the help of, come to the rescue of; assist, succor, render assistance.* [subvention.

succēdō, -cēdere, -cessī, -cessūrus, [**sub + cēdō**], 3, *come up, approach, advance; succeed to another's place, take the place of, relieve, follow; become the successor* (VI.13); *prosper, succeed.*

succendō, -cendere, -cendī, -cēnsus, [**sub,** cf. **candeō**], 3, *set on fire, set fire to.*

succīdō, -cīdere, -cīdī, -cīsus, [**sub + caedō**], 3, *cut down.*

succurrō, -currere, -currī, -cursum est, [**sub + currō**], 3, *run to help, succor.*

sudis, -is, f., *stake, pile.*

Suēba, -ae, [**Suēbus,** cf. **Suēbī**], f., *a Swabian woman* (I.53).

Suēbī, -ōrum, m., pl., *the Swabians,* a powerful German people.

Suessiōnēs, -um, m., pl., a Belgic people north of the Matrona (*Marne*); the name survives in *Soissons.*

suffrāgium, -ī, n., *vote.* [suffrage.

Sugambrī, -ōrum, m., pl., a German people.

suī, sibi, sē or **sēsē,** nom. does not exist, reflex. pron., (**40b**), *himself, herself, itself, themselves, him, her, it.*

Sulla, -ae, m., *Lucius Cornelius Sulla,* consul 88, dictator 81-79 BC (I.21).

Sulpicius, -ī, m., *Publius Sulpicius Rufus,* a lieutenant of Caesar in Gaul (IV.22).

sum, esse, fuī, futūrus, irr., *be, exist* (**52**). [future.

summa, -ae, [**summus;** sc. **rēs**], f., *sum total, aggregate, whole* (I.29; VI.11, 34); *control, administration; determination* (VI.11). **summa imperiī,** *the supreme command.* [sum.

sumministrō, -āre, -āvī, -ātus, [**sub + ministrō,** *serve*], 1, *supply, provide, furnish.*

summittō, -mittere, -mīsī, -missus, [**sub + mittō**], 3, *send secretly; send as reinforcement, send as help.* [submit.

summoveō, -movēre, -mōvī, -mōtus, [**sub + moveō**], 2, *force back.*

summus, see **superus.**

sūmō, sūmere, sūmpsī, sūmptus, 3, *take* (I.7, 16); *take to one's self, take on, assume* (I.33; II.4); *put forth, expend, spend* (III.14). **dē aliquō supplicium sūmere,** *to inflict punishment on any one* (I.31).

sūmptuōsus, -a, -um, comp. **-ior,** [**sūmptus**], adj., *costly.* [sumptuous.

sūmptus, -tūs, [**sūmō**], m., *expense* (I.18). [sumptuary.

superbē, comp. **-ius,** sup. **-issimē,** [**superbus,** *proud*], adv., *haughtily.*

superior, see **superus.**

superō, -āre, -āvī, -ātus, [**superus**], 1, *conquer, overcome, vanquish, defeat; surpass* (VI.24); *rise above* (III.14); *prove superior* (III.14); *carry the day* (V.31); *survive* (VI.19).

supersedeō, -sedēre, -sēdī, [**super + sedeō,** *sit*], 2, *refrain from* (II.8). [supersede.

supersum, -esse, -fuī, [**super + sum**], irr., *remain, be left* (I.23; III.28; V.22); *survive* (I.26; II.27, 28).

superus, -a, -um, comp. **superior,** sup. **summus** or **suprēmus,** [**super**], adj., *above, on high.* Comp., **superior, -ius,** *higher, upper, superior;* of time, *former, earlier,* as **superiōre nocte,** *the previous night* (V.10). Sup., **sum-**

mus, a, -um, *highest; greatest, very great; most important, chief; all together, all* (V.17); often denoting a part, as **summus mōns,** *the top of the height* (I.22). As noun, **summum, -ī,** n., *top, end.* **ab summō,** *from the top* (II.18); *at the end; from the end* (VI.26). [superior, supreme.

suppetō, -petere, -petīvī or **-iī, -petītus,** [**sub** + **petō**], 3, *be at hand, be available.*

supplēmentum, -ī, [**suppleō,** *fill up*], n., *raw contingent,* a body of recruits under training, not yet assigned to the legions in which they will serve. [supplement.

supplex, -icis, m. and f., *suppliant* (II.28).

supplicātiō, -ōnis, [**supplicō**], f., *solemn thanksgiving, thanksgiving.* [supplication.

suppliciter [**supplex**], adv., *after the manner of a suppliant, humbly.*

supplicium, -ī, [cf. **supplex**], n., *punishment; death penalty, execution.*

supportō, -āre, -āvī, [**sub** + **portō**], 1, *bring up, transport, convey.* [support.

suprā, adv. and prep.: (1) As adv., *above; before, previously.* (2) As prep., with acc., *above;* of time, *beyond, before* (VI.19).

suscipiō, -cipere, -cēpī, -ceptus, [**subs,** for **sub,** + **capiō**], 3, *undertake, take up; take upon one's self, assume* (I.3). [susceptible.

suspectus, -a, -um, comp. **-ior,** adj., *under suspicion.* [suspect.

suspīciō, -ōnis, f., (**12c**), *suspicion; reason to suspect* (I.4). [suspicion.

suspicor, -ārī, -ātus, [cf. **suspiciō**], 1, dep., *suspect, mistrust, surmise.*

sustentō, -āre, -āvī, -ātus, [freq. of **sustineō**], 1, *sustain, endure, bear.*

sustineō, -tinēre, -tinuī, -tentus, [**subs,** for **sub,** + **teneō**], 2, *hold up; check, pull up* (IV.33); *hold out, bear, endure; hold out against, withstand.* [sustain.

sustulī, see **tollō.**

suus, -a, -um, [cf. **suī**], possessive pronominal adj., *his, her, its, their; his own, her own, their own,* etc.; with **locō, locīs,** *favorable* to himself, to themselves. As noun, **suī,** m., pl., *his, their friends, people, party, side;* **suum, -ī,** n., *their own* (I.43); **sua,** n., pl., *his, her, their property, possessions.* **sē suaque,** *themselves and their possessions* (I.11, II.31) (**41**).

T.

T. = **Titus,** a Roman first name.

tabernāculum, -ī, [**taberna,** *hut*], n., *tent, hut.* [tabernacle.

tabula, -ae, f., *board; writing-tablet; list* written on a tablet (I.29). [table.

taceō, -ēre, -uī, -itus, 2, *be silent, remain silent* (I.17); *say nothing of, pass over in silence* (I.17).

tacitus, -a, -um, [part. of **taceō**], adj., *silent,* (I.32). [tacit.

tālea, -ae, f., *stick, block; bar* (V.12). [tally.

tālis, -e, adj., *such.*

tam, adv., *so, so very.*

tamen, adv., *yet, still, for all that, nevertheless, however.*

Tamesis, -is, m., (**14c**), *the River Thames.*

tametsī [**tam,** = **tamen,** + **etsī**], conj., (**191a**), *although, though.*

tandem [**tam**], adv., *at length, finally;* in questions, *after all, pray* (I.40).

tangō, tangere, tetigī, tāctus, 3, *touch, border on* (V.3). [tact.

tantopere [**tantō opere**], adv., *so earnestly, with so great effort* (I.31).

tantulus, -a, -um, [dim. of **tantus**], adj., *so small, so slight, so trifling.*

tantum [acc. of **tantus**], adv., *only so much, so far, merely.* **tantum modo,** *only* (III.5).

tantus, -a, -um, adj., *so great, so large, so much, so extensive, so important.* **tantus . . . quantus,** *so great, so much, only so much . . . as.*

Tarbellī, -ōrum, m., pl., a people in Aquitania, near the Ocean (III.27).

tardē, comp. **-ius,** sup. **-issimē,** [**tardus**], adv., *slowly;* comp., *rather slowly* (IV.23).

tardō, -āre, -āvī, -ātus, [**tardus**], 1, *check, delay, impede, hinder.*

tardus, -a, -um, comp. **-ior,** sup. **-issimus,** adj., *slow.* Comp., *less active* (II.25). [tardy.

Tarusātēs, -ium, m., pl., a people in Aquitania (III.23, 27).

Tasgetius, -ī, m., a ruler of the Carnutes (V.25, 29).

Taximagulus, -ī, m., a British chieftain (V.22).

Tectosagēs, -um, m., pl., a division of the Volcae, in the Province; represented also by a group settled near the Hercynian forest (VI.24).

tēctum, -ī, [**tegō**], n., *roof* (I.36); *house.*

tegimentum, -ī, [**tegō**], n., *covering.*

tegō, tegere, tēxī, tēctus, 3, *cover* (V.43); *hide, conceal, protect.*

tēlum, -ī, n., general word for *missile; dart, spear.*

temerārius, -a, -um, [**temere**], adj., *rash, headstrong* (I.31; VI.20).

temere, adv., *blindly, recklessly, rashly* (I.40, V.28); *without good reason* (IV.20).

temeritās, -tātis, [cf. **temere**] 1, *rashness, recklessness.* [temerity.

tēmō, -ōnis, m., *pole, tongue,* of a wagon or chariot (IV.33).

temperantia, -ae, [**temperāns,** *temperate*], f., *moderation, self-control, sound judgment* (I.19). [temperance.

temperātus, -a, -um, comp. **-ior,** [**temperō**], adj., *moderate, temperate, mild* (V.12). [temperate.

temperō, -āre, -āvī, -ātus, [cf. **tempus**], 1, *control one's self, refrain* (I.7). [temper.

tempestās, -tātis, [**tempus**], f., *weather; bad weather, storm.* [tempest.

temptō, -āre, -āvī, -ātus, [freq. of **tendō**], 1, *try, attempt; make an attack on, attack.*

tempus, -oris, n., (**13f**), *period of time; time, period; season; occasion, circumstances.* **prō tempore,** *according to the emergency* (V.8). **in reliquum tempus,** *for the future, for all time to come.* [temporal.

Tencterī, -ōrum, m., pl., a German people.

tendō, tendere, tetendī, tentus, 3, *stretch, extend.* [tend.

tenebrae, -ārum, f., pl., *darkness.*

teneō, tenēre, tenuī, 2, *hold, keep, occupy; hold in, keep in, hold back, restrain, hem in; bind* (I.31). **sē tenēre,** *to keep one's self, to remain.* [tenet.

tener, -era, -erum, comp. **-ior,** sup. **tenerrimus,** adj., (**22e**), *tender, young* (II.17).

tenuis, -e, comp. **tenuior,** sup. **tenuissimus,** adj., *thin; poor; feeble, delicate* (V.40).

tenuiter, comp. **tenuius,** sup. **-issimē,** [**tenuis**], adv., *thinly* (III.13).

ter, num. adv., *three times, thrice.*

tergum, -ī, n., *back.* **ā tergō, post tergum,** *in the rear, on the rear.* **terga vertere,** *to flee.*

ternī, -ae, -a, [**ter**], distrib. num. adj., *by threes, three each.*

terra, -ae, f., *earth; land, ground; territory, country, region.* [terrace.

Terrasidius, -ī, m., an officer under Publius Crassus (III.7, 8).

terrēnus, -a, -um, [**terra**], adj., *of earth, earthy* (I.43). [terrain.

terreō, -ēre, -uī, -itus, 2, *frighten, terrify, alarm;* followed by **quō minus,** *deter, frighten* from an action.

territō, -āre, [freq. of **terreō**], 1, *frighten greatly, terrify.* **metū territāre,** *to fill with apprehension* (V.6).

terror, -ōris, [cf. **terreō**], m., *fear, fright.* [terror.

tertius, -a, -um, [**ter**], num. ord. adj., *third.* **tertius decimus,** or **XIII,** *thirteenth.* [tertiary.

testāmentum, -ī, [cf. **testor**], n., *will* (I.39). [testament.

testimōnium, -ī, [cf. **testis**], n., *proof, evidence.* [testimony.

testis, -is, m. and f., *witness.*

testūdō, -inis, [cf. **testa,** *potsherd*], f., (**12d**), *turtle; turtle-shell roof, testudo,* a covering formed by the soldiers' shields held above their heads and overlapping (II.6; V.9); *turtle-shell shed,* a movable shed to protect soldiers near the enemy's wall (V.42, 43, 52).

Teutonī, gen. **-um,** m., pl., *Teutons,* see **Cimbrī.**

tignum, -ī, n., *log, pile* (IV.17).

Tigurīnus, -a, -um, adj., *Tigurian.* As noun, **Tigurīnī, -ōrum,** m., pl., *the Tigurians,* one of the four divisions of the Helvetians (I.12).

timeō, -ēre, -uī, 2, *fear, be afraid, be apprehensive* (I.14, 41) Pres. part., as noun, **timentēs,** m., pl., *the fearful.*

timidē, comp. **-ius,** [**timidus**], adv., *timidly* (III.25; V.33).

timidus, -a, -um, comp. **-ior,** sup. **-issimus,** [cf. **timeō**], adj., *timid, cowardly* (I.39).

timor, -ōris, [cf. **timeō**], m., (**11d**), *fear, apprehension, alarm.* [timorous.

Titūrius, -ī, m., *Quintus Titurius Sabinus,* a lieutenant of Caesar.

Titus, -ī. m., a Roman first name; abbreviated **T.**

tolerō, -āre, -āvī, -ātus, 1, *bear, support, endure; sustain.* [tolerate.

tollō, tollere, sustulī, sublātus, 3, *lift, raise;* of an anchor, *weigh* (IV.23); *take on board* (IV.28); *puff up, elate* (I.15; V.38); *take away, remove* (VI.17); *do away with* (I.42).

Tolōsa, -ae, f., a city in the Province, now *Toulouse* (III.20).

Tolōsātēs, -ium, [**Tolōsa**], m., pl., a people in the territory of the Volcae Tectosages, in the Province, about Tolosa.

tormentum, -ī, [cf. **torqueō,** *twist*], n., *windlass;* as a military term, pl., *torsioners, engines, artillery; missile,* thrown by the torsioners (IV.25); *means of torture, rack, torture* (VI.19). [torment.

torreō, torrēre, torruī, tostus, 2, *roast; burn, scorch* (V.43). [torrid.

tot, indecl. num. adj., *so many.*

totidem [**tot**], indecl. num. adj., *just as many, just so many.*

tōtus, -a, -um, gen. **tōtīus,** adj., (**23**), *the whole, all, all the, entire.* [total.

trabs, trabis, f., (**17c**), *beam, timber.*

trādō, -dere, -didī, -ditus, [**trāns + dō**], 3, *hand over, give up, deliver, surrender; entrust, commit, confide; commend; hand down* (IV.7); *teach, impart* (VI.14, 17).

trādūcō, -dūcere, -dūxī, -ductus, [**trāns + dūcō**], 3, *lead across, bring over; lead, transport, transfer; win over* (VI.12).

trāgula, -ae, f., *dart, javelin,* perhaps having a barbed point, and hurled by means of a leather thong.

trahō, trahere, trāxī, trāctus, 3, *drag along* (I.53); *draw along.* [tract.

trāiciō, -icere, -iēcī, -iectus, [**trāns + iaciō**], 3, *throw across; strike through, pierce, transfix* (V.35, 44). [trajectory.

trāiectus, -ūs, [cf. **trāiciō**], m., *passage* (IV.21; V.2).

trānō, -āre, -āvī, [**trāns + nō,** *swim*], 1, *swim across* (I.53).

tranquillitās, -ātis, [**tranquillus,** *still*], f., *stillness, calm* (III.15). [tranquility.

trāns, prep. with acc. only, *across, over; on the further side of, beyond.*

Trānsalpīnus, -a, -um, [**trāns + Alpīnus,** from **Alpēs**], adj., *beyond the Alps, Transalpine.*

trānscendō, -scendere, -scendī, [**trāns + scandō,** *climb*], 3, *climb over;* of ships, *board* (III.15). [transcend.

trānseō, -īre, -iī or **-īvī, -itum est,** [**trāns + eō**], irr., *go over, go across, pass over, cross over; pass by, march through;* of time, *pass* (III.2).

trānsferō, -ferre, -tulī, -lātus, [**trāns + ferō**], irr., *carry across; transfer.* [transfer.

trānsfīgō, -fīgere, -fīxī, -fīxus, [**trāns + fīgō,** *fix*], 3, *pierce through, transfix.*

trānsgredior, -gredī, gressus, [**trāns + gradiōr,** *walk, go*], 3, dep., *pass over, go across, cross* (II.19). [transgress.

trānsitus, -ūs, [cf. **trānseō**], m., *going over, crossing* (V.55). [transit (noun).

trānslātus, see **trānsferō.**

trānsmarīnus, -a, -um, [**trāns + mare**], adj., *beyond the sea* (VI.24). [transmarine.

trānsmissus, -ūs, [cf. **trānsmittō**], m., *passage* (V.13).

trānsportō, -āre, -āvī, -ātus, [**trāns + portō**], 1, *carry over, convey across.* [transport.

Trānsrhēnānus, -a, -um, [**trāns + Rhēnus**], adj., *beyond the Rhine, on the other side of the Rhine* (V.2). As noun, **Trānsrhēnānī, -ōrum,** m., pl., *the people beyond the Rhine* (IV.16).

trānstrum, -ī, [**trāns**], n., *thwart, cross-beam* (III.13).

trānsversus [part. of **trānsvertō**], adj., *crosswise* (II.8). [transverse.

Trebius, -ī, m., *Marcus Trebius Gallus,* an officer under Publius Crassus (III.7, 8).

Trebōnius, -ī, m., *Gaius Trebonius,* quaestor 60 BC, tribune of the people 55 BC, a lieutenant of Caesar.

trecentī, -ae, -a, or **CCC,** [**trēs + centum**], num., *three hundred.*

trepidō, -āre, -āvī, -ātus, [cf. **trepidus**], 1, *hurry about anxiously* (V.33). [trepidation.

trēs, tria, gen. **trium,** or **III,** num., (**37b**), *three.*

Trēverī, -ōrum, m., pl., *Treverans,* a Belgic people near the Rhine.

Trēverus, -a, -um, adj., *Treveran, of the Treveri* (II.24).

Tribocēs, -um, or **Tribocī, -ōrum,** m., pl., a German people near the Rhine.

tribūnus, -ī, [**tribus,** *tribe*], m., *tribune.* **tribūnus mīlitum,** *military tribune.* **tribūnus plebis,** *tribune of the people.*

tribuō, -ere, -uī, -ūtus, [cf. **tribus**], 3, *assign, ascribe; allot, give, concede; grant, pay, render.*

tribūtum, -ī, [part. of **tribuō**], n., *tax, tribute* (VI.13, 14).

trīduum, -ī, [**tri,** = **trēs,** cf. **diēs**], n., *space of three days, three days.*

triennium, -ī, [**tri-,** = **trēs,** + **annus**], n., *period of three years, three years* (IV.4). [triennial.

trīgintā, or **XXX,** indecl. num., *thirty.*

trīnī, -ae, -a, [**trēs**], distrib. num. adj., (**37e**), *three each; three; threefold, triple* (I.53).

Trinovantēs, -um, m., pl., a tribe in Britain.

tripertītō, [**tripertītus, tri-** + **partītus**], adv., *in three divisions, in three columns.*

triplex, -icis, [**tri,** = **trēs,** cf. **plicō,** *fold*], adj., *threefold, triple.*

triquetrus, -a, -um, adj., *three-cornered, triangular* (V.13).

trīstis, -e, comp. **-ior,** sup. **-issimus,** adj., *sad, dejected, disconsolate* (I.32).

trīstitia, -ae, [**trīstis**], f., *sadness, dejection.*

Troucillus, -ī, m., *Gaius Valerius Troucillus,* a Gaul who acted as interpreter for Caesar (I.19).

truncus, -ī, m., *trunk* of a tree. [trunk.

tū, tuī, pl. **vōs, vestrum,** personal pron., (**39a**), *you.*

tuba, -ae, f., *trumpet.* [tuba.

tueor, tuērī, 2, dep., *gaze at, behold, watch; guard, protect, defend.*

tulī, see **ferō.**

Tulingī, -ōrum, m., pl., a people near the Helvetians.

Tullius, see **Cicero.**

Tullus, see **Volcacius.**

tum, adv., *then, at that time; thereupon; besides, moreover.* **cum . . . tum,** *both . . . and, not only . . . but also.*

tumultus, -ūs, m., *disturbance, confusion, disorder, uproar; uprising, rebellion* (I.40; V.26). [tumult.

tumulus, -ī, [**tumeō,** *swell*], m., *mound, hillock.* [tumulus.

turma, -ae, f., *troop, squadron* of cavalry.

Turonī, -ōrum, m., pl., a Gallic people, on the Liger (*Loire*).

turpis, -e, comp. **-ior,** sup. **-issimus,** adj., *ugly; disgraceful, shameful.*

turpiter, comp. **-ius,** sup. **-issimē,** [**turpis**], adv., *basely, disgracefully.*

turpitūdō, -inis, [**turpis**], f., *baseness, disgrace* (II.27). [turpitude.

turris, -is, f., (**14b**), *tower;* movable *tower,* built on wheels so that it could be moved up to the wall of a besieged city. [turret.

tūtō, comp. **tūtius,** [abl. of **tūtus**], adv., *in safety, safely, securely.*

tūtus, comp. **-ior,** sup. **-issimus,** [part. of **tueor**], adj., *safe, secure.*

tuus, -a, -um, [**tū**], possessive pronominal adj., (**41**), *your.* (V.44).

U.

ubi or **ubī,** adv., of place, *where;* of time, *when.* **ubi prīmum,** *as soon as.*

Ubiī, -ōrum, m., pl., *Ubians,* a German people.

ubīque [**ubī** + **-que**], adv., *anywhere, everywhere* (III.16). [ubiquitous.

Ubius, -a, -um, adj., *Ubian, of the Ubians.*

ulcīscor, ulcīscī, ultus, 3, dep., *take vengeance on* (I.14; IV.19; V.38); *avenge* (I.12).

ūllus, -a, -um, gen. **ūllīus,** adj., (**23**), *any.* As noun, *anyone, anybody* (I.8).

ulterior, -ius, [**ultrā**], adj. in comp. degree, *farther, beyond, more remote, more distant.* Sup. **ultimus,** *farthest, most distant, most remote; last.* As noun, **ulteriōrēs, -um,** m., pl., *those who were further off;* **ultimī, -ōrum,** m., pl., *the last* (V.43). [ulterior, ultimate.

ultrā, prep. with acc. only, *on the farther side of; beyond* (I.48, 49).

ultrō, adv., *to the farther side; besides, moreover, also* (V.28); *of one's own accord, voluntarily.*

ultus, see **ulcīscor.**

ululātus, -ūs, [**ululō,** *yell*], m., only in acc. and abl., *shouting, yell.*

umerus, -ī, m., *shoulder.*

umquam, adv., *at any time, ever.*

ūnā [**ūnus**], adv., *into one place; in the same place* (II.29); *at the same time; together, in company.* **ūnā cum,** *along with, together with.*

unde, adv., *whence, from which.*

ūndecim, or **XI,** [**ūnus + decem**], indecl. num., *eleven.*

ūndecimus, -a, -um, [**ūndecim**], num. ord. adj., *eleventh.*

ūndēquadrāgintā, or **XXXIX,** [**ūnus + dē + quadrāgintā**], indecl. num., *thirty-nine.*

ūndēvīgintī, or **XVIIII,** [**ūnus + dē + vīgintī**], indecl. num., *nineteen.*

undique [**unde + -que**], adv., *from all sides, on all sides, everywhere.*

ūniversus, -a, -um, [**ūnus + versus,** from **vertō**], adj., *all together, all, in a body; the whole of, entire.* As noun, **ūniversī, -ōrum,** m., pl., *all the men together, the whole body, all together.* [universe.

ūnus, -a, -um, gen. ūnīus, num. adj., (**23**), *one; one alone, only one, only, sole; one and the same.* Pl., **ūnī,** *alone, only.* **ūnō tempore,** *at one and the same time.* **ad ūnum omnēs,** *all to a man* (V.37). [unite.

urbānus, -a, -um, [**urbs**], adj., *of the city,* referring to Rome. [urban.

urbs, urbis, f., (**17b**), *city;* often *the city,* referring to Rome.

urgeō, urgēre, ursī, 2, *press;* pass., *be hard pressed* (II.25, 26). [urge.

Usipetēs, -um, m., pl., a German people.

ūsque, adv., *as far as, even.* **ūsque ad,** *as far as;* of time, *up to, until* (I.50; III.15).

ūsus, see **ūtor.**

ūsus, -ūs, [cf. **ūtor**], m., *use, practice, exercise, employment; experience, familiarity (with), skill; control; advantage, benefit; need, necessity.* **ex ūsū,** *of advantage.*

ut, utī, adv. and conj.: (1) As adv., interrogative, *how* (I.43, 46); relative, *as, just as.* (2) As conj., with indic., *as* (I.4); *when, as soon as* (I.31); with subj., *that, so that; in order that; though, although* (III.9).

uter, utra, utrum, gen. utrīus, pronominal adj., often used as subst., (**23**), *which of two, whichever, which.*

uterque, -traque, -trumque, gen. utrīusque, [**uter + -que**], adj., (**51, 169**), *each, both.* As subst., **uterque, utrīusque,** m., *both, each.* Pl., **utrīque,** *both sides, both forces* (IV.26; V.50); *both peoples* (II.16).

utī, see **ut.**

ūtilis, -e, comp. **-ior,** sup. **-issimus,** [**ūtor**], adj., *useful, serviceable* (IV.7); *helpful.*

ūtilitās, -ātis, [**ūtilis**], f., *usefulness, advantage, benefit.* [utility.

ūtor, ūtī, ūsus, 3, dep., (**131c**), *use, employ, adopt; avail one's self of, have, enjoy, find; observe, maintain; exercise, display, show.*

utrimque [**uterque**], adv., *on both sides.*

utrum, [**uter**], conj., *whether.*

uxor, -ōris, f., (**13d**), *wife.*

V.

Vacalus, -ī, m., *Waal,* an arm of the Rhine, which flows west into the Meuse (IV.10).

vacātiō, -ōnis, [cf. **vacō**], f., *exemption* (VI.14). [vacation.

vacō, -āre, -āvī, -ātus, 1, *be unoccupied.* [vacate.

vacuus, -a, -um, sup. **vacuissimus,** [**vacō**], adj., *empty, clear, vacant, unoccupied; destitute* (II.12). [vacuum.

vadum, -ī, n., *shoal, shallow* (III.9, 12, 13; IV.26); *ford, shallow place.*

vāgīna, -ae, f., *scabbard, sheath* (V.44).

vagor, -ārī, -ātus, 1, dep., *wander, wander about, roam about.*

valeō, -ēre, -uī, -itūrus, 2, *be powerful, be strong; have power, have influence; prevail.* [value.

Valerius, -ī, m.: (1) *Lucius Valerius Praeconinus,* a lieutenant defeated and killed in Aquitania a few years before 56 BC (III.20). (2) *Gaius Valerius Flaccus,* a Roman governor in Gaul (I.47). (3) *Gaius Valerius Caburus,* a Gaul who received the Roman franchise, 83 BC (I.47). (4) *Gaius Valerius Procillus,* son of (3); sent by Caesar as envoy to Ariovistus (I.53). (5) *Gaius Valerius Troucillus,* see **Troucillus** (I.19).

valētūdō, -inis, [cf. **valeō**], f., *health* (V.40).

vallēs or **vallis, -is,** f., *valley.*

vāllum, -ī, [**vāllus**], n., *rampart set with palisades, wall, entrenchment.* [wall.

vāllus, -ī, m., *stake, pole; rampart stake, palisade;* rampart stakes in position, *stockade.*

Vangionēs, -um, m., pl., a German tribe.

varius, -a, -um, adj., *different, diverse.* [various.

vāstō, -āre, -āvī, -ātus, [**vāstus**], 1, *lay waste, devastate.*

vastus, -a, -um, comp. **-ior,** sup. **-issimus,** adj., *vast, immense.* [vast.

vāticinātiō, -ōnis, [**vāticinor,** *predict*], f., *prophecy* (I.50).

-ve, enclitic conj., *or.*

vectīgal, -ālis, [cf. **vehō**], n., (**16d**), *tax, tribute* (V.22); *revenue* (I.18, 36).

vectīgālis, -e, [**vectīgal**], adj., *paying tribute, tributary* (III.8; IV.3).

vectōrius, -a, -um, [**vector,** cf. **vehō**], adj., *for carrying.* **vectōrium nāvigium,** *transport ship* (V.8).

vehementer, comp. **vehementius,** sup. **-issimē,** [**vehemēns,** *eager, violent*], adv., *vigorously, violently; exceedingly, greatly.*

vehō, -ere, vexī, vectus, 3, *carry.* **equō vectus,** *riding on horseback.* [vehicle.

vel, [**volō**], conj., *or.* **vel . . . vel,** *either . . . or.*

Velānius, -ī, m., *Quintus Velanius,* an officer under Crassus (III.7, 8).

Veliocassēs, -ium, and **Veliocassī, -ōrum,** m. pl., a small state north of the Sequana (*Seine*).

vēlōciter, comp. **vēlōcius,** sup. **vēlōcissimē,** [**vēlōx**], adv., *swiftly, quickly* (V.35).

vēlōx, -ōcis, comp. **-ior,** sup. **-issimus,** adj., *swift, fast* (I.48). [velox.

vēlum, -ī, n., *sail* (III.13, 14).

velut [**vel + ut**], adv., *just as.* **velut sī,** *just as if* (I.32).

vēnātiō, -ōnis, [cf. **vēnor,** *hunt*], f., *hunting, hunting expedition.*

vēnātor, -ōris, [**vēnor,** *hunt*], m., *hunter.*

vēndō, -dere, -didī, -ditus, [**vēnum,** *sale,* + **dō**], 3, *sell.* [vend.

Venellī, -ōrum, m. pl., a Gallic people, on the northwest coast.

Venetī, -ōrum, m. pl., *Venetans,* a seafaring Gallic people, on the west coast.

Venetia, -ae, f., *the country of the Venetans.*

Veneticus, -a, -um, [**Venetia**], adj., *of the Venetans, Venetan.* **Veneticum bellum,** *the war with the Venetans* (III.18; IV.21).

veniō, venīre, vēnī, ventum est, 4, *come.*

ventitō, -āre, -āvī, [freq. of **veniō**], 1, *come often, go often, keep coming.*

ventus, -ī, m., *wind.* [ventilate.

vēr, vēris, n., *spring.* [vernal.

Veragrī, -ōrum, m. pl., an Alpine tribe.

Verbigenus, -ī, m., *Verbigen,* a canton of the Helvetians (I.27).

verbum, -ī, n., *word.* **verba facere,** *to speak* (II.14). [verb.

vereor, -ērī, -itus, 2, dep., (**60**), *fear, be afraid; be afraid of, dread.*

vergō, -ere, 3, *lie, slope; be situated.* [verge.

vergobretus, -ī, m., [Celtic word, *"He that renders judgment"*; as a title, *"Dispenser of Justice"*], *vergobret,* title of the chief magistrate of the Aeduans (I.16).

veritus, see **vereor.**

vērō [abl. neuter of **vērus**], adv., *in truth, in fact, truly, certainly; but, but in fact, however.*

versō, -āre, -āvī, -ātus, [freq. of **vertō**], 1, *turn often; shift, change the position of* (V.44). Pass. **versor, -ārī, -ātus,** as dep., lit., *turn oneself about, move about* in any place; *dwell, live, be; be occupied, be engaged, be busy.* **in bellō versārī,** *to engage in war* (VI.15). [versatile.

versus, -ūs, [**vertō**], m., *line, verse* (VI.14).

versus, [part. of **vertō**], prep. and adv.: (1) As prep., with acc. only, sometimes following a word governed by **ad** or **in,** *towards, in the direction of.* **ad . . . versus, in . . . versus,** *towards.* (2) As adv., *turned, facing.* **quōque versus,** *in all directions* (III.23).

Verticō, -ōnis, m., a Nervian of rank.

vertō, vertere, vertī, versus, 3, *turn, turn about; change.* **terga vertere,** *to turn and flee, to flee.*

Verucloetius, -ī, m., a Helvetian who went as an envoy to Caesar (I.7).

vērus, -a, -um, comp. **-ior,** sup. **vērissimus,** adj., *true* (I.18, 20); *right, proper, fitting* (IV.8). As noun, **vērum, -ī,** n., *the truth.* **vērī similis,** *probable* (III.13).

verūtum, -ī, [**verū,** *spit* for roasting meat], n., *javelin, dart* (V.44).

Vesontiō, -ōnis, m., chief city of the Sequanians, on the Dubis (*Doubs*) river; now *Besançon* (I.38, 39).

vesper, -erī, m., (**7b**), *evening.* [vespers.

vester, -tra, -trum, [**vōs**], possessive pronominal adj., (**41**), *your, yours.*

vēstīgium, -ī, n., *footprint, track; spot, place* (IV.2); of time, *moment, instant.* [vestige.

vestiō, -īre, -īvī, -ītus, [**vestis**], 4, *clothe* (V.14); *cover.* [vestment.

vestītus, -ūs, [cf. **vestiō**], m., *clothing, garb.*

veterānus, -a, -um, [**vetus**], adj., *old, veteran* (I.24). [veteran.

vetō, -āre, -uī, -itus, 1, *forbid* (II.20). [veto.

vetus, -eris, sup. **veterrimus,** adj., (**26a**), *old, former; ancient, long-standing.*

vēxillum, -ī, [cf. **vēlum**], n., *banner, flag.*

vexō, -āre, -āvī, -ātus, [freq. of **vehō**], 1, *harass, assail* (I.14); *lay waste, overrun* (II.4; IV.15). [vex.

via, -ae, f., (**3**), *way, road; journey, march.* **bīduī via,** *a two days' march.*

viātor, -ōris, [cf. **via**], m., *traveler, wayfarer* (IV.5).

vīcēnī, -ae, -a, [**vīgintī**], distrib. num. adj., *twenty each, twenty.*

vīcēsimus, -a, -um, [**vīgintī**], num. adj., *twentieth* (VI.21).

vīciēs [**vīgintī**], num. adv., *twenty times.* **vīciēs centum milia passuum,** *two thousand miles* (V.13).

vicis, -is, f., nom., dat., and voc. sing. not in use; gen. and voc. pl. not in use, *change, succession.* **in vicem,** *in turn* (IV.1).

victima, -ae, f., *victim* (VI.16). [victim.

victor, -ōris, [**vincō**], m., (**11b**), *conqueror, victor.* As adj., *victorious* (I.31).

victōria, -ae, [**victor**], f., *victory.*

victus, see **vincō.**

vīctus, -ūs, [**vīvō**], m., *living* (I.31); *mode of life* (VI.24); *food, provisions* (VI.22, 23). [victuals.

vīcus, -ī, m., *village, hamlet.*

videō, vidēre, vīdī, vīsus, 2, *see, perceive, observe; understand.* Pass., generally as dep., **videor, vidērī, vīsus sum,** *be seen, seem, appear; seem proper, seem good, seem best.* [vision.

vigilia, -ae, [**vigil,** *watchman*], f., *watching, sleeplessness* (V.31, 32); *a watch, sentry duty* (**242c**). [vigil.

vīgintī, or **XX,** indecl. num., *twenty.*

vīmen, -inis, n., *pliant shoot, twig, withe* (II.33).

vinciō, vincīre, vinxī, vinctus, 4, *bind.*

vincō, vincere, vīcī, victus, 3, *conquer, overcome, defeat, subdue; exceed, surpass; carry one's point, have one's own way* (V.30). **victī, -ōrum,** part., used as noun; m. pl., *the conquered.*

vinculum, -ī, [**vinciō**], n., *chain, bond, fetters.* [vinculum.

vindicō, -āre, -āvī, -ātus, [cf. **vindex**], 1, *claim, demand; restore to liberty; inflict punishment* (III.16). [vindicate.

vīnea, -ae, f., *arbor-shed, sappers' hut* (**302**).

vīnum, -ī, n., *wine.*

violō, -āre, -āvī, -ātus, [**vīs**], 1, *do violence to, maltreat; invade, lay waste.* [violate.

vir, virī, m., (**7**), *man; husband* (VI.19). [virile.

vīrēs, see **vīs.**

virgō, -inis, f., (**12d**), *maiden.* [virgin.

virgultum, -ī, [**virga,** *a shoot*], n., *small brush; brushwood.*

Viridovīx, -īcis, m., a leader of the Venelli (III.17-18).

Viromanduī, -ōrum, m. pl., a Belgic people about the headwaters of the Samara (*Somme*) and the Scaldis (*Schelde*).

virtūs, -tūtis, [**vir**], f., (**10b**), *manliness; courage, bravery, prowess; vigor, energy; effort* (V.8); *worth* (I.47). Pl., *remarkable qualities, virtues* (I.44). [virtue.

vīs, acc. **vim,** abl. **vī,** pl. **vīrēs, -ium,** f., (**18a**), *strength; force, violence; influence, control* (VI.14, 17). Pl., *physical powers, strength.* [vim.

vīsus, see **videō.**

vīta, -ae, [cf. **vīvō**], f., *life.* [vital.

vītō, -āre, -āvī, -ātus, 1, *shun, avoid, try to escape.*

vitrum, -ī, n., *woad,* a plant used for dyeing blue (V.14).

vīvō, vīvere, vīxī, vīctūrus, 3, *live;* with abl., *sustain life, live on* (IV.1,10; V.14). [vivacious.

vīvus, -a, -um, [cf. **vīvō**], adj., *living, alive.* As noun, **vīvī, -ōrum,** m., pl., *the living* (VI.19). [vivisection.

vix, adv., *scarcely; hardly; with difficulty.*

Vocātēs, -ium, m., pl., a people in Aquitania (III.23, 27).

Vocciō, -ōnis, m., a king of the Norici.

vocō, -āre, -āvī, -ātus, [cf. **vōx**], 1, *call, summon; call for, demand; name, call* (V.21). [vocative.

Vocontiī, -ōrum, m., pl., a Gallic people in the Province (I.10).

Volcācius, -ī, m., *Gaius Volcacius Tullus,* an officer in Caesar's army.

Volcae, -ārum, m., pl., a Gallic people in the Province having two branches, **Arecomicī** and **Tectosagēs**.

volō, velle, voluī, irr., **(71)**, *be willing, wish, desire; mean, intend, purpose.*

voluntārius, -a, -um, [**volō**], adj., *willing; serving as a volunteer.* As noun, **voluntārius, -ī,** m., *volunteer* (V.56). [voluntary.

voluntās, -ātis, [**volō**], f., *will, wish, inclination, desire; goodwill, loyalty* (I.19; V.4); *consent, approval* (I.7, 20, 30, 39).

voluptās, -ātis, [**volō**], f., *pleasure, indulgence, enjoyment; amusement* (V.12). [voluptuous.

Volusēnus, -ī, m., *Gaius Volusenus Quadratus,* a military tribune.

Vorēnus, -ī, m., *Lucius Vorenus,* a centurion (V.44).

vōs, see **tū.**

Vosegus, -ī, m., a range of mountains in eastern Gaul, now *Vosges.*

voveō, vovēre, vōvī, vōtus, 2, *vow* (VI.16).

vōx, vōcis, f., **(10c)**, *voice* (II.13; V.30; IV.25); *utterance; word, reply* (I.32). Pl. **vōcēs,** *words, sayings, language, speeches, statements.* [voice.

Vulcānus, -ī, m., *Vulcan,* son of Jupiter and Juno, god of fire and of work in metals (VI.21). [volcano.

vulgō [**vulgus**], adv., *generally, commonly, everywhere* (I.39; II.1; V.33).

vulgus, -ī, n., **(6b)**, *common people; multitude, crowd;* of soldiers, *rank and file* (I.46). [vulgar.

vulnerō, -āre, -āvī, -ātus, [**vulnus**], 1, *wound, hurt.* [vulnerable.

vulnus, -eris, n., **(13e)**, *wound.*

vultus, -ūs, m., *countenance, features, expression of face* (I.39).

Maps and Plates

List of Maps and Plates

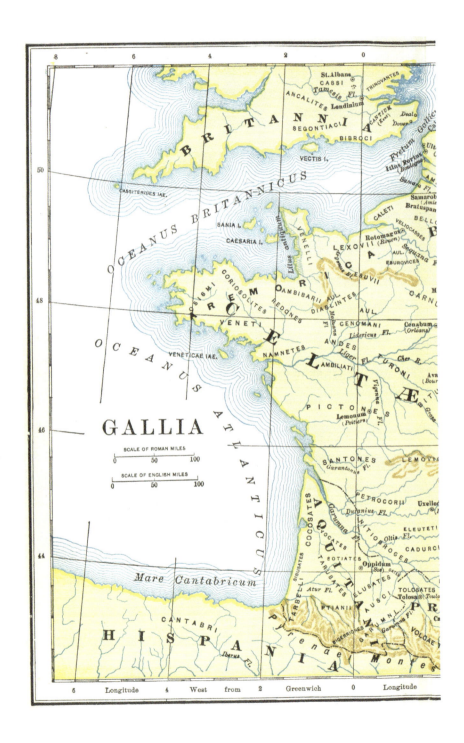

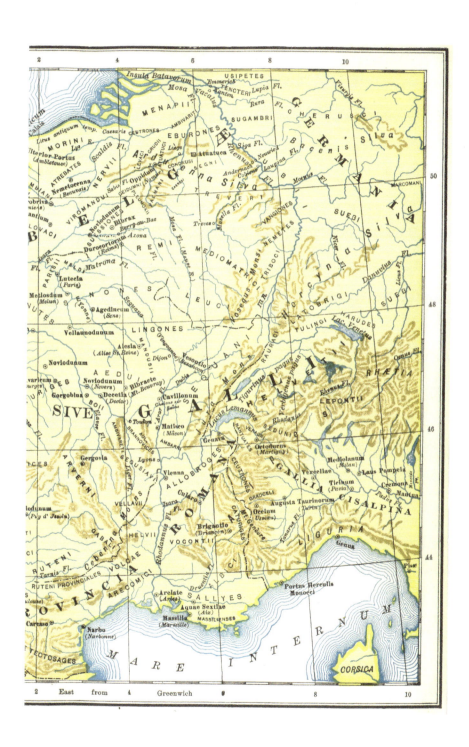

337

MAP I

CAMPAIGNS OF 58 AND 57 B.C.

Book I, 2–54 ; II, 1–33 ; III, 1–6

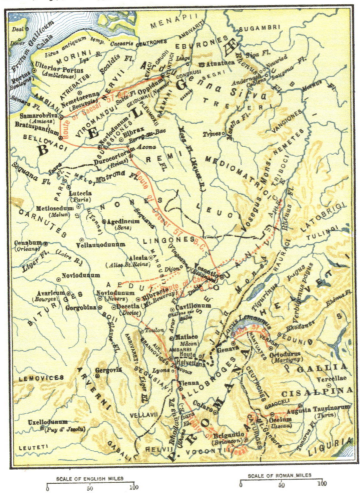

EXPLANATION

The route of the Helvetians to the Arar is indicated by a broken black line ; thence their line of march and Caesar's coincide, to Toulon.

MAP 2

CAESAR'S LINE OF WORKS ALONG THE RHONE FROM GENEVA TO MILL-RACE GORGE (PAS DE L'ÉCLUSE)

Book I, 8

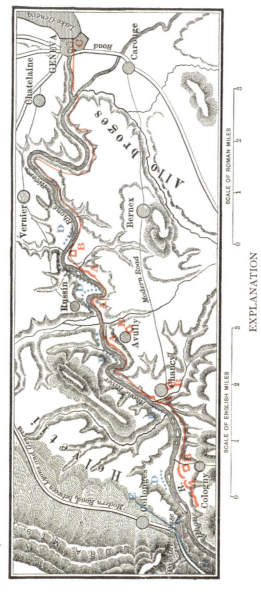

EXPLANATION

A, A. Places where strong fortifications were needed, such as are shown in Figure 34. The lighter red line between these places indicates where less extensive fortifying was required.

B, B. Redoubts, *castella* (chap. 8, l. 6).

C. Site of ancient Geneva, on the south side of the Rhone. The modern city spreads out on both sides of the river.

D, D. Places where the Helvetians probably gathered, in their attempts to force the crossing of the Rhone (chap. 8, ll. 12–16).

E–E. Route of the Helvetian host entering Mill-race Gorge.

339

MAP 3

THE BATTLE WITH THE HELVETIANS

Book I, 24–26

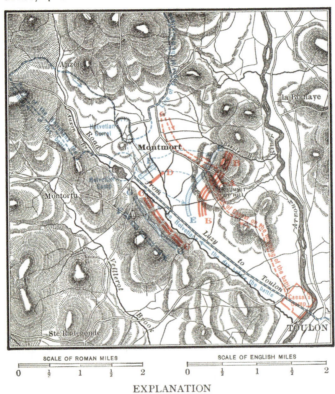

SCALE OF ROMAN MILES

SCALE OF ENGLISH MILES

0   ½   1   1½   2   0   ½   1   1½   2

EXPLANATION

On the day before the battle the Helvetians probably crossed the Arroux at Toulon and encamped near Montmort; a part of the site of the camp is now covered by a pond. Caesar, following, encamped near the Arroux.

A. Semicircular trench hastily dug by the XIth and XIIth legions on the hill (chap. 24, ll. 5–10).

B–B. The four veteran legions in battle order, three lines, first position.

C–C. First and second Roman lines, second position (chap. 25, ll. 21–23).

D. Third Roman line, second position, facing the Boians and Tulingians.

E–E. First position of the Helvetians (chap. 24, ll. 12–14).

F–F. Second position of the Helvetians, on a height (chap. 25, ll. 12–15).

G–G. Third position of the Helvetians, resuming the attack (chap. 25, ll. 18–20).

H. Boians and Tulingians (chap. 25, ll. 15–18).

MAP 4
The Battle with Ariovistus

Book I, 49–53

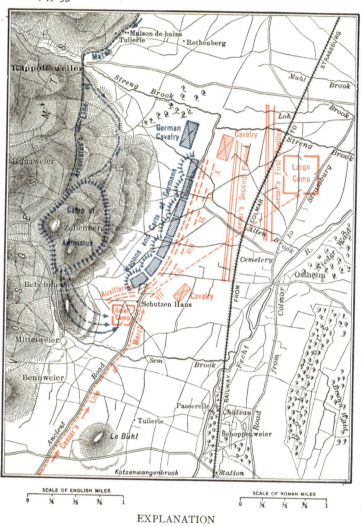

SCALE OF ENGLISH MILES

SCALE OF ROMAN MILES

EXPLANATION

Caesar, marching from the south, encamped north of Modern Ostheim (chap. 48, l. 2).   Ariovistus, marching from the north, encamped on Zellenberg.

MAP 5
The Battle at the Aisne (Axona)

Book II, 7–10

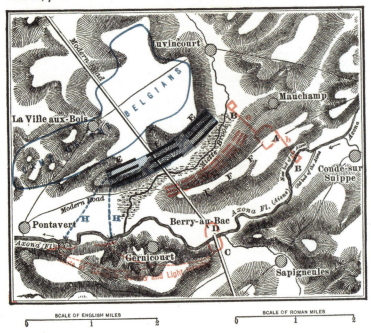

SCALE OF ENGLISH MILES

SCALE OF ROMAN MILES

EXPLANATION

Caesar, marching from the South, encamped on the north or right bank of the Aisne, on a long hill. As the camp was well protected by the streams and the low ground on the west, in order to secure the east side, he ran intrenchments from the corners to both the Aisne and the Miette. The widely extended Belgian camp was on the opposite side of the Miette (chap. 7, ll. 11–12).

A. Caesar's camp (chap. 5, l. 15 ; chap. 7, l. 9 ; chap. 8, l. 7).

a, b. Trenches, *fossae* (chap. 8, ll. 11–13).

B, B. Redoubts, *castella* (chap. 8, l. 13).

C. Redoubt at the south end of the bridge, *castellum*, held by Q. Titurius Sabinus (chap. 5, ll. 20–22 ; chap. 9, l. 11).

D. Guard at the north end of the bridge, *praesidium* (chap. 5, l. 20).

E–E. The Belgians in battle order (chap. 8, l. 20).

F–F. The six legions in battle order (chap. 8, l. 19).

H–H. Probable routes taken by the Belgians to the fords at the Aisne, where they were met by Caesar's light-armed troops and cavalry (chap. 9, ll. 8–15).

MAP 6

THE BATTLE AT THE SAMBRE (SABIS): FIRST PHASE

Book II, 18–22

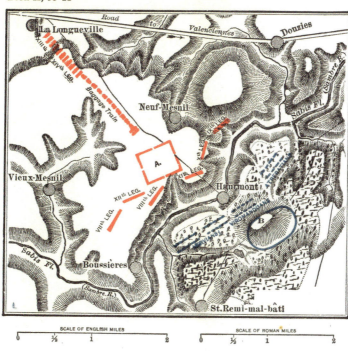

SCALE OF ENGLISH MILES

SCALE OF ROMAN MILES

EXPLANATION

Caesar's army, approaching the Sambre from the north, started to make a camp on a hill overlooking the river. The Belgian forces, comprising Nervians, Viromanduans, and Atrebatians, were lying in wait on the south side.

Supposing that each legion would be followed by its baggage train, the Belgians had planned to attack the first legion and destroy it before the others could come to the rescue, and in like manner to destroy the others one by one. Caesar, however, had placed six legions in light marching order first, then all the baggage, and two legions last, the XIIIth and XIVth; he sent cavalry, bowmen, and slingers in advance of the main column.

When the baggage train came into view, the Belgians hurled back the cavalry, bowmen, and slingers, rushed across the river and charged up the hill.

A. The Roman camp (chap. 18, ll. 1–7), with six legions forming in front.

B. The camp of the Belgians (chap. 26, ll. 10–12)

343

MAP 7

THE BATTLE AT THE SAMBRE (SABIS): SECOND PHASE

Book II, 23-27

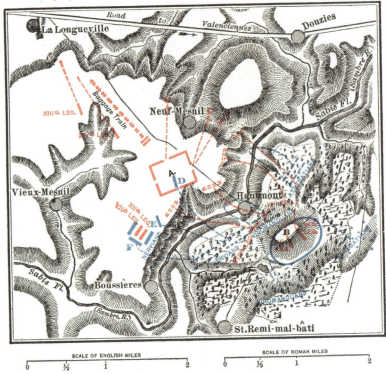

EXPLANATION

The Atrebatians, having crossed the river, were thrown back by the IXth and X[th] legions, and fled through the woods east of the Belgian camp. The IXth and X[th] legions entered the Belgian camp (**B**), which was on a hill.

In like manner the XIth and VIIIth legions routed the Viromanduans and crossed to the south side of the river in pursuit.

Of the Nervians, one division (**D**) made for the Roman camp (**A**) and entered it; the cavalry, bowmen, and slingers that had taken refuge there fled precipitately (**C**). Other divisions (**E, F**) started to surround the VIIth and XIIth legions, which by Caesar's order took up a position rear to rear.

Hearing the noise of battle the baggage train halted, and the XIIIth and XIVth legions hastened to the scene.

Caesar rushed into the front rank, and saved the day.

MAP 8

OPERATIONS AGAINST THE STRONGHOLD OF THE ATUATUCI

Book II, 29–33

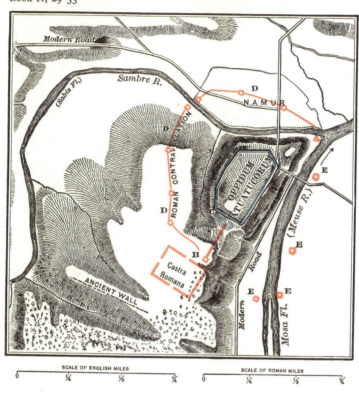

EXPLANATION

The Atuatuci abandoned their towns and gathered in a stronghold protected by steep cliffs except on one side, where there was an easy approach not more than 200 Roman feet wide.

Caesar blockaded the stronghold with a rampart and redoubts. Afterwards he ran an embankment up the inclined approach, and made ready to attack.

A. Incline along which Caesar-constructed his siege embankment, *agger*.

B. General's gate, *porta praetōria*, of Caesar's camp.

C. Upper end of the inclined approach, fortified with a double wall (chap. 29, ll. 8–10) and moat (chap. 32, ll. 9, 10).

D–D. Rampart, *vallum* (chap. 30, l. 3).

E–E. Redoubts, *castella* (chap. 30, l. 4).

MAP 9.

OPERATIONS OF THE YEAR 56 B.C.

Book III, 7–27

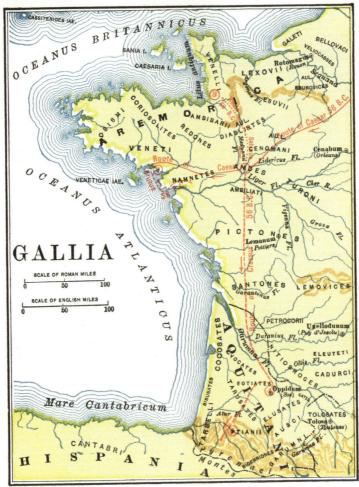

EXPLANATION

1. Base whence Caesar sent Sabinus north and Crassus south.   2. Sea-fight with the Venetans (chap. 13–15).   3. Battle of Sabinus (17–19).   4. Battle of Crassus with the Sotiates (20–22).   5. Final victory of Crassus (23–26).

MAP 10

SEA-FIGHT WITH THE VENETANS

Book III, 7–16

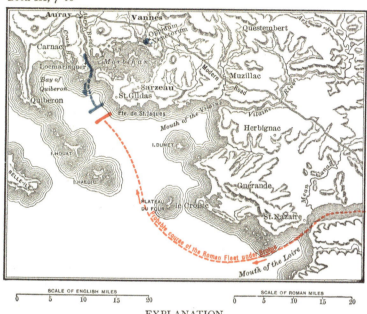

SCALE OF ENGLISH MILES

0   5   10   15   20

SCALE OF ROMAN MILES

0   5   10   15   20

EXPLANATION

Caesar's fleet was built on the Loire (Liger, chap. 9, ll. 2–4), and placed in command of Brutus. From the mouth of the Loire it followed a northerly course till it met the Venetan fleet (chap. 14).

MAP 10, A

OPERATIONS AGAINST A VENETAN TOWN
(III, 12)

a. Mainland.

b. Stronghold, *oppidum*, surrounded by water at high tide.

c. Parallel dikes over land submerged except at low tide. The dikes, or embankments, were high enough to keep out the water at high tide.

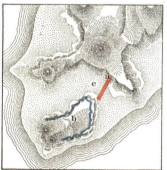

SCALE OF MILES

0   ¼   ½   ¾   1   1¼   1½

MAP 10, A

MAP II

OPERATIONS OF 55 AND 54 B.C.

Books IV, V.

EXPLANATION

MAP II

1, 2. Winter quarters, 56–55 B.C. (III.29).
3. Expedition into Germany, 55 B.C. (IV. 19).
4. March into Britain, 54 B.C. (V. 21).

MAP II, A

Heavy broken red line, route of main fleet in 55 B.C. (IV. 23).

Light broken red lines, route of transports with cavalry, part driven back, part driven down the channel (IV. 28).

Unbroken red line, route of fleet in 54 B.C. (V. 8).

MAP II, A

Detail of Caesar's crossings to Britain.

MAP 12

MAP OF BRITAIN AS CONCEIVED BY CAESAR

Book V, 13

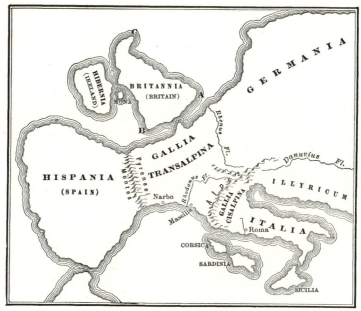

EXPLANATION

In view of the meagerness of Caesar's information, his statement about the geography of Britain is surprisingly near the truth in essential particulars. In this respect it compares favorably with the statements of modern travelers and explorers in regard to regions of which they have seen only a small part.

He knew that the Island was triangular in shape, and in his two expeditions he had himself seen a portion of the coast facing Gaul (chap. 13, l. 1). He could easily believe that one corner (**A**) faced east, another (**B**) toward the south. His language implies that he had a vague idea of a projection eastward (**C**) at the northern extremity (l. 18). He knew the location, and approximately the size, of Ireland (l. 7).

Caesar, as other ancients, found it more difficult to estimate distances north and south than east and west. He fell easily into the error of supposing that the northern end of Spain extended so far that it lay west of the southern part of Britain (l. 6); and his conception of the relative positions of the two Gauls, Italy and Illyricum, was probably very nearly as represented.

The strait between Italy and Sicily, now Strait of Messina, is called by Caesar *Fretum* (C. II, l. 3).

Plate I

CAESAR'S BRIDGE ACROSS THE RHINE, SECTIONS

Lib. IV., 17

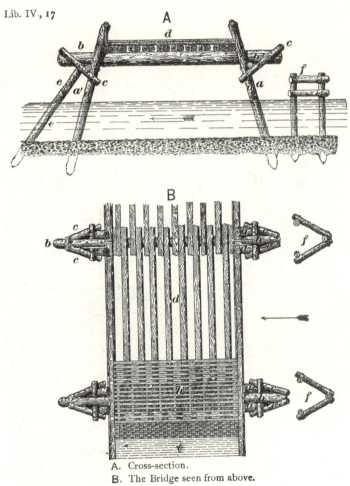

A. Cross-section.
B. The Bridge seen from above.

Plate II

CAESAR'S BRIDGE ACROSS THE RHINE

a, a'. Tigna bina sesquipedalia.
b, b. Trabes bipedales.
c, c. Fibulae.
d, d. Derecta materia, longuriis
cratibusque constrata.
e, e Sublicae ad inferiorem partem
fluminis oblique actae.
f, f. Sublicae supra pontem immis-
sae.   [positum.
g. Castellum ad caput pontis
h. Longurii.   i. Crates